Twenty-First-Century Peace Operations

Twenty-First-Century Peace Operations

Edited by William J. Durch

UNITED STATES INSTITUTE OF PEACE
and

THE HENRY L. STIMSON CENTER
Washington, D.C.

Photographs used in this work courtesy of UNMEE/Jorge Aramburu.

The views expressed in this book are those of the authors alone. They do not necessarily reflect views of the United States Institute of Peace or of the Henry L. Stimson Center.

UNITED STATES INSTITUTE OF PEACE
1200 17th Street NW, Suite 200
Washington, DC 20036-3011

First published 2006

Printed in the United States of America

The paper used in this publication meets the minimum requirements of American National Standards for Information Science—Permanence of Paper for Printed Library Materials, ANSI Z39.48-1984.

Library of Congress Cataloging-in-Publication Data
    Twenty-first-century peace operations / edited by William J. Durch.
      p. cm.
    Includes bibliographical references and index.
    ISBN-13: 978-1-929223-91-6 (pbk. : alk. paper) ISBN-10: 1-929223-91-9 (pbk. : alk. paper) ISBN-13: 978-1-929223-92-3 (alk. paper) ISBN-10: 1-929223-92-7 (alk. paper)
      1. Peace-building—History—21st century. 2. Conflict management—History—20th century. I. Durch, William J.
    JZ5538.T84 2006
    341.5'84—dc22
                                    2006016057

Contents

Illustrations

Foreword

We are pleased to introduce *Twenty-First-Century Peace Operations*, the most authoritative volume currently available on the most recent developments in peacekeeping. This is the third in a sequence of studies edited by William J. Durch that trace the evolution of UN peacekeeping and postconflict security. The study highlights the security tools developed over the past decade to help restore peace to war-ravaged lands and the lessons learned in applying them to six important and very different peace operations.

With a rising number of wars ending not in victory for one side but in stalemate, negotiated peace, or outside military intervention, many of the tools and lessons identified by Durch and the distinguished authors involve the deployment of international peacekeepers to help local parties get past the high-risk period that follows a decision to lay down arms. Indeed, as the international system grapples with the security challenges of the new century, peacekeeping has become an operational focus of more than just the United Nations: NATO, the European Union (EU), the new African Union (AU), and the Economic Community of West African States all have undertaken major operations. Regional peacekeeping is also newly on the agenda of the defense chiefs of the Association of Southeast Asian Nations, while the states of South Asia—with many troops in uniform but no regional security organization to manage their deployment—provide more than half of the soldiers now serving in record numbers in UN operations in sub-Saharan Africa. With many current conflicts as yet unresolved—and many more on the horizon—demand for capable peacekeepers will remain high.

Through their structured case studies of operations in Afghanistan, Bosnia and Herzegovina, the Democratic Republic of the Congo,

East Timor, Kosovo, and Sierra Leone, Durch and the authors place current peace operations in historical context, outlining the problems that have driven each conflict. They then examine the complex demands placed on the United Nations and other institutional managers of operations in these conflict zones, assessing how and why each operation succeeded, failed, or adapted to its environment. In so doing, Durch and the authors touch on a range of current policy concerns, providing constructive and practical guides for improving future interventions. Durch concludes this rich area of inquiry with reflections on how the nature of peace operations, their objectives, and their participants may change in ensuing years.

With a pragmatic rather than theoretical focus, the case studies and lessons offer some important insights. First, as this volume makes plain, today's peacekeepers often face formidable obstacles in complex environments where armed groups may splinter, coalesce, or change patrons and purposes with disorienting frequency. Indeed, the early success of impartial military cease-fire monitors—as envisioned by Lester B. Pearson, the father of the modern concept of peacekeeping—hung partially on the clear polarity of the Cold War and the clear-cut nature of most international boundaries. Today's peacekeepers do not share these advantages, but they do have the benefits of ever-growing field experience and a parallel body of peacekeeping scholarship. Unlike the first Pearson peacekeepers, today's forces can look to precedent and lessons learned from many recent operations—although each conflict environment is, like every other element of the human family, dysfunctional in its own way. As a much-needed contribution to this body of knowledge, *Twenty-First-Century Peace Operations* will inform tomorrow's peacekeepers and peacebuilders and serve as a critical guide in shaping their missions.

Second, peace operations are no longer simply about the provision of military and public security—although those remain primary goals—but also about political engineering and state building, sometimes without the consent of one or more conflicting parties. The decision of UN member states—at their September 2005 summit in New York—to endorse international responsibility for the protection of citizens from the worst excesses of their own governments portends future international interventions to stem genocide and other major crimes against humanity. At this writing, the international community's conflicted and dilatory response to ongoing, slow-motion genocide in Darfur, Sudan, shows that international will to act still tends to trail such expressions of principle, but a decade hence that will to act may be more evident, with heavy implications not only for military forces but also for any institutions that aspire to be serial keepers of the peace.

Third, since the early 1990s, the United Nations, in particular, has often been judged in the media and in policymaking circles by its peacekeeping scorecard. It is generally found wanting in effectiveness. Visible failures in the 1990s included the genocide in Rwanda and the massacres in and around Srebrenica, in Bosnia and Herzegovina. The early years of the newer missions in Sierra Leone and the Democratic Republic of Congo raised other questions about the training and discipline of UN-deployed troops and the UN's ability to meet the demands of a new era of "robust" peace operations. While Durch and the case authors pull no punches in their criticisms of certain UN decisions and are quick to point out sometimes tragic mistakes, the reader is left with an unavoidable and obvious conclusion: contemporary peacekeeping is very hard work for any institution and for the troops that it manages. By offering precise details on mission funding, politics, force levels, and organization, *Twenty-First-Century Peace Operations* demonstrates clearly that the United Nations can only be as powerful or effective as the support provided by the Security Council and by the rest of its member states. Neither the United Nations nor the peacekeepers it deploys operate in a political vacuum; it is, rather, a political vortex, and one that is becoming more, not less, intense with each passing year.

Twenty-First-Century Peace Operations is the most recent in a growing list of important and influential books and reports published by the United States Institute of Peace and by the Henry L. Stimson Center, the cosponsor of this volume. We are proud of our record of providing reliable information, authoritative analysis, and breadth of coverage, and our ability to offer practical, hardheaded lessons while also promoting and elaborating the latest scholarship. These are hallmarks of the kinds of work that both our institutions support and develop. Past Institute volumes on the United Nations and peacekeeping, published under the Institute's general congressional mandate, include *Angola's Last Best Chance for Peace,* by Paul Hare; *Council Unbound,* by Michael J. Matheson; *Mozambique,* by Richard Synge; *Peacemaking in International Conflict,* edited by William Zartman; and *The Quest for Viable Peace,* edited by Jock Covey, Michael Dziedzic, and Leonard Hawley.

The Stimson Center also has a distinguished record of publications in this field, including *The Evolution of UN Peacekeeping: Case Studies and Comparative Analysis* and *UN Peacekeeping, American Policy, and the Uncivil Wars of the 1990s,* both volumes edited by Durch; *Training for Peacekeeping: The United Nations' Role,* by Barry Blechman and J. Matthew Vaccaro, a report whose recommendations formed the core of the United Nations' first troop contributor training program; and *The Brahimi Report and the Future of UN Peace Operations,* by William Durch, Victoria Holt, Caroline Earle, and Moira Shanahan. This volume marked the third anniversary—and scored the UN's implementation—of the landmark August 2000 *Report of the Panel on United Nations Peace Operations,* an effort chaired by UN Undersecretary-General Lakhdar Brahimi, for which Durch served as project director.

In addition to its normal range of activities and publications, in 2005 the Institute formed—at the behest of Congress—a bipartisan Task Force on the United Nations to assess the efficacy of UN activities and to make actionable recommendations for UN reform. To date, the task force has published two reports on its findings: *American Interests and UN Reform* and *The Imperative for Action.* As the task force makes clear in these reports, the United Nations must undergo significant management reforms if it is to fulfill the purposes embodied in its charter and to meet the demands of the world's changing political realities.

In reading *Twenty-First-Century Peace Operations,* one is continually struck by one thought: despite the limitations and problems associated with its peace operations, the United Nations ultimately deserves more credit for what it has accomplished over the past decade in sometimes extremely adverse circumstances. As Durch and the authors lay out, UN peacekeepers often operate without sufficient funding, adequate or well-trained personnel, or even proper time to plan a fully formed strategy to stop violence or enforce peace. More significantly, the United Nations is often forced to undertake operations in hostile environments where "spoilers" seek to undermine the very peace it is trying to maintain or secure. While it is only natural to focus on what the United Nations has done wrong in drawing lessons for the future, we should also ask ourselves, what if there were no UN peacekeeping or peace support operations at all?

We trust you will find this volume an important contribution to the peacekeeping literature. We are grateful to its editor, William J. Durch, and to all the contributing authors for their fine work.

Richard H. Solomon, President   **Ellen Laipson, President and CEO**
United States Institute of Peace   Henry L. Stimson Center

Preface

Since the early 1990s, the international community has been increasingly involved in rebuilding war-torn states and societies, a role that, in this century, has included temporary governance of territories that have suffered large-scale and violent human rights violations. Most international support for peace implementation, however, followed an invite from the erstwhile combatants, who, having inked an agreement to end a stalemated conflict, sought outside help to do so.

Peace support operations (PSOs)—internationally authorized, multilateral, civil-military efforts to promote and protect such transitions from war to peace—are the subject of this volume, which treats six recent cases—Bosnia and Herzegovina under the Dayton Accords, Kosovo, East Timor, the Democratic Republic of Congo, Sierra Leone, and Afghanistan—in some detail. It does so using a common case structure that walks the reader into and through the problems that drive each case and the solutions derived to deal with them. The narrative and analytical focus, however, is specifically on the PSOs deployed in each case, on how they work and why they succeed, fail, drift, or recover. That particular, structured focus is this volume's principal contribution to the field, building on two similarly structured volumes that grew out of work at the Henry L. Stimson Center in Washington, DC.

Among the individuals whom I would like to thank for their contributions to this volume are, of course, the chapter authors, both for their research and writing and for their participation in an author's conference at Stimson following the first round of drafting. Their contributions reflect time borrowed from careers that take many of them into areas of conflict and conflict-transition routinely, some to analyze, report, and prod governments into action; others to provide humanitarian aid; and still others to champion human rights. The cases are therefore leavened, in many instances, by first-hand experience of the situations about which they write.

I would like to thank the United States Institute of Peace, its president, Richard Solomon, and its vice president for conflict analysis and prevention, Paul Stares, for their unstinting support of this project. I would also like to thank Ellen Laipson, president of the Stimson Center, and Cheryl Ramp, its chief operating officer, for their continuing confidence and institutional support. I would like to thank all of the foregoing individuals for their patience, given this project's rather long gestation.

Comments from the anonymous reviewers made this a better book and I thank them for the investment of time and effort involved. I deeply appreciate the work of the Institute's editorial and production team, in particular editors Nigel Quinney and Kurt Volkan, whose skill and patience each step of the way were essential to realizing a quality product in the end.

For invaluable research support, for key segments of chapter one, and for much-appreciated help in updating some of the cases, I would like to thank my research associate, Tobias Berkman, whose writing and analytic abilities will be missed by the Future of Peace Operations program. He is presently off to Cambridge (Massachusetts) to learn international law and public policy, after which we expect no bad guy in the world to feel safe. I would also like to thank Katherine Andrews for her unerringly accurate data gathering, keen organizing ability, and intuitive analytic skills.

Finally, I would like to thank my wife, Jane, for her love, friendship, enduring partnership and exquisite critical judgment. Without your support and advice I would be quite lost.

W. J. D.
Washington, DC
May 2006

Contributors

Tobias C. Berkman is a joint degree candidate in law and international security at Harvard Law School and the John F. Kennedy School of Government. Previously, he was a research associate and a Scoville Fellow at the Henry L. Stimson Center (2004–6). He came to Stimson from a semester of conflict resolution work at the Carter Center and several summers working at Seeds of Peace, an international coexistence program for youth from regions of conflict. He received his bachelor's degree cum laude in history and literature from Harvard University in 2002.

Eric G. Berman is managing director of the Small Arms Survey, a project of the Graduate Institute of International Studies at the University of Geneva. Previously, and during the time he worked on this manuscript, he was a visiting fellow at the Thomas J. Watson Jr. Institute for International Studies at Brown University in Providence, Rhode Island. He has also worked for the United Nations in Geneva, Nairobi, Phnom Penh, and New York. He has published widely on UN and African security issues, including: *Peacekeeping in Africa: Capabilities and Culpabilities*, Geneva: United Nations Institute for Disarmament Research, 2000 (coauthored with Katie E. Sams), and *Armed and Aimless: Armed Groups, Guns, and Human Security in the ECOWAS Region*, Geneva: Small Arms Survey, 2005 (coedited with Nicolas Florquin). His book on small arms in the Central African Republic will be published later this year.

Elizabeth Cousens is vice president of the International Peace Academy, having previously directed the Conflict Prevention and Peace Forum at the Social Science Research Council (2002–4), served with the Office of the United Nations Special Coordinator for the Middle East Peace Process, based in Gaza (2000–2), and as director of research at IPA (1997–2000). Her own research focuses on comparative peace processes, international implementation of peace agreements in civil wars, and UN peace efforts. She edited, with Chetan Kumar, *Peacebuilding as Politics* (Lynne Rienner, 2001) and also *Ending Civil Wars* (Lynne Rienner, 2002), with Donald Rothchild and Stephen Stedman. She received her DPhil and MPhil in international relations from the University of Oxford, as a Rhodes Scholar. She holds a BA in history from the University of Puget Sound and Princeton University.

Moreen Dee is a diplomatic and military historian and an editor on the *Documents on Australian Foreign Policy* series. She has written and published on peacekeeping and Australian foreign and defense relations with Southeast Asia: most recently, '*Not a matter for negotiation*': *Australia's support for Malaysia 1961–1966* (2005). She holds a master's degree in defense studies and a PhD in international relations from the University of New England.

William J. Durch is a senior associate at the Stimson Center, with stints as project director for the Panel on United Nations Peace Operations (2000) and scientific adviser to the U.S. Defense Threat Reduction Agency (1999, 2001). He has taught at Georgetown University (1989–90, 1999–2005) and at Johns Hopkins SAIS (1997–98). He was also assistant director of the MIT Defense Studies Program (1985–88); research fellow, Harvard Center for Science and International Affairs (1981–3); and foreign affairs officer at the U.S. Arms Control and Disarmament Agency (1978–81). He is coauthor of "The Economic Impact of Peacekeeping" with Michael Carnahan and Scott Gilmore (Peace Dividend Trust, 2006) and *The Brahimi Report and the Future of Peace Operations*, with Victoria K. Holt and others (Stimson, 2003). He edited and contributed to two previous peace operations case books from St. Martin's Press, and holds a BSFS from the Georgetown School of Foreign Service and a PhD in political science from MIT.

Michael J. Dziedzic has been a senior program officer at the United States Institute of Peace since June 2001. He was principal drafter of the "Standards for Kosovo" published in December 2003 by the UN Interim Administration Mission in Kosovo and strategic planner for UNMIK in 2000. A thirty-year U.S. Air Force career included postings as senior military fellow, Institute for National Strategic Studies, National Defense University (1995–9), where he headed the Peace Operations Team; faculty member, National War College (1994–5); air attaché, El Salvador (1992–4); political-military planner, Air Staff, the Pentagon (1992); tenured professor of political science, U.S. Air Force Academy; and visiting fellow, International Institute for Strategic Studies, London (1987–8). He coedited and contributed to *The Quest for Viable Peace* (USIP Press, 2005) with Jock Covey and Len Hawley, and *Policing the New World Disorder* (NDU Press, 1998) with Robert Oakley. He holds a PhD in government from the University of Texas at Austin.

David Harland is presently serving as director of change management in the UN Department of Peacekeeping Operations, where he previously directed the revival of the department's now highly regarded Best Practices Section. He has also served as senior policy adviser to the UN Office for the Coordination of Humanitarian Affairs in Geneva and in a series of UN field postings: as acting deputy special representative of the secretary-general for the UN Transitional Administration in East Timor; head of Civil Affairs, UN Mission in Bosnia and Herzegovina; and senior civil affairs officer, UN Protection Force, Sarajevo. He is author of *Killing Game* (Praeger, 1994) and has written a range of articles and op-ed pieces on international law, international relations, and peacekeeping that have appeared in the *International Herald Tribune* and elsewhere. He holds an MA from Harvard University and a PhD from the Fletcher School of Law and Diplomacy, Tufts University.

Melissa T. Labonte is assistant professor of political science at the University of Richmond. Her research and teaching focuses on international nongovernmental organizations, international organizations, multilateral peace operations, peacebuilding and conflict transitions, international law, and the politics of humanitarianism. In 2004–05, she was a visiting scholar with the Global Security Program at Brown University's Watson Institute for International Studies, and she has taught previously at Brown and at Providence College. Her recent publications include "Dimensions of Post-Conflict Peacebuilding and Democratization," *Global Governance* 9, no. 2 (2003) and "Humanitarian Actors and the Politics of Preventive Action: Is There Room in the Peace-Building Framework?" in *Building Sustainable Peace,* ed. W. Andy Knight and Tom Keating (University of Alberta Press, 2004). She holds a PhD in political science from Brown.

John Prendergast is a senior adviser at the International Crisis Group. He worked in the White House and the State Department in the Clinton Administration from 1996 to 2001 and has worked for a variety of nongovernmental organizations and think tanks in Africa and the United States, including the United States Institute of Peace, Human Rights Watch/Africa, the Fund for Peace, and UNICEF/Operation Lifeline Sudan. He has authored or coauthored seven books on Africa and given interviews or published articles and commentaries on African conflict issues and U.S. foreign policy in many major print and broadcast media, including the *Economist, Washington Post, New York Times, Los Angeles Times, Wall Street Journal, News Hour with Jim Lehrer,* and *Charlie Rose.* He holds a BA in urban policy from Temple University and an MA in international development from American University.

Philip Roessler is a doctoral candidate in the Department of Government and Politics at the University of Maryland and a David L. Boren Graduate Fellow. He has worked as a field analyst for the International Crisis Group and traveled extensively in parts of Africa. His publications include articles in the journals, *Comparative Politics* and *American Journal of Political Science.* He is currently working on a project on political authority and civil war in Africa and is based at the Woodrow Wilson International Center for Scholars as an Africanist Doctoral Candidate Fellow.

Since 2002, **"Mike" Smith** has served as chief executive officer of AUSTCARE, an independent, nonprofit humanitarian aid and development organization based in Australia. Previously, he served for thirty-four years with the Australian Defence Force, retiring in February 2002 with the rank of major general. His last posting was as deputy force commander for the UN Transitional Administration in East Timor

(2000–2), following other operational service in Papua New Guinea, Kashmir, and Cambodia. In 1998, he was team leader and principal author for the Australian Army's keystone strategic doctrine, *The Fundamentals of Land Warfare.* He is widely published on issues of national security, strategy, peacekeeping, leadership, military history, and defense assistance to regional countries. A graduate of the Royal Military College, Duntroon, the Australian Army Command and Staff College, and Australian Defence College, he holds a BA in history from the University of New South Wales and an MA in international relations from the Australian National University.

J Alexander Thier is senior rule of law adviser at the United States Institute of Peace. Previously, he directed the Project on Failed States at Stanford University's Center on Democracy, Development, and the Rule of Law. From 2002 to 2004, Thier was legal adviser to Afghanistan's Constitutional and Judicial Reform Commissions in Kabul, where he assisted in the development of a new constitution and judicial system. He worked as a UN and NGO official in Afghanistan during the civil war from 1993 to 1996, where he was officer-in-charge of the Kabul branch of the UN Office for the Coordination of Humanitarian Assistance to Afghanistan. He also served as coordination officer for the UN Iraq Program in New York. An attorney, Thier has a BA from Brown University, a master's degree in law and diplomacy from the Fletcher School at Tufts University, and a JD from Stanford Law School.

Glossary of Acronyms

Acronyms are generally based on an organization's name as expressed in the local language, which is translated into English for the glossary entry.

AACA   Afghan Assistance Coordination Authority (Afghan interim administration)

AAK   Alliance for the Future of Kosovo

AEC   Australian Electoral Commission

AFDL   Alliance of Democratic Forces for the Liberation of Congo (Laurent Kabila's coalition, 1997)

AFRC   Armed Forces Revolutionary Council (ousted Sierra Leone government, 1997)

AID   Agency for International Development (U.S.)

ALIR   Army for the Liberation of Rwanda (Rwandan armed group, eastern Congo, included *génocidaires* from 1994)

AMF   Afghan Militia Forces

ANA   Afghan National Army (new national army, 2002 onward)

AOR   Area of responsibility

APC   All People's Congress (ruling party, Sierra Leone, 1967–92)

APC   Congolese Popular Army (armed wing of RCD-K/ML)

APEC   Asia-Pacific Economic Cooperation

Apodeti	Timorese Popular Democratic Association (pro-integration political movement)
ASEAN	Association of Southeast Asian Nations
AU	African Union
BiH	Bosnia and Herzegovina
BPK	Banking and Payments Authority of Kosovo (central bank)
CAT-A	Civil Affairs Team–Alpha (U.S. in Afghanistan)
CCP	Commission for the Consolidation of Peace (Sierra Leone)
CDF	Civil Defense Force (local militias, Sierra Leone)
CFA	Central Fiscal Authority (Kosovo budget, treasury, and tax office)
CFC-A	Combined Forces Command–Afghanistan (U.S. Coalition forces from June 2003)
CIA	Central Intelligence Agency (U.S.)
CIMIC	Civil-military cooperation
CIU	Criminal Intelligence Unit (UNMIK police)
CJCMOTF	Coalition Joint Civil-Military Operations Task Force (Afghanistan)
CJTF-180	Combined/Joint Task Force 180 (Coalition forces in Afghanistan, to June 2003)
CMOC	Civil-Military Operations Center
CMRRD	Commission for the Management of Strategic Resources, National Reconstruction, and Development (Sierra Leone)
CNRT	National Council for Timorese Resistance (pro-independence political group)
COMISAF	ISAF commander
COMKFOR	KFOR commander
CPU	Civilian Police Unit (UN)
DAC	Development Assistance Committee, Organization for Economic Co-operation and Development

DDR	Disarmament, demobilization, and reintegration
DFAT	Department of Foreign Affairs and Trade (Australia)
DfID	Department for International Development (UK)
DPA	Department of Political Affairs (UN)
DPKO	Department of Peacekeeping Operations (UN)
DRC	Democratic Republic of the Congo
EASC	Election Appeals Sub-Commission (Bosnia and Herzegovina)
EC	European Community or European Commission
EC TAFKO	European Commission Task Force for the Reconstruction of Kosovo (EU)
ECOMOG	ECOWAS Cease-Fire Monitoring Group
ECOWAS	Economic Community of West African States
EO	Executive Outcomes (private security provider)
EU	European Union
EUFOR	European Union Force in Bosnia and Herzegovina
EUPM	European Union Police Mission in Bosnia and Herzegovina
FAC	Congolese Armed Forces (army of Laurent Kabila's regime)
Falintil	Armed Forces for the National Liberation of East Timor (pro-independence)
Falintil–FDTL	Defense Force of Timor-Leste (new national army, includes former Falintil)
FAR	Rwandan Armed Forces (Rwandan army, to July 1994)
FARDC	Armed Forces of the Democratic Republic of the Congo (new integrated army, post-2002)
FDLR	Democratic Forces for the Liberation of Rwanda (Rwandan Hutu rebel group based in DRC; subsumed ALIR)
FIPI	Front for Integration and Peace in Ituri (splinter group of UPC)
FNI	Nationalist and Integrationist Front (Ituri armed group, Lendu)

Fretilin	Revolutionary Front for an Independent East Timor (pro-independence)
FRY	Former Republic of Yugoslavia
G-8	Group of Eight
GDP	Gross domestic product
GPA	Governance and Public Administration (component of UNTAET)
HAER	Humanitarian Assistance and Emergency Rehabilitation (component of UNTAET)
HCIC	Humanitarian Community Information Center (humanitarian coordination mechanism, Kosovo)
HDZ	Croatian Democratic Union (nationalist Croatian political party)
HIRC	House International Relations Committee
ICC	International Criminal Court
ICFY	International Conference on the Former Yugoslavia (1992 peace talks)
ICTY	International Criminal Tribunal for the Former Yugoslavia
IDP	Internally displaced person
IEBL	Inter-Entity Boundary Line (separates Bosniac-Croat Federation from the RS)
IEMF	Interim Emergency Multinational Force (EU force in Bunia, DRC)
IFOR	Implementation Force (NATO force in Bosnia and Herzegovina)
IMATT	International Military Advisory and Training Team (British led, Sierra Leone)
IMF	International Monetary Fund
IMTF	Integrated Mission Task Force (UN)
INTERFET	International Force in East Timor (Australian-led multinational force)
IOM	International Organization for Migration
IPA	International Peace Academy

IPC	Ituri Pacification Commission (interim Ituri government, DRC)
IPTF	International Police Task Force (UN, Bosnia and Herzegovina)
ISAF	International Security Assistance Force (Afghanistan)
ISI	Inter-Services Intelligence (Pakistan's military intelligence agency)
JEMB	Joint Electoral Management Board (Afghanistan)
JIAS	Joint Interim Administrative Structure (Kosovo local governance structure)
JMC	Joint Military Commission (DRC)
JMG	Joint Monitoring Group (Sierra Leone)
JNA	Yugoslav People's Army
JPG	Joint Planning Group (UNMIK)
JVM	Joint verification mechanism (military officers from DRC and Rwanda)
KCB	Kosovo Consolidated Budget
KEK	Komitet Elektroprivredne Korporacije (Kosovo's electric company)
KFOR	Kosovo Force (NATO, Kosovo)
KLA	Kosovo Liberation Army (ethnic Albanian nationalist military organization)
KOPASSUS	Indonesian Special Forces Command
KPC	Kosovo Protection Corps
KPS	Commission on Peace and Stability (East Timor)
KPS	Kosovo Police Service
KVM	Kosovo Verification Mission (OSCE)
LDK	Democratic League of Kosovo (pro-independence)
MDTF	Multi-Donor Trust Fund (for DDR in Sierra Leone)
Milob	Military observer
MLC	Movement for the Liberation of Congo (DRC rebel group backed by Uganda)
MLO	Military liaison officer

MNB	Multinational Brigade (KFOR, SFOR)
MND	Multinational Division (IFOR)
MONUC	UN Organization Mission in the Democratic Republic of the Congo
MPR	People's Consultative Assembly (highest legislative body of Indonesia)
MPS	Military Planning Staff
NAC	North Atlantic Council (NATO)
NATO	North Atlantic Treaty Organization
NCC	National Consultative Council (East Timor)
NCDDR	National Committee for Disarmament, Demobilization, and Reintegration (Sierra Leone)
NDP	New defensive position (DRC)
NGO	Nongovernmental organization
NLA	National Liberation Army (ethnic Albanian nationalist military organization in Macedonia)
NMG	Neutral Monitoring Group (Sierra Leone, oversees withdrawal of forces, disarmament, and repatriation operations)
NPFL	National Patriotic Front of Liberia (Liberian rebel group led by Charles Taylor)
NPRC	National Provisional Ruling Council (Sierra Leone)
OAU	Organization of African Unity
OCHA	Office for the Coordination of Humanitarian Affairs (UN)
OHDACA	Overseas Humanitarian, Disaster, and Civic Aid (U.S. Department of Defense)
OHR	Office of the High Representative (chief civilian peace implementation agency in Bosnia and Herzegovina)
OIOS	Office of Internal Oversight Services (UN)
OSCE	Organization for Security and Co-operation in Europe
PCR	Postconflict reconstruction
PDK	Kosovo Democratic Party (main political successor of the KLA)

PDPA	People's Democratic Party of Afghanistan (Communist, took power in 1978)
PEC	Provisional Election Commission (Bosnia and Herzegovina, chaired by OSCE)
PIC	Peace Implementation Council (created by Dayton Accords for Bosnia and Herzegovina)
PIFWCs	Persons indicted for war crimes
PISG	Provisional Institutions of Self-Government (Kosovo)
PNTL	East Timor Police Service (national police)
POE	Publicly Owned Enterprise (Kosovo)
POLRI	Polisi Republik Indonesia (Indonesian police)
PRRP	Priority Reconstruction and Recovery Program (Bosnia and Herzegovina)
PRT	Provincial Reconstruction Team (Afghanistan, Coalition or NATO led)
PSO	Peace support operation
RCD	Congolese Rally for Democracy (DRC resistance movement)
RCD-Goma	Congolese Rally for Democracy–Goma (supported by Rwanda)
RCD-K/ML	Congolese Rally for Democracy–Kisangani/Liberation Movement (Kisangani faction of the RCD-ML)
RCD-ML	Congolese Rally for Democracy–Liberation Movement (breakaway faction of RCD-Goma, originally backed by Uganda)
RENAMO	Mozambican National Resistance
RPA	Rwandan Patriotic Army (Tutsi-dominated Rwandan army, since July 1994)
RPF	Rwandan Patriotic Front (expatriate Tutsi rebel faction, to mid-1994; formed new government in July 1994)
RRTF	Reconstruction and Return Task Force (Bosnia and Herzegovina, OHR)
RS	Republika Srpska (Serb-dominated territory of Bosnia and Herzegovina)

RSLAF	Republic of Sierra Leone Armed Forces (new national army)
RUF	Revolutionary United Front (Sierra Leone, rebel group)
SACEUR	Supreme Allied Commander Europe (NATO)
SADC	Southern African Development Community
SBS	State Border Service (Bosnia and Herzegovina, new service trained by UNMIBH)
SDA	Party for Democratic Action (Muslim political party, Bosnia and Herzegovina)
SDS	Serbian Democratic Party (Serbian nationalist political party in Croatia)
SFOR	Stabilization Force (NATO force in Bosnia and Herzegovina, after December 1996)
SFRY	Socialist Federal Republic of Yugoslavia
S-G	Secretary-General (UN)
SLA	Sierra Leone Army
SLP	Sierra Leone Police
SLPP	Sierra Leone People's Party
SOE	Socially Owned Enterprise (Kosovo)
SPU	Specialized Police Unit (UN)
SRSG	Special representative of the secretary-general (UN)
SSR	Security sector reform
TNI	Indonesian military
TRC	Truth and Reconciliation Commission (Sierra Leone)
UCPMB	Liberation Army of Presevo, Medvedje, Bujanovac (ethnic Albanian insurgents)
UDT	Timorese Democratic Union
UN	United Nations
UNAMA	UN Assistance Mission in Afghanistan
UNAMET	UN Mission in East Timor
UNAMSIL	UN Mission in Sierra Leone
UNDP	UN Development Programme
UNESCO	UN Educational, Scientific, and Cultural Organization

UNHCR	UN High Commissioner for Refugees
UNHOC	UN Humanitarian Operations Centre
UNICEF	UN Children's Fund
UNITA	National Union for the Total Independence of Angola (Angolan rebel movement)
UNITF	UN INTERFET Trust Fund
UNMEE	UN Mission in Ethiopia and Eritrea
UNMIBH	UN Mission in Bosnia and Herzegovina
UNMIK	UN Interim Administration Mission in Kosovo
UNMISET	UN Mission of Support in East Timor
UNOCHA	UN Office for the Coordination of Humanitarian Assistance to Afghanistan
UNOCI	UN Operation in Côte d'Ivoire
UNOMSIL	UN Observer Mission in Sierra Leone
UNOPS	UN Office for Project Services
UNOTIL	UN Office in Timor-Leste (UN political mission)
UNPOL	UN police
UNPROFOR	UN Protection Force
UNSMA	UN Special Mission to Afghanistan
UNTAET	UN Transitional Administration in East Timor
UPC	Union of Congolese Patriots (Ituri armed group, Hema)
UPDF	Uganda People's Defence Force (national armed forces)
WFP	World Food Programme
WHO	World Health Organization

Twenty-First-Century
Peace Operations

1

Restoring and Maintaining Peace

What We Know So Far

William J. Durch, with Tobias C. Berkman

According to scholars of global conflict, the incidence and magnitude of warfare, especially "societal" warfare—that which is primarily internal to states—climbed more or less steadily from the mid-1960s through the early 1990s, until the end of the Cold War, when it began to decline. The curve continued downward through the end of the 1990s and into the new century, to apparent levels of relative peace not enjoyed by humankind for forty years.[1] A rising proportion of these conflicts ended, however, not in victory for one side but in stalemate or outside intervention.

This book is about the international tools developed, largely since that curve turned downward, to deal with the aftermath of stalemated wars, especially internal/societal wars, the ones that halted with outcomes that were to no one participant's complete satisfaction or that were stopped by outside military force. It is thus about high-risk environments with imperfect deals (or deals sought after the fact), devastated economies, and governments that, in the past, likely provided little in the way of public services and listened very little to the voices of the governed. It is about international efforts to support (or guide, or control)

1

the difficult tasks of rebuilding and restructuring both governments and economies, almost always with the stated goal of leaving behind some semblance of functioning and sustainable market democracy. These tasks are usually undertaken with imperfect knowledge, limited resources, and uncertain prospects of success, because not to undertake them would be acquiescing in something worse—the creation of a terrorist haven or a drug transit zone, or the abandonment of the humanitarian and democratic principles that the West has been pressing upon the rest of the world for the past half-century. It is intellectually easy to write off a "failed or failing" state as a bad investment but, like a neglected and decaying neighborhood, dystopias have a way of spreading.[2]

In particular, this book is about the ongoing development of peace support operations (PSOs). These have evolved from largely UN-led military monitoring teams on disputed borders in the Middle East and South Asia, to enterprises that also engage the attention and resources of regional organizations such as the European Union and the African Union, of military alliances such as the North Atlantic Treaty Organization (NATO), and of powerful if temporary "coalitions of the willing."[3] The book is the third in a sequence of edited volumes growing out of work on peacekeeping and postconflict security undertaken at the Henry L. Stimson Center. Like its predecessors, it uses the method of focused, structured comparison of detailed cases, in the firm belief that broadly valid lessons about the complex problems of restoring peace in war-damaged lands can best be drawn out by using a common analytic structure applied to different sets of experiences.

Each of the six cases in the book briefly describes the geography and contemporary conflict history of the country (or other territory) of interest and then

- describes the process of negotiating the peace accord, if there was one, and summarizes what that accord called for in terms of outside implementation
- assesses support for that accord within the host country, among the country's immediate neighbors, and among the great powers
- summarizes the peace operation's mandate, how it may have changed over time, and what such changes meant for the operation and the country

- describes how the operation was funded, planned, and carried out
- assesses how well the operation accomplished its tasks and whether its mandate made sense in the circumstances
- offers broader conclusions about the operation's lessons or implications for efforts to implement peace elsewhere

Following the case studies, the final chapter summarizes lessons from them for future operations and offers some thoughts on how peace support operations, their objectives, and their participants may change over the next few years.

The remainder of this chapter briefly summarizes the history of peace operations through the late 1990s; examines the ongoing debate about how to define exactly what PSOs are and do; positions PSOs in the wider context of conflict and global assistance; reviews studies since the second volume in this series appeared that offer analytical frameworks for peace operations or structured lessons learned; and then provides an introduction to the "third surge" in PSOs that the cases in this volume address. The chapter annex offers details on an element of peace operations that governments always care about, namely, how much they cost and who pays for them.

Peacekeeping at the End of the Cold War

The first book in this sequence examined how UN operations through 1991 were planned and funded and offered twenty structured cases of UN peacekeeping from 1948 through mid-1991.[4] The last four years of that period saw the first surge in demand for peacekeepers, as the Cold War came to an end and external patrons and intervenors withdrew from some long-running struggles. UN observers watched the Soviet army leave Afghanistan and both Cuban and South African forces leave Angola. UN observers also patrolled the 870-mile border between Iran and Iraq at the end of those countries' bloody eight-year war. In 1989, the United Nations returned to complex peace operations—those having civil/political as well as military components—for the first time since leaving the chaotic ex–Belgian Congo in 1964, with a mission to support Namibia's transition to independence. This operation was widely considered successful, despite a somewhat rocky start, as UN officials monitored and promoted the vote for a constituent assembly and dogged the movements of the colonial government's special police units to reduce their harassment of would-be voters. In Central America, UN peacekeepers provided security for the disarming and disbandment of the Nicaraguan Contras, the insurgent force trained and equipped by the Reagan administration to undermine that country's leftist Sandinista government.

Back in Africa, a UN force prepared to repatriate thousands of refugees from Western Sahara as soon as a referendum determined whether that region would be independent from or merge into Morocco. When neither the government nor its Sahrawi adversaries would risk a vote whose outcome was uncertain, the referendum was postponed and as of this writing still has not been held, despite more than a decade of diplomatic effort. A UN observer mission still watches the sand berm that separates the two sides and runs through 2,000 miles of trackless desert. Finally, the United Nations became deeply involved in attempting to settle the civil war in Angola, a country that had known mostly war both before and after independence from Portugal in 1974. A modest UN observer mission could neither guarantee preelection disarmament of the opposing forces nor adequately monitor the fairness of the fall 1992 national elections, and the loser regrouped his forces and took them back to war. These results in Angola were a harbinger of disasters to come as the United Nations became involved in increasingly unstable conflict situations not only in Africa but also in Europe, where the Socialist Federal Republic of Yugoslavia (SFRY) was coming apart at the seams.

The second book in this sequence continued the story with the relatively brief but deadly "second surge" of operations in El Salvador, Angola, Mozambique, Cambodia, the SFRY (soon to be known as "the former Yugoslavia"), Somalia, and Rwanda from 1993 through 1995.[5] These were generally tougher cases than the earlier ones. The latter four involved either ongoing civil wars or wars that peace accords had interrupted but not solved, whose belligerent parties were committed only tenuously to peace or not committed at all. Although the United Nations had chalked up some successes in these cases by the mid-1990s—in El Salvador and Mozambique, and to some degree in Cambodia—its failures are better remembered. UN peacekeepers could not prevent the

1994 genocide in Rwanda or the 1995 Srebrenica massacre in Bosnia and Herzegovina; could not prevent the resumption of civil war (again) in Angola; and, not two months into their deployment in Somalia, found themselves at war with a powerful Somali faction, which led to intervention by U.S. special operations forces and thence to the firefight in Mogadishu chronicled in *Black Hawk Down*.[6] Frustrated by these failures, UN member states largely turned away from the organization as a manager of major peacekeeping initiatives. Thus, between 1995 and 1999, the United Nations launched just two robust peace operations, in eastern Croatia and in Haiti. Both were relatively short-lived, with the former viewed as a success, the latter ultimately not.[7] Meanwhile, most troop contributions, especially from developed states, went to operations run by NATO.

The Struggle to Define the Enterprise

"Peacekeeping" was the term coined to describe the tasks of UN-mandated troops deployed after the Suez Crisis of 1956. It gained official status of sorts when the UN General Assembly set up the Special Committee on Peacekeeping Operations in February 1965, just after UN forces finished their first operation in the former Belgian Congo.[8] It was not defined in any UN document, however, until *An Agenda for Peace* appeared in 1992.[9] In the meantime, scholars put forward their own definitions of UN practice.[10]

Evolving Typologies: Practice Meets Theory

Conceptual discord has grown as PSOs have added dimensions beyond military security. The discord reflects the elusive nature and boundaries of this field and the many disagreements about where to draw those boundaries. The number of moving parts in PSOs, their changeability over time and place, and these operations' susceptibility to the political whims of many different decision makers mean that analysts of PSOs deal with an open and changing set of variables, actors, and objectives (see table 1.1).

In 1992, John Mackinlay and Jarat Chopra recognized that peacekeeping was pushing beyond its traditional bounds. Their work on "second-generation multinational operations" incorporated many forms of military action that went beyond peacekeeping, particularly in the use of force. Their informal scale of operations bears a close family resemblance to what the U.S. military would later incorporate into "peace enforcement" under the rubric of "operations other than war." When Mackinlay and Chopra used the term "enforcement," however, they meant it in the original sense of Article 42 of the UN Charter, namely, the collective use of force to resist aggression and thereby maintain or restore international peace and security.[11]

William Durch parsed peace operations into four general categories but warned that the amount of force entailed by "humanitarian intervention" in particular can vary a great deal, ranging upward to become peace enforcement for humanitarian purposes. He also observed that the amount or intensity of force needed by an operation can vary significantly over time.[12] Daniel Byman and his coauthors reached a similar conclusion, stressing that military assistance to humanitarian aid providers may involve restoring order first, a potentially "unlimited, open-ended responsibility, which may be difficult to relinquish safely." Because the operational environment for humanitarian interventions can be so difficult, they argued, forces should both plan and be equipped to enforce their mandate and mission objectives, if necessary.[13]

Paul Diehl, Daniel Druckman, and James Wall developed a long taxonomy of "actual and potential" peacekeeping missions that they parsed into four "mission clusters" using quantitative methods. Diehl later summarized these clusters as "monitoring," "limiting damage," "restoring civil societies," and "coercive." He warned against giving multiple missions to one force, using Somalia as an example of a disastrous admixture of pacification and humanitarian assistance. "Divergent missions," he argued, "are best handled by different sets of personnel or separate operations."[14]

Trevor Findlay used a fairly standard mission typology in his work except for the term "expanded peacekeeping," by which he meant a "multifunctional operation linked to and integrated with an entire peace process." A multifunctional operation combines military force with non-military elements and objectives—human rights, elections, support for humanitarian relief—under a single chain of authority.[15] Charlotte Ku and the late Harold Jacobson developed a five-part classification

Table 1.1. Comparing Researchers' Typologies of Peace Operations

Use of Force (most to least likely, reading down)

Mackinlay and Chopra (1992)	Durch (1996)	Byman et al. (2000) (principal tasks)	Diehl (2001) (mission clusters)	Findlay (2002)	Ku and Jacobson (2002)	Bellamy, Williams, and Griffin (2004)
Enforcement	Peace enforcement ←	Restoring order	Coercive missions	Enforcement	Enforcement	Peace enforcement
Sanctions enforcement		Enforcing a peace agreement		Peace enforcement		Peace support operations
Guarantee of rights of passage		Protecting humanitarian assistance			Force to ensure compliance with international mandates	
Protecting delivery of humanitarian assistance	Humanitarian intervention					
Assisting in the maintenance of law and order	Multi-dimensional peace operations		Restoring civil society	Expanded peacekeeping (including humanitarian operations)		Wider peacekeeping
Supervising a cease-fire between irregular forces						
Preventive peacekeeping		Humanitarian assistance	Limiting damage (humanitarian aid and preventive deployment)		Peacekeeping plus state building	Managing transitions
Traditional peacekeeping	Traditional peacekeeping			Traditional peacekeeping	Traditional peacekeeping	Traditional peacekeeping
Conventional observer missions			Monitoring		Monitoring and observation	

Sources: See chapter endnotes 11–17.

scheme in their study of democratic accountability and the use of force.[16] What Durch called multidimensional peace operations, and Diehl called restoring civil society and Findlay called expanded peacekeeping, Ku and Jacobson called "peacekeeping plus state-building." Their term "force to ensure compliance with international mandates" encompasses all coercive uses of force short of war, while war, in their taxonomy, as in Mackinlay and Chopra's, is represented by "enforcement."

Finally, Bellamy, Williams, and Griffin offered a mission typology whose first step up from traditional peacekeeping is "managing transitions," complex but consent-based operations to implement intrastate peace agreements in situations of relative calm. The next step, "wider peacekeeping," involves situations of relative chaos, with military forces deployed in situations of ongoing violence but still bound by the rules of traditional peacekeeping (consent, impartiality, and nonuse of force); indeed, the category conveys a sense of "bridging" missions asked to do too much with too little. In contrast, the authors defined "peace support operations" as enforcing a political agreement, "the substance of which has been *dictated by the interveners* and supports the establishment of liberal democracy" (emphasis added). This definition leans more heavily on the imposition of outcomes than, say, NATO's definition of the same term. Finally, the authors used the term "peace enforcement" in the same way that Mackinlay and Chopra, Findlay, and Ku and Jacobson used the single word "enforcement." Their usage comports closely, however, with the most recent evolution of British doctrine.[17]

This debate notwithstanding, a consensus has emerged regarding the need for competent and effective security forces to stabilize the local situation. Peacekeepers provide interim security and stability in a situation that is formally postwar (where there is agreement on peace) but actually still in transition from war to peace; not all factions' behavior may as yet be compliant with the agreement, and splinter factions may deny its validity. The peacekeepers protect the peacebuilders, who work for institutional, political, and economic changes that will prevent the recurrence of conflict. The August 2000 *Report of the Panel on United Nations Peace Operations* (also known as the Brahimi Report) emphasized that without successful peacebuilding, the outside security providers could be stuck in that role indefinitely.[18] The Brahimi Report defined peacebuilding as activities undertaken on the far side of conflict to reassemble the foundations of peace and provide the tools for building on those foundations something that is more than just the absence of war. Thus, peacebuilding includes but is not limited to reintegrating former combatants into the civilian economy; strengthening the rule of law (for example, through training and restructuring of local police, and judicial and penal reform); and improving respect for human rights through monitoring, education, and investigation of past and present abuse; providing technical assistance for democratic development (including electoral assistance and support for free media); and promoting conflict resolution and reconciliation techniques.[19]

When peacebuilding accomplishes such ends, and promotes within local institutions the capacity to sustain them, the peacekeepers can go home. But if the Brahimi Report's authors hoped to add final definitional clarity to the concept of peacebuilding, their effort failed. Nearly five years later, a study commissioned by the UN Department of Political Affairs concluded that "peacebuilding" continued to lack consensus definition both inside and outside the UN system.[20] Some countries, agencies, and organizations prefer different terms entirely, eschewing "peacemaking," "-keeping," "-building," or "-enforcing" in favor of such terms as "nation building," "state building," "stabilization," "reconstruction," "conflict transition," or "conflict transformation." Indeed, in some leading U.S. government circles at mid-decade, "peace" seemed to have become, somewhat ironically, a fighting word.

PSOs and the Larger International Environment

PSOs can be readily situated within a much larger environment of international relations and programs to prevent and mitigate conflict (long-term, via political, economic, and human development; and short-term, via diplomatic and other interventions intended to keep crises in check, plus efforts to control terrorist organizations and activities). Figure 1.1 locates the components of peace operations within this larger environment.

The horizontal axis is a nominal timeline running from peacetime ("preconflict") through wartime to the difficult period of recovery from war. The vertical axis situates activities according to their level of

Figure 1.1. Peace Operations and the Larger International Environment

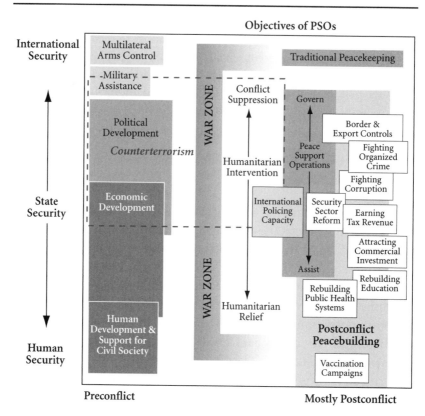

Objectives of PSOs

International Security — State Security — Human Security

Multilateral Arms Control

-Military- Assistance

Political Development

Counterterrorism

Economic Development

Human Development & Support for Civil Society

WAR ZONE

WAR ZONE

Conflict Suppression

Humanitarian Intervention

Humanitarian Relief

Govern

Peace Support Operations

International Policing Capacity

Security Sector Reform

Assist

Traditional Peacekeeping

Border & Export Controls

Fighting Organized Crime

Fighting Corruption

Earning Tax Revenue

Attracting Commercial Investment

Rebuilding Education

Rebuilding Public Health Systems

Postconflict Peacebuilding

Vaccination Campaigns

Preconflict   Mostly Postconflict

focus and effect: on international security (top of the chart), state security (middle), and human/personal security (bottom).

All of the activities on the left-hand side of the chart can be considered conflict preventive in some broad sense, from controlling armaments and the trade in them to building more responsive and democratic government, public order, and the rule of law ("political development"); strengthening economies and promoting equitable growth ("economic development"); and promoting civil society, education, health, and human rights ("human development").

Peace operations map onto this chart from the center rightward. Some, characterized in figure 1.1 as "humanitarian intervention," attempt to suppress conflict (as did NATO in Kosovo, 1999) or provide palliative aid while fighting continues (as did the United Nations in Bosnia, 1992–95). The security elements of peace operations (military forces and police contingents) may take over responsibility from an intervention force and support peacebuilding across a broad spectrum of activities. Elements of PSOs may monitor, advise, restructure, or temporarily replace the local law enforcement sector and/or other sectors of government, depending on the mission mandate.

Many of the boxes within the larger environment of peacebuilding overlap on the chart, and do so even more in reality. Thus, reform of the local security sector (military, police, courts, prisons) may be essential to fighting corruption, and fighting corruption may be essential to effective and lasting reform. Organized crime also feeds corruption, while effective border and export controls can be key tools in fighting such crime, especially those gangs that specialize in regional or even global commodities smuggling and human trafficking.

Some of the elements of peacebuilding that usually lie outside the ambit of PSOs are mapped onto figure 1.1 for illustrative purposes as they may occur contemporaneously. These include attracting outside investment, rebuilding educational and public health systems, and conducting internationally managed campaigns to vaccinate infants and children against infectious diseases. Not indicated on the chart are the many private actors (both commercial contractors and nonprofit organizations) that are almost always simultaneously engaged in parallel with PSOs, sometimes following their own agendas and sometimes executing the policies and programs of national or international aid and development agencies.

Framing the Problem, Seeking Success: The Recent Literature

The realization that restoring durable peace required much more than just ending overt fighting generated a growing literature on complex PSOs. Since contemporary PSOs aspire to be problem-solving ventures, the literature has tended to illuminate and seek solutions to the most recent and vexing problems encountered in the field. Through the mid-1990s, these included the new and sensitive problem of protecting humanitarian relief, which begged the further question of what, if anything, to do for those who received it. Both fighting (Somalia) and not fighting (Bosnia) on behalf of recipients seemed to produce less than desirable outcomes.

Much discussion and debate also was devoted to the problem of civil-military coordination in complex PSOs; to the problem of tardy deployments of military and police contingents for such operations; to problems of troop and police quality, especially among forces provided to UN operations; and to strategies for dealing with would-be "spoilers" of peace processes.[21] Over time it became clear that any PSO facing possible violent spoiler actions needed to be able to deter or, if necessary, defeat such actions. Indeed, as the veto-wielding Western members of the Security Council (the United States, the United Kingdom, and France) became more involved in peace operations in the 1990s, they reconceptualized the endeavor as, essentially, very low intensity conflict with a "hearts-and-minds" annex.

French doctrine evolved first, in the mid-1990s, but all three powers now see peacekeeping and peace enforcement as waypoints on a single continuum that runs from non-use to maximum use of force. Although U.S. and British doctrine retain an emphasis on winning hearts and minds, only British doctrine seems to value UN mandates as furthering the international legitimacy of peace operations.[22] These three states, which possess most of the world's military expeditionary capabilities, heavily influence NATO PSO doctrine. Two are key contributors to European Union (EU) doctrine, and all are likely to have a hand in shaping African Union (AU) doctrine, via their respective bilateral aid programs and through the Global Peace Operations Initiative approved at the 2004 Sea Island Summit of the Group of Eight (G8).

Astute military analysts, meanwhile, recognized that military forces could not avoid at least initial involvement in the politics and public security dilemmas of the places where they deployed, because the military almost always deploys faster than international police or civilian PSO personnel.[23] As interim security forces, however, militaries face a number of choices they would prefer to avoid, such as whether to protect threatened civilians and, if so, under what circumstances; whether to prepare for and engage in riot and crowd control;

and whether to seek out indicted war criminals, fight smugglers, or confront organized crime.

In the rest of this section we focus on works that attempted to shape lessons from "peace implementation" into evaluative or predictive frameworks intended to give guidance to future policymakers contemplating involvement in other peoples' war zones. We emphasize materials published since the appearance of the previous volume in this series.

Searching for the Sources of "Situational Difficulty"

Civil wars last longer, on average, than wars between states. While acknowledging the contributions of "contested values and identities that underlie many protracted conflicts," Charles King (1997) argued that the structure of internal conflicts also contributes substantially to their duration.[24] Structural variables include: faction leaders' personal commitments to the struggle; the difficulty of assessing the true battlefield situation and whether victory really is unattainable; the relatively weak command and control structures of many belligerent groups, which make leaders' commitments hard to enforce upon the rank and file; fears that compromises made to reach an accord may splinter the group and leave the weaker shards more vulnerable to individual defeat; leaders' and groups' reluctance to forgo the economic spoils of war; the desire to avenge the dead and make good other sunk costs of conflict; and the security dilemma, whereby giving up the fight without guarantees that opponents will do likewise exposes the peace-minded to the risk of ambush and encourages hedging behavior.[25]

External powers, King argued, can influence many of these factors in ways that favor an end to fighting, by providing services that the local belligerent parties cannot provide for themselves or that peace requires but that they would not voluntarily seek. The latter "services" include the curtailing of direct outside aid to the belligerents and/or curtailing their ability to sell war-financing commodities (such as gems, precious metals, or drugs) in collusion with neighboring states and smuggling networks. The former sorts of services include breaking the security dilemma by providing credible and reliable information about all sides' implementation of their commitments under the peace accord; provision of personal security guarantees to specific elites; and provision of impartial security at disarmament and demobilization sites, where groups are most vulnerable to attack. If equipped and mandated to do so, they may enforce the peace against a party that reneges on its commitments.[26]

Michael Doyle (2001), like King, focused on characteristics of the belligerent parties as key to understanding the dynamics of conflict and its termination. Doyle treated three characteristics—the number of parties, their relative mutual hostility, and their in-group coherence or ability to control their adherents—as the dimensions of five "conflict ecologies" of starkly varying difficulty. The ecology most conducive to peace implementation, Doyle argued, would be one with just a few factions, all of whom were coherent and largely reconciled. The least peace-conducive and most difficult environment would be one with many factions, all mutually hostile, and all incoherent and thus prone to freelance action or to splintering.[27]

Stephen Stedman (1997) emphasized that outsiders may need to enforce peace agreements against the activities of "spoilers" (his coinage), signatories who violate the terms of a peace accord for any of three purposes.[28] A total spoiler sees his struggle as zero-sum and, like Jonas Savimbi, the leader of the National Union for the Total Independence of Angola (UNITA), may take his forces back to war if he cannot achieve his aims by political means (and still has forces to call upon). A greedy spoiler like Foday Sankoh, the leader of the Revolutionary United Front (RUF) in Sierra Leone, will do what he can to maintain his wartime resource flows even after the fighting formally ends, and he may return to violence if it looks as though the flow will be turned off. A limited spoiler like Alphonse Dhlakama, the leader of the so-called Mozambican National Resistance (RENAMO), may stake out an ostensibly hard-line position but relent in return for the right payoff. Stedman proposed political-operational strategies to deal with each.[29]

A 1997 study by DFI International for the Pentagon's Office of Peacekeeping and Humanitarian Affairs, in which the author participated, adopted Stedman's terminology and also looked at structural issues and internal conflict. It stressed, however, that "the situations into which peace forces typically are sent are . . . unfinished wars. Militarily exhausted or not, local leaders often are dissatisfied politically. Short of an opposed entry into hostile territory, interventions in civil conflicts can be the most dangerous situations that the military forces of most countries, let alone their civil servants, will ever encounter."[30] The study, "Effective Transitions from Peace Operations to Sustainable Peace," therefore emphasized the importance of correctly gauging the situational difficulty that a new peace force could expect to encounter.[31]

Of the eight factors the study used to measure situational difficulty, the two most important to sustainable peace appeared to be the willingness of neighboring states to support the peace process, and the willingness of all faction leaders to compromise in the interest of peace, at the risk of losing power. The two variables correlated highly with one another as well as with sustainable peace. This made intuitive sense (shifty neighbors frequently aid and abet the war-sustaining contraband trade of recalcitrant warlords[32]), but would have packed more punch if the study team had been better able to measure faction leaders' attitudes in the absence of knowing how peace was progressing on the ground and those leaders' role in it. Intentionally or not, such knowledge may have shaped judgments about leaders' attitudes and thus promoted a higher than warranted correlation between that variable and the study's measure of sustainable peace.

The chapter by Downs and Stedman (2002) in the Stanford-International Peace Academy (IPA) study, *Ending Civil Wars,* also assessed factors thought to render peace implementation more difficult: many warring parties; a missing or coerced peace accord; likelihood of spoilers; collapsed state; more than 50,000 soldiers involved in the war; availability of disposable natural resources; presence of hostile neighbors; and secession demands on the part of one or more belligerent parties. The more factors present in a given situation, the authors argued, the more difficult the situation for peace implementation. Analysis indicated that three of the eight variables—spoilers, disposable natural resources, and hostile neighbors—were particularly important in defining situational difficulty. Paralleling the problems encountered by the DFI team, Downs and Stedman acknowledged the difficulty of measuring spoiler likelihood, as opposed to behavior, so as to better predict and plan for trouble.[33]

The Correlates of Success

Effective Transitions measured several dozen variables drawn from practitioner interviews and the relevant literature that were thought important to a PSO's success. These included variables related to local military forces, public security, governance, the economy, human rights, and freedom of speech, movement, and press. Fifteen of these variables, designed to be measured at the time a PSO ended its mission, correlated well with the study's dependent variable and, of these, five appeared key to an effective transition: demobilizing fighters, cantoning heavy weapons, restarting the economy, working for open and honestly-elected government, and developing a nonpolitical police force.[34] The dependent variable, intended to measure a country's degree of success in transitioning from conflict to sustainable peace, was an average of three measures: residual military conflict, quality of public security, and integrity of the political system. These were to be measured at the end of the first political cycle (that is, the first national election) after the PSO's departure.[35] This composite variable gave Effective Transitions a more sensitive outcome measure than the binary war/no war measure used by many recent quantitative studies of the duration of war and peace.[36] Because the passage of time dilutes the causal impact of any action on subsequent events, the project chose to limit the period for measuring relative success to that one political cycle; beyond that, it is increasingly difficult to sort out the impact of a peace operation from the effects of any number of other variables that continue to operate long after the PSO has shut down.[37]

Downs and Stedman evaluated international support for peace implementation as a key to successful peace implementation, finding great-power interests to be stronger drivers of their engagement than either costs of implementation or estimated risks to their troops (although how these latter variables were scored was not well-defined in text). The cases studied in *Ending Civil Wars* were cross-plotted by mission difficulty and great-power support. Failed cases, those in which peace collapsed either while a PSO was deployed or within two years of its departure, tended to cluster toward the "harder case, less support" quadrant of the plot. Successful cases clustered mostly in the "easier case, more support" corner, while "hard cases with high support" were either partially successful or failed. The authors concluded that, while great-power support for peace implementation might not be enough to guarantee success, its absence in hard cases virtually guaranteed the failure of implementation.[38]

The Importance of Government Legitimacy, Competence . . . and Democracy?

Better known in the practitioner community than to academic researchers, Max Manwaring and his colleagues at the U.S. Army War College and the National Defense University have been building a body of literature on the requirements of effective peace operations that grows out of their work on limited war, and specifically the Small Wars Operations Research Directorate (SWORD) model, developed for the U.S. Southern Command in the 1980s as a counterinsurgency tool. Possibly due to these origins, this work is cited infrequently in the academic literature. In this review, we focus on summative chapters from two books that follow the Manwaring paradigm, which is, by present standards of public policy and strategy in particular, refreshingly astute, humanistic, and lacking in hubris.

The first of these chapters, written by Manwaring and Kimbra Fishel (1998), argued that postconflict military security and economic development cannot be sustained once peacekeepers depart unless there is left behind in national institutions the basic "political competence" needed to *deliver* continuing security, growth, and other essential public services. They portrayed this requirement in what they acknowledged to be an overly simplified equation: Stability equals Military Security plus Economic Development times Political Competence $[S = (M + E)PC]$. The equation says that low political competence will undermine whatever one tries to build up in security and the economy.[39] Nothing that outsiders build—whether armies, police forces, or structures of investment and taxation—will long survive their departure unless the host government is competent to maintain them. Haiti exemplifies a situation where such competence was lacking. The Congo is a case that risks replicating the Haitian example on a much larger scale unless the government develops serious political competence quickly.

Manwaring and Fishel were inclined to be pessimistic about how much change outsiders can actually induce: "Probably the best an outside power or coalition of powers can do is to help establish a temporary level of security that might allow the carefully guided and monitored development of the ethical and professional political competence underpinnings necessary for long-term success."[40] This sentiment is worth keeping in mind when pondering other authors' requirements for building a complete latticework of modern democratic governance and a well-regulated market economy before the international community lets go of a war-torn state.[41]

In the second chapter of interest, Manwaring and Edwin Corr (2000) placed greater stress on the need for legitimacy, or moral authority, in a host government, both to protect against conflict and to speed postconflict recovery. They observed that insurgencies have been "nourished by the alienation of the governed from the government," and argued that the Batista and Somoza regimes in Cuba and Nicaragua, respectively, collapsed in the face of insurgent pressure in part because their regimes continued to focus, despite budding insurgencies, on their "personal enemies and legitimate internal political opposition." They did so, moreover, with a "lack of concern for any kind of human rights for detainees—innocent or not. . . . Consequently, the sacrifices necessary to press a fight against insurgents who promised reform were not readily forthcoming from either citizen or soldier. . . ."[42]

The actors of concern to Manwaring and Corr included the host government and its internal foes, the external powers that support the host government, and the external actors (governments or not) that support the host government's foes. In their conflict model, these players interact in seven distinct but simultaneous and interdependent "wars," or continuing, organized struggles. Only one of these is a shooting war. The others are a "legitimacy war" to "attack or defend the moral right of the incumbent regime to exist"; a war "to isolate belligerents from their internal and external support"; a war "to stay the course," or maintain the political, policy, and public backing needed for "consistent and long-term support to a supported host government"; "information and intelligence wars," which involve intense public diplomacy, on the one hand, and efforts to "locate, isolate, and neutralize" those who "lead, plan, execute, and support a given conflict," on the other. The final war is for "unity of effort": overcoming bureaucratic interests, cultural factors, and other obstacles to ensure common focus and the conduct of operations "in a manner acceptable to the populace. And that equates back to legitimacy."[43]

In the environment of peace operations, the real enemy in the Manwaring-Corr model becomes violence itself, and the objective of struggle, the equivalent of victory, is a sustainable peace.[44] The notion of seven interlocking struggles emphasizes that while robust fighting capability may always be useful, no peace support force (or government), however powerful, can expect to just shoot its way to sustainable peace.

Like Manwaring and Fishel, Elizabeth Cousens (2001) warned that committing to seemingly desirable objectives that prove unreachable can leave both donors and recipients worse off than if they had committed to lesser objectives that were more readily achievable.

> Peacebuilding . . . should not be equated to the entire basket of postwar needs. . . . Rather, it should be seen as a strategic focus on conflict resolution and opening political space, to which these other needs may or may not contribute. What are frequently conceived as peacebuilding activities—demobilization, economic reconstruction, refugee repatriation, human rights monitoring, community reconciliation—are not inherently equivalent to peacebuilding unless they design themselves to be.[45]

Cousens argued that in selecting its peacebuilding objectives, the international community should be "ruthlessly modest about its ambitions" and seek only to leave behind a self-enforcing peace with governmental institutions that offer "authoritative and, eventually, legitimate mechanisms to resolve internal conflict without violence." To attempt much more, for example, attempting to inculcate democracy or work out a society's problems in the realms of justice or equity, would be to invite frustration and failure.[46]

In the introduction to *Ending Civil Wars*, Stephen Stedman argued that the goal of peace implementation should be "the ending of violence and the conclusion of the war on a self-enforcing basis: when the outsiders leave, the former warring parties refrain from returning to war."[47] These are very similar to the goals for peacekeeping set out by Paul Diehl in his 1993 book.[48] Most analysts agree that peace is prerequisite to all other elements of conflict transformation but by seeking no more than a self-enforcing peace, Stedman and Cousens imply that *reinforcing* a thuggish prewar government may be as good as reforming or changing it.[49] During the Cold War, autocratic outcomes were routinely hailed (indeed, engineered) as stabilizing but, when they failed, they tended to fail violently.

Jack Goldstone and Jay Ulfelder (2005), drawing on the results of a multi-year, multi-author, government-funded study of state failure and political risk, concluded that stability is "overwhelmingly determined by a country's patterns of political competition and political authority," but also that "the key to maintaining stability appears to lie in the development of democratic institutions" that promote fair and open competition, deter factionalism, and constrain the power of the chief executive.[50] A subsequent paper from the same authors and their colleagues on the Political Instability Task Force reaffirmed that, "It is these conditions, not elections as such, and certainly not a mythic and utopian notion of 'democracy,' that should guide policymakers seeking greater stability in the world."[51] Peace and stability, in their view, require more than just efficient or even honest authoritarians, but more than a simple winner-take-all election, as well.

These studies both clarify and re-complicate the peacebuilding problem, which they define as political power and how it is exercised. If, according to one camp, outsiders cannot and should not expect to build a fully-institutionalized democracy but, according to the other, they cannot expect stability to last without it, what is to be done? It may turn out that, while democracy must indeed be built from within, it can be reinforced from without; that training, capacity-building, monitoring, verifying and other characteristically western liberal impulses can be tied to penalties in aid and trade, targeted sanctions, and other tunable gateways to global access, to help ensure that democracy is not hijacked, even if the result is occasionally bruised nationalist feelings. As the Task Force team argues, "The risks of such a slide from full to factionalized democracy are not merely a matter of the loss of some democratic character. Instead, they are more realistically viewed as a massive increase in the risks of political catastrophe, including civil war, genocide, and ethnic slaughter."[52]

The twin requirements to monitor peace deal signatories' behavior over some years and to trigger penalties for poor compliance raise the question of who or what should perform these functions. As of late 2005, UN member states were groping toward a mutually acceptable structure and job description for a new UN Peacebuilding Commission, to be a "subsidiary body" of the Security Council. Early feedback suggested an institution too weak to meet the need for commitment monitoring, let alone consistent implementation or enforcement, but neither could one rule out its potential for growing into these tasks.

The Management (and Limitations) of State and Nation Building

Whatever their ultimate objectives, international efforts to support war-to-peace transitions need to be competently run and effectively funded, with some notion of strategic direction (what to do when, with what priority, linked how to other issues). Jarat Chopra (1998–99) anticipated the legal and political requirements of transitional civil administration (the UN's term for temporary governance) in several articles and a book published just in time to be tested in the field. (Chopra was one of the earlier members of the civil administration team of the UN Transitional Administration in East Timor.)[53] The sort of international administration that Chopra had in mind in his writings involved an even more thoroughgoing program of political change than the missions in Timor and Kosovo were geared to produce. For Chopra, the main task of such missions is not state building per se but human security and human development; hence sovereignty loomed not so much as a quality of the state to be restored but as an obstacle to be surmounted en route to rebuilding human dignity.

Chopra delineated three phases of transitional tasks: immediate, medium-term, and long-term. Immediate tasks were about getting set up, imposing order as necessary, disarming factions, clearing landmines, and establishing law enforcement mechanisms. Medium-term tasks included direct public administration, training and structuring of local security forces, rebuilding basic infrastructure, and otherwise facilitating the transition back to local control. Long-term tasks included national reconciliation, "empowering civil society," and other actions to consolidate peace. Chopra was one of the first authors to advocate a "UN 'off the shelf' criminal law and procedure" code as "essential in any peace-maintenance arsenal" to enable it to deal quickly with the most serious of violent criminal offenses. This issue was taken up the following year by the United Nations' *Brahimi Report*. In late 2001, Chopra,

James McCallum, and Alexander Thier applied Chopra's peace maintenance framework to post-Taliban Afghanistan.[54]

Among the few authors to assign priorities to the major elements of postconflict reconstruction was Graham Day (2001), at the time a senior fellow at the United States Institute of Peace between postings as a UN civil administrator.[55] In "Policekeeping: Law and Order in Failed and Emerging States," Day agreed with most analysts that intervenors should stop warfighting first, with military commanders leading the international effort and other components supporting. He went on to argue that establishing law and order was the next priority, with the civilian elements of the administering PSO in the lead and the military supporting. Only when a reasonable semblance of governance had been restored, including judicial enforcement of contracts, could one expect to restore the economy and attract outside investment. The economic development phase should be led by the international development banks and funds, with the PSO's civil component "regulating" the effort and other components in support. Finally, with the war stopped, basic government functioning, the economy coming back, and jobs appearing, the international community could and should turn to implementing transitional justice and nurturing civil society (the latter effort led by NGOs). Day did not arrange these priorities linearly but in a kind of overlapping cascade, the next beginning once the preceding one was well under way.[56]

No sectoral specialist wants to be the one whose sector is consigned to the second, third, or fourth tier in the national recovery plan; all will argue that their sector must be active at the earliest possible moment, and they all will have valid arguments to make. But in internal wars, what matters to peace is power on the ground and who holds it. As military stability ebbs and flows, so will government services and any semblance of law enforcement. Local-area markets will function, in turn, based on buyers' and sellers' assessments of their personal security. Day's logic is, in short, basically sound: war can destroy all efforts to rebuild; a semblance of law and order over a fairly wide area is necessary if longer-range markets and trade are to function; and reconciliation is easier if people have work.

Simon Chesterman (2003) took a highly critical look at transitional administration, building on the proceedings of a conference of practitioners convened by the IPA in October 2002. He focused on oft-repeated mismatches between the stated ends of transitional administration and the means applied to achieve them, which he found to be, in various ways, inconsistent, inadequate, and inappropriate.[57]

Means were *inconsistent* insofar as outsiders talked "local ownership" going into a mission but would not be doing the mission if local capacity were up to the tasks of governing; hence talk of local ownership is, in his view, at best a mollifying smokescreen.

Means were *inadequate* because international resources tended to be supply- rather than demand-driven, reflecting donors' domestic politics or whatever happened to be popular with donors at the moment, which may not be what the society in question needed most. Funding and other resource shortfalls hampered the fulfillment of ambitious mandates. A paucity of UN police and related rule-of-law personnel, for example, meant that public security needs could be only partially met, leaving wide gaps for criminal elements or local political actors to exploit.

Means were *inappropriate* insofar as interventions created locally unsustainable institutions or imported technologies that could not be maintained once internationals left, due to either lack of skills or lack of funds. Conversely, standards of restored governance and institutional development that met external actors' needs and interests might fall well short of local parties' expectations of the government they were to inherit.

International administrators, Chesterman argued, should invite and embrace rather than avoid or dismiss local criticism, and see it as representative of the sort of open political environment that the United Nations hopes to foster in a war-torn state. Similarly, administrators should encourage local consultation but should not pretend that power sharing is happening if it really is not.

The author-editors of *Quest for Viable Peace* (2005) dug deeper into the management of transitional administration but drew their lessons and recommendations primarily from years of personal experience with various aspects of operations in Kosovo.[58] The volume developed a distinctive framework for peacebuilding that focused on requirements for rebuilding local capacity in public security, governance, and economics so that the international community might withdraw and leave behind a sustainable peace. The volume was co-edited by the author of the Kosovo chapter in this volume; readers can refer to that chapter's conclusions for a set of lessons and recommendations that parallel those in *Quest.*

Until September 11, 2001, the Bush administration ranged from indifferent to hostile toward what Washington tends to call "nation building." After 9/11, the administration reengaged the question through the lens of the "war on terrorism" and Washington became a more receptive market for lessons learned in this field. U.S. troops had been helping keep the peace in Bosnia since 1995 and in Kosovo since 1999 but their post-9/11 engagements placed much greater emphasis on war-fighting and counterinsurgency. In neither Afghanistan nor Iraq was organized resistance to U.S. intervention completely eliminated, however, necessitating simultaneous build-fight strategies. Subsequent lessons learned compendia aimed at U.S. policymakers tended therefore to address situations in which outsiders have responsibilities that are all but overwhelming, requiring power and resources far beyond those called for in even the most vigorous implementation of voluntary peace agreements.

The first post-9/11 report to reach policymakers was "Play to Win: Report of the Bipartisan Commission on Post-Conflict Reconstruction" (2003), co-sponsored by the Center for Strategic and International Studies (CSIS) and the Association of the U.S. Army. It defined what would become the canonical "pillars" of post-conflict reconstruction (PCR) for the Washington community: security, justice and reconciliation, social and economic well-being, and governance and participation. A companion "task framework" defined the operational elements of each pillar and, like Chopra, described tasks for each of three phases of intervention: the initial response, transformation, and fostering sustainability. Transformation, for CSIS, meant rebuilding or reforming local and national institutions and sustainability meant national authorities capable of shouldering all responsibility for running the government.[59] A book-length follow-up report, *Winning the Peace* (2004), fleshed out recommendations for the U.S. government initially sketched in "Play to Win":[60]

- Operations need coherent military leadership and good core troops (most easily provided by a single lead nation).

- The international community must have a coherent PCR strategy that addresses problems "holistically," prioritizes and sequences assistance; timing and phasing of operations must be driven by events and conditions on the ground.

- PCR is a fundamentally political process and intervention therefore must be designed with the interests of all key actors in mind, including the local parties, who must "own" the PCR process and eventually be its prime movers. Outsiders should therefore "avoid undermining" local leaders, institutions, and processes.

- Only a small team of external actors, working in-country, can leverage international resources and create change; resources, power, and authority should devolve to them.

- The international community needs mechanisms for mobilizing resources rapidly, and for maintaining accountability once deployed.

Robert Orr, editor and coauthor of *Winning the Peace,* noted that outsiders' approaches to rebuilding government may be guided initially by expatriates who have long-standing personal agendas, as will all local actors, and outsiders' failure to learn and account for those interests "may empower spoilers and disempower legitimate actors."[61] Advice from the more competent members of the old regime, Orr argued, should not therefore be automatically rejected.

As both U.S. and UN experiences in the field have repeatedly demonstrated, any devolution of authority and resources to the field must be joined at the hip to smart, strict, and well-enforced measures of accountability for both use of funds and personal behavior. And while rapid deployment can be and often is key to postconflict stability, haste opens windows for corruption if most of the necessary supporting contracts are not let well in advance, when competitive vetting can be done in the absence of extreme time pressure.

Where international presence derives from clauses in a peace accord, the templates for postwar leadership, institutions, and processes may already have been drafted by negotiators. The internationals who subsequently deploy will be the implementers, not the engineers or architects, of peace. *Winning the Peace* does not address this scenario, which is the standard one for most UN-led peace operations.

A RAND Corporation study published in 2005 focused on select UN operations. *The UN's Role in Nation-Building, from the Congo to Iraq,* was the second in a two-volume series that used case studies to review and, ultimately, compare the United States and the United Nations as nation builders.[62] Both volumes defined nation building as "the use of armed force in the aftermath of a conflict to promote a transition to democracy."[63] Cases not built around the use of force were therefore to be excluded. In addition, cases where U.S. troops deployed in any number at any time and any sequence were classified as "U.S. led."

The lessons learned chapter in *UN's Role* speaks with the voice of experience (perhaps that of lead author, former U.S. ambassador and diplomatic troubleshooter James Dobbins) in an engaging historical narrative. It highlights some of the known problems with UN operations at or before the turn of the century, including lengthy deployment delays, under-resourcing and difficulty managing violent challenges, but also notes some of the UN's achievements. This chapter is more or less divorced from the remaining thematic chapters of the study, however, whose conclusions depend heavily on the study's selection of cases, which is itself problematic.

RAND analyzed nine countries for *UN's Role:* the Congo (for operations 1960–64), Namibia, El Salvador, Cambodia, Mozambique, Croatia (Eastern Slavonia), Sierra Leone, East Timor, and Iraq. Of the nine, UN operations had forceful mandates in just four; in two other cases the United Nations released *local* forces to contest violations of peace accords. These were South African troops in Namibia and Cambodian factions other than the Khmer Rouge, which opted out of the peace process. There were no such episodes in Mozambique, no armed UN troops at all in El Salvador, and while the Security Council may have blessed the presence of coalition forces in Iraq from September 2003 onward, the relative handful of non-Iraqi UN personnel on the ground there were decidedly not using force to promote democracy.

RAND did not include on its UN case list either the UN Protection Force (UNPROFOR) in Croatia and Bosnia (1992–95) or the UN's operations in Angola, Somalia, Rwanda, or Haiti. Where the selected cases (even Congo) were comparatively successful, these latter cases are generally considered failures (Haiti not so much operationally as strategically). No case chapter in either volume mentions UNPROFOR, although it was the United Nations' largest operation and one of its most troubling, operationally and ethically. Together with Somalia (treated as a U.S. case), it was pivotal to the decisions of most Western states to forego future UN troop contributions.[64] The UN's major Somalia operation replaced U.S. coalition forces in May 1993 and was specifically mandated to promote a transition to democracy and authorized to use force if necessary. That summer, 110 troops from countries other than the United States lost their lives in combat in an ultimately futile effort to enforce that mandate. Before fighting ended, U.S. forces under U.S. command also suffered 25 dead, a trauma sufficient to help dissuade U.S. political leaders from making any military effort to halt the genocide in Rwanda the following spring.[65] The UN operation in Rwanda at that time, with a mandate and force comparable to the UN operation in Mozambique, dissolved as the genocide mounted. These issues of case selection and assignment in turn skew the conclusions drawn in the volume's final two chapters with regard to U.S. versus UN mission duration, success rate, combat deaths, and so forth.

In suggesting that the United Nations can do nation building as RAND defines it, albeit on a scale smaller than the United States, the RAND studies suggest that the organization can be a reliable junior partner able to hold together failing states that don't quite qualify for extreme political makeovers. This is a dangerous position for the United Nations to be in, not least because the corollary is that UN operations go where great power attention is least focused, yet great power attention has proven to be an essential ingredient for successful peacebuilding. Without that attention, the United Nations' many chaos-straddling missions are condemned at best to stalemate, yet the institution itself, not those who have given it these missions without the requisite political support, will be called to account for the lack of success.

This review has shown that there is considerable disagreement in the literature on peacebuilding and postconflict reconstruction, about how much democracy is needed or desirable for sustainable peace and, within that desirable level, about how much can be induced from the outside. There is disagreement regarding how much emphasis to place on economics and whether growth should be nurtured or just allowed to happen; disagreement on how much to press human rights concerns, accountability for wartime behavior, and formal mechanisms of reconciliation; and disagreement on how much transparency is necessary to promote accountability in postwar government.

There is agreement, however, on the need to get the difficulty of the implementation environment right; agreement that local actors will maneuver for advantage within the peace process after implementation begins; agreement that local actors' access to supporting resources gives them greater incentive and ability to resist and even to bolt the peace process; and agreement that, the longer it takes to get a transition started, the greater the prospect that the process will go awry. Finally, there is agreement that tangible support for implementation on the part of neighboring states and at least one great power is essential if difficult transitions are to have any hope of succeeding. Unfortunately, there is also agreement that, in most instances, great-power attention and money will be difficult to sustain long enough to create sustainable peace.

Complex Peace Support Operations in the Twenty-first Century

Except for the long-running effort in Bosnia, all of the operations detailed in this volume were launched between 1999 and 2001 and constituted the third surge in peace operations since the end of the Cold War. Four of these operations are ongoing as of this writing, so their stories, although updated for the most part to mid-2005, are by definition incomplete.

The third surge seems predictable in hindsight, but in early spring 1999 no one would have guessed that the Security Council would soon give the UN Secretariat another go at managing complex civil-military operations in dangerous and volatile, not-quite-postconflict settings. The growing crisis over Kosovo through most of 1998 and the winter of 1999 drew NATO ever closer to launching air strikes against the Serb-dominated Yugoslav army and its associated paramilitary police. These forces, pursuing the self-styled Kosovo Liberation Army (KLA), increasingly visited violence upon Kosovo's largely ethnic Albanian population, whose aspirations for independence the KLA themselves advanced by violent means. When the NATO bombing campaign began in March 1999, betting persons would have wagered that postwar security and administration tasks would be assigned to Europe's regional institutions. They would have been partly right: NATO got the military tasks, the European Union got the job of rebuilding Kosovo's economy, and the Organization for Security and Co-operation in Europe got the job of building democracy. The overall job of civil administration, however—providing police, power, water, and schools—went to the United Nations, whose personnel were roughly as surprised and alarmed as anyone else at their having gotten the job.

The Kosovo bundle-on-the-doorstep was not the United Nations' only new responsibility, however. In May 1999, the organization was invited by the president of Indonesia to manage a plebiscite in East Timor, the former Portuguese colony seized by Indonesia in 1975 and held for twenty-four years without recognition from the United Nations or from any country save Australia. East Timorese voters were expected to favor political independence and, despite months of violent harassment by Indonesian army–sponsored private militias, they did so—only to watch as the militias were unleashed to pillage, burn, and kill. Frantic diplomatic initiatives and serious international arm twisting led the Indonesian government to agree to the rapid dispatch of an Australian-led intervention force, which restored order quickly, but not before most of East Timor had been stripped and burned to the ground. In October 1999, the Security Council created a UN operation to replace the Australian force and, as in the case of Kosovo, gave it governing authority. At about the same time, the council also dispatched a UN force to Sierra Leone to help that beleaguered government implement a peace accord signed, under international pressure, with a rebel group best known for its diamond smuggling and atrocities against civilians.

The DRC was, to a great degree, the mission that the system feared the most, because of its potential to expand. The DRC is huge, the United Nations had been mired there before, and four decades of political decay, economic stagnation, and population growth made it an even more daunting venue in which to keep the peace or even monitor it. The Security Council decided, in February 2000, that the UN military observers already deployed there needed protection, and so voted for a guard force of 5,000 troops. The war in the DRC involved a half-dozen African armies, their local proxies, and assorted militias, which engaged in a kind of desultory war that did not kill so many soldiers but generated piles of precious gems and metals for officers to cart home. The war also contributed to the deaths of nearly four million ordinary Congolese.[66] Driven from their homes and fields by the many marauding bands, they starved or succumbed to disease in the bush.

As the UN Secretariat struggled to plan, staff, and deploy these new operations in November–December 1999, Secretary-General Kofi Annan released two reports, one on the Srebrenica massacre that had been requested by the General Assembly in November 1998, and the other on the UN role in Rwanda during the 1994 genocide, which Annan himself had commissioned in March 1999. Both reports were highly critical of the United Nations, reopening old wounds and creating new doubts about its ability to carry out the missions it had just been given.[67]

It was against this background in March 2000 that Kofi Annan took the initiative to appoint the Panel on United Nations Peace Operations, instructing it to "present a clear set of specific, concrete and practical recommendations to assist the United Nations in conducting [peace and security] activities." The panel, chaired by Undersecretary-General Lakhdar Brahimi, issued its report the following August, in time for submission to the Millennium Summit. The UN Secretariat subsequently engaged member states for three years to implement key elements of the panel's recommendations. The impacts of that process of change and renewal on the United Nations' ability to support and conduct peace operations are still being felt at UN headquarters and in the field.[68] Readers should bear in mind, however, that the operations chronicled in the chapters of this volume began before the *Brahimi Report* was commissioned and, in their early years, were themselves elements of the crisis that caused it to be commissioned. Most of these operations benefited from the post-Brahimi reforms, but not until the fourth surge in UN operations, in 2003–4, could the effects of reform on new missions be assessed. Those operations brought UN peacekeepers into Liberia, Côte d'Ivoire, Burundi, Haiti, and southern Sudan. Their stories are still unfolding.

Annex I: Paying for Peace Operations

Although peace support operations (PSOs) are cheaper than war, they are still not cheap. Developed states fund about 92 percent of assessed UN peacekeeping costs, pay most of their own real costs of participating in UN operations, and may subsidize other states' participation in non-UN operations. Except for operations led by the United Nations, the costs of PSOs are not easy to calculate, as there is no standardized cost reporting (some states may report the total cost of troops deployed, while others report just the marginal, or added, costs of deploying troops) or central repository of such data. Only the United Nations has a functioning system for reimbursing operational costs based on assessments levied on its member states. The Economic Community of West African States (ECOWAS) has a nominal system of member state taxation to support peace operations but has not managed to collect much toward that end. The lack of effective funding mechanisms led to the transfer of several African operations (including those in Sierra Leone, Liberia, Côte d'Ivoire, and Burundi) to UN management.

In a major departure, the report of the UN secretary-general's High-Level Panel on Threats, Challenges, and Change recommended that UN funding and equipment procurement channels be opened to regionally managed African peace operations on a case-by-case basis, in parallel with other, state-to-state programs to build up the region's peacekeeping and peacebuilding capacity.[69] Not mentioned, but necessary to ensure both transparency in expenditures and the upholding of global human rights standards by regional forces, would be mandatory measures to monitor field performance, for example, by using UN military observers with troop contingents and civilian counterparts in such operations' headquarters. The UN Department of Peacekeeping Operations might welcome being spared the hassle of mission management, but if UN financial norms and rules applied, UN-funded regional operations would be no less costly than those managed by the United Nations itself. If different, cost-saving norms and rules applied, however, the United Nations would risk charges of discrimination and perhaps racism. Thus, the advantage of the proposal would rest largely in its shifting of the operational management burden to the region, a burden that the African Union, ECOWAS, and other institutions are several years away from assuming effectively. As they become more capable, however, such a shift might well be in order.

NATO and the European Union cover some "common" costs, such as support for headquarters, infrastructure, identification marking, and medical support for the forces as a whole, "negotiated on an operation-by-operation basis."[70] Both organizations require their member states to cover their own operational costs (the rather mordant phrase being "costs lie where they fall"). Coalition operations also function on a pay-as-you-go basis unless the lead nation or some generous third party offers to defray a troop contributor's costs (as the United States did in support of Turkey's leadership of peacekeepers in Kabul in 2002). For all of these reasons, it is not easy to create global annual spending totals for peace operations. Thus the numbers discussed here should be treated as rough estimates.

The Costs of Non-UN Peace Operations

Non-UN mission costs are the hardest to calculate. Table 1.A.1 presents the results of a late-1999 cost survey, undertaken by the U.S. Congressional Research Service (CRS), of countries that were contributing troops to NATO's Kosovo Force. It also contains CRS data for American operating costs in Bosnia, Kosovo, and Macedonia, and British costs for Kosovo. When these data are combined with troop deployment numbers drawn from the International Institute for Strategic Studies' annual *Military Balance*, annual per capita troop costs for each contributor can be estimated. These costs averaged $128,600 (give or take $60,000) for members of the Development Assistance Committee (DAC) of the Organization for Economic Co-operation and Development. DAC membership is used here to define the developed states, that is, states with sufficient economic surplus that they can and do offer development aid to others. As Table 1.A.1 notes, the reported averages exclude the highest- and lowest-cost entries in each category, on the assumption that the extremes reflect less reliable or less consistently reported data.

Costs averaged $80,000 for non-DAC European troop contributors (give or take $20,000, again excluding the extremes). Assuming an overall inflation rate of 3 percent per year in Europe, these numbers

Table 1.A.1. Estimated Annual per-Soldier Costs of Non-UN Peace Operations in the Balkans, in Current Dollars

Average annual cost per soldier, NATO allies, Kosovo, 1999[a]	
$128,600	OECD/DAC[b] members
$79,300	Non-DAC members
$111,800	Both

Average annual cost per soldier, United States, 1996–2002	
$212,800	Bosnia and Kosovo only
$168,600	Bosnia, Kosovo, and FYROM (Macedonia)
$51,600	FYROM (Macedonia) only

[a]Averages exclude "outliers," or the most and least costly entries in each category.
[b]Organization for Economic Co-operation and Development, Development Assistance Committee.

Sources: Carl Ek, "NATO Burdensharing and Kosovo: A Preliminary Report," no. RL30398 (Washington, DC: Congressional Research Service, January 3, 2000), 14–15. International Institute for Strategic Studies (IISS), *The Military Balance* (Oxford: Oxford University Press for IISS, 1999, 2000, 2001, and 2002). Nina M. Serafino, "Peacekeeping: Issues of U.S. Military Involvement," no. IB94040 (Washington, DC: Congressional Research Service, August 6, 2003), 16. Kenneth Bacon, "DOD Press Briefing, March 16, 1999" (Washington, DC: Office of the Assistant Secretary of Defense for Public Affairs). UK Ministry of Defence, "Kosovo: The Financial Management of Military Operations," report by the Comptroller and Auditor General (London: The Stationery Office, June 2000).

would be closer to $145,000 and $89,000 in 2003.[71] (Unless otherwise noted, all dollar figures given in this book are in U.S. dollars.)

Reported U.S. operational costs are equally variable, especially if one includes the U.S. contribution to the UN Preventive Deployment in Macedonia, where reported annual U.S. costs averaged $50,000 per soldier, in current dollars, from 1996 to 1999. Even if this number reflects prior deductions of the reimbursements the U.S. government would have received from the United Nations for participating in a UN operation, reported U.S. operating costs in Macedonia would still be less than a third of reported U.S. costs for Bosnia and Kosovo, which averaged about $213,000 from 1996 through 2002, in current dollars (excluding the highest- and lowest-cost mission years).[72]

The Costs of UN Peace Operations

The United Nations reports publicly on the costs of its PSOs in far greater detail than does any other entity, national or multinational. Since 1973, the organization has paid a fixed rate of reimbursement per soldier, in part to avoid the kind of wildly varying claims for compensation that arose from its 1960–64 operation in the Congo.[73] Not finalized then and still subject to ongoing haggling among the United Nations' member states are the reimbursement rates for wear and tear on vehicles and other "contingent-owned equipment" that troop contributors bring with them to a UN operation. The standard troop reimbursement, initially $500 to $650 per month (the latter for specialties such as communications and engineering), was $1,100 to $1,400 by 2002. Periodic surveys of UN troop contributors, to determine actual operational costs, have confirmed that UN member states' actual costs vary widely but in many cases exceed reimbursement rates. An early 1989 survey, with responses from eleven of the thirteen states (all but four of them developed states) then contributing troops to UN operations, showed average monthly per capita costs of $2,300, with a high of $4,400 and a low of $280. A late 1996 survey generated responses from twenty-six of forty-three troop contributors (still a broad mix of developed and developing states), showing average monthly costs of $3,806, with a high of $10,778 and a low of $774. A new survey presently languishes in the 259-member working group of member states that ponders reimbursement issues. The group has not been able to reach consensus on changing the reimbursement formula, so the new survey should not be expected to see the light of day until around 2008.[74] Table 1.A.2 shows average per capita UN costs for troops in formed units in two of its peace operations: on the Ethiopia-Eritrea border and in the Democratic Republic of the Congo (DRC). The DRC operation was more expensive because most of its transport was by air.

In 2003, UN and non-UN peacekeeping combined—not including the cost of the occupation and counterinsurgency operations in Iraq—probably totaled between $9.4 and $9.6 billion (see table 1.A.3). While a substantial amount of money, this sum is still equivalent to just 1 percent of global military expenditure in 2003.[75]

Table 1.A.2. UN Troop Costs

	Ethiopia-Eritrea[a]	Democratic Republic of the Congo[b]
Total UN cost per troop-year for troops in units, 2003–4:	$38,011	$50,335
U.S. share of UN peacekeeping costs, 2003–4: 26.9%	$10,208	$13,518

Note: All UN costs are inclusive of operations, transport, and other support.

[a]Border- and cease-fire-monitoring mission, largely ground-mobile.
[b]Complex operation with enforcement mandate in eastern provinces; large country, poor roads, airborne logistics.

Sources: Compiled from United Nations, *Performance Report on the Budget of the United Nations Mission in Ethiopia and Eritrea for the Period from 1 July 2003 to 30 June 2004—Report of the Secretary-General*, A/59/616, December 16, 2004. United Nations, *Performance Report on the Budget of the United Nations Mission in the Democratic Republic of the Congo for the Period from 1 July 2003 to 30 June 2004—Report of the Secretary-General*, A/59/657, March 4, 2005. United Nations, *Implementation of General Assembly Resolutions 55/235 and 55/236*, A/58/157, July 15, 2003.

The UN Peacekeeping Scale of Assessments

UN peace operations are funded primarily through the "peacekeeping scale of assessments," a system first informally adopted in 1973 that puts most of the burden of peacekeeping finance on those states with the greatest ability to pay. It places a special burden on the five permanent members of the Security Council (or P5: China, France, Great Britain, Russia, and the United States), reflecting their special responsibility under the charter for the maintenance of international peace and security. The added burden also reflects the desire of developing countries, who were relieved of an equivalent financial burden, to avoid having to pay for operations whose costs were unpredictable and potentially quite high (in the 1960s, for example, the first Congo operation cost several times more per year than the entire UN regular budget), and which mostly served Western Cold War interests in stability.

The P5 therefore pay roughly a 22 percent higher share of UN peacekeeping costs than they pay in regular UN dues, while developing

Table 1.A.3. Total Cost of Global Peace Operations, 2003 (excluding Iraq)

Estimated gross OECD Development Assistance Committee (DAC) members' peacekeeping costs	$6,600,000,000	at	$144,700	per troop-year; cost derived from table 1.A.1, inflated to 2003 dollars at 3 percent per year
Less reimbursement for UN operations	$73,741,200	at	$23,500	Average UN reimbursement per troop-year, including COE[a] and self-sustainment costs
Net DAC members' peacekeeping costs	$6,526,258,800		16%	Estimated percentage of DAC members' actual UN operations costs that UN reimburses
Cost of non-UN, non-DAC operations	$387,864,500	at	$41,800	per troop-year, assuming that non-UN, non-DAC operational costs are equivalent to UN's
or	$193,932,250	at	$20,900	per troop-year, assuming that non-UN, non-DAC operational costs are half of UN's costs
UN peacekeeping budget normed to calendar year 2003 (half of 2002–3 budget plus half of 2003–4 budget)	$2,671,760,300	of which	91%	contributed by DAC members
Total peacekeeping expenditure, 2003, using higher-cost assumption about non-UN, non-DAC troop contributors	$9,391,951,350			
Total peacekeeping expenditure, 2003, using lower-cost assumption about non-UN, non-DAC troop contributors	$9,585,500,000			

[a]COE is contingent-owned equipment, the combat and transport vehicles and other equipment that military contingents bring with them to an operation. Self-sustainment reimburses the cost of fuel and other consumables.

Sources: Table 1.A.1. IISS, *Military Balance, 2003–2004.* United Nations, *Review of Rates of Reimbursement to the Governments of Troop-Contributing Countries, Report of the Secretary-General, A/57/774,* April 3, 2003. United Nations, *Overview of the Financing of the United Nations Peacekeeping Operations: Budget Performance for the Period from 1 July 2002 to 30 June 2003.* United Nations, *Budget for the Period from 1 July 2004 to 30 June 2005, Report of the Secretary-General, A/58/705,* February 9, 2004.

states receive a peacekeeping discount. The original peacekeeping scale had just four contributing categories: P5 (Group A); developed states (Group B); developing states (Group C, with an 80 percent dues discount); and least developed states (Group D, discounted 90 percent). Under this arrangement, the P5 and the twenty-six members of Group B funded 98 percent of peacekeeping-related costs from 1973 through 2000. The 157 members of Groups C and D funded 2 percent.

In 2000, however, U.S. ambassador to the United Nations Richard Holbrooke led a successful campaign to formalize the peacekeeping scale (it had, up until then, simply been applied to each new mission budget by custom). Holbrooke not only managed to increase the payments made by wealthier developing states but also won agreement to peg states' membership in an expanded number of payment groups to national per capita income. As states grow richer or poorer, their share of UN peacekeeping will rise or fall. Moreover, Holbrooke managed to get the U.S. contribution to the regular UN budget cut from 25 to 22 percent, and the nominal U.S. share of UN peacekeeping cut from 30–31 percent to about 26.5 percent, a combined savings to U.S. taxpayers, at the 2004 tempo of UN peacekeeping, of roughly $169 million per year. In turn, the U.S. Congress temporarily lifted a 25 percent ceiling on all U.S. contributions to the United Nations that it had imposed in the mid-1990s (reinstating it in mid-2005). Table 1.A.4 compares the old system with the new one, under which the wealthier among the developing states now pay for almost 5 percent of UN peacekeeping.

The forty-nine members of Group J—the poorest countries in the world—still receive a 90 percent discount on their peacekeeping dues and paid, on average, about $6,700 apiece toward UN peacekeeping costs in 2003. The eighty-one members of Group I, with an 80 percent discount, paid an average of $488,000 apiece. Were UN peacekeeping costs apportioned like the regular UN budget, those numbers would have been $67,000 and $2.4 million apiece, respectively. Whether such higher payments would be affordable is a matter of legitimate debate, but it is worth noting that in 2003, countries in Group J spent, on average, 12,000 times as much for their national militaries as they dropped in the United Nations' peacekeeping cup, while countries in Group I spent nearly 7,000 times as much.[76] (See table 1.A.5 for the average spending ratios of the other peacekeeping payment groups.) Some

Table 1.A.4. Old and New Peacekeeping Scales of Assessments

As of January 1999

Old Groups	Payment Relative to Regular Scale	Percentage Group Criteria	Number of Members	Funded by Each Group
A	121.1%	P5[a]	5	46.89%
B	100.0%	Developed	26	51.09%
C	20.0%	Developing	60	2.01%
D	10.0%	Least developed	97	0.02%

As of January 2005

New Groups	Payment Relative to Regular Scale	Group Criteria (per capita income)	Number of Members	Percentage Funded by Each Group
A	122.5%	P5	5	45.25%
B	100.0%	Developed	32	50.13%
C	92.5%	N/A	5	0.82%
D	80.0%	<$10,188	1	1.51%
E	60.0%	<$9,169	3	0.01%
F	40.0%	<$8,150	2	0.29%
G	30.0%	<$7,131	4	0.34%
H	30.0%	<$6,112	9	0.28%
I	20.0%	<$5,094	81	1.38%
J	10.0%	Least developed	49	0.01%

[a]P5 are China, France, Great Britain, Russia, and the United States.

Sources: United Nations, *Financing of the United Nations Transition Assistance Group,* A/RES/43/232, March 3, 1989. United Nations, *Scale of Assessments for Apportioning the Expenses of the United Nations,* A/RES/52/215, January 20, 1998. United Nations, *Implementation of General Assembly Resolutions 55/235 and 55/236, Report of the Secretary-General,* A/58/157/Add.1, December 17, 2003.

Table 1.A.5. Dollars of Defense Spending in 2003 per Dollar of
UN Peacekeeping Dues in 2004

	Average	Median	Standard Deviation
P5	$642	$423	$525
Developed States	$178	$150	$110
Groups C through H	$902	$832	$689
Group I	$6,907	$3,461	$8,766
Group J	$12,365	$9,580	$9,358

Sources: IISS, *The Military Balance, 2004–2005.* United Nations, *Implementation of General Assembly Resolutions 55/235 and 55/236, Report of the Secretary-General,* A/58/157/Add.1, December 17, 2003.

countries with very high ratios of military spending to peacekeeping dues (such as Pakistan, India, Bangladesh, Ethiopia, and Jordan) are also top troop contributors to UN operations, but many high spenders are not. Moreover, five of the top ten troop contributors in mid-2004 (Ghana, Nigeria, Kenya, South Africa, and Uruguay) managed to contribute brigade-sized units to UN operations despite below-average military spending ratios. The UN reimbursements system makes that possible.

Notes

1. Monty G. Marshall, "Global Trends in Violent Conflict," in *Peace and Conflict 2005,* ed. Monty G. Marshall and Ted Robert Gurr (College Park, MD: Center for International Development and Conflict Management, 2005), 11.

2. Not everyone buys Robert D. Kaplan's pessimistic assessments, but he does take the time to go out and look. See his *The Ends of the Earth: A Journey to the Frontiers of Anarchy* (New York: Vintage, 1997).

3. For an in-depth assessment of what each brings to peace operations and how they support one another, see William J. Durch and Tobias C. Berkman, *Who Should Keep the Peace? Providing Security for Twenty-first Century Peace Operations* (Washington, DC: Henry L. Stimon Center, 2006).

4. William J. Durch, ed., *The Evolution of UN Peacekeeping: Case Studies and Comparative Analysis* (New York: St. Martin's, 1993). The cases in this

volume include two complex operations, the original UN Operation in the Congo (1960–64) and the UN Temporary Executive Authority in West New Guinea (1962–63).

5. William J. Durch, ed., *UN Peacekeeping, American Policy, and the Uncivil Wars of the 1990s* (New York: St. Martin's, 1996).

6. Mark Bowden, *Black Hawk Down: A Story of Modern War* (New York: Atlantic Monthly, 1999). See also William J. Durch, "Introduction to Anarchy: Humanitarian Intervention and 'State-Building' in Somalia," in *UN Peacekeeping*, ed. Durch.

7. The UN Transitional Administration for Eastern Slavonia (UNTAES) supervised the transfer back to Croatia of districts bordering on the Former Republic of Yugoslavia that had been seized and occupied by the Yugoslav army, and then monitored by UN peacekeepers, after Croatia broke away from its parent federation in 1991. An operation with 5,000 well-equipped troops and substantial authority to manage the political transition, UNTAES also benefited from the presence of NATO forces in Bosnia as potential reinforcements. Initiated in January 1996, UNTAES ended in January 1998 roundly viewed as a success. See the information pages on UNTAES maintained by the UN Department of Peacekeeping Operations, www.un.org/Depts/dpko/dpko/co_mission/untaes.htm.

Haiti held its first democratic elections in 1990, but its first elected president was ousted by the army in late 1991. Its people then suffered under three years of international sanctions that hurt its ruling elites not much at all. U.S. military intervention in September 1994 was motivated as much by a desire to stop waves of Haitian refugees from flooding U.S. shores as by any interest in restoring Haiti's elected government. Its elected president, Jean-Bertrand Aristide, was viewed with a mix of uncertainty and alarm in Washington. American forces shifted from intervention to peacekeeping more or less in mid-deployment when, at the eleventh hour, the military government agreed to resign. A UN peace operation took over from U.S. forces in March 1995, with a U.S. force commander and 2,400 U.S. troops. The full UN force (7,000 strong) was replaced just one year later by a force one-fourth as large, which was replaced in turn after two years by a small contingent of police trainers. None of these missions touched Haiti's political, economic, or judicial structures, and the newly trained police force, standing virtually alone in an otherwise unreformed government, soon sank into the sort of disrepair that characterized the rest of the country. Interest in Haiti had faded by 1998, as outsiders grew frustrated with the country's growing political gridlock. By early 2004, Haiti once again exhibited visible symptoms of state failure, with militias brandishing arms against an incapacitated government. A coalition intervention force led by the United States deployed there briefly in the spring of 2004, replaced in short order by a Brazilian-led UN operation. For further details, see Chetan Kumar, "Peacebuilding in Haiti," in *Peacebuilding as Politics: Cultivating Peace in Fragile Societies,* ed. Elizabeth Cousens and Chetan Kumar (Boulder, CO: Lynne Rienner, 2001). See also Janice Stromsem and Joseph Trincellito, "Building the Haitian National Police," Haiti Papers, no. 6 (Washington, DC: Trinity College Haiti Program, 2003); and Robert Maguire, "U.S. Policy toward Haiti: Engagement or Estrangement?" Haiti Papers, no. 8 (Washington, DC: Trinity College Haiti Program, 2003).

8. Indar Jit Rikhye, *The Theory and Practice of Peacekeeping* (New York: St. Martin's for the International Peace Academy, 1984), 1.

9. Boutros Boutros-Ghali, *An Agenda for Peace* (New York: United Nations, 1992).

10. Charles C. Moskos, Jr., *Peace Soldiers: The Sociology of a United Nations Military Force* (Chicago: University of Chicago Press, 1976), 2–3. See also Rikhye, *Theory and Practice of Peacekeeping,* 1–2; and Alan James, *Peacekeeping in International Politics* (New York: St. Martin's, 1990), 1–8, 298.

11. John Mackinlay and Jarat Chopra, "Second Generation Multinational Operations," *Washington Quarterly* (Summer 1992): 116–17. See also United Nations, *Supplement to an Agenda for Peace,* A/50/60-S/1995/1, January 25, 1995, 7–18.

12. William J. Durch, "Keeping the Peace: Politics and Lessons of the 1990s," in *UN Peacekeeping,* ed. Durch, 3–7.

13. Daniel Byman et al., *Strengthening the Partnership: Improving Military Coordination with Relief Agencies and Allies in Humanitarian Operations,* MR-1185-AF (Santa Monica: RAND, 2000), 39.

14. Paul F. Diehl, "Forks in the Road: Theoretical and Policy Concerns for 21st Century Peacekeeping," in *Politics of Global Governance,* ed. Paul F. Diehl, 2nd ed. (Boulder, CO: Lynne Rienner, 2001), 217–19.

15. Trevor Findlay, *The Use of Force in UN Peace Operations* (Oxford: Oxford University Press, 2002), 3–7.

16. Charlotte Ku and Harold Jacobson, "Broaching the Issues," in *Domestic Accountability and the Use of Force in International Law,* ed. Charlotte Ku and Harold Jacobson (Cambridge: Cambridge University Press, 2002), 19–24.

17. Alex J. Bellamy, Paul Williams, and Stuart Griffin, *Understanding Peacekeeping* (Cambridge: Polity, 2004), 5–6. For the most recent iteration of

British doctrine for peace support operations, see UK Joint Doctrine and Concepts Centre, *The Military Contribution to Peace Support Operations,* Joint Warfare Publication 3-50, 2nd ed. (Shrivenham: UK Ministry of Defence, 2004).

18. United Nations, *Report of the Panel on United Nations Peace Operations* (Brahimi Report), A/55/305-S/2000/809, August 21, 2000, paras. 12, 28.

19. Ibid., para. 13.

20. Charles Call, "Institutionalizing Peace: A Review of Post-conflict Peacebuilding Concepts and Issues," a policy review for the United Nations Department of Political Affairs, New York, January 2005, 3–6.

21. The term derives from the piece by Stephen John Stedman, "Spoiler Problems in Peace Processes," *International Security* (Fall 1997), 5–53.

22. On French doctrine, see Thierry Tardy, "French Policy towards Peace Support Operations," *International Peacekeeping* 6, no. 1 (Spring 1999); and Joseph P. Gregoire, "The Bases of French Peace Operations Doctrine" Carlisle Papers in Security Strategy Series (Carlisle, PA: U.S. Army War College, Strategic Studies Institute, September 2002). On U.S. doctrine, see U.S. Army, *Peace Operations,* Field Manual 100-23 (Fort Leavenworth, KS: U.S. Army Training and Doctrine Command, December 1994); U.S. Army, *Stability Operations and Support Operations,* Field Manual FM 3-07 (Fort Leavenworth, KS: U.S. Army Training and Doctrine Command, February 2003); and U.S. Joint Forces Command, *Stability Operations Joint Operating Concept* (draft, September 2004), 3, www.dtic.mil/jointvision/finalstab_joc.doc. On British doctrine, see Philip Wilkinson, "Sharpening the Weapons of Peace: Peace Support Operations and Complex Emergencies," in *Peacekeeping and Conflict Resolution,* ed. Tom Woodhouse and Oliver Ramsbotham (Portland, OR: Frank Cass, 2000); and UK Ministry of Defence, Joint Doctrine and Concepts Centre, *The Military Contribution to Peace Support Operations,* Joint Warfare Publication [JWP] 3-50, 2nd ed. (Shrivenham, UK: 2004). Of the other two permanent members of the Security Council, Russia has long treated peacekeeping as low-intensity conflict but without the hearts-and-minds annex. See Kevin P. O'Prey, "Keeping the Peace in the Borderlands of Russia," in *UN Peacekeeping,* ed. Durch (New York: St. Martin's, 1996), 412–15. China has not been deeply involved operationally in peacekeeping, although that is beginning to change.

23. Colonel Michael Kelly, "Military Force and Justice," in *From Civil Strife to Civil Society: Civil and Military Responsibilities to Disrupted States,* ed. William Maley, Charles Sampford, and Ramesh Thakur (New York: United Nations University Press, 2003), 229–54. See also Michael Dziedzic,

"Introduction," in *Policing the New World Disorder,* ed. Robert B. Oakley, Michael J. Dziedzic, and Eliot M. Goldberg (Washington, DC: National Defense University Press, 1998), 6–15.

24. Charles King, *Ending Civil Wars,* Adelphi Paper no. 308 (London: International Institute for Security Studies, 1997). Others have addressed civil war duration, especially from the perspective of comparative national statistics (see, for example, Paul Collier, Anke Hoeffler, and Mans Soderbom, "On the Duration of Civil War," *Journal of Peace Research* (Oslo) 41, no. 3 [May 2004], 253ff). None, in my view, has addressed duration in a fashion as operationally useful to policymakers as King.

25. King, *Ending Civil Wars,* 29–52.

26. Ibid., 55–83.

27. Michael W. Doyle, "War Making and Peace Making: The United Nations' Post-Cold War Record," in *Turbulent Peace: The Challenges of Managing International Conflict,* ed. Chester A. Crocker, Fen Osler Hampson, and Pamela Aall (Washington, DC: United States Institute of Peace Press, 2001). Doyle uses only one of the four possible combinations with "many" factions, namely, hostile and incoherent.

28. Stedman, "Spoiler Problems."

29. Dhlakama had little choice but to settle for cash. RENAMO, created by the white minority regime in Rhodesia and sustained after that regime's demise by apartheid-era South Africa, ravaged Mozambique for fifteen years, only to lose its external support when South Africa abandoned apartheid. On the long-running conflict, see Alex Vines, *RENAMO: Terrorism in Mozambique* (Bloomington: Indiana University Press, 1991). With no substantial internal resources to trade for money or guns, RENAMO lacked the leverage to be a greedy spoiler.

30. See Barry Blechman et al., "Effective Transitions from Peace Operations to Sustainable Peace, Final Report" (report prepared for the Office of the Assistant Secretary of Defense for Strategy and Resources, Office of Peacekeeping and Humanitarian Affairs), Washington, DC: DFI International, September 1997, 10.

31. The DFI study modeled situational difficulty using eight variables, each with content scaled from +5 to −5, or from least to most problematic for peace, as judged by the authors. The first variable measured combatants' war objectives, ranging from "control of the state" (+5) to "secession from the state" (−5), with power sharing and autonomy goals ranked in between. The second variable measured the motives of the combatants, from political (seeking a redistribution of power, at +5) to ideological/religious (promoting a new order of power, at –5). The third reflected the amount of damage done to government in the course of the war (from not much, at +5, to complete collapse, at –5). The fourth and fifth reflected the breadth and depth of the peace agreement, respectively. The sixth measured the willingness of local faction leaders to place their hold on power at risk in the course of implementing the peace accord (for example, by gracefully losing an election). The seventh measured whether neighboring states' attitudes toward peace were, on balance, supportive, indifferent, or hostile, while the eighth was a comparably scaled measure of great-power involvement in the peace process. Ibid., 10–13.

32. See, for example, the report of the original panel of experts appointed to investigate the breaking of sanctions against the Angolan rebel group UNITA. It was known as the "Fowler Report," after Robert Fowler, the Canadian ambassador to the United Nations who chaired the Security Council committee overseeing the panel's work. United Nations, *Letter Dated 10 March 2000 from the Chairman of the Security Council Committee Established Pursuant to Resolution 864 (1993) Concerning the Situation in Angola Addressed to the President of the Security Council,* S/2000/203, March 10, 2000. There have since been more than thirty reports from comparable investigative panels.

33. George W. Downs and Stephen John Stedman, "Evaluation Issues in Peace Implementation," in *Ending Civil Wars: The Implementation of Peace Agreements,* ed. Stephen John Stedman, Donald Rothchild, and Elizabeth M. Cousens (Boulder, CO: Lynne Rienner, 2002), 56.

34. Ibid., 20–28.

35. A politically viable state is a key objective of war-peace transitions. Virtually all of the peace processes studied involved elections. A state that could not sustain itself for even one electoral cycle after a PSO's departure would be hard to define as viable. In most cases, the electoral cycle was four to six years. The tripartite-variable also credits the survival of a structurally democratic government in the face of resumed warfare and/or disturbance of public order (as in the case of Colombia), while it lowers the score of a country where war is over but elections are stolen.

36. Most of the quantitative studies use survival models with a dependent variable coded 0 or 1, indicating the presence or absence of war for a particular case and time period. See, for example, Virginia Page Fortna, "Does Peacekeeping Keep Peace? International Intervention and the Duration of Peace after Civil War," *International Studies Quarterly* 48 (2004): 269–92. For a useful critique of the limits of aggregate data models, see Nicholas Sambanis,

"Using Case Studies to Expand Economic Models of Civil War," *Perspectives on Politics* 2, no. 2 (June 2004), 259–79.

37. Downs and Stedman used an even more constrained timeline for measuring success in peace implementation: If peace lasts for two years after peacekeepers depart, then it should be considered self-enforcing and the mission a success. If peace fails after two years and two months, the mission should still be coded a success. A specific rationale for the two-year timeline was not given, however. "Evaluation Issues in Peace Implementation," in *Ending Civil Wars,* ed. Stedman, Rothchild, and Cousens, 51.

38. Ibid., 43–60.

39. Max Manwaring and Kimbra Fishel, "Lessons that Should Have Been Learned: Toward a Theory of Engagement," in *The "Savage Wars of Peace": Toward a New Paradigm of Peace Operations,* ed. John T. Fishel (Boulder, CO: Westview Press, 1998), 207–8.

40. Manwaring and Fishel, "Lessons that Should Have Been Learned," 209.

41. See, for example, Jack A. Goldstone and Jay Ulfelder, "How to Construct Stable Democracies," *Washington Quarterly* 28, no. 1 (Winter 2004–5): 9–20.

42. Max G. Manwaring and Edwin G. Corr, "Defense and Offense in Peace and Stability Operations," in *Beyond Declaring Victory and Coming Home: The Challenges of Peace and Stability Operations,* ed. Max G. Manwaring and Anthony James Joes (Westport, CT: Praeger Publishers, 2000), 22, 25.

43. Ibid., 21.

44. Ibid.

45. Elizabeth Cousens, "Introduction," in *Peacebuilding as Politics: Cultivating Peace in Fragile Societies,* ed. Elizabeth Cousens and Chetan Kumar (Boulder, CO: Lynne Rienner, 2001), 13.

46. Ibid., 4, 15.

47. Stephen John Stedman, "Introduction," in *Ending Civil Wars,* ed. Stedman, Rothchild, and Cousens, 2.

48. Paul F. Diehl, *International Peacekeeping* (Baltimore: Johns Hopkins University Press, 1993), 33–39.

49. For comparable warnings about the risks of attempting to instill democracy from abroad, see Roland Paris, *At War's End: Building Peace after Civil Conflict* (New York: Cambridge University Press, 2004) and Francis Fukuyama, *State-Building: Governance and World Order in the 21st Century* (Ithaca, NY: Cornell University Press, 2004).

50. Jack A. Goldstone and Jay Ulfelder, "How to Construct Stable Democracies," *The Washington Quarterly* 28, no. 1: 9–20.

51. Jack A. Goldstone, Robert H. Bates, et al., "A Global Forecasting Model of Political Instability," paper presented at the annual meeting of the American Political Science Association, Washington, DC, September 3, 2005, 31. Online at globalpolicy.gmu.edu/pitf/pitfp5.htm.

52. Ibid., 30.

53. Jarat Chopra, ed., *The Politics of Peace Maintenance* (Boulder, CO: Lynne Rienner, 1998), which originally appeared as a special issue of the journal *Global Governance* (January–March 1998). Chopra et al., "The Politics of Peace Maintenance," *Small Wars and Insurgencies* 10, no. 2 (Autumn 1999); Chopra, *Peace-Maintenance: The Evolution of International Political Authority* (New York: Routledge, 1999); and Chopra, "The UN's Kingdom of East Timor," *Survival* 42, no. 3 (Autumn 2000): 27–39.

54. Jarat Chopra, Jim McCallum, and Alexander Thier, "Planning Considerations for International Involvement in Post-Taliban Afghanistan," *Brown Journal of World Affairs* 8, no. 2 (Winter 2002): 43–60.

55. Day served with the United Nations in Central America, the Balkans, and Iraq and had just completed a tour with UNTAET as administrator of the Oecusse enclave, an extrusion of East Timor notched into the northwest coast of the island and surrounded, therefore, by Indonesian West Timor. Day went on to be deputy high commissioner in Bosnia, based in Banja Luka. See www.usip.org/specialists/bios/archives/day_graham.html.

56. Graham Day, "Policekeeping: Law and Order in Failed and Emerging States" (mimeo), March 29, 2001.

57. Simon Chesterman, "You, the People: The United Nations, Transitional Administration, and State-Building," Project on Transitional Administrations, Final Report (New York: International Peace Academy, 2003).

58. Jock Covey, Michael J. Dziedzic, and Leonard R. Hawley, eds., *The Quest for a Viable Peace: International Intervention and Strategies for Conflict Transformation* (Washington, DC: United States Institute of Peace Press, 2005). An excellent compendium on peacebuilding that offers more breadth on nonsecurity issues, but does not provide a consolidated framework of lessons or recommendations, is *From Civil Strife to Civil Society,* ed. Maley, Sampford, and Thakur.

59. "Play to Win: Report of the Bi-partisan Commission on Postconflict Reconstruction" (Washington, DC: Center for Strategic and International Studies [CSIS] and Association of the U.S. Army, January 2003). For a comparable but more detailed task framework for the military in postwar Iraq that does a more fine-tuned job of assigning priorities within major substantive categories, see Conrad C. Crane and W. Andrew Terrill, "Reconstructing Iraq: Challenges and Missions for Military Forces in a Post-Conflict Scenario," Strategic Studies Institute, U.S. Army War College, Carlisle, PA, January 29, 2003, www.strategicstudiesinstitute.army.mil.

60. Robert C. Orr, "Constructing a Cohesive Strategic International Response," in *Winning the Peace: An American Strategy for Post-Conflict Reconstruction,* ed. Orr (Washington, DC: CSIS Press, 2004), 19–36.

61. Ibid., 21.

62. James Dobbins et al., *The U.S. Role in Nation-Building: From the Germany to Iraq* (Santa Monica: RAND, 2004), and Dobbins et al., *The UN's Role in Nation-Building: From the Congo to Iraq* (Santa Monica: RAND, 2005).

63. Dobbins et al., *The UN's Role in Nation-Building,* 2.

64. For a case history see William J. Durch and James A. Schear, "Faultlines: UN Operations in the Former Yugoslavia," in *UN Peacekeeping, American Policy,* ed. Durch, 194–254.

65. The unusually frank report of the UN commission of inquiry on the summer 1993 war in Somalia is essential reading on this subject. United Nations, *Report of the Commission of Inquiry Established Pursuant to Security Council Resolution 885 (1993) to Investigate Armed Attacks on UNOSOM II Personnel Which Led to Casualties among Them,* S/1994/653, June 1, 1994.

66. The International Rescue Committee conducted several mortality surveys in the DRC, beginning in late spring 2000. The first found excess mortality of 1.75 million since the start of the regional war in August 1998; the latest, reflecting data collected between January 2003 and April 2004, found 3.8 million excess deaths. See Ken Coghlan et al., *Mortality in the Democratic Republic of Congo: Results from a Nationwide Survey* (New York, Kinshasa, and Bukavu: International Rescue Committee, 2004), iii.

67. United Nations, *Report of the Secretary-General Pursuant to General Assembly Resolution 53/35, The Fall of Srebrenica,* A/54/549, November 15, 1999; and United Nations, *Report of the Independent Inquiry into the Actions of the United Nations during the 1994 Genocide in Rwanda, Letter from the Secretary-General Addressed to the President of the Security Council,* S/1999/1257, December 16, 1999, www.un.org/Depts/dpko/dpko/reports.htm.

68. The full details on the implementation of the Brahimi Report can be found in William J. Durch, Victoria K. Holt, Caroline R. Earle, and Moira K. Shanahan, *The Brahimi Report and the Future of Peace Operations* (Washington, DC: Henry L. Stimson Center, 2003).

69. UN High-Level Panel on Threats, Challenges, and Change, *A More Secure World: Our Shared Responsibility* (New York: United Nations, 2004), 85–86.

70. See "Funding for Post-conflict Operations: NATO and the EU" (Washington, DC: Henry L. Stimson Center, March 2004), www.stimson.org/fopo/Factsheet_FundingPostConflictOperations.pdf. See also Michele A. Flournoy et al., "European Defense Integration: Bridging the Gap between Strategies and Capabilities" (Washington, DC: Center for Strategic and International Studies, October 2005), 62–63, www.csis.org/media/csis/pubs/0510_eurodefensereport.pdf.

71. The annual inflation rate for U.S. military outlays averaged 2.6 percent between 1999 and 2004, while the increase in the U.S. consumer price index for the same period averaged 1.9 percent. General rates of inflation in Europe during that period also averaged about 1.9 percent per year, and European armed forces operate at lower economies of scale than U.S. forces, so 3 percent annual inflation in military costs is a reasonable assumption for the militaries of other DAC members. See U.S. Department of Defense, *National Defense Budget Estimates for FY 2005* (Washington, DC: Office of the Comptroller, March 2004), table 5-1. For European Union inflation rates, see InfoBASE Europe News Service, "InfoBASE Europe Data Record," www.ibeurope.com/Records/8600/8608.htm.

72. All of the numbers cover ground operations only. The sources of such great variation in cost are not clear, although U.S. forces in Macedonia were light infantry deployed mostly in static positions, while the other forces were mechanized and used their equipment to patrol their zones of responsibility.

73. William J. Durch, "Paying the Tab: The Financial Crises," 41–42, and "The UN Operation in the Congo," 331, in *Evolution of UN Peacekeeping*, ed. Durch.

74. United Nations, *Review of the Rates of Reimbursement to the Governments of Troop-Contributing States, Report of the Secretary-General* (A/45/582, October 10, 1990, 3; A/54/763, February 21, 2000; and A/57/774, April 3, 2003). The 1996 survey was not reported until February 2000.

75. International Institute for Strategic Studies, *The Military Balance, 2004–2005* (Oxford: Oxford University Press, 2004), 358.

76. These numbers exclude the two countries in each group with the highest military-spending-to-UN-peacekeeping-spending ratios. For Group J, these are Angola and Myanmar (each roughly $250,000:$1); and for Group I, North Korea (roughly $98,000:$1) and Armenia ($72,500:$1).

2

Post-Dayton Bosnia and Herzegovina

Elizabeth Cousens and David Harland

Introduction

By mid-2005, the ambitious international effort to implement peace in Bosnia had gone on twice as long as the war itself. In the nine-plus years since war ended, considerable progress had been made on multiple fronts. The cease-fire established prior to the Dayton Agreement remained inviolate, even as the size of the Stabilization Force, led by the North Atlantic Treaty Organization (NATO), was progressively drawn down. Much of Bosnia's damaged infrastructure had been repaired. Out of an estimated 2.2 million refugees and displaced persons, about 1 million had returned home or been resettled.[1] Major wartime figures had been sent to The Hague for prosecution, including the former president of Serbia, Slobodan Milosevic. Four rounds of general elections had been held in relative calm and the Bosnian Constitutional Court, in a landmark decision, actually revised provisions in the Dayton constitution that had reinforced monoethnic authorities.

As the postwar situation stabilized, the international presence was downscaled. International troop strength had fallen below 7,000 from a post-Dayton high of nearly 60,000, and responsibility for those troops had shifted from NATO to the European Union (EU); Bosnian elections were being conducted by national bodies as of 2002; the United Nations mission dedicated to police restructuring and reform had been phased out; and an EU police mission served in its stead.

The "report card" for Bosnia was mixed, however. The results of ethnic cleansing had not been reversed; indeed, they had largely been consolidated. And while military confrontation between the parties no longer posed a significant threat, few argued that the peacekeepers should leave altogether. Moreover, Bosnia and Herzegovina was not yet a viable and self-supporting state. The supposedly unifying state institutions still worked sluggishly and appeared, according to numerous polls, to have earned negligible trust from significant segments of the population.[2] In fact, efforts to foster a postwar national identity to transcend ethnic allegiances were often thwarted by the structure of these very institutions. Meanwhile, the international community had arrogated to itself sweeping powers, provoking charges of a new colonialism.[3] The economy was heavily aid dependent, increasingly lagged behind others in central and eastern Europe and, most worrying, was becoming heavily criminalized.[4] Increasingly, early concerns about consolidating peace were yielding to anxieties about Bosnia's possibly more challenging transition to a postsocialist, democratic market economy.

Origins of International Involvement

The major historical divisions of Europe had also cleaved Bosnia and Herzegovina. When the Roman Empire was divided into eastern and western halves in the third century, the line of division passed along the river valleys and mountain ranges of northern and eastern Bosnia. The later schism that divided Western Christianity from Eastern Orthodoxy also passed through it. Bosnia's northern and western borders were, during the later centuries of the Ottoman rule, the line that divided the sultan's realm from the Hapsburg Empire.

Centuries at the crossroads of empires and faiths, combined with a topography of densely wooded mountains and deep valleys, left an imprint on the people of Bosnia and Herzegovina. Although they were largely indistinguishable from each other ethnically and linguistically, identities based on confessional differences were prominent. Prior to the Ottoman conquest of the fifteenth century, Western Christianity, the Serbian branch of Orthodox Christianity, and a distinct Bosnian Church all found adherents in Bosnia and Herzegovina. Under Ottoman rule in Bosnia, unlike in most other Ottoman-ruled territories in Europe, there were widespread conversions to Islam. This took place even in the absence of any significant Turkish settlement or intermarriage. For several centuries, Muslims and Serbian Orthodox were roughly equal in number, with a slightly smaller percentage of the population adhering to the Western Christianity of the Croats.

The last census of the population of Bosnia and Herzegovina (see figure 2.1), undertaken in 1991 just prior to the eruption of conflict, found a total population of 4.3 million, of which 43.7 percent identified themselves as Muslims, 31.4 percent as Serbs, and 17.3 percent as Croats, with the remaining 7.6 percent, including large numbers of people from mixed marriages, identifying themselves as "Yugoslavs and others."[5] Each community was widely dispersed geographically.

Despite earlier periods of independence and, as some argue, a distinct identity, Bosnia and Herzegovina had no modern experience as an independent state.[6] Austria-Hungary wrested it from the Ottoman Empire in 1876 and later incorporated it into the Double Monarchy. After World War I, Bosnia formed a part of the Kingdom of Serbs, Croats, and Slovenes and, later, the Kingdom of Yugoslavia. During World War II it was annexed to the pro-Nazi Independent State of Croatia, and was the principal battleground both for anti-Nazi resistance and for fighting between the various ethnoreligious communities. Following the victory of the Yugoslav Partisans under Tito, Bosnia and Herzegovina became one of the six republics of the Socialist Federal Republic of Yugoslavia (SFRY).[7]

The end of the Cold War and a growing economic crisis saw the disintegration of Yugoslavia along ethnoreligious (or "national") lines. Nationalist politicians swept to victory in a series of elections in 1990 and 1991. This period brought to power in all six Yugoslav republics the individuals and political parties who would soon prosecute the wars of Yugoslavia's breakup. Serbia elected President Slobodan Milosevic as a champion of the Serb people, whose fears of comparative vulnerability within Yugoslavia he actively stoked. Croatia elected Franjo Tudjman,

Figure 2.1. Map of Bosnia and Herzegovina

Source: UN Cartographic Section

whose new political party—the Croatian Democratic Union (HDZ)—was the bellwether of nationalist (and anti-Serb) revival in Croatia. In Bosnia, Alija Izetbegovic, who had been imprisoned under Tito for his Islamist writings, became president of a new Muslim-dominated Party for Democratic Action (SDA). Meanwhile, hard-line Croatian Serbs began to mobilize within Croatia, founding their own Serbian Democratic Party (SDS), and sister parties of both the Serb SDS and Croat HDZ were soon established within Bosnia. In each case, nationalist leaders sought independence or autonomy for those territories in which their conationals lived.

As the integrity of SFRY was beginning to fray, the international community actively tried to mediate a settlement. European countries took the lead, with EU foreign policy chief Jacques Poos memorably claiming that this was "the hour of Europe."[8] The United States took a back seat, with Secretary of State James Baker remarking that the United States didn't "have a dog in this fight."[9]

Slovenia and Croatia made separate declarations of independence on June 25, 1991.[10] Slovenia was the most fortunate of the former Yugoslav republics: its borders included only tiny numbers of non-Slovenes, ensuring that it would not be the object of territorial claims by others. Ljubljana reached a settlement with Belgrade after only ten days of skirmishing between separatist forces and the Serb-dominated Yugoslav People's Army (JNA). Under the terms of the Brioni Agreement, Slovenia, as well as Croatia, was obliged to respect a three-month moratorium on further moves toward independence.[11] Brioni also called for the deployment of a European Community Monitoring Mission of up to fifty personnel to monitor the situation in Slovenia.[12] In August, the European Community (EC) additionally established an arbitration commission, known as the Badinter Commission, to determine the criteria under which Yugoslav successor states could gain European recognition, and a peace conference for Yugoslavia (under the chairmanship of Lord Peter Carrington).[13]

The situation on the ground in Croatia and Bosnia was rapidly overtaking diplomatic efforts, however. Since 1990, Croatia had been steadily establishing the foundation for eventual independence, including a series of sharply nationalistic constitutional amendments.[14] When the Croat majority under Tudjman's leadership declared independence in June 1991, Croatia's Serb minority tried to secede from Croatia. Backed by the JNA and Serbian paramilitary groups, Serbs took control of approximately one-third of Croatian territory, establishing a "Republic of Srpska Krajina" and expelling Croats as they did so.

Meanwhile, the Badinter Commission issued its first ruling in December. Contentiously applying the principle of *uti posseditis,* the commission ruled that each of the six republics could be recognized as independent states provided that they met certain minimum conditions.[15] These included constitutional protection of minorities and demonstrated popular support for independence through referenda. The prospect that each of the seceding republics could be recognized within its previously internal borders was especially alarming to Serbs, roughly two million of whom (some 26 percent of the total) lived outside Serbia proper.[16] Before the Badinter Commission could issue its subsequent rulings specific to each republic, however, Germany unilaterally recognized Croatia, soon followed by other EC member states.[17]

The first phase of fighting ended in Croatia in January 1992 with the signature of an agreement brokered by former U.S. secretary of state Cyrus Vance, European recognition of Croatia, and the introduction of a United Nations Protection Force (UNPROFOR) to stabilize the cease-fire.[18] UNPROFOR's headquarters was established in Sarajevo, in neighboring Bosnia and Herzegovina—which was seen then as a suitable neutral location—though its operations, for the time being, were restricted to Croatia.

As the most ethnically mixed of the Yugoslav republics, Bosnia and Herzegovina was also the most vulnerable to conflict. After a brief period of cooperation in 1990 and 1991, when they had joined hands to oust the ruling communists, the new nationalist leaders in Bosnia and Herzegovina had fallen out. Broadly, each community sought to ensure that it would not be a minority in a state dominated by any of the others. The Muslims—later known as "Bosniacs"—were the most numerous community and sought to retain a unified Bosnian state.[19] Bosnian Serbs, headquartered in the town of Pale just miles from the capital, Sarajevo, sought first to keep Bosnia within a rump Yugoslavia, in which Serbs would be preponderant. When that option was closed they, like the Serbs in Croatia, sought to establish their own territory, "Republika Srpska," which would separate from Bosnia and Herzegovina as soon as Bosnia separated from Yugoslavia. Following the Badinter Commission rulings, Bosnia held a referendum on February 29 and March 1, 1992, in the midst of escalating tensions and violence. Though boycotted by the Serbs, strong Bosniac and Croat turnout carried the referendum.[20] On April 6, Bosnia and Herzegovina declared independence and was recognized by Europe and the United States. Almost immediately, Bosnian Serbs stepped up efforts to carve out their own independent territory.[21]

The Dynamics of War

The war in Bosnia and Herzegovina was by far the largest and bloodiest of the wars of Yugoslav succession. During the initial phases of the war, the Bosnian Serbs—backed by rump Yugoslavia and a range of Serbian paramilitary groups—were overwhelmingly successful. By the summer of 1992, they controlled some 70 percent of the territory of the country. From that territory, approximately one million non-Serbs were expelled, or fled, in a tactic that came to be known as ethnic cleansing. Several thousand women were held captive and raped. Sarajevo and a number of other cities came under siege. Although the official casualty figure of 200,000 is not well substantiated, it is certain that several tens of thousands of Bosnians—mostly Bosniac, and mostly civilians—lost their lives during the conflict.[22]

Diplomatic efforts did not yield quick results. The peace talks that had begun in 1991 under European auspices were joined in 1992 by the United Nations in a new International Conference on the Former Yugoslavia (ICFY). ICFY produced a series of plans and variation on plans, but none secured the agreement of all parties. Certain measures, such as the insertion of UNPROFOR, had some stabilizing effect and facilitated the provision of humanitarian assistance, but did not advance the prospects of lasting peace. Other measures, such as the arms embargo imposed on all belligerents, probably reinforced the position of the Serbs, who held most of the weapons.[23] The imposition of sanctions on the rump Yugoslavia was not sufficient, in the short term, to induce Belgrade's cooperation. (Over time, the sanctions regime did elicit some of the intended responses from Milosevic, though at the cost of accelerating the criminalization of the Serbian economy.)

Nonetheless, by the end of 1992, the broad contours of the final settlement in Bosnia and Herzegovina were clear to the major international players, and came to define the goals of the belligerents themselves. Bosnia and Herzegovina would exist as a single state, at least in name, with each community enjoying significant autonomy within defined territories. The relative authority of the single state vis-à-vis its component parts remained contentious, but the basic structure of a political resolution was understood.[24] By 1993, the scope of the territorial arrangements was also broadly accepted: all three sides and international mediators recognized that the final peace settlement would leave the Serbs with something close to 49 percent of the territory of the country, and the Bosniacs and Croats with 51 percent between them.[25] This formula did not change significantly over time except for tactical parrying in the context of negotiations.[26] Indeed, the military campaigns of 1995 that enabled a final settlement, though exacting a heavy toll in terms of casualties, were largely designed to bring de facto territorial holdings into line with this understood allocation.

Seeking to improve their positions in an eventual peace settlement, the three sides all played to their strengths. After initial successes in the first half of 1992, Serb strategy was a conservative one. They sought to apply "pressure" on their enemies to accept peace terms favorable to the Bosnian Serb leadership. That pressure included holding territory they intended ultimately to trade back for peace, restricting the flow of humanitarian assistance to surrounded cities, and inflicting casualties, mainly on civilians, by using snipers at close range and by bombardment with heavy weapons at longer range.[27]

The three-and-a-half-year siege of Sarajevo came to exemplify the brutality of this mode of warfare: sustained deprivation became a way of life, while a limited flow of humanitarian assistance ensured that few starved or died of cold.[28] Meanwhile, some 500,000 shells were fired, often with no real military purpose, and some 10,000 people, mostly Bosniac civilians, were killed.[29]

The Serbs tolerated UNPROFOR. They were opposed to its mission, which they correctly saw as bringing some relief to their enemies. Yet, aware that the alternative to the UNPROFOR peacekeeping mission could be NATO military support for their enemies, they stopped short of forcing its withdrawal. They imposed the tightest restrictions on what UNPROFOR could transport across Serb-held territory into the Bosniac-held enclaves. They harassed, manipulated, and humiliated the force, occasionally even taking hostages, but took care never to go so far as to cause it to withdraw altogether.[30]

For Bosniacs, the situation was reversed. Being weak militarily, they focused much of their effort on securing international support, primarily from the United Nations, Western powers, and the Islamic world. At the United Nations, the Bosniacs, who controlled the internationally recognized rump government of the Republic of Bosnia and Herzegovina, waged a high-profile campaign. Aware that public opinion in much of the Western world was outraged by the Serb war against civilians, the Bosniacs stressed—and sometimes even deliberately contributed to—the suffering of the civilian population of Sarajevo and elsewhere.[31] The leadership also emphasized the largely fictitious "multi-ethnic, plurireligious" nature of their administration.[32] Combined with solid support from the Islamic world, these efforts produced a majority in the Security Council and a slew of supportive resolutions. But the moral outrage did not bring an end to the arms embargo that had been in place since 1991, nor did it bring direct external military assistance, nor did it even bring UNPROFOR firmly over to the Bosniacs' side. UNPROFOR, in the words of its Bosnia and Herzegovina commander, was not willing "to cross the Mogadishu line" between peacekeeping and warfighting.[33]

For the Bosnian Croats, the smallest of the three main communities in Bosnia and Herzegovina, the articulation of a single coherent strategy was difficult. In western Herzegovina—compact, overwhelmingly Croat, bordering the Republic of Croatia, and closely tied to the ruling party in Zagreb—commitment to a united Bosnia and Herzegovina was minimal. In Sarajevo, central Bosnia, and Posavina, where Croat communities lived scattered among larger Bosniac and Serb communities, the idea of some sort of federal arrangement was attractive. The Croats' eight-month war against the Bosniacs in 1993, even when supported by the armed forces of the Republic of Croatia, was largely a failure.[34] Chastened by this, the Croats played only a limited role in the remainder of the war until, in 1995, Croatian government forces crossed the border and inflicted major reversals on the Serbs.

The Dynamics of Peace

There were five principal efforts to bring about a lasting settlement in Bosnia and Herzegovina. The two main peace initiatives of 1992 and early 1993—known as the Cutileiro plan and the Vance-Owen peace plan—envisaged a Bosnia and Herzegovina in which ethnic cleansing would largely be reversed: the country would be divided into "cantons," or provinces, each of which was configured broadly to reflect the distribution of population prior to the displacements of the war. Yet the Vance-Owen plan was denounced by Bosniac supporters, especially in the United States, for being too accommodating to ethnic cleansing. It was rejected entirely by the Serbs for the opposite reason. In the absence of firm commitment to the plan from any of the main actors in the conflict, it foundered.[35]

The next three peace plans—known as the HMS *Invincible* Plan, the Contact Group Plan, and the Dayton Agreement—were sponsored by different constellations of international actors. Each offered the parties the same amount of territory. The constitutional arrangements envisaged in the latter two plans were also similar, with a decentralized state divided into two "entities." According to a separate agreement brokered in 1994 by the United States and Germany, Bosniacs and Bosnian Croats would unite in a postwar federation. This federation would, in turn, be divided into cantons—some Bosniac-majority, some Croat-majority, and some mixed.[36] The counterpart for the federation would be a uniquely autonomous "Republika Srpska" in which Serbs would retain much of the territory they had ethnically cleansed, but to which non-Serb refugees would have the right to return, at least in theory.

Two factors created the preconditions for peace in Bosnia and Herzegovina by the summer of 1995: military reversals for the Serbs, in the absence of which they had little incentive to settle; and an international initiative capable of overcoming the divisions and disarray within the international community that had undermined previous efforts.

By late 1994 and early 1995, the Bosnian Serb leadership had come to believe that their basic military strategy of holding territory and terrorizing the enemy into submission was failing. They dominated the territory of Bosnia and Herzegovina, but time was now against them.

First, with the cessation of hostilities between Bosniacs and Croats in 1994, these two communities were able to focus on fighting the Serbs, aided by unofficial U.S. military support.[37] Second, the Bosniacs were beginning to receive enough outside help to turn their numerical superiority into military advantage. Third, and most ominously for the Serbs, the Republic of Croatia was clearly preparing for the military destruction of the Croatian Serb statelet of Republika Srpska Krajina, an eventuality that would leave the long western and northern borders of Republika Srpksa exposed to attack from Croatia proper. The Bosnian Serb leadership resolved to accelerate the pace of their military operations, in the first instance by eliminating the Bosniac enclaves of Srebrenica, Zepa, and Gorazde, thus freeing Serb troops for other operations.[38]

On July 11, 1995, Serb forces overran the Bosniac enclave of Srebrenica. Heavily outnumbered Dutch UNPROFOR troops provided no resistance, and no significant use was made of NATO air power. In the four days that followed, more than 7,000 Bosniacs were killed. In Kravica, several hundred captives were herded into a concrete warehouse, locked in, and then killed by grenades and small-arms fire directed through the windows. In Bratunac, captives were called out by name and beaten to death with shovels and picks. In the majority of cases, however, captives were bound, transported by truck and bus to execution sites, and shot in batches of twenty to fifty. Earth-moving machinery was then brought in to hide the results of what was the largest massacre in Europe since the end of World War II.[39]

The fall of Srebrenica had far-reaching consequences. It led France and the United Kingdom, which had hitherto opposed the widespread use of military force against the Serbs, to support more aggressive plans for the use of air power to curb future Serb outrages. For the United States, it focused attention on the possible need for NATO to support evacuation of UNPROFOR—a possibility that threatened to draw the United States into a large-scale military operation in the Balkans, and led President Clinton to support a major peace initiative.[40] NATO had, in fact, already begun to consider the possibility of an extraction of UN peacekeepers in its Operation Plan 40-104, drawn up in the spring of 1995, and had already started to deploy elements of a Rapid Reaction Force before Srebrenica fell.[41] The broader context was one of deep questioning about the future role of NATO and, indeed, the architecture of European security generally, which raised considerably the stakes of resolving the Bosnian war.

As these international processes were ripening, the Republic of Croatia launched Operation Storm, eliminating Republika Srpska Krajina in the first week of August 1995, and then following up with advances into Serb-held territories in western Bosnia. Bosniac forces in the far west of the country, no longer pinned down by Croatian Serb forces in the rear, also went on the offensive.

On August 28, as these events were unfolding, a mortar shell landed in Sarajevo's Markale marketplace, killing thirty-seven people, mostly Bosniac civilians. UNPROFOR investigators concluded "beyond any reasonable doubt" that the shell had been fired by the Serbs.[42] The same evening, the UNPROFOR commander, Lieutenant General Rupert Smith, "turned the key," clearing the way for major NATO air attacks.[43]

The Croatian attack into Bosnia, the Bosniac breakouts in the west, and NATO air attacks in the north and east combined to break the Serbs. Richard Holbrooke, leading the U.S. negotiating effort, encouraged Bosniac and Croatian forces to continue their advances against the Serbs—at least until each side held roughly the territory it could expect to be ceded in a formal peace agreement.[44] At the request of the United States, UNPROFOR provided daily updates of the front lines, calculating precisely the percentage of the territory held by each force. As the percentages grew closer to the agreed balance of 51:49, UNPROFOR provided twice-daily updates.[45] By October 6, UNPROFOR reported that the 51:49 balance had been reached. The Serbs, fearing a total collapse, began to sue for peace.

After three and a half years of fighting, the war in Bosnia and Herzegovina ended much as it had begun: in confusion and sporadic local fighting, with nothing clearly resolved and no one side clearly dominant. The last fighting took place on October 11, 1995. Croatian government forces, advancing from the south and west, paused after capturing the Serb-held town of Mrkonjic Grad. Farther west, Bosniac forces, having broken out of the Bihac enclave, captured Serb-held Sanski Most, but then stalled prior to an anticipated assault on Prijedor. Apart from the ethnic cleansing of the Serb populations who had not fled in time, there was little further violence.

Shortly thereafter, the three sides in the conflict, under the supervision of UNPROFOR, began a demarcation of the front lines and a progressive disengagement of the belligerent forces. There were no significant cease-fire violations, and by late October UNPROFOR, essentially for the first time, was able to function as a true peacekeeping force: interposing itself along front lines and confirming that agreed withdrawals had taken place.

On November 1, peace negotiations began at the Wright-Patterson Air Force Base in Dayton, Ohio, culminating on November 21 with the initialing of a General Framework Agreement for Peace and its eleven annexes, a 130-page document that constitutes the Dayton Agreement.[46] Almost a month passed before the agreement was officially signed (in Paris on December 14) and endorsed by the UN Security Council (on December 15).[47] Only on December 20, with guns silent, the forces disengaged, and the peace agreement signed, did the first elements of the NATO-led Implementation Force (IFOR) deploy into Bosnia and Herzegovina. Meanwhile, a new Peace Implementation Council, bringing together key donor capitals and other interested governments, met in London and designated an international High Representative to lead the civilian component of the peace effort. Carl Bildt, who had been the EU mediator since June, arrived in Sarajevo on December 21, 1995. The implementation of the peace agreement had begun.

Content of the Agreement

Dayton's mediators claimed that the agreement was meant to achieve three objectives: to end the fighting for good; to establish a viable Bosnian state; and to restore the multiethnic fabric of Bosnian society. They assumed that that these three objectives would be compatible and mutually reinforcing: an enduring cease-fire would create the enabling conditions for state building and for large-scale return of refugees and internally displaced persons; reversing mass displacement would, in turn, restore a multiethnic constituency for a unitary democratic state; and a nonethnicized state would be the best guarantee against a resumption of violence.

Military Provisions

The agreement's military provisions (Annexes 1A, Military Aspects; 1B, Regional Stabilization; and 2, Inter-Entity Boundary Line and Related

Issues) provided for the insertion of the powerful IFOR, along with related measures, to secure the Inter-Entity Boundary Line (IEBL) that was to separate the 51 percent of territory allocated to the Bosniac-Croat Federation from the 49 percent awarded to Republika Srpska (see figure 2.1). The parties accepted a detailed calendar of obligations to cease hostilities and draw down forces within six months, the bulk of their commitments occurring in the first thirty days.[48] In addition to regular military forces, the drawdown included "armed civilian groups, national guards, army reserves, military police and Ministry of Internal Affairs Special Police," who, collectively, had been in the vanguard of the ethnic cleansing campaigns, as well as all "foreign forces," including some 2,000 mujahideen fighters.[49]

The settlement was territorially vulnerable at two major points. First, the Bosniac-majority town of Gorazde, which had been a UN-designated Safe Area during the war, was connected to the Federation by only a narrow spit of land.[50] Second, the northern town of Brcko, to which both Serbs and Bosniacs laid claim, sat astride the even narrower Posavina land corridor that connected western and eastern Republika Srpska. Gorazde was treated within Annex 1A largely as a matter of territorial demarcation that would be guaranteed by outside implementers.

Brcko required a more intricate solution. The town had been seized and held by Bosnian Serbs since the spring of 1992, when they drove out the bulk of the Bosniac and Croat population and sought—unsuccessfully—to expand the three-mile-wide corridor linking the two halves of the Serb republic. Before the war, Brcko's nearly 90,000 residents were mixed: 44 percent Muslim, 25 percent Croat, and 21 percent Serb. Afterward, this population was displaced and divided: only one-third remained in the town, which was now 99 percent Serb.[51] The area was perceived as strategically critical for both sides: to take Brcko from the Serbs would effectively cut Republika Srpska in half; to give it to them would, beyond sanctioning ethnic cleansing, deprive the Federation of access to the Sava River and the trade and communications links that it represented. Because negotiations were unable to settle the Brcko question at Dayton, the dispute was remanded to an international arbitrator to resolve within one year (Annex 2).

The parties also agreed to a package of regional arms control and confidence-building measures. They committed to reach agreement on arms and troop levels that would reduce overall armaments as well as establish a ratio of forces between the Bosnian parties and their regional patrons: specifically, 40 percent (the Federal Republic of Yugoslavia) to 30 percent (Croatia) to 30 percent (Bosnia), with Bosnia's military capabilities, in turn, divided in a 2:1 ratio between the Federation and Republika Srpska. It was understood, but nowhere described in the agreement itself, that within these ceilings, the United States would provide support to the Bosniac armed forces, ostensibly in order to create an internal balance of power to deter future attacks by Bosnian Serbs.

On broader issues of public security, Dayton said comparatively little. In the context of the military annexes, however, the parties did pledge to maintain a "safe and secure environment for all persons in their respective jurisdictions," and they further committed to cooperation with all international personnel, expressly including those working with the International Criminal Tribunal for the Former Yugoslavia (ICTY).[52]

Civilian Provisions

The civilian provisions (Annexes 3–11; see table 2.1) covered all other aspects of keeping the peace. Annex 3 (Elections) promised free and fair elections within nine months, provided that "politically neutral" conditions could be established.[53] The first round of balloting would cover at least executive and legislative offices at state and entity levels: the three-person presidency of Bosnia; president of Republika Srpska; and the respective legislatures of Bosnia, the Federation, and Republika Srpska, as well as legislative assemblies in the Federation's ten cantons. It held open the possibility that elections might also be held for the country's 100-plus municipalities.

Annex 4 (Constitution) detailed an elaborate architecture for power sharing among Bosnia's three parties and two entities within a single state. The two entities retained significant autonomy under these arrangements, with exclusive authority over their own armed forces, internal affairs and police, judiciary, and a wide range of social sectors. Republika Srpska and the Federation also controlled taxes and duties collected on their own territory, which made the Bosnian state dependent upon fiscal transfers from the entities.[54]

Table 2.1. General Framework Agreement (Dayton Agreement), Annexes with Key Implementers

Annex	Title	Key Implementers
1A	Military Aspects	NATO-Led Implementation Force
1B	Regional Stabilization	Organization for Security and Co-operation in Europe (OSCE)
2	Inter-Entity Boundary Line and Related Issues	International Arbitrator
3	Elections	OSCE
4	Constitution	European Court of Human Rights, International Monetary Fund
5	Arbitration	N/A
6	Human Rights	OSCE, Council of Europe
7	Refugees and Displaced Persons	UN High Commissioner for Refugees
8	Commission to Preserve National Monuments	UN Educational, Scientific, and Cultural Organization
9	Bosnia and Herzegovina Public Corporations	European Bank for Reconstruction and Development
10	Civilian Implementation	Office of the High Representative
11	International Police Task Force	United Nations

Annex 5 (Arbitration) committed the parties to arbitration as a means of dispute resolution.[55]

Annex 6 (Human Rights) committed Bosnian authorities to a full range of international human rights conventions and established new mechanisms for monitoring Bosnia's compliance with them. The constitution incorporated fifteen international conventions, including the European Convention for the Protection of Human Rights, into Bosnian domestic law.

Annex 7 (Refugees and Displaced Persons) promised all 2.2 million of Bosnia's refugees and internally displaced persons (IDPs) that they could return to their "homes of origin," thereby reversing the ethnic cleansing that had been both a goal and a tactic of the war.[56] To enable this right of return, Dayton obliged the parties to an extensive array of minority protection measures, from repeal of discriminatory legislation and suppression of hate speech to agreement to refrain from intimidation and to prosecute any public authority engaged in it.[57] Dayton also called for the parties to establish a commission to consider property claims and their just compensation.[58]

Annex 8 (Commission to Preserve National Monuments) aimed to involve the parties in protecting or rebuilding the country's national patrimony.

Annex 9 (Public Corporations) provided for the establishment of joint bodies to operate public facilities in areas such as transportation, energy, utilities, post, and telecommunications.

Finally, as discussed further below, Annexes 10 (Civilian Implementation) and 11 (International Police Task Force) covered two additional dimensions of international assistance: the first establishing the office of an international High Representative to oversee civilian implementation and the second establishing a UN civilian police mission to monitor, advise, and train Bosnia's extensive police forces.

Political Support for Peace

Negotiations at Dayton were conducted almost exclusively by the United States, with representatives of the five-member Contact Group[59] and the European Union present but without a decisive role. With the exception of NATO, other international organizations that would be asked to implement parts of the agreement, including the United Nations, were not significantly involved in the Dayton process.

Two of the parties did not negotiate on their own behalf; the Bosnian Croats and Bosnian Serbs were represented by Croatia and Serbia, respectively. In fact, both regional parties went to considerable effort to keep their conationals in the dark. Croatia and Serbia both had their own interests at Dayton. Croatian president Tudjman was eager to gain Serbian recognition of Croatia's borders, especially as this affected Eastern Slavonia,[60] and President Milosevic was desperate to get economic sanctions on the Federal Republic of Yugoslavia lifted.

Both leaders proved willing to sacrifice some interests of Bosnian Croats and Serbs in service of their own. All parties were also smarting from the battlefield. The Serbs had lost most of their territorial holdings in both Croatia and Bosnia in a matter of weeks. The Bosniacs—and, to a lesser extent, the Bosnian Croats—were frustrated that their advance on Serb holdings had been halted when they regained 51 percent of Bosnian territory, far short of the more thorough rout of Bosnian Serbs that some among them felt was within reach.

Despite the narrow negotiating base, the Dayton Agreement won broad political support in the international community. There was little alternative. Four years of high-level European engagement in the peace process for the former Yugoslavia had failed to make meaningful headway, and the Europeans were now ready to accept the leadership of the United States.[61] The agreement was also structured to give major implementing roles to a range of interested nations and organizations. For example, military implementation would be handled by a NATO-led force under U.S. command, while a senior European official would be named the High Representative to oversee arrangements on the civilian side. Critical responsibilities were also parceled out to other international organizations. The United Nations, largely discredited in the eyes of Washington, found its role limited to the return of refugees and the reform of Bosnia's police force. Several potential roles for the United Nations were rejected, even in areas where the organization had considerable institutional experience, such as conducting elections.[62]

Shortly before the agreement was signed, an ad hoc group of fifty-plus interested states—including international donors who had felt excluded from the much smaller Contact Group—constituted itself as a Peace Implementation Council (PIC) to guide and support the implementation effort to come.[63] Initially, the PIC limited itself to appointing the High Representative. As time passed, however, the council became a unique feature of the peace process in Bosnia and Herzegovina, assigning to the High Representative executive powers unforeseen in the Dayton Agreement, if without clear legal basis. Through this instrument, some of the structural weaknesses in the Dayton Agreement were eventually addressed, and implementation, which had largely slowed by 1997, was able to proceed more rapidly thereafter.

Political support for the agreement within Bosnia and Herzegovina, and among neighboring states, was more convoluted. For many of these actors, the agreement and the peace process that followed were viewed as an opportunity for the continuation of war by other means.

The Serbs, in particular, appeared to view the negotiation process, peace agreement, and implementation that followed as vehicles by which to consolidate and subsequently resume pursuit of some of their war aims. Faced with what was becoming a rout on the battlefield, the Serbs had been the most eager for negotiations to begin. At Dayton, the Serb negotiators felt that many of their basic war aims had been secured. Under the provisions of the agreement, they would retain control of a continuous band of territory covering almost half of the land area of Bosnia and Herzegovina, including the entire border with Serbia and Montenegro, and large tracts of land in which, prior to the war, Bosniacs had constituted a majority. They would keep the ethnically identifying name "Republika Srpska," and a clear administrative boundary would separate them from the Bosniac-Croat Federation. The central state apparatus would be weak to a vanishing point. And within their own territory, they would retain an unusual level of autonomy, including the maintenance of their own armed forces, which would be deployed chiefly along the internal border with the Federation rather than outward along the international border.[64]

Leaving Dayton, two issues still troubled the Bosnian Serbs. The first was the requirement that they cede most of the areas they held around Sarajevo to the Federation. These areas, in which approximately 100,000 Serbs lived, were symbolically important to the Pale leadership. Second, there was anxiety about the provision for the return of refugees. The population of the territory that had been allocated to Republika Srpska had been somewhat less than 50 percent Serb prior to the war, and any large-scale return of non-Serb refugees promised to undermine Serb control of those areas.[65]

For the Bosniacs, as ever, the situation was the opposite. The state of Bosnia and Herzegovina would be preserved, which many Bosniacs saw as important, yet it would be divided ethnically, administratively, and even militarily. They negotiated hard to be given control of the town of Brcko, which connected Serb-majority areas in the west of the country to those in the east. In this they failed, though a complicated arrangement ensured that neither side would fully control that area.[66] Some also believed—as did Bosnian Croats—that their forces had been on the verge of victory over the Serbs when the United States vigorously appealed to them to stop short of retaking the western flank of Republika Srpska. The Bosniac leadership thus accepted the Dayton deal with misgivings and only after promises were made to heavily invest in Bosnia's postwar reconstruction and to equip and fully train Bosnia's still-young army.[67]

For the Croat leadership, the Dayton negotiations were a frustration. Having formed themselves into a federation with the Bosniacs at American urging, they were unable to negotiate the territorial and constitutional autonomy that were to be enjoyed by the Serbs, despite their recent battlefield successes. In a conflict in which each national community sought to avoid being a minority in any given political structure, the Croats enjoyed none of the minimal confidence felt by either of the other communities. So deep were these concerns that the Bosnian Croat representative at the peace talks resigned, leaving it to the representatives of the Republic of Croatia to initial the agreement in his stead.[68]

Mandate

The Dayton Agreement entailed a robust mandate on the military side, vested in a single, powerful organization—IFOR—versus a weak and decentralized mandate on the civilian side, with authority vested in several separate and autonomous organizations, as noted earlier. These efforts were to be loosely coordinated by the Office of the High Representative (OHR), though the office was not empowered with any line authority over implementing organizations or authority over the parties to the agreement. At Dayton, an overriding concern of senior U.S. military officials appeared to be that the central role of the U.S. military in the implementation process should not be subject to interference from nonmilitary or non-U.S. actors.[69] This view prevailed.

Military Responsibilities
Military provisions were to be supervised by IFOR. Authorized under Chapter VII of the UN Charter, IFOR reported to the North Atlantic Council (NAC), was 60,000 strong at first deployment, and was supposed

to complete its work by December 1996. IFOR's primary function was to separate armed forces, oversee cantonment of troops and heavy weapons, and stabilize the cease-fire, all fairly traditional peacekeeping tasks.[70] IFOR's main distinction from conventional peacekeeping lay in its robust capability, expressed willingness to deter military violations by the parties, and clear signal of strong U.S. backing.

IFOR also had multiple secondary functions, most related to dimensions of public security. In principle, IFOR was authorized to ensure that the parties complied with their obligations to protect civilians in their respective jurisdictions, to establish and preserve freedom of movement (specifically, "to observe and prevent interference with the movement of civilian populations, refugees, and displaced persons, and to respond appropriately to deliberate violence to life and person"), and to broadly support other components of implementation, with specific reference to the return-related responsibilities of the UN High Commissioner for Refugees (UNHCR). The agreement also asked IFOR to facilitate cooperation with the International Criminal Tribunal at The Hague, which many hoped would result in the force acting to apprehend "persons indicted for war crimes" (PIFWCs).[71]

In addition, the IFOR commander was given "final authority in theatre" to interpret all military aspects of the settlement and add to or subtract from the force's role "without interference or permission of any Party."[72] This provision reflected a U.S. concern with avoiding the "dual key" arrangement that, according to many critics, had inhibited NATO action during the war. Under the Dayton regime, military planners insisted that there be a unified, U.S. command free of civilian interference in tactical decisions.[73]

IFOR's mandate was renewed in December 1996, and the force was renamed the Stabilization Force (SFOR). Troop levels were gradually drawn down in the ensuing eight years, culminating in a handover to a European-led force in December 2004. There was no major change in the force's formal mandate in that time, and the only substantive change to the operation was addition of a 350-man specialized police battalion in mid-1998, specially trained and equipped to deal with public order and security.[74] However, there was a marked shift to a more assertive interpretation of the mandate after 1997. This was particularly notable with regard to apprehension of PIFWCs and public security.

Civilian Responsibilities

Civilian provisions were much less coherent and robust. Some tasks had single agency leads—for example, refugee return (UNHCR), elections (Organization for Security and Co-operation in Europe, or OSCE), and civilian policing (UN Department of Peacekeeping Operations). Other tasks had multiple agencies committed to their undertaking—for example, human rights (the collective responsibility of the OSCE, Council of Europe, UN High Commission on Human Rights, and European Court of Human Rights). Some agencies had multiple roles—for example, the OSCE (elections and regional arms control). Still others not mentioned in the agreement were understood to be central to its implementation; for example, the World Bank and the European Commission were expected to take the lead in postwar reconstruction.

Elections

National elections were to be held within nine months of the agreement's signing, provided that "a politically neutral environment" could be established in order to ensure a comparatively free and fair ballot.[75] The agreement specifically referred to freedoms of association, movement, expression, and the press and to absence of fear or intimidation.[76]

In Annex 3, the OSCE was asked to prepare, conduct, and supervise all aspects of the elections, including verification of acceptable conditions for holding them. This was a new responsibility for an organization that had never fielded an electoral mission before. Its head of mission would chair a Provisional Election Commission (PEC) composed of both international and Bosnian members that would establish all electoral rules and regulations until Bosnia could establish a permanent election commission of its own. Each of the three main ethnic groups was represented on the PEC, though its chair could designate additional members and his decisions were final and binding.[77] PEC rulings overrode preexisting national laws, and the body could take remedial action should any person or party violate the electoral rules it had established.[78] Acting through the PEC, the OSCE would formulate rules governing eligibility and registration of political parties and candidates, eligibility and registration of voters, method of voting, codes of campaign conduct, and the role of domestic and international observers.

The PEC could also establish subsidiary bodies, and it soon created a potent network of election-related offices.[79] These included a judicial Election Appeals Sub-Commission (EASC), set up in May 1996 to enforce compliance with the PEC's rules and regulations;[80] a National Election Results Implementation Commission, established in December 1996 to monitor implementation of election results, especially at the municipal level; and a Media Expert Commission, created in 1996 to regulate electronic media, which in 1998 was renamed the Independent Media Commission and put under the authority of the High Representative.

Between 1996 and 2001, the OSCE oversaw six rounds of balloting: three at the national and entity levels (in 1996, 1998, and 2000); one special election for the Republika Srpska National Assembly (in 1997); and two at the municipal level (in 1997 and 2000). In August 2001, the Bosnian legislature finally adopted a permanent election law and replaced the PEC with a new national Election Commission, which oversaw a fourth round of national elections in October 2002.[81]

While the OSCE eventually ended its oversight of Bosnian elections in 2002, the High Representative became more involved over time, starting with his establishment of a commission in 1998 to speed up the process of drafting the election law. With its passage, the High Representative remained engaged in the elections process through his authority to appoint the four national members of the Election Commission.[82]

Return of the Displaced

A staggering 50 percent of Bosnia's population was forcibly displaced during the conflict, a demographic shift that Dayton proposed to reverse. The agreement went beyond existing standards or practices to promise that the displaced could be repatriated not just to their home country but to their "home of origin" within it.[83]

Lead responsibility for return was assigned to the UN High Commissioner for Refugees in Annex 7. UNHCR's primary tasks were to plan, coordinate, and implement refugee repatriation and IDP return. In the process, the agency also became involved in a wide range of related activities involving additional agencies and nongovernmental organizations, such as providing temporary and permanent housing and tracing missing persons as well as providing medical assistance, distributing food, and protecting those who had been displaced.

Over time, the High Representative assumed a role on return issues as well, largely through the creation of a Reconstruction and Return Task Force (RRTF) in January 1997. The RRTF's mission was to work toward better integrating refugee returns with economic rehabilitation efforts in recognition of the impediment to returns posed by a lack of economic opportunities available to returnees.

International Police Task Force

In December 1995, a UN assessment team estimated that the number of police active in Bosnia had grown to three times prewar levels, to about 44,750.[84] This represented an approximate police-to-civilian ratio of 1:73, which was especially worrying given the paramilitary nature of much of the police forces and the heavy involvement of police in prosecution of the war effort.[85]

In Annex 11, the United Nations was asked to field an international civilian police mission to help downsize these forces and bring their conduct into line with "internationally recognized standards and with respect for internationally recognized human rights and fundamental freedoms."[86] This International Police Task Force (IPTF), which would be built out of the remnants of UNPROFOR, was subsequently christened the UN Mission in Bosnia and Herzegovina (UNMIBH).[87]

IPTF's precise mandate was to monitor, advise, and train Bosnian law enforcement agencies, with UNMIBH's larger role being to provide direction and support to the IPTF. The United Nations and IPTF's responsibilities evolved over time. They increasingly emphasized training in addition to monitoring, including human rights components for which UNMIBH established its own human rights unit. In 1996 IPTF also acquired independent investigatory powers,[88] and in 1998 UNMIBH began focusing on judicial reform.[89] Additional tasks included implementing law enforcement aspects of the Brcko settlement (S/Res/1103 in 1997); specialized training of police in drug control and organized crime (S/Res/1168 in 1998); and monitoring the courts and assisting judicial reform efforts (S/Res/1184 in 1998).

The mandate posed one immediate challenge: that there was no text, convention, or otherwise recognized statement regarding what "internationally recognized standards of law enforcement" actually entailed. IPTF found itself having to draft rules and standards to which Bosnian police—and international police monitors themselves—would subsequently be held accountable.[90]

The mandate also encoded a basic internal tension. On the one hand, IPTF was to advise and train local law enforcement, which required establishing trust and confidence with Bosnian police. On the other hand, especially after December 1996, IPTF was to monitor police behavior and investigate questionable conduct, putting it in a potentially adversarial position.

Other Civilian Roles

A few of Dayton's military provisions were actually assigned to civilian organizations. Dispensation over Brcko—which was treated in the agreement as a matter of territorial clarification of the IEBL and thus fell within the "military" sections of the agreement (Annex 2)—was remanded to international arbitration, which was meant to result in a final and binding decision within one year. Complementary to Dayton's principal military tasks, arms control and confidence-building measures were assigned to the OSCE (Annex 1B).

More consequentially, international actors and experts were also assigned roles within multiple new bodies that flourished in the postwar period, and were usually invested with decision-making authority (see table 2.2). The Provisional Election Commission and Election Appeals Sub-Commission have already been noted. In addition, three of nine seats on Bosnia's Constitutional Court were reserved for non-Bosnians, who were to be appointed to five-year terms by the European Court of Human Rights. Bosnia's Central Bank was to be headed for its first six years by a non-Bosnian governor appointed by the International Monetary Fund. The ombudsman for the new Human Rights Commission was to be an OSCE-appointed non-Bosnian for the first five years, and eight of fourteen members of the Human Rights Chamber, including its president, were to be appointed for five-year, renewable terms by the Council of Europe. Three of nine members, including the chair, of the Commission on Real Property Claims would be appointed for five-year, renewable terms by the European Court of Human Rights. Two of five members of the Commission on Public Corporations were

Table 2.2. International Representation on Select Governing Bodies of Bosnia and Herzegovina

Body	International Representatives	Key Roles and Authority	Selection Process	BiH Reps (State-Fed-RS)
Joint Interim Commission	OHR chairs			0-4-3
Provisional Election Commission, ended 2002	4 of 7 (later 16), including chair	OSCE chairs; decisions binding		1-1-1 (later 4-4-4)
Election Commission, from 2002	3 of 7		Bosnian members appointed by OHR	1-1-1, plus 1 other
Election Appeals Sub-commission	1 of 4	OSCE chairs, can over-ride splits; decisions binding, no appeal	Appointed by OSCE	1-1-1
Constitutional Court	3 of 9, five-year term		Parliamentary Assembly can amend after five years	0-4-2
Central Bank	1 (the governor), six-year term, renewable	International governor	Appointed by International Monetary Fund	N/A
Human Rights Chamber	8 of 14, including president; five-year term, renewable		Appointed by Council of Europe Committee of Ministers	0-4-2

Human Rights Ombudsman	1 (the ombudsman)	International president	Appointed by OSCE chair-in-office; after five years, appointed by BiH president	N/A
Commission on Real Property Claims	3 including chair, five-year term, renewable	International chair	Appointed by European Court of Human Rights	0-4-2
Independent Media Commission	3 including director-general	International director-general		0-1-1
Commission on Public Corporations	2 including chair, five-year term, renewable	International chair	Appointed by European Bank for Reconstruction and Development	0-2-1
Commission to Preserve National Monuments	2 including chair, five-year term, renewable	International chair	Appointed by UNESCO	0-2-1

to be appointed by the European Bank for Reconstruction and Development. And two of five seats on the Commission to Preserve National Monuments were to be appointed by UNESCO. In addition, the High Representative was authorized to establish any new mechanisms or bodies he found necessary for civilian implementation.

Civilian Coordination

The civilian OHR was designated to help coordinate this wide range of civilian tasks, with strategic oversight meant to come from the new PIC and its Steering Board. Despite high expectations, the OHR had minimal initial leverage either on the parties or on other implementers. The High Representative did enjoy a textually coequal status to the IFOR commander in being designated the "final authority in theatre" to interpret Dayton's civilian provisions; however, in practice, he was able to exercise negligible authority in the critical start-up phase of implementation.

From the beginning, OHR focused heavily on the establishment and implementation of Bosnia's new joint political institutions. Though this was not an express part of OHR's fairly generic mandate, the task was not assigned to any other organization, despite the fact that getting these new institutions to function was presumably central to the state-building project envisioned by Dayton. The importance of these issues had also long been a theme of the first High Representative, Carl Bildt, who lamented their comparative neglect during the negotiations at Dayton.[91] Over time, OHR incorporated into its coordination mandate an increasingly substantive portfolio, especially in the areas of human rights and rule of law, economic recovery, and refugee return.

Tensions and Challenges in the Mandate

One important weakness of the Dayton Agreement was the timetable. Political considerations within the United States—namely, the uphill battle faced by the Clinton administration to get domestic support for a sustained military commitment while in the shadow of Somalia and with a presidential election the following year—led negotiators to build into the Dayton Agreement a one-year deadline for the pullout of military peacekeepers. Getting a U.S. troop commitment was particularly important to European governments, who refused to join any postwar implementation force without U.S. participation, given their experience with UNPROFOR. This temporal fiction, as it was widely recognized at the time, necessitated a parallel commitment that internationally supervised elections also be held within the year.

The main weakness of the mandate, however, was structural and twofold: first, in the division between military and civilian wings of implementation, and second, in the decentralization among civilian tasks with a weak coordination mandate for the High Representative. OHR's initial ineffectiveness was exacerbated by the lack of institutional support and, indeed, accountability, as it reported to the ad hoc PIC, which had no institutional structure of its own.

The chief vehicle for overcoming these tensions, though not anticipated at the time, became the augmentation of the authority and powers of the high representative. This gradual empowerment involved an increasingly stark trade-off between results and "ownership." Exercise of the High Representative's so-called Bonn powers made it easier for the international community to accomplish a variety of objectives in the face of obstruction from uncooperative domestic actors. The price, however, has been a pattern of proconsul-like intrusion in Bosnian domestic politics and a lack of international accountability to Bosnian citizens. Over time, this pattern bred cynicism and disaffection in Bosnian society even as it proved necessary to move the implementation process forward.

Funding

The Bosnian peace operation would become one of the most expensive in the international community's experience. While it is difficult to gather comparable data about budget expenditures from different implementing agencies, some rough estimates can be credibly made (see table 2.3).[92] The military component of implementation, not surprisingly, was the most expensive. Estimates of IFOR and SFOR costs range up to $31 billion from inception in late 1995 through completion in late 2004, or 75 to 80 percent of the total international support effort for Bosnia during that period.[93] Economic reconstruction and humanitarian aid, at roughly $5 billion through 2001, accounted for barely more than 16 percent of international spending in those years.

Table 2.3. Costs of Key Elements of International Implementation, 1996–2004
(in millions, rounded to nearest million)

	1996	1997	1998	1999	2000	2001	Subtotal	Yearly Average	% of Total	2002	2003	2004	Subtotal
IFOR and SFOR[a]	$6,301	$4,441	$4,389	$4,149	$3,076	$3,133	$25,489	$4,248	79.2%	$2,530	$1,772	$1,175	$30,996
UNMIBH[b]	$37	$118	$157	$170	$152	$146	$780	$130	2.4%	$131	$74	N/A	$985
OSCE[c]	$104	$104	$75	$64	$72	$45	$464	$77	1.4%	$35	$42	$41	$582
OHR	$20	$36	$41	$54	$46	$41	$238	$40	1.1%				
Subtotal	$6,462	$4,699	$4,662	$4,437	$3,346	$3,365	$26,971	$4,495	83.8%				
Economic Aid[d]	$989	$701	$884	$803	$421	$417	$4,215	$703	13.1%				
Humanitarian Aid[e]	$398	$290	$172	$110	$20	$14	$1,004	$167	3.1%				
Subtotal	$1,387	$991	$1,056	$913	$441	$431	$5,219	$870	16.2%				
Total	$7,849	$5,690	$5,718	$5,350	$3,787	$3,796	$32,190	$5,365	100%				

a Combines U.S. incremental costs, as reported by Serafino, with estimates of average non-U.S. troop contributors' costs, calculated from expenditures reported by Ek for first-year deployments in Kosovo, adjusted for assumed 3 percent/year inflation.

b Actual expenditures, calculated from UN documents. Figures keyed to end-year based on UN fiscal year of July–June. First and last entries are part-years: December 1995 (start-up date) through June 1996; and July–December 2002 (when the mission ended, halfway through the 2002–3 peacekeeping fiscal year).

c OSCE and OHR include operating budgets plus cost of staff secondments estimated at $10,000 per secondee per month, which is probably low.

d 1996–98 data from European Commission and World Bank; 1999–2001 data estimated from EC, World Bank, and U.S. Agency for International Development (AID) trends for these years.

e Data from the three largest humanitarian donors in Bosnia: UN High Commissioner for Refugees, European Commission Humanitarian Aid Office, and AID.

Sources: Nina M. Serafino, "Peacekeeping: Issues of U.S. Military Involvement," no. IB94040 (Washington, DC: Congressional Research Service, August 6, 2003), 16. Carl Ek, "NATO Burdensharing and Kosovo: A Preliminary Report," no. RL30398 (Washington, DC: Congressional Research Service, January 3, 2000), 14–15. UN data from UN Department of Peacekeeping Operations, summary budgets and performance reports. OSCE, OHR, and AID data from Aurora Ferrari.

The cost of UNMIBH, about $780 million through 2001, was 2.4 percent of the total. The costs of two of the larger civilian presences in the country—the OHR and OSCE—were 2.1 percent of the total. OHR's budget averaged $40 million per year and the OSCE's $77 million, including estimated costs of staff secondments. The overall allocation of international resources in Bosnia remained heavily skewed toward the military, even with the progressive drawdown in the size of SFOR.

Given the economic and institutional challenges that persistently inhibited Bosnia's postwar recovery, it is worth examining the early expenditures on economic assistance (estimated at $4.2 billion between 1996 and 2001; see table 2.4). To the extent that resource allocation reveals implicit priorities, the numbers are telling. Nearly half of international economic assistance delivered between 1996 and 2001 was devoted to infrastructure repair, whereas other sectors of activity arguably were more critical for lasting economic recovery. Just over one-fifth of economic assistance to Bosnia was devoted to restarting Bosnian productive activity, another one-fifth came as fiscal support for the new state, and only one-tenth was devoted to social assistance (a low figure even if some of this support, particularly for refugees, is counted under humanitarian assistance).[94]

Planning and Deployment

The experience of planning and deployment mirrored the split between military and civilian implementation and the much higher relative priority accorded the former. IFOR also benefited from an early reliance on UNPROFOR assets, as did those elements of civilian implementation that already had a presence on the ground and could therefore get a postwar operation up and running more quickly.

Command and Control

The most salient feature of post-Dayton international operations in Bosnia was the division between military and civilian chains of command. IFOR (and subsequently SFOR) would be made up of both NATO and non-NATO troops, but would operate under the political direction of the NAC through the NATO chain of command. Overall military authority lay with NATO's Supreme Allied Commander

Table 2.4. Breakdown of Economic Aid, 1996–2001
(in millions)

	1996[a]	1997	1998	1999	2000	2001	Subtotal	Yearly Average	Percentage of Total
Infrastructure[b]	$526.00	$357.00	$363.00	$329.88	$172.85	$171.26	$1,919.99	$320.00	45.5%
Productive Sector	$148.00	$197.00	$208.00	$189.02	$99.04	$98.13	$939.19	$156.53	22.3%
Social Sector	$104.00	$88.00	$86.00	$78.15	$40.95	$40.57	$437.68	$72.95	10.4%
Fiscal Support	$211.00	$59.00	$227.00	$206.29	$108.09	$107.10	$918.47	$153.08	21.8%
Total	$989.00	$701.00	$884.00	$803.34	$420.93	$417.06	$4,215.33	$702.56	100.0%

[a]Data for 1996–98 from EC and World Bank, "1996-1998 Lessons and Accomplishments: Review of the Priority Reconstruction and Recovery Program," May 1999. Exchange rate calculated on January of each year. Data for 1999–2001 estimated based on EC, World Bank, and AID trends for these years.
[b]Infrastructure includes transport, telecommunications, energy, water and sanitation, housing, and landmine clearing. Productive sector includes industry and finance, agriculture, and employment generation. Social sector includes health and education.

Europe (SACEUR)—George Joulwan in the critical start-up phase of the operation; Wesley Clark from 1997 to 2000; Joseph Ralston from 2000 to 2003; and James Jones from 2003 to the time of this writing. It was understood that the NATO force would always be commanded by an American.[95] In the start-up of IFOR, the force commander of UNPROFOR, General Bernard Janvier, was designated deputy commander of IFOR in order to facilitate handover.[96] Bosnia was effectively divided into three geographical zones of operation under the respective command of the United States (based in Tuzla), the United Kingdom (based in Banja Luka), and France (based in Mostar), though each "multinational division" (MND) included troops from several countries.

In addition to the multiple specifications in Annex 1A regarding the IFOR commander's tactical latitude, Annex 10 underscored that there would be no civilian oversight of IFOR operations. Specifically, "the High Representative shall have no authority over the IFOR and shall not in any way interfere in the conduct of military operations or the IFOR chain of command."[97] His role was instead circumscribed to maintaining "close contact" and "appropriate liaison arrangements" with the force.[98]

Meanwhile, on the civilian side, reporting lines were almost completely decentralized, with the High Representative asked to coordinate civilian agencies while "respect[ing] their autonomy within their spheres of operation" and giving only "general guidance." According to Carl Bildt, the weakness of the High Representative's mandate on the civilian side also reflected primarily a U.S.—more specifically, a U.S. military—concern. He cites an early American draft at Dayton—when the role was designated a mere "implementation coordinator"—proposing that the coordinator "would not have any authority over any international organizations, voluntary organizations or functions in the host country."[99]

A novel aspect of IFOR was the inclusion of a Russian brigade. Russia fielded approximately 2,000 troops as part of IFOR (and approximately 1,200 under SFOR) and was the largest non-NATO troop contributor. A unique command and control arrangement was devised whereby a Russian general was named special deputy to the SACEUR, through whom the Russian brigade would receive NATO orders.[100] Russian troops were assigned to MND-North, and it was recognized that they would be under the tactical control of the commanding U.S. general. Russian participation was valuable for multiple reasons. The Serbs had insisted that Russians participate in IFOR, and their presence was an important negotiating chip. More broadly, cooperation between Russia and the United States in Bosnia was a kind of test case for evolving political and security relations in Europe after the end of the Cold War.[101]

Security Components

IFOR was authorized at a strength of 60,000 troops, including ground, air, and maritime units. In early December, NATO fielded an Advance Enabling Force of 2,600 troops to establish headquarters in Sarajevo and necessary communications and logistics support. UNPROFOR equipment and assets were made available to NATO, and it was expected that a large segment of UNPROFOR units would "rehat" and transfer to IFOR, both of which would help speed IFOR's deployment.[102] IFOR deployment was activated on December 15 after the NAC approved the operational plan (designated Operation Joint Endeavor). The formal transfer of authority from UNPROFOR to IFOR occurred on December 20.

The international military presence in Bosnia downsized from 60,000 to approximately 32,000 when SFOR took over from IFOR, and it eventually shrank to about 7,500 in November 2004 (see table 2.5). Throughout, it retained a three-part structure, though it evolved as the force shrank from multinational divisions to multinational brigades, with headquarters in Tuzla (approximately 1,800 personnel), Mostar (approximately 1,800 personnel), and Banja Luka (approximately 2,000 personnel). There were also 350 personnel at SFOR headquarters in Sarajevo and about 1,000 "theater troops" based at various other locations in Bosnia.[103]

Based on its assessment of police strength in Bosnia, the UN secretary-general initially recommended a total of 1,721 unarmed police monitors in order to achieve a monitor–to–local police ratio of 1:30, including supervisory personnel.[104] (See table 2.6.) These would be supported by approximately 49 civil affairs and related officers to provide broader advice and guidance both to IPTF and to the head of UNMIBH.[105] The secretary-general's original recommendation was for an operational structure that had regional headquarters colocated

Table 2.5. Troop-Contributing Countries for Peace Operations in Bosnia and Herzegovina

	IFOR	SFOR			EUFOR
	March 1996	August 1998	January 2002	January 2004	August 2005
Albania	—	35	70	70	71
Argentina	—	68	10	—	2
Australia	—	—	10	—	—
Austria	300	230	10	2	202
Belgium	300	850	10	4	58
Bulgaria	—	58	190	25	36
Canada	1,000	1,250	1,500	800	85
Chile	—	—	—	—	20
Czech Republic	850	640	20	14	89
Denmark	800	747	330	4	—
Egypt	400	270	—	—	—
Estonia	25	41	90	1	2
Finland	850	341	100	—	183
France	7,500	2,500	2,280	1,500	402
Germany	—	2,470	1,720	1,000	1,180
Greece	1,000	280	120	250	181
Hungary	500	310	130	154	122
Ireland	—	50	50	50	52
Italy	2,100	1,970	1,370	979	1,004
Jordan	—	10	—	—	—
Latvia	25	39	10	1	3
Lithuania	25	40	10	97	1
Luxembourg	36	36	—	23	1
Morocco	650	650	270	270	133
Netherlands	2,000	1,080	1,440	1,000	430

Table 2.5. *(cont.)*

	IFOR	SFOR			EUFOR
	March 1996	August 1998	January 2002	January 2004	August 2005
New Zealand	—	10	26	14	—
Norway	750	615	20	125	17
Poland	600	400	280	287	226
Portugal	900	320	360	330	231
Romania	221	221	150	106	110
Russia	1,400	1,400	640	—	—
Slovakia	—	—	10	29	4
Slovenia	—	57	10	158	153
Spain	1,250	1,550	1,210	935	467
Sweden	800	510	30	7	80
Switzerland	—	—	—	—	25
Turkey	1,200	1,520	760	1,200	345
Ukraine	150	380	—	—	—
United Kingdom	13,000	5,000	1,890	1,100	727
United States	16,500	7,400	3,100	839	—
Total in BiH	55,132	33,338	18,210	11,386	6,656

Sources: **IFOR:** "Operation Joint Endeavor Fact Sheet No. 006-B," December 11, 1995, www.dtic.mil/bosnia/fs/fs006b.html, compared with Steven R. Bowman, "Bosnia: U.S. Military Operations," Issue Brief no. IB93056 (Washington, DC: Congressional Research Service, updated July 8, 2003), 8–10. **SFOR:** U.S. General Accounting Office, "Bosnia Peace Operation: Missions, Structure, and Transition Strategy of NATO's Stabilization Force," GAO/NSIAD-99-19 (Washington, DC: October 1998), 34–35; Bowman, "Bosnia: U.S. Military Operations"; International Institute for Security Studies, *The Military Balance, 2004-05* (Oxford: Oxford University Press, 2004). United Nations, *Letter dated 1 March 2004 from the Secretary General of the North Atlantic Treaty Organization addressed to the Secretary-General*, S/2004/174, Annex, March 4, 2004, gives a total force of 11,280 in January 2004. **EUFOR:** European Union, "EUFOR Troop Strength 10 August 2005" (Web chart, updated monthly), www.euforbih.org/organisation/050810_strength.htm.

Table 2.6. Composition of the International Police Task Force

Contributing Country	June 1996	June 1999	May 2002	Contributing Country	June 1996	June 1999	May 2002
Argentina	40	35	16	Kenya	—	11	7
Austria	17	39	13	Lithuania	—	2	—
Bangladesh	36	33	26	Malaysia	43	47	25
Bulgaria	20	44	34	Nepal	141	41	18
Canada	—	29	9	Netherlands	50	45	54
Chile	—	29	6	Nigeria	—	22	6
China	—	—	15	Norway	—	24	12
Czech Republic	—	—	5	Pakistan	134	98	93
Denmark	36	28	30	Poland	26	49	50
Egypt	25	34	47	Portugal	41	53	31
Estonia	9	5	—	Romania	—	20	18
Fiji	—	5	15	Russian Federation	35	34	38
Finland	11	21	11	Senegal	53	20	19
France	100	95	114	Spain	47	57	30
Germany	85	114	153	Sweden	39	56	30
Ghana	90	99	98	Switzerland	5	4	10
Greece	9	9	11	Tunisia	7	2	—
Hungary	31	37	13	Thailand	—	5	5
Iceland	—	3	3	Turkey	26	18	36
India	77	102	95	Ukraine	16	32	35
Indonesia	28	31	27	United Kingdom	—	80	76
Ireland	31	27	35	United States	156	168	46
Italy	—	22	23				
Jordan	98	191	148	Total	1,562	1,920	1,588

Sources: UN Security Council, *Report of the Secretary-General Pursuant to Resolution 1035 (1995)*, S/1996/460, June 21, 1996. UN Security Council, *Report of the Secretary-General on the United Nations Mission in Bosnia and Herzegovina*, S/1999/670, June 11, 1999. UN Security Council, *Report of the Secretary-General on the United Nations Mission in Bosnia and Herzegovina*, S/2002/618, June 5, 2002.

with IFOR in addition to deploying police monitors in each of Bosnia's 109 municipalities. It quickly became clear that replicating Bosnia's prewar police structure in the UN mission would be administratively burdensome and operationally unnecessary, as many municipalities were close enough to one another to be monitored effectively from one central location. The first IPTF commissioner therefore reduced the number of IPTF stations from 109 to between 50 and 60.[106]

More than forty countries contributed civilian police personnel, the first of whom began to deploy in January 1996, adding their numbers to civilian police already in the field as part of UNPROFOR.[107] In line with previous missions, the United Nations asked that police meet certain basic requirements including English fluency, driving ability, and eight years' experience in their home country. Later in the mission, greater emphasis would be placed on additional, specialized skills such as training and administration. Unfortunately, also in keeping with previous missions, many civilian police arrived in theater who could not meet even the minimal standards. ("The number of those who failed to meet the criteria and to pass the required elementary tests upon arrival in theater has risen to alarming levels.")[108] By the end of February, a mere 400 of the authorized strength of 1,721 had arrived in theater, 80 of whom had to be returned to their governments.[109] Police standards also varied considerably among the contributing countries, which ranged from Argentina to Nigeria to the Ukraine to the United Kingdom.[110] This was a particular weakness given the objective of training Bosnian police in standards of "democratic policing." There were also problems posed by different rotation rates among different contributors (for example, French and German police served for only six months).

Other Components

Most agencies experienced a similar difficulty in recruiting staff with appropriate skills as well as delays in getting staff into the field, poor information flow, and resource scarcity.[111] For agencies with a foothold on the ground—for example, UNHCR, which had been extensively involved in providing humanitarian assistance during the war—establishing a postwar presence presented comparatively fewer difficulties. UNMIBH drew on UNPROFOR civilian personnel to staff up the new mission, but many of the old mission's physical assets were transferred to IFOR, leaving IPTF to begin almost from scratch.[112]

OHR faced perhaps the most dramatic difficulties as a new mission without an established larger organization for support. Carl Bildt was able to draw some staff from ICFY—including the German diplomat Michael Steiner, who was his first principal deputy—but he and his small team had to build an office from the ground up.[113] No funds were quickly available, as most capitals would not release monies without a budget that had been approved by the PIC. After energetic lobbying, Bildt managed to secure a quick initial infusion of cash from the European Union (specifically the European Commission and the Parliament), and he describes flying from Brussels to Sarajevo with the 300,000 deutschmarks in his pocket that he would soon use to rent office space, hire staff, and begin work. His staff describe an early winter of working with gloves on as snow blew through the windows of OHR's first office.[114]

Field Operations: Implementing the Mandate

Dayton implementation proceeded in three fairly distinct phases, characterized broadly by three different strategies. In the first year and a half, the story was one of progress on military components of implementation, with severe frustration of civilian and political aims. The hard-line nationalist leadership among Serbs, Bosniacs, and Croats, whose dominance had been established during the war, found and used virtually every opportunity to renege or stall on their commitments, from providing safety for civilians (particularly the displaced when these were not conationals) to building a set of common (or at least cooperative) state institutions. Not coincidentally, such moves also strengthened their respective domestic positions. By the end of 1997, the three monoethnic political parties—the Serb SDS, Bosniac SDA, and Croat HDZ—had consolidated their control militarily, politically, administratively, and even economically. This control both contributed to and was reinforced by continuing population movements that further consolidated the shift to ethnically homogeneous territories that had been so brutally begun during the war.

Frustrated by manifest lack of progress politically, implementers embarked on a more interventionist course starting in mid-1997, which included SFOR's greater willingness to support the political side of implementation and OHR's assumption of powers only barely implicit in the Dayton Agreement. This second main phase of implementation was characterized by a new assertiveness on the part of the PIC, OHR, and SFOR that reinforced continuing activism at the OSCE on electoral and related matters. The result was not just activism but an increasingly heavy "footprint" of implementation, especially in civilian and political affairs, that began to draw considerable criticism on both legal and practical grounds.

By 2001, many international implementers were beginning to explicitly consider exit strategies, partly under pressure from crises elsewhere in the world that were beginning to tug on donor and institutional resources, and partly with a view to placing Bosnia's continued transition in the broader context of European integration. At the time of this writing, however, this phase had not yet concluded, and it was likely that a significant international role would continue for some years to come.

Implementation by Suasion (through mid-1997)

The approach adopted in the first phase of implementation was largely predetermined by the decision to split military and civilian roles, and by the political constraints that this represented. Civilian aspects of implementation were already comparatively less well resourced. IFOR's reticence to embrace the full measure of its mandate meant that civilian implementers had no coercive levers to pull, which left them with few tactical options beyond suasion.

Security

At the end of the war, Bosnia was de facto divided among three authorities backed by three respective armed forces. The first, most immediate task was to complete the military disengagement, thereby stabilizing the territorial allocation between the Federation and Republika Srpska, and to further draw down and canton the armies. Between Serb and Federation forces, this was fairly straightforward since it involved separating forces across either side of the new Inter-Entity Boundary Line. Within the Federation, disengagement was more confused. Although Bosniac and Croat forces had been ostensibly at peace since 1994, much of central Bosnia was a patchwork of towns and villages held respectively by one or the other—and sometimes divided between them. The longer-term goal was to ensure that no party's army would have either the capability or the incentive to return to war.

To bolster this force separation strategy, the United States and other supporters of the Bosniacs proposed to "train and equip" Bosniac and Croat armies outside of the Dayton framework (the plan was also, importantly, part of the bargain struck between the Clinton administration and Bosnia hawks in the U.S. Congress to gain the latter's support for the Dayton Agreement). The expressed rationale of the train-and-equip program was to ensure military parity between the parties in order to send "an unmistakable message of deterrence" against renewed violence.[115] It was also meant to be a vehicle for integrating Bosniac and Croatian forces within a common army. Early fears that the program would embolden Bosniac forces to try to retake Serb territory turned out to be misplaced. In practice, the main outcome of the train-and-equip program was to equip more than to train. More disappointingly, it accomplished little with regard to helping unify Bosniac and Croat forces.

The main military elements of Dayton proper were, however, implemented successfully. Significant force separation had been accomplished by UNPROFOR even before IFOR arrived in theater. IFOR thus embarked on its mission in a comparatively "benign" environment.[116] Under its supervision, the parties' main military obligations were fulfilled according to schedule and have since held. Federation and Serb military forces were progressively demobilized.[117] Mujahideen by and large left the country.[118] The Inter-Entity Boundary Line was also quickly stabilized, with a buffer zone of just over a mile on either side (known as the Zone of Separation) along which international troops were heavily deployed, with no subsequent incidents of military-on-military violence or uses of force by one entity against the other. At the regional level, the Bosnian parties and their neighbors also reached an arms control agreement within six months that set numerical ceilings on heavy weapons.[119] In short, where U.S. and NATO leadership devoted resources, the military provisions of the Dayton Agreement were fully implemented.

Secondary security tasks, meanwhile, were neglected, leaving what U.S. general Wesley Clark described as a "huge gap in the Bosnia food chain."[120] Critical among these was the need to extend the cease-fire to

civilians and ensure that they were no longer targets of organized violence, particularly given that demographic reordering had been both a
goal and an instrument of the war. In the critical first months of peace
implementation, only IFOR had the mandate or capacity to take on
such issues, which would have required dealing with extramilitary belligerents ("all personnel and organizations with military capability,"
including reservists, internal security forces, paramilitaries, and armed
civilian groups);[121] helping to apprehend PIFWCs; and extending a
security umbrella over, in particular, returning refugees and displaced
persons. Yet leaders in key capitals did not have the stomach for asking
IFOR to embrace the full implications of its mandate. This was particularly true in Washington, where the specter of "mission creep" and concerns about force protection threatened to undermine an already fragile
base of political support for U.S. engagement.

Dramatically illustrating this gap was IFOR's failure to prevent the
flight of some 60,000 to 100,000 Serbs from Sarajevo just three months
after the peace agreement was signed. This episode sent a powerful signal to Bosnians that the country's prewar pluri-ethnicity was a thing of
the past. During the month in which several long-held Serb suburbs
were to be handed over to Federation authority, resident Serbs were
intimidated or otherwise encouraged to vacate. The Pale leadership
launched what the United Nations described as "an overt and insidi-
ous campaign of pressure to induce them [Serb residents] to leave," including harassment, threats, truck convoys to transport them out of
Sarajevo, arson, and destruction of existing infrastructure ("hospital
clinics, schools, water, electricity and gas plants and factories were left
completely stripped"). Federation authorities, meanwhile, gave Serbs
little reassurance, while Bosniac gangs contributed to their flight by
robbing and looting apartments in the confusion.[122]

During the actual IFOR-managed handover, the suburbs were
gutted and burned. The Sarajevo Serbs who fled were largely resettled
in the former homes of Bosniacs in Srebrenica and elsewhere, effectively blocking large-scale returns to those areas.

IFOR's narrow interpretation of its own mandate was all the more
problematic since the IPTF was neither mandated nor able to fill the
breach. Even had its force been at full strength during the burning of
the suburbs, IPTF was in no position to respond. As it was, there were

150 police monitors when the transfer began. As the secretary-general argued, it was "not feasible to assign to this unarmed force the task of enforcing law and order in a country awash with weapons, all the more so when it has no legal authority to do so."[123]

During this initial phase, IPTF did accomplish some of its main tasks, such as drawing down the number of police and providing training for those who remained in the forces.[124] It was less successful in monitoring human rights abuses or preventing violence against civilians—both ethnic minorities and political opposition figures—in which local police were either directly or indirectly involved.[125] Efforts to integrate police forces, or otherwise render them responsive to citizens beyond their own ethnic group, also produced poor results. Ultimately, IPTF—unarmed and lacking executive powers—was an inappropriate vehicle for contending with extramilitary armed groups, including segments of Bosnia's police forces.

Return of Refugees and IDPs

Partly due to this absence of public security, the first phase of implementation was also characterized by frustrated progress on the return of refugees and IDPs. When the war ended, more than half of Bosnia's 4.3 million citizens had been forcibly displaced, either as refugees in other countries (1.2 million) or as IDPs within Bosnia (1 million).[126] In the immediate aftermath of the war, further displacement, such as that from the Sarajevo suburbs, only deepened the ethnic segregation of the population. The settlement of returnees in "majority" areas rather than in the refugees' real place of origin was, in fact, a policy that was actively pursued by both the Croat and Serb political leaderships, and that reinforced the largely monoethnic holdings of the three communities.[127]

Dayton proposed to reverse these trends. The agreement stipulated an unqualified right of return for refugees and displaced persons to their "home of origin," setting a benchmark for success that extended beyond existing standards or practices for the rights of the displaced. The parties were, in turn, obligated to establish security, legal, and other conditions necessary for peaceful repatriation and reintegration, particularly for so-called minority returns. The monoethnic parties, having strengthened their hold on power during the war, however, were not especially interested in a remixing of populations that would dilute their political power.

For UNHCR, this created a vexing problem beyond the range of the usual logistical challenges faced in a major repatriation effort. Immediately after the war, security concerns and restricted freedom of movement gave the agency little choice but to repatriate the displaced to areas where they belonged to the ethnic majority. Postwar, the overwhelming majority of Bosnians lived and moved exclusively in one of three ethnically cleansed zones controlled by the army of that ethnicity. The few who attempted to travel beyond these circumscribed zones were frequently intercepted by police or vigilante forces and subjected to violence or harassment. In the absence of a better security environment, which only the parties or IFOR could meaningfully provide, UNHCR thus found itself in the uncomfortable position of facilitating further ethnic separation through supporting majority returns. UNHCR did what it could to offset restricted movement among minorities, introducing, for example, an interentity bus service to facilitate safe inspection visits by potential minority returnees.[128] IFOR and IPTF also undertook a concerted campaign to remove illegal checkpoints that had been used to frustrate freedom of movement, and IPTF endeavored to curtail police harassment.

In addition to the problem of free movement, the legal and administrative legacy of the former Yugoslavia presented a slew of obstacles to minority returns, affording local authorities a wide range of instruments with which to withhold property rights, deny employment, and restrict benefits.[129] Compounding the situation, early donor assistance went mostly to the Federation. Between 1995 and 1997, Republika Srpska (RS) received less than 8 percent of total donor funds expended in Bosnia.[130] While this made sense on multiple levels—greater destruction in the Federation, higher population, and a desire to withhold support from hard-line Serb leadership—it further isolated the RS and did not contribute to rendering the economic environment conducive for Bosniac and Croat return.

As a result, return results were disappointing in this first phase. While more than 431,000 displaced persons resettled in Bosnia between 1996 and 1997 (208,000 refugees and 223,000 IDPs), the vast majority were Bosniacs and Croats returning to the Federation. Just over 45,000 of the total, or about 11 percent, were minority returns, meaning that approximately 385,000 people returned to areas where they were in the ethnic majority.[131] Thus the clear trend of ethnic segregation begun by the war was consolidated in the early years of the peace. In what was now territorially defined as the RS, the Serb population rose from 54 percent in 1991 to 97 percent by 1997, while the Bosniac population dropped from 29 to 2 percent, the Croat from 9 to 1 percent, and "other" from 8 percent to zero. The Federation was little better; there the Bosniac population rose from 52 to 73 percent while the Serb population dropped from 18 to 2 percent, "other" dropped from 8 to 2 percent, and the Croat population stayed the same at 22 percent.[132]

Elections

The most critical election was the first national ballot that Dayton committed the parties to hold within nine months of the agreement's signing, or by September 1996. The prospects for a successful round of elections less than a year after the war ended were slim, given the displacement of more than half of the voting population and the sway held by wartime leaders. The timetable was unavoidable, however, if IFOR were really to pull out by December of that year.

There was considerable debate over whether the elections should be postponed, even with IFOR's mandate theoretically ending. On the one hand, there was a manifest absence of "politically neutral" conditions. The prevailing environment was still one of generalized insecurity and partisanship, with indicted war criminals dominating political life, opposition politician figures and minority communities targeted for intimidation and attack, and minimal freedom of media and movement. There were also real operational concerns (for example, voter registration for refugees did not begin until June, and a full set of rules governing electoral conduct was published only in July, barely two months before the ballot). The OSCE's chair-in-office and many others predicted that holding national elections in such circumstances would restore to power the wartime leaders least likely to commit themselves to peace, only this time with democratic legitimacy. There were also confusions created by the debate: the OSCE itself seemed to speak with contradictory voices, with conflicting messages coming from the chair-in-office and the Bosnia-based head of mission and even from the latter's own public statements.[133]

On the other hand, many diplomats viewed elections as the essential first step in getting Bosnia's new joint institutions off the ground and establishing Bosnian interlocutors for reconstruction, even at the risk of strengthening nationalist political parties. This seemed all the more necessary in the absence of a mandate for international implementers to exercise transitional authority. On this point, there was unusual agreement between Carl Bildt and the United States. Both the OHR and the United States agreed that elections were vital for launching joint institutions, which were in turn deemed essential both to Bosnian state building and to eventual international exit.

There was, further, considerable political pressure to go ahead, especially from the United States, where 1996 was a presidential election year. Having barely won domestic support for an American military presence in Bosnia by promising that U.S. troops would be out by December, the Clinton administration was eager to see elections proceed on schedule. The OSCE was, consequently, under enormous pressure to stay on the Dayton clock. The case for early elections was reinforced in July 1996 when Richard Holbrooke was able to broker a deal to remove Radovan Karadzic from the public political scene, thereby giving the goal of politically neutral conditions a modest boost.[134]

The elections were thus held in September, with operational problems of debatable extent and impact.[135] Voter registration for the displaced was particularly complex, and few good solutions were available given the time constraints. To enable refugees and IDPs to vote, provisions were made for them to register in municipalities to which they had not yet returned, or in which they had never lived at all. The flexibility in these provisions made them easy to manipulate and enabled the three main nationalist political parties to consolidate votes in core areas, thereby providing a legal framework for the results of ethnic cleansing. The extent of rigging in the registration process was sufficiently known in advance that this became a chief reason for the postponement of municipal elections, although the national ballot was allowed to proceed.

The results of the elections surprised no one. Boosted by evident manipulation and authentic polarization of the population, the three leading nationalist political parties won by large margins in all offices. For the Bosnian presidency, 80 percent of the Bosniac vote went to the SDA's Izetbegovic, 89 percent of the Bosnian Croat vote to the HDZ, and 67 percent of the Bosnian Serb vote to the SDS. For the RS presidency, 59 percent of the vote went to the SDS. Similar results were obtained in the respective legislative bodies.[136]

Joint Institutions

The Dayton constitution laid out the structure and powers of the new Bosnian state and its two entities, the Bosniac-Croat Federation and Republika Srpska, ironically in a form not dissimilar to that of the former Yugoslavia or the Bosnian republic within it. This created a fundamental tension between the powers of a central state—which represented aspirations for a unified Bosnia—and a centrifugal pull to the entities and, below them, cantons and municipalities. In the first two years of implementation, the ruling parties consistently resisted efforts to strengthen the central state, except on the Bosniac side, where the federal state offered institutions, offices, and resources that they believed they could dominate. Perhaps correctly, those who held power feared that genuine integration would reduce their respective power and privileges. As frustrations with their obstruction mounted, implementers increasingly recognized that they would need to develop instruments for overruling Bosnian recalcitrance. They would also have to deal with the limitations of the Dayton constitution, which included provisions that actually presented an impediment to overcoming wartime divisions.

The state structure established by Dayton was exceedingly complex (see figure 2.2). Bosnia would have a rotating, three-person presidency (one Bosniac, one Croat, and one Serb—no provision was made for the substantial minority of Bosnians who identified with none of these communities) and a bicameral parliament with a 2:1 ratio of Federation to Serb members, but no independent judiciary. Republika Srpska and the Federation had their own entity-level executive and legislative branches (the Federation had two of the latter). The Federation in turn was divided into ten cantons—some Croat, some Bosniac, and some mixed—which also had legislative assemblies; and both entities were also composed of municipalities, totaling slightly more than a hundred, each with its own assembly. The weakest of these

Figure 2.2. State Structure of Bosnia and Herzegovina

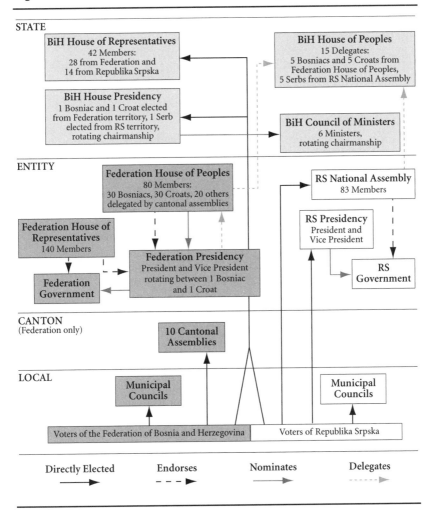

levels of government was the state. It was dependent on budgetary transfers from the entities, lacked an army, police, or judiciary of its own, and had relatively little leverage over lower levels of government. Meanwhile, the Federation was weak vis-à-vis its ten cantons, which had taxing power as well as exclusive authority over police, internal security, and judicial matters.[137] In practical terms, most political and economic power in the Federation was wielded by a range of informal, parallel political structures established by the ruling Bosniac and Croat political parties.

The OHR took the lead in pushing the institutional agenda, but getting the joint institutions to function even minimally was an ordeal. The sheer complexity of the system and constant rotation of roles between representatives of the three main ethnic groups made it easy for parties to obstruct the functioning of various offices. Every issue, from the timing of meetings to their location and agenda, became an opportunity for resistance. Meetings were boycotted, as when the newly elected Serb member of the Bosnian presidency, Momcilo Krajisnik, was absent at his own inauguration ceremony in Sarajevo in 1996, or when Croat members walked out of the inaugural session of the Sarajevo canton assembly.[138] Legislative progress was quickly stymied when drafts would be left unadopted or in need of further implementing legislation that would, in turn, require strenuous cajoling, lobbying, and pressuring by OHR.

Similarly unsuccessful at this early stage were efforts to integrate Bosnian armed forces. Despite the U.S.-sponsored train-and-equip program, common exercises between the Bosniac and Croat armies were superficial, leaving the forces separate in all significant respects—finance, administration, command, doctrine, and training. Each force was tied to its respective party leadership, with doctrine, capabilities, and intentions relatively opaque to one another and to the international community. Cooperation, let alone integration with the Serb army, was a chimera.

IPTF negotiations on police integration fared little better (and they, of course, had far fewer resources with which to work than did the train-and-equip program and IFOR). Significant staff time and resources were expended trying to get common uniforms for Federation police, joint patrolling, and coordinated command, but there was relatively little at this stage to show for those efforts beyond agreements to cooperate that were then reneged upon.[139]

Economic Reconstruction

The task of revitalizing the Bosnian economy was daunting. The country was dealing with a double transition—recovery from war and transformation from a socialist to a market economy—and it had not had a healthy economy for some time.[140] Bosnia had been the second poorest of the Yugoslav republics (beating only Macedonia), with a gross domestic product (GDP) 32 percent lower than the Yugoslav national average and an unemployment rate of 20 percent before the war even started.[141] It had been heavily dependent on exports within Yugoslavia and to the Eastern bloc; unlike Croatia or Slovenia, for whom independence from Yugoslavia promised economic rewards, Bosnia had stood only to lose.

The war dealt a devastating blow to this already vulnerable economy. The conflict seriously damaged or destroyed much of Bosnia's infrastructure, industrial base, and capacity for productive activity. The war also took a toll on human capital: beyond those killed, wounded, or forcibly displaced, tens of thousands of Bosnians with the greatest mobility—largely, the best educated and highest skilled among the population—left the country. By 1995, Bosnia's per capita GDP had dropped to less than $500, or about 20 percent of its prewar levels, and unemployment had reached 80 percent.[142]

The international community pledged extraordinary levels of assistance to rebuild the country, initially through a Priority Reconstruction and Recovery Program (PRRP) with a price tag of $5.1 billion. Shortly after Dayton (in December 1995), the first of a series of major donor pledging conferences was held in Brussels; through mid-1997, these would yield nearly $3 billion in pledges.[143] Per capita aid during the first two years after the war was approximately $1,400, compared to $800 in Kosovo and less than $100 in Afghanistan (or postwar Japan) during equivalent time frames.[144] External assistance constituted more than 35 percent of Bosnia's GDP in the initial postwar period.[145]

International implementers, preoccupied by immediate physical needs, put comparatively little emphasis on jump-starting Bosnia's economy in this first phase. Approximately two-thirds of the PRRP was expected to be allocated to physical reconstruction, with far lower amounts expended on institutional development and transition, economic recovery, or peace implementation.[146] Other efforts, such as establishment of a central bank and currency board to curb inflation, focused mainly on macroeconomic stability, arguably at the cost of neglecting basic requirements for sustained economic recovery such as the need for fresh capital, microeconomic restructuring, and some protection from an influx of cheap goods from abroad.[147] Several initiatives also were counterproductive. A customs tariff established early on to raise badly needed revenue for entity governments, for instance, largely generated funds for local mafia rather than for the public sector.[148] Many funds helped shore up institutions that should have been left to collapse, and the disproportionate spending on physical reconstruction tended to redound to the benefit of sitting authorities (not usually the most receptive to the Dayton agenda). Moreover, aid distribution, particularly in the beginning of the reconstruction process, was poorly coordinated, enabling local authorities to go "donor shopping," encouraging corruption, and discouraging growth.[149]

A further challenge was finding a way to reconcile competing approaches to conditionality. The World Bank tended to avoid political conditionality as a muddying of what should be a technical exercise in matching resources to needs. Bilateral donors tended to be more comfortable with the conditioning of assistance upon compliance with Dayton. In the absence of a reasonably systematic way of defining what this meant, it tended to mean that the bulk of early assistance—98 percent in 1996–97—went to the Federation rather than the RS.

Assertive Implementation (mid-1997 through 2001)

The second phase of Dayton implementation emerged from the frustrations of the first. Increasingly, implementers recognized that the parties would continue to stall efforts at rebuilding a common country, a project in which the elected leaderships appeared to have no great interest. Those voices within Bosnian politics and society who were genuinely committed to the Dayton project simply didn't have the institutional resources, political base, or coercive power with which to make greater headway. The implication was that the international community would have to take charge of moving the Dayton process forward, even over the backs of most of Bosnia's elected politicians.

Importantly, there was greater receptiveness among key governments and donors to a more activist role as time passed. Partly, this was due to mounting frustration and an unwillingness to let years of investment in Bosnia fail. The way was also paved by changes in key capitals and institutions. By 1997, Clinton had been reelected, choosing as his second-term secretary of state Madeleine Albright, who had long been a Bosnia hawk; Tony Blair and Robin Cook, their counterparts in Britain, were also both long advocates of international activism in Bosnia; and General Wesley Clark had replaced the more conservative George Joulwan as SACEUR. Bosnia's parties did not become particularly more compliant; however, international implementers acquired new capacities and a new unity of purpose to try to contend with them.

By the end of 2001, visible progress was made on multiple fronts, including joint institutions, freedom of movement, the percentage of minority returnees (though the higher percentage was of increasingly smaller numbers of absolute returns), integration of Bosnian police (especially through the establishment of a new State Border Service) and, though it required OHR/OSCE intervention, adoption of a Bosnian electoral law that would enable the OSCE to hand off the running of future elections to Bosnians.[150] Most major accomplishments had required heavy international action, however, raising concerns that further progress would come only through international imposition.

Sintra, Bonn, and New Powers for the High Representative

In May 1997, the PIC Steering Board met at Sintra, Portugal. It castigated the parties for obstructing efforts at integration and outlined a range of issues on which the High Representative could override local intransigence. These went beyond symbolic issues, such as a common flag and national anthem, to include more consequential items such as the continued lack of a common currency, a joint telephone system, uniform car registration, citizenship laws, and an agreed mechanism for appointing Bosnian ambassadors. When the full PIC met in December in Bonn, they were even bolder and vested in the High Representative an extraordinary range of new decision-making powers—the so-called Bonn powers. With strong international backing, if dubious legal authority, the High Representative could now develop and enact laws; issue binding directives across the spectrum of political, judicial, legal, economic, and media activity; and take enforcement action against any public party, including dismissing public officials who were not abiding by the terms of Dayton.[151] Added to the already extensive powers of the OSCE, which had been certifying and decertifying Bosnian politicians for some time, these powers were extraordinary and were abundantly used.

Between 1997 and 2001, OHR issued 263 directives on matters relating to the economy, media, judiciary, property rights, the Federation, and Bosnian state symbols and institutions, including the state constitution. The OHR also removed or suspended eighty-one officials from public office, ranging from judges to mayors to a minister of finance and an entity president. A particularly dramatic episode was the March 1999 removal of the elected president of Republika Srpska, Nikola Poplasen. Poplasen had refused to accept as prime minister the more moderate Milorad Dodik, who had Serb parliamentary support and was favored by the West. The visibility of Western support for Dodik contributed to rising cynicism about the international community's impatience with due process, with obvious implications for the legitimacy of postwar institutions.[152]

NATO

OHR's activism was significantly buttressed by the greater willingness of IFOR's successor, SFOR, to take on the secondary tasks in its mandate. These included extending a security umbrella to critical civilian activity, from implementation of election results to some return efforts, and selectively lending coercive backup to OHR decisions.

The opening salvo in SFOR's new activism was its seizure in mid-1997 of Serb radio and television transmitters that were broadcasting violent and inciting messages, particularly against SFOR and other international personnel.[153]

SFOR soon moved on to the hunt for Hague indictees (PIFWCs), finally acknowledging that its mandate to provide a "safe and secure environment" could be undermined by their fairly open presence. In contrast to the IFOR period, when patrols routinely avoided areas where they might accidentally encounter indictees, SFOR actually sought them out, in some cases energetically.[154] In NATO's first use of force for this purpose, UK forces moved against two major figures in July 1997, killing one and wounding another.[155] Until that point, all indictees had either surrendered voluntarily, been arrested by national police forces, or remained at large. By 2001, SFOR had detained twenty-three PIFWCs (not including seventeen detained outside of Bosnia, two who died in detention, and twenty-two who surrendered). All together, these accounted for two-thirds of publicly announced indictees, including

Momcilo Krajisnik, the Bosnian Serb leader and first Serb member of the Bosnian presidency.[156]

SFOR also began to monitor Interior Ministry "special police" units in Republika Srpska after August 1997. Special police had long been suspected of holding secret stores of heavy weapons. They also threatened to be a base of opposition to the new RS president, Biljana Plavsic, in whom the West placed particular hope in mid-1997.[157] At that time, a rift had developed within the Serb leadership, which the United States and others sought to exploit in order to replace Radovan Karadzic and his SDS party with a more moderate alternative. Until that time, international isolation of the Serb entity was near total: Serbs received all of the opprobrium for having started the war and virtually none of the humanitarian or economic assistance flowing into Bosnia after it. By 1997, it was becoming clear that implementation depended on a new approach. If Serb areas were not opened up politically or economically, there was little hope of getting movement toward the development of Bosnia's joint institutions or toward non-Serbs being able to return to their original homes. Plavsic's break with the SDS created new security concerns: she had to be shored up against hard-liners, who enjoyed substantial support among Serb security forces, and international personnel had to be protected from possible retaliation by Serb militants.

Even with the Bonn powers and somewhat greater SFOR activism, problems remained. Most progress on Bosnia's joint institutions had come only through international intervention. Even the PIC, which was the authorizing agent of such intervention, expressed "concern" in mid-1998 that "almost all progress has required continued and intensive efforts from the international community . . . and that Bosnia and Herzegovina [had to] take responsibility for its future and prepare to stand on its own."[158]

There was even greater difficulty in integrating Serb and Federation armed forces. OHR and NATO both appealed publicly in mid-2000 for a single, joint army, but without success. Indeed, the division among the country's three militaries remained a major obstacle to building common institutions for the postwar Bosnian state. Dayton had empowered NATO to decide where Bosnia's armies deployed and from which areas they withdrew, meaning that NATO forces could have helped sever the link between military control of territory and political jurisdiction. Instead, their early force separation efforts only contributed to consolidating this nexus, which would subsequently be extremely difficult to reverse.

UNMIBH

The new powers allocated to the High Representative and the new activism in SFOR gave UNMIBH and the IPTF new resources on which to draw in reforming and restructuring the police forces of Bosnia. In August 1997, the IPTF and SFOR launched a series of weapons inspections at local police stations around the country. Of 563 inspections conducted in the program's first five months, 121 yielded contraband weapons, including 3,500 long-barreled weapons (such as assault rifles), 25 grenade- and rocket-launchers, 1,350 grenades, and "over 504,000 rounds of ammunition"—military-pattern arsenals typical of the old regime's police.

In October 1997, UNMIBH established a human rights office and assigned 120 officers to the IPTF to investigate rights violations perpetrated by local law enforcement. Those investigations could and did result in the removal from office of local police officials.[159] Not only were those officials failing to take their UN-mandated "human dignity" training to heart, but nearly four years after Dayton, "nationalist political agendas" continued to "infect policing at every level." The inspections program also confirmed a separate policing structure maintained by Bosnian Croat police ("parallel budgets and . . . personnel systems, undeclared police personnel, [and] separate crime databases") despite the United Nations' efforts to integrate Croat and Bosniac police into a single Federation force.[160]

To keep closer watch on its charges, in 1998 UNMIBH began colocating UN police monitor-advisers with their charges, which required the sort of senior and experienced officers that were the hardest to find and to retain. The colocation effort accelerated substantially in 1999, such that by the end of the year, about half of the IPTF had been colocated with local police. Even the normally critical International Crisis Group acknowledged that colocation appeared to decrease "incidents of police misconduct."[161] Citations for serious noncompliance with international policing standards could result in "decertification" by the

IPTF, although in practice it was difficult to ensure that decertified officers were in fact dismissed.[162]

The Madrid PIC meeting in December 1998 instructed UNMIBH to create a unified, multiethnic State Border Service (SBS) to begin to check the smuggling and trafficking in humans that supported organized crime in Bosnia, and to do so not later than October 1, 1999.[163] UNMIBH encountered much resistance at all levels of government in trying to carry out this mandate, if only because an effective and uncorrupt border service could interrupt many lucrative arrangements. Ultimately, the force had to be established by OHR decree in January 2000 when the Bosnian parliament failed to act. The first SBS officers, who were Austrian trained, were stationed at Sarajevo airport. The force plateaued for a while at less than 400 officers, due to lack of funds. Eventually international support and a little creative reallocation of the national budget provided enough support to expand the SBS to three-fifths of Bosnia's border crossings by June 2001 and three-quarters by November.[164]

In late 2000, UNMIBH developed a two-year "mandate implementation plan" emphasizing six core programs of police reform, police restructuring, police and criminal justice cooperation, institution building and interpolice force cooperation, public awareness, and support for Bosnian "participation in the UN system, in particular UN peacekeeping."[165] Reform focused on building a Law Enforcement Personnel Registry that reflected close vetting of police officers, prison guards, and court police to weed out undesirables. Restructuring focused on increasing minority representation in the respective entity police forces, which by the end of 2001 was roughly 11 percent in the Federation but just 3 percent in Srpska.[166] Criminal justice cooperation addressed, in particular, the need to provide protection for judges and witnesses in organized crime and corruption prosecutions—five years after Dayton mechanisms to provide such protection still did not exist.[167] Interpolice cooperation focused on intelligence sharing and joint programs to stem illegal immigration and trafficking, with mixed results.[168] The peacekeeping participation initiative saw Bosnia send a dozen police to the UN operation in East Timor and a handful of military observers to the UN Mission in Ethiopia and Eritrea (UNMEE) by April 2001. By June 2005, a total of forty-four Bosnian peacekeepers (thirty police and fourteen military observers) were working in Haiti, Liberia, and the Congo as well as with UNMEE.[169]

Elections and Democratization

Aided by new assertiveness at OHR, the OSCE supervised four further rounds of elections between 1997 and 2001, two at the national level and two at the municipal level.[170] At each stage, the security situation improved, the OSCE made technical improvements, and moderate political parties made steady if small inroads, posting their best showing in the municipal ballot of April 2000. The OSCE also was eventually able to establish a regulatory framework to provide a more solid, legal foundation for Bosnia's continuing political transition, including through the election law eventually ratified in 2001.[171]

On balance, however, democratization was not faring well. The sheer complexity of the electoral system, even taking into account simplifications that were made over time, tended to alienate voters. More than seventy political parties and nearly 600 candidates were represented in the 1998 national elections, for example.[172] The large numbers of parties representing very small constituencies tended to lead to fragmented, divisive electioneering and a perception among bewildered voters that the new system was unresponsive to their interests. Even the so-called reformers who comprised the victorious "Alliance for Change" in the 2000 elections were widely perceived as more committed to personal than reform agendas and were able to achieve much less than expected, further alienating the electorate.[173]

The constitutional framework established at Dayton posed a more fundamental challenge. Insofar as many offices could be elected only by residents of one entity or the other, politicians had no incentive to build a base that crossed ethnic lines. The Dayton constitution thus inhibited the formation of nonnationalist constituencies and thereby the electoral success of nonnationalist parties.

Not surprisingly, mononational elites manifestly dominated political life at every level of government except the weak and unwieldy national state. In the 1997 municipal elections, for example, few minority candidates secured seats in municipal assemblies, and those who did were rarely able to travel to the locations of their new offices or take up their new duties, even in the one municipality—Srebrenica—

where Bosniac candidates took 52 percent of the vote. In these cases, the OSCE refused to certify the ballot pending meaningful acceptance of its results. SFOR had to deploy to especially problematic areas simply to enable newly elected minority officials to get to work, and "special envoys" were even appointed to try to break resistance in particularly recalcitrant municipalities.[174]

The situation in the entities was even more dramatic. In the RS, although 25 percent of RS National Assembly members were non-Serb, all twenty-one ministers were Serb. Nearly 98 percent of judges and prosecutors were Serb, compared to barely more than 2 percent Bosniac and Croat (all nine of whom were based in internationally administered Brcko). Ninety-four percent of RS police were Serb compared to 6 percent Bosniac and Croat. In the Federation, the patterns were similar, with 72 percent of judges and prosecutors being Bosniac, 23 percent Croat, and only 5 percent Serb; and 69 percent of police being Bosniac, 30 percent Croat, and 1 percent Serb.[175]

Partly in response to this persistent exclusion of minorities, Bosnia's Constitutional Court issued a ruling in July 2000 that would require both the RS and the Federation to amend the entity constitutions and to take additional steps to ensure equal status of each of Bosnia's three "constituent peoples."[176] The "Constituent Peoples" decision, as the ruling came to be known, was notable mainly as the first serious effort, and the first by a Bosnian state institution, to tackle tensions within the Dayton Agreement, in this case between group and individual constitutional rights. Importantly, the court based its reasoning on Dayton itself.[177] This suggested that Dayton would not have to be junked in order to remedy its flaws, but that improvements could be sought within the Dayton framework by means of creative reinterpretation.

Although this landmark decision was taken by a Bosnian institution, its ruling required heavy international involvement. The court's five-to-four ruling was based on three international judges voting with the two Bosniac judges against dissenting opinions from the two Serbs and two Croats on the court. The ruling was also followed by two years of intensive negotiations brokered by OHR, the United States, and the European Union to get the entities to implement it. This eventually resulted in a deal in early 2002 (the "Sarajevo

Agreement"), though with considerable room for continued back-sliding within the entities.

Return and Freedom of Movement

Significant energy was thrown into efforts to increase minority return during this phase. In the context of greater SFOR presence in public security and OHR use of Bonn powers as leverage against obstructionist authorities, international implementers experimented with a range of carrots and sticks to give incentives to local authorities to co-operate (e.g., through the "Open Cities" initiative, designed to prioritize international assistance to mayors who accepted minority returns). They also attempted to bring reconstruction efforts into line with return strategies (for example, through the Reconstruction and Return Task Force established within OHR) and to reform property laws to enable recovery.

A related development was the decisive breakthrough in freedom of movement with the introduction of a common vehicle registration plate. Previously, Bosniac, Croat, and Serb authorities had issued their own distinctive plates, which allowed the authorities of one community to identify and intercept vehicles coming from areas controlled by either of the other communities. The few drivers who did attempt to cross from one zone to another were regularly subjected to harassment and abuse. Following the Sintra PIC decision of May 1997, establishing that "action must be taken to establish a uniform system of car registration throughout the country," Bosnians were informed that no vehicles bearing the old, ethnically identifiable plates would be allowed to cross into western Europe.[178] The project, which was implemented by OHR and UNMIBH's Civil Affairs office, met with heavy initial resistance from the political leaderships on all three sides, but was popular among the bulk of Bosnians of all nationalities. As the new plates were introduced, in 1997 and 1998, freedom of movement surged and was never again significantly restricted, despite sporadic efforts from the political leaderships.

Despite this and other achievements, however, the pattern of returns did not significantly undo the effects of ethnic cleansing. Most of those who originally fled from their homes during the war would have had to return as "minority returnees." Yet, as described above,

Table 2.7. Returns Summary, 1996–2004

Year	Refugees	IDPs	Subtotal	Minority Returns	Minority Percentage
1996	88,039	164,741	252,780	45,523	18.0%
1997	120,280	58,295	178,575	—	—
1998	110,000	29,570	139,570	41,191	29.5%
1999	31,560	43,385	74,945	41,007	54.7%
2000	18,607	59,347	77,954	67,445	86.5%
2001	18,693	80,172	98,865	92,061	93.1%
2002	37,134	70,775	107,909	102,111	94.6%
2003	14,012	40,303	54,315	44,868	82.6%
2004	2,532	17,948	20,480	14,199	69.3%
Total	440,857	564,536	1,005,393	448,405	44.6%

Source: UNHCR Sarajevo through January 1, 2005.

mononational authorities still controlled institutions, such as the police and judiciary, that could block minority return (or, alternatively, promote majority return) and maintained control over the distribution of socially owned property among other forms of patronage. A series of OHR decisions that aimed to block allocation of property only to political clients and conationals failed to stem the abuse.[179]

Although official figures for minority return appeared to show dramatic improvement in percentage terms, the total figures for 1996–2001 were disappointing. Between 1996 and 2001, 535,000 majority returns had taken place, against 287,000 minority returns (see table 2.7).[180] Moreover, many minority returnees were returnees only in name —returning to take possession of property, and then selling it to majority-community buyers. This appeared to be the dominant pattern with minority returnees to the Federation (compared to the RS, where most minority returnees were elderly villagers).[181] And many of those who did not return at all were those who would have been minority returnees—Bosniacs to eastern Bosnia, Croats to Posavina, Serbs to Sarajevo.

Exit or Stalemate (2002 onward)

In the final phase of implementation, still ongoing at the time of this writing, the question of international exit weighed heavily on the minds of the peace operation's stakeholders. Most of the basic military tasks had been accomplished. Domestic elections had been handed over to Bosnian authorities (although the first full-domestic election netted only 55 percent turnout, indicating to most observers a general cynicism about the political process).[182] The return process had largely exhausted itself; most displaced persons who had not already returned to Bosnia had found a durable solution elsewhere.

Aside from its unrealistic one-year IFOR mandate, however, the Dayton Agreement was largely silent about the end state of the implementation process. Moreover, irrespective of the political concerns that had produced that one-year mandate, there was, from the start, a general feeling among international officials that it would be mistaken to set an early date for departure. By 1997, the catchphrase became "end state before end date," and this sentiment did not substantially change over time.[183]

For some time, there was little serious discussion of exit strategies, as the desired "end state" of a self-sustaining peace was not clear. After the assumption of the Bonn powers, however, two considerations changed this. First, the broad outlines of the end state came into view: real progress was made in the creation of the legislation, institutions, and facts on the ground that could lead to a self-sustaining peace. Second, and related to the first, Bosnia and Herzegovina was developing a morbid dependence on outsiders. In the political sphere, Bosnian politicians had a degree of authority, but they were able to transfer responsibility for most of the difficult decisions onto internationals. It suited Bosnian politicians to let the High Representative enact unpopular legislation, and to criticize that legislation rather than tackle such jobs themselves.

Among the major implementers, each approached the question of exit strategy differently.

NATO and EUFOR

Although U.S. and NATO authorities consistently signaled that SFOR would stay on the ground as long as necessary, by mid-2002 it had shrunk to about 12,000 troops and, by mid-2004, to just 8,500. Consistent with Bush administration desires to reduce U.S. troop commitments in the Balkans, the U.S. presence shrank faster than did the rest of the force, from about 30 percent of the total in 2000 to less than 10 percent in 2004. The May 2003 agreement among all Bosnian armed forces on a common military doctrine was an important milestone toward eventual NATO exit, although major outstanding issues remained, such as ambiguity about the command relationship between the Bosnian presidency and the armed forces, and failure to carry out planned joint exercises.[184]

Decisions about NATO's continued presence in Bosnia were shaped by larger debates on such issues as the role of the United States in peacekeeping in Europe, the relationship between NATO and the European Union, the future relationship between the countries of the former Yugoslavia and the European Union, and NATO enlargement.[185] Within the context of these wider discussions, it was decided that the NATO-led force would hand over its peacekeeping responsibilities in late 2004 to an EU-led force of 6,500 troops. NATO kept a headquarters unit in Sarajevo, however, to promote the creation of a single, integrated, professional Bosnian military of 9,000 to 10,000 troops (or about half the size of the separate entity armed forces permitted under Dayton), organized into entity-oriented regiments.[186]

Owing to RS refusal to arrest indicted war criminals, in 2004 NATO twice refused to admit Bosnia into its Partnership for Peace program. The second rejection followed news that General Ratko Mladic, the architect of the Srebrenica massacre, had been on the Serbian army payroll until 2001 and the RS army payroll until 2002, and had been sheltered at a hidden RS military compound until July 2004. The European Union Force in Bosnia and Herzegovina (EUFOR) inspected that facility shortly after starting operations and resolved to shut down and seal all underground facilities "not required for civil or military use."[187] That such facilities would continue to exist after a decade of de facto international occupation is startling and troubling, as are the amounts of arms and ammunition still being collected (EUFOR picked up 1,300 small arms, 2,000 grenades and mines, a staggering 400 kilograms of explosives, and 200,000 rounds of ammunition in its first two months on the job—in the dead of winter).[188]

UNMIBH

Of the major implementing organizations, UNMIBH was the first to think seriously in terms of an exit strategy and the steps necessary to achieve it. The operation fulfilled key aspects of its mandate: Police numbers had fallen from the 1995 peak of 45,000 largely paramilitary police to some 16,000 fully vetted and certified civilian police who were no longer a major impediment to the return of refugees. Freedom of movement had largely been restored through the common license plate project. Agreement had been reached, within the Federation and in Republika Srpska, as to the structure and ethnic makeup of entity police forces. Police academies, operating according to international standards, had been established. Work had begun on the establishment of minimum national-level police functions, such as the State Border Service, which had expanded to cover all of Bosnia's major border crossing points by the end of 2002, when UNMIBH's mission ended.

EU Police Mission

In January 2003, following the closure of UNMIBH, a new European Union Police Mission (EUPM) was established with 500 police officers and a three-year mandate.[189] Having the European Union take over the security-related functions of the international presence in Bosnia served several purposes. It provided graceful exits from Bosnia for NATO (and thus U.S.) ground forces and for UNMIBH. The European Union got the chance to run a midsized peacekeeping operation in a relatively safe and stable environment that was not really even out of area, given the extent of EU expansion by 2003. Finally, dual-hatting the High Representative as EU special representative allowed the European Union to develop and test concepts and operating procedures for its version of an integrated peace operation, with the intention of eventually supplanting the High Representative.

   The EUPM deployed as a monitoring and mentoring force but also needed to be capable of catalyzing and managing a major restructuring of Bosnia's entity police forces into a single police service for the country. The limitations of its mandate and its reluctance to exercise its remaining powers to remove tainted police officers stood in relatively stark contrast to the IPTF, which looked increasingly effective in retrospect to close observers like the International Crisis Group.[190] EUPM did assist in the creation of a second state-level police force, the State Investigation and Protection Agency, to focus on organized crime, money laundering, terrorism, and the apprehension of war criminals. But neither IPTF nor EUPM could make the political-level changes—altering police command and control structures—that were needed to complete police reform.

The impetus for high-level change came from the European Union in late 2003 in the form of the sixteen "priority areas"—reforms required before Bosnia could begin negotiations toward the Stabilization and Association Agreement that is a precursor to EU membership. By mid-2005, the only unchecked requirement on the list was to give the police a single, state-run structure that met EU standards. In the spring of 2004, EUPM proposed a structure with five local police areas defined according to such criteria as total population and crime rate, without regard to cantonal or entity boundaries, de facto diluting political influence over police operations. That proposal served as a starting point for the work of the Police Restructuring Commission established by OHR in July 2004. Chaired by a former prime minister of Belgium and a former police inspector from the U.K, the commission comprised nine full and four associate members drawn from the Bosnia, Federation, and RS cabinets; from cantonal and city administrations; and from state- and entity-level police forces. Because the RS politicians on the commission refused to countenance a single, state-run police force, the chair issued the commission's report in December over his own signature, offering options for police restructuring to OHR. The RS National Assembly rejected the proposal that OHR subsequently put forward as well as any other attempt to do away with entity-based police forces, even though such rejection jeopardized Bosnia's eligibility for EU membership. International Crisis Group interviews indicated that Serb politicians in the eastern RS, in particular, envisioned Serbia offering independence to Kosovo in exchange for annexation of some or all of the RS—in effect completing the Greater Serbia project that the ethnic cleansing campaigns of 1992–95 had initiated.[191]

OSCE

The OSCE appeared not to have an exit strategy from Bosnia at all, morphing from one new role to another as necessary. The OSCE effectively got out of the election business with the adoption of Bosnia's electoral law and, importantly, with the continued efforts of OHR to nudge domestic processes when they remained sluggish. By 2002 the OSCE was turning attention to human rights and education issues, which related intimately but less visibly to Bosnia's continued transition. Arguably, more concentrated efforts on these issues earlier might have been a wiser strategy than beginning with elections, which did not demonstrably contribute to the postwar peace process. Human rights efforts were notoriously underresourced in both funds and personnel, and despite early interest at OHR in trying to redress the persistence of parallel national curricula for Bosnia's schoolchildren, little headway was made.

The longer-term achievements of OSCE efforts in Bosnia's democratization are difficult to assess. The 2002 elections appeared not to bode well, with the main nationalist parties sweeping back into power (although there was an alternative interpretation that the nationalist victories represented a "protest vote" against the international presence). Over the next two years, OSCE continued its long slog toward legislative process reform, education reforms, property law reform, and restitution for property lost during the war (completed in 120 of 129 municipalities as of November 2004).[192]

UNHCR

From the outset, one of the explicit reasons for international engagement with Bosnia and Herzegovina had been to reverse the process of ethnic cleansing. This intention had, at least rhetorically, driven the U.S. peace initiative that produced the Dayton Agreement. Despite a stream of optimistic reporting from the Office of the High Representative, however, the return process did not reverse the pattern of ethnic cleansing. On the contrary, as of mid-2003, the ethnic consolidation favored by nationalist leaders on all sides remained the principal demographic feature of the country.

A decade after the ethnic cleansing campaigns of 1992, Republika Srpska, the prewar population of which territory was approximately half Serb, remained, in spite of some much-publicized returns, well over 90 percent Serb, ensuring comfortable Serb majorities in almost all elections. A similar situation was apparent in Sarajevo. At the time of the

1991 census, slightly more than 40 percent of the population of Sarajevo had declared themselves to be Muslim. Although there was continued resistance to conducting a new census, sampling of local community rolls indicated that by 2002 Bosniacs accounted for some 90 percent of the resident population of Sarajevo. The campaigns of ethnic cleansing had succeeded, and neither the end of the war nor almost nine years of vigorous peace implementation significantly reversed it.

The returns process, such as it was, can be viewed as comprising at least three distinct dynamics. Taken together, they have produced a Bosnia and Herzegovina that is, for the first time in its history, largely divided into ethnoconfessional zones.[193]

The first and largest stream of returnees were refugees from abroad. Of these, the great majority returned to areas where they would be part of the ethnic majority, either returning to their original homes or going to new ones.

The second group of returnees consisted mainly of IDPs returning to homes close to the Inter-Entity Boundary Line. The first major returns to Republika Srpska, for example, took place in 1998 when Bosniacs from the municipality of Brcko moved from temporary accommodation just south of the IEBL to their original homes just north of the IEBL.[194] Similarly, many Serbs originally from Sarajevo returned to the city to reclaim property while commuting from nearby communities in Republika Srpska. Other return communities of this sort grew up, during 1998 and 1999, on the Serb side of the IEBL in the municipality of Zvornik, and between Bosniac- and Croat-controlled areas of the Federation.[195]

The third process of return was that of returnees going back to their original homes with the intent to sell and then relocate to majority areas with the proceeds. This became possible during 2000 and 2001, with the Property Law Implementation Plan, a major effort to create a legal framework for property repossession, and with corresponding improvements in the quality of the local police forces.[196] The large discrepancy between registered minority returns to Sarajevo and the actual number of non-Bosniac residents may, to a significant degree, reflect this pattern of "return."

By the end of 2002, UNHCR was refocusing its Bosnia strategy. It newly emphasized protection issues, as violence and intimidation continued to plague returnees, especially minorities.[197] It also proposed to focus on building national capacity to handle return-related tasks, including through a new strategy endorsed by the PIC in December 2002.[198] In 2004, UNHCR reduced its presence from ten offices to four (Banja Luka, Tuzla, Sarajevo, and Mostar), as refugee returns slowed to a trickle. The number of international agency staff in Bosnia dropped below twenty, and the total operation, including national hires, numbered just ninety.[199] In April 2005, UNHCR completed the first reregistration of persons displaced within Bosnia since 2000. The survey determined that nearly 40 percent of the previously registered IDP population had dropped off the rolls, having returned without assistance or decided to resettle where they were, leaving 186,500. There were, in addition, roughly 20,000 refugees from Croatia and Kosovo, mostly located in the RS.[200]

OHR

The toughest question regarding exit was OHR's.[201] Paddy Ashdown, the High Representative from mid-2002 on, faced a fundamental dilemma upon assuming office. Much of the political and civilian progress since 1997 had come through the intercession of that office. In the years since 1996, OHR had become a de facto transitional administrator and assumed extraordinary powers of decision making, adjudication, and sanction in virtually every domain of Bosnian public life. From the beginning of the Bonn powers era, no one argued that this pattern did not come at the expense of Bosnian ownership and responsibility. Rather, the internal debate centered on whether this trade-off was worth it. The challenge for Ashdown was whether and how OHR could disengage without risking what had already been achieved.

In 2003, the debate focused on a public critique lodged by two long-standing Bosnia watchers, Gerald Knaus and Felix Martin, in an article in the *Journal of Democracy*.[202] Describing the OHR role in Bosnia and Herzegovina as akin to a new European Raj, they depicted OHR as a neoimperial institution: operating largely without legal authority in a foreign land; prone to move the goalposts at which the Bosnian authorities were aiming, thereby necessitating OHR's own expansion; negligibly accountable to anyone but itself; and producing a syndrome of free riding among Bosnian authorities that was deeply worrying for long-term, indigenous democratization.[203]

Ashdown was publicly candid about these issues. In a revealing speech to the Bosnian Parliamentary Assembly in September 2003, he urged the members to take responsibility for the future of their own country. The speech described a "half full, half empty" situation in which further reform would languish unless Bosnian leadership assumed greater ownership. The tone of the speech—half pleading, half hectoring—indicated how vexed the question of the relative ownership of continuing reform had become: "If you vote it [a series of reforms] through, *you* take the credit. If you vote it down, *you* bear the responsibility." "Please note, this agreement [a recent tax reform] was made by *your* representatives . . . , not—I repeat *not*—by the international community." Regarding the fact that Bosnia's performance paled in comparison to other recent aspirants to the new Europe: "They [Poland and Hungary] stuck [to] the course. . . . And it is precisely because they didn't get a free ride."[204]

The question by 2003 was whether Bosnia had really "turned a chapter," in Ashdown's words, in which the international civilian presence could be significantly downscaled.[205] In January, OHR had proposed a form of wind-down through a new Mission Implementation Plan, modeled on that of UNMIBH, which included increasing the proportion of Bosnian staff in the office and focusing it heavily on Bosnia's move toward Europe.[206] In various public statements, Ashdown noted that the trend in OHR interventions to impose legislation and dismiss officials had already declined, that its budget and size had dropped, and that it would transition into a "more normal, European Mission, supporting Bosnia on the next stage of her journey towards EU membership."[207] Yet most analysts of Bosnian developments acknowledge that European membership was a distant objective, given the state of the country's economy and institutions.[208]

In his introduction to the third iteration of the Implementation Plan, in March 2005, Ashdown emphasized the accomplishments of the international community over nine years in Bosnia—rebuilt physical infrastructure, returned refugees, a peacekeeping force one-tenth the size of the force that rumbled into the country in December 1995, new state-level defense structures, and the prospect of Bosnia's membership in the political and economic structures of Europe. Blocking that prospect, however, was the "fundamental obstacle" of Republika

Srpska's failure to cooperate fully with the war crimes tribunal in the Hague. Perhaps looking toward the end of his three-year tenure as High Representative, Ashdown warned again that Bosnia faced "declining donor resources" in the face of "pressing priorities vying for the international community's attention," and that it was not "the job of OHR to oversee BiH to the point that it becomes a wholly modern economy. . . ."[209] That, it would seem, is the European Union's self-appointed task, as the problem of Bosnia-Herzegovina comes full circle to rest once again on Europe's doorstep.

Assessment and Conclusion

The Bosnian case presents international peacemakers and peacekeepers with three fundamental, tough questions and object lessons that are still ongoing. The first question is whether the Dayton Agreement was implementable from the start. The map was unwieldy, the parties to the conflict were dubiously ready to make peace, and the political resolution was close to unworkable if it depended on voluntary compliance. Short-term trade-offs required by some parties to reach agreement, such as a virtually powerless central government and a constitution based on ethnic or "constituent" identities rather than a national polity, would unavoidably stymie longer-term implementation and peacebuilding, playing into the hands of ethnic nationalists and frustrating efforts to build popular support for a more broad-based Bosnian identity. Even with an unpromising beginning, the second question is whether the implementation effort itself compounded these difficulties, on which this chapter has largely focused. The third question is that posed by Knaus and Martin, among others, about the longer-term implications of the international community's chosen methods for overcoming weaknesses in the agreement and recalcitrance among the parties.

The implementation of the Dayton Agreement began in the face of substantial constraints: parties unlikely to act in good faith, a peace agreement that contained internal tensions and ambiguities that would have to be worked out on the ground, and serious tension between capitals and institutions about relevant roles and responsibilities, particularly regarding the relationship between military and civilian components of implementation. These factors were closely interrelated. In particular, the acknowledged constraints on troop and resource mobilization from the capitals and institutions that would supply them largely determined the implementation model proposed in the agreement. This was, in other words, very much "supply-side" peace implementation.

What implementers could offer, and the way in which they could operationalize it—for example, strict segregation between military and civilian command—did not match what the postwar environment needed, especially in the face of predictable obstruction from the parties. Particularly hobbling was the decision to create the implementers' own "zone of separation" between military and civilian responsibilities and, further, to decentralize critical civilian tasks with no mechanism for coordination and joint strategy. This may have been a necessary compromise, but it was one that carried a substantial cost.

More fundamentally, the military-civilian division reflected contradictory strategies in the agreement. On the one hand, there was a military strategy to separate forces, with the deployment of what, in a Bosnian context, would be an overwhelming international force. On the other hand, the civilian strategy entailed the remixing of the population from the grass roots through the return of refugees and displaced persons and building joint institutions. To make matters more complicated, there were internal contradictions between major civilian elements of Dayton such as reintegration, on the one hand, and a constitutional division of powers that by and large reinforced the claims of monoethnic political parties, on the other. Thus Dayton stabilized lines of confrontation and derived political rights from them while it simultaneously aspired to override such divisions from above and below.

These tensions played themselves out in early missteps, the main consequence of which was to require ever greater international intervention in order to make further progress. Early elections, along with the persistent territorial hold of ethnic militaries, consolidated the power of the nationalist political parties. The focus on elections—seven rounds in seven years—further distracted international actors from attending to deeper issues such as organized crime, corruption, and weak rule of law.[210] Failure to establish a more conducive environment for return facilitated the movement of hundreds of thousands to majority areas, which was numerically, electorally, and symbolically counterproductive. Aid conditionality against the RS delayed its economic recovery by at least two years, with obvious impact on the viability of return. Some months after the RS regime opened up in November 1997, aid began to flow to the west, but it continued to be withheld from the eastern RS due to allegations that it was harboring war criminals. Economically, the heavy emphasis on physical reconstruction also empowered ruling authorities, who controlled contracts and labor markets.

The eventual resort to augmented international authority through OHR accomplished a great deal. But it also complicated the question of exit by establishing a pattern in which Bosnian authorities were able to avoid taking real responsibility for tough decisions. It is worth speculating, too, about the impact of adopting a "trusteeship" strategy incrementally versus starting with one from the outset. In Bosnia, implementers lost time for want of more robust civilian capabilities. They also sent mixed signals to Bosnian parties and the population at large about democratic process and legitimacy: if due process does not yield results, override it—at least, if one has the political backing to do so. When the implementers shifted to the trusteeship strategy to accomplish one set of implementation objectives, they risked undermining others, principally those of fostering institutions and a culture of democratic accountability.

Particularly worrying for the long haul, Bosnia has steadily fallen behind otherwise comparable economies in eastern Europe. The official unemployment rate in 2004 was in the "mid-20s," according to the International Monetary Fund, down from perhaps 40 percent two years earlier (with the highest rates among the young).[211] The World Bank estimated that 18 percent of the population lived below the poverty line in 2003, and that per capita GDP was $2,040.[212] The price of international implementation also continued to dwarf Bosnia's own economic production, and the economy remained heavily dependent on foreign assistance, uncompetitive in domestic and foreign markets and rife with corruption and "the organized misuse of financial assistance."[213] The criminalization of Bosnia's economy set in motion by the war—as is commonly the case—has become even more rampant, with illegal activity ranging from drugs transshipment to customs fraud to human trafficking.[214]

Perhaps most troubling, malaise among the population remained deep-seated, both about economic prospects and about politics. A revealing poll conducted by Mark Thompson in 2002 depicted deep discouragement, especially in the RS. He described a "pathological depression" and paranoia in Serb areas, where fully 89 percent of the population believed that decisions affecting their future will be made by outsiders, 61 percent expected the economy to worsen, only 14 percent wanted to join the European Union, and most were "sweepingly distrustful" of the international community.[215] The most trusted institutions were, instead, the Serbian Orthodox Church and the army—both, among other things, stalwarts of the nationalism that had fueled the war. Even in the Federation, which Thompson described as "a society in the midst of arduous post-conflict normalization," 43 percent of the population thought Bosnia was on the wrong track.[216]

Bosnia is often seen—accurately—as having been the beneficiary of comparative largesse from the international community: 60,000 troops at highest peacekeeping deployment and more than $5 billion in postconflict aid for a country of four million people. Compare this to peacekeeping in the Democratic Republic of the Congo (DRC): with more than twelve times as many people, fifty times as much territory, and every bit as violent and complex a conflict, the DRC received one-tenth the number of troops deployed to Bosnia. Put another way, for every peacekeeper in Bosnia, there were 67 Bosnians; for every troop member in the DRC, there were 8,333 Congolese (see table 2.8). Five years into its mission, NATO was able to scale back its Bosnia force by two-thirds, while the United Nations, five years into the Congo operation, needed to more than double the size of its force and give it greater authority and capacity to fight.

Whether one sees the glass in Bosnia as half full or half empty, this contrast should give pause. The resources expended in Bosnia to reach a vastly improved but still frankly disappointing outcome nearly ten years after the fighting ended reveal severe limitations in the international community's capacity to keep and build peace after civil wars. First, the level of international engagement in Bosnia is unlikely to be replicated in many other contexts, particularly where the strategic interests of key states and organizations are not seen to be heavily at stake. Second, even with this level of commitment, and despite many notable achievements, the overall outcome in Bosnia has lagged. In our view, this relates less to absolute resources than to how resources

Table 2.8. Bosnia and Herzegovina Compared to the
Democratic Republic of the Congo

	DRC	BiH	BiH as Percentage of DRC
Population	50,000,000	4,000,000	8%
Physical area (square miles)	905,600	19,700	2%
Initial number of peacekeepers	6,000	60,000	1,000%
Initial ratio of peacekeepers to population	1:8,333	1:67	
Number of peacekeepers five years into mission	16,500	20,000	121%
Ratio of peacekeepers to population five years into mission	1:3,030	1:200	

Sources: Calculations from World Bank, "Bosnia and Herzegovina Data Profile 2004," http://devdata.worldbank.org/external/CPProfile.asp?PTYPE=CP&CCODE=BIH, and "Congo, Dem. Rep. Data Profile 2004," http://devdata.worldbank.org/external/CPProfile .asp?PTYPE=CP&CCODE=ZAR. UN Security Council Resolution 1417 (2002) authorized 5,537 peacekeepers for the UN Mission in the Democratic Republic of the Congo.

are deployed in the service of an overall strategy to consolidate peace. Third, what the Bosnia case acutely reveals is the constraining effect on implementation of political dynamics within and among key capitals —especially within Washington, D.C., and between the United States and the European Union—and within organizations. The implementation strategy in Bosnia, particularly in the critical first years, derived less from the needs of this particular case than from bargains struck among the intervenors in relation to organizational and domestic political imperatives. It was an approach that was necessary, perhaps, but not auspicious in relation to future wars and operations.

Notes

The authors wish to thank Nils Mueller for excellent research assistance.

1. UN High Commissioner for Refugees (UNHCR) in Bosnia and Herzegovina, "Statistical Summary as of 30 June 2005," www.unhcr.ba/

return/Summary_30062005.pdf. Official figures count slightly more than 451,000 of these as "minority" returnees, although, as we argue later, this number deserves serious scrutiny. Regularly updated UNHCR return statistics can be found at www.unhcr.ba/return/index.htm.

2. See, for example, UN Development Programme (UNDP), "Early Warning System: Bosnia and Herzegovina," *Annual Report 2002;* and Mark Thompson, "South Eastern Europe: New Means for Regional Analysis," Policy Brief no. 2 (Stockholm: International Institute for Democracy and Electoral Assistance, May 2002).

3. Gerald Knaus and Felix Martin, "Travails of the European Raj," *Journal of Democracy* 14, no. 3 (July 2003): 60–74.

4. Among others, James Dobbins notes the "nexus between organized crime and political extremism" as one of the chief lessons learned from the Bosnia experience. See James Dobbins et al., *America's Role in Nation-Building: From Germany to Iraq* (Santa Monica, CA: RAND, 2003), xxi, 107–8.

5. Figures from the 1991 census, cited in Susan L. Woodward, *Balkan Tragedy: Chaos and Dissolution after the Cold War* (Washington, DC: Brookings Institution, 1995), 32–33.

6. Robert J. Donia and John Fine, Jr., *Bosnia and Hercegovina: A Tradition Betrayed* (New York: Columbia University Press, 1994); Rusmir Mahmutcehajic, *The Denial of Bosnia* (University Park, PA: Pennsylvania State University Press, 2000); and Noel Malcolm, *Bosnia: A Short History,* rev. ed. (New York: New York University Press, 1996).

7. The other republics were Croatia, Serbia, Slovenia, Montenegro, and Macedonia. Yugoslavia also included two semiautonomous provinces linked to Serbia (Kosovo and Vojvodina) and recognized six constituent nationalities (Croatian, Serbian, Slovenian, Montenegrin, Macedonian, and Muslim, the last of which became an official Yugoslav nationality with constitutional amendments in 1974).

8. See "Balkan Report," Radio Free Europe/Radio Liberty (RFE/RL), October 27, 2000, www.rferl.org/reports/balkan-report/2000/10/80-27100 0.asp.

9. Richard Holbrooke, *To End a War* (New York: Random House, 1999), 27.

10. Both invoked the results of popular referenda that showed overwhelming support for independence. In Slovenia, 89 percent had voted for independence in a plebiscite held in December 1990. In Croatia, 83 percent of the electorate voted in May 1991 (with the notable exception of Serbs in Krajina, who boycotted the referendum), of which 94 percent approved

independence. See Government of Slovenia, Public Relations and Media Office, "Path to Slovene State," www.uvi.si/10years/path; and Chuck Sudetic, "Croatia Votes for Sovereignty and Confederation," *New York Times,* May 20, 1991, A3.

11. The *Common Declaration on Peaceful Solution of the Yugoslav Crisis* was reached at Brioni on July 7, 1991, between Slovenia, Croatia, and SFRY, under the auspices of the European Community.

12. In August, the European Community Monitoring Mission was expanded to 500 personnel and extended to Croatia.

13. The arbitration commission was chaired by French jurist Robert Badinter and consisted also of the presidents of the constitutional courts of Belgium, Germany, Italy, and Spain.

14. These included, in June 1990, replacing the Yugoslav national symbol with a Croatian emblem that was last associated with the Croatian puppet state allied to Nazi Germany and, in December 1990, declaring Croatia the national state of Croats, thus effectively demoting Serbs from a constituent nationality to a national minority.

15. *Uti possidetis* had previously been applied only in decolonization contexts and was intended to ensure stability by requiring that newly independent states keep the same external borders as former colonies.

16. Carl Bildt, *Peace Journey: The Struggle for Peace in Bosnia* (London: Weidenfeld and Nicolson, 1998), 372.

17. For discussion of the German position, see Woodward, *Balkan Tragedy,* 183–89. The Badinter Commission did issue specific rulings on January 11, 1992, which concluded that Slovenia and Macedonia fulfilled requirements for recognition, whereas Croatia and Bosnia had to take further steps, Croatia needing to amend its constitution regarding national minorities and Bosnia needing to hold a referendum. Despite this opinion, on January 15 the EC announced that it would begin the process of recognition with Slovenia and Croatia (though not Macedonia, because of Greek opposition).

18. UN Security Council Resolution 743, S/RES/743, February 21, 1992.

19. The term "Bosniac" had supplanted "Muslim" as the official designation by late 1993. Despite some precise differences, the two terms are basically interchangeable. This text uses "Muslim" with reference to events before 1993 and "Bosniac" thereafter.

20. Of the 63.4 percent who voted, 99.7 percent supported independence. Woodward, *Balkan Tragedy,* 194. See also Chuck Sudetic, "Turnout in Bosnia Signals Independence," *New York Times,* March 2, 1992, A3.

21. This effort had in fact already begun as early as January 1992, with the declaration of a Serbian Republika BiH (later Republika Srpska) and the transfer of Bosnian Serbs in the JNA back to Bosnia from Croatia in anticipation of hostilities.

22. Estimates of the death toll from the conflict in Bosnia range widely, from 60,000 to 250,000. The most commonly cited figure of upwards of 200,000 has been acknowledged by Bosnia's then foreign minister, Haris Silajdzic, to have been fictional. Meeting with David Harland and Harriet Martin, Sarajevo, May 13, 1999.

23. The arms embargo was established under UN Security Council Resolution 713, S/RES/713, September 25, 1991, in response to the outbreak of war in Croatia.

24. Bildt, *Peace Journey*, 97.

25. The January 1993 Vance-Owen peace plan offered the Serbs 43 percent of Bosnian territory in a unified state, while the subsequent HMS *Invincible* and Contact Group plans specified a 49:51 ratio. See David Owen, *Balkan Odyssey* (New York: Harcourt Brace, 1995), 121.

26. As when the Bosniacs presented an initial map at Dayton claiming 67 percent of territory for the Federation, a position from which they quickly backed away. See Bildt, *Peace Journey*, 140.

27. See International Criminal Tribunal for the Former Yugoslavia (ICTY), Milosevic Trial (IT-02-54, November 5, 2003), Testimony of David Harland, 28628–709, www.un.org/icty/transe54/031105ED.htm, for discussion of general Serb strategy. See especially 28653–54, 28656–57, 28668–70, 28696–99, 28701.

28. Michael Rose, *Fighting for Peace* (London: Harvill, 1998), 39, 170, 246.

29. Ibid., 1.

30. Ibid., 243, 246.

31. Ibid., 172–73. See also United Nations, *The Fall of Srebrenica*, A/54/549, November 15, 1999, para. 39.

32. Including through the visibility of moderate figures, such as then foreign minister Haris Silajdzic, who would later come under attack by SDA hard-liners in postwar Bosnia. See Jovan Kovacic, "Assault on Bosnian Leader Highlights Tension," *Reuters World Service,* June 16, 1996. See also UNPROFOR, BiH Command, "Weekly Report," October 25, 1993.

33. Rose, *Fighting for Peace*, 184.

34. U.S. Central Intelligence Agency (CIA), *Balkan Battlegrounds: A Military History of the Yugoslav Conflict, 1990–1995* (Washington, DC: CIA Office of Public Affairs, 2002), 189–200.

35. See Owen, *Balkan Odyssey,* for a thorough discussion of the Vance-Owen peace plan.

36. The Federation constitution of 1994 provided for ten cantons, which represented a level of government between municipalities (at the lowest level) and entities and state (at the higher levels). See UN Office of the High Representative (OHR), *Bosnia and Herzegovina: Constitution of the Federation* (March 18, 1994), www.ohr.int/const/bih-fed.

37. This included the involvement of the private contractor Military Professional Resources Incorporated as well as Washington's turning "a blind eye to substantial Iranian arms deliveries" to the Bosniacs in violation of the UN arms embargo. Bildt, *Peace Journey,* 19.

38. ICTY, Milosevic Trial (IT-02-54, October 9, 2003), Testimony of General Rupert Smith, 27301, lines 18–25; 27302, lines 1–7. See also UNPROFOR, Correspondence, Military Assistant to Force Commander, Sarajevo, March 7, 1995.

39. See United Nations, *Fall of Srebrenica.* The report includes firsthand accounts from ICTY testimony by some who participated in the massacre, such as Drazen Erdemovic (80).

40. Holbrooke, *To End a War,* 74.

41. Ibid., 65–66.

42. NATO, "Statement by the Secretary General of NATO" (press release [95] 73, August 30, 1995), www.nato.int/docu/pr/1995/p95-073.htm.

43. Needing to allay the fears of the Serbs, however, while UNPROFOR evacuated troops from Serb-held territory, Smith announced to the press that it was unclear who had fired the mortar shell that had devastated the Markale marketplace. This has given rise to erroneous speculation that the Bosniacs might have fired the bomb themselves. See ICTY, Milosevic Trial (IT-02-54, November 5, 2003), Testimony of David Harland, 28689.

44. Holbrooke, *To End a War,* 73, 160.

45. See United Nations, *Fall of Srebrenica,* paras. 449, 462.

46. United Nations, *General Framework Agreement for Peace in Bosnia and Herzegovina* (GFAP), S/1995/999, November 30, 1995.

47. UN Security Council Resolution 1031, S/RES/1031, December 15, 1995.

48. Measured from the date of official transfer of authority from the United Nations to NATO on December 20, 1995.

49. GFAP, Annex 1A, Art. II, para. 1.

50. The UN Security Council designated six so-called Safe Areas in 1993 to protect civilians and enable delivery of humanitarian relief. These were Srebrenica—the first so designated—and Sarajevo, Tuzla, Zepa, Bihac, and Gorazde. UN Security Council Resolution 819, S/RES/819, April 16, 1993, paras. 1–4; UN Security Council Resolution 824, S/RES/824, May 6, 1993, paras. 3–4.

51. Prewar estimate from internal document, UN Civil Affairs, Brcko. Postwar estimates of the population in Brcko town from Task Force Eagle, Memorandum for Record, "Brcko Assessment," May 22, 1996; in the wider Brcko municipality from UNHCR, "Brcko Municipality," March 1996, 3.

52. GFAP, Annex 1A, Art. II, para. 3.

53. GFAP, Annex 3, Art. II, para. 2.

54. Dayton included a side agreement on the Bosniac-Croat Federation that had been established under the Washington Agreement in 1994. See *Dayton Agreement on Implementing the Federation of Bosnia and Herzegovina,* November 10, 1995.

55. Possibly with some skepticism, given experience with European disregard for the findings of its own Badinter Commission.

56. We use the general term "displaced" when there is no need to distinguish between refugees and internally displaced persons.

57. GFAP, Annex 7, Art. I, paras. 1–3.

58. GFAP, Annex 7, Art. VII, para. 1. Now called the Commission on Real Property Claims, this body was originally named the Commission on Displaced Persons.

59. The Contact Group, comprising the United States, France, Germany, Russia, and the United Kingdom, was expanded to six members in 1996 to include Italy.

60. These discussions were carried on separately, culminating in the Basic Agreement reached between Tudjman and Milosevic on November 11, 1995. The agreement provided for restoration of Croatian sovereignty while safeguarding Serb minority rights, and it established a UN Transitional Authority to oversee the process. Holbrooke, *To End a War,* 264–68.

61. Nevertheless, tensions in the relationship between U.S. and European negotiating teams flared, revealing competing interests in and approaches to the negotiations. See Bildt, *Peace Journey,* 118; and Holbrooke, *To End a War,* 186, 201, 242.

62. Cousens interviews with OHR and UN officials, Sarajevo, November 1996.

63. The Peace Implementation Council (PIC) also has a smaller Steering Board consisting of the Group of Eight, or G-8 (which is equivalent to the former Contact Group plus Japan and Canada), the OSCE chairman-in-office, and the EU president. The PIC was created out of the remnants of the International Conference on the Former Yugoslavia, which was set up in August 1991.

64. Harland interview with Jovan Zametica, former adviser to Radovan Karadzic, Pale, January 1996.

65. Ibid.

66. Holbrooke, *To End a War,* 308, 358.

67. See Roger Cohen, "Terms of Muslim-Croat Alliance Are Set at Dayton Talks," *New York Times,* November 11, 1995, 3; and Cohen, "Bosnia Asks U.S. Army Aid as Part of Any Peace Accord," *New York Times,* November 19, 1995, 10.

68. "Bosnian Croat Leader Dissatisfied with Dayton Talks," *Open Media Research Institute Daily Digest* II, no. 225, November 17, 1995.

69. Harland interview with Carl Bildt, Washington, DC, May 7, 2003.

70. Related provisions for arms control and confidence building were assigned to the Organization for Security and Co-operation in Europe (OSCE).

71. An International Criminal Tribunal for the Former Yugoslavia was established by the Security Council in 1993 to prosecute persons indicted for violations of international humanitarian law and grave breaches of the laws of war.

72. GFAP, Annex 1A, Art. VI, para. 4.

73. The dual-key command and control arrangement required UNPROFOR commanders to consult NATO and UN authorities before calling in NATO air support, and vice versa.

74. Steven Lee Myers, "NATO Sends in the Foreign Police in Bosnia," *New York Times,* October 6, 1998, A9.

75. GFAP, Annex 3, Art. I, para. 1.

76. Portions of the 1990 Conference on Security and Co-operation in Europe "Copenhagen Document" were reproduced in the Annex, further detailing these conditions. See "Document of the Conference on the Human

Dimension of the CSCE," Copenhagen, 1990, www.osce.org/documents/odihr/1990/06/13992_en.pdf.

77. The PEC initially had seven members and expanded to a maximum of sixteen in 1998.

78. GFAP, Annex 3, Art. III, para. 2(d).

79. GFAP, Annex 3, Art. III, paras. 2(b)–(c).

80. The EASC has consisted of four judges, all appointed by the OSCE head of mission: one international, one representing the Bosnian state, one the Federation, and one the Republika Srpska (RS). Its decisions must be consensual, though the chair can decide in the event of a split. All decisions are final, binding, and not subject to appeal.

81. See OSCE, Office for Democratic Institutions and Human Rights, "International Election Observation Mission, 2002 General Elections—Bosnia and Herzegovina, October 6, 2002, Statement of Preliminary Findings and Conclusions," www.osce.org/documents/odihr/2002/10/1189_en.pdf.

82. The commission had seven members: one Bosniac, one Croat, one Serb, one "other," and three representatives of the international community.

83. Though there is some disagreement, the dominant interpretation of Annex 7 is that compensation is offered *in addition to* return rather than as an alternative to it. Whatever its relation to compensation, Dayton's conception of return is a subnational one, premised on return to villages and towns from which people were driven. See Howard Adelman, "Refugee Repatriation," in *Ending Civil Wars: The Implementation of Peace Agreements,* ed. Stephen John Stedman, Donald Rothchild, and Elizabeth Cousens (Boulder, CO: Lynne Rienner, 2002), 273–302, especially note 49.

84. United Nations, *Report of the Secretary-General Pursuant to Security Council Resolution 1026,* S/1995/1031, December 13, 1995, para. 22.

85. The police-to-civilian standard in Europe is 1:330. On European standards and IPTF generally, see Michael J. Dziedzic and Andrew Bair, "Bosnia and the International Police Task Force," in *Policing the New World Disorder: Peace Operations and Public Security,* ed. Robert B. Oakley, Michael J. Dziedzic, and Eliot M. Goldberg (Washington, DC: National Defense University Press, 1998), 264.

86. GFAP, Annex 4, Art. III, para. 2c.

87. The IPTF was authorized by UN Security Council Resolution 1035, S/RES/1035, December 21, 1995.

88. The issue of IPTF investigations arose at a PIC Steering Board meeting in December 1996 and was added to the IPTF mandate with UN

Security Council Resolution 1088, S/RES/1088, December 12, 1996. See also United Nations, *Conclusions of the Peace Implementation Conference,* S/1996/1012, December 6, 1996, para. 77.

89. UN Security Council Resolution 1168, S/RES/1168, May 21, 1998. This new emphasis centered primarily on a program of judicial monitoring.

90. Cousens interview with Peter Fitzgerald, IPTF commissioner, Sarajevo, November 11–19, 1996.

91. Bildt, *Peace Journey,* 133 and 139 passim.

92. Most data in text and table come from Aurora Ferrari, "The Cost of Intervention: A Preliminary Inter-sectoral Analysis" (unpublished manuscript, 2000). Where Ferrari's sources account in different currencies, she calculates based on an exchange rate at January 1 of the relevant year.

93. Stephen John Stedman estimated a cost of $20 billion from inception through 2000, for an average cost of $4 billion per year. Stedman, "Ending Civil Wars: The Implementation of Peace Agreements" (presentation at the International Peace Academy, New York, November 15, 2002). As SFOR was downsizing fairly steadily, an average cost of $2 billion per year is a reasonable extrapolation from these numbers for 2001–4, for a total of $28 billion. U.S. Congressional Research Service reports suggest a similar, slightly higher cost of roughly $31 billion over the life of these operations. See Nina M. Serafino, "Peacekeeping: Issues of U.S. Military Involvement," Issue Brief no. 94040 (Washington, DC: Congressional Research Service, updated August 6, 2003), 16; and Carl Ek, "NATO Burdensharing and Kosovo: A Preliminary Report," no. RL30398 (Washington, DC: Congressional Research Service, January 3, 2000), 14–15.

94. Author calculations based on Ferrari data.

95. IFOR had two commanders in its one year of operation: Admiral Leighton Smith and Admiral Joseph Lopez. Under SFOR, commanders generally served for one year: General William Crouch (November 1996–July 1997), General Eric Shinseki (July 1997–October 1998), General Montgomery Meigs (October 1998–October 1999), Lieutenant General Ronald Emerson Adams (October 1999–September 2000), General Michael L. Dodson (September 2000–September 2001), Lieutenant General John Sylvester (September 2001–October 2002), Lieutenant General William Ward (October 2002–October 2003), Major General Virgil L. Packett II (October 2003–October 2004), and Brigadier General Stephen Schook (October–December 2004), who continued as head of NATO Headquarters Sarajevo after SFOR handed operations to the European Union.

96. United Nations, *SG Report on SC Resolution 1026,* S/1995/1031, para. 10.

97. GFAP, Annex 10, Art. II, para. 9.

98. Ibid., paras. 2, 4–7.

99. Bildt, *Peace Journey,* 131.

100. Holbrooke, *To End a War,* 214.

101. Bildt, *Peace Journey,* 114.

102. United Nations, *SG Report on SC Resolution 1026,* S/1995/1031, paras. 7, 9–11.

103. SFOR Web site, www.nato.int/sfor/organisations/sfororg.htm. Data as of June 2004.

104. United Nations, *SG Report on SC Resolution 1026,* S/1995/1031, para. 26. The number of monitors was subsequently increased to an authorized strength of 2,027 under Security Council Resolution 1103, S/RES/1103, March 31, 1997; and Security Council Resolution 1107, S/RES/1107, May 16, 1997.

105. For a description of the role of Civil Affairs officers within UNMIBH, see United Nations, *Report of the Secretary-General Pursuant to Security Council Resolution 1035,* S/1996/1017, December 9, 1996, paras. 14–17.

106. United Nations, *Report of the Secretary-General Pursuant to Security Council Resolution 1035,* S/1996/210, March 29, 1996, para. 7.

107. Ibid.

108. Ibid., para. 8.

109. Ibid., paras. 6, 9.

110. Lists of country contributions can be found in the quarterly reports of the secretary-general to the Security Council pursuant to the council's resolutions 1035 and 1088, respectively.

111. Cousens interviews with OHR, UNMIBH, OSCE, and UNHCR officials, Sarajevo, November 1996. See United Nations, *SG Report on SC Resolution 1035,* S/1996/210, paras. 3–5, for a description of difficulties faced by UNMIBH in its start-up phase.

112. See Dziedzic and Bair, "Bosnia and the International Police Task Force," in *Policing the New World Disorder,* ed. Oakley, Dziedzic, and Goldberg, 275.

113. The Spanish diplomat Carlos Westendorp (1997–99), the Austrian diplomat Wolfgang Petritsch (1999–2002), and the UK politician Paddy Ashdown (2002–present) followed Bildt as High Representative.

114. Bildt, *Peace Journey,* 173–74; and Cousens interview with senior OHR staff Earl St. Aubin Scarlett and Michael Maclay, Sarajevo, November 11–19, 1996.

115. Briefing on Train-and-Equip Program for the Bosnian Federation, Ambassador James W. Pardew, Jr., Special Representative for Military Stabilization in the Balkans, July 24, 1996, www.state.gov/www/regions/eur/bosnia/724brief_bosnia_federation.html.

116. Michele Zanini and Jennifer Morrison Taw, *The Army and Multinational Force Compatibility* (Santa Monica, CA: RAND, 2000), 62.

117. Active-duty troops were reduced according to schedule from a wartime high of more than 300,000 to 86,000 in 1997, in a ratio of 2 (Federation) to 1 (Republika Srpska).

118. Some remained in Bosnia and came to renewed attention as a security threat after September 11, 2001. According to Bosnian officials, at least seventy of these fighters remained in Bosnia as of 2001, most having been granted citizenship after marrying Bosnian women. See Robert Macpherson, "Bosnia Suspect Has 'Direct Links' to bin Laden: NATO Secretary-General," *Agence France-Presse,* September 29, 2001. See also "George Tenet's al-Qaida Testimony," *Guardian Unlimited,* October 18, 2002, www.guardian.co.uk/september11/story/0,11209,814731,00.html.

119. *Agreement on Sub-regional Arms Control* (Florence Agreement), June 14, 1996, modeled on the Conventional Forces in Europe Treaty.

120. Holbrooke, *To End a War,* 252.

121. GFAP, Annex 1A, Art. II, para. 1; Art. III; Art. II, para. 3.

122. United Nations, *SG Report on SC Resolution 1035,* S/1996/210, paras. 30–35.

123. Ibid., para. 42.

124. This number was reduced from an estimated 44,750 at the end of the conflict (see United Nations, *SG Report on SC Resolution 1026,* S/1995/1031, para. 22) to a target of 20,000 by early 1999 (11,500 for the Federation and 8,500 for the RS). See United Nations, *Report of the Secretary-General on the United Nations Mission in Bosnia and Herzegovina [UNMIBH],* S/1999/284, para. 11.

125. Most violence evidently enjoyed the support of local security forces. Indeed, "Most of the violations of human rights which occur in Bosnia and Herzegovina (by some estimates as many as 70 percent) are the work of police forces of the Entities themselves," according to the United Nations. See United Nations, *Report of the Secretary-General Pursuant to Security Council*

Resolution 1035, S/1996/1017, para. 15; and OHR, "Political Declaration from Ministerial Meeting of the Steering Board of the Peace Implementation Council, Sintra, 30 May, 1997," published as S/1997/434, May 30, 1997, para. 55.

126. UNHCR Sarajevo, "Statistical Summary," November 1998.

127. Reports by International Crisis Group (hereafter referred to as Crisis Group) detail these practices, including "Minority Return or Mass Relocation?" May 14, 1998; "Preventing Minority Return in Bosnia and Herzegovina: The Anatomy of Hate and Fear," August 2, 1999; and "The Continuing Challenge of Refugee Return in Bosnia and Herzegovina," December 13, 2002. All Crisis Group reports are at www.crisisgroup.org.

128. By 1997, the bus service had transported 460,000 Bosnians across the IEBL—an average of nearly 9,000 people per week. See U.S. Committee for Refugees, "Country Report: Bosnia and Herzegovina," *World Refugee Survey 1998,* www.refugees.org/world/countryrpt/europe/1998/bosnia_herce.htm. A different initiative—a pilot return project to swap Bosniac and Croat IDPs within the Federation by reciprocally exchanging the populations of designated towns—largely failed due to obstruction by local authorities.

129. Crisis Group has an especially good report on this subject, titled "Going Nowhere Fast: Refugees and Internally Displaced Persons in Bosnia," April 30, 1997.

130. Z. Hurtic, A. Sapcanin, and S. L. Woodward, "Bosnia and Herzegovina," in *Good Intentions: Pledges of Aid for Postconflict Recovery,* ed. Shepard Forman and Stewart Patrick (Boulder, CO: Lynne Rienner, 2000), 348.

131. UNHCR, "Returns Summary to Bosnia and Herzegovina from 01/01/1996 to 09/30/2003."

132. Constitutional Court of Bosnia and Herzegovina, "Partial Decision of July 1, 2000 in Case U 5/98, Request for Evaluation of the Constitutionality of Certain Provisions of the Constitution of Republika Srpska and the Constitution of the Federation of Bosnia and Herzegovina," paras. 86 and 130, www.ccbh.ba/?lang=en&page=decisions/byyear/2000.

133. The OSCE has a rotating chair-in-office, elected on an annual basis from among its members (roughly equivalent to the EU presidency or UN Security Council and General Assembly presidents), that is distinct from the organization's secretariat and field missions. In 1996 Switzerland held the OSCE chair-in-office, most visibly embodied by the minister of foreign affairs, Flavio Cotti. See, for example, Chris Hedges, "Swiss Diplomat Resists U.S. on Certifying Bosnian Vote," *New York Times,* June 8, 1996, A4.

134. Through Milosevic, Holbrooke engineered to have Karadzic removed from the presidency of the Republika Srpska and from public political activities. He remained a widely acknowledged, active presence behind the scenes, however. See, for example, Elaine Sciolino, "U.S. to Send Holbrooke to Discuss Indicted Bosnian Serb Leaders," *New York Times,* July 14, 1996; Raymond Bonner, "U.S. to Tell Serbs They Face New Sanctions," *New York Times,* July 17, 1996; and Jane Perlez, "Top Bosnian Serb Agrees to Resign," *New York Times,* July 20, 1996.

135. Crisis Group, "Elections in Bosnia and Herzegovina," Bosnia Report no. 16, September 22, 1996.

136. Chris Hedges, "Bosnia's Nationalist Parties Dominate Election Results," *New York Times,* September 21, 1996, A12. For a breakdown of election results by position and by party, see OSCE, "General Elections 1996," www.oscebih.org/electionsimplementation/pdf/96results/general_elections_96.pdf. Percentages are author calculations based on OSCE data.

137. Constitution of the Federation, III. Division of Responsibilities between the Federation Government and the Cantons, Art. 2, points (d), (e), (f), and (g).

138. For some time, the HDZ continued to resist cooperation with parliamentary and presidential bodies, demanding a renegotiation of power-sharing arrangements with the SDA that would give them a legal status within Bosnia closer to that of the RS.

139. See, for example, United Nations, *Report of the Secretary-General on UNMIBH,* S/1997/468, June 16, 1997, paras. 8–10.

140. Arguably, Bosnia was facing a triple transition if one includes the challenge of democratization.

141. David Woodward, *The IMF, the World Bank and Economic Policy in Bosnia* (Oxford: Oxfam, 1998), 11; and Economist Intelligence Unit, *Country Profile: Bosnia-Herzegovina, 1994–1995* (London: Economist Intelligence Unit), 16.

142. Bosnia's 1990 per capita GDP is estimated at $1,900. See World Bank, "Towards Economic Recovery: Discussion Paper no. 1" (prepared by the World Bank, European Commission, and European Bank for Reconstruction and Development for the Second Donors' Conference, April 2, 1996), 3, 9.

143. By May 1999, two further pledging conferences brought the total donor aid pledged to $5.25 billion. Hurtic, Sapcanin, and Woodward, "Bosnia and Herzegovina," in *Good Intentions,* ed. Forman and Patrick, 325–26.

144. Figures are in constant 2001 dollars. Dobbins et al., *America's Role in Nation-Building,* 158.

145. Ibid.

146. European Commission and World Bank, *Bosnia and Herzegovina, 1996–1998 Lessons and Accomplishments: Review of the Priority Reconstruction and Recovery Program and Looking Ahead towards Sustainable Development,* A Report Prepared for the May 1999 Donors Conference Co-hosted by the European Commission and the World Bank, 1.

147. Ibid., 92, 97–98.

148. Dobbins et al., *America's Role in Nation-Building,* 105.

149. UNDP Bosnia and Herzegovina, "Bosnia and Herzegovina Human Development Report/Millennium Development Goals 2003," 89.

150. Because the Bosnian parliament failed to ratify the law on its own, OHR enacted it de facto by incorporating it into the existing PEC rules and regulations.

151. Bonn Peace Implementation Conference, "Conclusions," December 10, 1997, Section XI, paras. 2, 2(b), and 2(c), www.oscebih.org/documents/61-eng.pdf.

152. OHR, "Removal from Office of Nikola Poplasen" (press release, March 5, 1999).

153. See, for example, "NATO Troops Stop Hard-Line Bosnian Serb Broadcasts; Transmitters to be Turned Over to Karadzic's Rival," *CNN,* October 1, 1997, www.cnn.com/WORLD/9710/01/nato.serbia.

154. The first PIFWC apprehension actually took place in Eastern Slavonia under the UN Transitional Administration for Eastern Slavonia on June 27, 1997. See Coalition for International Justice, www.cij.org/index.cfm?fuseaction=indictees&tribunalID=1#foot5.

155. The two were picked up in Prijedor. For details about the arrest, see Institute for War and Peace Reporting, *Tribunal Update 36: Last Week in The Hague (July 7–12, 1997).* For coverage of Prijedor's politics, see also Human Rights Watch/Helsinki Report, *The Unindicted: Reaping the Rewards of 'Ethnic Cleansing,'* January 1997, www.hrw.org/reports/1997/bosnia.

156. SFOR, "Persons Indicted for War Crimes" (fact sheet, November 2001), www.nato.int/sfor/factsheet/warcrime/t001116i.htm. As of October 2003, ICTY had tried or detained ninety-one PIFWCs. See ICTY, "Detainees and Former Detainees," www.un.org/icty/glance/detainees-e.htm.

157. In a sobering lesson about handpicking moderates to back in immoderate climates, Biljana Plavsic later surrendered to The Hague in 2001, pleading guilty on counts of "persecutions on political, racial and religious grounds as a crime against humanity" and is currently serving an eleven-year sentence in Sweden. See ICTY, "Detainees."

158. OHR, "Declaration of the Ministerial Meeting of the Steering Board of the Peace Implementation Council," Luxembourg, June 9, 1998, para. 5, www.ohr.int/pic. See also Susan Woodward, "Compromised Sovereignty to Create Sovereignty: Is Dayton a Futile Exercise or an Emerging Model?" in *Problematic Sovereignty: Contested Rules and Political Possibilities,* ed. Stephen D. Krasner (New York: Columbia University Press, 2001).

159. United Nations, *Report of the Secretary-General on UNMIBH,* S/1997/966, December 10, 1997, 3–4.

160. United Nations, *Report of the Secretary-General on UNMIBH* (S/1999/989, September 17, 1999, para. 23; and S/1999/1260, December 17, 1999, para. 5).

161. Crisis Group, "Is Dayton Failing? Bosnia Four Years after the Dayton Agreement," Balkans Report no. 80, October 29, 1999, 44.

162. United Nations, *Report of the Secretary-General on UNMIBH,* S/2001/1132, November 29, 2001, para. 5.

163. United Nations, *Situation in Bosnia-Herzegovina,* S/1999/492, April 30, 1999, Annex, 34–35.

164. United Nations, *Report of the Secretary-General on UNMIBH* (S/2000/212, March 15, 2000, para. 11; S/2001/571, June 2001, paras. 22–23; S/2000/1137, November 30, 2000, paras. 16–17; S/2001/1132, para. 17).

165. United Nations, *SG Report on UNMIBH,* S/2000/1137, para. 3.

166. United Nations, *SG Report on UNMIBH,* S/2001/1132, para. 14.

167. United Nations, *SG Report on UNMIBH,* S/2000/1137, para. 15.

168. Human Rights Watch, "Hopes Betrayed: Trafficking in Women and Girls to Post-conflict Bosnia and Herzegovina for Forced Prostitution," November 2002, with documentary updates posted on June 14, 2004, at www.hrw.org/english/docs/2004/06/14/bosher8815.htm.

169. UN Department of Peacekeeping Operations, "Monthly Summary of Contributions (Military Observers, Civilian Police and Troops) as of 30 June 2005," www.un.org/Depts/dpko/dpko/contributors/2005.

170. Specifically, these were national and entity elections (September 1998, November 2000) and municipal elections (September 1997, April 2000).

171. Improvements made in this context included open party lists, assignment of some parliamentary offices to fixed constituencies, a preferential ranking for election of the Bosnian presidency, a ban on candidates who occupied property belonging to refugees or displaced persons, and tight regulation of campaign expenditures.

172. Cousens interview with OSCE officials, Sarajevo, August 1998. "Bosnia Ballots Too Bewildering for Many: NGOs," *Agence France-Presse,* October 1, 1998.

173. See Crisis Group, "Bosnia's Alliance for (Smallish) Change," Balkans Report no. 132, August 2, 2002, for a thorough discussion of the reasons for the Alliance's shortcomings.

174. See OHR, "More Information about Special Envoys Offices," September 9, 2002, www.ohr.int/ohr-dept/s-envoys/default.asp?content_id=27873.

175. Constitutional Court, Partial Decision of July 1, 2000, paras. 92, 93, 136.

176. The court was ruling on a case brought by Izetbegovic in 1998 as a challenge to the constitutionality of the entity constitutions. It issued four partial rulings on this case, beginning in January 2000, but the main ruling is that of July 1. For analysis of the court decision, see Crisis Group, "Implementing Equality: The 'Constituent Peoples' Decision in Bosnia & Herzegovina," Balkans Report no. 28, April 16, 2002, 6.

177. "Hence, despite the territorial delimitation of Bosnia and Herzegovina by the establishment of the two Entities, this territorial delimitation cannot serve as a constitutional legitimation for ethnic domination, national homogenization or a right to uphold the effects of ethnic cleansing." See Constitutional Court, Partial Decision of July 1, 2000, para. 61.

178. OHR, "Steering Board of the Peace Implementation Council: Sintra Declaration Communiqué," May 30, 1997, para. 60, www.ohr.int/pic.

179. In fact, by instituting a cumbersome system of vetting property transactions, it had the perverse effect of penalizing compliant authorities, who had to wait on the outcome of an overwhelmed bureaucratic process— as of mid-2002, OHR had processed only 470 of more than 1,300 requests— while enabling noncompliant authorities to proceed generally unpunished. See, for example, OHR, "Decision on Re-allocation of Socially Owned Land, Superseding the 26 May 1999 and 30 December 1999 Decisions," April 27, 2000; and "Decision on Suspending the Power of Local Authorities in the Federation and the RS to Reallocate Socially Owned Land in Cases Where the Land Was Used on 6 April 1992 for Residential, Religious, Cultural, Private Agricultural or Private Business Activities," May 26, 1999, both at www.ohr.int/decisions.

180. In percentage terms, minority returns as a percentage of total returns rose steadily from a low of 11 percent between 1996 and 1997 to 30 percent of the total in 1998, 55 percent in 1999, 87 percent in 2000, and 93 percent in 2001. The percentage remained as high in 2002 and 2003, when another 162,000 returns were logged by UNHCR, of whom 90 percent (147,000) were counted as minority returnees. In numerical terms, however, this still left a cumulative imbalance between 1996 and end-2003 of 550,707 majority returns to 435,347 minority returns, the latter number to be further discounted given the phenomenon of "name-only" minority returns described in the text. Author calculation from UNHCR statistics at www.unhcr.ba/return.

181. "Povratak u Federaciju dvostruko veci [Return to the Federation Twice as Great]," *Oslobodjenje*, March 21, 2002, cited in Crisis Group, "Implementing Equality," 4.

182. OSCE, "International Election Observation Mission, 2002."

183. See, for example, statements made by U.S. secretary of state Madeleine Albright and NATO officials during the North Atlantic Council meetings of December 16–17, 1997, in Linda D. Kozaryn, "Albright Says Follow-on Force Serves U.S. Interests," *American Forces Press Service*, www.defenselink.mil/news/Dec1997/n12171997_9712172.html.

184. SFOR, "Transcript of Press Conference, May 27, 2003," www.nato.int/sfor/trans/2003/t030527a.htm.

185. See, for example, "Growing the Alliance," *Economist*, March 11, 1999.

186. Ahto Lobjakas, "Bosnia-Herzegovina: NATO Aims to Merge Rival Armies into Single Bosnian Force," *RFE/RL* online, August 18, 2005, www.rferl.org/featuresarticle/2005/08/8ebdcec9-5698-4783-864f-c56b1d396701.html.

187. Crisis Group, "Bosnia's Stalled Police Reform: No Progress, No EU," Europe Report no. 164, September 6, 2005, 2–3.

188. United Nations, *Letter Dated 4 April 2005 from the Secretary-General Addressed to the President of the Security Council*, S/2005/236, April 5, 2005, Enclosure (report of the European Union military mission in Bosnia and Herzegovina).

189. The EUPM was endorsed by both the PIC Steering Board and the UN Security Council.

190. Crisis Group, "Bosnia's Stalled Police Reform," 12.

191. Ibid., 5–11.

192. OSCE in Bosnia and Herzegovina, "Statement of the Head of Mission to the Permanent Council," February 17, 2005, www.oscebih.org/public/default_asp?d=6&article=show&id=943.

193. On Bosnia's ethnic structure pre–twentieth century, see Donia and Fine, *Bosnia and Hercegovina: A Tradition Betrayed.*

194. Crisis Group, "Minority Return or Mass Relocation?" Bosnia Report no. 33, May 14, 1998, 32–34.

195. Ibid., 23–24.

196. See Crisis Group, "The Continuing Challenge of Refugee Return in Bosnia and Herzegovina," Balkans Report no. 137, December 13, 2002, 9–11.

197. UNHCR, "UNHCR's Concerns with the Designation of Bosnia and Herzegovina as a Safe Country of Origin," July 2003, www.unhcr.ba/publications/B&HSAF~1.pdf.

198. UNHCR, "Strategy of BiH for the Implementation of Annex VII" (press release, March 18, 2003), www.unhcr.ba/press/2003pr/180303.htm.

199. At its peak, the agency deployed 380 personnel in Bosnia and spent $250 million. Its program for 2005 was budgeted at $11 million. See UNHCR, "Global Appeal 2005," 281; UNHCR, Executive Committee, 48th Session, "Update on Regional Developments in the Former Yugoslavia," April 2, 1998 (EC/48/SC/CRP.10), para. 29; UNHCR, Executive Committee, 47th Session, "Update on Regional Developments in the Former Yugoslavia," April 9, 1997 (EC/47/SC/CRP.18), para. 10.

200. UNHCR, "Bosnia and Herzegovina: Re-registration Shows Substantial Drop in IDP Numbers" (briefing notes, April 15, 2005). See also UNHCR, "Country Operations Plan, Bosnia and Herzegovina, Planning Year 2005," www.unhcr.ch/cgi-bin/texis/vtx/country?iso=bih.

201. For Paddy Ashdown's description of these dilemmas, see "We Want to Achieve Legislation Stamped 'Made in Bosnia,'" *Frankfurter Allgemeine Zeitung,* July 10, 2003, www.esiweb.org/ pdf/esi_europeanraj_reactions_id_3_b.pdf.

202. Knaus and Martin, "Travails of the European Raj."

203. Ibid., 61.

204. Paddy Ashdown, Speech to the BiH Parliamentary Assembly, Sarajevo, September 10, 2003, www.esiweb.org/pdf/esi_europeanraj_reactions_id_23.pdf (emphasis in the original).

205. Paddy Ashdown, "Bosnia Turns a Chapter," *Wall Street Journal,* October 24, 2003.

206. OHR, "Mission Implementation Statement," January 30, 2003, www.ohr.int/print/?content_id=29145.

207. Ashdown, "Made in Bosnia."

208. Susan L. Woodward, "Background Note: The Situation in the Balkans," Conflict Prevention and Peace Forum (unpublished note to the UN Department of Political Affairs, November 7, 2002), 7.

209. Paddy Ashdown, "Introduction," in OHR, *OHR Mission Implementation Plan for 2005,* March 7, 2005, www.ohr.int/print/?content_id=34144.

210. Paddy Ashdown, "What I Learned in Bosnia," *New York Times,* October 28, 2002, A25.

211. The "real" scale of unemployment is probably considerably less than the official figure, given the magnitude of the gray economy in which many Bosnians find supplemental, if not primary, livelihood. See Joe Ingram, "What Is the Real Unemployment Rate in Bosnia?" *Nezavisne novine,* May 17, 2002; International Monetary Fund (IMF), "Bosnia and Herzegovina, 2004 Article IV Consultation, Mission Concluding Statement, December 17, 2003," para. 3; and IMF, "Executive Board Concludes 2005 Article IV Consultation with Bosnia and Herzegovina," June 15, 2005, para. 2.

212. World Bank, "Bosnia and Herzegovina Country Brief 2005" (online report) www.worldbank.org/ba. The IMF estimated the poverty rate in 2004 at "over 30 percent," however. See IMF, "Executive Board," para. 2.

213. UNDP Bosnia and Herzegovina, "Millennium Development Goals 2003," 89–92.

214. Paddy Ashdown, "Corruption and Crime Are the Worst Legacy," *Novi Reporter,* April 9, 2003.

215. Mark Thompson, "South Eastern Europe," 6.

216. Ibid., 7.

3

Sierra Leone

Eric G. Berman and Melissa T. Labonte

Introduction

The people of Sierra Leone have had the great misfortune to reside in a country rich in diamonds that others needed to bankroll a war. The quickest path to those diamonds was large-scale armed robbery, fronted by an insurgency best known for its atrocities. The outside world took years to make the connection between Sierra Leoneans' missing hands and limbs and the country's missing gems, and more years to decide that the bandits were not trustworthy bargaining partners. That epiphany occurred only after a misguided peace accord, inked at American insistence, had all but collapsed, nearly taking with it an ill-prepared UN peacekeeping operation that succeeded an ill-conceived West African force. When Revolutionary United Front (RUF) rebels took more than 400 UN peacekeepers hostage in May 2000, not only that operation but also UN peacekeeping as a whole faced a critical choice: learn to use force effectively against those who violently disrupt the peace, or find another line of work.

Many factors other than diamonds contributed to the war in Sierra Leone, of course, including extreme poverty resulting from decades of economic underdevelopment and mismanagement; unprofessional and dispirited armed forces; government disregard of the needs of all but the political elite and their patronage networks living in the capital,

Figure 3.1. Map of Sierra Leone

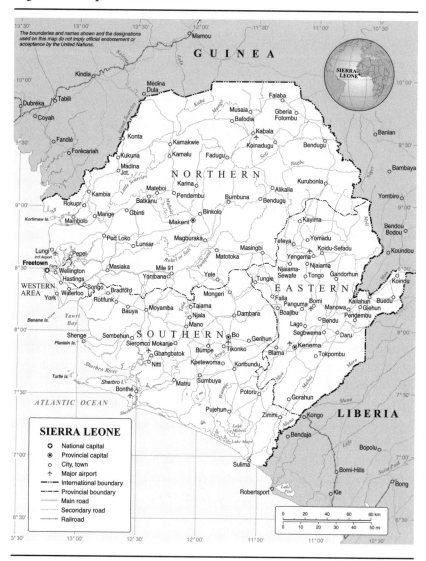

Source: UN Cartographic Section

Freetown; endemic corruption throughout society; and a civil war next door, in Liberia. The international community's initial response to the atrocities committed by the RUF was not just inadequate but destructive, rather than confronting the rebel group, the outside world bestowed legitimacy on it. There was real fear that Sierra Leone would join other failed states in Africa. That this did not happen provides important lessons for future peace operations.

This chapter reviews the four different peace operations that were active in Sierra Leone from 1998 to 2005 (see figure 3.1). These included the Economic Community of West African States (ECOWAS)[1] Cease-Fire Monitoring Group (ECOMOG), from 1997 to 2000; the United Nations Observer Mission in Sierra Leone (UNOMSIL), from 1998 to 1999; the United Nations Mission in Sierra Leone (UNAMSIL), from 1999 to 2005; and the military intervention by the United Kingdom in 2000. The chapter focuses on codeployment challenges encountered in simultaneous missions; disarmament, demobilization, and reintegration (DDR) of ex-combatants; transitional justice and accountability; the 2002 national and parliamentary elections; and the drawdown of peacekeepers as UNAMSIL prepared to complete its mandate in 2005.

Origins of the Operations

Having gained its independence from the United Kingdom in April 1961, Sierra Leone enjoyed a peaceful transition from colonial rule. Its population comprises some five million people, and its territory spans 27,000 square miles, approximately the combined size of Belgium and the Netherlands. The Temne and Mende ethnic groups each represent about 30 percent of the population, with some twelve other groups constituting the remaining 40 percent.[2] Although other countries in the region have experienced long-standing ethnic tensions, Sierra Leone's ethnic groups have coexisted relatively peacefully. Religious tensions have also been infrequent. Muslims constitute about 60 percent of the population, while Christians and people practicing indigenous beliefs constitute 10 and 30 percent, respectively.[3] Historically, Sierra Leone had no major diplomatic disputes with Guinea and Liberia, the two countries with which it shares borders.[4]

Until 1991, the greatest threat to the state was internal. Political corruption and repression, as well as military coups and countercoups, characterized the first thirty years of independence. Siaka Stevens and his All People's Congress (APC) party won general elections in March 1967, replacing the Sierra Leone People's Party (SLPP), which had been led since independence first by Milton Margai and then his brother, Albert—although Stevens did not assume power until April 1968 after a series of coups.[5] Joseph Momoh succeeded Stevens in November 1985, ensuring the APC's continued domination over a country left impoverished by its misrule,[6] despite vast mineral wealth.[7] Popular discontent with and alienation from the central government in Freetown was not just socioeconomic in nature. The capital, which rests on a small peninsula, is physically isolated from the rest of the country, and even separated by miles of water from the country's international airport.

In March 1991, a small group of individuals calling themselves the Revolutionary United Front invaded Sierra Leone from neighboring Liberia. Their leader, Foday Sankoh, was a former corporal in the Sierra Leone Army (SLA). He received training and support in Libya alongside Charles Taylor, an Americo-Liberian who launched an attack from Côte d'Ivoire on the government of Liberian president Samuel K. Doe in December 1989. Taylor's National Patriotic Front of Liberia (NPFL) failed to seize Liberia's capital, Monrovia, in August 1990 because ECOWAS dispatched a peacekeeping force—ECOMOG—to Liberia. Taylor's assistance to Sankoh and his group of about a hundred men, many of whom were reportedly members of the NPFL, was an effort to distract and undermine ECOMOG, as Sierra Leone was a troop contributor and served as a logistical support base for the mission.[8]

The RUF quickly made inroads in Sierra Leone; the country was faring poorly after thirty years of nepotistic, corrupt, and ineffective rule. Sankoh tapped into the growing resentment and disenfranchisement, especially among the rural jobless youth, offering to represent these neglected areas and the country's interior. The RUF garnered some popular support and additional recruits, and soon captured important diamond-mining towns in the country's southeast. Even though Sankoh was a Temne from the north, his anti-APC message appealed to Mendes in the country's south and east. Northern influence in the APC was considerable, and Mende and southern agricultural interests had received little support during the reign of Stevens and Momoh. In the early days of the war, before the RUF resorted to large-scale forced conscription (including the conscription of children) and engaged in a reign of terror, many families willingly gave their sons to Sankoh's rebellion.[9]

President Momoh managed to curtail the RUF's advance, but in so doing set in motion developments that would lead to his own downfall.[10] He quickly doubled the strength of the SLA, from approximately 2,500 to 5,000, without properly planning how to support and supervise them. The armed forces, historically kept small and poorly equipped so as to reduce the military threat to the government, lacked proper leadership, training, and pay. The SLA's better-trained troops were serving in ECOMOG, and a small number were in the Gulf supporting the U.S.-led Operation Desert Storm.[11] Even had they been present in the country during this time, however, the army still would have lacked both the human and the material resources to effectively counter the RUF advance. In May 1992, a group of junior officers led by Captain Valentine Strasser mutinied and drove Momoh from power.[12] Strasser assumed the presidency and attempted to consolidate his power by creating a National Provisional Ruling Council (NPRC), expanding the armed forces to 12,000, dissolving the legislature, and ruling by decree.

Unlike Momoh, who had relied exclusively on force to deal with the RUF, Strasser pursued a dual-track approach. On the political front, he formally requested the good offices of UN secretary-general Boutros Boutros-Ghali in November 1994, leading to the appointment of Berhanu Dinka as UN special envoy to Sierra Leone. Dinka was tasked with facilitating a dialogue between the Strasser government and the RUF that would lead to national elections.[13] On the military front, Strasser did not rely primarily on the SLA but rather counted on local militias, which together constituted a Civil Defense Force (CDF) organized loosely along tribal or ethnic lines.[14] Strasser also hired private security companies. He first brought in Gurkha Security Guards Limited, a UK firm, to help repel the RUF, but that initiative proved short-lived when the Gurkhas' commander was killed.[15] Strasser subsequently contracted with Executive Outcomes (EO), a South African firm, which is largely credited with performing ably against the RUF and helping the government recover territory.[16] In 1995, Strasser also concluded an agreement with the Nigerian government to expand the presence of that country's armed forces in Sierra Leone with additional troops, including military trainers.[17]

In January 1996 Strasser's chief of defense staff, Julius Maada Bio, launched a successful coup. Bio justified the coup on the basis of Strasser's purported unwillingness to step down after upcoming democratic elections. Although he had the support of regional leaders for delaying the ballot,[18] Bio deferred to public opinion and held national elections in February and March 1996.[19] The RUF stepped up its campaign of terrorizing the populace; as a result, the elections process was marred by large-scale human rights violations, mutilations, and amputations.[20] Despite such intimidation as well as voting irregularities, the international community judged the elections to be moderately free and fair and supported the winner, SLPP candidate Ahmad Tejan Kabbah.[21]

President Kabbah continued Bio's effort to pursue a negotiated settlement to the five-year-old civil war, an effort that the RUF appeared to welcome. Several years earlier Strasser had offered the RUF a place in a coalition government, but Sankoh had refused. Executive Outcomes had successfully reclaimed diamond mines from the RUF, but Strasser never gave them the means to defeat the rebels decisively. He and his senior officials benefited from the status quo; ending the war was not in their interests. Under Kabbah, however, EO made significant progress in its military operations. It also trained the CDF, which proved a more dangerous adversary than the SLA to the RUF.[22] By the fall of 1996, Sankoh's position had weakened considerably. He agreed to a cease-fire and entered into peace negotiations with the government.

The Abidjan Agreement, ECOMOG, and UNOMSIL

The Kabbah government and the RUF signed the Abidjan Agreement on November 30, 1996.[23] Politically, Abidjan was shepherded by key individuals from Côte d'Ivoire, the Organization of African Unity (OAU), and ECOWAS. ECOWAS as an organization was not directly involved in the negotiations, however, and an ECOMOG-type peacekeeping mission was not discussed, as ECOWAS was, at the time, preoccupied with the ECOMOG mission in Liberia. Moreover, several countries were unwilling to engage ECOWAS because of the actions of its chair, Nigerian military dictator General Sani Abacha.

Under the agreement, the RUF would be transformed into a political party, amnesty would be offered to all combatants, and a DDR program would be established. All foreign military forces and Executive Outcomes personnel would leave the country. A Joint Monitoring Group (JMG), including representatives of the government and the RUF, would monitor withdrawal of forces and combatant disarmament. A Demobilization and Resettlement Committee, in conjunction with a Neutral Monitoring Group (NMG), would oversee disarmament of combatants, the withdrawal of Executive Outcomes, and the repatriation of all foreign troops from Sierra Leone. The United Nations was to provide the sixty military observers constituting the NMG for an initial period of eight months, to oversee the DDR program and monitor the cease-fire.

If the peace agreement held, troop units under the command of the United Nations were to be deployed at a later date.[24] The timetable for implementing Abidjan was ambitious and optimistic, placing a great deal of faith in the warring parties' commitment to peace. Disarmament and encampment of the RUF was to begin within seventeen days of the signing, and UN military observers were to deploy within sixty days. The DDR program was to be completed, foreign troops were to be repatriated, the Republic of Sierra Leone Military Forces[25] were to be demobilized, and all remaining peace agreement provisions were to be completed within 240 days of the signing.

Abidjan's timetables were not met. Instead, Sierra Leone experienced further political turmoil and conflict, demonstrating that the country's rebel factions were not committed to peace.

Political Support for Peace, and the Lack of It

Sankoh's (and therefore the RUF's) commitment to the peace process quickly became suspect. In early January 1997, President Kabbah hosted a UN assessment team to discuss joint efforts to implement the peace agreement. The RUF expressed distrust of Special Envoy Dinka and called into question the sequencing of the Abidjan provisions. Sankoh was willing to receive neutral international monitors but emphasized that peacekeepers were not necessary, provided that all other combatants were disarmed and demobilized before the RUF was.[26] Skeptics rightly questioned Sankoh's fidelity to the accord. Evidence surfaced that the RUF leader never intended to abide by the agreement and had decided to continue the armed struggle, using the accord to gain tactical advantage. This intent was confirmed in March 1997, when Sankoh was arrested at a Nigerian airport with illegal weapons in his car.

On May 25, a group of SLA officers calling themselves the Armed Forces Revolutionary Council (AFRC) overthrew the Kabbah government. Major Johnny Paul Koroma, in jail at the time of the coup, was made head of the AFRC. He invited the RUF to form an alliance, an offer Sankoh accepted from detention in Nigeria. Although the UN Security Council continued to tout the viability of the peace accord,[27] this had more to do with supporting a diplomatic process in the face of continued warfare than with proclaiming particular fidelity toward any specific document.[28] The Abidjan Agreement had been effectively terminated.

In the wake of the May 1997 coup d'état, there was near-universal support for President Kabbah. The OAU, which convened its annual summit meeting the following week in Harare, Zimbabwe, roundly condemned the coup, called for the immediate restoration of President Kabbah, and looked to ECOWAS to take the lead in this regard.[29] The Security Council debated the coup two days later and issued a presidential statement echoing the OAU position.[30] Most governments closed their embassies in Freetown and moved their personnel to the Guinean capital, Conakry, where Kabbah and his government established temporary residence.[31] It was Kabbah who addressed the UN General Assembly in September in New York, and who was invited to attend the Commonwealth Summit of heads of state in October in Edinburgh, Scotland.

The international community by and large favored a diplomatic resolution to the conflict. ECOWAS foreign ministers met in Conakry in June and established a Committee of Four to discuss with Koroma the AFRC's role in restoring the Kabbah government.[32] Negotiations with the junta were unsuccessful. In August, ECOWAS heads of state and government agreed to impose a series of military and economic as well as diplomatic sanctions, and authorized ECOMOG, then in Liberia, to reinstate the legitimate Sierra Leone government.[33] In October, the

Security Council authorized its own sanctions under Security Council Resolutions 1132 (October 8, 1997) and 1156 (March 16, 1998).[34]

Shortly thereafter, Koroma formally agreed to relinquish power. Meeting with representatives of regional and international organizations in the Guinean capital in October 1997, Koroma signed the Conakry Agreement, which called for Kabbah to be reinstalled by April 1998.[35] The wide array of sanctions have been credited with contributing to Koroma's decision, and the threat by ECOWAS to intervene militarily may also have weighed on the AFRC chairman. Soon after the Conakry Agreement was concluded, however, it became apparent to many that Koroma could not hold up his end of the bargain; he had lost influence with the hard-liners in his coalition. But even after Koroma began to talk openly of a much longer transition to democratic rule, most ECOWAS member states remained firmly committed to finding a diplomatic resolution to the crisis.

Nigeria, which had stationed troops in Sierra Leone since 1991, was the country with the greatest interest in resolving the crisis through military means. It soon decided, unilaterally, to use military force to reinstall Kabbah. After an abortive early effort to reverse the coup, Nigeria's President Abacha conducted a round of shuttle diplomacy and select consultations with regional leaders. He received Kabbah's go-ahead for further military action in early 1998.[36] Diplomats from ECOWAS countries based in Conakry and the Nigerian capital of Abuja apparently were told nothing of the pending offensive, however, and seemed genuinely surprised when it was launched in early February.[37]

Notwithstanding international support for ECOMOG, there remained a general distrust of the Nigerian-led mission, which largely explains the creation of UNOMSIL. The United Kingdom took the lead in preparing the conditions for the observer mission by first proposing the deployment of a team of ten military liaison officers to Sierra Leone. Paris, which had an unwritten understanding with London that each country would support the other's interests in the Central African Republic and Sierra Leone, respectively, was perhaps the other driving force behind the creation of the subsequent, larger UN observer mission.[38] Whereas numerous African countries had remained ambivalent, if not hostile, toward a UN mission in Liberia, ECOWAS member states were generally supportive of a similar arrangement in Sierra Leone.[39]

Mandate

The provision of an ECOWAS mandate for ECOMOG in Sierra Leone can best be understood as an uneasy compromise between Nigeria and most other members of the regional organization, rather than as outright support for Nigeria's position. The August 1997 enabling resolution by ECOWAS heads of state and government warned that military force would be a last resort and favored sanctions to impress upon Koroma their seriousness of purpose. Numerous factors diminished enthusiasm for the intervention, among them financial considerations, distrust of Nigeria, regional rivalries, and, in the case of Burkina Faso and Liberia, implicit support for the coup.

ECOMOG's principal focus was to stabilize the country. The force was to deploy throughout Sierra Leone, control select entry points into Sierra Leone in connection with the embargo, and monitor roadblocks and the movement of arms and ammunition. ECOMOG was to oversee the disarmament of ex-combatants at designated areas, and to conduct patrols with an eye toward establishing freedom of movement and governmental authority. The peacekeeping mission was to provide security for key individuals, including UN and nongovernmental organization (NGO) personnel, and to assist in protecting refugees and internally displaced persons (IDPs).[40]

In April 1998, the Security Council authorized deployment of ten military liaison officers to Sierra Leone with a ninety-day mandate to assist ECOMOG with planning.[41] In June Secretary-General Kofi Annan proposed creation of UNOMSIL, and the council authorized it in July. The seventy-strong observer force (including an additional small medical unit) was intended to complement—but not supplant—ECOMOG. Headed by Francis Okelo, the special representative of the secretary-general (SRSG), UNOMSIL focused largely on observing ECOMOG activities. Formally, it was to assess the country's overall military and security situation and monitor the disarmament, demobilization, and arms collection processes. UNOMSIL observers would be responsible for reporting on voluntary disarmament in CDF strongholds. The secretary-general also proposed—and the council approved—augmenting the Office of the Special Envoy (who became SRSG) with police advisers (to help the government and local police officials with police practice, training, and recruitment); human rights officers (to report on human rights and international humanitarian law violations and to assist the government in upholding these laws); and information and political officers. Annan also raised the possibility of fielding a highly mobile unit of armed UN peacekeepers to provide additional protection to the observers but did not recommend that the council take such action.[42]

Funding

ECOWAS was unable to finance the mission independently and relied essentially on a single country, Nigeria, for support. Although there were some voluntary contributions to a special international trust fund and bilateral ad hoc funding from donor countries to troop contributors, ECOWAS was nearly totally dependent on Nigeria. Abuja complained about the huge cost it was incurring in fielding the mission, but there was widespread belief that Abacha was using the mission to claim phantom expenditures while money was diverted elsewhere. Nigeria's claim that it was spending $1 million a day on its operations in Sierra Leone may have been inflated. Nonetheless, the Nigerian government did assume the greatest financial burden and received little assistance in its bid to enforce the sanctions and then to oust the AFRC.

The United Nations attempted to address this problem by raising additional funds to support ECOMOG's efforts. In response to a request by the Security Council, Secretary-General Annan established in March 1998 a special Trust Fund to Support United Nations Peace-keeping-Related Efforts in Sierra Leone.[43] By the end of 1998, only two countries—the United Kingdom and Japan—had contributed to this voluntary fund. They gave a total of $1.79 million, of which only $100,000 had been disbursed. At the time, the Netherlands pledged $1 million to the fund as well, but it is unclear whether this money was ever delivered.[44]

Some countries did provide low-level support outside these funding mechanisms. The United States, for example, contributed $3.9 million in 1998 to fund improvements in ECOMOG logistics, although this exhausted all State Department funds available at the time for peace operations in Africa.[45] Western assistance to ECOMOG operations in Sierra Leone became more generous in 1999, following the RUF's siege of Freetown in December 1998 and January 1999. The United Kingdom provided some $18 million, and Canada, Italy, the Netherlands, and the United States also contributed assistance.[46]

Funding for UNOMSIL came from the assessed contributions of UN member states to the peacekeeping budget. In June 1998, the secretary-general requested appropriations of $18.3 million for the first six months of UNOMSIL.[47] The General Assembly appropriated $22 million for the first year, July 1998 through June 1999. The secretary-general later sought $40.7 million for 1999–2000, but the creation of UNAMSIL in October 1999 supplanted this request, as UNOMSIL personnel were absorbed into the new mission.[48]

Planning and Deployment

Even though ECOWAS authorized the mission in Sierra Leone, neither its secretariat nor a coalition of its member states contributed meaningfully to the mission's initial plans. Nigeria did receive assistance from the British company Sandline International in conceiving the February 1998 offensive. Sandline provided ECOMOG with intelligence and strategic planning until it departed Sierra Leone in March.[49] With mid-level support in the British government, Sandline also attempted to provide material assistance to reinstate Kabbah—in violation of the UN arms embargo, which applied to both the AFRC and the Kabbah government and which London had taken the lead in drafting. The materiel reportedly did not arrive until after Freetown had been secured, however, and the offensive may well have succeeded without any outside help. Nevertheless, the incident, known as the Sandline Affair, created a stir in the United Kingdom when the story came to light.[50]

In early 1998, the United States agreed to transfer American-supplied vehicles, in service with Nigerian units in Liberia, to Sierra Leone. The Netherlands, similarly, gave permission for Dutch-supplied vehicles to be transported. By mid-January, Nigeria had significantly increased the transfer of men and materiel from Liberia in preparation for the February offensive, but neither the Americans nor the Dutch appear to have been informed of the pending plans for this operation.[51]

The ECOMOG mission for Sierra Leone was to number 15,000 troops, deployed across four sectors: western, northern, southern, and eastern. Seven battalions, an aviation unit, and an artillery brigade were to constitute the western sector troops, covering Freetown, Lungi, and

Hastings. The northern sector would include a brigade headquarters in Makeni, with separate battalions in Port Loko, Magburaka, and Kabala. Battalions were planned for Moyamba, Pujehun, and Kenema as part of a southern sector, with brigade headquarters in Bo. The eastern sector, the most difficult deployment given the high concentration of RUF rebels, would require battalions headquartered at Yengema, Zimmi, and Kailahun. The mission also required naval assets. Subsequently, ECOWAS sought to increase the strength of ECOMOG to about 18,000 troops.[52]

The number of ECOWAS peacekeepers that were actually deployed in Sierra Leone is very difficult to ascertain, however. By one account, the initial ECOMOG (read Nigerian) force for Sierra Leone that ousted the AFRC from Freetown in February 1998 numbered some 4,000 men.[53] Nigeria listed Guinean troops stationed in Sierra Leone under a bilateral agreement with the government as part of what Abuja called the ECOMOG Task Force for Sierra Leone, but they maintained operational autonomy from and did not share information with Nigerian troops. On the eve of the February 1998 offensive, Guinean troops codeployed with Nigerians outside the city center withdrew to their area of operation in the hinterland.[54] A Guinean battalion of 600 troops later became a full member of ECOMOG, as did a 600-strong Ghanaian battalion, shortly after Kabbah was reinstalled. (The few Ghanaian soldiers in Sierra Leone before then were technicians serving at Lungi airport in support of ECOMOG operations in Liberia.) Mali also provided 500 troops, with Western support. Commitments from Benin, Côte d'Ivoire, the Gambia, and Niger did not materialize.[55]

According to Secretary-General Annan, ECOMOG's force strength by June 1998 was around 12,000, which would imply a Nigerian contingent of at least 10,000, although, as noted, these numbers may have been inflated.[56] Regardless, there is consensus that ECOMOG expanded significantly in response to the RUF's attempted siege of Freetown at the end of 1998. According to the ECOMOG force commander, Major-General Timothy Shelpidi, Nigeria dispatched five more battalions to Sierra Leone after Freetown came under attack.[57]

Meanwhile, the United Nations moved to deploy UNOMSIL observers at seven locations: a headquarters in Freetown; three locations where former SLA troops were being detained (two on the capital's peninsula and one across the peninsula at Lungi); and the three ECO-MOG brigade headquarters (at Hastings, on the capital's peninsula, and at the provincial capitals of Bo and Makeni). Annan envisaged deploying the remaining thirty or so observers of the anticipated seventy-strong force outside of Freetown, security permitting, in two additional phases, August/September and October 1998.[58]

The United Nations was able to field initial components of the mission quickly. By August it had concluded the prerequisite status of mission agreement with the government of Sierra Leone, and twenty-seven military observers from eight countries, under the command of Brigadier-General Subhash C. Joshi of India, arrived in Freetown. Deployment was made somewhat easier by the "rehatting" of the eight UN military liaison personnel already in the country since May.[59] By September the remaining fourteen observers and the fifteen-member medical team had arrived, thus completing the first deployment phase. Ten countries provided personnel to the mission.[60] They deployed as planned, as well as in Kenema, where ECOMOG maintained an additional brigade headquarters.[61]

The security situation prevented the mission from deploying fully, however; indeed, most of the force was withdrawn to Guinea after the Freetown siege. As late as June 1999, the mission consisted of only twenty-two observers and a two-person medical team.[62] It was expanded to 210 observers in response to the July 1999 Lomé Agreement (discussed at length in a later section). About half of these had deployed when UNOMSIL was replaced by a larger peacekeeping operation.[63]

Field Operations: Implementing the Mandate

Nigerian troops first moved against Koroma's junta in early June 1997, only eight days after it had taken power. Operation Sandstorm failed for a variety of reasons, not least because of insufficient logistical support and insecure communications that resulted in the junta's receiving advance warning of the attack. In mid-June, however, Nigerian forces did gain control of the strategic town of Lungi, including the international airport. Well before ECOWAS leaders authorized what they called ECOMOG II in August 1997, Nigeria took to calling its Operation Sandstorm the ECOMOG Task Force in Sierra Leone, incorporating SLA and, later, Guinean troops. Continuing skirmishes and mounting Nigerian casualties were trying Abuja's patience. Matters came to a head in early 1998, when a single landmine explosion killed seventeen Nigerian soldiers.[64]

In February 1998, Nigerian troops led by the ECOMOG Task Force commander, Colonel (soon to be Brigadier-General) Maxwell Khobe, launched an assault on rebel-held Freetown.[65] Koroma and the AFRC were driven from power by the end of February, and Kabbah returned to Freetown on March 10, 1998. The West African force did not fully neutralize the AFRC and RUF threat, however, and fighting continued in the eastern and northern parts of the country.[66] By December, the RUF was advancing from the east toward Freetown, and the Kabbah government again faced a rebel assault. Some accounts mention only the RUF role in the subsequent siege of Freetown, but numerous credible sources credit the ex-SLA/AFRC with organizing the attack, in which some RUF troops participated. More than 5,000 civilians were killed.[67]

An infusion of Nigerian troops and firepower helped dislodge the rebels from the capital and hastened their withdrawal to the hinterland. The military campaign, which the Nigerians called Operation Death before Dishonor, was criticized by human rights advocates for excessive use of force and serious human rights abuses.[68] Several Western states provided additional support to troop-contributing countries to facilitate the deployment of peacekeepers. ECOMOG succeeded in opening resupply routes connecting the capital to Kambia in the northwest and to Kenema in the southeast but often had to rely on secondary roads and contend with sporadic RUF raids. While ECOMOG maintained positions in Bumbuna and Kabala, in Tonkolili and Koinadugu districts, the RUF continued to dominate the northern and eastern provinces.[69]

Major General Shelpidi argued that his troops lacked the appropriate equipment to undertake successful counterinsurgency operations. Unfamiliarity with the terrain also hampered operations, and the Ghanaian and Guinean battalions operated independently and did not coordinate their activities with their Nigerian counterparts. Moreover, outside assistance for the force was slow in coming and not particularly generous.[70] As a result, Nigerian troops often had to deploy alongside SLA units that included rebel elements or sympathizers who sabotaged ECOMOG operations.[71]

Yet Nigeria itself contributed to ECOMOG's problems. Nigerian troops were underpaid or went unpaid for long periods; this adversely affected morale and discipline. Shelpidi also grossly overestimated his troops' control of the countryside and allowed many officers to return to Nigeria before Christmas in December 1998 to celebrate that holiday and the new year.[72] This compounded the problem of command and control when it became clear that the optimistic security reports were baseless and the capital came under siege.[73]

The embargo and sanctions against the RUF were not well implemented, due, in large part, to the ineffective role played by ECOMOG and to resistance on the part of Liberia. ECOMOG lacked the capacity to carry out extensive border patrols, smuggling was common, and efforts to coordinate border patrols with neighboring states were largely unsuccessful. Reports of illegal arms being channeled across the Sierra Leone–Liberia border were a regular feature of Security Council presidential statements and the secretary-general's reports.[74] Moreover, ECOMOG could not patrol or blockade Sierra Leone ports effectively, so embargoed items continued to enter the country by sea. Liberia openly defied the embargo and used its border with Sierra Leone's RUF-controlled eastern districts to transport shipments of arms and other munitions to the rebels. It is alleged that the RUF itself exploited Resolution 1132's vague provisions concerning military assistance by contracting military technical training from Liberia and mercenaries from Ukraine.[75]

DDR was a critical component of both the Abidjan and Conakry agreements, and the guidelines established therein served as the benchmarks for the DDR program following Kabbah's restoration. Prior to the signing of the Abidjan agreement, the government of Sierra Leone established a DDR program unit within the Ministry of National Reconstruction, Resettlement, and Rehabilitation. In July 1998, the ministry was replaced by the National Committee for Disarmament, Demobilization, and Reintegration (NCDDR), which recommended the disarmament process. The NCDDR prepared an overall strategy for DDR and tasked UN-assisted NGOs with establishing assembly sites. ECOMOG was assigned to be the primary implementing actor. The committee's goal was to disarm some 32,000 combatants between July 1998 and January 2000, including elements from the SLA, the

AFRC, the RUF, the CDF, and child soldiers.[76] Combatants were directed to report to designated reception centers, where they would be disarmed and encamped pending entry into resettlement and reintegration programs. UNOMSIL military observers, recently deployed, monitored the process.

Security problems in the countryside made implementation slow and sporadic. Screening and registration of combatants began at Lungi, but participation rates were low.[77] Predischarge orientation programs quickly ran out of money and ceased by the end of 1998, and the siege of Freetown then erased what little progress had been made. The World Bank evaluated the DDR program in early 1999 and recommended relaunching it, with a pilot effort again beginning at Lungi. The bank suggested that a national DDR program be postponed until a new peace treaty was executed. The NCDDR estimated that nearly 3,200 combatants were disarmed from September to December 1998 (2,994 AFRC and ex-SLA, 187 RUF, and 2 CDF). Of this total, 189 were child soldiers.[78]

Assessment (1996–99)

ECOMOG's initial utility to the international community and the United Nations in Sierra Leone was as an instrument for reinstating the democratically elected government of Ahmad Tejan Kabbah. ECOMOG forces found themselves taking up new and potentially more dangerous duties, however, when it became clear that the AFRC and the RUF remained dedicated to violence to secure their objectives. ECOMOG carried out offensive operations to protect the government in Freetown, while the United Nations attempted diplomatic pressure to bring the combatants to the negotiating table.

ECOMOG's failure to rout the rebels completely in February 1998 meant that fighting continued and imposed high material and human costs on the main troop-contributing nation, Nigeria. The use of force seemed to bolster a previously unsuccessful diplomatic process, and the United Nations appeared to view this, erroneously, as a sign that the political process was working. But the rebels had not bought into the process and ECOMOG failed to protect it, owing to a mix of incompetence, corruption, poor intelligence, and poor communications as well as disunity of effort among ECOMOG's national contingents. Together, these factors resulted in the AFRC/RUF assault on Freetown to coming as a complete surprise to both ECOMOG and the United Nations.

It is questionable whether the embargo and travel ban mandated under Security Council Resolution 1132 helped push the military junta to the negotiating table. Almost certainly, the sanctions put in place under Resolutions 1132 and 1156 did not constrain the junta materially and played little or no role in attempts to negotiate a stable settlement. Some analysts have claimed that Sierra Leone should have been "highly vulnerable to sanctions . . . with only three seaports and four usable airports" and heavy dependence on mineral resources whose exports are relatively easy to control and trace.[79] Monitoring and enforcement of the embargo by ECOMOG were ineffective. Guinea, a strong Kabbah and UN ally, attempted to enforce the sanctions and embargo but had only limited success, owing to a lack of resources and the sheer amount of terrain to be monitored. Liberia engaged in what could be characterized as "lip service" discussions with the secretary-general regarding the development of joint border patrols but failed to resolve issues of financing the patrols. The matter became moot because the AFRC/RUF maintained near total control of the Sierra Leone–Liberia border from early 1999 to summer 2000. Yet the Security Council did not do much more to address the problem than continue to remind member states of their obligations to comply with the two resolutions and suggest that investigations be conducted into reported violations.

What little progress there was in DDR in 1998 was quickly negated by the return to conflict at the end of that year, when the RUF and the AFRC attacked Freetown. In addition, the program's scope and procedural mechanisms were vague. Little guidance was available to implementers in such key areas as how to determine the level and nature of reintegration support to be offered and the process for providing reinsertion allowances.[80] Indeed, the necessary implementation funds—estimated at $14 million—were never raised. Even if funding had been secured, program goals were overly optimistic and did not provide for contingencies such as a return to combat by one or more parties. Nor did the program substantially alter incentives for ex-combatants who saw violence as their "primary survival alternative in a country with high levels of urban unemployment."[81] The RUF had offered to change the fortunes of many disaffected youths through the lure of diamond mining profits and "gang-like" bonding. Many perceived violence as the way to reverse the inequalities of their lives, and the DDR program offered nothing to alter that perception.[82] Ultimately, as soon as fighting resumed, recently disarmed soldiers broke open the weapons depots, rearmed themselves, and returned to the bush.

Finally, neither ECOMOG nor UNOMSIL succeeded in fulfilling their mandated responsibility to provide information about the security situation throughout the country. On the eve of the AFRC/RUF attack on Freetown at the end of 1998, UNOMSIL (almost totally dependent on ECOMOG for security assessments) was reporting to other UN agencies, UN headquarters, and NGOs that the RUF was taking up defensive positions in the center and eastern districts. The lack of communication and, as some analysts have claimed, abundance of misinformation severely damaged the mission's credibility and put other UN and aid agency staff, as well as civilians, at great risk.[83]

Throughout this initial period of ECOMOG and UN involvement in Sierra Leone, neither the military nor the political strategy was well coordinated or accepted by all the key actors involved in the conflict. The RUF was able to capitalize on the absence of international resolve, an incoherent strategy, a poorly designed peacekeeping mission command and control structure, and discordant agendas. It repeatedly manipulated the political process to its benefit. These factors had a significant impact on the lessons the United Nations ultimately learned from the Sierra Leone conflict about the limits of diplomacy and negotiating with warlords.

The Lomé Agreement and ECOMOG's Handover to UNAMSIL

During the first months of 1999, the prospects for durable peace in Sierra Leone appeared remote. The Kabbah government had lost legitimacy domestically and was unable to provide either basic security for its citizens or social services such as public health care and education. Fighting was widespread. The Sierra Leone courts had recently sentenced Sankoh to death, causing much anger and outrage among his RUF supporters.[84]

However, by midyear, the government and the RUF had signed two negotiated settlements. The international community, particularly the United States and important ECOWAS member states such as Guinea and Nigeria, exerted significant pressure on Kabbah to end the war through diplomatic means. In an effort to get the peace process back on track, Kabbah offered Sankoh a considerable carrot: he would rescind Sankoh's death sentence if Sankoh would commit the RUF to a peaceful end to the civil war. Sankoh accepted.[85] Peace negotiations commenced in Togo, whose president was then chairing ECOWAS, and produced a May 1999 cease-fire and the July 1999 Lomé Agreement.[86]

The Lomé Agreement was wide-ranging and controversial. It allotted the rebels four cabinet positions, a series of public-sector directorships, and several ambassadorial posts. It also guaranteed the departure of Nigerian troops from Sierra Leone, a long-standing RUF objective. Sankoh was appointed chair of the Commission for the Management of Strategic Resources, National Reconstruction, and Development (CMRRD).[87] Koroma, who was not present at the negotiations, was appointed chair of the Commission for the Consolidation of Peace (CCP). The agreement also included provisions for the monitoring of the cease-fire, the transformation of the RUF into a political party, and the review (and possible revision) of the constitution. Much to the disappointment of the United Nations and human rights groups, the accords also granted the RUF an amnesty for human rights abuses and other criminal acts committed between November 1996 and July 1999.[88] Although new peacekeeping roles for ECOWAS and the United Nations were included in the agreement, they were left unspecified, and there was considerable uncertainty and concern over Nigeria's future role. As an interim measure, in late August 1999 the Security Council added 140 military observers to UNOMSIL. Two months later, it decided to replace UNOMSIL with an armed and much larger peacekeeping force known as the UN Mission in Sierra Leone (UNAMSIL). The council intended this new force to function in parallel with ECOMOG, which it believed would continue to assume the main role in providing security. This assumption proved faulty.[89]

Political Support for Peace

While Foday Sankoh remained in charge of the RUF, it continued to be an unreliable partner for peace. In the months following Lomé, the

RUF became increasingly obstructionist, restricting the movement of UN troops and humanitarian staff in the rebel-controlled eastern and northern parts of the country. Cease-fire violations were common.

Renewed international support for ECOMOG was short-lived following the 1998 siege of Freetown.[90] Even ECOWAS member states' support had begun to wane. Only four of the regional bloc's then sixteen members (Ghana, Guinea, Mali, and Nigeria) provided troops for the mission. Although the ECOWAS states gave ECOMOG a new mandate in August 1999, a number of its members supported a stronger role for the United Nations in Sierra Leone.

After Sankoh's capture and arrest, however, and a change in RUF leadership (discussed further, below), the situation slowly improved. On November 10, 2000, the government and the RUF concluded the Abuja Cease-Fire Agreement (Abuja I). They reaffirmed their commitment to Lomé and to UNAMSIL's central role in overseeing the cease-fire, promised it unimpeded access throughout the country, and pledged to participate in disarmament and demobilization programs.[91] In January 2001, the RUF suffered unaccustomed and significant casualties in border clashes with the Guinean armed forces, which weakened it.[92] In early May 2001, the RUF and the government met again in Abuja, together with UN and ECOWAS representatives, to take stock of progress made in implementing the cease-fire. As a result of this meeting (Abuja II), the government affirmed its willingness, "after careful screening," to recruit demobilized RUF personnel into the national army and police. For its part, the RUF pledged to return the weapons and equipment it had seized from UNAMSIL and ECOMOG, and to disarm simultaneously with the CDF. The rebel group dropped its demand that the Sierra Leone Army be included in the DDR program. Collectively, the government and the RUF agreed to dismantle all roadblocks in their respective areas. Two weeks after Abuja II, and as agreed at that meeting, a new joint committee on DDR, including representatives of UNAMSIL, the government, the CDF, and the RUF, met in Freetown, "the first high-level meeting" of all these parties since May 2000.[93]

Contributing to this transformation was Issa Hassan Sesay, an RUF battle group commander who emerged as Sankoh's successor. The government, UNAMSIL, and the international community all cultivated relationships with Sesay to reinforce his pursuit of a diplomatic resolution to the conflict. The Sierra Leone government released some seventy RUF members from prison in early 2001 in recognition of the RUF's progress in moving toward peace.[94] Thereafter, the United Nations, ECOWAS, and the government implemented a number of direct confidence-building measures to bring the rebels more fully into the peace process, and responded meaningfully to a number of RUF concerns. These included the timetable for disarmament and the transitioning of the RUF into a political party in preparation for national elections.[95]

In addition to a series of resolutions that expanded and strengthened UNAMSIL, the UN Security Council passed several measures intended to strengthen the Sierra Leone government, weaken the RUF, and punish the government of Liberia. Resolution 1306 (July 2000) called upon the government of Sierra Leone to establish a certificate-of-origin regime for trade in diamonds and called on member states to prohibit the direct import of all rough diamonds from Sierra Leone.[96] In March 2001, the council laid out a series of sanctions—including embargoes on imports of Liberian diamonds, exports of arms to Liberia, and international travel by Liberian government and military officials and their families—that were to take effect after two months unless Charles Taylor expelled all members of the RUF, ceased all support to the RUF, and froze RUF assets and funds. Although Taylor claimed to have ended his support of the RUF, the sanctions took effect as scheduled.[97]

Washington reassessed its Sierra Leone policy following the election of Olusegun Obasanjo as Nigeria's president in May 1999. Washington had long acknowledged ECOMOG's and Nigeria's shortcomings as peacekeepers but felt that the operation could be reformed and strengthened. Moreover, ECOMOG troops could take forceful and somewhat unsavory measures to counter the RUF that UN blue helmets could not. While some U.S. officials dismissed Obasanjo's campaign pledge to bring Nigerian troops home from Sierra Leone as populist rhetoric, doubts remained as to whether the international community could pay Nigeria enough to sustain its commitment to ECOMOG, absent a peace deal.[98] Thus the Clinton administration pressed Kabbah and the RUF to reach a negotiated settlement.[99] In so doing, Washington portrayed Sankoh and Taylor as honest brokers and focused on mainstreaming the RUF as a political party.[100] After the UNAMSIL mission's near collapse in May 2000, the United States provided financial support and military expertise to train and equip African peacekeepers from three ECOWAS countries for duty in UNAMSIL under Operation Focus Relief. The program cost about $90 million and ran from October 2000 to December 2001.[101]

The United Kingdom's policy toward Sierra Leone was essentially constant and clear. London did not believe that a Nigerian-led ECOMOG could restore peace and instead promoted a UN peacekeeping force for Sierra Leone. When UN peacekeepers ran into trouble, London responded militarily within days with a noncombatant evacuation operation, Operation Palliser, which quickly developed into a separate, if short-term, peace operation working alongside UNAMSIL (discussed in more detail in "Field Operations," below).

Several factors played into that decision: the safety and well-being of British nationals; Sierra Leone's status as a former British colony and member of the Commonwealth with close ties to London; and the legacy of the Sandline Affair, which had made British policymakers more sensitive to events in Sierra Leone.[102] Moreover, Britain did not want Nigeria and ECOMOG to rescue or replace the United Nations. Once Sierra Leone's immediate peace implementation crisis had been resolved, British military personnel settled in to train a renamed Republic of Sierra Leone Armed Forces (RSLAF), serving under the banner of the International Military Advisory and Training Team (IMATT).

Mandate

Even after the Security Council established UNAMSIL in October 1999, ECOMOG continued to play the lead role on the ground. It was responsible for the security of government officials, UN staff, and humanitarian agency and NGO personnel, as well as cantoned ex-combatants awaiting demobilization at designated disarmament centers. The West African force also established safe corridors and suitable locations for refugee and IDP resettlement, conducted security patrols, and guarded strategic locations, including weapon storage sites associated with the DDR process.[103]

UNAMSIL's mandate was initially rather limited. The force was to monitor the cease-fire and assist the government in national and parliamentary elections and support the DDR program. UN blue helmets were to complement ECOMOG efforts to secure key locations throughout the country, including disarmament and demobilization reception centers, and to assume responsibility for security of UN staff in the mission area.[104]

The council amended and expanded UNAMSIL's mandate in February 2000, in preparation for ECOMOG's withdrawal from Sierra Leone. The mission assumed responsibility for security at key locations and government buildings, especially in Freetown, at the airports, along major roadways, and at DDR sites. It was to guard and arrange for the destruction of all weapons, ammunition, and equipment turned in at disarmament centers. UNAMSIL was also tasked with facilitating the free flow of people, goods, and humanitarian assistance, and with coordinating with and assisting local law enforcement authorities in the discharge of their duties.[105]

On May 19, 2000, the council raised UNAMSIL's troop ceiling to 13,000.[106] In August, in the wake of the hostage crisis (described below), the council formally considered Lomé to have broken down and authorized the mission to help extend the government's authority countrywide, with priority given to Freetown and Lungi (the site of the country's international airport) and to strategic lines of communication. UNAMSIL also was instructed to "deter and, where necessary, decisively counter the threat of RUF attack by responding robustly to any hostile action or threat of imminent and direct use of force."[107] Later that month, the secretary-general recommended that UNAMSIL develop a strategy to support upcoming elections, and the Security Council authorized it to assist the Special Court for Sierra Leone (see "Justice and Accountability," below).[108]

After Abuja I, the force was given significant additional tasks. These included supervising and monitoring the cease-fire; investigating and reporting alleged violations; securing the return of all weapons and equipment seized by the rebels during the hostage crisis of May 2000, in which the RUF detained more than 400 UN peacekeepers; extending government authority throughout the country; and reestablishing the DDR program. In March 2001, the secretary-general presented a revised concept of operations that would extend UNAMSIL exercises into RUF-controlled areas in the north and east. The council approved his request for a larger force, raising UNAMSIL's troop ceiling to 17,500.[109] Although UNAMSIL deployed to RUF strongholds, including the diamond districts, it was not authorized to interfere with the widespread, illicit mining activities in these areas.

After the May 2001 review of Abuja I, conditions on the ground steadily improved. In turn, UNAMSIL's mandate was transformed from dealing primarily with security concerns to focusing on peacebuilding and national recovery activities that would integrate the civilian and military aspects of the mission. Its responsibilities included cooperating with the Sierra Leone government on the reintegration of ex-combatants, coordinating with the government and Commonwealth states on reforming the Sierra Leone Police (SLP), and assisting the work of the Special Court and the Truth and Reconciliation Commission (TRC).[110] The 2002 national and parliamentary elections, for which UNAMSIL provided highly visible, "robust umbrella security" in partnership with the SLP, helped to sustain earlier progress in stabilizing the security environment.

The mission's mandate focused increasingly on "assessment, drawdown, and withdrawal."[111] The drawdown plan had a series of benchmarks, the achievement of which would trigger subsequent stages of withdrawal. These benchmarks included the following:

- strengthening the capacity of the SLP and RSLAF to prevent a security vacuum as the UN mission withdrew from various parts of the country
- completing reintegration of ex-combatants
- reestablishing and consolidating government authority countrywide
- reestablishing government authority in the diamond mining districts

As of 2005 the benchmarks remained essentially the same, with the addition of helping to consolidate the deployment of UN forces in neighboring Liberia.[112]

Funding

UNAMSIL was funded primarily by assessed contributions from UN member states. Additional support came from voluntary funds for DDR, national and parliamentary elections, and other peacebuilding activities such as rebuilding roads, bridges, health clinics, and schools. Other voluntary funding mechanisms supported the work of the Truth and Reconciliation Commission (TRC) and the Special Court.

The funding history of UNAMSIL reflects the changes in its mandate. In its first two years expenditures almost doubled, from $263 million in 1999–2000 to $521 million in 2000–2001, as the mission grew from 6,000 troops to an average of 12,500. Spending peaked in 2001–2 at $618 million, reflecting average troop levels of 17,500 and increased numbers of civilian personnel, including new components to work on elections and DDR.[113] As military and political conditions on the ground stabilized, expenditures decreased, to $603 million in 2002–3 and $449 million in 2003–4. Appropriations for 2004–5 dropped to $292 million, and for 2005–6 to $113 million, of which $18 million was earmarked for liquidation of the operation and its assets.[114] Altogether, the United Nations spent about $2.86 billion in assessed funds on peace operations in Sierra Leone from mid-1999 through mid-2006.

In addition to assessed funding, several special voluntary funds were created in conjunction with Sierra Leone peace operations programs, the TRC, and the Special Court (see table 3.1). At the time of this writing, comprehensive figures on donor pledges and on percentages of pledged resources committed and delivered are difficult to ascertain. The data presented in table 3.1 should thus be treated as macrolevel estimates for these special funds.

Mission Planning and Force Structure

The Security Council initially envisaged UNAMSIL as a supplement to ECOMOG. The 6,000-strong force was to have six infantry battalions, four being rehatted ECOMOG units already serving in Sierra Leone and two coming from Kenya and India, with India also providing various support elements.

The first new UN troops—a company of 130 from Kenya—arrived in the mission area on November 29, 1999, five weeks after the council authorized the operation. The force commander (India) and SRSG (Nigeria) joined the mission in the second week of December. By early January, five of the six battalions were in place, as were 220 of UNAMSIL's 260 authorized military observers.[115]

The Secretariat had a difficult time fielding the necessary force when the council authorized an additional 5,100 blue helmets for the mission on February 7, 2000. Zambia was to provide one battalion, while Bangladesh, Jordan, and Nigeria each pledged two. As of early March 2000, only the Nigerian troops had deployed. Ten weeks later, the mission was still waiting for the two Bangladeshi battalions. It proved equally difficult to find many of the additional support elements that the mission required.

The delay in fielding the mission is especially difficult to comprehend because the United Nations had advance warning of Nigeria's plans to withdraw its troops. As noted, President Obasanjo had pledged repeatedly during his campaign to bring Nigerian troops home from Sierra Leone. After winning the election, he officially informed the UN secretary-general in August of his intention to repatriate Nigerian soldiers at the rate of some 2,000 a month and to complete the process before the end of 1999.[116] Everyone understood that an ECOMOG force in Sierra Leone without Nigerian participation was not viable. Why did the United Nations not plan more urgently for this contingency?

The explanation rests in part with Nigeria's willingness to be persuaded to stay and in part with a UN peacekeeping staff whose resources were severely overstretched at the time. Obasanjo was willing to keep his troops in Sierra Leone under ECOMOG's banner if sufficient financial and material resources were forthcoming. Washington attempted to accommodate Abuja in this but ultimately failed.

Meanwhile, the UN Department of Peacekeeping Operations (DPKO) was struggling to find troops and staff not only for UNAMSIL but also for other complex new missions in Kosovo, East Timor, and the Democratic Republic of the Congo. The UN peacekeeping force in southern Lebanon was also undergoing significant changes and a temporary buildup as Israel withdrew its troops from that country.[117] The situation at DPKO had been made more difficult by the loss of several dozen "gratis military personnel" who had been attached to the department but were required by the General Assembly to return to their home countries in early 1999.[118]

Yet the rate at which the United Nations fielded troops for UNAMSIL was arguably less significant than several other shortcomings that plagued the mission. One was logistical support. Having learned

Table 3.1. Special Funds for UNAMSIL and Related Activities

Fund or Institution	Administering Institution	Activities Funded	Time Period	Donors (partial list)	Estimated Budget	Committed Funds
Special Trust Fund	UN Secretariat	• UNAMSIL-related activities • Quick-impact projects • Short-term support to war-affected people	1999–2002	Japan, UN Development Programme	N/A	$2,500,000
Multi-Donor Trust Fund	World Bank	• Disarmament, demobilization, and reintegration of combatants	1999–2002	Canada, European Union, Germany, Italy, Norway, Sweden, UNICEF, United Kingdom, United States, World Bank, World Food Programme	N/A	$36,900,000
Elections Trust Fund	UN Development Programme	• National and parliamentary elections • Training ECOWAS and OAU election observers, local observers, and political party representatives	2001–2002	Canada, Germany, government of Sierra Leone, UN Development Programme	$11,600,000	$9,300,000
Truth and Reconciliation Commission (TRC)	UN High Commissioner for Human Rights	• All TRC operations (staff salaries, logistics, communications, administration, and security)	2003–2004	Denmark, European Union, Germany, government of Sierra Leone, Norway, Sweden, United Kingdom, United States	$5,000,000	$4,500,000

| Special Court for Sierra Leone (SCSL) | Management Committee of the SCSL[a] | • All court operations (staff salaries, logistics, communications, administration, and security) | 2002–2005 | Australia, Belgium, Canada, Chile, China, Cyprus, Czech Republic, Denmark, Finland, Germany, Greece, Ireland, Italy, Japan, Lesotho, Liechtenstein, Luxembourg, Malaysia, Mauritius, Mexico, Netherlands, Nigeria, Norway, Oman, Philippines, Senegal, Singapore, South Africa, Spain, Sweden, United Kingdom, United States | $57,000,000 | $40,000,000 |

[a]The Management Committee is constituted of donors and representatives from the UN Secretariat and the government of Sierra Leone. It meets monthly to address budgetary and administrative issues for the court.

Sources: United Nations, *Report of the Secretary-General on the UN Mission in Sierra Leone* (S/1999/1223, December 6, 1999; S/2000/751, July 31, 2000; S/2001/228, March 14, 2001; S/2001/627, June 25, 2001; S/2001/857, September 7, 2001; S/2002/267, March 14, 2002; and S/2002/987, September 5, 2002). Priscilla Hayner, *The Sierra Leone Truth and Reconciliation Commission: Reviewing Its First Year* (New York: International Center for Transitional Justice, 2004). 3. International Crisis Group, "The Special Court for Sierra Leone: Promises and Pitfalls of a 'New Model,'" Africa Briefing no. 16, August 4, 2003, 4–9. *First Annual Report of the President of the Special Court for Sierra Leone for the Period 2 December 2002 to 1 December 2003* (Freetown: Special Court for Sierra Leone, 2004); and *Second Annual Report of the President of the Special Court for Sierra Leone for the Period 1 January 2004 to 17 January 2005* (Freetown: Special Court for Sierra Leone, 2005).

painful lessons in the mid-1990s about the cost and difficulty of being the parts, fuel, and maintenance supplier to dozens of troop contributors with hundreds of unique pieces of equipment, DPKO decided to require that troop contributors be self-sustaining in terms of major equipment, spare parts, related minor equipment, and other mission-critical elements such as communications within the contingent, with reimbursement to troop contributors at prenegotiated rates.[119] UNAMSIL was the first operation to which these new "wet-lease" arrangements applied. With the exception of the Kenyan and Indian battalions, however (both of which satisfied or exceeded military planning expectations for materiel), none of the new units met the United Nations' self-sustainment requirements. For example, contingents re-hatted from ECOMOG lacked not only logistics and communications assets but also basic military equipment.[120]

This situation put significant stress on the mission's force commander, Major-General Vijay Kumar Jetley of India, who was being asked to meet increasingly demanding challenges without proper resources. It may also have contributed to Jetley's belief that to get things done, he had to rely excessively on his own Indian troops. Whether this belief created or worsened tensions between Indian headquarters staff and other contingent commanders, it is clear that, aside from his countrymen, Jetley had relatively few admirers within the mission.

Continuing tensions between the force commander and the mission's other top officials—including Oluyemi Adeniji, the SRSG, and Brigadier-General Mohammad Garba, the deputy force commander (both from Nigeria)—also hurt the mission. Although President Obasanjo may have accepted, as a compromise, the secretary-general's decision to award the mission's top military spot to New Delhi rather than Abuja, it is clear that many officers within the Nigerian military did not. Adeniji and Garba displayed utter disdain for Jetley, and allegations have been raised (but never fully investigated) that they purposely undermined the force commander, thus placing the entire mission's effectiveness at risk.

In May 2000, tensions escalated yet again when the RUF took more than 400 UN peacekeepers hostage. When the worst of the crisis had abated (see "Field Operations," below), the secretary-general sent an assessment team to Sierra Leone led by Manfred Eisele, a former

DPKO assistant secretary-general. The Eisele mission delved deeply into UNAMSIL operations, procedures, management style, and internal communications; went into the field to talk with military contingents; and spoke to government officials, ambassadors, and other UN agencies working in Sierra Leone. Its findings, never publicly released, were summarized in the secretary-general's July 2000 quarterly progress report to the Security Council. The Eisele mission found

> a serious lack of cohesion within the Mission . . . no commonly shared understanding of the mandate and rules of engagement . . . serious problems related to internal communication and coordination between the civilian and military components, as well as within each component . . . a lack of integrated planning and logistic support [and] insufficient sharing of information with United Nations agencies, nongovernmental organizations, and diplomatic missions in Freetown. Some military units showed a lack of training and others had serious shortfalls in equipment. Essential military support units were lacking. . . .[121]

Since this was the sanitized, public version of its findings, it is reasonable to characterize the Eisele Report as a scathing indictment of UNAMSIL leadership, management, and procedures, and of the competence of some of its forces to carry out the operation's mandate.

In the wake of the Eisele Report, the Secretariat and UNAMSIL worked to put the operation's house in order. Its military headquarters established a joint operations cell that included members from each of the operation's troop contingents. Between May and December 2000, the number of military staff officers supporting the operation increased nearly sixfold, doubling the military staff at Freetown military headquarters and establishing separate military staffs in each of the operation's new sector headquarters.[122]

Personal animosities among the top leadership continued to plague the mission, however, and boiled over in September 2000. It was then that a private memo of Jetley's, which detailed the operation's shortcomings and called into question Nigeria's commitment to the peace agreement, was leaked to the newspaper the *Guardian*. Abuja made it clear that Jetley had to be replaced. The head of Nigeria's army at the time, General Victor Malu, said, "We are not going to serve under [Jetley] in whatever circumstances. If he is not removed, he will not get our co-operation, and we are the largest contingent in the force."[123] By not coming to Jetley's defense, Secretary-General Annan essentially sided with Nigeria, and within a week of Malu's comments, India told the United Nations that it would be pulling its troops from UNAMSIL. Annan may well have been right in his long-term view that the mission and the region needed Nigerian buy-in, yet Jetley's allegations were never shown to be false and an opportunity was missed to investigate them fully.[124]

In June, Behrooz Sadry, an Iranian international civil servant with significant UN peacekeeping experience, joined the mission as deputy SRSG for operations and management. He was joined the following January by Alan Doss, a UK national who had been director of the European Office of the UN Development Programme (UNDP) in Geneva. Doss was appointed deputy SRSG for governance and stabilization and was also made UN humanitarian coordinator/resident coordinator. In this latter role, he headed the United Nations' humanitarian and developmental activities (the "UN Country Team") in Sierra Leone, which facilitated more effective coordination in these areas. For example, biweekly UNAMSIL and UN agency meetings were introduced, where vital security and humanitarian coordination information was exchanged. In addition, the mission established a five-day training program for all new mission staff. On the military side, the mission set up an internal training program on the rules of engagement.[125]

The Security Council, meanwhile, wanted to ensure that the mission had substantially augmented force protection and force projection capabilities, as well as installing compatible personalities at the top. The rank and nationality of the force commander changed in late November 2000 with the arrival of Lieutenant-General Daniel Ishmail Opande from Kenya. Major-General Martin Agwai of Nigeria subsequently replaced Garba. A much-chastened Adeniji remained in his post. Both Opande and Agwai were capable professionals, and they developed a good working relationship with Adeniji. At the same time, Brigadier-General Alastair Duncan (United Kingdom) was appointed UNAMSIL chief of staff.[126]

Between May and July 2000, the United Nations delivered assets from Brindisi, other peacekeeping operations, and other sources to help bring its former ECOMOG troops closer to expected levels of readiness. Canada, Germany, the Netherlands, Russia, and the United States also helped airlift other countries' troops to the mission area.[127]

Still, UNAMSIL continued to experience delays in fielding additional troops, in particular specialized units such as logistics and signals.[128] Its situation became more difficult in the fall of 2000, when India and Jordan decided to withdraw their troops (about 3,000 and 1,750, respectively) from the mission. These countries' troops were among the best-trained and -equipped contingents in UNAMSIL at the time. Amman was ultimately persuaded to remain engaged in the mission and provided a Level III medical facility in Freetown, but UNAMSIL still had to find almost 5,000 troops to replace the departing Indian and Jordanian peacekeepers, and another 4,500 beyond that to reach its new authorized strength of 17,500.[129] Bangladesh had already deployed three battalions to Sierra Leone by March 2001, helping to replace the Indian troops, and sent a fourth battalion, plus support units, to bring its total contribution to 4,200 by June 2001. The first battalion from Pakistan, a new troop contributor, deployed in early August, and 4,200 Pakistani troops were deployed by September.[130] Together, the two countries accounted for nearly half of the expanded force (see table 3.2).

Force levels were more or less stable, at or near peak strength, from September 2001 to September 2002 (see figure 3.2), when plans were put into place for the gradual drawdown and eventual withdrawal of the force. The Secretariat dispatched a military team to Sierra Leone in June 2002 to help UNAMSIL develop an exit strategy keyed to development of the government's capacity to provide national and public security.[131] An Integrated Planning Group within UNAMSIL was established to evaluate all information related to the security benchmarks, and collaborative mechanisms with the government of Sierra Leone were set up to plan and monitor the transition. These included the National Security Coordination Group, which took stock of overall security and identified potential threats to state security, and the Steering Committee, which coordinated the training and reform of the SLP.

To support the work of the Steering Committee, in September 2002 the Security Council increased UNAMSIL's police contingent to 170 officers—mostly for training and operations, functions

Table 3.2. UNAMSIL Military and Police Contributions, December 2001

Country	Military Observers	Staff Officers	Troops in Units	Sector HQ Staff	Military Total	Police
Bangladesh	12	19	4,180	65	4,276	7
Bolivia	6	—	—	—	6	—
Canada	5	—	—	—	5	2
China	6	—	—	—	6	—
Croatia	10	—	—	—	10	—
Czech Republic	5	—	—	—	5	—
Denmark	2	—	—	—	2	—
Egypt	10	—	—	—	10	—
France	1	—	—	—	1	—
Gambia	24	—	—	—	24	2
Ghana	6	10	850	58	924	7
Guinea	12	5	776	—	793	—
India	—	—	—	—	—	2
Indonesia	10	—	—	—	10	—
Jordan	10	2	118	—	130	3
Kenya	11	17	992	63	1,083	4
Kyrgyzstan	2	—	—	—	2	—
Malaysia	10	—	—	—	10	3
Mali	8	—	—	—	8	—
Nepal	10	2	797	—	809	5
New Zealand	2	—	—	—	2	—
Niger	—	—	—	—	—	2
Nigeria	10	20	3,222	65	3,317	3
Norway	—	—	—	—	3	3
Pakistan	10	10	4,204	50	4,274	—
Russia	15	5	109	—	129	—
Senegal	—	—	—	—	—	1
Slovakia	2	—	—	—	2	—
Sri Lanka	—	—	—	—	—	2
Sweden	3	—	—	—	3	—
Tanzania	12	—	—	—	10	2
Thailand	5	—	—	—	5	—
Ukraine	5	5	618	—	628	—
United Kingdom	15	8	—	—	23	—
Uruguay	11	—	—	—	11	—
Zambia	10	4	815	5	834	4
Zimbabwe	—	—	—	—	—	4
Total	260	107	16,681	306	17,354	56

Source: United Nations, *Twelfth Report of the Secretary-General on the UN Mission in Sierra Leone,* S/2001/1195, December 13, 2001, Annex. United Nations, Department of Peacekeeping Operations, data table on monthly troop and police contributions, countries by mission; online at http://www .un.org/Depts/dpko/dpko/contributors/2001/November2001_3.pdf .

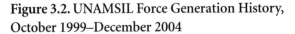

Figure 3.2. UNAMSIL Force Generation History,
October 1999–December 2004

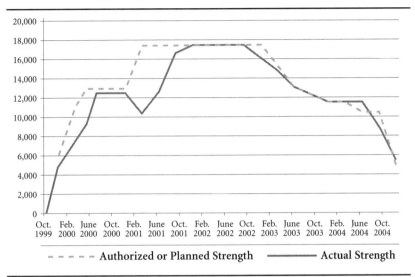

that required experienced personnel. Recruiting that number of officers for Sierra Leone was not easy; by the following June, the operation had 32 police trainers and 83 officer-mentors deployed at seventeen team sites across the country, plus 11 officers at headquarters to manage these efforts.[132]

The drawdown process, proceeding in four phases, required elaborate deployment adjustments in all sectors. In Phase 1, UNAMSIL troops vacated several key districts, including Bonthe, Koinadugu, and Port Loko, and forces stationed in Kambia were reduced.[133] In Phase 2 (December 2002 to May 2003), roughly 3,500 troops from Bangladesh, Ghana, Guinea, Kenya, Nigeria, and Pakistan returned home.[134] Phase 3 began with 700 Nigerian troops leaving Makeni, followed by 800 Bangladeshi troops departing Magburaka. Sector Center was fully vacated on schedule in late May 2004, leaving UNAMSIL with 10,800 troops deployed in two restructured northern and southern commands, headquartered in Freetown and Koidu, respectively. Departures included all headquarters staff of Sector Center, a Bangladeshi medical unit and signals company, the Nepalese battalion, and the last Bangladeshi battalion. Between June and early December 2004, UNAMSIL troop strength was reduced from 10,800 to about 5,150 (plus roughly 170 military observers; see table 3.3). UNAMSIL maintained a limited security response capability in the form of an air-mobile force reserve, to ensure ready access to recently vacated sectors. The northern and southern command headquarters were closed at the end of the year, all UN forces thereafter being commanded from force headquarters in Freetown.[135]

On March 30, 2004, the Security Council unanimously adopted Resolution 1537, which agreed to a "residual" UNAMSIL presence, initially slated for the first six months of 2005, with three battalions of approximately 3,250 military personnel. These were deployed in and near Freetown to support the Special Court for Sierra Leone and provide backup for the Sierra Leone Police; in Kenema, in the east, to help national forces bolster border security with Liberia; and at Bo, in between the two, to serve as a quick-reaction reserve. A military observer contingent of about 140 officers continued to serve as the mission's eyes and ears, and 80 UN police personnel continued to help train the national police.[136]

UNAMSIL's drawdown schedule was tied, however, to capacity-building benchmarks for the SLP and RSLAF. When those forces continued to suffer from a lack of equipment, basing, and accommodations, the transition slowed down, and the residual mission was extended to the end of 2005. By April 2005, UNAMSIL had reached its residual force level.[137] By mid-2005, UNAMSIL officials were thinking in terms of a follow-on political mission with a minimal, company-sized military presence dedicated to providing security for the Special Court, with all other military units and observers to depart by the end of 2005.[138]

Field Operations: Implementing the Mandate

Initially UNAMSIL was preoccupied with simply deploying its forces, in Freetown, Hastings, Lungi, and Port Loko in the west; in Bo, in the south-central part of the country; and in Kenema and Daru, in the east.[139] UNAMSIL forces also codeployed with ECOMOG troops in Freetown and at DDR sites in Bo and Moyamba. Military observers were segmented into teams ranging in strength from twelve to twenty-five and deployed to each locale alongside infantry forces to assist with DDR activities.[140] From these positions, UNAMSIL was expected to extend its deployment as rapidly and robustly as possible throughout

Table 3.3. UNAMSIL Military and Police Contributions, December 2004

Country	Military Observers	Staff Officers	Troops in Units	Military Total	Police
Bangladesh	8	17	456	481	2
Bolivia	3	—	—	3	—
Canada	5	—	—	5	3
China	3	—	—	3	—
Croatia	6	—	—	6	—
Czech Republic	2	—	—	2	—
Denmark	1	—	—	1	—
Egypt	9	—	—	9	—
Gambia	15	—	—	15	4
Germany	—	—	16	16	—
Ghana	5	9	775	789	10
Guinea	5	1	—	6	—
India	—	—	—	—	6
Indonesia	6	—	—	6	—
Jordan	6	4	121	131	2
Kenya	6	10	188	204	6
Kyrgyzstan	2	—	—	2	—
Malawi	—	—	—	—	4
Malaysia	5	—	—	5	4
Mali	7	—	—	7	—
Mauritius	—	—	—	—	2
Namibia	—	—	—	—	4
Nepal	5	3	—	8	4
New Zealand	2	—	—	2	—
Nigeria	7	12	1,581	1,600	8
Norway	—	—	—	—	2
Pakistan	11	15	1,287	1,313	2
Russia	7	4	110	121	2
Senegal	—	—	—	—	6
Slovakia	1	—	—	1	—
Sri Lanka	—	—	—	—	6
Sweden	1	—	—	1	4
Tanzania	12	—	—	12	—
Thailand	3	—	—	3	—
Turkey	—	—	—	—	7
Ukraine	2	3	617	622	—
United Kingdom	12	6	—	18	10
Uruguay	6	—	—	6	—
Zambia	7	5	—	12	14
Zimbabwe	—	—	—	—	6
Total	170	89	5,151	5,410	118

Source: United Nations, *Twenty-fifth Report of the Secretary-General on the UN Mission in Sierra Leone,* S/2004/965, December 10, 2004, Annex.

Sierra Leone, in accordance with Lomé. Key objectives included positioning UNAMSIL forces in areas that ECOMOG troops were vacating; enabling government authorities to reassert control in key provincial cities; securing the diamond mining areas and other territory that the RUF controlled; and creating the conditions under which national and parliamentary elections could be held.

The drawdown and ultimate withdrawal of ECOMOG between February and May 2000 substantially complicated UNAMSIL's mission. Its deployment area was expanded and reorganized into four sectors: the Freetown peninsula; Lungi/Port Loko; Makeni/Magburaka/Koidu; and Bo/Kenema/Kailahun. Each sector was to have three infantry battalions and a sizable headquarters staff. Some sixty UN police advisers were deployed to DDR sites to assist and consult with the SLP, which assumed responsibility for these sites from departing ECOMOG forces.[141]

The peace process, meanwhile, was deteriorating; cease-fire violations were common, and little progress on disarmament had been made. Although security improved in government-controlled areas, the RUF retained control of much of the east and north, where it restricted the movements of UNAMSIL troops and humanitarian agency staff.[142] RUF-UN relations would soon worsen.

The Hostage Crisis

Throughout April 2000, RUF elements harassed and interfered with UNAMSIL operations, blocking entrances to DDR facilities and occasionally taking shots at UN positions or patrols. On May 1, the RUF commander in Makeni demanded that the United Nations return a small number of RUF soldiers who had volunteered for DDR. UNAMSIL refused to comply. A political and military standoff ensued. RUF troops laid siege to DDR centers in Makeni and Magburaka. UNAMSIL headquarters received reports that there had been casualties among UN peacekeepers and that the Kenyan contingents in Makeni and Magburaka were running dangerously low on ammunition. Meanwhile, a patrol of twenty-three Indian peacekeepers had been detained by the RUF while en route to the Indian contingent at Kailahun, whose 200 troops, plus military observers from more than a dozen countries, were encircled by RUF forces. The RUF also attacked a company of Nigerian peacekeepers in Kambia, who surrendered their weapons and equipment.[143]

Force commander Jetley came under harsh criticism, much of it undeserved, for his part in the crisis. To assist the Kenyans in Magburaka, he sent the Indian quick-reaction force. To relieve the besieged Kenyans in Makeni, he dispatched a battalion of Zambian infantry troops. Jetley was later accused of using the Zambians essentially as cannon fodder, paying insufficient regard to their well-being, but they were the only battalion not yet deployed. Although some elements of the Zambian contingent had arrived in Sierra Leone only days before, most had deployed in stages over the previous weeks. Rather, what happened to the Zambians en route to Makeni was symptomatic of the deeper command, control, and capacity issues plaguing UNAMSIL at that time.

The force commander's intent was for the Zambian battalion to depart at dawn and arrive in Makeni before dusk on the same day. UN military observers familiar with the political-military situation and terrain were to accompany the Zambians and keep the convoy on the proper roads. Several people familiar with Jetley's plan agree that it was viable and that it was taken with the best interests of the Kenyans and the mission in mind. That plan was not followed, however. The Zambian battalion made it only as far as Lunsar before dusk fell on the first day. The following account is based on firsthand observations of the deployment:

> [The plans] would have been viable if the Zambians had been prepared for combat operations but they were . . . a mix of artillerymen and infantry and armor . . . [who] were not used to working as a combat grouping. . . . They had been due to move up country in a few weeks time in any case and their attitude was essentially that the move had been brought forward. There was a lack of everything. I remember lending my map to the front armored car. Initially the plan was for the Indian Contingent to lead on the Rogberi Junction-Lunsar-Makeni route with the Zambians moving behind in support [together with] the Sierra Leone government [helicopter] gunship. . . . Then at the last moment the Indians were told or elected to go by a different route via Mile 91 to secure Magburaka. The gunship was not deployed and the Zambians were given the task of securing Makeni[,] where the strongest concentration of RUF were deployed not only in the

town but in a series of well-prepared checkpoints and ambushes on the Western approach to the town. . . . With no air cover this was going to be a very dangerous operation. Thus the Zambians took the view that as they were there as a UN peacekeeping force, their best course of action was to negotiate with the RUF commanders rather than confront them with violence.

At dusk we reached Lunsar. There were reports of RUF within a few kilometers of the town and the place was full of fleeing refugees from Makeni. There was a conversation between the Kenyan Colonel (appointed as the Sector Commander) and the HQ UNAMSIL[,] during which Jetley urged the unit to move on in the dark so as to get to Makeni as soon as possible. But everyone was very nervous about pushing down the road in the dark and entering an RUF ambush zone. So it was decided that the unit would stay put and then push for Makeni before daybreak next day.[144]

The rescue mission therefore spent the night in Lunsar against Jetley's orders. This pause gave the RUF additional time to defend itself. Aspects of what happened the following day remain unclear, but somehow the Kenyan sector commander and the Zambian contingent commander separated from the column of peacekeepers. It is likely that they attempted to meet with a local RUF commander to negotiate one of the many rebel checkpoints on the road from Lunsar to Makeni. The RUF detained them and subsequently took the other 436 Zambian peacekeepers hostage as well, relieving them of their weapons and vehicles.

On May 9 the head of UN peacekeeping, Bernard Miyet, flew to Sierra Leone to observe what was happening. The same day, the Kenyans in Makeni and Magburaka, together with the Indian quick-reaction force, broke through RUF lines and moved to secure areas. Neither the Kenyans nor the Indians surrendered weapons or equipment. The RUF released their UN hostages in stages in May and June. In July, a reinforced Indian contingent successfully launched Operation Khukri, with support from Nigerian and Ghanaian troops and logistical assistance from the United Kingdom, to relieve the besieged peacekeepers in Kailahun.[145]

On May 17, supporters of Johnny Paul Koroma captured Sankoh near his home in Freetown and turned him over to the government. As mentioned above, the RUF's and Sankoh's commitment to the peace process had become suspect, and in spite of his denials, Sankoh was perceived as having given the green light to take UN troops hostage.

The British Interventions

The United Kingdom had drawn up plans for a noncombatant evacuation operation in Sierra Leone well in advance of the May 2000 crisis.[146] Indeed, London had authorized a similar mission in December 1998 in response to the siege of Freetown. Military planners undertook two fact-finding and reconnaissance missions to Sierra Leone in 1999 to familiarize themselves with the terrain and to get to know government officials, ECOMOG units, and UN peacekeeping personnel.

Deployment of British forces occurred within days of the decision. Royal Marines training in southern France and British naval assets, already in the Mediterranean Sea, were tasked with going to Sierra Leone. The first members of Operation Palliser arrived in Freetown on May 6. The initial eight-person reconnaissance and liaison team was joined the next day by aviation assets and paratroopers. All told, some 4,500 British soldiers, sailors, and marines participated in the mission, on land and offshore.

Palliser quickly achieved its objectives, which then expanded significantly. British troops secured Lungi airport along with a staging area to evacuate noncombatants. Shortly after their arrival, however, it became clear that the UN mission was in dire straits. The United Kingdom decided about two weeks into the mission to formally extend its deployment and assist the government of Sierra Leone and UNAMSIL in shoring up security until troops from other countries arrived to reinforce the mission and the crisis was resolved.

The significance of the UK intervention resonated well beyond the termination of Operation Palliser on June 15. Some UK military assets and personnel remained behind to train the RSLAF and provide assistance to UNAMSIL and, notably, Operation Khukri. The United Kingdom maintained an offshore presence and conducted frequent, highly visible military patrols in Freetown.

A subsequent UK military undertaking further bolstered UNAMSIL, the government, and the people of Sierra Leone both psychologically and strategically. In August 2000 a British security patrol was taken hostage by the West Side Boys, an offshoot of the AFRC that had terrorized civilians for months with near impunity, attacking vehicles passing between the capital and the rest of the country. In the course of rescuing their comrades, UK special forces killed at least twenty-five West Side Boys and captured the group's leader, suffering one fatality in turn. The West Side Boys ceased to be a cohesive fighting force thereafter, and their attacks largely ended. Many opted to enter the DDR program. Moreover, the robust military response received substantial publicity. Although this episode, coming several months after the arrest of Foday Sankoh, did not directly affect the RUF, it is reported to have further undermined the rebel movement's morale.

Reinventing UNAMSIL

After the hostage crisis, UNAMSIL drew back from the northern province and from most of the eastern province, consolidating its forces in relatively few sites outside the western area. They remained there through March 2001. Beginning that spring, and particularly following Abuja II, UNAMSIL began to redeploy anew into RUF-held areas, striving to take full control over main access routes. By June, UN contingents had moved back into Makeni and Magburaka. From there, they "maintained a continuous patrol presence" in Koidu, in the east, and patrolled as far north as Kamakwie and Kabala.[147]

By September 2001, UNAMSIL had deployed to the key diamond districts of Kailahun, Kono, and Tonga. Air patrols were conducted along Liberian and Guinean border areas. By December 2001, UNAMSIL had positioned its largest contingents in the eastern provinces and had deployed successfully to all districts in Sierra Leone.[148]

These deployment activities were coordinated with a series of political steps to strengthen the RUF's commitment to the peace process. In contrast to his earlier objective of positioning forces in as many areas as possible and in as timely a manner as possible, the secretary-general now emphasized that UNAMSIL should deploy with due care and preparation. This would require both sufficient numbers (battalion strength, or 800 to 1,000 troops, wherever possible) and sufficient military means to deter attacks and, if necessary, respond decisively to any hostile action or intent.[149]

Security Council Resolution 1389 (January 16, 2000) tasked UNAMSIL to secure and support the May 2002 national and parliamentary elections. In preparation for its role, the mission realigned its military sector boundaries to coincide with electoral district boundaries, deploying in thirty-nine locations countrywide. Thirty additional UN police were authorized to join UNAMSIL and work with the SLP in developing plans to post 4,400 police personnel to voting centers around the country. UNAMSIL also coordinated the logistical programs of the National Election Commission and its partner agencies (many UNAMSIL sectors received additional equipment to assist in transporting electoral materials).[150]

National and parliamentary elections were held on May 10 and 14, 2002. The military voted on May 10; the civilian population voted on May 14. During the elections, mission personnel visited 4,700 of the 5,256 polling stations to monitor events, assessed the transparency and fairness of what they saw, and reported on these matters to UNAMSIL headquarters. Some 11,000 troops were temporarily deployed to 200 "high-risk" areas. Afterward, the mission provided security to ensure stability as the voting results were publicly released.[151]

Public Information: Radio UNAMSIL

Keeping the public informed is especially difficult in settings that are transitioning away from conflict. The public and private institutions that typically perform these duties are often decimated by war. In the case of Sierra Leone, the population's perception and understanding of both the foreign military force on the ground in their country and the state of public security in general was driven by widespread misinformation and rumor. The low rate of literacy (36 percent) among the adult population diminished the utility of print media as a primary source of public information.[152] Using television would have been prohibitively expensive, and its impact would have been questionable given the country's unreliable infrastructure, including electricity, and each television transmitter's limited signal reach. Therefore, radio was the alternative preferred by the international community to communicate with the civilian population in Sierra Leone.

Radio UNAMSIL, funded through the operation's assessed budget, was launched on May 22, 2000. It represented one of at least seven radio stations then operating in the country. Operated by a team of international and Sierra Leonean staff, "Radio U" balanced entertainment and music formats with news, public information, and phone-in segments covering various aspects of the peace process. The station's initial four-hour broadcasts were eventually expanded to twenty-four-hour programming.[153] Gradually, Radio UNAMSIL's signal coverage expanded from the immediate Freetown area to the entire country. Originally donated to the United Nations by Denmark in 1998, its transmitter had been recycled from Radio MINURCA (the UN operation in the Central African Republic). A shortwave transmitter, added in November 2000, gave the station's signal national reach. In addition, FM transmitters established in spring 2002 in Magburaka and Bo rebroadcast a satellite feed from Freetown to the rest of the country in time for the May 2002 national and parliamentary elections.[154]

Radio UNAMSIL played an important role in several of the mission's peacebuilding activities, broadcasting timely and critical information about the work of the Special Court, the TRC, and the withdrawal of UNAMSIL troops from various sectors of the country. Airtime was also made available for weekly programs by local and international NGOs, the NCDDR, and other agencies. Before the national and parliamentary elections, the radio station played a critical role in voter education, provided information about polling stations and voter registration, and offered airtime to all political parties in the presidential election. Finally, the station established a forum where local citizens could engage in exchanges with one another and with political candidates about election issues. On election day, Radio UNAMSIL aired live coverage from reporters stationed in every electoral district of the country.[155]

Disarmament, Demobilization, and Reintegration

The Sierra Leone government was responsible for developing a national strategy for demobilization and reintegration through the NCDDR, which President Kabbah chaired. The committee worked in partnership with the World Bank and the UK Department for International Development to establish DDR guidelines that were then implemented by other actors, including UNAMSIL, UN agencies such as the UNDP, and local and international NGOs. UNAMSIL's primary role in the initial stages of this process, in accordance with both the provisions of Lomé and UNAMSIL's own successive mandates, was to assist the government in implementing this DDR program.

A false start: 1999–2000. Disarmament progress was irregular and slow from July 1999 until the program's suspension in May 2000 following the hostage crisis. A number of constraints limited its effectiveness. For example, the articles of Lomé that dealt with disarmament (Articles XVI and XXX) were generous to the rebel groups, who could withdraw from the process at any time without penalty and effectively stall or derail it. Certain classes of weapons, such as hunting rifles and single- and double-barreled shotguns—weapons used mainly by the CDF—were initially exempted, which created disarmament imbalances between the CDF and the RUF. This exemption was rescinded in October 2000.

Moreover, the quality of weapons handed in was poor, and the ratio of combatants to weapons surrendered was more than 2:1. In the program's first seven months, only about half the projected number of combatants came forward to disarm.[156] Reintegration efforts were delayed several times for lack of funds, and no plans were developed to assist the dependents who often accompanied combatants to reception centers.[157] UNAMSIL and its partner institutions also failed to establish programs to respond to the needs of the estimated 12 percent of combatants who were female.[158]

Following its trip to the region in October 2000, the UN Security Council strongly recommended that the DDR program be thoroughly overhauled and reoriented.[159] That fall, only 706 combatants (138 RUF, 554 AFRC, 14 CDF) came forward to disarm, and the NCDDR completely halted the distribution of transitional safety allowances.[160] UNAMSIL turned its attention instead to ensuring that the majority of the Abuja I cease-fire provisions were secured before relaunching DDR. Under Abuja's terms, several conditions had to be fulfilled by the rebels before the overall peace process and DDR proceeded. These included respecting the terms of the cease-fire, ensuring the unhindered movement of UNAMSIL troops throughout the country, and returning all equipment and munitions taken from UNAMSIL during the May 2000 hostage crisis. The terms were largely met. There were substantially fewer cease-fire violations, and most UNAMSIL materiel was recovered—although severely damaged.

Representatives from the interagency team for DDR met in New York in early May 2001 to develop a new program and plan its implementation under Abuja II. The time frame for planning was very short, as the team wished to capitalize on the newfound commitment to peace by the parties to the conflict. Therefore, despite the inadequacies of the local institutional infrastructure, weak logistical capacity on the part of the government, and serious financial shortfalls on the part of the United Nations and the World Bank, the program was officially relaunched on May 18. The government established a joint committee, with representatives from the government, the RUF, the CDF, and UNAMSIL, to consult regularly on implementation. The government also augmented the renewed disarmament and demobilization efforts with a six-month reintegration program that began in August 2001.

A revitalized DDR program. UNAMSIL played a greatly enhanced role in the revitalized program. The DDR Coordination Section of the mission in effect oversaw the entire disarmament and demobilization effort and appointed two UNAMSIL military observers to act as a liaison with NCDDR.[161] UNAMSIL's responsibilities included providing security at DDR sites; receiving, screening, and processing ex-combatants; collecting and disabling weapons and ammunition; transporting ex-combatants from disarmament sites to demobilization centers; and arranging for the destruction of collected weapons and ammunition. UNAMSIL military observers assisted in the coordination and management of demobilization centers.[162]

The new DDR program also benefited from greater cooperation and transparency among various actors. For example, ECOWAS member states and UNAMSIL officials met regularly and shared information. NCDDR and UNAMSIL coordinated on two levels, and both appeared to work effectively during the final phases of DDR. The political level involved monitors from the Sierra Leone government, the RUF, the CDF, UNAMSIL, and donor countries, and dealt mainly with tracking progress in disarmament. The technical level involved a committee of national and international NGOs, humanitarian agencies, the Sierra Leone media, and UNAMSIL. It dealt with issues such as sensitization of combatants to the disarmament and demobilization process, updating disarmament policy guidelines, coordinating food delivery to demobilization centers, and coordinating registration by ex-combatants in reintegration programs. UNAMSIL troops and military observers also provided oversight and reported back to the government and ECOWAS, and Radio UNAMSIL was used extensively for public outreach and education.

Disarmament proceeded apace and without significant incidents. The first districts to be disarmed were Port Loko (CDF) and Kambia (RUF). Surprisingly, the RUF's response in Kambia was overwhelming, and the quality of weapons turned over at the reception center (Rokpur) was high.[163] Turnout at the Port Loko site was quite low, however, reportedly due to CDF mistrust of the process. When disarmament in one set of districts approached completion, planning would begin for the next districts. By the end of October 2001, the pace of the program had increased to meet its goal of completion before the May 2002 elections.[164] One district was disarmed approximately every two weeks, a pace twice as fast as initially planned.

In contrast to the relatively smooth disarmament process, demobilization was beset with challenges. For example, the government did not reliably process and distribute reinsertion packages and transition allowances, so ex-combatants lingered with their units near disarmament centers instead of returning to their home communities. There were few suitable demobilization facilities to accommodate combatants and/or their dependent family members. Violence broke out sporadically at several demobilization reception centers, and UNAMSIL was called upon to intervene and restore calm. Various mission contingents also helped negotiate between combatant groups in unstable districts.[165]

The unexpectedly high turnout at reception centers led the DDR Coordination Section of UNAMSIL to rethink its overall reintegration strategy. While UNAMSIL had expected 27,000 combatants from the CDF and the RUF to participate in the program, the actual caseload exceeded 47,000.[166] The decision was made to demobilize and reintegrate combatants in their home communities rather than at disarmament reception centers. A Reintegration Opportunities Program was established to provide ex-combatants with community-based educational, vocational, agricultural, or entrepreneurial support. One- to six-month subsistence allowances, along with vocational tool kits, were also offered to ex-combatants.

The Reintegration Opportunities Program had a number of perceived benefits. First, it would enhance the access of the implementing partners (national and international NGOs) to demobilized soldiers. Second, it would create incentives for them to return home faster than if they received reinsertion allowances at demobilization sites. Distributing reintegration resources at the community level rather than at the individual level also helped mitigate the perception that DDR was, in effect, privileging the welfare of ex-combatants over that of the civilian population. Third, by relocating ex-combatants quickly, it would reduce pressure on crowded demobilization centers. Fourth, it would provide a viable mechanism for managing the return to local communities of significant numbers of ex-combatant dependents (including "war brides" and their children). Fifth, the return of ex-combatants to their home communities would let UNAMSIL, the United Nations, and the government turn their attentions to coordinating the May 2002 elections and would facilitate national voter registration.

The decision to reintegrate fighters in their home communities also created new challenges, however. Fighters from some districts controlled by the RUF, such as Kailahun, Kono, and Makeni, did not reintegrate into their communities of origin and instead remained together in the bush. Some former RUF and SLA/AFRC combatants were recruited to fight in Liberia's civil war.[167] The CDF, in spite of having participated in disarmament, reportedly had, in 2002, maintained a number of its battalions (an estimated 10,200 fighters).[168] An August 2003 preliminary "lessons learned" exercise conducted by the DDR Coordination Section of UNAMSIL concluded that, in many cases, ex-combatants chose to self-reintegrate rather than participate in NGO- or UN agency–sponsored programs. Still others applied to enter the Military Reintegration Program and thus were no longer eligible for reintegration benefits.[169]

The special case of children associated with fighting forces. All parties to the conflict in Sierra Leone, but especially the RUF and the CDF, used child combatants. The UN Children's Fund (UNICEF) and other child protection agencies have estimated that between 7,000 and 10,000 child soldiers (those under the age of eighteen) fought in Sierra Leone.[170] Some were reportedly younger than ten (although most villagers find it difficult to establish dates of birth with accuracy). Many were used as combatants, but others, especially RUF children, served as bush camp laborers, porters, spies, miners in the eastern diamond districts, sex slaves, or war brides.

In the early part of the civil war, many child fighters joined with the approval of their families. As the conflict wore on, however, they often were taken involuntarily from their families or joined a rebel group after their family members were killed. Following the December 1998 siege of Freetown, some 4,800 children (more than half of them female) went missing; it is believed that many were taken by the fleeing AFRC/RUF forces. The primary "advantages" of enlisting children to fight were twofold: they did not need to be paid, and they followed orders better than adults. Many children were plied with drugs, forced to commit atrocities against their communities (thus estranging them from those communities), and threatened with violent retribution against their families if they failed to fight.

The Lomé Agreement required that all rebel groups demobilize their child combatants, but only about 1,700 were disarmed between July 1999 and May 2000. As the RUF renewed its offensive across the country in 2000, it targeted many interim care and rehabilitation centers for children. The RUF forcibly re-recruited many children from these centers, which neither UNAMSIL nor UNICEF had the capability to defend.[171]

Although by July 2003 approximately 98 percent of registered former child combatants had been reintegrated back into their home communities and families, a number of ongoing social and financial challenges continued to impede reintegration efforts.[172] First, relatively little attention was given to the needs of female child combatants, especially those who were sexually abused. The latter are particularly difficult to reintegrate and are often ostracized from their home communities. UNAMSIL established a program to teach vocational skills to young girls formerly abducted by rebel groups, but plans for government-sponsored trauma healing centers and a national advocacy agenda for war-affected boys and girls had not been fully realized as of this writing.[173] An interim program of health services and psychosocial counseling for former child combatants was organized by UNICEF in collaboration with several NGOs, but it was available to child ex-combatants only until they were reunited with their families.[174] Second, it has been difficult to reintegrate former RUF child combatants. Some between the ages of ten and fifteen continue to be exploited as cheap labor on the streets of Freetown, while others toil in the diamond mines. Former RUF child soldiers fearing revenge attacks have also been reluctant to return to communities that have been ravaged by the RUF and where they themselves may have committed atrocities.[175] (Whether these fears are well founded is unclear.) Third, funding shortfalls have undercut critical education and vocational skills training projects.

Meanwhile, all levels of society vigorously debated whether to treat child soldiers as victims or perpetrators. In many cases children played both roles. Some saw child combatants as unwilling participants forced to commit horrific crimes in order to survive; others argued that such crimes had to be punished if healing and reconciliation were to occur at both the local and the national levels. For example, children as young as eleven were granted the rank of brigadier, and had leadership and authority roles within their militias. It appears unlikely that children under the age of eighteen will meet the Special Court's criteria for prosecution (prosecutions have been limited to "those bearing the greatest responsibility" for abuses),[176] but they can be called to testify.[177]

After DDR. Disarmament and demobilization was officially completed in January 2002 (see table 3.4). The NCDDR reported in August that 72,500 combatants, 4,370 of them children, had been disarmed since December 1998, when DDR officially began. The national structures overseeing reintegration, including the NCDDR, were phased out at the end of 2003.

Establishing whether the NCDDR achieved its goals is difficult. The outstanding caseload of ex-combatants awaiting placement in reintegration programs was reduced very slowly, and as of March 31, 2004, when the reintegration program was officially closed, some 2,800 eligible ex-combatants still awaited placement. They were instead given one-time assistance packages the following June,[178] and responsibility for their cases was transferred to the National Committee for Social Action and various line ministries, including the labor ministry.

Moreover, there is a dearth of sustainable programming related to female ex-combatants and former war brides who have reintegrated, or attempted to reintegrate, into their home communities. Assistance

Table 3.4. Disarmament and Demobilization Statistics,
October 1999–January 2002

Time Frame	RUF	CDF	AFRC/ ex-SLA	Other	Total
October 1999–April 2000	4,130	8,800	4,495	1,473	18,898
May 2000–May 17, 2001	768	524	1,038	298	2,628
May 18, 2001–January 2002	19,267	28,051	0	463	47,781
Total	24,165	37,375	5,533	2,234	69,307

Sources: National Committee for Disarmament, Demobilization, and Reintegration (NCDDR), August 2002; Mark Malan et al., *Sierra Leone: Building the Road to Recovery,* ISS Monograph Series, no. 80 (Pretoria: Institute for Security Studies, 2003), 33.

programs have tended to focus on male ex-combatants and on material needs. Community sensitization programs and psychological counseling resources for ex-combatants and their dependents are virtually nonexistent. The quality of reintegration programs was also affected early on by weaknesses in coordination and planning. For example, programs administered by the World Bank, UNDP, and the United Kingdom's Department for International Development, and those administered by NGOs and the NCDDR, were initially weakly coordinated, and this led to program overlap and redundancy.[179] To some degree, coordination improved between 2003 and 2004. For example, the World Bank estimated that by September 2003, 85 percent of registered ex-combatants had received some form of reintegration services, either through training and employment programs implemented by NGOs or through UNDP-organized "stopgap" projects. Interministerial cooperation and coordination in the national reintegration effort lagged, however, and this will undoubtedly affect the long-term impact of DDR across the country.[180]

Financial difficulties hampered the DDR program. The Multi-Donor Trust Fund (MDTF), established and managed by the World Bank to cover the expenses of the DDR program (see table 3.1), remained undersubscribed during the course of the civil war. Repeated donor appeals yielded few pledges. Successive reports of the secretary-general indicated that the gap between delivered pledges and the budgetary needs of DDR continued to widen in 2001, and the MDTF reportedly verged on bankruptcy in August 2002.[181]

Perhaps the biggest challenge to the long-term stability of demobilization and reintegration in Sierra Leone, however, is the current state of the national economy. For several years Sierra Leone has ranked last or nearly last among all countries in all aspects of sustainable human development, according to the Human Development Index in the UNDP's *Human Development Report.*[182] Despite a gross domestic product real growth rate of 5.9 percent, GDP per capita is approximately $520, and 57 percent of the population lives on less than $1 per day. Economic and professional opportunities remain limited for most citizens (ex-combatants and noncombatant civilians alike) because nearly 70 percent are illiterate and most lack employable skills.[183]

Justice and Accountability

One of the most vexing concerns of the government and the United Nations has been how to create justice and accountability in response to the massive human rights violations perpetrated during the civil war. Two institutions were established to deal with these issues: the Truth and Reconciliation Commission and the Special Court for Sierra Leone. UNAMSIL has played a role in both mechanisms.

The Lomé Agreement provided for a TRC, which was duly established by an act of parliament in February 2000, although it did not begin its work for more than two years.[184] An independent body, the TRC had a fifteen-month mandate (a three-month start-up phase and one year of operations) and consisted of seven commissioners (four Sierra Leone nationals and three foreigners) appointed by a consensus of the SRSG of UNAMSIL, the government, and the UN High Commissioner for Human Rights. The TRC headquarters were in Freetown, with satellite offices in the interior districts of Makeni, Bo, and Kenema. Much of the commission's work was conducted from Geneva rather than in Sierra Leone, however, in offices provided by the High Commissioner. The UNDP in Freetown served as the local administrative partner for the commission, but the structural split of the commission into two sites delayed operations and reduced efficiency at times.

While the commission was not a judicial body per se, it possessed broad investigatory and seizure powers.[185] Its primary objective was to create an impartial historical record of violations and abuses of human rights and international humanitarian law related to the country's recent period of armed conflict. Its goals included promoting reconciliation among the civilian population and preventing such abuses from occurring in the future. The commission's mandate covered the period from March 1991 to the signing of the Lomé Agreement in July 1999. It established an interim secretariat in March 2002 and was officially inaugurated on July 5. It did not begin its work until October 2002, while an overarching strategy for the first year of operations was developed. In October 2003, President Kabbah granted the commission a six-month extension to complete its work; the commission ultimately required even more time.[186]

The TRC's work proceeded in three phases. In the first phase, staff were deployed across the country, and more than 8,000 individuals offered their testimonies either in writing or in person before the commission. Both public and confidential hearings were held in the second phase, which commenced in April 2003.[187] In the third and final phase, the TRC prepared a report for submission to the government of Sierra Leone and the United Nations. That report, which was presented to President Kabbah in early October 2004, was released in electronic form three weeks later. Its eighty-two pages of findings, organized by group (RUF, AFRC, SLPP, and others), emphasized group responsibility rather than associating specific activities with specific individuals. Its 100-page recommendations chapter covered a wide range of issues, from women's rights to a broken-down justice system and pervasive corruption in government, exhorting Sierra Leone's "civil society organisations and activists" to vigorously monitor "the performance of government and its agencies in the implementation of the recommendations."[188]

The government agreed to evaluate the TRC's recommendations and incorporate them into its national transitional justice program, and issued a white paper on implementation in June 2005. Civil society organizations criticized the white paper, however, as "vague and noncommittal."[189]

UNAMSIL's assistance to the TRC was multifaceted. The mission provided significant levels of logistical support to the interim secretariat and the secretariat. It also cooperated closely with UNICEF to develop TRC guidelines for the appropriate treatment and protection of children as victims, witnesses, and perpetrators.

Initially the TRC was slow in disseminating public information about its work, resulting in poor public understanding of its purposes and how they differed from those of the Special Court. For example, nearly one-fifth of ex-combatants learned about the TRC and the Special Court via rumors and thought they would be arrested if they turned in their weapons.[190] In 2001, however, UNAMSIL and the TRC collaborated to increase civic awareness of the commission. UNAMSIL administered regional workshops for civilians and paramount chiefs,[191] in partnership with the National Forum for Human Rights (a twenty-seven-group coalition), and published illustrated information leaflets and a fact sheet on the TRC process, which were distributed widely. Sensitization workshops were also organized specifically for the RUF from June to October 2001 in Makeni, Bombali, Koidu, and Kabala, which were then RUF strongholds. Radio UNAMSIL broadcast weekly radio programs about the TRC.[192]

The second mechanism for postwar justice and accountability was the Special Court for Sierra Leone. Despite the blanket amnesty provided to the rebels by the 1999 Lomé Agreement, many in the international community supported punitive justice for those who had committed war crimes. Following nearly two years of negotiations and an agreement between the United Nations and the government, the Special Court was inaugurated in 2002 as an independent judicial body possessing international jurisdiction to prosecute those "who bear the greatest responsibility" for war crimes, crimes against humanity, and other serious violations of international humanitarian law.[193]

The court's jurisdiction began on November 30, 1996 (the date of signing of the Abidjan Agreement), and is open-ended. Sitting officials are not immune from prosecution by the Special Court, and double jeopardy is possible in select cases in which an individual was initially tried by the national courts of Sierra Leone but prosecution was not diligently pursued.[194] Three of the Special Court's eight justices are appointed by the government and five by the UN secretary-general. The secretary-general appointed the special prosecutor, David Crane, a U.S. national; the government of Sierra Leone appointed the deputy prosecutor, Desmond de Silva, a Sri Lankan–UK national. In May 2005, De Silva was appointed by the secretary-general to replace Crane as the chief prosecutor.

The Special Court's most innovative features included the application of both national and international law in its proceedings, as well as specific provisions for cases involving juveniles. The court has also attempted to deal squarely with the issue of amnesty for combatants, which it and other international legal scholars have determined cannot be granted with respect to international crimes. Article 10 of the court's statute denies the legal effect of the Lomé Agreement's amnesty provision (Article IX), noting its illegality under international law.[195] The court was also the first of its kind to operate in the same country where the crimes it is prosecuting have been committed.

Operating a court or tribunal in the same country where crimes against humanity were perpetrated posed a number of concerns regarding witness intimidation and protection. The court responded to these challenges by revising its rules of procedure and evidence and establishing a Victims and Witness Support Unit to provide short- and long-term protection for adult and child witnesses, along with other services such as counseling and trauma rehabilitation. It also created a Defence Office, headed by a principal defender, to coordinate the defense of indictees—a first among existing ad hoc tribunals. Moreover, the court can now delegate directly to police or other government agencies for execution, without having to first pursue diplomatic channels for approval. Such capacity does not exist in the statutes of either the International Criminal Tribunal for the Former Yugoslavia or the International Criminal Tribunal for Rwanda, and it has expedited the Special Court's work.[196]

UN member states have been encouraged to cooperate with the Special Court in areas such as extradition and obtaining documents and evidentiary material. Unlike the ad hoc tribunals for Rwanda and the former Yugoslavia, however, the Special Court as established lacks Chapter VII powers to compel states to respect its jurisdiction.[197] It was given concurrent jurisdiction with and primacy over the national courts of Sierra Leone, but not over the national courts of third-party states.[198] The court issued its first group of indictments and arrests under Operation Justice between March and September 2003.[199] All indictees were charged with crimes against humanity, war crimes, and serious violations of international humanitarian law. Three indicted members of the CDF were tried together, as were the grouped indictees from the RUF and the AFRC (see table 3.5). These trials began in June 2004, July 2004, and March 2005, respectively.[200]

As envisioned when the initial plans for the court were developed, UNAMSIL provided significant support to the institution.[201] The UN operation coordinated and oversaw all security arrangements for the court (two UNAMSIL platoons were permanently assigned to court premises), for prison facilities at Bonthe Island, and for staff, defendants, and witnesses. Because the Special Court's financial resources were limited, it relied on UNAMSIL in the early phases of operations to provide logistics, administrative support, transportation, communications, finance and procurement, and temporary accommodation for justices and staff. The mission's security assistance was scaled back as the court enlisted its own security contractors. UNAMSIL also provided assistance to court investigators, compiling a database of incidents of war-related sexual violence against women and girls. The data were to be used for future national programs and shared with the TRC as well as the Special Court.[202] UNAMSIL also conducted preliminary investigations of mass graves in Kailahun, Port Loko, Bombali, and Koinadugu and turned over to the Special Court an inventory of war-related killings.[203]

The United Nations and the government of Sierra Leone attempted to portray the TRC and the Special Court as complementary institutions that would help close the book on the war, the former by addressing the grievances of the victims, the latter by punishing the perpetrators. Their simultaneous functioning has set a precedent in international law and posed challenges that affected the ability of UNAMSIL to assist them effectively. For example, confusion persisted over whether the TRC and the court would share information, which affected the UNAMSIL-administered DDR program. RUF combatants had a distorted perception of the links between the TRC and the Special Court, fearing court indictment if they participated in DDR or agreed to testify before the TRC.[204] The Special Court announced that it would not use information from TRC hearings or testimonies to issue indictments; the prosecutor had the discretion to use public statements to the TRC made by individuals already indicted by the Special Court, however.[205] (This tension surfaced in connection with the case pending against Kamajor leader Sam Hinga Norman.[206]) Moreover, because the TRC lacked the legal status of a court of law, defendants submitting testimony to it could also be indicted by the Special Court.

Finally, the TRC and the Special Court have been reliant on UNAMSIL for the bulk of their respective security arrangements because they are so poorly funded. The budget for the TRC was $5 million for an eighteen-month term, having been cut in half from a proposed $10 million in 2001. Many of its initial planned activities were thus curtailed or eliminated; staff salaries went unpaid for long periods, and employee morale suffered as a result.

The Special Court was likewise financially troubled but was ultimately aided by direct funding from the UN regular budget. Its proposed budget, initially derived from voluntary contributions, was subjected to multiple downward revisions, from $114.6 million to $57 million over a three-year term. Its funding scheme was much leaner than those for the ad hoc tribunals for the former Yugoslavia and Rwanda, and it was authorized by the secretary-general to commence its work even though it had failed to meet the required financing conditions specified in his July 2001 letter to the Security Council.[207] The secretary-general advised consistently against a voluntary financing arrangement for the Special Court, noting that such an arrangement was risky and could expose the United Nations to legal liability if it were unable to honor the contractual commitment with the Sierra Leone government that it concluded on January 16, 2002.[208]

In March 2004, the secretary-general asked the General Assembly for $16.7 million in UN regular budget funds, to be used by the Special Court in the second half of 2004. The funds were granted, but due to a combination of spending controls, exchange rate shifts, $8 million in "unliquidated obligations" (deferred payments on outstanding bills), and the delayed trials for the AFRC defendants, the court was able to get through 2004 without the UN money, which was then rescinded at the end of the year. At that point, however, the court was nearly broke. The General Assembly therefore agreed, in January 2005, to provide $20 million for the first half of 2005 and, at midyear, $13 million for the rest of the year, transitioning the court, for one year, from voluntary

Table 3.5. Special Court for Sierra Leone, Indictments

Indictee	Role in Civil War	Status
Sam "Mosquito" Bockarie	Senior member, military junta government; battlefield commander, RUF; director, RUF operations while Sankoh imprisoned; adviser to Charles Taylor	Killed in Liberia Indictment withdrawn, December 2003
Alex Tamba Brima	Public liaison officer, AFRC; senior member, military junta government; commander, AFRC/RUF forces in Kono; a commander of AFRC/RUF forces in the January 1999 attack on Freetown	In custody; awaiting trial To be tried jointly with Kamara and Kanu
Moinina Fofana	National director of war, CDF; second in command to Sam Hinga Norman; Kamajor battalion commander	In custody; awaiting trial To be tried jointly with Kondewa and Norman
Augustine Gbao	Senior commander, RUF in Kailahun; overall security coordinator, AFRC/RUF; joint commander, AFRC/RUF Makeni/Bombali	In custody; awaiting trial To be tried jointly with Sesay and Kallon
Morris Kallon	Deputy area commander, RUF; battlefield inspector, military junta government; battlefield commander, RUF; battle group commander, RUF	In custody; awaiting trial To be tried jointly with Gbao and Sesay
Brima Bazzy Kamara	Public liaison officer, military junta government; commander, AFRC/RUF in Kono; a commander of AFRC/RUF forces in the January 1999 attack on Freetown	In custody; awaiting trial To be tried jointly with Brima and Kanu

Name	Role	Status
Santigie Borbor Kanu	Member, AFRC Supreme Council; senior commander, AFRC/RUF in Kono; commander, AFRC/RUF forces that attacked Koinadugu and Bombali; a commander of AFRC/RUF forces in the January 1999 attack on Freetown	In custody; awaiting trial. To be tried jointly with Brima and Kamara
Allieu Kondewa	High priest, CDF; responsible for all initiations of combatants, including child combatants; commander, special CDF missions	In custody; awaiting trial. To be tried jointly with Fofana and Norman
Johnny Paul Koroma	Former lieutenant colonel, SLA; chair, AFRC; head of state/president, military junta government	Not in custody; whereabouts unknown
Sam Hinga Norman	National coordinator, CDF; commander, Kamajor Defense Forces	In custody; awaiting trial. To be tried jointly with Fofana and Kondewa
Foday Sankoh	Vice chair, AFRC/RUF junta military government and leader of the RUF	Died in custody of natural causes, July 2003. Indictment withdrawn, December 2003
Issa Hassan Sesay	Senior officer, AFRC/RUF military junta government; area commander, RUF; battle group commander, RUF; battlefield commander, RUF; interim leader, RUF	In custody; awaiting trial. To be tried jointly with Gbao and Kallon
Charles Taylor	Former president, Liberia	Returned to court custody from Nigerian exile, March 2006

Source: Special Court for Sierra Leone Web site, www.sc-sl.org.

to assessed contributions. Its total spending to that point will have amounted to roughly $100 million over four years. In comparison, the two ad hoc war crimes tribunals for Rwanda and the former Yugoslavia have spent between $100 million and $150 million per year, essentially all of it assessed funds.[209]

Assessment (1999–2005)

The Lomé Agreement was a deeply flawed platform on which to base peace operations in Sierra Leone. Not only did it reflect the "desperation under which the central government negotiated and compromised the future of the country on the assumption that it would bring enduring peace,"[210] but it also rewarded RUF aggression and intransigence. Because the RUF's post-Lomé goals remained unchanged, there was no real peace to keep. Thus the basic premise of UNAMSIL's original mandate—that the United Nations would help implement a viable peace accord—was deeply unrealistic. Equally unrealistic was the assumption that ECOMOG would keep and, if necessary, enforce the peace more capably, once the United Nations deployed, than its record of several years in Sierra Leone would suggest. Moreover, by relying on ECOMOG, the Security Council was trying to keep peace on the cheap, and African leaders like Nigeria's Obasanjo were unwilling to oblige.

As a result, the Security Council and DPKO waited too long to assume responsibility for the mission. Faced with competing demands for troops in the Congo, East Timor, and Kosovo, UN headquarters knowingly accepted offers of troops that were ill prepared in terms of training, equipment, and levels of self-sufficiency. Once deployed, the troops failed to develop any sense of shared understanding of the mission's rules of engagement. In UNAMSIL's critical first months, command and control were severely compromised, due in part to poor leadership within the civilian and military components of the mission, and in part to improper individual or national agendas. UNAMSIL's original force commander was made the scapegoat for these early failures.

The early structural shortcomings in UNAMSIL explain why it continued to experience difficulties despite more than doubling its authorized strength in February 2000. The May 2000 hostage crisis underscored what was wrong with the mission.

The British intervention represented a much-needed infusion of military force and professionalism but also raised many concerns. While it is now clear that the crises in Makeni and Magburaka would not necessarily have spread to the capital, that was the fear at the time. British forces stayed on after meeting their initial objective of ensuring the safety of foreign noncombatants. By not placing its troops under UN command, however, the United Kingdom sent a message to troop-contributing countries from the developing world that "first-world" countries in general, and the five permanent members of the Security Council in particular, either did not trust and respect UN mission leadership or viewed affiliation with the United Nations as an avoidable drag on their decisions and field operations.

Fortunately, UNAMSIL was able to survive the departure of its best-equipped troops. The RUF was in disarray during the internal leadership transition from Sankoh to Sesay. U.S.-trained Nigerian troops performed more ably than those they replaced, and newly arrived troops from Pakistan, in particular, were well equipped and capable. The original force commander and deputy were replaced, and the new military leadership worked well together.

The mission's key stakeholders took other necessary steps to turn UNAMSIL around. In addition to establishing a joint operations cell to which all contingents in the mission contributed, mission leadership and contingent commanders organized field-level meetings and briefings, and the UN secretary-general began to hold regular meetings with troop-contributing countries' representatives in New York. Induction training programs were instituted for all new mission personnel, and all were familiarized with the mission's rules of engagement. Perhaps most importantly from the standpoint of mission management and impact on peacebuilding, two deputy SRSGs were appointed, in recognition that effective management and close coordination of all peacebuilding efforts in a transitional country are essential to creating sustainable peace.

The role of the United Kingdom in saving UNAMSIL and creating peace in Sierra Leone is often accorded greater significance by analysts than is warranted. Some commentators have suggested that the lesson to be learned is that a small first-world intervention force on its own can bring peace to a war-torn country quickly and relatively easily; this conclusion is erroneous. Several factors explain why the civil war in Sierra Leone ended: RUF leader Foday Sankoh was captured; the United States provided thousands of African peacekeepers with the tools necessary to do a much better job; the Security Council gave UNAMSIL a more robust and appropriate mandate, as well as sufficient numbers of well-trained and well-armed troops to get the job done; the international community took serious measures to control "conflict diamonds" and to counter the influence and power of Liberian president Charles Taylor; and Guinea attacked RUF positions to great effect.[211] Arguing that all it takes to make peacekeeping in Africa work is a few hundred Western troops for a short period is not just an oversimplification of peace operations' complexities; it sets up any future undertaking for failure by creating inappropriate expectations of a quick and relatively painless fix.

Disarmament and demobilization goals were largely achieved, in part via coordinated efforts to process new information about the local situation quickly and efficiently. This required a strong capacity to make rapid adjustments to the program and maintain operational flexibility in the field. Lessons learned from each district's disarmament experience were channeled into the plans for subsequent districts, providing a measure of continuity and learning throughout. The disarmament efforts undertaken during UNAMSIL were also reinforced in some instances by subsequent community arms collection programs.

Claims of success are harder to sustain with regard to reintegration, however. Proper and sustained levels of funding were needed but not forthcoming. When a peace operation is planned, DDR is commonly referred to and spoken of in terms of a three-part, interlinked, and coherent program. Its implementation in the case of Sierra Leone was anything but coherent, however. In order to be effective, reintegration of ex-combatants must be well planned, follow thoughtful and qualified assessment of conditions on the ground, and be sufficiently funded. Reintegration efforts in Sierra Leone were poorly planned and severely constrained in their implementation, in spite of the recognition that reintegration is critical to a sustainable postconflict transition. Coordination with local implementing partners was ill executed and should be improved for future missions if "coherence" is to be maintained. Moreover, donors and implementing partners (as well as governments) should ensure that disarmament, demobilization, and reintegration are assessed from the perspective of impact and qualitative achievement rather than simply that of deliverables or quantitative measures such as remaining caseload, educational scholarships offered, or number of tool kits distributed. Planning for DDR should also be flexible enough to accommodate ex-combatant dependents and bush wives if it is to be truly effective and sustainable over the long term.

As noted above, the Truth and Reconciliation Commission and the Special Court for Sierra Leone were portrayed by the United Nations as complementary exercises that would contribute to sustainable peace in Sierra Leone. While this may turn out to be true, much more could have been done to increase their effectiveness. Advance coordination should have been done more carefully, so as to avoid ambiguity and confusion among the TRC and Special Court staff and the general population. Stronger coordination and public outreach might have actually enhanced initial participation in DDR by clarifying the role of both institutions to combatants.

In addition, the funding mechanisms for the TRC and the Special Court were suboptimal. The decision to rely solely on voluntary funding for both was intended to endow these institutions with legitimacy and independence. Nonetheless, repeated but ill-coordinated appeals by the secretary-general and the High Commissioner for Human Rights generated relatively little donor support for the TRC and little more than half of what the Special Court required. The results were a dramatic scaling back of budget and operational objectives in the case of the TRC, and delayed trials in the case of the court. This phenomenon is fairly common when "loud" crises turn "soft" and donor interests shift toward other civil wars or complex emergencies.

Because the secretary-general pressed for assessed UN funding for the court, the General Assembly agreed to provide roughly eighteen months' financing. But financial planning for future postconflict justice and accountability processes must strike an early balance between the need to create legitimate and independent institutions and the need to ensure that these institutions are financially capable of carrying out their mandated responsibilities. The institutions, in turn, must demonstrate that they are capable of running a tight fiscal ship, which the Special Court did to the satisfaction of the United Nations' Advisory

Committee on Administrative and Budgetary Questions and other key UN decision-making bodies.

Some factors that promoted conflict remain insufficiently addressed: Unemployment rates continue to be high throughout the country, and economic growth prospects in the near term are low. Corruption is endemic and permeates all levels of society, especially government institutions. Popular support for and acceptance of the Special Court may be tested when it renders its final verdicts. Strident youth groups, which appeared in the eastern diamond mining districts as DDR released youthful former combatants into a market without jobs, may pose a continuing challenge to stability in those districts, where the government has struggled to reassert its authority. National revenues from diamond mining, which were a tiny $10 million in 2000, did rise to $76 million in 2003 and about $125 million in 2004; UN officials estimated, however, that the government should be deriving closer to $250 million in revenues from known diamond extraction activities, suggesting how much remains to be done both to legitimize diamond mining and to control the corruption associated with it.[212]

The Security Council's March 2004 decision to extend UNAMSIL's mandate through 2005 demonstrated a level of political will and commitment to see the mission succeed, but that additional commitment was needed because Sierra Leone's armed forces and police were not yet capable of providing for the country's internal and external security. The average Sierra Leonean seemed to echo those concerns, according to a UN-commissioned public opinion survey conducted from March to May 2005. It found Sierra Leoneans quite positively inclined toward the operation—especially its public works and Radio UNAMSIL— and reluctant to see its security presence removed before the 2007 presidential elections.[213] Respondents seemed to concur with many analysts that creating stable and sustainable peace in Sierra Leone will remain a challenge for some time to come.

Conclusions

The various peace operations in Sierra Leone underscore that the Security Council's enthusiasm for Chapter VIII of the UN Charter should be tempered as concerns Africa, at least until the continent better develops its regional capacity for peacekeeping and peacebuilding. ECOMOG's first intervention in Sierra Leone proved capable of uprooting the military junta from Freetown, but ECOWAS could not (and would not) support the sort of large, multifaceted peace operation needed to pacify the entire country. The small, unarmed UN observer mission accompanying ECOMOG did not fill that gap, nor did it have the political weight or the training capacity to make ECOMOG a better-behaved or more professional force. At best, regional organizations at a comparable phase of development can supply only short-term fixes to security problems—much as was done in Liberia in August 2003.

While UN missions have advantages over African regional forces, Sierra Leone showed that strength levels are, in and of themselves, poor indicators of likely performance. Proper equipment and the will and ability to use it are crucial factors in a peace operation's success. As initially conceived, the wet-lease program, which required that troop contingents provide their own major equipment, parts, and maintenance, expected too much of the United Nations' principal troop-contributing countries. The United Nations devised some fairly effective ad hoc fixes, but the nature of the problem is such that they will remain ad hoc.

The critical roles of personalities and effective oversight were made crystal clear in UNAMSIL. The breakdown in communication as well as command and control during the first half of 2000 should never have been allowed. For a mission to succeed, the SRSG must work closely with the force commander, and the latter must have the respect and support of his or her deputy. Moreover, an individual's success in one mission may be a poor indicator of likely performance elsewhere—even at the same leadership level—if mission circumstances are substantially different. Although a person's nationality is a legitimate factor to consider when filling a post, it must not be the overriding concern. Nationals of a single country should not hold more than one of the top two military and political positions. Just as a force commander's job necessitates a deputy, so must an SRSG rely on a deputy. Indeed, UNAMSIL showed that for a large and complex mission, two deputy SRSGs may well be needed. Finally, it should not take a hostage crisis to elicit a proper demand from DPKO for accountability in a mission headquarters.

The implementation of what were multiple and sometimes over-lapping peacekeeping and peace enforcement mandates over the course of Sierra Leone's civil war offers broader insights for future operations. First, although DDR experienced numerous setbacks, especially in reintegration, it appears that small arms and light weapons are not easily available in the capital or throughout the country. Johnny Paul Koroma's supporters tried (unsuccessfully) to steal weapons from the army engineer unit's depot in Wellington in January 2003. This suggests that weapons are not circulating freely or reentering the country easily from abroad. Second, UNAMSIL's role in the 2002 national and parliamentary elections was critical in ensuring that the vote was conducted peacefully. Third, the TRC's work has potential for healing society and reconciling differences between former combatants and civilians, especially if the government delivers on its promise to devote the necessary political capital and resources to implement the commission's findings. Fourth, the hybrid national-international Special Court may serve as a model for other states looking for ways to bring to justice the perpetrators of war crimes and other atrocities.

In some respects, Sierra Leone represented one of the United Nations' largest commitments to peacekeeping, peace enforcement, and peacebuilding since the end of the Cold War, demonstrating not only what can go wrong but also what can go right in such endeavors. More than three years after national and parliamentary elections, UN peacekeeping efforts in Sierra Leone are coming to an end, but a substantial UN presence will remain, along with bilateral donors, international and national NGOs, and other actors whose work has been and will be vital to the future stability of the country.

Notes

1. ECOWAS at the time comprised sixteen member states—nine Francophone, five Anglophone, and two Lusophone. Its membership was reduced to fifteen in 2000 with the departure of Mauritania.

2. See W. B. Ofuatey-Kodjoe, "Sierra Leone," in *Dealing with Conflict in Africa: The United Nations and Regional Organizations,* ed. Jane Boulden (New York: Palgrave Macmillan, 2003), 128–29.

3. U.S. Central Intelligence Agency (CIA), *CIA World Factbook,* www. cia.gov/cia/publications/factbook/geos/sl.html#People (accessed August 10, 2005). Many Sierra Leoneans practice a mixture of indigenous beliefs along with Islam or Christianity, so this breakdown should be seen as a particularly rough estimate.

4. The three countries together form the Mano River Union, a subregional organization that addresses economic, political, and—increasingly— security issues. For a brief overview of the union, see West Africa Network for Peace-Building and Forum on Early Warning and Early Response (FEWER), "The Mano River Union Regional Report" (London: FEWER Secretariat, 2003).

5. Both Margai brothers were Mende. The head of the country's armed forces at the time of the 1967 elections, Brigadier David Lansana, led a coup d'état that prevented Stevens from taking office. Lieutenant Colonel Andrew Juxon-Smith replaced Lansana two days later and formed the National Reformation Council, which ruled until a countercoup installed Stevens thirteen months later.

6. Both Momoh and Stevens were Limba. The Limba are the third-largest ethnic group in Sierra Leone and have traditionally allied themselves with the Temne from the north. Author telephone interview with Zainab Bangura, former coordinator, Sierra Leone, of the Campaign for Good Governance, December 2, 2003.

7. Besides diamonds, Sierra Leone has large deposits of bauxite and possesses nearly a quarter of the world's known deposits of rutile (titanium oxide), a metal ore used in the aerospace industry and high-tech alloys. Rutile is also used to enhance the properties of gemstones such as rubies and sapphires.

8. Personal as well as professional considerations may have motivated Taylor. Sierra Leone's president, Joseph Momoh, had once arrested him. For an accounting of these other motives, see William Reno, *Warlord Politics and African States* (Boulder, CO: Lynne Rienner, 1998), chap. 4; and Adekeye Adebajo, *Building Peace in West Africa: Liberia, Sierra Leone, and Guinea-Bissau* (Boulder, CO: Lynne Rienner, 2002), 82.

9. Moreover, Sankoh had SLPP credentials. In the 1970s he had run for office as an SLPP candidate from Tonkolili district. Author interview with Zainab Bangura, November 18, 2003.

10. For a comprehensive overview of the Momoh and Strasser regimes, see Reno, *Warlord Politics,* chap. 4.

11. Eric G. Berman, "Re-armament in Sierra Leone: One Year after the Lomé Peace Agreement," Occasional Paper no. 1 (Geneva: Small Arms Survey, December 2000), 20.

12. Personal interests motivated the coup. In an effort to take firmer control over the mining districts, the SLA under Momoh engaged in operations to rid the area of strongmen and illicit miners. These operations also disrupted the illegal activities of SLA soldier-rebels, or "sobels" (soldiers by day, rebels by night). Valentine Strasser and his army unit were among those adversely affected. See Reno, *Warlord Politics,* 123.

13. See United Nations, *Report of the Secretary-General on the Situation in Sierra Leone,* S/1995/975, November 21, 1995, paras. 9–11.

14. In addition to the Kamajors—the best-known members of the CDF, who were concentrated in the Bo district—other CDF units included the Tamaboros (Koinadugu district), the Donsos (Kono district), the Kapras (Tonkolili district), and the Gbethis (Port Loko and Tonkolili districts). In addition to being traditional hunters, many CDF members were farmers or students. It is generally agreed that these elements were not centrally coordinated and resisted such efforts, including those made by Kamajor chief Sam Hinga Norman. See United Nations, *Third Report of the Secretary-General on the Situation in Sierra Leone,* S/1998/103, February 5, 1998, para. 10; and United Nations, *Fifth Report of the Secretary-General on the Situation in Sierra Leone,* S/1998/486, June 9, 1998, para. 16.

15. For an account of Gurkha Security Guards' brief experience in Sierra Leone, see Alex Vines, "Gurkhas and the Private Security Business in Africa," in *Peace, Profit or Plunder? The Privatisation of Security in War-Torn African Societies,* ed. Jakkie Cilliers and Peggy Mason (Halfway House: Institute for Security Studies, 1999), 129–32.

16. See P. W. Singer, *Corporate Warriors: The Rise of the Privatized Military Industry* (Ithaca, NY: Cornell University Press, 2003), 101–18.

17. Nigeria had deployed about 450 troops in Sierra Leone since 1991. In 1995, this number was increased to 639 with the introduction of an artillery battery and two training teams. See R. A. Adeshina, *The Reversed Victory: Story of Nigerian Military Intervention in Sierra Leone* (Ibadan, Nigeria: Heinemann Educational, 2002), ix, 7.

18. Bio claimed that he had informed Nigeria of his intentions prior to seizing power and had received word that Abuja would warmly greet his putsch. According to Bio, both Nigerian president Sani Abacha and Ghanaian president Jerry Rawlings indicated that holding elections was not of paramount concern. See Adebajo, *Building Peace in West Africa,* 85.

19. In the first round of elections, neither the SLPP nor the APC received the 55 percent of the popular vote that would have been required to win. See International Crisis Group (hereafter cited as Crisis Group), "Sierra Leone: Ripe for Elections?" Africa Briefing no. 6, December 19, 2001; and Crisis Group, "Sierra Leone: Time for a New Military and Political Strategy," Africa Report no. 28, April 11, 2001, Appendix C. All Crisis Group reports are at www.crisisgroup.org.

20. Some have suggested that the RUF amputated the arms and hands of potential voters and their families as a perverse preelection disincentive, playing off the 1996 election slogan "The future is in your hands." Others note that citizens voted using their thumbprints to identify themselves and prevent election fraud, and that the RUF often amputated the limbs of voters easily distinguished by the indelible ink on their thumbs, regardless of whom they supported. Author interview with Zainab Bangura, November 18, 2003.

21. For example, there were allegations of voter fraud in the south, an SLPP stronghold, where more ballots were cast than there were voters registered. See John Hirsch, *Sierra Leone: Diamonds and the Struggle for Democracy* (Boulder, CO: Lynne Rienner, 2001), 46; and Crisis Group, "Sierra Leone: Ripe for Elections," 7. The Security Council endorsed the outcome in a Presidential Statement, S/PRST/1996/12, March 19, 1996.

22. Author telephone interview with UN official, October 9, 2003.

23. See *Peace Agreement between the Government of the Republic of Sierra Leone and the Revolutionary United Front of Sierra Leone (RUF/SL)* (Abidjan Agreement), November 30, 1996, www.sierra-leone.org/documents.html.

24. United Nations, *Report of the Secretary-General on Sierra Leone,* S/1997/80, January 26, 1997, Annex 1.

25. Over the past fifteen years, the government's national military forces have taken on various names: the Sierra Leone Army, the Republic of Sierra Leone Military Forces, and the Republic of Sierra Leone Armed Forces.

26. United Nations, *SG Report on Sierra Leone,* S/1997/80, para. 16.

27. See UN Security Council Resolution 1132, S/RES/1132, October 8, 1997.

28. Author interview with UK government official, October 3, 2003, London.

29. "Decisions Adopted by the Sixty-sixth Ordinary Session of the Council of Ministers of the Organization of African Unity, May 28–31, 1997, Harare, Zimbabwe," Docs. no. CM/2004 (LXVI) C and CM/Dec/357 (LXVI).

30. See UN Security Council, Presidential Statement, S/PRST/1997/29, May 27, 1997; and UN Security Council, Press Release, SC/6394, July 11, 1997.

31. Affairs of state were conducted in a former Chinese restaurant that the British government rented for the government of Sierra Leone. Author telephone interview with Peter Penfold, former UK high commissioner to Sierra Leone, October 3, 2003.

32. The Committee of Four consisted of representatives of Côte d'Ivoire, Ghana, Guinea, and Nigeria. The committee's membership was subsequently expanded to five in August 1997 with the addition of Liberia, and to six in December 1997 with the addition of Togo. See Eric G. Berman and Katie E. Sams, *Peacekeeping in Africa* (Geneva: UN Institute for Disarmament Research; Pretoria: Institute for Security Studies, 2000), 114–15.

33. See United Nations, *Letter Dated 97/09/08 from the Permanent Representative of Nigeria to the United Nations Addressed to the President of the Security Council*, S/1997/695, September 9, 1997, Annexes I and II.

34. UN Security Council Resolution 1132 (1997); UN Security Council Resolution 1156, S/RES/1156, March 16, 1998.

35. See *ECOWAS Peace Plan for Sierra Leone, 23 October 1997–22 April 1998*, www.sierra-leone.org/documents.html.

36. Author interview with Zainab Bangura, November 18, 2003.

37. Author interviews with UN official, September 2003, New York, and former U.S. government official, October 29, 2003, Providence, RI.

38. Author interview with Ambassador Bernard Miyet, former UN undersecretary-general for peacekeeping operations, September 2, 2003, Paris. France had been seeking Security Council authorization for a UN peacekeeping operation to replace the operation in the Central African Republic. The council authorized the mission, known as the United Nations Mission in the Central African Republic (MINURCA), in April 1998.

39. Author interview with UN official, September 2003, New York.

40. United Nations, *Fourth Report of the Secretary-General on the Situation in Sierra Leone*, S/1998/249, March 18, 1998, para. 21.

41. UN Security Council Resolution 1162, S/RES/1162, April 17, 1998, para. 5.

42. UN Security Council Resolution 1181, S/RES/1181, July 13, 1998, paras. 6–8.

43. UN Security Council, Presidential Statement, S/PRST/1998/5, February 26, 1998.

44. United Nations, *Third Progress Report of the Secretary-General on the UN Observer Mission in Sierra Leone [UNOMSIL]*, S/1998/1176, December 16, 1998, para. 70; and United Nations, *Special Report of the Secretary-General on UNOMSIL*, S/1999/20, January 7, 1999, para. 29.

45. United Nations, *Fifth SG Report on Sierra Leone*, S/1998/486, para. 28; and author interview with former U.S. government official, November 18, 2003, Washington, DC.

46. Berman and Sams, *Peacekeeping in Africa*, 125–26, 327.

47. United Nations, *Fifth SG Report on Sierra Leone*, S/1998/486/Add.1, July 1, 1998. All UN budget figures in this chapter are "gross," which refers to spending before income from the UN staff assessment—a tax equalization procedure—is taken into account. Rather than engage the intricacies of the staff assessment, we have reported the higher, gross spending numbers.

48. United Nations, *Seventh Report of the Secretary-General on UNOMSIL*, S/1999/836/Add.1, August 11, 1999, paras. 1–2.

49. Author telephone interview with Michael Grunberg, commercial adviser, Sandline International, November 22, 2003. See also Tim Spicer, *An Unorthodox Soldier: Peace and War and the Sandline Affair* (Edinburgh and London: Mainstream, 1999), 195–98.

50. The British parliament undertook a lengthy and expansive investigation into the affair, led by Sir Thomas Legg. The findings, known as the Legg report, are available at www.parliament.the-stationery-office.co.uk/pa/cm199899/cmselect/cmfaff/116/11602.htm (accessed October 26, 2003).

51. Adeshina, *Reversed Victory*, 22; and author interview with former U.S. government official, November 18, 2003.

52. United Nations, *Fourth SG Report on Sierra Leone*, S/1998/249, paras. 22–23; and United Nations, *Fifth SG Report on Sierra Leone*, S/1998/486, para. 18.

53. Festus B. Aboagye, *ECOMOG: A Sub-regional Experience in Conflict Resolution, Management and Peacekeeping in Liberia* (Accra, Ghana: Sedco, 1999), 246.

54. Adeshina, *Reversed Victory*, 22–23.

55. Berman and Sams, *Peacekeeping in Africa*, 121, 126.

56. United Nations, *Fifth SG Report on Sierra Leone*, S/1998/486, para. 18.

57. Shelpidi replaced Malu as ECOMOG force commander in January 1998. See Adebajo, *Building Peace in West Africa*, 96.

58. United Nations, *Fifth SG Report on Sierra Leone,* S/1998/486, paras. 69–77.

59. United Nations, *First Progress Report of the Secretary-General on UNOMSIL,* S/1998/750, August 12, 1998, paras. 17–18.

60. United Nations, *Second Progress Report of the Secretary-General on UNOMSIL,* S/1998/960, October 16, 1998, Annex. The ten member states were China, Egypt, India, Kenya, Kyrgyzstan, New Zealand, Pakistan, Russia, the United Kingdom, and Zambia.

61. United Nations, *First SG Progress Report on UNOMSIL,* S/1998/750, para. 20.

62. United Nations, *Sixth Report of the Secretary-General on UNOMSIL,* S/1999/645, June 4, 1999, Annex.

63. United Nations, *Eighth Report of the Secretary-General on UNOMSIL,* S/1999/1003, September 28, 1999, Annex. The ten countries that contributed observers initially were joined by ten others: Bangladesh, Bolivia, France, the Gambia, Jordan, Malaysia, Nepal, Norway, Slovakia, and Tanzania.

64. Adeshina, *Reversed Victory,* 14–17, 22.

65. The ECOMOG force commander at this time, with overall responsibility for ECOWAS peace operations in both Liberia and Sierra Leone, was a fellow Nigerian, Major General Victor Malu.

66. United Nations, *Fifth SG Report on Sierra Leone,* S/1998/486, 3.

67. Author interviews with former U.S. and Sierra Leone government officials, September 2003, New York, and October 29, 2003, Providence, RI.

68. The Nigerian excesses and abuses during this operation were captured in Sorious Samura's 2000 film, *Cry Freetown* (www.cryfreetown.org), and have been documented by Human Rights Watch, "Getting Away with Murder, Mutilation, Rape: New Testimony from Sierra Leone," July 1999, www.hrw.org/reports/1999/sierra/.

69. United Nations, *Sixth SG Report on UNOMSIL,* S/1999/645, paras. 18–19.

70. Berman and Sams, *Peacekeeping in Africa,* 119–20.

71. Perhaps because Nigerian troops mistakenly trusted their SLA "allies" and because of a possible reluctance to become further enmeshed in internal Sierra Leone politics, Shelpidi did not take full advantage of the CDF's skills and expertise. See Hirsch, *Sierra Leone: Diamonds and the Struggle for Democracy,* 74.

72. Author interview with U.S. government official, September 2003, Philadelphia.

73. Many Nigerian officials viewed Shelpidi as more than simply ineffective. Indeed, there was discussion at very high levels in the Nigerian military of court-martialing him for gross negligence. Author interview with former U.S. government official, October 23, 2003, Providence, RI. Shelpidi was replaced in March 1999 by Major General Felix Mujakperuo, who was in turn replaced by Major General Gabriel Kpamber in July 1999.

74. UN Security Council, Presidential Statements (S/PRST/1997/52, November 17, 1997; S/PRST1998/103, February 5, 1998; S/PRST/1998/13, May 20, 1998; S/PRST/1999/1, January 7, 1999; and S/PRST/1999/13, May 15, 1999).

75. David Cortright, George A. Lopez, and Richard W. Conroy, "Sierra Leone: The Failure of Regional and International Sanctions," in *The Sanctions Decade: Assessing UN Strategies in the 1990s,* ed. David Cortright et al. (Boulder, CO: Lynne Rienner, 2000), 172–74.

76. United Nations, *Fifth SG Report on Sierra Leone,* S/1998/486, especially paras. 55, 56, and 60; and United Nations, *First SG Progress Report on UNOMSIL,* S/1998/750.

77. For example, some 5,000 CDF troops were expected to disarm at Lungi and other sites in Magburaka and Gerihun, but the CDF refused to participate in the program. Disarmament of SLA soldiers was deferred because many had joined up with ECOMOG. See United Nations, *Second SG Progress Report on UNOMSIL,* S/1998/960, para. 17; and United Nations, *Third SG Progress Report on UNOMSIL,* S/1998/1176, para. 31.

78. Mark Malan et al., *Sierra Leone: Building the Road to Recovery,* ISS Monograph Series, no. 80 (Pretoria: Institute for Security Studies, 2003), 33–34.

79. Cortright, Lopez, and Conroy, "Sierra Leone," in *The Sanctions Decade,* ed. David Cortright et al., 167, 172. In 1997, when the embargoes were instituted, diamonds—more easily smuggled than most mineral resources—were not yet a focus of international interest as a factor in the conflict.

80. At different times during the DDR program these "reinsertion allowances" were known by other names, such as transition allowances, transitional safety allowances, and reinsertion packages. In some instances, these differed in terms of not only their labels but also their substance. A reinsertion allowance, for instance, included money, whereas a reinsertion package included money and, in some cases, tool kits or other basic provisions such as shelter materials or seeds.

81. Ibrahim Abdullah and Patrick Muana, "The Revolutionary United Front of Sierra Leone," in *African Guerrillas,* ed. Christopher S. Clapham (Bloomington, IN: Indiana University Press, 1998), 172.

82. For a comprehensive treatment of this subject, see Angela McIntyre, Emmanuel Kwesi Aning, and Prosper Nii Nortey Addo, "Politics, War, and Youth Culture in Sierra Leone: An Alternative Interpretation," *African Security Review* 11, no. 3 (2002): 7–15.

83. Toby Porter, *The Interaction between Political and Humanitarian Action in Sierra Leone, 1995–2002* (Geneva: Centre for Humanitarian Dialogue, 2003); and Marc Sommers, *The Dynamics of Coordination,* Occasional Paper no. 40 (Providence, RI: Watson Institute for International Studies, 2000).

84. Sankoh was imprisoned in Nigeria until late July 1998, when he was returned to Sierra Leone. He stood trial on October 29, 1998, on charges of treason and attempted overthrow of the government.

85. Author interview with former Sierra Leone government official, New York, September 24, 2003.

86. *Agreement on Ceasefire in Sierra Leone,* May 18, 1999, www.sierra-leone.org/ceasefire051899.html; and *Peace Agreement between the Government of Sierra Leone and the Revolutionary United Front of Sierra Leone* (Lomé Agreement), July 17, 1999, www.sierra-leone.org/lomeaccord.html.

87. Contrary to some claims, Sankoh was not a ranking government minister. See Abiodun Alao and Comfort Ero, "Cut Short for Taking the Short Cut: The Lomé Peace Agreement in Sierra Leone," *Civil Wars* 4, no. 3 (Autumn 2001): 124. Sankoh's and Koroma's powers were constrained in the new government. This may have contributed to Sankoh's decision to abandon the Lomé provisions in the spring of 2000. Author interview with former Sierra Leone government official, September 24, 2003, New York.

88. The United Nations lodged its official reservation with this provision of Lomé at the final signing of the agreement. See United Nations, *Seventh SG Report on UNOMSIL,* S/1999/836, July 30, 1999, para. 55. See also United Nations, *Report of the Secretary-General on the Establishment of a Special Court for Sierra Leone,* S/2000/915, October 4, 2000, para. 22.

89. UN Security Council Resolution 1260, S/RES/1260, August 20, 1999; UN Security Council Resolution 1270, S/RES/1270, October 22, 1999; UN Security Council Resolution 1289, S/RES/1289, February 7, 2000; and United Nations, *Eighth SG Report on UNOMSIL,* S/1999/1003, para. 37.

90. Hirsch, *Sierra Leone: Diamonds and the Struggle for Democracy,* 81.

91. United Nations, *Identical Letters Dated 2000/11/13 from the Permanent Representative of Mali to the United Nations Addressed to the Secretary-General and the President of the Security Council,* S/2000/1091, November 14, 2000, Annex: *Agreement on Cease-Fire and Cessation of Hostilities between the*

Government of Sierra Leone and the Revolutionary United Front of Sierra Leone (Abuja Cease-Fire Agreement), signed in Abuja, November 10, 2000. See also United Nations, *Eighth Report of the Secretary-General on the UN Mission in Sierra Leone* (hereafter cited as UNAMSIL), S/2000/1199, December 15, 2000.

92. Guinea's improving military fortunes against the RUF and Liberian forces led Conakry to withdraw its support for a regional peacekeeping force to be deployed along its border. See James Milner, "The Militarization and Demilitarization of Refugee Camps in Guinea," in *Armed and Aimless: Armed Groups, Guns, and Human Security in the ECOWAS Region,* ed. Nicolas Florquin and Eric G. Berman (Geneva: Small Arms Survey, 2005), 161, 163.

93. United Nations, *Tenth Report of the Secretary-General on UNAMSIL,* S/2001/627, June 25, 2001, paras. 2–13.

94. United Nations, *Eleventh Report of the Secretary-General on UNAMSIL,* S/2001/857, September 7, 2001, paras. 4–5.

95. Sesay was, however, subsequently indicted for war crimes by the Special Court for Sierra Leone (see table 3.5).

96. UN Security Council Resolution 1306, S/RES/1306, July 5, 2000. This regime was subsequently integrated into the Kimberley Process Certification Scheme to stop the trade in illicit diamonds, which was endorsed by Resolution 1385, S/RES/1385, December 19, 2001.

97. UN Security Council Resolution 1343, S/RES/1343, March 7, 2001, para. 2. See also United Nations, *Ninth Report of the Secretary-General on UNAMSIL,* S/2001/228, March 14, 2001, para. 27.

98. Author interview with former U.S. government official, October 29, 2003, Providence, RI.

99. Author interview with former U.S. government official, November 18, 2003, Washington, DC.

100. For critical accounts of U.S. policy and the Lomé Agreement, see Ryan Lizza, "Where Angels Fear to Tread," *New Republic,* July 24, 2000, 22–27; and Alao and Ero, "Cut Short for Taking the Short Cut," 117–34.

101. Eric G. Berman, "French, UK, and US Policies to Support Peacekeeping in Africa: Current Status and Future Prospects," NUPI Working Paper no. 622 (Oslo: Norwegian Institute of International Affairs, February 2002), 27–30.

102. Author interview with UK defense official, October 2003, London. Richard Connaughton notes these concerns and adds that criticism of the government's response to Mozambican floods in February of that year was also a contributing factor to the UK decision. See Connaughton, "The Mechanics and

Nature of British Interventions into Sierra Leone (2000) and Afghanistan (2001–2002)," *Civil Wars* 5, no. 2 (Summer 2002): 83.

103. United Nations, *Eighth SG Report on UNOMSIL,* S/1999/1003.

104. United Nations, *Letter Dated 99/05/19 from the Permanent Representative of Togo to the United Nations Addressed to the President of the Security Council,* S/1999/585, May 20, 1999, Annex: transmits the agreement on cease-fire in Sierra Leone, signed in Lomé, May 18, 1999; and UN Security Council Resolution 1270 (1999), especially paras. 8(a–i).

105. UN Security Council Resolution 1289 (2000).

106. UN Security Council Resolution 1299, S/RES/1299, May 19, 2000.

107. UN Security Council Resolution 1313, S/RES/1313, August 4, 2000.

108. United Nations, *Sixth Report of the Secretary-General on UNAMSIL,* S/2000/832, August 24, 2000, paras. 3–4, 40–41; and UN Security Council Resolution 1315, S/RES/1315, August 14, 2000.

109. UNAMSIL's revised concept of operations is laid out in the *Ninth SG Report,* S/2001/228, paras. 57–67. The RUF eventually returned most of the vehicles previously seized from UNAMSIL and ECOMOG, as demanded by the Security Council, but they had been vandalized and were inoperable. See ibid., para. 6.

110. United Nations, *Fifteenth Report of the Secretary-General on UNAMSIL,* S/2002/987, September 5, 2002, paras. 37–43.

111. UN Security Council Resolution 1370, S/RES/1370, September 18, 2001; UN Security Council Resolution 1436, S/RES/1436, September 24, 2002; United Nations, *Fifteenth SG Report on UNAMSIL,* S/2002/987, paras. 26–32; and United Nations, *Seventeenth Report of the Secretary-General on UNAMSIL,* S/2003/321, March 17, 2003, paras. 10–14.

112. United Nations, *Fifteenth SG Report on UNAMSIL,* S/2002/987; and United Nations, *Twenty-fifth Report of the Secretary-General on UNAMSIL,* S/2005/273, April 26, 2005. With three contiguous peacekeeping missions deployed in Sierra Leone, Liberia, and Côte d'Ivoire, the United Nations has placed increasing emphasis on cross-mission support and coordination. See also United Nations, *Report of the Secretary-General on Inter-Mission Cooperation and Possible Cross-Border Operations . . . ,* S/2005/135, March 2, 2005.

113. United Nations, *Financial Performance Report of UNAMSIL for the Period from 1 July 1999 to 30 June 2000, Report of the Secretary-General,* A/55/853, March 26, 2001, 1; United Nations, *Financial Performance Report for the Period from 1 July 2000 to 30 June 2001 . . . , Report of the Advisory Committee on Administrative and Budgetary Questions,* A/56/887/Add.3,

April 3, 2002, 2; and United Nations, *Financial Performance Report for the Period from 1 July 2001 to 30 June 2002 . . . , Report of the Advisory Committee on Administrative and Budgetary Questions,* A/57/772/Add.3, May 7, 2003, 1.

114. United Nations, *Performance Report on the Budget of UNAMSIL for the Period from 1 July 2002 to 30 June 2003,* A/58/660, December 22, 2003, 2; and United Nations, *Proposed Budget for the Period from 1 July 2005 to 30 June 2006 of UNAMSIL and Financial Performance Report for the Period from 1 July 2003 to 30 June 2004, Report of the Advisory Committee on Administrative and Budgetary Questions,* A/59/736/Add.9, April 28, 2005, 1.

115. United Nations, *First Report of the Secretary-General on UNAMSIL,* S/1999/1223, December 6, 1999, para. 30; United Nations, *Second Report of the Secretary-General on UNAMSIL,* S/2000/13, January 11, 2000, paras. 7 and 17, and Annex.

116. United Nations, *Eighth SG Report on UNOMSIL,* S/1999/1003, paras. 36–38.

117. United Nations, *Report of the Secretary-General on the United Nations Interim Force in Lebanon (for the Period from 17 January to 17 July 2000),* S/2000/718, July 20, 2000.

118. For a summary of the "gratis military personnel" issue, see William J. Durch et al., *The Brahimi Report and the Future of Peace Operations* (Washington, DC: Henry L. Stimson Center, 2003), 3.

119. The UN supply system normally provides food, water, laundry, and POL ("petrol, oil, and lubricants") and can also provide office, electrical, and tentage or other accommodation, as negotiated in its memorandum of understanding with the troop contributor. There are set reimbursement rates for situations in which the United Nations is unable to provide some or all of these items. For details on self-sustainment standards and options, see UN DPKO, *Manual on Policies and Procedures Concerning Reimbursement and Control of Contingent-Owned Equipment of Troop-Contributors Participating in Peacekeeping Missions,* 2002 ed., web.schq.mi.th/~matpmunny/UN%20document/COE/COE%202002%20Chapters%201-10.pdf.

120. DPKO looked for third states that might function as suppliers to some of the contingents, brought other essential materiel from the United Nations' logistics base at Brindisi, Italy, and developed a program of predeployment visits to determine specific deficiencies needing remedy before troops reached the field. From winter 2002 onward, joint UNAMSIL–UN Secretariat evaluation teams assessed the readiness status of all new contingents, identified deficiencies prior to troop deployment in the field, and tried to match troop-contributing countries with donor countries to remedy those deficiencies. See United Nations, *Fifth Report of the Secretary-General on UNAMSIL,* S/2000/751, July 31, 2000, paras. 57–58; United Nations, *Tenth SG Report on UNAMSIL,* S/2001/627, para. 68; United Nations, *Eleventh SG Report on UNAMSIL,* S/2001/857, para. 20; United Nations, *Twelfth Report of the Secretary-General on UNAMSIL,* S/2001/1195, December 13, 2001, para. 78; UN General Assembly, *Practical Aspects of Wet-Lease, Dry-Lease and Self-Sustainment Arrangements, Report of the Secretary-General,* A/57/397, September 11, 2002; and UN DPKO Best Practices Unit, *Lessons Learned from United Nations Peacekeeping Experiences in Sierra Leone* (New York: United Nations, August 2003), 45–48, www.un.org/Depts/dpko/lessons/.

121. United Nations, *Fifth SG Report on UNAMSIL,* S/2000/751, paras. 53–54.

122. Ibid.; United Nations, *Fourth Report of the Secretary-General on UNAMSIL,* S/2000/455, May 19, 2000, Annex; and *Eighth Report of the Secretary General on UNAMSIL,* S/2000/1199, December 15, 2000, 12.

123. Chris McGreal and Ewen MacAskill, "UN to Bolster Peacekeeping Force by 7,000," *Guardian,* September 13, 2000, www.guardian.co.uk/international/story/0,,367711,00.html.

124. Indeed, the previously cited study by the UN DPKO Best Practices Unit, *Lessons Learned from . . . Sierra Leone,* essentially avoids this topic.

125. United Nations, *Seventh Report of the Secretary-General on UNAMSIL,* S/2000/1055, October 31, 2000, paras. 38–39.

126. United Nations, *Eighth SG Report on UNAMSIL,* S/2000/1199, para. 23.

127. United Nations, *Fifth SG Report on UNAMSIL,* S/2000/751, paras. 57–58; and United Nations, *Fourth SG Report on UNAMSIL,* S/2000/455, para. 82.

128. United Nations, *Fifth SG Report on UNAMSIL,* S/2000/751, paras. 57–58.

129. New Delhi informed the secretary-general in September, and Amman informed him in October. See United Nations, *Seventh SG Report on UNAMSIL,* S/2000/1055, para. 48. Level III medical facilities provide the highest level of medical care available within a mission area, including surgery, anesthesiology, radiology, laboratory medicine, and care for UN mission civilian staff as well as blood and blood products. Level II medical facilities provide sector-level medical coverage for military personnel, including peripheral surgical care and physician support as well as holding and stabilization for seriously ill or injured troops. Level I medical facilities provide medical coverage to all company deployments in the form of specially trained medical personnel for emergency situations involving triage, stabilization, and resuscitation. See V. Joshi, "UN Mission in Sierra Leone: Medical Deployment and Experiences," *Indian Journal of Aerospace Medicine* 47, no. 1 (2003): 54.

130. United Nations, *Tenth SG Report on UNAMSIL*, S/2001/627, Annex; and United Nations, *Twelfth SG Report on UNAMSIL*, S/2001/1195, Annex.

131. United Nations, *Fourteenth Report of the Secretary-General on UNAMSIL*, S/2002/679, June 19, 2002, para. 16.

132. United Nations, *Eighteenth Report of the Secretary-General on UNAMSIL*, S/2003/663, June 23, 2003, paras. 9–10.

133. United Nations, *Sixteenth Report of the Secretary-General on UNAMSIL*, S/2002/1417, December 24, 2002, para. 2. Security in these "low risk" areas was turned over to the SLA/RSLAF and SLP.

134. For details, see United Nations, *Seventeenth SG Report on UNAMSIL*, S/2003/321, paras. 16–22; and United Nations, *Eighteenth SG Report on UNAMSIL*, S/2003/663, paras. 28–31.

135. United Nations, *Twenty-second Report of the Secretary-General on UNAMSIL*, S/2004/536, July 6, 2004, paras. 14–15; and United Nations, *Twenty-fourth Report of the Secretary-General on UNAMSIL*, S/2004/965, December 10, 2004, para. 8.

136. United Nations, *Fifteenth SG Report on UNAMSIL*, S/2002/987, paras. 26–36, describes the initial plans for the withdrawal. The revised plans are detailed in United Nations, *Twentieth Report of the Secretary-General on UNAMSIL*, S/2003/1201, December 23, 2003, paras. 2–4; and United Nations, *Twenty-first Report of the Secretary-General on UNAMSIL*, S/2004/228, March 19, 2004, paras. 72–91. See also UN Security Council Resolution 1537, S/RES/1537, March 30, 2004.

137. United Nations, *Twenty-fifth SG Report on UNAMSIL*, S/2005/273, 2 and Annex.

138. Interview conducted by William Durch at UNAMSIL headquarters, Freetown, July 18, 2005.

139. United Nations, *First SG Report on UNAMSIL*, S/1999/1223, para. 30.

140. The authorized level of military observers for UNAMSIL remained constant at 260. This level was more or less sustained from 1999 to 2002 but has decreased along with military and civilian staff reductions as part of the overall mission drawdown and withdrawal.

141. United Nations, *Second Report of the Secretary-General on UNAMSIL,* S/2000/13, January 11, 2000, para. 31.

142. Ibid.; United Nations, *Third Report of the Secretary-General on UNAMSIL,* S/2000/186, March 7, 2000; and United Nations, *Fourth SG Report on UNAMSIL,* S/2000/455.

143. United Nations, *Fourth SG Report on UNAMSIL,* S/2000/455, paras. 56–71.

144. Author written correspondence with former UNAMSIL military official, November 5, 2003.

145. For additional details on the hostage rescue and Operation Khukri, see United Nations, *Fifth SG Report on UNAMSIL,* S/2000/751, paras. 26–27; and the Indian Armed Forces Web site: indianarmy.nic.in/arunpk.htm.

146. This discussion of the British interventions draws from Richard M. Connaughton, "Organizing British Joint Rapid Reaction Forces," *Joint Force Quarterly* 26 (Autumn 2000): 92–93; and "Operation 'Barass,'" *Small Wars and Insurgencies* 12, no. 2 (Summer 2001): 110–19. Author interviews with UK defense officials, October 2003, London, and by telephone, November 5, 2003.

147. United Nations, *Tenth SG Report on UNAMSIL,* S/2001/627, paras. 19–20.

148. United Nations, *Twelfth SG Report on UNAMSIL,* S/2001/1195, paras. 2, 11–13.

149. United Nations, *Fourth SG Report on UNAMSIL,* S/2000/455, para. 100.

150. United Nations, *Twelfth SG Report on UNAMSIL,* S/2001/1195, para. 53; United Nations, *Thirteenth Report of the Secretary-General on UNAMSIL,* S/2002/267, March 14, 2002, para. 10; and United Nations, *Fourteenth SG Report on UNAMSIL,* S/2002/679, paras. 8–9.

151. United Nations, *Fourteenth SG Report on UNAMSIL,* S/2002/679, paras. 8–9.

152. See UNDP, *Human Development Report* (New York: Oxford University Press, 2004).

153. Sheila Patricka Dallas, "Radio UNAMSIL: A Weapon for Peace," *MediaChannel Reports,* July 6, 2000, www.mediachannel.org/originals/unradio.shtml. Dallas was Radio UNAMSIL's first general manager.

154. United Nations, *Tenth SG Report on UNAMSIL,* S/2001/627, para. 51; and United Nations, *Thirteenth SG Report on UNAMSIL,* S/2002/267, para. 36. See also Radio Netherlands Media Network, "Peace Radio: Sierra Leone," www2.rnw.nl/rnw/en/features/media/dossiers/sierra-leone-p.html.

155. United Nations, *Fourteenth SG Report on UNAMSIL,* S/2002/679, para. 9.

156. Adebajo, *Building Peace in West Africa,* 102.

157. United Nations, *Fourth SG Report on UNAMSIL,* S/2000/455, para. 34.

158. Dyan Mazurana and Khristopher Carlson, *From Combat to Community: Women and Girls of Sierra Leone* (Washington, DC, and Cambridge, MA: Women Waging Peace Policy Commission, 2003).

159. UN Security Council, *Report of the Security Council Mission to Sierra Leone,* S/2000/992, October 16, 2000, para. 54(e).

160. United Nations, *Seventh SG Report on UNAMSIL,* S/2000/1055, para. 23. Ex-combatants were to be given a financial allowance upon registering with a reintegration program. Initially these were called transitional safety allowances or reinsertion benefits and totaled approximately $150. They were replaced in mid-2001 by a transport allowance of approximately $15, which was designed to encourage ex-combatants to return to their home communities.

161. United Nations, *Eighth SG Report on UNAMSIL,* S/2000/1199, paras. 38–41.

162. United Nations, *Ninth SG Report on UNAMSIL,* S/2001/228, especially para. 77.

163. United Nations, *Tenth SG Report on UNAMSIL,* S/2001/627, para. 27.

164. RUF leader Issa Sesay interrupted the DDR program briefly in November 2001 to protest the National Election Commission's decision to adopt the district block voting system in the scheduled May 2002 elections. See United Nations, *Twelfth SG Report on UNAMSIL,* S/2001/1195, paras. 16, 33–34.

165. In Koidu, for example, CDF forces frequently crossed into Sierra Leone from Guinea and clashed with RUF units awaiting disarmament nearby. UNAMSIL responded by creating "hot spot DDR," which involved the physical transfer by UNAMSIL of combatants from a hostile disarmament district to other, less hostile locations, where disarmament would be effectively and rapidly carried out (in this case, moving the RUF from Koidu to Daru to be disarmed).

166. Author interview with former UNAMSIL official, New York, September 2003. For some discussion of the trade-offs involved in balancing combatant eligibility, individual versus group disarmament, and the need to recover as many weapons as possible, see UN DPKO Best Practices Unit, *Lessons Learned from . . . Sierra Leone,* 24–25.

167. Plans were developed by the governments of Sierra Leone and Liberia, in conjunction with UNAMSIL and the UN Mission in Liberia, to disarm and demobilize these individuals, who are estimated to number between 500 and 2,000, in Liberia rather than in Sierra Leone. These ex-combatants would then be eligible to participate in reintegration programs either in Liberia or in Sierra Leone. See United Nations, *Twenty-second Report of the Secretary-General on UNAMSIL,* S/2004/536, July 6, 2004, paras. 27–28.

168. United Nations, *Sixteenth SG Report on UNAMSIL,* S/2002/1417, paras. 19–21. There is disagreement regarding whether the CDF poses a credible threat to the government. See Florquin and Berman, eds., *Armed and Aimless,* especially 368–79.

169. The UNAMSIL DDR Coordination Section estimated that as many as 11,000 ex-combatants were unaccounted for. See *The DDR Process in Sierra Leone: Lessons Learned* (Freetown, Sierra Leone: DDR Coordination Section, UNAMSIL, August 2003), 7.

170. United Nations, *SG Report on Establishment of Special Court,* S/2000/915; United Nations, *Fourth SG Report on UNAMSIL,* S/2000/455; and Lansana Fofana, "Children—Sierra Leone: Militia Admits Recruiting Child Soldiers," *Inter-Press Service,* June 29, 1998, www.oneworld.org/ips2/jul98/13_41_045.html.

171. UNICEF, "Child Soldier Projects: Assistance to Child Soldiers in Sierra Leone," UNICEF, "Peace Process Falters for Child Soldiers of Sierra Leone" (press release, July 23, 2003), www.unicef.org/media/media_12200.html.

172. See *Witness to Truth: Report of the Sierra Leone Truth and Reconciliation Commission,* vols. 1–3, available at www.trcsierraleone.org/pdf/start/html; and the children's version, *Truth and Reconciliation Commission Report for the Children of Sierra Leone,* available online at www.unicef.org/infobycountry/files/TRCCF9SeptFINAL.pdf. The World Bank estimated that 6,845 children were disarmed, demobilized, and "discharged" over the course of the DDR program. See World Bank, "The World Bank–Administered Multi-Donor Trust Fund (TF022604) for the Sierra Leone Disarmament, Demobilization and Reintegration Program," Progress Report no. 13, June 20, 2003, 3.

173. United Nations, "UN Mission in Sierra Leone Sets Up Skills Training for Girl Victims of War" (press release, March 12, 2001). See also United Nations, *Twenty-second SG Report on UNAMSIL,* S/2004/536, para. 32.

174. UN DPKO Best Practices Unit, *Lessons Learned from . . . Sierra Leone,* 29.

175. Human Rights Watch, "Child Soldier Use 2003," January 16, 2004, www.hrw.org/reports/2004/childsoldiers0104/15.htm.

176. *Statute of the Special Court for Sierra Leone*, Art. 7; Special Court for Sierra Leone, "Special Court Prosecutor Says He Will Not Prosecute Children" (press release, November 2, 2002), www.sc-sl.org/press-2002.html.

177. William Schabas, "The Relationship between Truth Commissions and the International Courts: The Case of Sierra Leone," *Human Rights Quarterly* 25 (2003): 1035–66.

178. United Nations, *Twentieth SG Report on UNAMSIL*, S/2003/1201, para. 27; United Nations, *Twenty-first SG Report on UNAMSIL*, S/2004/228, para. 16; and United Nations, *Twenty-second SG Report on UNAMSIL*, S/2004/536, para. 26.

179. Poor reintegration opportunities, especially during the initial implementation efforts, were noted repeatedly as a weakness of this aspect of the DDR program. See, for example, United Nations, *Twelfth SG Report on UNAMSIL*, S/2001/1195, para. 89.

180. See Francis Kai-Kai, "NCDDR Executive Secretariat Report," March 2, 2004 (published by the National Committee for Disarmament, Demobilization, and Reintegration [NCDDR], Freetown); Bengt Ljunggren and Desmond Molloy, "Some Lessons in DDR: The Sierra Leone Experience," internal UN report, June 2004; P. C. Mohan, "Sierra Leone: Community Reintegration and Rehabilitation," *Findings: Good Practice Infobrief*, Africa Region, no. 112, May 2005; UN DPKO Best Practices Unit, *Lessons Learned from . . . Sierra Leone*, especially 26–28; and Jeremy Ginifer with Kaye Oliver, *Evaluation of the Conflict Prevention Tools: Sierra Leone*, Department for International Development [DfID] Evaluation Report EV 647 (London: DfID, March 2004), especially 15–16.

181. UN DPKO Best Practices Unit, *Lessons Learned from . . . Sierra Leone*, 27–28; United Nations, *Tenth SG Report on UNAMSIL*, S/2001/627, para. 34; and United Nations, *Eleventh SG Report on UNAMSIL*, S/2001/857, para. 24. Some $33 million was reportedly needed to fill this gap, which resulted in the cessation of the program that distributed reinsertion packages to ex-combatants. In March 2003, the shortfall was approximately $6 million; in June 2003, it had been reduced to approximately $3 million. See United Nations, *Seventeenth SG Report on UNAMSIL*, S/2003/321, para. 31; and United Nations, *Eighteenth SG Report on UNAMSIL*, S/2003/663, para. 18.

182. The Human Development Index measures country achievements in terms of life expectancy, educational attainment, and adjusted real income.

UNDP, *Human Development Report* (New York: Oxford University Press, 1999–2004). The 2005 *Human Development Report* ranked Niger last among 177 countries; Sierra Leone was ranked 176.

183. CIA, *CIA World Factbook,* www.cia.gov/cia/publications/factbook/geos/sl.html.

184. *Truth and Reconciliation Commission Act,* February 22, 2000, www.sierra-leone.org/trcact2000.html. See also Art. XXVI of the Lomé Agreement, www.sierra-leone.org/lomeaccord.html; United Nations, *Twenty-first SG Report on UNAMSIL,* S/2001/228, paras. 52–54; and United Nations, *Tenth SG Report on UNAMSIL,* S/2001/627, paras. 57–59, which describe the planning process.

185. See *Truth and Reconciliation Commission Act,* paras. 8(1)(a)–(h).

186. Priscilla Hayner, *The Sierra Leone Truth and Reconciliation Commission: Reviewing Its First Year* (New York: International Center for Transitional Justice, 2004).

187. "Sierra Leone: Civil Society Criticises a 'Vague' Government Plan for Postwar Reform," *UN Integrated Regional Information Networks (IRIN),* July 13, 2005, www.irinnews.org/print.asp?ReportID=48098.

188. Sierra Leone Truth and Reconciliation Commission, *Witness to Truth,* vol. 2, chap. 3, 121; available online at www.trcsierraleone.org/pdf/start/html.

189. "Sierra Leone," *IRIN.*

190. Post-conflict Reintegration Initiative for Development and Empowerment (PRIDE), *Ex-Combatant Views of the Truth and Reconciliation Commission and the Special Court in Sierra Leone,* research report in partnership with the International Center for Transitional Justice (Freetown, Sierra Leone: PRIDE, September 12, 2002).

191. The paramount chiefdom system represents local-level governance in Sierra Leone. Paramount chiefs are the principal administrators of chiefdoms, which are constituted by "sections"—themselves constituted by towns and villages.

192. United Nations, *Tenth SG Report on UNAMSIL,* S/2001/627, paras. 57–60, and S/2001/857, para. 44; and Crisis Group, "Sierra Leone's Truth and Reconciliation Commission: A Fresh Start?" Africa Briefing no. 12, December 20, 2002, www.crisisgroup.org/home/index.cfm?id=1391&l=1.

193. UN Security Council Resolution 1315 (2000); and United Nations, *Eleventh SG Report on UNAMSIL,* S/2001/857, para. 46. The secretary-general dispatched a planning mission for the Special Court for Sierra Leone

in January 2002. See United Nations, *Twelfth SG Report on UNAMSIL*, S/2001/1195, para. 71. The government subsequently ratified legislation in March 2002. See *Special Court Agreement, 2002 (Ratification Act)*, March 19, 2002, www.sierra-leone.org/specialcourtagreement.html.

194. *Statute of the Special Court for Sierra Leone*, Art. 6(1) and Arts. 9(1), 9(2), and 9(3), www.sierra-leone.org/specialcourtstatute.html. UN peacekeepers and ECOMOG troops are immune from prosecution by the Special Court; the troop-contributing state is responsible for taking legal action against alleged wrongdoing by its peacekeepers. See Art. 1(2).

195. United Nations, *SG Report on Establishment of Special Court*, S/2000/915, paras. 22 and 24. Article 10 of the *Statute of the Special Court for Sierra Leone* reads, "An amnesty granted to any person falling within the jurisdiction of the Special Court in respect of the crimes referred to in . . . the present Statute shall not be a bar to prosecution."

196. See Special Court for Sierra Leone, "New Rules of Procedure and Evidence Adopted" (press release, July 21, 2003), www.sc-sl.org/press-2003. html; *Rules of Procedure and Evidence of the Special Court for Sierra Leone* (especially Rules 8, 34, 45), www.sc-sl.org; and *Second Annual Report of the President of the Special Court for Sierra Leone for the Period 1 January 2005–17 January 2005* (Freetown: Special Court for Sierra Leone, 2005).

197. The Special Court can seek Chapter VII support from the Security Council, and in 2003 the president of the court, Geoffrey Robertson, formally requested such support. See Special Court for Sierra Leone, "No Country Found to Take Sankoh for Medical Treatment" (press release, June 11, 2003), www.sc-sl.org/press-2003.html.

198. United Nations, *SG Report on Establishment of Special Court*, S/2000/915, Annex, para. 10.

199. The indictments were signed by the prosecutor and approved by the judge on March 3 and 7, 2003, respectively. Eight indictments constituted the initial group; four additional indictments followed. The indictment of Charles Taylor was not disclosed until June 4, 2003.

200. United Nations, *Special Court for Sierra Leone: Completion Strategy*, A/59/816-S/2005/350, May 27, 2005, Annex, para. 12.

201. United Nations, *SG Report on Establishment of Special Court*, S/2000/915, paras. 66–67, and Annex, Art. 16.

202. United Nations, *Eighth SG Report on UNAMSIL*, S/2000/1199; United Nations, *Sixteenth SG Report on UNAMSIL*, S/2002/1417, para. 26; and United Nations, *Eighteenth SG Report on UNAMSIL*, S/2003/663, para. 6.

203. United Nations, *Fourteenth SG Report on UNAMSIL,* S/2002/679, para. 26; and United Nations, *Seventeenth SG Report on UNAMSIL,* S/2003/321, paras. 48–51.

204. Only 13 percent (1,000 out of 8,000) of the statements taken by the TRC were directly from combatants/perpetrators. See Hayner, *Sierra Leone Truth and Reconciliation Commission,* 4.

205. For example, it was possible that the entire TRC report would be entered into evidence to stipulate that a war took place in Sierra Leone. Author written communication with staff member of the Special Court for Sierra Leone, March 19, 2004.

206. Norman, being held pending trial by the Special Court, requested permission to testify in person at a public hearing before the TRC. The court denied his request but agreed to allow him to submit written testimony to the TRC. See Special Court for Sierra Leone, "The Special Court Responds to TRC Statement" (press release, December 3, 2003), www.sc-sl.org/press-2003. html; and *Decision on Appeal by the Truth and Reconciliation Commission for Sierra Leone . . . and Chief Samuel Hinga Norman JP against the Decision of His Lordship, Mr. Justice Bankole Thompson Delivered on 30 October 2003 to Deny the TRC's Request to Hold a Public Hearing with Chief Samuel Hinga Norman JP,* SCSL-2003-8-PT, November 28, 2003.

207. See United Nations, *Letter Dated 12 July 2001 from the Secretary-General Addressed to the President of the Security Council,* S/2001/693, July 13, 2001. The Special Court was to commence its activities once the secretary-general had sufficient contributions in hand to finance the establishment of the court and twelve months of operations, plus pledges equal to twenty-four months of anticipated expenses. Contributions beyond the third year were to be sought by the secretary-general in coordination with the government of Sierra Leone and the UN High Commissioner for Human Rights.

208. See United Nations, *SG Report on Establishment of Special Court,* S/2000/915, para. 70.

209. United Nations, *Special Court for Sierra Leone,* A/59/816-S/2005/350, paras. 57–58; United Nations, *Request for a Subvention to the Special Court for Sierra Leone. Report of the Secretary-General,* A/59/534/Add.2, December 7, 2004, paras. 7–10 and Annex; and United Nations, *Programme Budget for the Biennium 2004–2005, Report of the Fifth Committee,* A/59/448/Add.4, June 10, 2005, 4. Snapshots of the two ad hoc tribunals' budgets can be found in United Nations, *Second Performance Report of the International Criminal Tribunal for Rwanda . . . [and the] International Criminal Tribunal for the Former Yugoslavia for the Biennium 2002–2003, Report of the*

Advisory Committee on Administrative and Budgetary Questions, A/58/605, November 19, 2003.

210. Alao and Ero, "Cut Short for Taking the Short Cut," 124.

211. Amnesty International, "Guinea and Sierra Leone: No Place of Refuge," AFR 05/006/2001, October 24, 2001, web.amnesty.org/library/Index/ENGAFR050062001?open&of=ENG-GIN.

212. United Nations, *Twenty-first SG Report on UNAMSIL,* S/2004/228, para. 26; United Nations, *Twenty-fourth SG Report on UNAMSIL,* S/2004/965, para. 20; and Stimson Center interviews, Freetown, Sierra Leone, July 2005.

213. Jean Krasno, *Public Opinion Survey of UNAMSIL's Work in Sierra Leone,* external study for the UN DPKO Best Practices Unit (New York: United Nations, July 2005), 10, 14, 16, 25–26, www.un.org/Depts/dpko/lessons/.

4

Democratic Republic of the Congo

Philip Roessler and John Prendergast

Introduction

The war in the Democratic Republic of the Congo has been Africa's deadliest conflict, contributing to the deaths of more than three million persons since its start in August 1998. It has embroiled as many as nine African countries at one time and devastated a large swath of central Africa. With local, national, and regional dimensions, it has resisted conventional conflict resolution mechanisms. Progress in one dimension merely inflamed violence in another. The withdrawal of foreign troops from 2002 onward gave rise to flare-ups of ethnic cleansing and communal violence in the country's eastern region, which undermined attempts at creating a new national government and army. In the center of this quagmire was the United Nations Organization Mission in the Democratic Republic of the Congo (MONUC).

MONUC originated in response to the Lusaka Cease-Fire Agreement, which was signed by the Kinshasa government and the warring regional states on July 10, 1999, and by the Congolese rebel groups several weeks later. The Lusaka signatories thrust upon the United Nations, which had little direct involvement in the peace talks, a burden that it was not prepared to accept: namely, full responsibility for implementing and enforcing the peace agreement. The signatories wanted the United Nations to monitor the disengagement of the regional states and to track down and forcibly disarm foreign armed groups, including tens of thousands of Rwandan combatants who fled into eastern Congo after the 1994 Rwandan genocide and were scattered throughout the region by the Rwandan army after 1996. In essence, the African states were asking the United Nations to address a regional crisis that the Security Council had failed to deal with twice before—first, when it withdrew UN peacekeepers at the start of the Rwandan genocide, and second, when it failed to act as the *génocidaires* regrouped and rearmed within UN refugee camps in eastern Congo.

During the Congo crisis of the early 1960s, both the Security Council and the General Assembly, driven by Cold War tensions, authorized UN peacekeepers to end the secession of Katanga province.[1] Some 3,000 peacekeeping troops were made available within four days of the initial Security Council authorization, and more than 10,000 were deployed within three weeks.[2] In the late 1990s, in contrast, the Security Council lacked strategic interest in the Congo. This translated into the authorization of a peacekeeping force with a far too modest observation mandate, inadequate resources, a halting deployment, and little diplomatic follow-up or leverage in support of implementation.

The 1960s operation was not perfect, however. It rapidly became entangled in Congolese national politics, whose various factions each had the backing of an opposing great power. The experience led the United Nations to treat the Congo with great caution. In the 1990s, the diffidence of the Secretariat and the Security Council was matched by the Congolese government's initial refusal to let UN forces deploy beyond the capital, and by UN members' reluctance to place their troops in harm's way. As a result, MONUC took three years just to reach its initial authorized capacity of 5,537 peacekeepers, and much longer to begin to fulfill its mandate to protect civilians ("within its capabilities") from the imminent threat of violence.

The Lusaka signatories themselves helped ensure that peace would be a long time coming. Blatantly violating the Lusaka Agreement and subsequent disengagement plans, the governments of Rwanda, Uganda, Zimbabwe, and the Congo calculated that the benefits of war—unlimited exploitation of the country's riches—outweighed the domestic and international consequences of flouting formal peace commitments. Looting the Congo's natural resource wealth with impunity, they developed private networks, protected by militia proxies, to ensure exploitation continued long after their official armed forces withdrew in 2002.

At the end of 2002, the Congo's government and the fractious rebel groups reached an agreement on a transitional government. This political breakthrough, coupled with the withdrawal of most of the foreign forces, contributed to a reduction of violence in most of the country—except in the east, where proxy militias still waged economic and ethnic warfare and political allegiances frequently shifted. The continued fighting threatened to undermine the nascent interim government and to incite Uganda and Rwanda to refortify their positions in the Congo. Faced with particularly gruesome ethnic violence in the northeastern district of Ituri in the spring of 2003, the Security Council agreed to take enforcement measures: requesting help from a third party (a French-led European Union force), appointing an energetic new head of mission for MONUC (former U.S. diplomat William Lacy Swing), and authorizing a robust UN task force with Chapter VII authority to take over when the EU force left.

The Ituri crisis finally forced the Security Council to concede that MONUC's mandate and capabilities, relatively static since February 2000, were wholly incommensurate with the changing conditions on the ground. MONUC needed to transition from passive observation to proactive peacekeeping to help the Congo's transitional government extend its authority throughout the country, fill the security vacuum created by the withdrawal of the foreign forces, and eradicate the violent private networks that remained. Achieving these goals would be instrumental to the ultimate disarmament and repatriation of Rwandan and other foreign combatants, and the restoration of regional stability.

In the spring of 2004, the eastern Congo again became the site of horrific violence, following a cycle of killings in and around Bukavu that were caused by power struggles between ex-rebel and government commanders within the new, ostensibly integrated, Congolese army. The UN secretary-general requested, and the Security Council approved, more troops and a tougher mandate. Aggressive new tactics by MONUC in 2005 weakened the militias responsible for the violence but increasingly made the UN force itself a target. Moreover, the operation's rapid expansion contributed to disciplinary failures and a breakdown in military–civil society relations, including a sexual abuse scandal in 2004 that had repercussions not only for MONUC but for all UN operations.

The core, unresolved problem for the mission in mid-2005, however, remained what to do with the 8,000 to 10,000 Rwandan Hutu rebels, many of whom had been in the Congo since the Rwandan genocide. Their continued presence in 2005 underscored the failure of the African region and the broader international community to sufficiently address the more than decade-long regional crisis. As long as those militia remained, preying on local populations and provoking cross-border conflict with Rwanda, the war—and the killing—would continue.

Origins of the Operation

The Democratic Republic of the Congo[3] is the third-largest country in Africa, with an area roughly equivalent to the United States east of the Mississippi (about 905,000 square miles; see figure 4.1). The Congo River, about 2,900 miles in length, serves as the country's major artery, originating in the southeastern interior and flowing to the northwest before bending toward the southwest and emptying into the Atlantic Ocean. The Congo River basin covers 90 percent of the country and feeds its 580,000 square miles of equatorial rain forest. The land contains lucrative reserves of diamonds, gold, copper, zinc, cobalt, iron ore, and columbo-tantalite (coltan). These minerals have been more of a curse than a blessing for the Congolese people, however, having led to centuries of exploitation by foreigners and by the country's own leaders.

The Congo's postcolonial history was dominated by the thirty-two-year rule of Mobutu Sese Seko, who seized power in 1965, ending a turbulent first five years of independence. Personalistic, authoritarian, and repressive, Mobutu relied heavily on military and economic aid from the United States during the Cold War to stay in power. In the

Figure 4.1. Map of the Democratic Republic of the Congo

Source: UN Cartographic Section

first decade or so of his rule, he emphasized the importance of Zairean nationalism over tribalism and restructured the state's federal arrangement to dampen ethnic violence and secessionist sentiments.[4] In his last fifteen years in office, however, especially after the end of the Cold War, he increasingly played different ethnic groups against each other and manipulated the post–Cold War democratization process to maintain political control.

By the 1990s Mobutu held on to power only tenuously. After decades of neglect and misrule, Zaire's economy and infrastructure were in shambles. The country had only 1,500 miles of asphalted roads, while the once extensive national railway system was now limited to Katanga province, from which minerals were exported to southern Africa.[5] Thirty years of corruption and illegal expropriation by the president and his cronies had sapped economic growth, and the armed forces were in a state of decay after years of no pay. Mobutu was unable to project power much beyond the capital and lacked resources to buy off or repress political challengers. By the time of the Rwandan genocide in 1994, the country was ripe for a violent collapse.

From Rwandan Genocide to "Africa's First World War"

The Rwandan civil war began in October 1990 when the Rwandan Patriotic Front (RPF), a rebel group composed of mainly exiled Rwandan Tutsi, invaded the country from neighboring Uganda.[6] The initial RPF invasion was repelled by government forces, but guerrilla warfare continued for the next two years. In early 1993, the RPF launched a major attack and doubled the amount of territory under its control in northern Rwanda. In August 1993 the Rwandan government and the RPF signed the Arusha Accords, which called for a power-sharing regime and the merging of RPF forces into the national army.

Hutu hard-liners, who were excluded from the peace talks, resisted implementation of the Arusha agreement. Motivated by the ideology of "Hutu Power," which called for the exclusion of all Tutsi from Rwandan society and politics, the hard-liners set in motion a plan to annihilate all Tutsi and moderate Hutu. The assassination of Rwandan president Juvenal Habyarimana on April 6, 1994, signaled the start of the Rwandan genocide, which lasted roughly 100 days and left more than 800,000 Tutsi and moderate Hutu dead.[7] The genocide ended only with the RPF's capture of the capital, Kigali, and triggered the exodus of two million mostly Hutu refugees to eastern Congo, Tanzania, Burundi, and Uganda.

Among those fleeing were a significant number of former soldiers in the Rwandan Armed Forces (FAR) and their Interahamwe militia allies who had carried out the killings. Endowed with foreign exchange from the Rwandan treasury, equipment from the national army, and anything else "movable and of any value,"[8] these former government forces regrouped in the UN refugee camps of eastern Congo. There international relief efforts, including the American Operation Support Hope (July–September 1994), provided fresh water and other supplies. The exiled Rwandan government proceeded to reestablish the state structure in the camps, and then attempted to set up military bases from which its troops could make incursions back into Rwanda. It eventually assembled a potent political force in eastern

Congo that included some 50,000 fighters—former soldiers from the FAR as well as Interahamwe militia. Rwanda faced persistent attacks from this force, beginning sporadically in late 1994 and intensifying throughout the following year.

The Hutu forces continued their ethnic cleansing campaign, targeting Banyarwanda Tutsi[9] and Banyamulenge[10] living in eastern Congo, often with the support of the Zairean government, which had revoked the two groups' Congolese nationality in 1981 despite their long presence in the country. The government publicly called for expulsion of the Banyamulenge in 1996.

Reacting to the government's decree, the Banyamulenge rose in revolt in October 1996. Quickly, other antigovernment elements joined the uprising and coalesced to form the Alliance of Democratic Forces for the Liberation of the Congo (AFDL), with the aim of toppling Mobutu. The rebellion was backed by a broad coalition of African countries, including Rwanda, Uganda, and Angola. Rwanda, which accused Mobutu of supporting the Interahamwe in eastern Congo, provided tactical support, military supplies, and troops to guide the diverse and disorganized indigenous insurgency. Rwandan forces attacked refugee camps controlled by the ex-FAR and Interahamwe militias. Some of the fighters and their dependents were killed, but most were dispersed into the Congolese bush. The task of rounding up, disarming, and repatriating these large, armed, itinerant bands would later be foisted upon the United Nations by Congolese negotiators.[11]

After thirty years of corruption, repression, and patrimonial rule, many Zaireans welcomed the insurgency, even if they were wary of the involvement of foreign powers.[12] The poorly equipped and demoralized Zairean army barely put up resistance as the rebel alliance, led by Laurent Kabila, rolled toward Kinshasa. In May 1997 the Mobutu regime was overthrown and Kabila declared himself president.

Kabila, however, failed to learn from the mistakes of his predecessor. He rejected any thoughts of reviving the democratization process and became increasingly authoritarian and personalistic in his rule. He soon alienated nearly all of those who had rallied behind him: the democratic opposition groups, civil society, and many of his partners in the AFDL, including the Banyamulenge. Moreover, Kabila damaged relations with the Rwandan government when he dismissed his Rwandan military advisers and expelled Rwandan forces from eastern Congo in late July 1998. By early August, a new rebel group had materialized.

On the surface, the new insurgency was a coalition force composed of Kabila's former Tutsi allies in the AFDL, old Mobutu elites, and other officials who had become frustrated with Kabila's dictatorial rule. In reality, however, it was a narrow group supported and instigated by Rwanda in direct retaliation for the expulsion of the RPF. As one analyst noted, "There is no truth to the widely held view that Uganda and Rwanda intervened in support of a rebellion by Congolese Tutsi and their allies against President Kabila. . . . Rwanda and Uganda initiated the war that erupted on 2 August 1998, prior to the founding of the Rassemblement Congolais pour la Democratie [Congolese Rally for Democracy, or RCD]."[13]

With external support—particularly from Rwanda but also from Uganda—the RCD made dramatic military gains in the first week of the rebellion. (See the list of key rebel factions in table 4.1.) By the end of August, the RCD had captured Goma, Bukavu, and Kisangani, and was threatening Kinshasa. The swift intervention of Angola, Zimbabwe, and Namibia on behalf of the Kabila regime, however, thwarted a surprise rebel attack from the Bas-Congo region, west of the capital, and slowed the rebels' advance in the east. Sudan and Chad also backed the Kabila government, while Burundi dispatched troops to support the Tutsi insurgents. In early November 1998, a new rebel group, the Movement for the Liberation of Congo (MLC), emerged in the northwest, near Mobutu's hometown. By the end of 1998, what many called "Africa's first world war," with as many as nine foreign countries intervening, had engulfed the Congo. The conflict's intensity, level of devastation, and toll on civilians were unprecedented. According to one widely cited estimate, as many as two million people died in five provinces in eastern Congo in the first eighteen months of the conflict.[14] Even after the war officially ended, mortality rates remained high due to malnutrition, disease, and population displacement caused by the conflict. Total conflict-related deaths were estimated at 3.8 million by 2004.[15]

Motivation of the Parties

The regional war in the Congo had three root causes: foreign armed groups (e.g., Interahamwe and ex-FAR militias) using the country as a base to destabilize or overthrow neighboring governments; the intervention of foreign armies to defend the Kabila regime, and/or to pursue economic interests; and the failure of successive Congolese central governments, which pursued devastating divide-and-rule policies that provoked violent opposition. The regional countries' material exploitation of the Congo further protracted the conflict by entrenching foreign interests and sparking violent competition for lucrative territory.

Laurent Kabila seemed motivated purely by the desire to hang on to power. Recognizing his precarious security situation, Kabila turned to foreign and local forces to bolster the weak and unreliable Congolese Armed Forces (FAC). His regime depended heavily on troops and military assistance from Angola, Zimbabwe, and Namibia. In exchange, he offered these governments lucrative mining contracts or trade in precious commodities, including diamonds, coltan, and timber. Moreover, the government supported foreign nonstate actors, such as the ex-FAR and Interahamwe, and coopted local militias, including the Mai-Mai in the Kivus, to check the RCD and the MLC. The consequences of this divide-and-rule policy were devastating: the eastern part of the country was overwhelmed by vicious cycles of conflict and large-scale human rights violations. Relying on proxies or foreign forces to fight the war diminished Kabila's administrative control of the Congo, but he preferred "sharing the country to sharing power."[16]

At its inception, the RCD had broad and ambitious goals. Railing against Kabila's failure of governance, the RCD leadership espoused such political ideals as establishing a democratic government, granting equal rights to all citizens, and fighting personalistic rule.[17] Over the next five years, however, the RCD's track record would prove dismal. Unable to garner popular support from the Congolese population, it increasingly relied on violence and repression to administer the territories it controlled.

Human Rights Watch exposed the movement's hypocrisy in a report detailing systematic abuses committed by the rebels. The RCD "vowed to restore democracy and respect for human rights within the Democratic Republic of the Congo (DRC), but the RCD-Goma and its Rwandese allies have regularly slaughtered civilians in massacres and extrajudicial executions. . . . They seem in many cases to have

Table 4.1. Primary Rebel Factions and Militia in the Congo Conflict

Group	Description (including foreign sponsor, location, leadership, factions)
Congolese Rally for Democracy (RCD, RCD-Goma)	RCD first emerged in early August 1998 as the primary rebel organization in the war against Laurent Kabila's government. Concentrated in the Kivus, with its headquarters in Goma, the insurgency received military and financial support from Rwanda, Uganda, and, to a lesser extent, Burundi. RCD's failure to quickly overthrow Kabila and take Kinshasa led to leadership squabbles, fractionalization, and a falling-out between Uganda and Rwanda. Rwanda continued to back what became known as RCD-Goma, while Uganda offered assistance to the splinter movement RCD-ML and to the Movement for the Liberation of Congo (MLC). RCD-Goma's oppressive governing style and devastating human rights abuses provoked popular resistance from the Banyamulenge and other communities in eastern Congo—the very people the movement claimed to be protecting from the Kabila government and its Interahamwe allies. Lacking popular support and self-sufficiency, RCD-Goma remained dominated and controlled by Kigali.
Congolese Rally for Democracy-Liberation Movement (RCD-ML)	Supported at its inception by Uganda, RCD-ML emerged in September 1998 with its headquarters in Bunia, in northeastern Congo. It was founded by Wamba dia Wamba, who was forced out as the first president of RCD-Goma in the lead-up to the Lusaka negotiations. Wamba, however, had difficulties consolidating control of the splinter faction and was under constant threat from his deputies. Eventually, Wamba was superseded by Mbusa Nyamwisi, who controlled the movement's military wing, the Congolese Popular Army (APC). After seizing control of the movement, Nyamwisi resisted attempts by Uganda to merge the organization with the MLC and improved its relations with the Kinshasa government. Increasingly, RCD-ML cultivated ties with the Lendu ethnic group in Ituri while violently opposing the Hema militias and their Ugandan backers. RCD-ML also remained active in North Kivu, Nyamwisi's hometown, battling against RCD-Goma and the Mai-Mai in this region.

Movement for the Liberation of Congo (MLC)	Under the consistent leadership of Jean-Pierre Bemba since its founding in November 1998, MLC established control over much of northwestern Congo, with its central base in Gbadolite, Mobutu's hometown. Though heavily backed by the Ugandans, the MLC managed to generate popular support from the local populations. This assured the movement a certain degree of self-sufficiency and granted Bemba a fair amount of autonomy from the Ugandans. Bemba's and Kampala's bid to extend the MLC's control over the various rebel factions in Ituri and establish the united Front for the Liberation of Congo failed in 2001. In late 2002, Bemba turned his attention to the neighboring Central African Republic, where he sent 1,500 MLC troops to support the failing president, Ange-Felix Patasse.
Mai-Mai	The Mai-Mai first emerged as a military force in 1964 after one of Congo's many postindependence rebellions. Historically, these militias resented the migration of Rwandan Tutsi settlers into eastern Congo. With the invasion of the Rwandan Patriotic Front and the formation of RCD-Goma, the Mai-Mai were revived to repel the "invaders" and target Congolese Tutsi in the Kivus. Though some leaders were supported by Kinshasa, the Mai-Mai remained decentralized and fragmented, with different factions allying with various external sponsors, including Rwanda. Competition for control over gold and coltan reserves further divided the militias.

committed the abuses deliberately to punish civilians for their supposed support of enemies of the RCD."[18]

Throughout the conflict, the rebels remained primarily financed and controlled by the Rwandan government in Kigali, which used them as pawns in its attempt to overthrow Kabila and disarm the Interahamwe and ex-FAR forces.[19] Rwanda's manipulation and the disjointed nature of the movement fostered continuous leadership rivalries and several major splits. RCD-Goma, the remnant of the original RCD movement, has had four different leaders; the latest, Azarias Ruberwa, was appointed in June 2003. Ruberwa became a vice president in the transitional government, only to be marginalized later as party leaders such as Eugene Serafuli, the governor of North Kivu, gained influence.

In contrast to the RCD, the MLC enjoyed some local support in Equateur province and had consistent leadership throughout the conflict. Jean-Pierre Bemba, the son of a wealthy businessman and a former Mobutu associate, had been the sole leader of the MLC since its founding in November 1998. Uganda began to support the MLC after it became frustrated by divisions within the RCD and by Rwanda's oppressive influence. Bemba's primary objective was to overthrow Kabila, but when that goal proved elusive, the MLC attempted to consolidate its control of northwestern Congo, maximize its political and economic benefits, and strengthen Bemba's bargaining position. The MLC also briefly intervened in the conflict in the neighboring Central African Republic on behalf of its failing government, which was eventually overthrown.

Rwanda and Uganda supported the RCD and the MLC, respectively, to bolster security along their borders, to put direct military pressure on the "armed groups,"[20] and to gain access to Congolese resources. Rwanda had the most at stake because the remaining ex-FAR and Interahamwe fighters posed an ongoing security threat.[21] Kigali's invasion of the Congo was an attempt to neutralize and eliminate these threats to Rwandan security and install a "more accommodating regime" in Kinshasa.[22]

In support of its parallel efforts to exploit resources from eastern Congo and control the lucrative coltan and diamond markets, Rwanda pursued a policy of direct rule. It created a Congo Desk, to oversee its commercial and military operations in the neighboring country, which was distinct from Kigali's official national treasury and thus beyond the scrutiny of international financial institutions. It is estimated that the Congo Desk's budget, which was based entirely on the exploitation of Congo's resources, was as much as $320 million for 1999, or 20 percent of Rwanda's GNP.[23]

Uganda also had security interests in the Congo. Its troops entered the northern part of the country partly to prevent the Ugandan rebel Allied Democratic Forces from using this region for incursions into Uganda, but also to exploit resources that included coltan, diamonds, and gold. Uganda's strategy was less centralized and more indirect than that of Rwanda, but it was no less exploitative and devastating for the local Congolese population.

The Ugandan network was led by Lieutenant General (Ret.) Salim Saleh and Major General James Kazini of the Uganda People's Defence Force (UPDF).[24] The UPDF played a crucial role in exploiting the gold and other minerals from the Congo that contributed to Uganda's impressive economic growth in the 1990s. The surge in Ugandan gold exports in the late 1990s, for example, can be attributed to Kampala's exploitation of Congolese gold, there having been no concomitant increase in domestic production. The proceeds helped to offset the country's large trade deficit.[25] Disastrously, Uganda's extraction of mineral resources heightened the conflict in Ituri between the Hema and Lendu peoples (see "Violence in the Northeast" under Phase IV, below).

The task of controlling different Congolese proxies and operating with divergent strategies soon became a source of tension between the former allies. As early as December 1998, Ugandan and Rwandan forces clashed. Heavier fighting occurred over the strategic and lucrative town of Kisangani in August 1999, March 2000, and May 2000. The battle for Kisangani's diamond markets showed how economic motives paralleled or even trumped security considerations as reasons for Kigali and Kampala to keep a hand in the Congo.

There was greater solidarity among Zimbabwe, Angola, and Namibia, all of whom justified military involvement in the Congo as part of their duty to support a fellow member of the Southern African Development Community (SADC). Zimbabwean president Robert Mugabe ran into trouble, however, when he tried to obtain official sanction from SADC for the intervention. South African president Nelson

Mandela objected to the use of force by SADC, preferring a negotiated settlement to the Congolese war. In an attempt to circumvent Mandela, Mugabe, as chair of SADC's Organ for Politics, Defence and Security, announced after a meeting of defense officials in Harare on August 18 that SADC had "unanimously" agreed to intervene on behalf of the Congo, although only nine of thirteen SADC members had been represented and the Organ had no authority to mandate an intervention.[26] Mandela resented the move but dropped his opposition for the sake of SADC unity, announcing in early September that SADC was unanimous in its support of intervention. Nevertheless, animosity between Mandela and Mugabe continued to undermine the body's ability to play a constructive early role in helping to end the conflict.

Beyond diplomatic showmanship, Zimbabwe's intervention was motivated by economics. Mugabe exploited his strong personal relationship with Kabila to acquire lucrative contracts with the Kinshasa government. Eager to recoup money he had originally loaned to Kabila in his first year in office, and recognizing the potential for further enrichment, Mugabe offered military hardware and thousands of troops to the Kabila regime despite widespread domestic opposition and protests from international donors.[27]

Indeed, Zimbabwe's military intervention in the Congo was designated as "self-financing" in a September 1998 bilateral deal signed by Kinshasa and Harare.[28] As payment for its intervention, the Mugabe regime secured one of the largest timber concessions in the world, gaining rights to exploit more than eighty million acres of forests in the Congo;[29] a 37.5 percent share in the Congo's state mining company, Gecamines;[30] and ventures in other industries including electricity, agriculture, and civil aviation. Though the Zimbabwean state as a whole found itself in the red with its investments in the Congo, Mugabe cronies who allied with Congolese elites profited enormously. UN investigators determined that Zimbabwean and Congolese elites illegally transferred $5 billion of mining assets from the Congolese state to private companies from 1999 to 2002.[31] In essence, this amounted to stealing from the state the equivalent of the Congo's entire gross domestic product (GDP) for the year 2000.

Angolan leaders worried that the long-running insurgency of the National Union for the Total Independence of Angola (UNITA) would exploit a rebel victory in the Congo by opening bases throughout the country. Moreover, Angola became increasingly suspicious of UNITA's relationship with Rwanda and Uganda. Both were important transit routes for UNITA's diamond trade, and high-ranking UNITA leaders, including Jonas Savimbi, had made visits to Kampala and Kigali prior to the war.[32] If Kabila held on to power, Angola could concentrate on weakening UNITA's supply lines and denying the rebels use of bases in the Congo.

Namibia provided troops to support Kabila despite a constitutional provision proscribing the use of force by the government except in defense of national security.[33] Namibia's president, Sam Nujoma, had close personal ties with Kabila and Mugabe reaching back to the 1960s, when all were fighting colonial rule. Nujoma dismissed domestic criticism of the army's intervention and played up the importance of supporting a fellow SADC member facing external invasion. Nujoma's regime also seemed to benefit from various economic kickbacks; reports alleged that it received diamond mining rights in the Congo in exchange for its military support.[34]

Even though Zimbabwe and Rwanda withdrew most of their forces by late 2002, and Uganda followed suit by April 2003, elites connected to these governments continued to exploit the Congo's resources through covert and private means, inciting ethnic violence and sponsoring and arming militias. A UN Panel of Experts documented that the UPDF trained a paramilitary group to serve its interests in the Ituri district in anticipation of its own withdrawal.[35] Similarly, Rwanda restructured RCD-Goma to incorporate more Rwandans after the RPF left, while Zimbabwe created private military companies to continue its operations in the Congo after Zimbabwean forces left. This strategy of privatizing foreign exploitation intensified warlordism, ethnic violence, and attacks on civilians. In the end, the economic exploitation of the Congo deeply entrenched Rwanda, Uganda, and Zimbabwe in the country and added one more level of complexity to attempts to end the war, and ultimately to MONUC's struggles to implement the Lusaka Agreement.

The Road to Lusaka

Almost two dozen peace initiatives littered the Congo political scene in the first nine months of the conflict.[36] Many were not formal negotiations but peace consultations or discussions at the ministerial and presidential level. The early talks, spearheaded by SADC, began almost immediately after the war broke out but quickly reached an impasse due to divisions within the organization, SADC members' lack of neutrality, the Kabila government's distrust of South African motives, and Rwandan and Ugandan opposition to any mediation effort spearheaded by Mugabe. In September 1998, President Frederick Chiluba of Zambia assumed the mantle of lead mediator, representing SADC as a more neutral actor despite extant tension with Angola.

The failure of the early SADC initiative opened the door for other peace forums to address the conflict, including a meeting of defense ministers in Addis Ababa in September 1998, a Francophone summit in November 1998 in France attended by thirty-four African heads of state, and an Organization of African Unity (OAU) conference in Burkina Faso in December 1998. Although each initiative on its own failed to produce a comprehensive agreement, the parties made slow progress. The peace efforts maintained a degree of continuity and developed a common framework on which the later Lusaka Cease-Fire Agreement would ultimately be based.

A key obstacle to early success was Kabila's refusal to meet face-to-face with the MLC and the RCD. Reluctant to legitimize the rebel groups, whom he viewed as foreign invaders, Kabila at first rejected any type of dialogue with them. Thus, initiatives occurred with partial participation. A meeting in Windhoek, Namibia, on January 18, 1999, led to "significant progress," in which the sides committed themselves to signing a cease-fire agreement, but only Rwanda, Uganda, Namibia, Zimbabwe, Angola, and the RCD were represented. In Libya on April 19, 1999, Kabila and Ugandan president Yoweri Museveni signed a cease-fire agreement, but again the absent parties rejected it outright. Nonetheless, these partial agreements were significant in that they kept the peace process alive and sustained hope for a comprehensive agreement.

In June and July 1999, all of the sides were finally represented in Lusaka as Chiluba tried once again to forge consensus on a cease-fire agreement. At this time, the Kabila regime was under enormous military pressure. Rwandan forces had made significant gains in early 1999. They had crossed the Sankuru River, had captured the Kasai Oriental town of Lusambo, were on the verge of taking the diamond-rich capital of Mbuji Mayi, and were threatening to take Kananga, which would open the way to the capital. Faced with the imminent challenge at Mbuji Mayi and the potential Rwandan march to Kinshasa, Kabila made a tactical decision to seek a political settlement. Most significantly, he reversed his position that Rwanda and Uganda had to withdraw their forces before he would sign a cease-fire agreement. Instead, he permitted Rwanda and Uganda to keep troops in the Congo until the deployment of a UN peacekeeping force.[37] Kabila's commitment to a political solution effectively thwarted the advance of the Rwandan Patriotic Army (RPA) as international pressure compelled Rwanda and Uganda to sign the Lusaka Agreement and retreat to defensive positions on the battlefield. Furthermore, the negotiations granted Kabila and his allies time to rearm, reorganize, and prevent the RPA capture of Mbuji Mayi. Thus the Lusaka Agreement represented, not a genuine commitment by Kabila to end the war and share power, but a calculated decision to regain the military balance and survive politically.

On July 10, 1999, the Lusaka Agreement was signed by Congo, Angola, Zimbabwe, Namibia, Rwanda, and Uganda. Representatives of Zambia, the United Nations, the OAU, and SADC signed on to the agreement as witnesses. The United States and the European Union were present as observers.

Although each of the states involved in the war had solid political or tactical reasons to sign the Lusaka Agreement, the rebels, who had gained the military upper hand going into the talks, were reluctant to commit to a cease-fire. The MLC had made significant gains during the course of negotiations, capturing Gbadolite, the birthplace of former president Mobutu, and the town of Gemena. The MLC was popular in the areas it controlled, which imbued Bemba with a legitimacy not available to the other rebel groups and gave the movement, which was relatively unknown less than six months before the Lusaka talks, an equal place at the negotiating table. Bemba was eager to exploit this advantage at the future national dialogue and signed the Lusaka Agreement after a three-week delay. Nonetheless, even after the agreement was signed, the MLC pressed its military advantage; captured the town of Zongo, on the border with Central African Republic; and approached Mbandaka, a gateway to Kinshasa.[38]

Personality differences and power struggles within the RCD, between Emile Ilunga and Wamba dia Wamba, contributed to the rebel group's delay in signing the agreement. Wamba was replaced by Ilunga as RCD leader in May 1999 but continued to participate in the talks. As the official leader of the party, Ilunga refused to sign the accord if Wamba did so.[39] In addition, because Rwanda wanted RCD-Goma to be free to continue pursuit of the Interahamwe, it exerted little pressure on the rebel group to sign.[40] International pressure mounted, however, on RCD-Goma and Kigali, especially from South Africa and Tanzania. A compromise allowed fifty RCD representatives to sign the agreement, which they did on August 31.

Lusaka was purely a regional initiative and, at the time, gave great hope to those who sought African solutions for African problems. The role of both SADC and Chiluba in forging the agreement proved invaluable. As one analyst noted,

> For the first time in the modern history of the continent it was the African actors themselves taking the lead—and not the former European colonial powers, the superpowers or the United Nations. An African regional organization, SADC, with its fourteen member states from South Africa to the DRC, proved capable to transform (but not to stop) one of the world's major armed conflicts and the most deadly conflict in recent decades. This is no small achievement since the war in the Congo was the most internationalized conflict Africa has ever seen.[41]

As an African solution to the Congo war, Lusaka was impressive; yet it also represented abdication of responsibility by the signatories for the critical process of implementation (especially the disarmament, demobilization, and repatriation of foreign rebel groups), pawning it off on an unprepared and reluctant United Nations.

The Lusaka Agreement

The Lusaka Agreement attempted to address the key underlying issues of the conflict: the presence of foreign armed rebel groups ("negative forces") using the Congo as a base to destabilize and threaten regional neighbors, most notably Rwanda; the intervention of foreign militaries; and the breakdown of governance and the need to reform the Congo's political system to be more democratic and inclusive. As such, it was much more than a cease-fire. The peace agreement called for disarmament of the negative forces, disengagement and withdrawal of foreign armies, and reform of the Congo central government through an Inter-Congolese Dialogue, which was to be the main forum for the creation of a reformed and inclusive Congolese government.[42]

The agreement stipulated that the parties would cease all hostilities within twenty-four hours of the signing. This was to include military offensives, attacks on civilians, and transfers of ammunition and weaponry to the field. Furthermore, all parties agreed to end support for the negative forces and pledged to help identify and disarm them. The agreement tasked the United Nations with disarming the negative forces within thirty days of the signing, and required foreign states to disengage their armies from the front lines within fourteen days and withdraw all forces within 180 days. Thus, foreign armed groups were to be disarmed well before all foreign troops were to be withdrawn. Finally, the Inter-Congolese Dialogue was to begin forty-five days after the signing of the cease-fire. The Congolese government, the RCD, the MLC, the unarmed opposition groups, and Congolese civil society were to meet to craft a new political system with the help of a neutral mediator. Central to the reforms would be the formation of a national army, the strengthening of state administration throughout the country, and democratic elections.

The Lusaka Agreement mandated the creation of two security mechanisms to oversee its implementation and monitor the cease-fire. The first, a Joint Military Commission (JMC), would comprise the warring parties themselves and was to be set up within a week of the signing. It included two representatives from each signatory to the agreement and was to be led by a neutral chairman appointed by the OAU. Observers from OAU members such as Algeria, Nigeria, Senegal, and Malawi would support the JMC, which in turn would report to the Political Committee, a group comprising the Lusaka signatories' ministers of foreign affairs and defense.

The idea for the JMC originated in a proposal by South African president Thabo Mbeki, who accurately predicted that African states would have to bear some of the burden of keeping peace in the Congo because the UN Security Council would be reluctant to endorse a major military intervention.[43] The JMC's mandate included observing the cease-fire, establishing the location of armed groups and foreign armies, liaising between the belligerents, verifying the disengagement of the forces and the disarmament of the armed groups, and monitoring the withdrawal of foreign forces. The JMC was to complement the second security mechanism, a strong UN peacekeeping force.

Paragraph 11 of Lusaka states, "The United Nations Security Council, acting under Chapter VII of the UN Charter and in collaboration with the OAU, shall be requested to constitute, facilitate and deploy an appropriate peacekeeping force in the DRC to ensure implementation of this Agreement; and taking into account the peculiar situation of the DRC, mandate the peacekeeping force to track down all armed groups in the DRC. In this respect, the UN Security Council shall provide the requisite mandate for the peace-keeping force."[44] Working closely with the JMC, the peacekeeping mission was to observe and monitor the cease-fire; investigate cease-fire violations; supervise the disengagement of forces and their redeployment to defensive positions; collect and secure unauthorized weapons; supervise the withdrawal of foreign forces; and provide and maintain humanitarian assistance to civilians, including internally displaced persons and refugees. More controversially, the agreement asked the United Nations to deploy a peace-enforcement mission that would, after "tracking down" and disarming the negative forces, screen them for mass killers and war criminals, hand over *génocidaires* to the International Criminal Tribunal for Rwanda, and help repatriate the armed groups to their home countries.

Lusaka was an impressive peace agreement in that it covered all of the bases of the conflict. Unfortunately, it was practically impossible to implement within the artificial timetables specified, except under perfect conditions: absolute commitment from the signatories, the international community, and regional actors; swift identification and disarmament of the negative forces; flawless disengagement of foreign troops; and genuine political will to reform the central government. As timelines had to be extended, the agreement lost legitimacy. The parties incurred few costs for transgressing or obstructing it because it lacked an enforcement mechanism. The brevity of the initial timelines, in fact, created a culture of delay and violations. Within months the agreement was rendered nearly irrelevant.

Furthermore, despite warnings from U.S. and EU observers present at Lusaka that there was almost no chance the UN Security Council would adopt a Chapter VII mandate, the signatories passed the buck to the United Nations, which up until then had little involvement in the Congo conflict. As one senior representative to the United Nations noted, "The Congo file started in Africa, not in the United Nations. The Lusaka Agreement called for UN forces. They didn't know what they were writing. The UN wasn't there. The UN came in with a framework that wasn't theirs."[45] The disconnect between the Lusaka signatories and the world's major powers would contribute to the inadequate mandate provided by the UN Security Council in its initial authorization of MONUC.

Political Support for Peace

Essential for the success of the newly signed Lusaka Agreement was the political support of not only the signatories themselves but also the UN Security Council, which was designated as the key guarantor of the accord. Both camps abdicated their responsibilities. The Security Council, led by the United States, recognized that it had to authorize a peacekeeping force because the Congo conflict was too deadly and destabilizing to ignore. Lacking any strategic or political interest in the conflict, however, the Security Council developed a peacekeeping strategy that linked the deployment of peacekeepers to the actions of the parties themselves. If the Lusaka signatories wanted a UN peacekeeping mission, their military and political behavior would dictate the size and speed of its deployment. In short, the Security Council quickly passed the buck back to the Lusaka signatories, which were content to defy the United Nations because they faced almost no consequences for continuing to prosecute the war and loot the Congo of its riches.

International Actors: The Politics behind MONUC

Establishing a new peacekeeping mission in the shattered Congo was an uphill battle. At the time, the permanent members of the UN Security Council were devoting much attention and many resources to expensive and complicated missions in Bosnia and Kosovo. Furthermore, the United Nations was just establishing another large peacekeeping mission in Sierra Leone in October 1999, and the UN track record in Africa in the post–Cold War era was mixed, with failures in Somalia, Rwanda, and Angola overshadowing more successful interventions in Mozambique and Namibia. Cognizant of these facts but recognizing the costs of doing nothing, the newly appointed U.S. ambassador to the United Nations, Richard Holbrooke, working closely with Secretary of State Madeleine Albright and her assistant secretary for Africa, Susan Rice, took the lead in getting the United Nations to authorize a peacekeeping mission in the Congo.

Holbrooke was determined to see the United Nations and United States "get it right" in the Congo, though he was under no illusion as to the difficulties of the task ahead.[46] Mindful of the U.S. record in Africa in the past decade—the debacle in Somalia and the failure in Rwanda —and the political and operational difficulties of deploying a massive peacekeeping force, Holbrooke felt the Security Council had to act but needed to craft a precise and specific mandate. Moreover, he insisted that the United States would delay the deployment of any peacekeeping mission until the parties fully respected the cease-fire agreement. In December 1999 he, along with Howard Wolpe, President Clinton's special envoy for Africa, Senator Russell Feingold, and other American representatives visited nine countries in sub-Saharan Africa, including the Congo, Rwanda, Uganda, Angola, Namibia, Zimbabwe, and Zambia, to stress this message, making clear the preconditions for any UN peacekeeping force.

After Holbrooke returned from his multicountry African tour, the United States, as president of the Security Council, devoted the month of January 2000 to Africa. The countries involved in the Congo conflict were invited to meet several times with the Security Council, in the hope that they would sign a new accord called "Lusaka Plus."[47]

At the Security Council meetings on the Congo, the African leaders unanimously called for a robust peacekeeping force to be deployed immediately to disarm the negative forces. They advocated a force of between 15,000 and 20,000 UN troops. Meanwhile, France requested "the immediate deployment of 10,000 peacekeepers," arguing that a comprehensive cease-fire would remain elusive without the presence of UN troops.[48] These higher figures contrasted sharply with what Holbrooke and the U.S. administration envisioned.[49] Privately, Holbrooke and Secretary of Defense William Cohen questioned the United Nations' capacity to handle a large force in the Congo.[50] They felt the mission should be held to a maximum of 5,000 troops. Furthermore, the United States was wary of supporting a peace enforcement mission to the Congo to disarm nonstate actors, much to the disappointment of the African leaders.[51]

In early February, the United States introduced Security Council Resolution 1291, which called for a peacekeeping mission with a clear mandate to facilitate the implementation of Lusaka, while not acting as an interpositional force. Before the vote on the resolution, however, the Clinton administration had to persuade the U.S. Congress to approve funding for the mission. Several vocal domestic critics opposed it. In an interview before a special hearing of the Senate Foreign Relations Committee, Senator John Warner, a Republican from Virginia, commented, "Frankly, Holbrooke is putting this tremendous emphasis on Africa. I would have to express great concern if I saw a lot of funds that could now relieve this crisis situation in Bosnia and Kosovo being diverted to the African continent."[52] The *Washington Post*, in an editorial on February 14, 2000, questioned the wisdom of another peacekeeping commitment "when other major UN-led peacekeeping operations [e.g., Kosovo and East Timor] are ... faltering." Others similarly questioned whether the United Nations was capable of simultaneously handling major missions in Europe, Asia, and Africa.

In his testimony before the House International Relations Committee in mid-February, Holbrooke attempted to appease his domestic opponents. He made it clear that the proposed peacekeeping mission would not involve any U.S. troops, would not divert any funds from Kosovo, would not act as an interpositional force or act to forcibly disarm nonstate actors, would not entail an automatic transition to Phase III (support for demobilization and disarmament), and would not begin until key on-the-ground conditions were met, including security, access, and local cooperation with UN personnel.[53] Furthermore, he stressed that the Pentagon had worked closely with the United Nations to establish operational details for the mission.[54]

The Clinton administration, working with the Pentagon, insisted that the peacekeeping mission be structured appropriately before intervening and that the implementation of the peacekeeping force be contingent upon cooperative behavior from the warring parties. "The world can't just plant the UN flag first, and then worry about logistics, support, and mandate later," Holbrooke argued. "After months of rejecting unrealistic proposals for a UN peacekeeping force in the Congo, we have finally reached the point where the UN planners are now adopting a rational, phased approach to peacekeeping—one that tailors UN deployments to concrete actions by the parties to implement the peace agreement."[55] The phased approach would not only link deployment of peacekeepers to cooperation from the signatories, but also ensure that the size of the force would be politically feasible in Washington.

African countries, however, were frustrated by the minimalist and incremental approach proposed by the United States in Resolution 1291. Rwanda's UN envoy, Joseph W. Mutaboba, remarked that 5,000 troops was "a meaningless number" for a country the size of the Congo.[56] Others demanded that the peacekeeping mission in the Congo be on par with those in Kosovo and Bosnia. "Why does the UN act so quickly to [control] conflicts in Kosovo and East Timor but drags its feet when it comes to the DRC, Somalia and Rwanda?" asked Stan Mudenge, Zimbabwe's foreign minister. "One cannot but wonder if the racial composition is the reason."[57] Ambassador Robert R. Fowler, Canada's permanent representative to the United Nations, stated candidly that political and economic considerations were significant in deciding on a small force:

> There is a human security disaster unfolding in the DRC, which requires immediate attention. The Lusaka Agreement requires substantive support from the United Nations. There are few places in the world where civilians are more in need of protection than in the DRC. In situations as grave as this, there is an imperative to act and to do what is possible to relieve the suffering of the beleaguered people of the DRC. It is never easy to balance the requirements of immediate response with the sober consideration of longer-term consequences. Unfortunately, such considerations were not the only ones driving the decision on MONUC's force level. Other factors, such as cost-aversion and outside political realities, also influenced the Council's decision-making in this instance.[58]

Finally, as one senior UN official lamented about the size and mandate of the proposed force, "This is Bosnia all over again. These guys are not going to be able to protect anyone."[59]

The war in the Congo was too gruesome and devastating for the West to ignore, but too difficult and too low a priority to address seriously. As the *Washington Post* presciently commented in February 2000, "The UN presence will prove too small to accomplish much in the way of facilitating a peace, but too big to escape the blame when, say, civilians, are massacred in the vicinity of blue helmets. The United Nations then would be attacked as ineffectual, when the fair question would be whether the major powers inside the UN sought credit for an operation that they were reluctant to support in a meaningful way."[60] Without a more favorable environment in the Congo, or at least a cooperative government, the Security Council was not willing to assume the necessary political and economic costs to make a major investment in the country's security. Furthermore, at a time when other major UN missions were ongoing throughout the world, the Security Council was reluctant to pursue a robust intervention in the large and complex Congo crisis. Unlike during the Cold War, no strategic imperative warranted an aggressive response. It quickly became apparent that the UN peacekeeping mission in the Congo, with its limited mandate, could function only as an "observer" of the conflict and its ambitious ceasefire accord. Holbrooke tried to "get it right" both politically and operationally, but the two goals were clearly incompatible.

Although the Americans took the lead on Resolution 1291, their political support for the MONUC mission would fade over time. Nonimplementation by the warring parties undermined the United States' interest in the area. In its first years in office, the Bush administration gave little more than rhetorical support to MONUC. The appointment of William Lacy Swing as the secretary-general's special representative to the Congo in May 2003 signaled a change, however. Swing was a former U.S. ambassador to the Congo, well connected in the U.S. State Department. His leadership of the mission helped it garner more support from the United States, despite a number of serious challenges.

Through 2004 and 2005, it was unclear whether even Swing could generate the support for MONUC necessary for it to successfully shepherd the Congo through the final stages of the transition. As mentioned above, MONUC received a mandate for less than half of the additional troops it requested in August 2004 to address instability in eastern Congo. When a sexual abuse scandal involving peacekeepers in Bunia and elsewhere made headlines in the mainstream media in late 2004, the fallout threatened support for MONUC just as it began the difficult process of preparing for elections. The issue was addressed in at least three U.S. congressional hearings between March and July 2005, with many U.S. lawmakers questioning the value of continued U.S. funding for UN peacekeeping in general and MONUC in particular.[61]

The Warring Parties

Ultimately, the greatest obstacle to the success of MONUC in its first three years would prove to be not the inadequate mandate given to the mission by the Security Council or the council's evident lack of political will, but the warring parties' own violations of the Lusaka Agreement and their obstruction of the UN peacekeeping mission.

Laurent Kabila had much to lose with the implementation of the Lusaka Agreement. He depended heavily upon the foreign military help of Angola and Zimbabwe; domestically, he employed the Mai-Mai and other militias to counter RCD-Goma and other rebel groups. The withdrawal of the foreign armies would leave him vulnerable on the security front, while the Inter-Congolese Dialogue threatened his monopoly on political power. Any significant opening of the country's political system could spell the end of Kabila's regime. Consequently, he did everything he could to thwart the implementation of Lusaka. He systematically obstructed MONUC's deployment from day one and attempted to suppress the Inter-Congolese Dialogue. In the first year and a half of MONUC's existence, the Kabila government would do more to frustrate the peacekeeping mission than would any other warring party.

Laurent Kabila's assassination in January 2001 would prove a critical juncture in the Congo peacekeeping mission. Kabila's successor, his son Joseph, adopted a more accommodative posture toward MONUC. He favored revitalizing Lusaka and endorsed the Inter-Congolese Dialogue. The younger Kabila opened the door for political reconciliation and supported the installation of a transitional government in July 2003. Nonetheless, Joseph Kabila continued to rely on the ex-FAR and Interahamwe forces, the Mai-Mai, and other militias in the east. These groups undermined MONUC's attempts to carry out a disarmament, demobilization, repatriation, resettlement, and reintegration (DDR)[62] program, and to curtail violence in the Kivus and Ituri.

The main rebel groups, the MLC and the RCD, also flouted Lusaka and obstructed MONUC's deployment. The MLC continued its offensives toward Kinshasa and became ensnarled in fighting in the Ituri district. RCD-Goma refused for years to demilitarize the strategic city of Kisangani despite persistent demands by MONUC and the UN Security Council, and continued its offensive in the Kivus. After Amos Namanga Ngongi, the special representative of the secretary-general (SRSG), criticized the RCD's excessive crackdown on a mutiny in Kisangani in May 2002, the rebel movement declared him persona non grata in all RCD-controlled territories and labeled MONUC as biased in favor of the government. The fractionalization of the rebel groups and the proliferation of militias in the east made it even more difficult for MONUC to curb violence and implement the DDR program, because these splinter groups were not incorporated in the Inter-Congolese Dialogue and were not susceptible to political pressure.

Despite their fervent calls for the deployment of a robust UN peacekeeping force, regional intervenors failed to comply with the Security Council's demands and frustrated MONUC's deployment. Namibia and Angola were the least obstructionist of the regional powers. Namibia contributed the fewest troops (only 2,000) and was the first to withdraw. After Angolan government forces killed UNITA leader Jonas Savimbi in spring 2002, the rebel movement collapsed and Angola had little strategic imperative to keep its troops in the Congo, although it still played an influential, behind-the-scenes role in Congolese politics. Both countries were relatively supportive of the peacekeeping mission.

For Rwanda, Uganda, and Zimbabwe, on the other hand, the continuing material benefits of intervention outweighed the political costs of contravening Lusaka and the various demands put upon them by the Security Council. Rwanda and Uganda not only kept between 10,000 and 20,000 troops in the country[63] but also actively funded and armed Congolese rebel groups to maintain their control of lucrative territory. Their meddling further contributed to the spiraling of ethnic violence in the Kivus and Ituri, and undermined the DDR process. Only major political pressure, including threats in mid-2002

to suspend foreign aid, induced the two countries to sign bilateral agreements with Kinshasa to arrange their troops' withdrawal. Even then, both
countries continued to manipulate proxy militias and rebel groups to
maintain their influence in the Congo, further thwarting the peacekeeping mission.

In sum, the African actors involved in the Congo conflict had to
look no further than themselves to understand why MONUC struggled to get off the ground and fulfill its mandate. Although the Security Council limited the peacekeeping operation in the Congo because
of high costs and low strategic priority, it was disingenuous for the
Lusaka signatories to lay all blame on the United Nations. Almost all of
the Lusaka signatories were guilty of hamstringing MONUC and de-
flating international political will to enforce the agreement. Only when
their behavior changed could the peace—and the peacekeepers—
make any progress.

Funding

The Security Council's reluctance to deploy a robust peacekeeping
force in the Congo was a consequence not only of its lack of strategic
and political interest, but also of the exorbitant bill its members would
have to foot to finance any large, protracted mission in one of Africa's
largest and least developed countries. By peacekeeping fiscal year
2003–4, MONUC would be the most expensive UN peacekeeping
mission in the world.

The inertia in MONUC's mandate and troop size in its first four
years can be partially explained by the cost of expanding the mission.
The United States reportedly resisted increases in MONUC's troop
size in late 2002, for example, because it did not want its annual share
of the funding to increase from $160 million to $200 million.[64] And in
2004, the Security Council gave MONUC only 5,900 of the 13,100 additional troops it had requested, denying the mission a brigade planned
for the southeastern part of the country.

Consequently, MONUC found itself in a vicious cycle: the worse
the fighting became, especially the violence in eastern Congo, the greater
the need for an expanded peacekeeping force, but the more the Security
Council resisted strengthening the mandate or enlarging the force,

concerned (in part) about throwing money at an apparently intractable problem. This was a recurring predicament from day one, when Richard Holbrooke demanded that the warring parties obey the ceasefire before peacekeepers were deployed.

The size of the country and the abysmal state of its infrastructure combined to generate MONUC's high price tag per peacekeeper deployed. With the Congo's road network almost completely destroyed from decades of neglect and years of war, MONUC had to rely almost exclusively on air transport to ferry personnel and equipment around the country. Furthermore, in the absence of a functioning central government and national economy, nearly all supplies, from water purifiers to cargo aircraft, had to be brought in from the outside by the United Nations.

In the 2002–3 fiscal year, operational costs accounted for 49 percent of the mission budget, and air transportation was responsible for half of the total operational costs.[65] In contrast, at the peak of the UN mission in Sierra Leone in 2001–2, operational costs were just 35 percent of the total budget. Table 4.2 breaks out MONUC's annual costs from 1999 through mid-2005. In 2003–4, military and civilian personnel costs outpaced operational costs for the first time, as the number of troops doubled and the force benefited to a degree from logistical economies of scale. The General Assembly appropriated $954,766,100 for 2004–5, an almost 50 percent increase from 2003–4, and the operation received another $3.1 million in in-kind donations to operate Radio Okapi. For 2005–6, the General Assembly approved $383 million for the first quarter of the fiscal year, and $1.1 million in in-kind donations, with further appropriations pending as the operation continued to expand and take on new duties such as electoral support.

MONUC was funded primarily by assessed contributions from UN member states. In addition, the Secretariat started a voluntary trust fund in October 1999 to help finance the JMC and support the Inter-Congolese Dialogue. The trust fund had amassed only $1.4 million as of August 2005. The Congo's $200 million National Program for Disarmament, Demobilization, and Reintegration, launched in July 2004, was funded with $100 million from Multi-country Demobilization and Reintegration Program donors and a matching grant from the World Bank.[66]

Table 4.2. MONUC's Annual Costs
(in millions)

	Expenditures					Appropriations	
	1999–2000	2000–2001	2001–2002	2002–2003	2003–2004	2004–2005	2005–2006[a]
Military Observers	$6.0	$18.8	$38.2	$38.7	$41.3	$41.5	$13.2
Peacekeeping Troops	—	$10.9	$58.4	$115.4	$215.4	$333	$121.8
UN Police	—	—	$0.6	$2.8	$6.0	$9.3	$3.8
Civilian Personnel	$6.6	$31.1	$68.5	$93.5	$112.6	$149.2	$57.8
Operations	$42.7	$185.4	$222.4	$229.4	$260.2	$420.7	$186.3
Quick-Impact Projects	—	$0.3	$0.7	$0.1	$1.0	$1.0	$0.3
Budgeted Voluntary Contributions in Kind[b]	—	—	—	$1.8	$2.3	$3.1	$1.1
Total	$55.3	$246.5	$388.8	$481.7	$638.8	$957.8	$384.3

[a]First-quarter budget only (July–October 2005). Extrapolated full-year total: $1.54 billion.
[b]Radio Okapi.

Sources: United Nations, annual financial performance reports for MONUC (A/55/935, May 10, 2001; A/56/825, February 19, 2002; A/57/682, December 18, 2002; A/58/684, January 16, 2004; and A/59/657, March 4, 2005) and budgets for MONUC (A/55/779, April 14, 2005). (For full document titles, see bibliography.)

Operation Artemis, the EU-authorized military operation to pacify the Ituri district from June through August 2003, was funded by EU member states rather than the General Assembly. The Treaty on European Union specifies that contributions for any EU military operation are met on a "costs lie where they fall" basis. Thus, France, leading the Interim Emergency Multinational Force, footed most of the bill for the Ituri intervention. All EU member states contributed some funds, however, to cover the 7 million euros in common costs.[67]

Phases of the Operation

Given the lack of implementation commitment from the Lusaka signatories and the UN Security Council's lack of enthusiasm for robust peacekeeping in the Congo, the UN Secretariat approached Congo peacekeeping with extreme caution. It was under no illusion that this would be a cheap, straightforward, or easy mission. An earlier UN study in March 1999 estimated that a successful and credible peacekeeping force in the Congo would require upwards of 100,000 troops.[68] Immediately after Lusaka was signed, the secretary-general warned,

> In order to be effective, any United Nations peacekeeping mission in the Democratic Republic of the Congo, whatever its mandate, will have to be large and expensive. It would require the deployment of thousands of international troops and civilian personnel. It will face tremendous difficulties, and will be beset by risks. Deployment will be slow. The huge size of the country, the degradation of infrastructure, the intensity of its climate, the intractable nature of some aspects of the conflict, the number of parties, the high levels of mutual suspicion, the large population displacements, the ready availability of small arms, the general climate of impunity and the substitution of armed force for the rule of law in much of the territory combine to make the Democratic Republic of the Congo a highly complex environment for peacekeeping.[69]

Recognizing the risks involved and the challenges of operating in a hostile environment, the secretary-general internalized the Pentagon-recommended phased approach, which linked increased UN involvement to cooperation from the warring parties. Phase I would include the deployment of a small advance team to work with the JMC to liaise with the warring parties, determine the feasibility and logistics of the operation, and prepare for the deployment of military observers. Phase II would consist of 500 military observers, protected by 5,000 peacekeepers, who would oversee and monitor the disengagement of the warring parties from the front lines. Phase III would entail overseeing the withdrawal of the foreign forces and the initiation of the DDR program. In mid-2003 MONUC transitioned into a fourth phase, one not envisioned by the Secretariat in its original planning, when it evolved from a protected observer mission to a peacekeeping mission. Its focus shifted from observing the cease-fire and withdrawal of the warring parties to ending violence in the Ituri district and the Kivus and assisting the Congolese government in restoring its governing authority throughout the country. It was not until this fourth stage that MONUC had the means to take seriously its mandate to protect civilians under the imminent threat of attack.

Phase I: Advance Team

Phase I was merely a preparatory stage for the deployment of the larger peacekeeping force. It entailed positioning UN military personnel to liaise with the warring parties and arrange for the establishment of peacekeepers throughout the country, particularly along the cease-fire line. Yet, in a foreshadowing of the trouble to come, the United Nations met resistance from the warring parties, particularly the Kabila government, when sending out the liaison officers to conduct surveys of rebel-controlled areas to prepare for the peacekeeping mission.

Mandate

Wary of plunging headlong into monitoring a cease-fire for which the warring parties showed no signs of respect, the secretary-general advanced a cautious and limited first phase. Authorized by the UN Security Council in Resolution 1258 of August 6, 1999, Phase I included the deployment of up to ninety UN military liaison personnel, along with appropriate civilian, political, humanitarian, and administrative staff, to the capitals of the signatories to the Lusaka Agreement. If security permitted, liaison officers were also to be stationed in the rear military headquarters of the rebel groups. Their primary duties included establishing relations with the JMC and all parties to the agreement in order to guarantee security for the future deployment of military observers, to conduct conflict reconnaissance, and to report any cease-fire violations to the secretary-general.[70]

Deployment and Operations

As laid out by the Lusaka Agreement, the United Nations and the JMC were to work together to monitor the cease-fire agreement and oversee the disengagement of the warring parties. The JMC, composed of observers from the Lusaka signatories and other African countries, was created immediately after the signing of the Lusaka Agreement to monitor the cease-fire while the UN Security Council established an observer mission. To facilitate coordination between the United Nations, OAU, and JMC, UN liaison officers were sent to Addis Ababa and OAU officials visited New York to consult with the Secretariat in October 1999. A month later, the United Nations trained OAU observers and helped deploy them to three JMC regional offices in the Congo.

The OAU's lack of resources, however, hampered the OAU and JMC observers, who were incapable of effectively monitoring the cease-fire. Furthermore, because the group included the warring parties themselves, it lacked sufficient neutrality and cohesion. Mbeki and the negotiators in Lusaka may have envisioned that the JMC would act as a supplemental force to any UN peacekeeping mission, but it quickly became deeply dependent upon MONUC and eventually integrated into MONUC's command and control.[71] MONUC accepted the JMC into its fold because the United Nations saw the commission as an avenue through which it could apply direct leverage to the warring parties. When it needed political support from the belligerents, "MONUC would expect to be able to propose the convening of a [JMC] meeting and to initiate their agenda. Decisions would be taken by consensus. MONUC would then expect the parties to abide by the decisions taken by the Commission and to implement those decisions in the field under United Nations verification."[72] MONUC effectively used this structure to convene the Kampala disengagement meeting in April 2000 (see "Deployment and Operations" under Phase II, below), but subsequent meetings were not nearly as effective. Oftentimes representatives did not show up for the meetings, and rarely were agreements acted upon.

Whereas the JMC was paralyzed by its lack of financial resources, MONUC found itself thwarted by the warring parties, especially the Kabila regime, which perceived the peacekeeping mission as a threat to its political power. After all parties had signed the Lusaka Agreement, including the RCD and the MLC, the United Nations established its advance military headquarters in Kinshasa and sent liaison officers to the six capitals of the state signatories (Kinshasa, Kigali, Kampala, Harare, Windhoek, and Luanda) and to Bujumbura and Lusaka, the provisional seat of the JMC. The remaining liaison officers designated for deployment with the rebel groups were not initially dispatched because the Kabila government prevented the advance technical team from traveling outside of Kinshasa and surveying the rebel areas.[73]

A visit by the special envoy of the secretary-general for the peace process, Moustapha Niasse, to President Kabila in early November 1999 proved necessary to pave the way for the technical survey team to proceed and the military liaison officers to be deployed to seven rebel-held locations and one government-held area.[74] The time wasted, obstacles encountered, and energy exerted merely to deploy the technical survey team and establish military liaison officers throughout the Congo did not bode well for the deployment and operation of the larger peacekeeping mission. Moreover, the warring parties' frequent violations of the cease-fire agreement frustrated the liaison officers' attempts to achieve a secure environment and guarantee the Lusaka signatories' cooperation with the deployment of military observers.

Phase II: Protected Observation

Phase II involved a substantial expansion of MONUC's mandate and operations, particularly after the assassination of Laurent Kabila in January 2001. The more accommodating policies of his son and successor, Joseph Kabila, sparked new regional and international interest in pushing the peace process forward.

Mandate

On November 30, 1999, the Security Council passed Resolution 1279, which officially established MONUC. Resolution 1279 authorized the deployment of 500 military observers (milobs). To give them protection and tactical support in the Congo's hostile environment, the secretary-general requested an additional resolution approving the deployment of four reinforced infantry battalions totaling 3,400 troops.

After the heated January debate in the United Nations between the African nations and the Clinton administration, the Americans sponsored Resolution 1291 of February 24, 2000, which mandated the observer mission, backed by the infantry battalions, to begin Phase II of operations. It instructed MONUC to bring all warring parties together within forty-five days to craft an action plan for the implementation of the Lusaka Agreement. The military observers and infantry battalion groups were to monitor the disengagement of troops from the front lines and their redeployment to defensive positions. Beyond that, the armed infantry units were to have no active military role, although a provision granted MONUC the right to act under Chapter VII "in the areas of deployment of its infantry battalions and as it deems it within its capabilities, to protect United Nations and colocated JMC personnel, facilities, installations and equipment, ensure the security and freedom of movement of its personnel, and protect civilians under imminent threat of physical violence."[75] Other MONUC duties included demining, assisting the distribution of humanitarian assistance, and securing the release of prisoners of war.

Subsequently, Security Council Resolution 1355 of June 15, 2001, endorsed the creation of a MONUC police component to advise and help train a Congolese police force throughout the countryside, but especially in Kinshasa and Kisangani. Planning for the police component would commence under Phase II, while deployment would occur during Phase III.

Deployment and Operations

MONUC crafted a plan for the disengagement of troops from the front lines to MONUC-designated defensive positions. The JMC presented the plan to the Political Committee, which adopted it at a meeting in Kampala on April 8, 2000. The Kampala Disengagement Plan called for a comprehensive cease-fire beginning April 14 (D day); sharing of detailed military information by the belligerent parties with MONUC and the JMC starting April 21; and a fifteen-kilometer (roughly nine miles) pullback from either side of the front lines. The Kampala Plan was to be monitored and verified by MONUC observers from mid-May to mid-July (D+30 to D+86). The MONUC infantry battalions would start to deploy during this period to four sector headquarters at Kisangani, Kananga, Mbandaka, and Kalemie. The sector headquarters were to act as safe bases and logistical sites to which military observers could be evacuated by air if necessary.[76]

At the time of the signing of the Kampala Disengagement Plan, MONUC had only 111 military personnel on the ground—hardly enough military observers to monitor a cease-fire line of more than 1,200 miles. More troops were desperately needed, but MONUC required improved cooperation from the warring parties, especially the Kabila regime, in order to deploy them. Consequently, the UN Security Council sent a team, led by Holbrooke, to the region in early May to meet with Kabila and the other regional leaders to obtain their commitment to a set of ground rules for the deployment of the peacekeepers. An agreement between the United Nations and the intransigent Kabila regime became all the more important as the UN peacekeeping mission in Sierra Leone faltered that same week, when the Revolutionary United Front killed seven peacekeepers and took hundreds more hostage (see the chapter on the UN mission in Sierra Leone). The serious military setbacks in Sierra Leone threatened to undercut support for the deployment of UN troops in the Congo, which was considered a much more hostile and complicated peacekeeping environment.

Under pressure from the Security Council team, Kabila signed a status-of-forces agreement with MONUC on May 4, 2000. The Kabila regime promised to permit MONUC unfettered access throughout the country, to ensure security for UN personnel, and to accept South Africans in the peacekeeping force.[77] The United Nations hoped that with the April cease-fire and Kabila's renewed commitment, the first peacekeeping troops could be deployed by July or August.

Fading hopes: May–December 2000. Hope quickly faded, however, as the conflict escalated throughout the next year. In early May, devastating fighting erupted in Kisangani between Rwandan and Ugandan forces that caused widespread loss of life and destroyed housing occupied by MONUC military observers.[78] This blatant violation of the cease-fire agreement represented a clear challenge to the nascent UN peacekeeping mission because the first deployment of UN troop units was to have been at Kisangani.[79] MONUC acted to end the fighting by bringing the commanders of the Ugandan and Rwandan forces together to sign a demilitarization agreement. Both sides agreed to move their troops about sixty miles away from Kisangani and to have their compliance verified by MONUC observers. During the withdrawal process, however, tensions spiraled into open hostilities. On June 5, destructive fighting once again overwhelmed the city.

The upsurge of fighting in Kisangani was not the sole violation of the cease-fire agreement. In Equateur province, the MLC began a major southward advance along the Ubangi River, which led to a clash with government forces. Meanwhile, in Haut Plateau in the Kivus, substantial fighting continued between the ex-FAR and Interahamwe forces and the RCD and their allies. According to the UN Office for the Coordination of Humanitarian Affairs (OCHA), the fighting in Kisangani, the Kivus, and northern Equateur displaced 400,000 people and increased the total number of internally displaced persons in the Congo to 1.8 million.[80] By the end of 2000, the Congo found itself in a vicious cycle. The worse the fighting became, the more urgently UN peacekeepers were needed, and the less likely they were to be deployed.[81]

Despite the promises made to the Security Council assessment mission in May, the Kabila regime continued to obstruct MONUC's deployment and suppress the Inter-Congolese Dialogue. Kabila maintained flight restrictions on MONUC and insisted that flights be authorized on a case-by-case basis. The government refused to participate in preparatory meetings for the Inter-Congolese Dialogue, attempted to block participation by unarmed opposition groups in Kinshasa,[82] and criticized the UN-appointed facilitator, Sir Ketumile Masire, a former president of Botswana. Furthermore, between June 9 and 12, Congolese police stood by as hundreds of demonstrators attacked MONUC offices in Kinshasa.[83]

The breakdown of the cease-fire, the government's intransigence, and the demonstrations in Kinshasa dampened international interest in MONUC. On June 14, Kofi Annan was forced to announce a delay in the deployment of the peacekeepers because of "serious logistical deficiencies," including a lack of adequately trained troops and a shortage of armored vehicles and communications equipment. With the situation on the ground appearing as inflamed as ever, foreign governments were reluctant to provide MONUC with troops and equipment. Congressional Republicans in the United States froze the disbursement of a $41 million U.S. contribution to the mission. In light of concurrent troubles in Sierra Leone, the secretary-general felt it best to delay the deployment.[84]

Relations between the United Nations and the Kabila regime deteriorated even further when Kabila announced that he was terminating the Inter-Congolese Dialogue and banning Masire from the Congo because of the mediator's public criticism of the Congolese government. Kinshasa also withdrew from the JMC and increased its obstruction of MONUC, blocking the mission's access to government-held cities.

In August 2000, Annan considered aborting the entire peacekeeping mission. Kabila finally agreed to the deployment of peacekeepers in late August after Annan sent a special envoy, former Nigerian president General Abdulsalam Abubakar, to meet with the obstinate leader. The deteriorating security environment and logistical constraints, however, prevented the immediate deployment of infantry units. By the end of 2000 not more than 224 military observers and staff officers were deployed in and around the Congo.

With the Lusaka Agreement in dire straits, a flurry of diplomatic activity late in the year attempted to save the peace agreement. The secretary-general, in his September 21, 2000, report, and the UN Security Council, in Resolution 1323 on October 13, 2000, essentially issued ultimatums to the warring parties, giving them two months to revive the peace process or risk seeing MONUC's termination. As the secretary-general stated, "Lack of any progress in the peace process would make it difficult to justify not only the commencement of the second phase of United Nations deployment but also the continuation of the current level of the Mission's presence in the Democratic Republic of Congo. It is clear that United Nations peacekeeping operations cannot serve as a substitute for the political will to achieve a peaceful settlement."[85]

On December 6, 2000, all of the warring parties met in Harare, Zimbabwe, with the hopes of revitalizing the stalled Kampala Disengagement Plan. The Harare summit specified a clear sequence of steps to implement Phase II. First, the warring parties pledged to disengage and withdraw all forces to new defensive positions (NDPs); then the forces would be moved from the NDPs to designated assembly areas; and, finally, the forces would be repatriated to their respective countries. The Harare subplan was to be initiated on December 15, after which the troops would have forty-five days to undertake the fifteen-kilometer disengagement.

Intense fighting continued as the Harare subplan was crafted. RCD-Goma, backed by the Rwandan army, recaptured Pweto, in Katanga province, from Congolese government forces in early December. Thousands of civilians and government soldiers (including Zimbabwean soldiers) fled into Zambia.

Turning point: The assassination of Kabila père. On January 16, 2001, a member of the presidential bodyguard assassinated Laurent Kabila. Kabila's son, Major General Joseph Kabila, was appointed head of state and commander in chief of the Congolese Armed Forces (FAC) by a joint meeting of ministers and senior military officers. Kabila's death and his son's accession sent political shock waves through the country and marked a critical turning point in the peace process.

The younger Kabila pursued a more conciliatory diplomatic track than his father. In meetings with Kamel Morjane, the secretary-general's special representative, Joseph Kabila reversed his father's policies and endorsed MONUC and the Inter-Congolese Dialogue. In his inaugural address on January 26, he announced his commitment to ending the war and establishing regional stability: "We will examine ways and means to revive the Lusaka accord so that it can lead not only to an effective cease-fire, but also bring back peace to the Great Lakes region."[86] He repeated this message in meetings with President Chirac in France, with U.S. secretary of state Colin Powell in Washington, and with the UN Security Council in New York over the next few weeks. Remarkably, while in Washington in early February 2001, the new president had a face-to-face meeting with Rwandan president Paul Kagame. On February 15, Joseph Kabila accepted Masire as the lead facilitator of the Inter-Congolese Dialogue.

Kabila's death also prompted the secretary-general to revise MONUC's concept of operations in his February 12, 2001, report. As described above, the original concept of Resolution 1291, which called for the deployment of four reinforced infantry battalion groups totaling

3,400 troops to protect 500 military observers, proved extremely difficult to implement. The new plan called for "a gradual build-up of capability that encourages the parties to cease hostilities, positions MONUC to respond in a timely and effective manner once the parties begin the disengagement and redeployment process, and minimizes risks to United Nations personnel."[87] The revised plan reduced the total number of personnel from 5,537 to roughly 3,000, of which 1,900 would be armed troops, 550 military observers, and the rest auxiliary personnel. In place of infantry battalions, the secretary-general envisioned the deployment of much smaller and ostensibly more mobile "guard units" to protect UN "facilities, equipment and supplies against tampering or pilfering. . . . [They] will not be able to extract other United Nations personnel at risk, or accompany humanitarian convoys, nor will they be able to extend protection to the local population."[88] In sum, the altered concept of operations was an attempt to make the Harare subplan a reality by creating a more flexible and mobile force that could travel throughout the country to monitor and verify troop disengagement—that is, to complete Phase II, but at the cost of abandoning the protective elements of the mission's mandate.

The Security Council adopted the new concept of operations for MONUC when it passed Resolution 1341 on February 2, 2001, which called on the warring parties to begin disengagement on March 15 and, optimistically, hoped for total withdrawal of foreign troops by May 15. It also included a harsh condemnation of Rwanda and Uganda for their continued destructive presence in the Congo and demanded that they withdraw. The Kabila regime welcomed Resolution 1341 and the new concept of operations, while recommitting itself to the Inter-Congolese Dialogue.

With this change of strategy and a more receptive Kinshasa government, the first guard units (from Uruguay) were deployed to the Congo on March 29, 2001. Within two months a total of 1,869 troops were deployed to the respective sector headquarters, including 539 Senegalese troops dispatched to Kananga and Mbandaka, 614 Moroccans sent to Kisangani and Goma, and 220 Tunisians deployed to Kinshasa. South Africa contributed one aeromedical evacuation unit, an airfield crash/rescue unit, and six aircraft cargo-handling teams, and Uruguay supplied a riverine unit of 176 personnel.[89] In the next year, MONUC would open four coordination centers in Basankusu, Boende, Ilebo, and Manono to provide support to the military observers.

The disengagement of the foreign forces picked up momentum, because each country was keen to avoid being seen as the intransigent actor and thus suffering international isolation. Moreover, as the capture of Kinshasa was clearly out of reach for RCD-Goma and the MLC, the rebel groups and their external sponsors concentrated on consolidating power and extracting resources from the Kivus and Ituri. With the deployment of the first peacekeepers and in accordance with Resolution 1341, Rwanda, Uganda, Zimbabwe, Angola, Namibia, the RCD, and the FAC retreated to new defensive positions. Nevertheless, the MLC at first resisted disengagement, while the RCD obstructed the deployment of UN troops to Kisangani.

By October 2001, the secretary-general declared the disengagement phase near completion, since ninety-five out of ninety-six defensive positions had been verified.[90] MONUC had a total of 2,408 military personnel, including 1,868 armed troops, 397 military observers, and 143 staff officers in the Congo. As Phase II neared completion, the secretary-general proposed to accelerate the implementation of Phase III —disarmament of the negative forces and withdrawal of foreign forces. Disarming the negative forces was a particularly urgent issue, because much of the remaining fighting was between such forces and RCD-Goma in the Kivus. Between September and October 2001, the RCD and the negative forces exchanged control of the strategic towns of Fizi in South Kivu province and Kindu in Maniema.

Phase III: Oversee Withdrawal of Foreign Forces, Disarm the "Negative Forces"

During the implementation of Phase III, MONUC turned its attention to disarmament and attempted to relocate its center of operations from the cease-fire line, which split the country in half, to the troubled east. Although the Security Council boosted MONUC's troop levels by more than half during this phase, it resisted giving MONUC overall Chapter VII authority—that is, making it a mission with peace enforcement capabilities. Phase III saw the withdrawal of almost all foreign troops from the Congo, but the resulting security vacuums intensified ethnic conflict in Ituri and the Kivus, which largely stalled the DDR program.

Mandate

By late 2001, the secretary-general was eager to maintain "the momentum generated by the disengagement of forces" and push forward the idea of transitioning to Phase III and establishing the DDR program.[91] The Harare subplan linked the final withdrawal of foreign forces to the disarmament of armed groups and the holding of a national dialogue. Thus, it was essential that the United Nations make progress on these two fronts before the foreign forces would be withdrawn.

In Resolution 1376 of November 9, 2001, the Security Council supported the launch of Phase III and encouraged the stationing of MONUC "in the east of the Democratic Republic of the Congo . . . including in the cities of Kindu and Kisangani," if the conditions on the ground were favorable and the warring parties cooperated.[92] Resolution 1376 also demanded the demilitarization of Kisangani, then occupied by RCD-Goma, and affirmed MONUC's decision to extend the UN police training program to the city.[93]

Insecurity in the east and lack of cooperation from Rwanda and the Congolese government halted the start of DDR for months. A breakthrough occurred, however, on July 30, 2002, when the governments of Rwanda and the Congo signed an agreement in Pretoria, South Africa, under which Kinshasa promised to dismantle ex-FAR and Interahamwe forces within its borders and Rwanda promised to withdraw its troops from the country. A similar accord was signed between the Congo and Uganda on September 6. By October, Rwanda had withdrawn almost all of its troops from the country. In response, the Security Council passed Resolution 1445, which expanded MONUC to 8,700 personnel and affirmed the new concept of operations for DDR in the east, where a phased deployment of two task forces, headquartered in Kisangani and Kindu, would be conducted and multiple DDR reception centers would be established. Because the DDR program was to be voluntary, Resolution 1445 did not expand MONUC's Chapter VII authority or responsibility. Sadly, MONUC's mandate once again proved inadequate to the task, as violence in the Kivus continued to thwart voluntary disarmament.

Deployment and Operations

Logistical difficulties and the volatility of eastern Congo, where the majority of the negative forces were located, led the secretary-general to advocate a step-by-step approach to moving MONUC farther east.[94] The secretary-general made it clear that MONUC could not coerce the negative forces into disarming:

> The tracking down of armed groups and their disarmament by force are not peacekeeping functions. [There is] no military solution to the problems posed by the armed groups. . . . Any recommendation I make concerning the assistance MONUC can provide to the disarmament, demobilization, reintegration, repatriation or resettlement process will be based on the assumption that MONUC will not be called upon to use enforcement action. In some cases, it is anticipated that armed groups/elements serving with allied forces may present themselves to MONUC for voluntary disarmament and demobilization. MONUC may be called upon to assist accordingly.[95]

Establishing forward support. MONUC originally planned to establish a forward support base in Kindu, sustained by a staging and transit camp in Kisangani. The initial deployment at Kindu would include 400 military personnel, who would work to establish the base and prepare for future deployments. Then an additional 1,200 troops, including a headquarters unit, an infantry battalion, an aviation regiment, and an 800-person forward force support unit would be sent to bolster MONUC's military presence in the region. In Kisangani, the secretary-general envisaged the positioning of 1,100 total military personnel.[96]

Before the United Nations could use Kisangani, however, RCD-Goma forces needed to leave. In December 2001, MONUC's SRSG, Amos Ngongi, traveled to Goma to pressure the rebels to abide by previous Security Council resolutions and leave Kisangani. The rebels linked their withdrawal from the city to the training of 4,000 armed policemen by MONUC to protect the local population.[97] In February 2002, the secretary-general indicated that MONUC would extend its police program to Kisangani. Furthermore, it would deploy additional military personnel to help maintain law and order in exchange for RCD's withdrawal and the Congolese government's promise not to provoke the situation by deploying its security forces in the city.[98]

RCD-Goma nonetheless kept its troops in Kisangani. On May 14, 2002, a group of RCD-Goma soldiers mutinied, took over the Kisangani radio station, and broadcast anti-Rwandan statements. Loyalist

RCD-Goma troops brutally suppressed the mutineers, brought in reinforcements, and orchestrated a campaign of rape, looting, and systematic reprisal killings against civilians and military personnel suspected of involvement in the uprising.[99] Over the next several days, as many as fifty people died. MONUC, which had around 1,000 peacekeepers and dozens of military observers in the city, refused to intervene militarily, using only diplomatic pressure to staunch the human rights abuses. RCD-Goma responded by banning Ngongi from RCD-Goma territories and declaring the United Nations biased in favor of the Kinshasa government.[100] The mutiny and subsequent crackdown stalled the establishment of the DDR task force and the implementation of the UN police program in Kisangani.

Even if the circumstances for DDR in the Congo had been ideal, however, the sheer scale of the task would have remained enormous. As Phase III began, the Congo was still host to a kaleidoscope of well-armed, sizable, and potentially hostile militias, Congolese and foreign, totaling 30,000 to 50,000 fighters.[101] By April 2002, UNITA had no organized presence in the Congo, and only 200 to 300 fighters of one Ugandan armed group—the Allied Democratic Forces—were active there, but the Forces for the Defense of Democracy from Burundi had between 3,000 and 4,000 troops in eastern Congo. The remnants of the former Rwandan army and the Interahamwe formed the most substantial foreign armed groups in the country. The Army for the Liberation of Rwanda (ALIR) I, with 4,000 to 6,000 troops, included the majority of the *génocidaires* who had fled Rwanda in 1994. It had tried (and failed) to invade Rwanda in May and June 2001. ALIR II was a more robust fighting force of 4,000–6,000 troops, many of them younger nonparticipants in the 1994 genocide. An umbrella organization, the Democratic Forces for the Liberation of Rwanda (FDLR), was formed in September 2000 and emerged publicly a year later, subsuming ALIR I and II and the latter's postgenocide recruits. FDLR was closely allied with the Congolese government, took a hard-line stance against DDR, and called for political negotiations with Kigali. In early 2003, the International Crisis Group estimated the number of "forces operating under the FDLR banner in the Kivus [at] between 15,000 and 20,000."[102]

Although not considered an official negative force by the Lusaka Agreement, the indigenous Mai-Mai group was a diverse and large coalition of Congolese community-based fighters who were very active in eastern Congo. The Mai-Mai leaders' interests varied, and they allied with different national governments, including the Congo and Rwanda. The United Nations estimated their overall size as between 20,000 and 30,000 fighters.

MONUC lacked the capacity to undertake the enormous task of disarming and repatriating these armed groups. By mid-June 2002, it had only limited numbers of peacekeepers in Kisangani and Kindu. The arrival of additional Uruguayan guard units in Kisangani raised the troop level there to 1,150. At the same time, 400 Uruguayan troops set up base in Kindu with support from elements of an Uruguayan engineering company. Such small forces, however, could not guarantee a secure and safe environment for DDR.[103]

The Kamina incident. The broader shortcomings of MONUC's DDR program showed clearly in the disastrous attempt to repatriate the first group of ex-FAR fighters, who were cantoned in Kamina. In April 2001, the Congolese government notified MONUC that thousands of ex-FAR fighters were quartered in Kamina in southeastern Congo but denied the United Nations access to Kamina for months. Not until November did MONUC begin screening the irregular forces to verify their nationality and military affiliation.[104] By the end of the year, MONUC had finished screening 1,981 Hutu combatants and identified them as closely allied with the FDLR. Consistent with the political agenda of the FDLR, the quartered fighters indicated that they would return home only if an inter-Rwanda political dialogue was begun. This last fact, the linking of disarmament with political change in Rwanda, added a new level of complexity to the disarmament process that neither MONUC nor the rest of the international community had previously considered.[105]

Although the cantoned soldiers were confirmed to be Rwandans and ex-FAR combatants, they could not be demobilized because they refused to reveal their personal identities or otherwise cooperate with MONUC officials.[106] Thus they remained idle in the camps in Kamina for months. To entice them to disarm and go home, the United Nations sent an initial group of sixty-nine demobilized ex-FAR combatants and ten dependents to Rwanda to assess the conditions for their return. Upon arrival in Rwanda, many ex-combatants seemed genuinely happy to return home, experiencing emotional reunions with their families. MONUC videotaped these reunions and showed them to the remaining soldiers in Kamina as a way to persuade the rest of them to voluntarily return to Rwanda.

In the midst of this repatriation program, however, in November 2002 the governments of the Congo and South Africa attempted to forcibly repatriate eight FDLR leaders from Kinshasa to Rwanda. In response, most of the Rwandan combatants in Kamina rose up against their Congolese army guards and tried to seize a weapons cache.[107] Seven Congolese soldiers were killed, and all but 200 Rwandan combatants dispersed toward the north and east. After this incident, MONUC reiterated publicly that it favored only voluntary repatriation of foreign combatants in the Congo. Of the 1,700 Rwandans who fled Kamina, MONUC managed to repatriate 402 combatants and 333 dependents to reintegration camps in Mutobo, Rwanda. The Kamina incident also soured the FDLR leadership on the disarmament process and fed into its propaganda campaign to dissuade Rwandan combatants from returning home.

MONUC's experience in Kamina highlighted the difficulties of a DDR program that was more complicated than most because its targets were foreigners who feared returning home but who, for cultural, linguistic, and ethnic reasons, had trouble assimilating in eastern Congo. They were stuck in eastern Congo but unwelcome, all the more so for preying on the local populations.

MONUC, which struggled in its attempts to liaise with the negative forces because of language barriers and personnel shortages, had no choice but to pursue a voluntary disarmament process. The UN peacekeeping mission had little capability to handle the backlash that forcible disarmament and repatriation would provoke. Unable to establish stable and secure DDR reception centers, MONUC resorted to pursuing "austere DDR": approaching armed combatants individually and trying to persuade them to return home. Even if this strategy were successful, it would take decades to disarm and demobilize, one by one, the thousands of armed combatants marauding in eastern Congo. Ultimately, the establishment of the transitional government and the bolstering of MONUC's presence in the east proved crucial to accelerating the DDR process.

Political breakthroughs and foreign troop withdrawals. Although the first attempt at DDR was a failure, diplomatic progress and growing success with the Inter-Congolese Dialogue created extraordinary opportunities to push the disarmament process forward. Presidents Kabila and Kagame signed the Pretoria Peace Agreement on July 30, 2002, with South African president Thabo Mbeki and UN secretary-general Kofi Annan signing on as witnesses. The bilateral accord tackled two of the main obstacles to peace in the Congo: the disarmament of ex-FAR and Interahamwe forces and the withdrawal of foreign troops. The agreement stipulated that the Congo would locate and disarm the negative forces in its territory, work with MONUC and the JMC to disband the organizational structures of the ex-FAR and Interahamwe, and repatriate all Rwandan ex-combatants to Rwanda.[108] In return, the government of Rwanda would withdraw all of its troops from the Congo "as soon as effective measures that address its security concerns, in particular the dismantling of the ex-FAR and Interahamwe forces, have been agreed to."[109] The United Nations and South Africa committed themselves to verifying and monitoring the agreement as part of a third-party verification mechanism. Furthermore, MONUC was called upon to complete Phase III deployment and facilitate the DDR process. All of the above provisions were to be completed within ninety days.

Under intense international pressure, Rwanda withdrew 21,000 of its troops from the Congo by early October 2002. By the end of the month, the Kinshasa government had announced the official departure of the armies of Angola, Namibia, and Zimbabwe. With the withdrawal of almost all foreign troops, except Uganda in the northeast, and in light of MONUC's verification duties designated by the Pretoria Agreement, the secretary-general once again adopted a new concept of operations to try to kick-start the disarmament process. Rather than setting up the forward support base in Kindu, MONUC planned to establish a forward mission headquarters in Kisangani, which would "enable MONUC to shift the 'centre of gravity' of its activities gradually towards the eastern Democratic Republic of the Congo."[110] Two robust task forces of 1,700 troops each were to be based in Kindu and Kisangani, with the capacity to dispatch up to three company groups to different disarmament and demobilization sites. The main duties of the task forces, according to the secretary-general, were to "provide 'point security' at disarmament and demobilization sites for the conduct of the disarmament, demobilization and reintegration process, support the engineering preparation of disarmament and demobilization sites, destroy weapons and munitions, and provide limited demining capability."[111] The mobile task forces would be equipped with helicopters and armored personnel carriers. In addition, multidisciplinary civilian/military DDR teams were dispatched to the eastern MONUC offices of Bukavu, Butembo, and Kalemie, as well as Kindu.

The secretary-general proposed that MONUC, working with the World Food Programme, the World Health Organization, and the United Nations Children's Fund, open mobile reception centers throughout eastern Congo where the ex-combatants could be disarmed and demobilized and then returned to Rwanda. The Secretariat estimated that MONUC could operate two to four mobile reception centers simultaneously, while a total of ten to twelve would be needed for the entire DDR process. Upwards of 90,000 ex-combatants and dependents were expected to pass through the camps. To handle this caseload, the Secretariat sought to more than double the size of the peacekeeping force, adding 4,340 troops and 120 military observers to the then-current deployment of 3,600 troops and 640 military observers.[112]

On December 16, 2002, MONUC opened its first DDR reception center in Lubero, in North Kivu. MONUC hoped that the 3,000 to 4,000 Rwandan combatants in the area would be disarmed, demobilized, and repatriated from this center, but had little initial success. Hard-line leaders of the FDLR, suspicious of MONUC and fearful of returning to Rwanda, were obstructing the process and broadcasting antidisarmament messages that helped persuade rank-and-file members not to participate in the DDR program.[113]

Rwanda also deserved a large portion of the blame for the lackluster initial results. With the support of the country's military, RCD-Goma carried out a series of offensives in North Kivu in the first half of 2003, despite ongoing cease-fire talks with a rival rebel faction in Burundi. An attack near the Lubero reception center dispersed 200 to 300 Rwandan combatants waiting to enter the DDR program.[114] In June, RCD-Goma actually captured Lubero, displacing most of its people and deterring many ex-FAR and Interahamwe combatants from entering the disarmament program.[115] RCD-Goma's campaigns caused some of the worst human rights violations in the Congo in 2003.[116]

Rwanda was content to stoke the conflict in eastern Congo every so often to ensure that the Kivus remained in a permanent state of emergency. This strategy served two purposes. First, it justified Rwanda's presence in the region and allowed mineral exploitation to continue. Second, it ensured that the DDR process did not progress so far that ex-FAR and Interahamwe soldiers were once again sitting in camps demanding that Kigali liberalize the country's political system and initiate an inter-Rwandan dialogue before they returned home. A failed DDR program, in other words, kept pressure for domestic political reform at manageable levels.

At the same time as RCD-Goma's offensives in Lubero, MONUC was overwhelmed by ethnic cleansing in Ituri (see "Violence in the Northeast" under Phase IV, below). Consequently, it was able to devote only one task force to DDR in the Kivus, while the second relocated from Kisangani to Bunia. The South Africans made up the bulk of MONUC Task Force I in the Kivus, deploying more than 1,200 troops to Kindu in May 2003, with smaller units deployed in Goma, Bukavu, and Lubero. Task Force I began "robust patrols" in an attempt to create a more secure environment, communicate with the foreign armed combatants, and coax them into disarming.

Accompanied by microlevel mediation efforts between armed factions and by the formation of the transitional government in Kinshasa, MONUC hoped that its proactive patrolling would boost the disarmament process in the Kivus. Through October 2003, however, only 400 more Rwandan combatants repatriated (together with 700 dependents and others), raising total Rwandan repatriations to about 2,700.[117] The number repatriated had increased dramatically by March 2004, however, to about 9,700 (including noncombatants) due to the inauguration of the interim Congolese government, the ongoing integration of the Congolese armed forces, and MONUC's updated mandate and troop presence. With the acceleration of the repatriation process, however, the leaders of the FDLR, who know they could be tried for war crimes or prosecuted by the Rwandan government if they left the Congo, acted to forcibly prevent their members from returning to Rwanda, leaving them even more isolated and vulnerable.[118] In the spring of 2004, the United Nations estimated that 10,000 ex-FAR and Interahamwe members still remained in eastern Congo, and Rwandan government estimates were two to three times that number.

Phase IV: Operation Artemis and Expansion in the East

As instability and continued violence in the east frustrated MONUC's attempts to implement voluntary DDR, it became apparent that the formation and inauguration of the transitional government would be necessary prerequisites for the DDR program to succeed. The Inter-Congolese Dialogue had been revived after Laurent Kabila's death in January 2001, but the initial political negotiations in Addis Ababa at the end of 2001 broke down after the government walked out, claiming there was insufficient representation from the other belligerents to make any progress.

New talks over power sharing and a transitional government started in Sun City, South Africa, in February 2002. The Sun City talks included serious discussion and compromise on the division of power between Kabila's government and Jean-Pierre Bemba's MLC, but led only to a partial agreement because RCD-Goma refused to enter into the negotiations. Rwandan army withdrawal from the Congo, however, increased the pressure on RCD-Goma to engage in the talks or risk even greater international and domestic isolation.

Toward the end of 2002, talks between the government, the MLC, RCD-Goma, and the unarmed opposition intensified. In mid-December, these parties signed an all-inclusive peace agreement for the first time since the start of the Inter-Congolese Dialogue, leading to the division of power among the four parties and a call for a two-year interim period before national elections.[119] Subsequent technical talks in 2003 paved the way for a new constitution and the unification of the army.

These landmark agreements necessitated reunification of the polity and the extension of the central government's authority to all regions of the country, especially the east. Nevertheless, the Security Council balked at strengthening or amending MONUC's mandate to correspond with the changing political and conflict dynamics. UN Security Council Resolution 1468 of March 20, 2003, welcomed the signing of the all-inclusive political agreement and encouraged MONUC to continue its deployment in the east to help the new transitional government assert its authority in these troubled regions, but it did not boost the peacekeeping mission's capacity commensurate with the task ahead. Though the conclusion of the Inter-Congolese Dialogue decreased conflict in most of the country, the withdrawal of Ugandan forces from the northeast and Rwandan forces from the Kivus resulted in an escalation of violence in these regions. It would take spiraling ethnic violence in Ituri to focus worldwide attention on the Congo and encourage the Security Council to substantially strengthen MONUC's mandate.

Violence in the Northeast

In 2003, Uganda remained the lone foreign power with a substantial force still in the Congo. Its soldiers were concentrated in the Ituri district, in the northeastern corner of the country near the Ugandan border. As early as February 2001, the United Nations had identified the situation in Ituri as "highly explosive," but MONUC managed to position only ten military observers in the region over the next year.[120] As long as the Ugandans and Rwandans remained in the eastern Congo, fomenting but also limiting the extent of ethnic violence, the Security Council could tolerate the status quo. The slow burn in eastern Congo —millions of civilians dying of malnourishment and disease, with the occasional massacre—did not provoke a serious international response.

The UPDF justified its presence in Ituri as necessary to keep peace between the Hema and Lendu, but its paramount motive was economic. Ituri is rich in gold, diamond, cobalt, timber, and oil reserves, and Uganda stoked ethnic tensions in the region to ensure control of these lucrative resources. Although it armed and trained whichever side served its interests, the UPDF sided predominantly with Hema businessmen, causing a backlash among the Lendu that led to a spiral of violence between the two ethnic groups. At least 60,000 people died in Ituri between 1999 and 2003 as a result. As Human Rights Watch concluded, Uganda "played the role of both arsonist and fireman with disastrous consequences for the local population."[121]

The tribal rivalry between the Hema and Lendu was longstanding. Favored by the Belgian colonialists, the minority pastoralist Hema dominated economic and political affairs in the region at the expense of the agriculturalist Lendu. Various minor conflicts over land had occurred between Hema landholders and Lendu communities in the first four decades of independence, but since 1999 intergroup violence had spiraled out of control. The UPDF intervention, the presence of Congolese rebel groups, a ready supply of weapons, the deterioration of the economy, and the rising salience of ethnicity to security all contributed to the militarization of Hema-Lendu relations.[122]

The first major escalation came in June 1999 after Brigadier General James Kazini, commander of the UDPF in the Congo, appointed a Hema extremist as governor in Ituri and Hema landholders tried to seize Lendu land with falsified property documents.[123] The dispute evolved into large-scale fighting as both sides organized militias. The Hema paid Ugandan soldiers to intervene on their behalf, and the UPDF raided Lendu villages. The Ugandan soldiers' intervention and their use of high-powered weapons increased the devastation and the death toll. As many as 7,000 civilians were killed and 150,000 displaced after the first wave of violence.[124] Eventually, mediation efforts cooled the conflict as the Hema governor was replaced, Ugandan soldiers involved in the fighting were removed, and the UPDF bolstered its presence.[125]

Tensions between the groups persisted, however. The UPDF sponsored various ethnic militias to ensure its control over natural resources and to maintain its commercial network, but did little to protect civilians.[126] Moreover, persistent leadership squabbles, political infighting, and fractionalization plagued the main Congolese rebel group operating in Ituri (RCD Liberation Movement—RCD-ML). The MLC attempted to extend its control to Ituri, leading to more fighting. In an effort to reduce the violence, Uganda tried to merge the MLC and RCD-ML into a new rebel movement, the Front for the Liberation of Congo, led by Bemba. RCD-ML officials rebuffed Bemba and the merger failed. Meanwhile, the political wrangling sparked another wave of large-scale violence between Hema and Lendu militias.

In November 2000, Mbusa Nyamwisi, a businessman from the Nande tribe, emerged as the acting leader of RCD-ML. He formed a military wing, the Congolese Popular Army (APC), to advance his interests. Nyamwisi garnered backing from both Nande and Lendu. In June 2002, a group of Hema militias led by Thomas Lubanga broke away from RCD-ML, formed the Union of Congolese Patriots (UPC) and, with the support of the UPDF, captured Bunia in August. On September

5, the APC and Lendu militias retaliated with a slaughter of 1,000 Hema civilians in the town of Nyankunde that the UPDF did little to stop.[127]

On September 6, Uganda and the Congo signed an agreement in Luanda, Angola, that gave Uganda one hundred days to complete the withdrawal of its final two battalions from Bunia, in exchange for normalization of relations with Kinshasa, which promised to secure its border with Uganda. Later that month, the two countries established the Ituri Pacification Commission (IPC) to govern Ituri after Uganda's withdrawal, but its implementation stalled in the face of sundry militia infighting. Although MONUC eventually brokered a cease-fire, Lubanga's UPC not only failed to sign it but also aligned itself with RCD-Goma and therefore, implicitly, Rwanda. The UPC also splintered into several militia groups, the most notable of which was the Front for Integration and Peace in Ituri (FIPI), which the Ugandans backed.

Kampala undertook to drive Lubanga and the UPC out of Bunia and replace them with FIPI and other, more friendly militias. In March 2003 Ugandan troops did so, and their assertion of control enabled the launch of the Ituri Pacification Commission. In early April, under the auspices of MONUC, the IPC met and established arrangements to pacify Ituri, including the formation of a local assembly, an interim executive, and various human rights and conflict prevention committees that were to form the new Ituri interim administration. Crucial to its success was MONUC's commitment to deploy a sizable force to Ituri.[128]

MONUC scrambled to send peacekeepers to Bunia but, despite the troop ceiling increase to 8,700 in December 2002, only 4,700 had deployed by April 2003 (see table 4.3), and no extra troops were available. Crucially, a brigade from South Africa that "certainly would have been an appropriate military asset for the tasks required in Bunia," according to the UN Department of Peacekeeping Operations (DPKO), Peacekeeping Best Practices Unit, had been delayed by logistical difficulties and thus was not available to MONUC for deployment in Ituri.[129] Instead, MONUC had to use a reserve battalion from Uruguay of only 700 troops, trained for static guard duty, to attempt to stabilize the Ituri district, a region roughly the size of Sierra Leone. MONUC's 700 military guards in Bunia were not prepared to deal with the security vacuum created by the sudden withdrawal of 7,000 Ugandan soldiers.[130]

Table 4.3. MONUC, Contributors of Uniformed Personnel, April 2003

Country	Troops	Military Observers	Police	Total
Uruguay	1,594	28	—	1,622
Morocco	657	1	—	658
Senegal	482	10	9	501
Ghana	405	18	—	423
Tunisia	259	23	—	282
China	219	9	—	228
Bolivia	205	2	—	207
South Africa	184	3	—	187
Kenya	16	30	—	46
Pakistan	17	26	—	43
Bangladesh	25	13	—	38
Russia	2	28	5	35
India	9	24	—	33
Jordan	5	26	—	31
Benin	1	22	6	29
Egypt	4	24	1	29
Romania	—	27	1	28
Mali	1	25	1	27
Nigeria	4	23	—	27
Zambia	4	17	—	21
Malawi	—	20	—	20
Nepal	4	15	—	19
Niger	2	13	4	19
Malaysia	11	7	—	18
Ukraine	2	13	3	18
Paraguay	2	15	—	17
Burkina Faso	—	11	2	13
Indonesia	4	9	—	13
Algeria	1	10	—	11
Ten or fewer per country: Argentina, Belgium, Bosnia-Herzegovina, Cameroon, Canada, Côte d'Ivoire, Czech Republic, Denmark, France, Guinea, Ireland, Italy, Mongolia, Mozambique, Norway, Peru, Poland, Portugal, Spain, Sri Lanka, Sweden, Switzerland, Turkey, United Kingdom	40	33	19	92
Total	4,159	525	51	4,735

Source: UN Department of Peacekeeping Operations (DPKO), "UN Missions, Contributions by Country," April 2003. Updated monthly. www.un.org/Depts/dpko/dpko/contributors/ 2003.

As the UPDF started to pull out, the United Nations realized that MONUC was incapable of securing order in Bunia. Kampala offered to keep its troops in Ituri to stabilize the situation, but only if the United Nations formally authorized its presence. The United Nations had already implicitly recognized Ugandan occupation of Ituri when it exhorted Kampala, as an occupying power, to protect civilians under its control as specified in the fourth Geneva convention.[131] Such implicit recognition, however, was already a dangerous precedent that could encourage states to foment discord and anarchy in neighboring countries, then benefit from that disorder through the exploitation of resources, and finally threaten an even greater crisis by hastily departing and leaving a security vacuum. The disconnect between the international diplomatic pressure to force the Ugandan forces out of Ituri and MONUC's limited capacity to replace them was extraordinary, and was representative of the Security Council's failure to craft a coherent political and military strategy to deal with the Congo crisis.

Once the Ugandans left, unchecked militias ravaged Bunia. Lendu militias conducted a series of revenge killings against Hema. UN offices outside the MONUC sector headquarters compound were looted. Two MONUC soldiers were killed, while others withdrew to the UN compound. Several thousand civilians also converged on the UN compound, scaling walls and fences to do so, but not being turned out once inside. The Uruguayan troops on hand functioned under stringent orders from home not to shoot except in self-defense.

On May 12, the UPC recaptured Bunia and reprisal killings continued—this time with Lendu as targets. The UPC established control of the town and used the radio to broadcast threats against Lendu. An estimated 400 people were killed in two weeks.

Amnesty International and Human Rights Watch issued a joint letter calling for the UN Security Council to deploy a robust force to stop the calculated violence.[132] In mid-May, Kofi Annan called for a rapid reaction force to be created and deployed in northeastern Congo. By the end of May, France answered the secretary-general's plea and agreed to lead the force into Ituri provided that other countries also contributed troops and resources, that there was a precise and limited operation timeline, and that the regional troublemakers, Rwanda and Uganda, supported the intervention.[133]

Mandate

In Resolution 1484 of May 30, 2003, the UN Security Council author-
ized the deployment of an Interim Emergency Multinational Force
(IEMF) to pacify the town of Bunia, despite objections from Rwanda.
Specifically, the UN Security Council mandated the IEMF to work

> in close coordination with MONUC, in particular its contingent
> currently deployed in the town, to contribute to the stabilization
> of the security conditions and the improvement of the humani-
> tarian situation in Bunia, to ensure the protection of the airport,
> the internally displaced persons in the camps in Bunia and, if the
> situation requires it, to contribute to the safety of the civilian pop-
> ulation, United Nations personnel and the humanitarian presence
> in the town.[134]

The IEMF was granted a full Chapter VII mandate—the right to employ all necessary means to carry out its mission. The Security Council envisaged that the French-led force would act to stop the spiraling
violence in Ituri until MONUC could bolster its presence in the
region. On June 5, 2003, the European Union sanctioned the French-
led intervention as an EU military operation—Operation Artemis—
the first of its kind outside of Europe. The operation was to last three
months, with a self-imposed September 1 withdrawal deadline.

Recognizing that Operation Artemis was only a temporary measure and that fighting also continued to rage in the Kivus, the Security
Council acted to strengthen MONUC as well. On July 28, 2003, the
council adopted Resolution 1493, which increased MONUC's troop
strength to 10,800 and authorized the use of "all necessary means" to
carry out its mandate—including protection of civilians—in Ituri and
the Kivus. The Security Council also instituted an arms embargo,
declaring that "all States, including the Democratic Republic of the
Congo, shall . . . take the necessary measures to prevent the direct
or indirect supply, sale or transfer, from their territories or by their
nationals, or using their flag vessels or aircraft, of arms and any related
materiel, and the provision of any assistance, advice or training related
to military activities, to all foreign and Congolese armed groups and
militias operating in the territory of North and South Kivu and of Ituri,
and to groups not party to the Global and All-inclusive agreement, in

the Democratic Republic of the Congo."[135] Resolution 1493 neglected to give the embargo an enforcement mechanism, an omission the council partially rectified nine months later. Resolution 1533 of March 12, 2004, established a Security Council Sanctions Committee and a Group of Experts on the Congo to monitor the embargo and report on violations. The same resolution gave MONUC the authority "to use all means, within its capabilities, to [enforce the embargo] ... and in particular to inspect, without notice as it deems it necessary, the cargo of aircraft and of any transport vehicle using the ports, airports, airfields, military bases and border crossings in North and South Kivu and in Ituri."[136]

Deployment and Operations

Operation Artemis included approximately 1,500 personnel, with more than 1,000 troops deployed in Bunia. France served as the "framework" (lead) nation and hosted the operational headquarters in Paris. The force headquarters was based in Entebbe, Uganda, with an advance position in Bunia.[137] A reconnaissance unit of ten to fifteen personnel was sent to Bunia on June 6 to secure the airport and prepare for the deployment of the larger force. On June 8 and 9 a contingent of 700 French soldiers, along with sixty Canadians and a dozen Belgian soldiers, arrived in Uganda, with onward deployment to Bunia the next day. By early July more than 1,000 French soldiers were in Bunia. Germany contributed 350 troops to Operation Artemis, providing logistical and medical assistance from Entebbe.[138]

Equipped with helicopter gunships, heavy armor, and the ability to call on fighter aircraft operating from French bases in Chad,[139] the IEMF had an immediate impact on the conflict dynamics in Bunia. It swiftly devised a plan to demilitarize Bunia and canton all militias outside the city. The force quickly demonstrated that it was not afraid to use force. During the mission's first week, IEMF soldiers killed two Hema militiamen after being fired upon.[140] As calm was restored to Bunia, however, fighting flared in other parts of Ituri, where the French-led forces were not patrolling. For example, twenty-two civilians were slaughtered in Nizi, a village fourteen miles north of Bunia, on July 22, and fighting persisted from mid-July until late August in Fataki, a town thirty-seven miles northwest of Bunia, where hundreds of people were killed.[141] One assessment counted at least sixteen massacres outside of

Bunia in the period between June and August 2003.[142] As a whole, however, the mission was judged successful in achieving its limited mandate:

> Ultimately, the IEMF re-established security in Bunia and weakened the military capabilities of the rival Lendu and Hema militias, including by cutting off military supplies from abroad, through monitoring of airfields. As a result, the political process in Ituri was allowed to resume some activity as political offices reopened in Bunia and the town population began to return. To a certain extent, economic and social activities were resumed.[143]

By July 16 the first reinforcements of a 4,800-strong UN replacement force, known as Task Force II or the Ituri Brigade, arrived in Bunia in preparation for taking over control of the town from the IEMF. One month later, EU peacekeepers started to hand over control of checkpoints to Bangladeshi troops who had arrived as part of Task Force II. By September 1, 2,400 UN peacekeepers from Uruguay, Bangladesh, India, Pakistan, and Indonesia were in Bunia. UN troops on the ground reported excellent cooperation with the IEMF, as the two forces coordinated operations and exchanged information in an open manner.[144] Upon request from the UN Security Council, the French-led IEMF agreed to leave some personnel in Bunia for another two weeks to assist with the transition. By November, Nepal and Pakistan each had deployed a battalion, bringing the troop levels close to 4,500. Task Force II was equipped with heavy firepower, including attack helicopters, as well as armored personnel carriers.

Tension increased with the departure of the French-led force, and the security situation deteriorated slightly. Nonetheless, the Ituri Brigade maintained aggressive patrolling and displayed a willingness to use force. After the departure of the French, the UPC immediately began testing MONUC's Task Force II to see if it would respond robustly. In early October, a massacre of sixty-five Hema roughly sixty miles northeast of Bunia accelerated the Ituri Brigade's deployment outside Bunia town limits. In early November, MONUC sent 150 troops to intervene in a clash between the UPC and a rival Hema militia in Tchomia, twenty-eight miles southeast of Bunia.

Though massacres still continued outside Bunia and tension ratcheted up within the town following the EU withdrawal, the UN peacekeepers took a more proactive military stance than in the past, demonstrating that MONUC had begun to take its Chapter VII mandate seriously. The United Nations also sought to go further than the IEMF by attempting to extend its authority throughout the region and to disarm the militias. It engaged in robust patrols and cordon-and-search operations, and deployed to seven locations in the Ituri interior in addition to Bunia. At the same time, MONUC's more aggressive stance in Ituri increasingly made it the target of violent attacks by militia groups. Between December 2003 and March 2004, the United Nations reported twenty violent attacks on MONUC in Ituri alone.[145] By late 2004 the frequency of attacks had roughly doubled, as the United Nations reported forty incidents of direct fire against MONUC between September 1 and December 15.[146]

MONUC recognized that crucial to establishing any permanent stability in the region would be the extension of the interim Congolese government's authority. As MONUC consolidated control of Bunia and extended its military presence throughout the Ituri district, it began working with the transitional government in Kinshasa to prepare for the positioning of newly trained Congolese police officers and integrated army units in the region.

William Lacy Swing, newly appointed as the secretary-general's special representative in May 2003, deserves credit for helping MONUC make the transition from an observer mission to a Chapter VII peacekeeping force. Swing instilled MONUC's operations with an aggressiveness that was lacking under the direction of his predecessor, Amos Ngongi. As a former U.S. ambassador to the Congo, with local and regional expertise and connections back in Washington, Swing was able to help bridge the divide between the military component of the mission and the diplomatic track, which for years had led to an incoherent and badly coordinated military and political strategy.

With the deployment of Task Force II, MONUC was showing signs in Ituri of becoming the force it should have been over the previous four years—one that could protect civilians, support the delivery of relief aid, and undertake DDR. The operation's fifth and sixth sector headquarters were created in 2003 at Kindu and Bunia, respectively. From October 2004 onward, Kisangani became eastern division headquarters following the expansion and restructuring of MONUC that was authorized in Resolution 1565. The real challenge would be expanding MONUC's reach to the Kivus and other parts of the east and tackling disarmament of the Interahamwe and ex-FAR forces, whose presence in the Congo since 1994 had helped ignite the regional conflict.

Renewed Tensions in the Kivus

Soon after MONUC completed deploying the Ituri Brigade, an upsurge of violence in Bukavu, the capital of South Kivu, once again tested the mission's capacity and willingness to use force. The conflict in Bukavu originated in power struggles between RCD-Goma and Kabila's faction relating to army integration, but on a deeper level it involved jousting between Kinshasa and Kigali over lucrative natural resources in the Kivus and the continued presence of the FDLR in eastern Congo.

As Kinshasa attempted to extend its authority over the Kivus and integrate the rebel groups operating there into its new armed forces, tensions between competing factions quickly surfaced. In September 2003, a number of dissident officers from RCD-Goma refused their nomination by Kinshasa to posts in the new national army, knowing that many of the RCD-Goma officers who had already joined up felt excluded from positions of influence. Former rebel officers who had integrated into the new army received the same salaries as their soldiers and would not receive confirmation of their military rank until September 2004.[147] Kigali may also have exerted its influence over these officers and encouraged their insubordination.[148]

In early 2004 the regional commander of South Kivu, stationed in Bukavu, was General Prosper Nabyolwa, a former FAC officer allied with the central government. The dissident officers from RCD-Goma refused to acknowledge Nabyolwa's authority and began smuggling weapons into the region, in cooperation with the governor of South Kivu. In February 2004, Nabyolwa raided the dissidents' houses in search of weapons, seized stockpiles of ammunition, and arrested one officer. In response, Nabyolwa's deputy commander, Colonel Jules Mutebutsi, allied himself with the dissidents and attacked Nabyolwa's house, killing two bodyguards and forcing Nabyolwa to flee.

Shortly thereafter, the UN secretary-general announced the expansion of Task Force I into a brigade-sized force for the Kivus. The brigade would total 3,500 troops for both North and South Kivu, with a base in Bukavu. It would utilize MONUC's existing resources, including South African–led Task Force I units in North Kivu and a battalion of Uruguayans redeployed to South Kivu.[149]

The next regional commander sent by Kinshasa to South Kivu was General Mbuza Mabe, who had little more success in quelling unrest among the dissidents. On May 26, Mutebutsi's troops mutinied against Mabe, clashing with troops loyal to Mabe and the transitional government. Although MONUC had cantoned Mutebutsi's forces by May 29, the clashes sparked exaggerated accusations by General Laurent Nkunda, one of the original dissident RCD-Goma officers, that troops of Mabe's Armed Forces of the Democratic Republic of Congo (FARDC), the new integrated army of the transitional government, had harassed and even committed genocide against Bukavu's Banyamulenge population.[150] Nkunda assembled a force of 1,000 to 1,500 men and marched on Bukavu from Goma. National army troops had established a buffer zone outside Bukavu to stem Nkunda's advance, but they quickly abandoned their posts as his forces approached. Meanwhile, Mutebutsi's troops confronted the small number of Uruguayan troops stationed to guard them and broke out of their UN cantonment, fully armed. The UN troops deployed outside Bukavu similarly failed to forcibly intercept Nkunda's men as they approached the city, marching through UN checkpoints. Despite orders by the UN deputy force commander in charge of Bukavu, General Jan Isberg, to defend the Bukavu airstrip with force if necessary, an Uruguayan commander gave up the airstrip to Nkunda's troops without a fight.[151]

Over the course of the next week, the armies of Nkunda and Mutebutsi laid siege to Bukavu, engaging in a campaign of murder, rape, and pillage and causing more than 2,000 civilians to seek shelter at the MONUC compound. Nkunda and Mutebutsi eventually agreed to withdraw under intense diplomatic pressure on June 6 and June 8, respectively. A subsequent UN investigation found that they had received support from Rwanda in the form of weapons, ammunition, and permission to use its territory as a rear base.[152] While Nkunda's forces remained in the Congo, setting up camp between Bukavu and Goma, Mutebutsi crossed into Rwanda on June 21 along with 300 of his troops.[153]

Following Mutebutsi's and Nkunda's withdrawal, Mabe's forces engaged in their own campaign of abuse against Bukavu's civilian population. Members of the Banyamulenge community, blamed for supporting or sympathizing with the mutineers, were now the primary victims, and almost 3,000 of them fled to Rwanda.[154]

In addition to its ethnic dimensions and complex relationship to turf battles in Kinshasa, fighting in the Kivus in 2004 was also about resources. Rwanda's economic stake in the Kivus remained high, despite the formal departure of its armed forces. Before the crisis in Bukavu, resources and profits from the mines in the Kivus flowed primarily north to Goma and then east into Rwanda. Following the crisis in May and June 2004, these profits increasingly began their journey to international markets by flowing south to Bukavu.[155] As of June 2005, Rwanda was exporting more than five times as much cassiterite (a metal used to produce tin) as it produced domestically, resulting in revenue of more than $10 million. The excess exports almost certainly came from cassiterite originally mined in the Kivus, then illegally shipped to Rwanda without the payment of export tariffs.[156]

MONUC had 450 troops in the Bukavu area when fighting began in late May. It had redeployed 350 more troops by the time Nkunda's forces arrived on May 29, and another 204 troops by June 1, to bring the total to 1,004.[157] The troops also could have called on a fleet of armored vehicles and air support in the form of Indian Mi-25 attack helicopters. Despite this substantial force capacity, the United Nations opted to step aside and allow Nkunda and Mutebutsi to take the city. An internal UN report would later criticize MONUC for its passive response to the crisis.[158]

Although it is not entirely clear what led MONUC to decline to defend Bukavu, part of the problem was a disconnect between MONUC's military leadership on the ground and its political leadership in Kinshasa and New York. General Isberg was prepared to turn Nkunda away by force if necessary, but confusion and uncertainty in New York and Kinshasa led to last-minute instructions that he stand aside. MONUC's leadership initially appeared unsure of Nkunda's political allegiances and whether he was an illegitimate mutineer or represented a faction of the transition. MONUC's inaction was therefore motivated by a fear of choosing sides, abandoning neutrality, and alienating influential leaders in the transitional government. UN spokes-man Fred Eckhard argued, "When war breaks out, the role of peace-keepers ends."[159] By choosing not to act, however, MONUC alienated not only various members of the transitional government but also the Congolese civilians it was mandated to protect.

The events in Bukavu and the United Nations' decision not to intervene led to large-scale, violent demonstrations against the United Nations in Kinshasa and elsewhere, the destruction of more than $1 million worth of UN equipment and property by angry mobs of protesters, and the deaths of a number of civilian demonstrators. Meanwhile, relations between the Banyamulenge and other ethnic groups in the Kivus remained tense, and deteriorated even further after an August 13 massacre of 160 Banyamulenge refugees in Gatumba, Burundi.

Although the Burundian rebel National Liberation Forces claimed responsibility for the Gatumba killings, Ruberwa blamed Mabe and Kabila. Subsequent UN investigations found no evidence of involvement by Mabe, Kabila, or the FDLR, but the event nevertheless galvanized opposition to the transitional government within RCD-Goma and in Kigali. On August 23, Ruberwa announced the suspension of RCD-Goma's participation in the transition (a decision that was eventually reversed). The MLC similarly threatened to withdraw from the transition in January 2005, as a result of similar turf battles in Kinshasa over the control of lucrative state-controlled enterprises.

A Stalled DDR Campaign

Even as struggles over army integration brought ethnic tensions in the Kivus to the boiling point, the FDLR continued to foment instability by preying on Congolese civilians and staging cross-border raids into Rwanda. Rwandan president Kagame charged that the FDLR attacked Rwanda eleven times in 2004, although only three of these incidents could be independently verified by the United Nations. With support from MONUC, in September 2004 the Congo and Rwanda signed the terms of reference for a joint verification mechanism (JVM) to monitor and investigate military activity along the Congo/Rwanda border. The JVM comprised both Rwandan and Congolese military officers, who were to work together to determine the veracity of claims of cross-border incursions. Another initiative aimed at quelling regional tensions was the tripartite agreement signed by the Congo, Rwanda, and Uganda in Kigali in October 2004. In the agreement, the three states outlined their commitments to facilitating peace in the Congo and co-operating to resolve conflict in the Great Lakes region as a whole. The agreement also established the Tripartite Commission, made up of high-level representatives from the three states, which continued discussions on regional peace and security in a meeting hosted by the U.S. government in February 2005.

The FARDC, with support from MONUC, engaged in several halting efforts to disarm FDLR elements in 2004 without much success. Although voluntary DDR had progressed at a reasonable pace before the crisis in Bukavu (according to the United Nations, the rate had quadrupled between December 2003 and April 2004), it slowed significantly in the latter months of 2004 and into 2005 due to heightened tensions in the Kivus. By June 27, 2005, 11,729 foreign combatants and their dependents had registered as having returned from the Congo to their home countries.[160] An estimated 8,000 to 10,000 FDLR troops remained, as well as roughly 30,000 dependents.

The new integrated national army began military action against the FDLR in South Kivu in April 2004, deploying three integrated brigades to the region and engaging in joint planning with MONUC on disarmament operations. The first major operation took place in the city of Walungu on November 8. Despite a promising start, however, the commander of the FARDC contingent claimed that he was never told to attack the FDLR, and many FARDC actually *cooperated* with the FDLR troops they were supposed to be disarming, jointly engaging in roadblocks and "tax" collection.[161]

On November 23, following the disarmament debacle in Walungu, Kigali announced its intention to launch a "surgical strike" into the Congo to pursue the FDLR.[162] Although Rwanda denies ever actually having entered the country, the transitional government issued a complaint to the JVM on November 29 that thousands of Rwandan troops had been present in the Kivus since January 2004. (A JVM team sent to investigate was unable to confirm the Rwandans' presence.)[163] In response to Rwanda's threats, Kabila sent 10,000 troops to North Kivu, ostensibly to guard against a potential Rwandan invasion, without informing the RCD-Goma leadership of his actions. By early December,

Kabila's troops were clashing with militia forces in North Kivu, leading to numerous atrocities against civilians and large-scale population displacements. Many feared the region was on the brink of another all-out war. Diplomatic pressure led Kigali to rescind its threat of invasion on December 19, although the region as a whole remained unstable and abuses against civilians continued.[164]

Phase V: A New MONUC?

In response to the Bukavu crisis and heightened instability in the Kivus, the United Nations once again attempted to reshape MONUC. The mission received new troops and a new mandate, promulgated a new concept of operations, reoriented existing forces to address the volatile situation in the east, and adjusted its command and control structure. By the time the transformation was complete (or appeared complete—another troop increase was on the horizon in connection with Congolese elections), MONUC had become one of the more forward-leaning UN peacekeeping operations in terms of the use of force.

In August 2004, the secretary-general asked the Security Council to increase MONUC's troop ceiling from 10,800 to 23,900. The new troops would give the Ituri Brigade a rapid reaction reserve force, constitute a new brigade for the Kivus (so that North and South Kivu would each have its own brigade), and support a new brigade for Katanga and the Kasais. The secretary-general's report proposed establishing an eastern division headquarters, headed by a major general, at either Kisangani or Kindu, with operational control over all UN troops in the east. The report also sought a civilian-military joint mission analysis cell to function as an information clearinghouse for the mission.

To address the Congo's wide-ranging needs in a comprehensive manner, MONUC proposed the formation of three joint commissions to work in cooperation with the transitional government—on essential legislation, security sector reform, and elections. In addition, the secretary-general requested that the Security Council clarify the degree of force that MONUC should use in pursuing its mandate: "Should the Security Council provide a mandate, under Chapter VII of the Charter, for MONUC to assist in the creation of stability in areas other than Ituri, the conditions under which MONUC should use force to deter dissident elements from using violence to derail the political process must be clearly defined."[165]

The secretary-general's request offered a glimpse of the United Nations' evaluation of its failings during the Bukavu crisis, which went beyond simple troop capacity shortfalls. The formation of an eastern division headquarters, for example, was intended to put more military decision-making power in the hands of those with a working knowledge of events on the ground. Likewise, the formation of a joint mission analysis cell could improve decision makers' understanding of peace opponents' behavior and avoid the type of confusion that had permitted the advance of Nkunda's army. The secretary-general's report remained wary, however, of raising unrealistic popular expectations regarding MONUC's abilities to support peace in the Congo, regardless of the deployment of additional troops and improvements in the mission's command and control structure.

> The expectations of the Congolese people, and some international observers, of the role MONUC can play under a Chapter VII mandate far outweigh what any external partner could ever do to assist a peace process. In that connection, all concerned must be clear about one thing: MONUC cannot implement the transitional process on behalf of the Transitional Government, it can only assist. Likewise, MONUC cannot create stability; it can only assist the Transitional Government in doing so.[166]

Despite such caveats, the report thoroughly reconceptualized MONUC's role, going beyond Resolution 1493, which established the Ituri Brigade. Gone was the pretense that MONUC could function as a mere observer mission, or even a force providing robust if limited security to key locations in pursuit of DDR. Its immediate and urgent primary tasks were to augment the capacity of the nascent Congolese central government and to encourage intransigent militia groups to disarm by disrupting their operations. MONUC eventually came to interpret its mandate as allowing the use of preventive force to thwart rebel groups that would prey on civilians and attack UN troops.

Mandate

In Resolution 1565 of October 2004, the Security Council gave MONUC a reinforced mandate and general affirmation of its new concept of operations, but far fewer troops than the secretary-general had sought. While mandating MONUC to deploy to key regions of instability, deter violence in the Kivus and elsewhere, monitor and help enforce the arms embargo, assist with DDR and security sector reform, engage in active and robust operations in support of the DDR of foreign combatants, support elections, and protect civilians, among other tasks, the resolution authorized the deployment of only 5,900 of the 13,100 additional troops requested. An entire brigade, which would have deployed to Katanga and the Kasais, was eliminated. Nevertheless, since MONUC's new concept of operations included the large-scale redeployment of existing forces to the east, Resolution 1565 marked the beginning of one of the largest and most rapid reconfigurations of an existing UN mission ever attempted. Between the end of October 2004 and the end of February 2005, DPKO deployed almost 5,500 new MONUC personnel and successfully shifted both troops and resources to the east (for contributors, see table 4.4).

Deployment and Operations

As outlined in the secretary-general's request, MONUC's new structure included an eastern division headquarters and a division commander with operational and tactical control of the forces in his area of operation. Major General Patrick Cammaert of the Netherlands, a former military adviser to the UN secretary-general, was appointed to the post, and the headquarters became operational on February 24, 2005.

A Joint Commission on Essential Legislation was formed, chaired by MONUC, to help the transitional government develop and enact the legislation necessary to hold elections and to coordinate donor assistance. Items on the legislative agenda included the formation of a new constitution and laws on nationality, voter registration, referendums, decentralization, and elections. The new Joint Commission on Security Sector Reform included MONUC and representatives from key donor states, who were to help in the integration, reform, and training of the Congolese armed forces and the provision of technical assistance. Finally, the Electoral Technical Committee consisted of representatives from MONUC, the Independent Electoral Commission (the Congolese body in charge of organizing and conducting electoral operations, established in June 2004), and international elections

Table 4.4. MONUC, Contributors of Uniformed Personnel, April 2005

Country	Troops	Military Observers	Police	Total
Pakistan	3,735	25	—	3,760
India	3,508	36	—	3,544
Uruguay	1,719	26	—	1,745
South Africa	1,394	3	—	1,397
Bangladesh	1,269	16	—	1,285
Nepal	1,127	19	—	1,146
Morocco	804	1	4	809
Senegal	474	9	25	508
Tunisia	471	23	—	494
Ghana	462	23	—	485
China	220	10	—	230
Bolivia	221	4	—	225
Indonesia	179	9	—	188
Guatemala	104	4	—	108
Kenya	14	29	—	43
Mali	1	27	14	42
Niger	1	18	22	41
Nigeria	4	29	3	36
Jordan	6	24	5	35
Benin	1	20	13	34
Russia	1	22	3	26
Egypt	15	9	—	24
Malawi	—	24	—	24
Zambia	5	19	—	24
Romania	—	22	1	23
Burkina Faso	—	12	10	22
Guinea	—	—	22	22
France	8	1	11	20
Paraguay	—	18	—	18
Malaysia	12	5	—	17
Ukraine	1	13	—	14
Algeria	—	11	—	11
Turkey	—	—	11	11
Ten or fewer per country: Argentina, Belgium, Bosnia-Herzegovina, Cameroon, Canada, Chad, Côte d'Ivoire, Czech Republic, Denmark, Ireland, Mongolia, Mozambique, Peru, Poland, Portugal, Serbia and Montenegro, Spain, Sri Lanka, Sweden, Switzerland, United Kingdom	34	35	31	100
Total	15,790	546	175	16,511

Source: UN DPKO, "UN Mission's Contributions by Country," April 2005, www.un.org/Depts/dpko/dpko/contributors/2005.

experts, who would coordinate assistance and planning for elections, originally scheduled to take place in June 2005 but soon delayed.

In late 2004, MONUC quickly began deploying its best-trained, most combat-ready forces east to the Kivus. A brigade from India made its headquarters in Goma, while a brigade from Pakistan set up in Bukavu. As MONUC's new deployments neared completion in early 2005, the mission began to take on more challenging, robust operations, proactively targeting spoilers and enforcing the arms embargo. Pakistani troops in South Kivu engaged in Operation Night Flash, an effort to bring security to Congolese villages being preyed upon by rebel groups. Using night patrols and radio communication, the Pakistanis responded rapidly to reports of nighttime rebel attacks on villages, confronting the rebels and apprehending or dispersing them, by force if necessary. The Pakistanis and Indians also conducted aggressive cordon-and-search operations and, while not actually engaging in forcible disarmament, made FDLR survival in the Kivus more difficult, flushing it out of its bases and forcing it deeper into the bush. On July 14, Operations Falcon Sweep and Iron Fist destroyed six empty FDLR camps, following warnings to the militia to leave the premises.[167]

The actual job of forcible disarmament and repatriation belonged not to MONUC but to the FARDC, which as of mid-2005 remained significantly underprepared for the complexity and dangers of the task at hand. On March 31, 2005, following negotiations with Kabila in Rome, the FDLR leadership announced its intention to return to Rwanda, provided the Rwandan government created a political opening for the movement upon its return.[168] The FDLR leadership renounced the use of force against Rwanda and condemned the 1994 Rwandan genocide. The timetable for returns, however, remained unspecified, and the FDLR's requirements for political reform in Kigali appeared particularly unlikely to be fulfilled. As of August 2005, there had been no significant increase in the rate of FDLR repatriation.

At the same time, international efforts to train the FARDC continued, and in July 2005 the transitional government committed itself to taking forcible action to disarm the FDLR. The African Union (the successor to the OAU) spoke of plans to create a force of 6,000 to 7,000 to assist with forcible disarmament, although given its commitments in Darfur, Sudan, as well as its limited troop capacity, it was unclear how much assistance it could offer in practice.[169]

From early 2005, MONUC forces in Ituri operated with almost unprecedented force for a UN peacekeeping mission. Following a late February ambush north of Bunia by militia of the Nationalist and Integrationist Front (FNI), which killed nine Bangladeshi peacekeepers, the Ituri Brigade engaged in a large-scale cordon-and-search operation involving troops from Pakistan, Nepal, and South Africa, supported by Indian attack helicopters. The operation dismantled an FNI base in the town of Loga, northeast of Bunia. After FNI fighters began firing on UN troops, the UN forces responded by killing fifty to sixty rebels. A number of peacekeepers were also injured during the firefight, one of the largest that UN-led forces had engaged in since Somalia in 1993.

Major General Cammaert, the eastern division commander, told his troops that MONUC would no longer back down from such provocations: "If we have an opponent that engages you or misbehaves, he will feel the consequences. It's very simple." The FNI reportedly used human shields during the battle, and a number of civilians may have died as a result. Following their actions in Loga, UN forces staged robust cordon-and-search operations elsewhere, dismantling militia bases, seizing weapons and ammunition, and in general reducing the militia groups' "capacity for nuisance."[170]

The forceful UN actions appeared to speed up DDR in Ituri. SRSG Swing gave all armed groups in Ituri an ultimatum to disarm or integrate into the national army by April 1, 2005, or face disarmament by force. Before this, only 2,000 Ituri militia fighters had disarmed.[171] When the UN transit centers closed in late June, however, roughly 15,600 had voluntarily given up their weapons.[172] Meanwhile, the United Nations continued robust operations against militia fighters who refused to disarm, estimated to number 1,200.[173]

In addition, MONUC appeared to improve its enforcement of the arms embargo over time. The first report by the Group of Experts tasked with monitoring the arms embargo, in January 2005, observed that MONUC was failing to conduct regular ad hoc inspections of aircraft or monitor key centers of illicit arms trafficking, such as the Ubwari peninsula on Lake Tanganyika.[174] The second report, in July 2005, noted that MONUC had made monitoring the arms embargo one of the primary tasks of its new joint mission analysis cell, was producing a daily arms embargo report, and was collecting information on aviation traffic at key airports and serial numbers of weapons captured or surrendered. The report also noted, however, that MONUC still lacked capacity for "deployment on the borders and in the airports of the Democratic Republic of the Congo to support existing national customs structures" and "monitoring of airspace and airport activities."[175]

A further security hurdle loomed in the form of national elections and the instability likely to attend them, as formerly warring parties jockeyed for influence and those excluded from the political process maneuvered to undermine it. In late May 2005, the secretary-general sought a temporary expansion of MONUC by 2,590 troops (the brigade for Katanga that the Security Council had declined to authorize in October 2004) and 841 UN police, including 625 officers organized in five formed police units with military-type equipment to help keep public order. In early September, the council authorized deployment of all the requested police but not the Katanga brigade.[176]

Sexual Exploitation and Abuse

In addition to being the largest, most expensive, and arguably most challenging UN peacekeeping operation currently in existence, MONUC had the distinction of generating the worst instances of sexual exploitation and abuse by peacekeepers to have surfaced in recent years. Press accounts first emerged in 2004, stimulating MONUC to take action against a problem that some within the mission had been aware of, to some degree, for at least two years. MONUC had issued a code of conduct in 2002, but senior leadership at the time reportedly did little to enforce it or to investigate rumors of abuse.[177] UN DPKO circulated disciplinary directives for its operations in July 2003, and the secretary-general issued a bulletin to UN staff in October 2003 that defined and prohibited sexual exploitation and abuse. The secretary-general published further, more detailed guidance on gender issues in peace operations in July 2004.[178]

In the spring of 2004, MONUC began to address the abuse issue seriously. MONUC's personnel conduct officer collected initial case reports, which were given to the United Nations' Office of Internal Oversight Services (OIOS). An OIOS team spent June through September 2004 in Bunia conducting a preliminary investigation of the problem; of the seventy-two allegations it examined, the team was able to fully

substantiate just eight cases. In the others, physical evidence was frag-
mentary, or witnesses were reluctant to testify or had difficulty identifying their alleged abusers. For the substantiated military cases, the United
Nations sent the OIOS report to the troop-contributing country in
question and asked that it take appropriate disciplinary action.

Beyond the substantiated cases, however, OIOS found circumstan-
tial evidence of widespread abuse in Bunia within a general climate of
impunity. Abuses continued even while the investigators worked. A
special investigative team headed by Assistant Secretary-General Angela
Kane arrived in December 2004 to examine allegations of abuse throughout the mission. The special team evolved into a new UN headquarters
Office for Addressing Sexual Exploitation and Abuse, established on
March 1, 2005. Between December 2004 and June 2005, this group investigated seventy-seven allegations, substantiating forty-six. About 40 percent of the new allegations involved civilian personnel, while 60 percent
involved military personnel. One in five involved paternity claims. By
August 2005, seventeen military personnel had been repatriated on disciplinary grounds, and UN disciplinary proceedings had been initiated against eight civilian personnel.[179]

Another team was led by Prince Zeid Ra'ad Zeid al Hussein, Jordan's permanent representative to the United Nations, who visited the
Congo in October 2004 and was appointed the secretary-general's special adviser on sexual exploitation and abuse upon his return. A veteran
of UN peacekeeping himself, one of his duties was to encourage troop-
contributing countries to act on allegations of abuse by their nationals
serving in UN operations. His report, issued in late March 2005, offered
practical recommendations on how to more effectively apply UN codes
of conduct, deter violations, and investigate and punish violations.[180]
Its recommendations included more secure perimeter fencing, closer
supervision of off-duty personnel, drawing military police units from
countries not providing other military units to an operation, better
provision for troops' recreation, improved and universal training of all
UN personnel in expected standards of conduct for peacekeepers, and
repatriating military contingent and unit commanders who failed to
enforce UN behavioral rules among their troops.[181]

The United Nations also established a senior-level, headquarters-
based task force on sexual exploitation and abuse that met weekly to

draft new policies and provide new guidelines to MONUC, and MONUC implemented a number of measures designed to prevent exploitation and abuse beginning in late 2004. These included a curfew, declaring problematic areas off-limits for peacekeepers, requiring that military personnel wear their uniforms at all times, and installing improved perimeter fencing and lighting around military compounds. MONUC military police and security personnel conducted patrols to enforce these measures.[182] MONUC also began to train all new civilian personnel, military observers, staff officers, and civilian police on issues related to exploitation and abuse, and disseminated an updated, more stringent code of conduct on the subject in November 2004.

Assessment

Of all the United Nations' peacekeeping operations, MONUC best exemplifies what can go wrong with peace implementation when there is serious deficiency in local leaders' willingness to support the peace, marginal international political will to take risks for peace, and equally little willingness to expend the necessary resources to create it. As a result, during MONUC's deployment, there were the largest number of war-related civilian deaths ever to occur in a country where UN blue helmets were deployed.

The Congo is a very difficult logistical environment in which to work. The country is huge, its roads and railways in abysmal repair. All MONUC equipment and personnel had to be flown from one part of the country to the other. This increased MONUC's price tag per mission member by comparison with operations in smaller countries or those with better ground transport infrastructure. The more expensive the mission, the more reluctant the United States and other permanent members of the UN Security Council are to authorize or expand it.

The difficulty of recruiting states to participate in MONUC, especially developed countries, was another major problem. Sweden was the only western European country to contribute troops to MONUC—ninety personnel as part of an airfield services unit. Every other UN operation in Africa involving internal conflict also experienced this problem, however.

From the beginning of the Congo conflict, little international political will existed to do much about it. Not strategically important to the five permanent members of the Security Council, the Congo got a peacekeeping operation designed for a conducive conflict environment —respect for the cease-fire by the warring parties, a cooperative and consensual central government, and voluntary disarmament by the foreign armed groups. The Security Council was not prepared to have the United Nations shoulder the de facto combat tasks thrust upon it by the Lusaka signatories. But neither did the council impose aid conditionality or engage in more assertive diplomacy on behalf of peace.

In place of a coherent strategy, the Security Council and DPKO adopted a phased approach that used the *prospect* of outside support to encourage positive developments in the field. Such a phased approach to peacekeeping had already been discredited in neighboring Angola only a few years earlier, having demonstrably failed to alter the course of the war despite a series of nominal peace accords. In Congo, by giving the warring parties the ability to control peacekeeper deployments merely by continuing to violate the cease-fire, kill civilians, and line their pockets, the phased approach had the opposite of its intended effect.

When the warring parties failed to implement the bargain they had struck at Lusaka, and the government of Laurent Kabila refused to let the United Nations implement even its limited initial mandate, the phased approach was shown to lack all political leverage. It degenerated into piecemeal peacekeeping that the warring parties could use as a further excuse to flout the Lusaka Agreement and subsequent accords. Once the regional intervenors finally did begin withdrawing their forces after the Pretoria Agreement, the United Nations failed to anticipate the security vacuum that would be left behind. Poor coordination between Security Council diplomacy and MONUC's deployment left the operation scrambling for options when international pressure led Uganda to leave Ituri before MONUC had an adequate force on the ground to secure the region.

The crisis in Ituri marked a low point for MONUC. The need for an outside intervention force clearly exposed the UN operation's limitations as an observer mission with a weak mandate. Helping the interim government consolidate its political control and extend its authority to eastern Congo would require a substantially strengthened peacekeeping force with a much more aggressive mandate.

After years of resisting such a robust phase of the mission because of its costs and size, the Security Council found itself forced by the Ituri crisis to respond to events on the ground. It was compelled to give the operation a mandate and force capacity commensurate with its responsibilities. One could argue that the council had been waiting for the agreement on the transitional government to establish internal power sharing and thus bound the enforcement problem, but only the systematic violence and widespread war crimes in Bunia seemed to prod the council into effective action. That it took a month of ethnic cleansing in Bunia to compel the council to bolster MONUC's mandate and capability was symptomatic of the Security Council's entire approach to peacekeeping in the Congo: responding to events on the ground rather than crafting diplomacy and deploying a robust peacekeeping force to shape them.

The absence of a strong regional organization to support the United Nations in the Congo contributed to its struggles and to its temporary reliance on the French-led multinational force. The OAU was not disposed to undertake robust peacekeeping, and the successor African Union was still building its institutions and capacity when the Ituri crisis erupted. Moreover, most members of the Southern African Development Community were directly involved in the conflict itself. The American and EU observers at the negotiations told the Lusaka signatories that there would be limits to the UN role in post-Lusaka Congo. In response, the signatories created their own monitoring entity in the JMC, but that entity merely comprised the warring parties themselves and had neither adequate funding nor any independent enforcement capability. In the end, the United Nations was left with the daunting task of managing the Congo war by itself.

The sluggishness with which international donors and the United Nations addressed the foreign dimension of the disarmament problem contributed to the long-running misfire of the DDR program. The disarmament of the foreign armed groups was not just a matter of finding the right mix of economic incentives but a political issue that required serious reform in the Congo and Rwanda, and a workable peace accord in Burundi. The Rwandan combatants in particular had little motivation to disarm without greater reassurance about what awaited them back home. UN efforts to dispel those fears in 2002 were sabotaged by Kinshasa's forced repatriation of some Rwandan rebel leaders. Burundi's government, on the other hand, refused repatriation of rebels who agreed to demobilize in early 2003. Between late 2003 and April 2004, disarmament and repatriation of foreign forces accelerated, but was derailed again by the intra-Congolese fighting in and around Bukavu. Sluggish financial contributions to the DDR program also contributed to its long-running malaise. Such examples point to the danger and futility of trying to resolve a complex internal-cum-regional war without a regionwide political strategy that has the backing, attention, and financing of the international community.

Even more than the Security Council, however, the Lusaka signatories deserve blame for repeatedly agreeing to hopelessly unrealistic objectives and timelines for peace implementation; for repeatedly flouting those objectives; and for creating an environment that was hostile to peacekeeping. No peacekeeping mission can succeed without the cooperation of the host country. For the first year and a half, Laurent Kabila did everything he could to paralyze MONUC. His regime obstructed MONUC's deployment of troops, restricted the travel of its personnel, and suppressed the Inter-Congolese Dialogue. Rwanda and Uganda, in turn, funded and armed a deadly kaleidoscope of militias in the Kivus and Ituri, which complicated MONUC's attempts to pacify the east and initiate the DDR program, which was supposed to benefit these very countries.

The economic dimension of the conflict complicated the United Nations' DDR efforts. Disarming the armed groups in the Congo did not promise to benefit Rwanda and Uganda as much as did the flow of illicit gems and industrial minerals from the Congo. Demobilizing and repatriating the negative forces would have helped the postwar Congolese government assert control over its border areas and ultimately over its national mineral production, to the detriment of the exploiters. The international community needed to increase the costs of Rwandan and Ugandan meddling in the Congo.

The United Nations took a step in the right direction by forming a Panel of Experts to monitor illegal exploitation of the Congo. Its investigations clearly exposed the two neighbors' campaigns to steal the Congo's wealth with no regard for the local populations. Reports from groups such as Human Rights Watch and Amnesty International detailed how mineral exploitation contributed directly to widespread atrocities in Ituri and to the spiraling of violence in the Kivus. Yet Kigali and Kampala suffered no consequences for their wrongdoing. International donors were wary of placing strong pressure on two of Africa's fastest-growing economies. States eventually put diplomatic pressure on Uganda and Rwanda to withdraw their forces but turned a blind eye toward their incitement of ethnic violence and suborning of militias to secure their commercial networks. Even an expanded MONUC could not hope to stem the violent exploitation of Congolese resources, and as of mid-2005, it had no mandate to do so.

Conclusion

Any peacekeeping mission is shaped and influenced by the cooperation of the warring parties, specifically by their commitment to the peace agreement or cease-fire that initiated the establishment of the peacekeeping force. When the parties are strongly committed to the underlying peace agreement, peacekeeping is more likely to succeed. But when the end of the war may jeopardize the warring parties' political, economic, or security positions, they have little incentive to cooperate unless international pressure alters their cost-benefit calculus. The Security Council can exert such leverage in two ways: robust intervention, which attempts to deter transgressions with the threat of violence; and political pressure, threatening to punish the parties through economic sanctions, international shaming, or isolation. In a case such as the Congo, a balance of both strategies is superior.

If the international community is not willing to commit the resources needed for a robust operation, then perhaps no operation should be undertaken, because a weak operation still creates the impression, among the local population, that something is being done to protect civilians and keep the peace, when in fact that is not the case. It was not the case for the first three years of MONUC, with the result that hundreds of thousands died in the Congo despite the presence of peacekeepers.

Disarmament, demobilization, and repatriation or reintegration of former fighters poses a fundamental challenge to the reconstitution of war-torn societies. If not done correctly, it may even reinforce structural problems that support systemic violence and predation by militias and militaries, whose members are often left both unchecked and unsupported. To be effective, DDR operations must be made an integral part of a peace operation's assessed budget so that they are fully funded from the outset and can be seamlessly integrated into operational strategy.

Demand for peacekeeping in hostile environments with limited global strategic value poses a fundamental challenge to the Security Council, and the council and the UN system at large still have not found a satisfactory approach to meet this challenge. Richard Holbrooke hailed the phased approach, when it was first adopted, as the way the United Nations could get peacekeeping right in these types of environments. From the standpoint of the war's civilian victims, however, it is instead dead wrong. It is a way to ensure that costs and risks are shifted only very late and very minimally from the victims of war to their tardy rescuers.

Notes

1. See William J. Durch, "The UN Operation in the Congo: 1960–1964," in *The Evolution of UN Peacekeeping: Case Studies and Comparative Analysis*, ed. William J. Durch (New York: St. Martin's, 1993), 315–52.

2. Brian Urquhart, "A Force Behind the UN," *New York Times*, August 7, 2003, A23.

3. In 1965 Mobutu Sese Seko changed the name of the country from the Republic of the Congo to Zaire. Upon becoming president in 1997, Laurent Kabila changed the name of the country from Zaire to the Democratic Republic of the Congo. Before 1997, the country will be referred to as Zaire; afterward, as the Democratic Republic of the Congo, the DRC, or the Congo.

4. Crawford Young, *The Politics of Cultural Pluralism* (Madison: University of Wisconsin Press, 1976), chap. 6.

5. Economist Intelligence Unit (EIU), "Democratic Republic of Congo: Country Profile" (London: EIU, June 15, 2003).

6. About 85 percent of Rwandans belong to the Hutu group, and about 15 percent are Tutsi. The Tutsi were initially favored by the Belgian colonial administration and during the colonial period dominated the Hutu

politically and economically. Right before independence, however, Hutu groups, led by the Parmehutu (Party of the Hutu Emancipation Movement), mobilized in an attempt to challenge Tutsi dominance. Violence flared between Hutu and Tutsi, and the Belgian colonial authority intervened to stop the bloodshed. In an effort to appease the Hutu parties, the Belgians replaced about half of the Tutsi local administrators with Hutu. Taking advantage of their improved political status and ethnic majority, the Hutu parties would go on to win elections in 1960 and 1961, consolidate their control of the government, and dominate the postcolonial Rwandan state at the expense of the Tutsi minority.

7. Alison Des Forges, *Leave None to Tell the Story* (New York: Human Rights Watch, 1999).

8. William Cyrus Reed, "Guerrillas in the Midst," in *African Guerrillas,* ed. Christopher Clapham (Cambridge: Cambridge University Press, 1999), 139.

9. Banyarwanda are Kinyarwanda-speaking people, including both Hutu and Tutsi, who migrated from Rwanda to the Congo between the eighteenth century and the present. The 1994 Rwandan genocide and the subsequent refugee crisis in Zaire undermined the unity and collective identity of the Banyarwanda, who increasingly divided along Hutu and Tutsi lines. See Mahmood Mamdani, *When Victims Become Killers: Colonialism, Nativism, and the Genocide in Rwanda* (Princeton: Princeton University Press, 2001).

10. Banyamulenge includes the group of ethnic Tutsi who migrated from Rwanda and Burundi to South Kivu in eastern Congo between the sixteenth and mid-nineteenth centuries. See Catherine Newbury, *The Cohesion of Oppression: Clientship and Ethnicity in Rwanda 1860–1960* (New York: Columbia University Press, 1988).

11. Kevin C. Dunn, "A Survival Guide to Kinshasa," in *The African Stakes of the Congo War,* ed. John Clark (New York: Palgrave Macmillan, 2002), 57; and Howard Adelman, "The Use and Abuse of Refugees in Zaire," in *Refugee Manipulation: War, Politics, and the Abuse of Human Suffering,* ed. Stephen John Stedman and Fred Tanner (Washington, DC: Brookings Institution, 2003), 95–134.

12. Abbas H. Gnamo, "The Rwandan Genocide and the Collapse of Mobutu's Kleptocracy," in *The Path of a Genocide: The Rwandan Crisis from Uganda to Zaire,* ed. Howard Adelman and Astri Suhrke (New Brunswick: Transaction Publishers), 335.

13. Georges Nzongola-Ntalaja, *The Congo: From Leopold to Kabila* (London: Zed, 2002), 227–28.

14. Les Roberts et al., "Mortality in Eastern Democratic Republic of the Congo: Results from Eleven Mortality Surveys" (New York: International Rescue Committee, 2001).

15. Ben Coghlan et al., "Mortality in the Democratic Republic of Congo: Results from a Nationwide Survey Conducted April–July 2004" (Melbourne and New York: Burnet Institute and International Rescue Committee, December 2004).

16. International Crisis Group (hereafter cited as Crisis Group), "Scramble for the Congo: Anatomy of an Ugly War," Africa Report no. 26, December 20, 2000, 40.

17. Osita Afoaku, "Congo's Rebels: Their Origins, Motivations, and Strategies," in *African Stakes of the Congo War,* ed. Clark, 117.

18. Human Rights Watch, "Eastern Congo Ravaged: Killing Civilians and Silencing Protest," May 2000.

19. Afoaku, "Congo's Rebels," in *African Stakes of the Congo War,* ed. Clark.

20. The Lusaka Agreement defined armed groups, also referred to as negative forces, as foreign rebel groups that were using bases in the Congo to attack neighboring countries. They included the following: from Rwanda, the former Rwandan Armed Forces (ex-FAR) and the Interahamwe militias; from Uganda, the Allied Democratic Front, the Lord's Resistance Army, the former Ugandan National Army, the Uganda National Rescue Front II, and the West Nile Bank Front; from Burundi, the Forces for the Defense of Democracy; and from Angola, the National Union for the Total Independence of Angola (UNITA).

21. John Prendergast and David Smock, "Putting Humpty Dumpty Together: Reconstructing Peace in the Congo" (special report, United States Institute of Peace, August 31, 1999).

22. Senior Rwandan official cited by Crisis Group, "Africa's Seven Nation War," Africa Report no. 4, May 21, 1999, 25–26.

23. UN Security Council, *Final Report of the Panel of Experts on the Illegal Exploitation of Natural Resources and Other Forms of Wealth of the Democratic Republic of the Congo (DRC),* Letter from the Secretary-General to the President of the Security Council, S/2002/1146, October 16, 2002, para. 71.

24. Ibid., para. 98.

25. Crisis Group, "Scramble for the Congo," 31.

26. Eric G. Berman and Katie E. Sams, *Peacekeeping in Africa: Capabil-*

ities and Culpabilities (Geneva: UN Institute for Disarmament Research, 2000), 175–83.

27. Crisis Group, "Zimbabwe in Crisis: Finding a Way Forward," Africa Report no. 32, July 13, 2001, 9–10.

28. Crisis Group, "Scramble for the Congo," 60.

29. Global Witness, "Branching Out: Zimbabwe's Resource Colonialism in DRC," 2nd ed. (London: Global Witness, February 2002).

30. Crisis Group, "Scramble for the Congo," 60.

31. UN Security Council, *Report on Exploitation of Natural Resources,* S/2002/1146, para. 22.

32. Crisis Group, "Scramble for the Congo," 54; and Thomas Turner, "Angola's Role in the Congo War," in *African Stakes of the Congo War,* ed. Clark, 85.

33. EIU, "Namibia: Country Report" (London: EIU, October 5, 1998).

34. The UN Panel of Experts investigating the illegal exploitation of the Congo noted that Kabila's allies convened the Windhoek summit in January 1999 to seek compensation from Kabila for their military support. UN Security Council, *Addendum to the Report of the Panel of Experts on the Illegal Exploitation of Natural Resources and Other Forms of Wealth of the DRC,* S/2001/1072, November 13, 2001, paras. 87–90; and "Defence Defends Congo Kinshasa Mine," *Namibian,* February 28, 2001.

35. UN Security Council, *Report on Exploitation of Natural Resources,* S/2002/1146, para. 14.

36. Crisis Group, "The Agreement on a Cease-Fire in the Democratic Republic of the Congo: Analysis of the Agreement and Prospects for Peace," August 20, 1999, Annex A.

37. EIU, "Country Report: Democratic Republic of the Congo," (London: EIU, August 2, 1999).

38. Crisis Group, "Agreement on a Cease-Fire," 12–13.

39. Ian Fisher, "Congo Peace Accord Ailing as Rivals Jockey for Position," *New York Times,* August 1, 1999, A10.

40. Crisis Group, "Agreement on a Cease-Fire," 16.

41. Christian P. Scherrer, *Genocide and Crisis in Central Africa: Conflict Roots, Mass Violence, and Regional War* (Westport, CT: Praeger, 2002), 278.

42. United States Institute of Peace Library, Peace Agreements Digital Collection, "Lusaka Cease-Fire Agreement," www.usip.org/library/pa/drc/drc_07101999.html.

43. Crisis Group, "Scramble for the Congo," 70.

44. United States Institute of Peace Library, "Lusaka Cease-Fire Agreement."

45. Clifford Bernath and Anne Edgerton, "MONUC: Flawed Mandate Limits Success" (Washington, DC: Refugees International, May 2003), 5.

46. U.S. Department of State, Office of International Information Programs, "January 2000 'Month of Africa' for UN Security Council," January 6, 2000, usinfo.state.gov/regional/af/unmonth/.

47. Some questioned the utility of bringing the warring parties together at the United Nations in January 2000 and forcing them to sign a new agreement, as it seemed to widen the divisions between the belligerents and conveyed the appearance that Holbrooke was hijacking the Lusaka initiative. Holbrooke apparently believed that the meeting was necessary to strengthen the credibility of the Lusaka Agreement after months of postagreement fighting. (The reaffirmation of Lusaka would also make it easier to sell a peacekeeping mission for the DRC to the U.S. Congress.)

48. "African Leaders Call for Action in Security Council," *UN Wire,* January 24, 2000, www.unwire.org.

49. The secretary-general, in line with the thinking of the U.S. Department of Defense, which was advising the UN Department of Peacekeeping Operations in the design of the DRC mission, called for the deployment of 5,537 troops and observers. United Nations, *Report of the Secretary-General on the UN Operation in the DRC (MONUC),* S/2000/30, January 17, 2000.

50. Colum Lynch, "Senator Warner Urges UN to Put Balkans Missions Ahead of Africa," *Washington Post,* January 22, 2000, A20.

51. U.S. Congress, House International Relations Committee (HIRC), *Peacekeeping in the Democratic Republic of the Congo,* Hearing before the Subcommittee on Africa, 106th Cong., 2nd sess., February 15, 2000. Testimony of Ambassador Richard Holbrooke.

52. Lynch, "Senator Warner Urges UN."

53. HIRC, *Peacekeeping in the Democratic Republic of the Congo.*

54. Ben Barber, "Pentagon Advises UN on Congo," *Washington Times,* February 17, 2000.

55. Ambassador Richard C. Holbrooke, "Statement at the Woodrow Wilson Center" (USUN press release no. 18(00), February 7, 2000), www.un.int/usa/00_018.htm.

56. Barbara Crossette, "U.S. Offers U.N. Resolution For 5,500-Troop Congo Force," *New York Times,* February 9, 2000, A5.

57. Michael Dynes, "West Faces Calls to Keep Peace in Congo," *Times* (London), January 24, 2000.

58. "Statement by Ambassador Robert R. Fowler (permanent representative of Canada) in the United Nations Security Council on the Situation Concerning the Democratic Republic of the Congo," February 24, 2000, www.un.int/canada/securitycouncilspeeches.htm.

59. Colum Lynch, "U.S. to Support Sending U.N. Team to Congo," *Washington Post,* January 28, 2000, A14.

60. "Another UN Commitment?" *Washington Post,* February 14, 2000, A16.

61. Two such hearings were held by the HIRC Subcommittee on Africa, Global Human Rights, and International Operations on March 1 and May 18, 2005. For online transcripts, see wwwc.house.gov/international_relations/afhear.htm. See also Senate Foreign Relations Committee, "Hearing on United Nations Peacekeeping Reform," July 27, 2005. Details available at www.foreign.senate.gov/hearing.html.

62. For consistency with other chapters in this volume, we will use the common acronym DDR (for "disarmament, demobilization, and reintegration") rather than the longer, awkward DDRRR, which captures each element of the DRC's program but risks self-caricature in the process.

63. Crisis Group, "Scramble for the Congo," Appendix C.

64. Bernath and Edgerton, "MONUC: Flawed Mandate Limits Success," 28.

65. United Nations, *Performance Report on the Budget of MONUC for the Period from 1 July 2002 to 30 June 2003,* Report of the Secretary-General, A/58/684, January 16, 2004, 12.

66. "DRC: World Bank Approves U.S. $100 Million Grant," *UN Integrated Regional Information Networks (IRIN),* May 28, 2004, www.irinnews.org/report.asp?ReportID=41314.

67. European Union Council Secretariat, "Fact Sheet: EU-Led Military Operation in the Democratic Republic of Congo, Operation 'Artemis,'" July 2003, ue.eu.int/pesd/congo/index.asp.

68. Crisis Group, "The Agreement on a Cease-Fire," 27.

69. United Nations, *Report of the Secretary-General on the UN Preliminary Deployment in the DRC,* S/1999/790, July 15, 1999.

70. UN Security Council Resolution 1258, S/RES/1258, August 6, 1999.

71. United Nations, *SG Report on MONUC,* S/2000/30, 5.

72. United Nations, *Second Report of the Secretary-General on MONUC,* S/2000/330, April 18, 2000, 6.

73. "DRC: UN Mission Grounded," *IRIN,* October 25, 1999, www.irin news.org.

74. United Nations, *SG Report on MONUC,* S/2000/30, 4.

75. UN Security Council Resolution 1291, S/RES/1291, February 25, 2000, para. 8.

76. Crisis Group, "Scramble for the Congo," 75.

77. Barbara Crossette, "Congo Grudgingly Accepts Ground Rules for Peacekeepers," *New York Times,* May 5, 2000, A14.

78. United Nations, *Third Report of the Secretary-General on MONUC,* S/2000/566, June 12, 2000, 2–3.

79. Ibid., 4–5.

80. "Humanitarian Situation Continues to Deteriorate," *IRIN,* September 19, 2000.

81. "Briefing by U.S. Envoy to the UN Richard Holbrooke on Africa," *IRIN,* June 30, 2000.

82. The main parties of the Congolese political opposition were the Union for Democracy and Social Progress (UDPS), led by Etienne Tshisekedi; Party of the United Lumumbaists (PALU), led by Antoine Gizenga; Renovating Forces for Union and Solidarity (FONUS), led by Joseph Olenghankoy; Movement of Congolese Nationalists (MNC-L), led by François Lumumba; and the G4 group of four parties, led by Mbwebwe Kabamba.

83. United Nations, *Third SG Report on MONUC,* S/2000/566, para. 11.

84. Colum Lynch, "UN Holds Back Observer Mission for Congo, Citing Logistical Woes," *Washington Post,* June 15, 2000, A27.

85. United Nations, *Fourth Report of the Secretary-General on MONUC,* S/2000/888, September 21, 2000.

86. "Kabila Pledges to Revive Lusaka," *IRIN,* January 29, 2001.

87. United Nations, *Sixth Report of the Secretary-General on MONUC,* S/2001/128, February 12, 2001, 10.

88. Ibid., 11.

89. United Nations, *Eighth Report of the Secretary-General on MONUC,* S/2001/572, June 12, 2001, 4.

90. United Nations, *Ninth Report of the Secretary-General on MONUC,* S/2001/970, October 16, 2001, para. 28.

91. United Nations, *Eighth SG Report on MONUC,* S/2001/572, para. 85.

92. UN Security Council Resolution 1376, S/RES/1376, November 9, 2001.

93. MONUC personnel of the UN police component were first deployed to Kinshasa on October 28, 2001, where they were tasked with planning UN police operations throughout the country. UN Security Council Resolution 1355, S/RES/1355, June 15, 2001.

94. United Nations, *Ninth SG Report on MONUC,* S/2001/970, paras. 73–91.

95. United Nations, *Seventh Report of the Secretary-General on MONUC,* S/2001/373, April 17, 2001, para. 103.

96. United Nations, *Ninth SG Report on MONUC,* S/2001/970, para. 80.

97. "RCD-Goma Sets Conditions for Kisangani Withdrawal," *IRIN,* December 14, 2001.

98. United Nations, *Tenth Report of the Secretary-General on MONUC,* S/2002/169, February 15, 2002, para. 42.

99. Human Rights Watch, "War Crimes in Kisangani: The Response of Rwandan-Backed Rebels to the May 2002 Mutiny," August 2002.

100. "MONUC Counters RCD-Goma Charges of Partiality," *IRIN,* May 29, 2002.

101. UN Security Council, *First Assessment of the Armed Groups Operating in the DRC,* S/2002/341, April 5, 2002, Annex.

102. Ibid., paras. 19–26. The report noted that Rwandan government estimates of the number of ALIR I fighters in the DRC was substantially higher, between 13,000 and 15,000. See Crisis Group, "The Kivus: The Forgotten Crucible of the Congo Conflict," Africa Report no. 56, January 24, 2003, 8.

103. United Nations, *Eleventh Report of the Secretary-General on MONUC,* S/2002/621, June 5, 2002, para. 27.

104. "UN Screens Rwandan FDLR Troops in Kamina," *IRIN,* November 15, 2001.

105. Crisis Group, "Disarmament in the Congo: Jump-Starting DDRRR to Prevent Further War," December 14, 2001, 18–19.

106. United Nations, *Twelfth Report of the Secretary-General on MONUC,* S/2002/1180, October 18, 2002, para. 30.

107. It is disputed whether the mutiny in Kamina was a spontaneous reaction by the Rwandan combatants to the forced repatriation of their leaders from Kinshasa or was provoked by the Congolese army after it also tried to forcibly repatriate the combatants cantoned in Kamina. See Crisis Group, "Rwandan Hutu Rebels in the Congo: A New Approach to Disarmament and Reintegration," Africa Report no. 63, May 23, 2003.

108. "Kabila, Kagame Sign Peace Pact," *IRIN,* July 30, 2002.

109. "Text of the Pretoria Memorandum of Understanding," *IRIN,* July 31, 2002.

110. United Nations, *Special Report of the Secretary-General on MONUC,* S/2002/1005, September 10, 2002, para. 45.

111. Ibid., para. 49. Though a step in the right direction, the new plan was criticized by the Crisis Group for using Kindu and Kisangani as task force bases because of their distance ("hundreds of kilometers") from the field operations, "which will neither deter the militias nor influence them to negotiate, let alone opt to disarm." See Crisis Group, "The Kivus: The Forgotten Crucible," ii.

112. United Nations, *SG Special Report on MONUC,* S/2002/1005, para. 54.

113. United Nations, *Thirteenth Report of the Secretary-General on MONUC,* S/2003/211, February 21, 2003, para. 19.

114. United Nations, *Second Special Report of the Secretary-General on MONUC,* S/2003/566, May 27, 2003, para. 22.

115. "Follow-up Committee Urges RCD-Goma to Withdraw from Lubero," *IRIN,* June 20, 2003.

116. See details of summary executions, torture, mass killings, and other war crimes committed by RCD, often in the context of battling the Mai-Mai, in U.S. State Department, "Democratic Republic of the Congo," Country Reports on Human Rights Practices, 2003, available at www.state.gov/g/drl/rls/hrrpt/2003/27721.htm.

117. United Nations, *Fourteenth Report of the Secretary-General on MONUC,* S/2003/1098, November 17, 2003, para. 19.

118. United Nations, *Fifteenth Report of the Secretary-General on MONUC,* S/2004/251, March 25, 2004, para. 40.

119. The all-inclusive agreement followed a cumbersome but necessary power-sharing formula that included one president and four vice presidents, each with responsibility for a different government portfolio. Joseph Kabila remained president during the two-year interim period, while each party to the talks—the government, the MLC, RCD-Goma, and the political opposition—received a vice presidency. RCD chaired the political commission; MLC chaired the economic and finance commission; the government chaired the reconstruction and development commission; and the political opposition chaired the social and cultural commission. A transitional parliament was created that included a 500-person national assembly and a 120-person senate. All representatives would be appointed by the respective signatories until elections could be held at the end of the transitional period.

120. Human Rights Watch, "Ituri: 'Covered in Blood,'" July 8, 2003.

121. Human Rights Watch, "Uganda in Eastern DRC: Fueling Political and Ethnic Strife," March 2001, www.hrw.org/reports/2001/drc.

122. Crisis Group, "Congo Crisis: Military Intervention in Ituri," Africa Report no. 64, June 13, 2003, 3.

123. "Focus on Hema-Lendu Conflict," *IRIN*, November 15, 1999.

124. Human Rights Watch, "Uganda in Eastern DRC."

125. "Special Report on the Ituri Clashes [part 2]," *IRIN*, March 3, 2000.

126. UN Security Council, *Report on Exploitation of Natural Resources*, S/2002/1146, para. 101.

127. Crisis Group, "Congo Crisis," 5.

128. UN Security Council Resolution 1468 of March 20, 2003, encouraged MONUC to play an active role in helping to create the Ituri Pacification Commission and to "assist the work of this commission as consistent with MONUC's current mandate." In private, MONUC representatives "repeatedly assured the delegates that by the time the UPDF withdrew, it would have brought in an alternative force to guarantee security in the town of Bunia and support the [disarmament and reintegration] work of the interim administration." See Crisis Group, "Congo Crisis," 11.

129. UN DPKO, Peacekeeping Best Practices Unit, *Operation Artemis: The Lessons of the Interim Emergency Multinational Force*, October 2004, 6, www.un.org/Depts/dpko/lessons.

130. Crisis Group, "Congo Crisis."

131. "DRC: Special Report on Tensions in the Northeast," *IRIN*, February 19, 2002; and Human Rights Watch, "Ituri: 'Covered in Blood.'"

132. Amnesty International and Human Rights Watch, "Democratic Republic of Congo: UN Should Deploy a Rapid Reaction Force in Ituri" (joint press release, May 20, 2003).

133. Crisis Group, "Congo Crisis," 13.

134. UN Security Council Resolution 1484, S/RES/1484, May 30, 2003.

135. UN Security Council Resolution 1493, S/RES/1493, July 28, 2003.

136. UN Security Council Resolution 1533, S/RES/1533, March 12, 2004, paras 3–4.

137. EU Council Secretariat, "Fact Sheet: EU-Led Military Operation."

138. "French General Inspects Soldiers in War-Ravished Bunia," *Pan African News Agency*, July 4, 2003; and "Chronology of EU Operation Artemis in DR Congo," *Agence France-Presse*, August 16, 2003.

139. EIU, "Country Report: Democratic Republic of the Congo."

140. "Multinational Force Shoots Dead Two Militiamen in Bunia," *IRIN*, June 17, 2003.

141. "22 Civilians Killed and Mutilated in Nizi, Ituri District," *IRIN*, July 22, 2003; and "Fataki Deserted, Houses Looted and Burnt," *IRIN*, September 1, 2003.

142. Forum for Early Warning and Early Response (FEWER), "Ituri: Stakes, Actors, Dynamics" (London: FEWER Secretariat, October 2003).

143. UN DPKO, Peacekeeping Best Practices Unit, *Operation Artemis*, 13.

144. Ibid., 14.

145. United Nations, *Fifteenth SG Report on MONUC*, S/2004/251, para. 25.

146. United Nations, *Sixteenth Report of the Secretary-General on MONUC*, S/2004/1034, December 31, 2004, para. 11.

147. Crisis Group, "The Congo's Transition Is Failing: Crisis in the Kivus," Africa Report no. 91, March 30, 2005, 10.

148. Ibid., 5.

149. United Nations, *Fifteenth SG Report on MONUC*, S/2004/251, para. 33.

150. Crisis Group, "The Congo's Transition Is Failing," 11.

151. Ibid., 24.

152. Ibid., 6.

153. United Nations, *Third Special Report of the Secretary-General on MONUC*, S/2004/650, August 16, 2004, para. 45.

154. Human Rights Watch, "DR Congo: War Crimes in Bukavu" (briefing paper), June 2004, 30.

155. Interview with member of the UN Group of Experts on the DRC, May 23, 2005.

156. Global Witness, "Under-Mining Peace: The Explosive Trade in Cassiterite in Eastern DRC" (Washington, DC: Global Witness Publishing, June 2005), 30.

157. United Nations, *Third Special SG Report on MONUC,* S/2004/650, para. 36.

158. Crisis Group, "The Congo's Transition Is Failing," 24.

159. Susannah Price, "Peacekeepers Powerless in DR Congo," *BBC Online,* June 3, 2004.

160. United Nations, *Eighteenth Report of the Secretary-General on MONUC,* S/2005/506, August 2, 2005, para. 44.

161. Crisis Group, "The Congo's Transition Is Failing," 20.

162. United Nations, *Sixteenth SG Report on MONUC,* S/2004/1034, para. 17.

163. Ibid., para. 18.

164. Ibid., para. 21.

165. United Nations, *Third Special SG Report on MONUC,* S/2004/650, para. 76.

166. Ibid., para. 119.

167. United Nations, *Eighteenth SG Report on MONUC,* S/2005/506, para. 34.

168. Crisis Group, "The Congo: Solving the FDLR Problem Once and for All," Africa Briefing no. 25, May 12, 2005, 7.

169. Ibid., 5.

170. "UN Peacekeeping Patrols Seize Weapons in Eastern DR of Congo," *UN News Service,* March 17, 2005.

171. Stephanie Wolters, "Is Ituri on the Road to Stability?" (online report, Pretoria: Institute for Security Studies, May 12, 2005), www.monuc.org/downloads/ASAP_Sit_Rep_Ituri.pdf, 7.

172. Mohammad A. Wahab, "MONUC Ituri Brigade Chases Militias" (MONUC press release, July 18, 2005), www.monuc.org/Story.aspx?storyID=536.

173. United Nations, *Eighteenth SG Report on MONUC,* S/2005/506, para. 25.

174. UN Security Council, *Letter Dated 25 January 2005 from the Chairman of the Security Council Committee Established Pursuant to Resolution 1533 (2004) Concerning the DRC Addressed to the President of the Security Council,* S/2005/30, January 25, 2005, paras. 230, 232.

175. UN Security Council, *Letter Dated 26 July 2005 from the Chairman of the Security Council Committee Established Pursuant to Resolution 1533 (2004) Concerning the Democratic Republic of the Congo Addressed to the Pres-*

ident of the Security Council, S/2005/436, July 26, 2005, paras. 18, 114.

176. United Nations, *Special Report of the Secretary-General on Elections in the Democratic Republic of the Congo,* S/2005/320, May 26, 2005, paras. 45–46, 56–57; and UN Security Council Resolution 1621, S/RES/1621, September 6, 2005.

177. Jane Rasmussen, "MONUC: Sexual Exploitation and Abuse, End of Assignment Report" (online report, UN DPKO, Peacekeeping Best Practices Unit, February 25, 2005), 1, www.un.org/Depts/dpko/lessons.

178. United Nations, *Special Measures for Protection from Sexual Exploitation and Sexual Abuse,* Secretary-General's Bulletin, ST/SGB/2003/13, October 9, 2003. The *Gender Resource Package* can be downloaded from www.un.org/Depts/dpko/lessons.

179. United Nations, *Eighteenth SG Report on MONUC,* S/2005/506, paras. 72–73.

180. UN General Assembly, *A Comprehensive Strategy to Eliminate Future Sexual Exploitation and Abuse in United Nations Peacekeeping Operations,* A/59/710, March 24, 2005, paras. 15–22, 32–35, 41.

181. Ibid., paras. 47–49, 60.

182. United Nations, *Eighteenth SG Report on MONUC,* S/2005/506, para. 71.

5

Kosovo

Michael J. Dziedzic

Introduction

Kosovo's peace operation was a product more of force than of diplomacy. When the Kosovo Verification Mission withdrew under duress in March 1999, diplomacy had run its course. A scorched-earth campaign by Serb security forces rapidly ensued. Some 850,000 members of Kosovo's ethnic Albanian community were driven to seek refuge, mostly in neighboring Macedonia and Albania; several hundred thousand more were displaced from their homes inside Kosovo.[1] A seventy-eight-day coercive bombing campaign by the North Atlantic Treaty Organization (NATO) was the instrument that compelled Serb leader Slobodan Milosevic to capitulate. When the NATO-led Kosovo Force (KFOR) eventually embarked upon its UN-mandated peace mission on June 12, the casus belli, Kosovo's political status, remained unresolved.

KFOR would have little peace to keep. As refugees spontaneously flooded home, assaults on Kosovo's Serb minority began erupting on a regular basis. Ultimately, nearly half of that community fled into exile. Initially some left of their own accord, but a climate of violence and intimidation quickly ensued that posed a threat to the very existence of the Serb community.

While the bombing was unfolding during the spring of 1999, uncertainty reigned about how the international community would deal with the outcome. The UN Secretariat received the lead role in organizing the international civilian presence in Kosovo on June 10, 1999, under Security Council Resolution 1244. With virtually no advance warning, it would be required to exercise the sovereign prerogatives of a state. The United Nations was hard pressed to cobble together a governmental bureaucracy for this purpose. One particularly demanding aspect of the mandate of the UN Interim Administration Mission in Kosovo was the requirement to exercise "executive" law enforcement authority. This challenge was vastly compounded by the lack of a functioning local judicial and penal system. More than 4,000 armed international police had to be recruited to perform the gamut of public security functions required of a governing body, along with hundreds of civil administrators. A severely understaffed UN bureaucracy struggled for many months to mobilize the required personnel from its member states, which, with few exceptions, were also totally unprepared for such a demand.

Responsibility for other crucial civilian tasks was divided between the European Union and the Organization for Security and Co-operation in Europe (OSCE). The European Union (EU) assumed responsibility for rehabilitating Kosovo's economy, while the OSCE developed basic institutions of governance and nurtured civil society.

In sum, Kosovo presented the international community with the most demanding combination of peace implementation challenges yet confronted; it required the simultaneous capacity to make peace, enforce peace, and build peace while also performing the multitudinous functions of governance.

Origins of the Operations

Kosovo is, officially, a province of Serbia and Montenegro, known in 1999 as the Former Republic of Yugoslavia, or the FRY (see figure 5.1). At 4,200 square miles, Kosovo is about as large as Los Angeles County, California. It is mostly a high plateau, 1,200 feet above sea level, ringed by mountains and hills. Its summers are hot and dry, its winters cold and snowy.

Kosovo's history has produced a legacy that is of symbolic significance to the Serb nation, but its population is predominantly Albanian.

Figure 5.1. Map of Kosovo

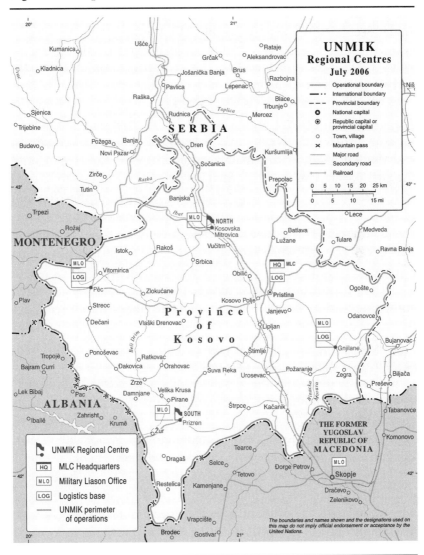

Source: UN Cartographic Section

(In 1991, at the time of the last census, its population of nearly two million was 82 percent ethnic Albanian, 10 percent Serbian, and 8 percent other.[2]) As the location of major Orthodox monasteries and the site of the mythic Serb defeat by the Ottomans in the Battle of Kosovo Polje (1389), Kosovo helped to define the Serb nation. Accordingly, Serbs regard it as the cradle of their civilization.

Albanian nationalism is also rooted in Kosovo, dating from the 1878 League of Prizren, which sought the unification of Albanian-speaking peoples residing in present-day Albania, Kosovo, Macedonia, and Montenegro. Kosovo remained part of the Ottoman Empire until the First Balkan War in 1912, when Serbia and its allies asserted control. After World War I, Kosovo was governed as part of the Kingdom of Serbs, Croats, and Slovenes. Albanians were forced to either assimilate or emigrate. This situation was reversed under Italian occupation during World War II when Kosovo was annexed to Albania, producing a Serb exodus and restoration of Albanian dominance.

Under Josip Broz Tito's rule (1945–80), Kosovo was accorded autonomous status within the Serb Republic, one of the six republics that made up the Socialist Federal Republic of Yugoslavia (SFRY). Albanians were recognized as a minor nationality with rights to education in their own language. Political control was reinforced via economic subsidies and ultimately the apparatus of a police state. Demonstrations in 1968 prompted the Yugoslav government to grant Albanians increased freedoms. The Constitution of 1974 significantly enhanced Kosovo's status, recognizing it as an autonomous province with its own legislative assembly, judiciary, police force, and central bank.

Kosovo was the poorest part of Yugoslavia, and federal investment in the 1970s and 1980s had only begun to transform its agrarian economy when Yugoslavia went into persistent economic decline. Kosovo felt the gravest impact, with its unemployment rate rising to more than 20 percent by the late 1980s.[3]

Conflict

In 1981, a year after Tito's death, Kosovo Albanians agitated for recognition as one of Yugoslavia's constituent republics, a move that provoked repressive action by federal security forces. Restiveness persisted throughout the 1980s. The minority Serb population perceived its situation as increasingly tenuous, a feeling that surfaced in the form of a public memorandum in 1986 calling for a reversal of the decline in Serb influence in Kosovo. In the estimation of historian Noel Malcolm, "With good reason, this Memorandum has been seen in retrospect as a virtual manifesto for the 'Greater Serbian' policies pursued by Belgrade in the 1990s."[4] In a visit to Kosovo the following year, Slobodan Milosevic recognized that incitement of Serb nationalism would propel him into unassailable control of government in Serbia.

In 1989, the 600th anniversary of the Battle of Kosovo Polje, Milosevic revoked Kosovo's autonomy and reimposed direct rule from Belgrade. The Kosovo Assembly was disbanded, and thousands of additional troops and police were deployed to maintain order. Kosovo Albanians were denied rights to education in their own language, and tens of thousands were dismissed from government positions. Kosovo Albanians responded by establishing a parallel governing structure and education system under Ibrahim Rugova and the Democratic League of Kosovo (LDK), which espoused a nonviolent path to independence.

The fabric of Yugoslavia's multiethnic society was shredded in 1990 by Milosevic's drive to unite all Serbs under one state and form a "Greater Serbia." This was a decisive turning point, according to Louis Sell, involving "a new strategy aimed at using armed force to create a separate Serb state, with the full knowledge that this would cause the disintegration of Yugoslavia and war."[5] The Dayton Agreement, which ended hostilities in Bosnia, failed to address Kosovo's status, discrediting Rugova's nonviolent approach and initiating the radicalization of the population. Impetus for a violent resistance movement, the Kosovo Liberation Army (KLA), began to build.

By 1997, the KLA was openly claiming responsibility for attacks against Serb police. When Albania imploded that same year, the insurgent movement gained access to an arsenal that included crew-served weapons in addition to small arms. After the KLA shifted to systematic violence against Serb police and officials, Milosevic responded by launching an offensive in early 1998 using Interior Ministry police and the Yugoslav army. Their scorched-earth tactics were a replay of many previous episodes in Yugoslavia's progressive dissolution under Milosevic.

Diplomacy Backed by Suggestions of Force

The international community began to search in earnest for a means to avert another cycle of ethnic cleansing in the Balkans. In March 1998, the UN Security Council passed Resolution 1160, imposing an arms embargo on Yugoslavia, including Kosovo, that was to remain in effect until Belgrade entered into a "meaningful dialogue" with the leaders of Kosovo aimed at achieving a political solution to the issue of Kosovo's status. The resolution suggested that such an agreement be based on principles of territorial integrity for the Federal Republic of Yugoslavia and "an enhanced status for Kosovo which would include a substantially greater degree of autonomy and meaningful self-administration."[6]

Milosevic responded by reinforcing his military posture in Kosovo. In May NATO announced that it was developing military options and was willing to act to deter further violence. The deterrent effect was tempered, however, by a warning from the UN secretary-general that military intervention required a UN mandate.[7]

Any resolution seeking to authorize the use of force by NATO, however, faced a certain Russian veto and was also opposed by China. NATO members, moreover, were far from prepared to act in the absence of a UN mandate. Unconstrained by an effective deterrent, Serb offensives and intermittent massacres continued into September. Between 200,000 and 300,000 Albanians were forced from their homes, and a groundswell of recruits was driven to join the KLA. With winter approaching and the cycle of violence spinning out of control, the specter of an impending humanitarian catastrophe loomed large.[8]

On September 23, 1998, the UN Security Council adopted Resolution 1199, which called for a cease-fire, withdrawal of Serb forces of repression, monitoring by an international presence, return of refugees and displaced persons, and a dialogue to resolve the issue of Kosovo's political status. Although the Security Council acted under Chapter VII of the charter, the resolution did not provide authorization to enforce its provisions. In the event that its provisions were disregarded, the resolution merely threatened "to consider further action and additional measures."[9] Russia made it clear that it would veto any future resolution that permitted the use of force.

NATO had already completed advanced planning for various military options if a cease-fire could not be attained. The North Atlantic Council (NAC) had also authorized NATO planners to begin contacting alliance members to determine what capabilities they would be prepared to commit to prospective air operations.[10] With the passage of Resolution 1199, NATO's credibility was on the line. Accordingly, on September 24, the NAC took the additional step of issuing an "activation warning" directing NATO commanders to identify the forces they needed to carry out two options: limited air strikes and a major air campaign.[11] This meant that the alliance had taken all the steps necessary to act, short of the political decision to do so.

In spite of continuing political divisions within NATO over the legal requirement for a UN mandate, the alliance's increasing display of resolve provided leverage for U.S. envoy Richard Holbrooke to reach an agreement with Milosevic. When NATO ultimately issued an "activation order" on October 13 that authorized execution of an air campaign, an agreement swiftly emerged.[12] International monitoring by NATO reconnaissance aircraft and a 2,000-member Kosovo Verification Mission (KVM) would verify compliance with Resolution 1199.[13] The KVM, established under the aegis of the OSCE, became operational in December.

The KVM was not a cure for Kosovo's crisis. It was merely an opportunity for diplomacy to begin addressing the core issue: Kosovo's status. The crux of the matter remained the absence of any on-the-ground enforcement mechanism. Indeed, the presence of international monitors actually deterred the use of force by NATO, since KVM members could easily have been taken hostage by Serb forces. The KVM was quickly sabotaged by the KLA's exploitation of its presence to recoup territory lost in earlier Serb offensives and by renewed attacks on civilians by Serb security forces. A massacre at Racak on January 15, 1999, in which more than forty ethnic Albanians were killed, left the chief of the KVM, Ambassador William Walker, with no choice but to verify the obvious.[14] For this he was declared persona non grata by Milosevic, effectively vitiating the mission even though the KVM continued to operate with Walker at the helm.

As a result of the Racak massacre, UN secretary-general Kofi Annan met with the North Atlantic Council on January 28, declaring that force could well be necessary when all other means had failed, and in Kosovo that point was nearing.[15] NATO secretary-general Javier Solana reaffirmed the alliance's readiness to use force. The Contact Group on Kosovo (France, Germany, Italy, Russia, the United Kingdom, and the United States) met in London on January 29 and demanded that the Serb and Kosovo Albanian leadership attend peace talks at Rambouillet, France, on February 6.

The plan presented at Rambouillet called for the KLA to disarm within three months and for the Serbs to withdraw all but a small contingent of security forces.[16] Kosovo would enjoy autonomous self-governance, as it had prior to 1989, and after three years an international mechanism was to be established to resolve its final status. Compliance with the agreement was to be enforced by a 30,000-member NATO force. After two weeks of negotiations, only the Kosovo delegation showed any inclination to accept the package, but they insisted on first returning to Kosovo for consultations. The United States made it clear that the bombing option would not be exercised unless they signed the agreement. This was intended to place Milosevic in the position of having the last clear option for avoiding the use of force. When the parties reconvened on March 18, the Kosovo delegation signed while the Serbs remained intransigent. With tens of thousands of Serb forces massing on the border, the KVM was ordered to evacuate. As it withdrew on March 20, the Serbian offensive, Operation Horseshoe, was already in motion. The strategic aim was to defeat the KLA by depriving it of a support base. As Daalder and O'Hanlon argue, in the process, Milosevic sought "both to alter the ethnic balance in Kosovo in the Serbs' favor and to destabilize Kosovo's neighbors, who had to cope with the large influx of refugees."[17]

Force Backed by Diplomacy

On March 24, NATO launched Operation Allied Force, an air campaign against targets in Serbia and Kosovo, in an attempt to achieve through force what had been unattainable through diplomacy. The expectation was that a few days of bombing would persuade Milosevic to accept the bargain proffered at Rambouillet. The use of ground troops to drive Serb security forces out of Kosovo was publicly disavowed by President Clinton in his address to the nation on the eve of the bombing.[18] Serbian forces proved to be undeterred, however, by bombs dropped from an altitude of 15,000 feet (a limitation NATO imposed on itself to avoid politically damaging aircraft losses). A door-to-door ethnic cleansing campaign rapidly unfolded that produced the exodus of roughly half the Kosovo Albanian population, primarily to refugee camps in Albania and Macedonia. Public support within NATO nations began to waver. Bombing alone appeared unlikely to deter Milosevic from achieving his military objectives and then suing for peace. NATO's solidarity was clearly at risk.

Force and diplomacy ultimately came together as planning for a ground offensive combined with incorporation of the Russians into the negotiating process to resolve the crisis. A diplomatic overture to Russia initiated by the German government provided an opening for a negotiated outcome. President Boris Yeltsin appointed Viktor Chernomyrdin as his envoy. While options for a ground invasion were being developed by NATO, President Clinton reciprocated by appointing Strobe Talbott to spearhead consultations for the United States. At a meeting involving the two negotiators in Washington, D.C., on May 4, the decision was made to add Finnish president Marti Ahtisaari to the team, representing the European Union. The following day, President Clinton was briefed on the initial results of NATO's planning for an invasion.[19]

A May 6, 1999, meeting of the Group of Eight (G-8), a body that includes both the United States and Russia, called for the establishment of an interim administration in Kosovo and the "deployment . . . of effective international civil and security presences, endorsed and adopted by the United Nations, capable of guaranteeing the achievement of the common objectives."[20] This proposal was one component of the diplomatic formula for ending the crisis; the other was acceptance of the following NATO conditions by Milosevic before military operations would be terminated:

- a verifiable halt to Serb violence and repression against the Albanians
- withdrawal of all Serb security forces from Kosovo
- deployment of an international military force
- return of all refugees and internally displaced persons
- acceptance of the Rambouillet accords as the basis for a political framework to resolve Kosovo's status[21]

The trio of Ahtisaari, Chernomyrdin, and Talbott would have to resolve whether any Serb forces would be allowed to remain in Kosovo, whether the bombing would cease immediately after an agreement was reached or only after Serb troops had begun a rapid withdrawal, whether international military forces would be under NATO or UN command, and whether the international force would include nations that had participated in the bombing and how those forces would be deployed.[22] NATO would not budge on the necessity for a total Serb withdrawal and a unified NATO command structure. On May 27, Chernomyrdin communicated to Milosevic that he would either have to accept these conditions or be prepared to be invaded. The clock was indeed ticking, since NATO calculated that a decision on the ground force option was needed by June 1 in order to complete the campaign by winter. Milosevic sought to impose conditions about the composition and command and control of the force, but Russia and the United States decided to resolve these issues themselves. Once this agreement had been reached, Ahtisaari and Chernomyrdin informed Milosevic on June 2 that he would have to accept the basic conditions established by NATO and the G-8, which he did. This left the technical details of the Serb withdrawal and the deployment of KFOR to be worked out by the Supreme Allied Commander Europe, General Wesley Clark, and Yugoslav army commanders. The resulting Military Technical Agreement was signed on June 9, and Serbia completed withdrawal on June 20.[23]

Political Support for Peace

Since Kosovo's "final status" remained unresolved, continued conflict between Serbs and Albanians was the predominant concern of the international community as it moved to take temporary control of the territory. The UN Interim Administration Mission in Kosovo (UNMIK) did not anticipate, however, that it would have to prevent a civil war from erupting within the Kosovo Albanian community itself, between the triumphant KLA and followers of Ibrahim Rugova. Nor did NATO anticipate that its forces would face a greater security challenge from Albanian violence against the Serbs than from armed resistance by Serb forces.[24]

Internal Actors

Initially, Kosovo's "peace process" was little more than the continuation of warfare by other means, with politically motivated violence continuing to play a dominant role along two dimensions of conflict: between Kosovo's Albanian and Serb communities and within the Kosovo Albanian population. As NATO troops began arriving in June 1999, about a hundred civilians were being killed each week, mostly Serbs. Although vengeance played a part, most of these killings were carried out by shadowy KLA extremists who were determined to set the stage for a Kosovo completely liberated from Serb influence.

The Serbs who remained in Kosovo felt more betrayed than defeated. The war was continuing, as far as they were concerned, and they were unrepentant for Serb oppression and atrocities. Milosevic encouraged resistance, and parallel governing structures in Serb-dominated areas were sustained by Belgrade. This was the case particularly in areas where Serbs were the dominant majority—in the three northern municipalities adjacent to the FRY and that portion of Mitrovica north of the Ibar River. Serbs saw Mitrovica as the place to take an uncompromising stand against Albanian domination.

At the same time, KLA fighters considered the LDK's military arm[25] to be nearly as much an enemy as the Serb special police. During the war the KLA had secretly assaulted Rugova's followers, and in its immediate aftermath KLA extremists sought to eliminate the LDK militia. Indeed, from the KLA's perspective, the main conflict was not with the defeated Serbs but between the KLA and the LDK for the military and political domination of Kosovo. In the aftermath of the war, the KLA immediately filled the power vacuum created by the withdrawal of Serb authorities and declared itself the "provisional government."

To advance the peace process, therefore, the looming civil war within Kosovo's Albanian community would have to be averted, and the Milosevic regime would have to be removed from power. Until these underlying sources of conflict had been addressed, little headway could be made in attenuating the conflict between Kosovo's Serb and Albanian communities.

External Actors

The principal external actors involved in defining the fate of Kosovo were the United States, the Russian Federation, the "Quint" (the United States, the United Kingdom, France, Germany, and Italy), the Contact

Group (the Quint plus Russia), neighboring Macedonia and Albania, the European Union, and the OSCE.

President Clinton identified four challenges for U.S. policy in Kosovo when he addressed the nation at the conclusion of the seventy-eight-day bombing campaign:

- ensuring that Serbian authorities fulfilled their commitments
- returning Kosovar refugees safely to their homes
- building peace and stability in Kosovo and throughout the region
- encouraging Serbia to join "this historic journey, to a peaceful democratic united Europe"[26]

Clinton also referenced two other interests that were entangled in the effort to stabilize Kosovo: the strength and solidarity of the NATO alliance, and the tenor of the U.S. relationship with Russia.

The United States was the indispensable source of momentum for the peace process, mobilizing resources to sustain the operation and garnering support from other international actors for policy initiatives. When the European Union, for example, failed for many months to provide the funding it had pledged to regenerate economic activity, key figures in the Clinton administration and Congress took the Europeans to task for shirking their commitments. U.S. leadership was also needed to establish an international consensus that a review of Kosovo's progress toward compliance with international standards should take place in 2005. This was intended to trigger a process to determine Kosovo's future political status once sufficient progress toward meeting international standards had been achieved.

Russian national interests coincided with the Serb desire to retain sovereignty over Kosovo, owing to the parallels with Russia's own rebellion in Chechnya. The precedent of an independent Kosovo emerging in the wake of an armed insurrection was perceived by the Russian government as potentially threatening to its own territorial integrity. As the principal international benefactor of the Serbs, moreover, its own stature was at issue when Milosevic capitulated to NATO's use of force. The injury to national pride was assuaged by Russian forces' cross-country dash into Pristina airport ahead of KFOR and the inclusion of Russian troops as part of KFOR.

During the early stages of the mission, Russian diplomacy was stridently protective of Belgrade's sovereign prerogatives. Russia's UN delegation caused the UN Secretariat to make incessant requests for information about UNMIK's operations. Scathing Russian complaints during open debates in the Security Council eventually subsided, however, as shared interests in regional stability provided a basis for allowing the peace process to move forward.

The **Quint countries** had already established the practice of coordinating their policies within NATO, including Bosnia policy, prior to the intervention in Kosovo. This process was simply replicated on the ground in Pristina and on a rotating basis in national capitals. Given that the Quint countries were the lead nations for the five multinational brigades of KFOR, periodic meetings were especially useful for dealing with overarching security-related issues of concern to both civilian and military leaders. Consultations among the Quint were also useful to establish a consensus prior to meetings of the Contact Group.

A peace operation faced with serious unresolved sources of conflict needs the support (or at least acquiescence) of the major powers affected by the situation to drive the overall process forward. The **Contact Group** served as the mechanism for political consensus building in support of UNMIK. When difficult policy choices had to be made, it was invaluable to be able to demonstrate to the parties that UNMIK had their endorsement. It met at a senior policymaker level on a rotating basis in one of the national capitals, or at the United Nations when there was a need to establish a consensus on major policy initiatives. In the words of Jock Covey, UNMIK's principal deputy special representative of the secretary-general (SRSG) under Bernard Kouchner, "When difficulties arose, we could turn to the Contact Group, describe our situation, explain our preferred strategy, and urge its support of our efforts. For the most part, it was a powerful and reliable advocate for UNMIK."[27]

Although the Russian representative to the United Nations made life difficult for UNMIK, his counterpart in the Contact Group was more moderate, since Russia enjoyed being included among the major powers. The Contact Group could also work as a constraint on the United States. Early on, U.S. policy greatly favored the development of a constitution for Kosovo. UNMIK's leadership preferred to remain ambiguous about potentially explosive isues such as power sharing among the parties.[28] UNMIK officials consulted with other members of the Contact Group, who were also troubled by the idea. UNMIK then encouraged the United States to present the proposal to the Contact Group, with the result that it went nowhere.

The conflict in Kosovo posed an existential threat to **Macedonia** over which it had no control. Were its own substantial ethnic Albanian community (22 percent of the total population) to be drawn into the fighting, Macedonia risked disintegration.[29] This did not stop venal national politicians from seeking to profiteer from the situation by imposing customs duties on relief supplies flowing into Kosovo in 1999, creating a monumental traffic tie-up that stretched from the border all the way to Skopje. The conflict did eventually spill over the border in 2001 but was contained through international intervention.

Solidarity with the plight of ethnic Albanians in Kosovo was the basic posture of the population of **Albania**, at a time when its government was largely unable to assert control over national territory. Albania therefore served as a conduit for smuggled weapons and trafficking in illicit commodities that fueled subversive activity on Kosovo's periphery.

Although there was little enthusiasm in European capitals about the prospect of Kosovo's ultimate independence, the region's long-term stability would require incorporating it in some fashion into the political and economic structures of Europe. "The challenge, from a European perspective, was to ensure the province's long-term stability and regional integration by establishing the conditions for sustainable economic development."[30] The role of the **European Union** was to provide the bulk of the funding for and management of the economic rebuilding effort.

Owing to its experience conducting the Kosovo Verification Mission, the **OSCE** harbored expectations that it would lead the international civil administration mission. Even though there was initial disappointment about having to take a back seat to the United Nations when UNMIK was created, the OSCE played an invaluable role because of its ability to mobilize former KVM personnel rapidly to staff the new mission and because of the staff's familiarity with local conditions.

Since the promotion of human rights was a vital part of the heritage of the OSCE, it was institutionally accustomed to operating as an external critic of state authorities. Owing to serious defects in Kosovo's legal system initially, both the KFOR commander and the SRSG felt compelled to use extended extrajudicial detentions for particularly dangerous suspects. This unleashed a stream of public criticism from the OSCE's legal system monitors, even though they were themselves part of UNMIK.

Mandate

On June 10, the Security Council passed Resolution 1244. The resolution did not prescribe Kosovo's future political status, but it did direct the international civil presence to facilitate "a political process designed to determine Kosovo's final status, taking into account the Rambouillet accords." It granted authority for NATO-led KFOR to establish a safe and secure environment under Chapter VII, and authorized the international civil presence to establish an interim administration aimed at producing "substantial autonomy and meaningful self-administration for Kosovo."[31]

Paragraph 9 of Resolution 1244 itemized the tasks that the international security presence was expected to perform related to establishing a secure environment:

a. Deterring renewed hostilities, maintaining and where necessary enforcing a cease-fire, and ensuring the withdrawal and preventing the return into Kosovo of Federal and Republic military, police and paramilitary forces . . . ;

b. Demilitarizing the Kosovo Liberation Army (KLA) and other armed Kosovo Albanian groups . . . ;

c. Establishing a secure environment in which refugees and displaced persons can return home in safety, the international civil presence can operate, a transitional administration can be established, and humanitarian aid can be delivered;

d. Ensuring public safety and order until the international civil presence can take responsibility for this task;

e. Supervising demining until the international civil presence can, as appropriate, take over responsibility for this task;

f. Supporting, as appropriate, *and coordinating closely with* the work of the international civil presence; [emphasis added]

g. Conducting border monitoring duties as required;

h. Ensuring protection and freedom of movement of itself, the international civil presence, and other international organizations...[32]

KFOR's mission was further defined by the Military Technical Agreement signed between KFOR and the FRY, which established the process of Serb withdrawal from Kosovo and the relationship between KFOR and FRY security forces. The agreement between KFOR and the KLA, known as the "Undertaking," signed by Hashim Thaci, the commander in chief of the KLA, on June 21, 1999, provided for the demilitarization of the KLA after ninety days. Finally, UNMIK Regulation 1999/8 established the Kosovo Protection Corps. Together, these basic documents formed the "mandate" of the "international security presence" and guided the operations of KFOR.[33]

This mandate provided the authority for KFOR to secure Kosovo against outside threats, remove the means for Albanian paramilitary leaders to continue the war, and present a credible security presence using assertive peace enforcement tactics.

Resolution 1244 required that the United Nations exercise the sovereign prerogatives of a state for the first time. It authorized UNMIK to establish an interim civilian administration under which the people of Kosovo could progressively enjoy substantial autonomy. In particular, paragraph 11 assigned UNMIK responsibility for

a. Promoting the establishment, pending a final settlement, of substantial autonomy and self-government in Kosovo . . . ;

b. Performing basic civilian administrative functions where and as long as required;

c. Organizing and overseeing the development of provisional institutions for democratic and autonomous self-government pending a political settlement, including the holding of elections;

d. Transferring, as these institutions are established, its administrative responsibilities while overseeing and supporting the consolidation of Kosovo's local provisional institutions and other peacebuilding activities;

e. Facilitating a political process designed to determine Kosovo's future status, taking into account the Rambouillet Accords (S/1999/648);

f. In a final stage, overseeing the transfer of authority from Kosovo's provisional institutions to institutions established under a political settlement;

g. Supporting the reconstruction of key infrastructure and other economic reconstruction;

h. Supporting, in coordination with international humanitarian organizations, humanitarian and disaster relief aid;

i. Maintaining civil law and order, including establishing local police forces[,] and meanwhile through the deployment of international police personnel to serve in Kosovo;

j. Protecting and promoting human rights;

k. Assuring the safe and unimpeded return of all refugees and displaced persons to their homes in Kosovo . . .[34]

This mandate was unprecedented in its scope and complexity. It was also open ended. Thus UNMIK was not constrained by insufficient authority. It *was* hampered, however, by the lack of advanced preparation to mobilize the qualified personnel and financial resources that would be required, and also by the early reluctance and limited capacity of UN Secretariat legal advisers to allow UNMIK to exercise fully the authority provided in the mandate.

Funding

The United Nations had well-established funding mechanisms for dealing with humanitarian emergencies and typical peacekeeping activities. NATO similarly had standing arrangements among alliance members that prescribed how the expenses of military operations would be borne. UNMIK's responsibility to serve as a substitute government was unprecedented, however. No international mechanism existed to generate grants to offset the expenses of running a foreign government. UNMIK had to employ upwards of 55,000 Kosovan civilians but had no sources of revenue, such as customs fees or other local taxes, with which to pay local salaries and fund the functions of the Kosovan bureaucracy. Eventually the capacity to generate revenue would be established and funds would flow into the Kosovo Consolidated Budget (KCB).[35] By 2004 the KCB was able to cover all operating expenses of the Kosovo government (the Provisional Institutions of Self-Government) (see table 5.1).

Table 5.1. Funding for Kosovo Consolidated Budget and UNMIK (in millions)

Kosovo Consolidated Budget

	2000	2001	2002	2003	2004	2005
	DM562	€380	€374.1	€516.9	€632	€736.8

UNMIK

Pillar	Function	Lead Agency	Funding Source	1999–2000	2001	2002	2003	2004	2005
I	Humanitarian Assistance (1999–2001)	UN High Commissioner for Refugees	Donor contributions	$1,447[a]					
I	Police and Justice (2001–present)	UN Department of Peacekeeping Operations	Member states; annual UN General Assembly resolutions	$361.8	$383.5	$360.2	$330	$315.5	$294.5
II	Interim Civil Administration								

| III | Democratization and Institution Building | Organization for Security and Co-operation in Europe | Member states[b] | 1999: €75.1 2000: €88.3 | €73.4 | €64[c] | €45 | €44[d] | €33.6 |
| IV | Reconstruction and Economic Development | European Union | EC funds (and funds from other sources) managed by the European Agency for Reconstruction[e] | €541.7 | €140 | €155 | €33.5 | €25 | €4 |

[a] Includes first and second donor conferences.
[b] Source: OSCE Permanent Council Resolutions, http://www.osce.org/kosovo.
[c] Includes supplement for 2002 Municipal Elections.
[d] Includes supplement for Kosovo Police School.
[e] Source: European Agency for Reconstruction Annual Reports, http://www.ear.eu.int/publications/publications.htm. All figures as of January 31, 2006.

During the first months of the mission, however, when the delivery of basic public services was an urgent priority, none of this existed. Finance ministers in potential donor nations initially refused to consider direct grants to support Kosovo's budget out of a philosophical aversion to creating a dependency on external handouts. They insisted that Kosovo's government should be self-sufficient. The failure to provide basic services directly affected UNMIK's credibility among all Kosovan groups.

The initial Kosovo donors' conference, attended by officials from a hundred donor countries and international organizations, took place in Brussels on July 28, 1999. Conferees pledged $1.4 billion for humanitarian assistance and, by that October, had committed nearly the full amount and spent $831 million. They pledged another $722 million for urgent reconstruction and, by October, had committed $270 million but spent only $76 million. For local civil administration ("budget assistance"), however, only $34 million was pledged, $23 million committed, and $14 million spent.[36]

With the mission on the verge of collapse in late 1999, political reality finally overcame this resistance. At the second donors' conference in November 1999, participants pledged $34 million for humanitarian aid, $47 million for "peace implementation," $884 million for reconstruction, and $88 million for local budget assistance.[37]

Compounding their financial difficulties was the fact that Kosovo itself was not a sovereign entity, which precluded the World Bank and International Monetary Fund from providing loans, although the bank financed a series of relatively modest grants, totaling roughly $100 million through 2005, to support economic reform, job creation, and infrastructure rehabilitation.[38]

The European Union assumed primary responsibility for funding reconstruction programs, but it was unable to deliver on its commitments for the better part of a year. This left urgent infrastructure repair requirements, such as power generation, water, waste management, and transport, unmet. In part this was due to the novelty of the demand, but the inherent sluggishness of the EU bureaucracy was also a contributing factor.

In 1999, the European Union allocated €127 million through the European Commission Task Force for the Reconstruction of Kosovo

(EC TAFKO), which was established in August 1999. In February 2000 it was replaced by the European Agency for Reconstruction, which spends the vast majority of its Kosovo funds in the fields of energy, housing, transport, water, agriculture, and enterprise development.[39]

Finally, troop-contributing countries by and large financed their own deployments with KFOR. Although budget data are hard to come by, knowledgeable estimates suggest that KFOR cost about $5 billion a year initially, decreasing to about $2.5–3 billion in 2003 as troop strength dropped from 57,000 (including nearby support troops) in September 1999 to 16,600 in 2005. Total spending on KFOR through 2003 was on the order of $20–22 billion, constituting 75 to 85 percent of all international and domestic public spending for Kosovo during that period. Although international civil administration and postconflict reconstruction are costly, using modern military forces for public security is costlier still.[40]

Planning and Administration

In May 1998, as NATO began to develop coercive options to support a diplomatic resolution to the crisis, it also initiated planning for enforcement of an eventual agreement. NATO planners anticipated two potential outcomes. One was NATO enforcement of a cease-fire agreement reached by the parties that would require maintaining an environment conducive to negotiating a final peace settlement; this option was estimated to require 50,000 NATO troops. The other option was NATO enforcement of a peace settlement reached by the parties; this would have required 28,000 NATO troops.[41] Thus, a full year before the 50,000-strong Kosovo Force was deployed to provide a safe and secure environment pending the determination of Kosovo's future status, NATO had taken steps to prepare for such a mission.

On the civilian side, however, even as KFOR was on the brink of intervention in June 1999, no decision had been made about which international organizations would assume responsibility for peace implementation in Kosovo. Due to its experience with the Kosovo Verification Mission, the OSCE had anticipated a mandate and was preparing for functions relating to the rule of law and civil administration. It had conducted assessments and developed a concept for reestablishing the police force well in advance of the passage of Resolution 1244. When the decision was made at a G-8 meeting in May to have the United Nations take the lead instead, there was virtually no time remaining for planning.[42] Nor was the Department of Peacekeeping Operations adequately staffed to respond, since member states had recently ended the practice of providing personnel to the department on a gratis basis. "Strategic planning was not possible in this environment."[43]

Planning and Deploying KFOR

The route by which NATO planned to send forces into Kosovo led through Macedonia. In late 1998, a French-led "extraction force" of 2,000 was deployed at Kumanovo, along the Macedonian border with Serbia, to provide assistance, if necessary, to the Kosovo Verification Mission. These troops could be converted to support either of the peace enforcement options being contemplated by NATO. Realistically, this small contingent was capable of acting only in a "permissive" environment, as opposed to in a typical hostage-taking scenario. Accordingly, the task of preparing a more robust response was assigned to Lieutenant General Michael Jackson, commander of the Allied Command Europe Rapid Reaction Corps.[44] Lieutenant General Jackson and KFOR were deployed to Macedonia in February and March 1999 in response to the deteriorating situation in Kosovo. In addition to assisting with the ensuing refugee crisis, KFOR figured in the planning for a ground invasion via Macedonia and Albania. As NATO drew closer to a decision about an invasion, KFOR's capabilities were further augmented. Thus KFOR was already in position to implement the peace enforcement option immediately upon conclusion of the bombing campaign. By May, NATO had approximately 13,000 troops on standby in Macedonia, with an additional 2,000 supporting humanitarian missions in Albania.[45]

Command and Control in KFOR

The United States and its NATO allies insisted that KFOR operate under the alliance's unified command structure. Russia and the Serbs sought a UN-controlled force and a separate Russian sector. UN command was totally unacceptable to the United States and NATO, however, after their experience in Bosnia with the UN Protection Force. A

Russian sector, which undoubtedly would have been located in the predominantly Serb municipalities of northern Kosovo, would have meant a de facto partitioning of the province.

Although NATO prevailed in both cases, these issues remained in contention until the final negotiations to end the bombing. The issue of a Russian sector remained in play even during the early days of the deployment. After Russian troops seized control of Pristina airport on June 11 (see "Deployment of KFOR," below), U.S. and Russian negotiators hammered out an arrangement similar to the one used in Bosnia. As explained by U.S. secretary of defense William Cohen, "Russian troops[,] like all of those who are participating in the KFOR mission[,] would be under the tactical control of KFOR. But Russia, in terms of its operational control . . . they would be answerable to the national command authorities of Russia."[46] This paved the way for a Russian contribution of a maximum of 3,600 troops, distributed among several brigade sectors.[47]

Each of these sectors became the responsibility of a multinational brigade, or MNB. Command of the MNBs was assigned to the five leading troop contributors. Often referred to as the "confederation of KFOR," the MNBs operated largely as autonomous sectors. Although the KFOR commander (see table 5.2) had nominal direct command over them, each of his lower-ranking generals had the right to consult with his national government whenever he chose to do so. Each nation also reserved the right to place "caveats" on the rules of engagement that its forces would follow. KFOR main headquarters could be effective, however, at joint planning for activities that crossed MNB boundaries, as will be seen.

Deployment of KFOR

The Military Technical Agreement, signed on June 9, defined the nature of the relationship between KFOR and Serb security forces, a necessary step before the Security Council could provide the mandate for the "international military presence." After the passage of Resolution 1244 on June 10, KFOR was authorized to begin deployment, but the first unit to arrive was a rogue contingent of 200 Russian soldiers assigned to the Stabilization Force in Bosnia that seized control of Pristina airport on June 11. NATO sensed that this was a precursor to an

Table 5.2. KFOR Commanders, 1999–2005

KFOR Commander	Period of Service
Lieutenant General Sir Mike Jackson, United Kingdom	March–October 1999[a]
General Dr. Klaus Reinhardt, Germany	October 1999–April 2000
Lieutenant General Juan Ortuño, Spain	April–October 2000
Lieutenant General Carlo Cabigiosu, Italy	October 2000–April 2001
Lieutenant General Thorstein Skiaker, Norway	April–October 2001
Lieutenant General Marcel M. Valentin, France	October 2001–October 2002
Lieutenant General Fabio Mini, Italy	October 2002–October 2003[b]
Lieutenant General Holger Kammerhoff, Germany	October 2003–September 2004
Lieutenant General Yves de Kermabon, France	September 2004–September 2005
Lieutenant General Giuseppe Valotto, Italy	September 2005–

[a]Lieutenant General Jackson deployed to Macedonia as KFOR commander in March 1999 and led the force into Kosovo in June.
[b]See NATO, "Biographies of KFOR Commanders," www.nato.int/kfor/kfor/bios/default.htm.

airlift of a much larger force that would then take control of northern Kosovo and proclaim it the Russian sector. This ploy was effectively thwarted by denial of overflight authorization by countries surrounding Serbia, allowing the KFOR deployment to proceed without a major confrontation. On June 12, the first KFOR elements entered Kosovo, and within five days some 20,000 troops were on the ground.[48]

The withdrawal of Serb forces proceeded without incident, allowing KFOR to announce on June 20 that all FRY military and police units had departed. By July 26, the number of KFOR troops in Kosovo had reached 35,000, which included some 1,500 Russian troops. If logistics support forces stationed in Macedonia are included, the KFOR troop total at that point was 43,000. Virtually the entire contingent was fielded by late September (see table 5.3).[49]

Planning and Deploying UNMIK

A planning void was created at the start of the Kosovo mission because of the uncertainty about which international organization would take the lead. This gap was filled in part by the advanced political-military planning effort that had been taking place in Washington and other key capitals throughout the bombing campaign. Once international consensus was achieved that the United Nations should take charge, the United States provided a draft strategic plan to the UN Secretariat and, in the estimation of Jock Covey, principal deputy SRSG, "it proved to be about 80% applicable to what turned out to be required."[50]

As KFOR was deploying in early June 1999, a UN advance party headed by UNMIK's interim SRSG, Sergio Vieira de Mello, arrived in Pristina to conduct assessments and develop the approach the United Nations would take to the mission. Within thirty days, the UN secretary-general was able to publish a realistic concept of operations for UNMIK.[51] There was an immediate need for thousands of police to curb the wave of violence that was unfolding against the Serb population and for hundreds of professional staff to establish an interim administration. This was a severe challenge that the UN Secretariat and UN member states were not equipped to address.

Without an opportunity to conduct advance planning, the United Nations' Civilian Police Unit (CPU) had to estimate the number of international police that would be required simply by using a numerical ratio of police to inhabitants. This seriously underestimated the actual need, in part because the United Nations had never had a mission with executive policing authority before. There was little appreciation outside the CPU that such authority would require much more than equipping police officers with a pistol. Recruitment thus largely left to chance whether personnel with the range of specialized skills required by a major police force would in fact turn up in Kosovo. The factors used to establish the level and type of support and equipment required were based on those used in traditional monitoring missions. As a result, very basic items of equipment were lacking for the first

Table 5.3. KFOR End-Strengths, 1999, 2003, and 2005

Force Structure	Troop Contributors (Years as lead nation)	Troop Strength Sept. 1999[a]	Troop Strength Aug. 2003[a]	Troop Strength Aug. 2005[a]
Multinational Task Force North	Belgium	1,142	500	500
	Denmark	868	540	540
	France (1999–2005)	6,126	3,800	2,400
	Greece	—	(850)	(850)
	Latvia	—	—	12
	Luxembourg	—	26	26
	Morocco	—	279	279
	Russia	(6–800)	—	—
	United Arab Emirates	996	—	—
Multinational Task Force Center	Canada	1,162	800	3
	Czech Republic (2005)	158	409	410
	Finland (2003)	707	820	510
	Hungary	319	325	—
	Ireland	103	104	104
	Norway	562	980	60
	Russia (logs)	(750)	—	—
	Sweden	81	703	650
	United Kingdom (1999)	6,264	1,400	1,400
Multinational Brigade East	Armenia	—	—	34
	Greece	1,290	(850)	(850)
	Lithuania	10	30	30
	Poland	754	574	574
	Romania	—	—	(113)
	Russia	(6–800)	—	—
	Ukraine	240	325	325
	United States (1999–2005)	7,443	2,250	1,800

year, including handcuffs, forensic equipment, and automatic weapons for close protection of dignitaries.

UN planners did anticipate a need for a crowd control capability, based on experience in Bosnia, where implementation of the Dayton Agreement had been stymied by orchestrated civil disturbances. As a result, UNMIK police included ten Specialized Police Units (SPUs), in

Table 5.3. *(cont.)*

Force Structure	Troop Contributors (Years as lead nation)	Troop Strength Sept. 1999[a]	Troop Strength Aug. 2003[a]	Troop Strength Aug. 2005[a]
Multinational Brigade Southwest[b]	Argentina	—	113	113
	Azerbaijan	—	34	34
	Georgia	—	140	140
	Hungary	—	—	294
	Romania	—	226	(113)
	Slovenia	—	2	2
Former MNB South[b]	Austria	169	535	532
	Germany (1999)	6,013	3,100	3,900
	Netherlands	1,706	—	—
	Russia	(1,000)	—	—
	Slovakia	38	100	100
	Switzerland	35	220	220
	Turkey	977	940	940
Former MNB West[b]	Italy (1999–2005)	6,286	3,780	2,530
	Portugal	350	313	313
	Spain	1,258	1,300	800
Totals:	+Support: 8,000 in 1999[c]	48,207 +HQ: 759	26,368 +HQ	c. 21,500 +HQ

[a]Data in parentheses are estimated distributions of contingent troop totals.
[b]Multinational Brigades (MNBs) South and West merged into MNB Southwest in 2002.
[c]Support troops based in Greece, Albania, and Former Yugoslav Republic of Macedonia.

Sources: KFOR, "The International Security Presence in Kosovo," September 27, 1999. Online at www.afsouth.nato.int/operations/kfor/backgrounder.html. International Institute for Strategic Studies, *The Military Balance, 2003–04,* and *2005–06* (London: IISS, 2003, 2005), data as of August, both years.

addition to individual patrol officers. Each SPU had 115 men equipped with riot control gear, body armor, and armored vehicles.[52]

One vital step taken to facilitate the planning process in the field was the establishment of a Joint Planning Group (JPG). The JPG worked for UNMIK's senior leadership "to prepare a broad strategy to accomplish mission objectives, integrate UNMIK's component parts, and

Table 5.4. UNMIK Special Representatives of the Secretary-General

SRSG	Period of Service
Sergio Vieira de Mello (Brazil)	June 1999 (interim)
Bernard Kouchner (France)	July 1999–January 2001
Hans Haekkerup (Denmark)	February–December 2001
Michael Steiner (Germany)	January 2002–July 2003
Harri Holkeri (Finland)	August 2003–June 2004
Søren Jessen-Petersen (Denmark)	July 2004–

Note: See UNMIK, "UNMIK at a Glance," www.unmikonline.org/intro.htm.

bring capabilities to bear on the major emerging challenges to the mission."[53] The JPG sought to anticipate crucial decision points far enough in advance that UNMIK and KFOR could conduct joint planning to address them.

Command and Control of UNMIK

Owing to the sweeping nature of the mandate, no single international organization had the capacity to carry it out. Thus, UNMIK was the first UN mission designed with other multilateral organizations as full partners. It was built around four pillars, under the leadership of an SRSG who managed the overall mission and coordinated the activities of the UN agencies and other international organizations that made up UNMIK (see table 5.4).[54] The pillar concept was adopted by the United Nations from the initial political-military plan developed by the U.S. government. Each pillar had its own deputy SRSG, and each was to be responsible for one major component of the mission.[55]

It was not always possible to resolve contentious issues that arose among UNMIK's various pillars through a deliberate planning process. In these instances, as described by Jock Covey:

> You could not bring the EU, the OSCE, UNHCR [United Nations High Commissioner for Refugees], a group of UN civilians and senior NATO military officers all together to have a policy-making

discussion on controversial and complex issues and get agreement. . . . We began to articulate a policy that described the actions we had already taken and were continuing to take. We essentially distilled the policy from our actions after the fact. This backward approach worked in the UN system because if we had declared the policy at the outset, we would have created substantial opposition well before we had even started.[56]

Pillar I (Humanitarian Assistance) was led by the UNHCR. Its responsibilities included repatriation and resettlement of refugees and internally displaced persons. Since the vast majority of ethnic Albanian refugees returned during 1999, during the following year UNHCR was able to scale its activities back to the point that Pillar I was disbanded in June 2000.

A new Pillar I (Police and Justice) was created in May 2001 when UNMIK Police and the Department of Judicial Affairs were combined. This brought all operations relating to the rule of law together in an effort to maximize the coordination of police investigations with prosecution within the criminal justice system. UNMIK police exercised full "executive policing" authority and were responsible for the gamut of public security and law enforcement functions required of any major governing body. The July 12, 1999, *Report of the Secretary-General* established that "two main goals will define UNMIK's law and order strategy in Kosovo: provision of interim law enforcement services, and the rapid development of a credible, professional and impartial Kosovo Police Service (KPS)."[57] The Security Council originally authorized a police force of 3,110, including international civilian police officers, border police, and ten Specialized Police Units. In October 1999, the council approved an increase to 4,718.[58] The function of the Department of Justice was to develop "a multi-ethnic, independent, impartial and competent judiciary, while ensuring in the shorter term that inter-ethnic and organised crime are addressed through international judges and prosecutors who can act, and be seen to act, without fear or favour."[59] The department also administered the penal system.

Pillar II (Interim Civil Administration) was the responsibility of the Department of Peacekeeping Operations. It oversaw five regional administrators, thirty municipal administrators, and administrative functions and services, including such areas as health and education, banking and finance, post and telecommunications, and, until May 2001, law and order. Initially, 1,148 international staff members were authorized; however, by mid-2000, this figure had been increased to 1,339.

Pillar III (Democratization and Institution Building) was run by the Organization for Security and Co-operation in Europe. Its mandate included building human capacity in the areas of justice, police, and public administration; democratization and governance, human rights monitoring and institutional development; organizing and monitoring elections; and strengthening the institutions of civil society, particularly the media. With 450 international staff, it was the largest of all the OSCE's field missions.

Pillar IV (Reconstruction and Economic Development) was managed by the European Union. It was concerned with rebuilding Kosovo's physical and economic infrastructure, reactivating public services and utilities, and creating the foundation for a market-based economy. It had sixty-four international staff.

Inadequate police and civil administration staffing severely constrained UNMIK's effectiveness throughout the first year. The first SPUs did not begin deploying until spring 2000, and it was not until mid-May 2000 that UNMIK police reached even 75 percent strength.[60] Similarly, the United Nations had managed to hire only two-thirds of the 1,339 international staff it needed to help administer the territory by the time the standard one-year field employment contracts of many staff members were due to expire. Initially, staffing delays were attributable to the inability of member states to provide the types of skilled personnel in the numbers required, but the United Nations' own "inflexible procedures related to the secondment of suitable qualified personnel from OSCE and UN member states unnecessarily prolonged shortages of key staff."[61]

By mid-2000, the mission was on the verge of collapse. This crisis compelled the United Nations to permit the mission to hire directly from the field, rather than relying on an understaffed and rules-bound UN Secretariat to do the hiring for it. After this authority was delegated to UNMIK, personnel were recruited fairly quickly. The European Union was even more dilatory in mobilizing personnel. Indeed, for more than a year the bulk of its personnel were hired under a contract funded by the U.S. Agency for International Development.[62]

An assessment of the pillar's performance by King's College London noted, "A senior official acknowledged that the European Union 'had failed miserably' by not mobilizing funding and human resources more quickly."[63] The OSCE, in contrast, was able to draw upon former members of the Kosovo Verification Mission to staff its operations efficiently.

Once UNMIK was well established, SRSG Bernard Kouchner and the heads of all the pillars met every morning. These sessions were often contentious, owing in part to the differing organizational objectives and cultures represented and to the autonomy of each international organization involved. The relationship between UNMIK and KFOR during Kouchner's stewardship, in contrast, was characterized by close and generally effective collaboration (see "Field Operations," below).

Humanitarian Information

A significant innovation in international coordination was the Humanitarian Community Information Center (HCIC), established in August 1999 with funds from UNICEF and the Office of the UN Coordinator for Humanitarian Assistance. The HCIC provided "open access to information and data that will support organizations as they plan and implement relief and rehabilitation projects."[64] It exploited information technology, principally geographic information systems, to integrate digital maps with data needed to organize relief and peacebuilding activities. This made possible the development of a "who does what where" database, detailed election support, and an atlas of Kosovo including digitized city plans for use in specialized functions like crime mapping. The HCIC actively promoted information sharing by providing advice on standardization of data collection; by collating existing information and connecting it visually with specific locales; and by producing encyclopedias on compact disc about Kosovo and the international activities unfolding there.

As Paul Currion, manager of the HCIC from April to September 2000, observed,

> HCIC services were available to anyone who needed them—including local people, who could come in off the street to ask for advice on where they might receive shelter assistance or food aid. ... But the most important lesson learned by the HCIC is relatively

simple: that effective coordination of humanitarian work is greatly aided by effective information management, both within and between organizations.[65]

Researchers from King's College London concluded that the center served as "a vital information-sharing and co-ordination hub between humanitarian agencies, KFOR military, and the interim administration."[66] The essential contributions of the HCIC concept to peace operations led to its replication in Afghanistan (as the Afghanistan Information Management System) and Iraq (as the Humanitarian Information Center for Iraq).[67]

Field Operations

Initially, KFOR focused on the withdrawal of Serb forces, as stipulated in the Military Technical Agreement, and on preventing a renewal of Serb-Albanian hostilities. Thus, the configuration and operational deployment of its forces were oriented toward a conventional threat from the Serb military establishment. Nevertheless, SRSG Bernard Kouchner and KFOR's first commander, Lieutenant General Mike Jackson, appreciated that KFOR's active support of UNMIK was essential, especially during the emergency period, when UNMIK was struggling to establish its presence.

KFOR

Even though Serb forces withdrew as agreed, KFOR had little peace to keep. The power vacuum left by departing Serb forces was quickly filled by returning KLA members, who unleashed a wave of violence against the Serb population, other minorities, and their perceived rivals within the Kosovo Albanian community. Serbs who had been actively involved in the war were prime targets, but most had fled to Serbia. Suspected collaborators among the other ethnic communities were also among the victims, as were Kosovo Albanians regarded as having been too cooperative with Serbs. The massacre of fourteen Serb farmers working in their fields near Pristina on July 23, 1999, was the most gruesome assault in a continuing campaign of intimidation and brutality against residents of Serb communities.[68] Vengeance was not the only motive, however. A pattern of intimidation developed in which warning letters, assaults, and bombings were used to coerce Serbs to sign over property rights. If this failed, their dwellings were liable to be torched. The clear intent was to drive Serbs from Kosovo. In two months, the number of Serb inhabitants in Pristina alone plunged from 20,000 to 2,000. Thus the gravest challenge to KFOR's mission was not a conventional threat from regular Serb military units but an unconventional threat from paramilitary forces, especially former KLA combatants.

There was no strictly military solution for this threat. Extremist elements of the KLA could have readily gone underground, continuing to conduct disruptive operations and subverting the emergence of moderate political leadership. The price of a direct confrontation with the KLA, at a minimum, would have been loss of local consent. Nor was demobilization an option, since the KLA regarded itself as the victor in the war against the Serbs, as well as the future national army of an independent Kosovo. Diplomacy rather than force was required, and UNMIK took a novel approach. The KLA was transformed into a 5,000-man Kosovo Protection Corps (KPC), an unarmed civilian organization devoted to responding to humanitarian emergencies and other civilian tasks. The formal "demilitarization" process was completed on September 19, 1999, and KFOR assumed the responsibility for providing day-to-day operational direction to the KPC. Key KLA leaders were brought into the peace process as a result. KFOR and UNMIK jointly decided how to respond to transgressions or acts of noncompliance by KPC members.

The creation of a "halfway house" for the KLA was a major milestone for the peace process, but it was not the end of violent political conflict. Extremist elements on both sides of Kosovo's ethnic schism continued to employ force in the form of civil disturbances, politically motivated killings, and cross-border insurrection to promote their uncompromising agendas. The most serious instability unfolded in the divided city of Mitrovica and in predominantly Albanian regions contiguous to Kosovo: the Presevo Valley in southern Serbia, and Macedonia.

The Ibar River bisecting Mitrovica soon became a flashpoint. North of the river, the city was predominantly Serb, as were the three municipalities between Mitrovica and the boundary with Serbia. A substantial community of ethnic Albanians lived in northern Mitrovica, however. Authorities in Belgrade refused to cede authority to UNMIK in this region, maintaining parallel structures of government that continued to provide health care, schooling, administrative services, and a court system. A paramilitary entity that came to be called the Bridge-watchers emerged in 1999. They sought to prevent Albanians from crossing into northern Mitrovica[69] and were adept at surveillance, intimidation, muggings, and the instantaneous orchestration of unruly demonstrations. Essentially a gang of thugs, the Bridge-watchers also resisted efforts by UNMIK police to assert their authority in Serb-populated areas.

The early international response to interethnic violence and rioting in Mitrovica involved short-term surges in the security presence. This merely dealt with the symptom of the problem, however. Getting to the source proved elusive. Owing to French concerns about the viability of the Serb population in Kosovo, commanders in MNB-North made an early strategic decision to avoid confronting the Bridge-watchers. In spite of efforts by UNMIK police to establish joint mechanisms with MNB-North for communication and backup support, on various occasions French troops simply observed while international police were violently assaulted. The most serious confrontation involved a grenade and sniper assault in April 2002 that left twenty-six international police injured.

For various reasons, therefore, curtailing the source of violent resistance could be accomplished only if Belgrade cooperated. Even after Milosevic had been deposed, it took more than a year for the government to assert that its financial support to the Bridge-watchers would end. It was not until late 2002 that UNMIK obtained an agreement to unify Mitrovica under international administration. The Bridge-watchers were allowed to apply for the Kosovo Police Service, but they had to satisfy the entry requirements. As had been the case previously with former KLA applicants, many had difficulty doing this. A December 2003 assault on Kosovo's prime minister, Bajram Rexhepi,[70] and visitors from the World Bank while dining in northern Mitrovica demonstrated that rogue elements in the Serb community continued to pose a persistent menace.[71]

The American- and German-led brigades in MNB-East and MNB-South had to contend with insurrections fostered by former KLA extremists. The population of the Presevo Valley of southern Serbia, adjacent to the U.S.-led MNB-East, was predominantly Albanian. As had been the case in Kosovo, this community was excluded from power and deprived of economic opportunity. The Military Technical Agreement of June 1999 had compelled Serb military units to withdraw from a three-mile-wide ground security zone on the periphery of Kosovo.[72] Much of the Presevo Valley fell within the zone, thus creating a de facto sanctuary that was exploited by KLA militants to mobilize an insurgent force, the Liberation Army of Presevo, Medvedje, Bujanovac, known by its Albanian acronym as the UCPMB.[73] As Bob Churcher notes in a study of the conflict that ensued there, this activity was "part of wider pan-Albanian aims, or at least part of the aims of radical nationalists who saw success in Kosovo as only the start of regaining control of all Albanian inhabited lands."[74]

In early 2000, the UCPMB began to conduct sporadic, low-level assaults on Serb police forces in the Presevo Valley. It was not until late that year, however, after Milosevic had been deposed, that serious fighting broke out. KFOR responded with a mixture of force and diplomacy. U.S. troops, aided by the deployment of a British strategic reserve contingent, eventually tightened control of the boundary. By February 2001, 80 to 100 UCPMB partisans had been detained by MNB-East, out of a force that was estimated to number 700 to 1,000.[75] If the UCPMB had been seeking to provoke Serb atrocities and thereby draw NATO into the conflict on its behalf, just as the KLA had done in Kosovo, these actions helped to disabuse it of such notions.

The unequivocal opposition of the United States and NATO to the rebellion encouraged a diplomatic resolution to the conflict. NATO-led negotiations with the new Serbian leadership resulted in a formula for the phased removal of the Ground Security Zone. This was made contingent on demonstration of restraint by the Serb army as it gradually returned. UCPMB insurgents from Kosovo were allowed to lay down their weapons and return home, Albanians were recruited into a reformed local police force, and steps were taken to address underlying political and economic grievances.[76]

The search for a solution to the unrest in southern Serbia became urgent during the spring of 2001 when adjoining portions of Macedonia also began to descend into turmoil. The proximate cause was a border demarcation agreement between the Federal Republic of

Yugoslavia and the Macedonian government that ceded a portion of Kosovo, including a portion of the village of Tanusevci, to Macedonia. Owing to its strategic location adjacent to the Presevo Valley, Tanusevci had served as a "funnel" for arms smuggling to both the KLA and the UCPMB.[77] Ensuing incidents there ignited smoldering tensions within Macedonia's broader Albanian population. Although spontaneous, this uprising opened the door for extremist KLA factions that sought to foment rebellion aimed at forging a "Greater Albania." Indicative of this linkage with elements of the former KLA, the National Liberation Army (NLA) that quickly emerged displayed "a high degree of competent and effective control and thinking from the beginning."[78] Another reputed bond among the NLA, the KLA, and the UCPMB was a linkage with the criminal underworld. As Philip Gounev explains, there is reason to believe that

> the conflict in Macedonia was a criminalized "spillover" of the war in Kosovo and the conflict in the Presevo Valley . . . [and] that it was inspired more by Albanian criminal networks, conducting illicit cross-border activities, especially trafficking in drugs and human beings, who sought to preserve or expand their interests by inciting ethnic conflict.[79]

The spread of fighting to Macedonia put pressure on MNB-South as well as MNB-East to prevent Kosovo's use as a support base and sanctuary for subversion. Their counterinsurgency efforts resulted in the detention of hundreds of suspected rebels. KFOR's role helped, once again, to pave the way for a negotiated resolution to interethnic conflict on Kosovo's border. In this case, the Ohrid Framework Agreement of August 2001 addressed various forms of discrimination against Albanians and granted greater powers of self-government and recognition of Albanian as a national language.[80]

Through a combination of counterinsurgency operations by KFOR and international diplomacy, these two attempts to export rebellion from Kosovo to its neighbors were effectively parried. They did not eradicate the threat, however. Although the UCPMB and NLA were formally disbanded, another subversive organization, the Albanian National Army, soon sprang up, and high-profile assaults on the Serb population of Kosovo continued.

Some MNBs displayed greater sophistication at coping with this paramilitary threat than others, but MNB-Center, under British command, was especially effective. Having honed their skills in the crucible of Northern Ireland, British commanders instinctively understood the need for joint military-police operations. This involved creating an operational framework of police stations, fixed and mobile checkpoints, and coordinated patrolling. These efforts were guided by an integrated intelligence gathering effort that combined military and police sources. Indeed, to deal with the paramilitary threat to peace in Kosovo, the capabilities of KFOR and UNMIK had to be brought together.

KFOR and UNMIK

KFOR was responsible for law enforcement until sufficient international civilian police could be deployed to assume this function in a phased manner across Kosovo.[81] This deployment took far longer than the three to four months initially estimated. The emergency judicial system also struggled, throughout the summer and fall of 1999, merely to conduct hearings for the detentions made by KFOR in response to violence against Serbs. After six months, detainees had to be either indicted or released. UNMIK drafted a regulation extending to one year the period of pretrial detention for serious offenses, and the KFOR commander (COMKFOR) adopted a similar practice called "COMKFOR holds." The human rights community vigorously criticized these actions, but this situation was indisputably an indication of local judicial incapacity.

Even after UNMIK assumed responsibility for police patrolling and investigations from KFOR, individual international police armed with nothing more than a pistol were no match for the sophisticated campaign of violence against the Serb population or for the paramilitary Bridge-watchers in Mitrovica. Although KFOR could impose stability in specific locations, it could not unilaterally create conditions for a lasting peace. It could seek to disrupt subversive activities temporarily, and it could deter assaults on Serb communities by its presence. Such actions merely addressed the symptoms, however, not the sources of insecurity and disruption of the peace process.

Beginning in the spring of 2000, UNMIK planners recognized that a strategy had to be developed that would identify and neutralize the sources of interethnic violence and obstruction. Ultimately a secure environment could be created only by establishing a system of justice capable of incarcerating Kosovo's most ruthless and violent elements. KFOR and UNMIK would eventually have to acquire the full spectrum of capabilities, from intelligence to incarceration, that would enable the dismantling of political-criminal power structures in both the Kosovo Albanian and Serb communities.

To do that required the integrated efforts of KFOR and UNMIK. During the initial phase of the mission, SRSG Bernard Kouchner and KFOR commander Lieutenant General Michael Jackson met on a daily basis. Their principal deputies held weekly Joint Security Executive Committee meetings to anticipate and direct civil-military planning for matters affecting the security environment. UNMIK's senior leadership used a basic national security planning paradigm (i.e., interests, objectives, and options) to guide KFOR's operational planning cycle. Military and civilian planners worked together using a common methodology to plan for major operations. KFOR had vital contributions to make across the entire spectrum from intelligence to incarceration. It was vital for UNMIK to employ its regulatory authority actively to provide a suitable legal framework for gathering criminal evidence and to establish an effective organizational structure to carry out investigations and prosecute crimes.

Applicable law. One of the first issues that UNMIK confronted was the determination of which penal code it would enforce. The existing "Serb" code was odious to Kosovo Albanians because it implied continuing subordination to Belgrade. They preferred the code that had been in existence prior to 1989, when Kosovo had enjoyed autonomous status. The UN Secretariat was reluctant to appear to infringe on FRY sovereignty in this matter. Consequently, UNMIK Regulation 1 in July 1999 stipulated that the applicable law would consist of "the laws applicable in the territory of Kosovo prior to 24 March 1999."[82]

The vast majority of judges who were expected to administer this body of law, however, were ethnic Albanians. They simply refused to apply existing "Serb" law. UNMIK staff proposed that the SRSG use his regulatory authority to establish a temporary code.[83] The United Nations was unwilling to act, however, until the issue reached the crisis stage in December. Paralysis in the legal process was overcome with the adoption of Regulation 1999/24, reverting to the law in force in Kosovo in 1989. The United Nations' initial choice about the applicable law had created a legal vacuum at the inception of the mission that took many months to overcome.

Criminal intelligence. A basic requirement of law enforcement in Kosovo was to identify the major sources of interethnic violence. In early 2000, the Quint countries agreed to create a Criminal Intelligence Unit (CIU) within UNMIK police in order to pool relevant KFOR intelligence with information gathered by UNMIK police on the organized crime threat. Eventually intelligence started flowing into the CIU. Over time, UNMIK and KFOR evolved an understanding of the various political-criminal power structures at play in Kosovo and the threat that they posed to the peace process.

Criminal investigation. UNMIK's early efforts to gather criminal evidence ran afoul of obstacles in the applicable law, which ruled inadmissible any evidence gathered by covert means such as video cameras or wiretaps. Witness protection was unheard of, and Kosovo's pre-1989 legal code contained no provisions against terrorism or kidnapping. Even after these deficiencies in the legal code were overcome through the use of UNMIK's regulatory authority, many investigative means used by police elsewhere remained unavailable. The United Nations opposed the payment of informants, for example, and it delayed the delivery of surveillance equipment for at least a year after the United States provided funding for its acquisition. Years also passed before a forensics lab was established. As a result, prosecutors were primarily reliant on witnesses. Although a witness protection program was created, the resources needed to operate it effectively were lacking, so witnesses remained vulnerable to intimidation.

In mid-2002 UNMIK police expanded the Kosovo Organized Crime Bureau to include specialists in various investigative disciplines, including the use of technical devices. These were supplemented as necessary by KFOR's surveillance capability. The integrity of the organization was maintained through the use of polygraphs and periodic internal surveillance on its own personnel. To focus international investigative resources decisively on the political-criminal centers of gravity, KFOR and UNMIK formed an Operational Planning Group composed of the head of the UNMIK Department of Justice, the UNMIK police commissioner, and the deputy commander of KFOR.

High-risk arrest. As the number of UNMIK police grew in 1999 and into 2000, it became possible to assemble a team of highly trained police who specialized in high-risk arrests. The proficiency of the high-risk arrest team was demonstrated throughout 2002 with the apprehension of scores of former KLA members suspected of involvement in a range of violent crimes, particularly murdering rival Kosovo Albanians during and after the war.

Crowd control. Initially there was resistance at senior levels within UNMIK to the use of either the Specialized Police Units (SPUs) of UNMIK or the Multinational Specialized Unit of KFOR for crowd control, owing to the fragility of the peace process and uncertainty about how they would perform. As a result, the SPUs were initially used primarily to supplement UNMIK police, providing protection for Serb enclaves, support for the close protection and high-risk arrest units, prisoner escort, and point security for high-priority locations such as courthouses, prisons, and other critical facilities.

In early 2002 UNMIK began arresting former KLA members, and this provoked the sort of orchestrated civil disturbances encountered previously in Bosnia, including violent assaults on UNMIK police. The SPUs helped to contain these disturbances and de-escalate the potential for confrontation. In one of the earliest encounters, demonstrators grew so frustrated that they attacked city residents in downtown Pristina restaurants because they had not joined the protest.

International judges and prosecutors. The need to involve international judges directly in the legal process was raised at the inception of the mission but rejected by the United Nations' Office of Legal Affairs. During the first half of 2000, serious disruptions of the peace process compelled UNMIK to begin incorporating international judges and prosecutors in an ad hoc manner into Kosovo's judicial system. The triggering event took place that February when a military-style assault on a Serb bus precipitated a rampage against Kosovo Albanians in northern Mitrovica. Armed members of the Kosovo Protection Corps were arrested by UNMIK police and KFOR for firing their unauthorized weapons at French troops and Serb apartments. The suspects were immediately released by the ethnic Albanian judge. UNMIK acted with unusual dispatch to promulgate Regulation 6/2000, authorizing the emergency appointment of an international judge and prosecutor to the district court in Mitrovica with authority to become involved in any case under the court's jurisdiction. A few months later, Serb prisoners who had been in jail without trial for a year went on a hunger strike, demanding that international judges be assigned to hear their cases. This caused the expansion of appointments of international judges and prosecutors to all five district courts in Kosovo.[84]

At the district courts level, to which most international judges were assigned, judicial panels had five members. Initially only one international judge was assigned to these panels, which meant that they were simply outvoted. Innocent Serbs began to be convicted, with apparent international involvement. To remedy this, UNMIK promulgated Regulation 2000/64 in December 2000, allowing for the formation of special three-member judicial panels—composed of at least two international judges—to hear cases involving interethnic violence, political violence, organized crime, or war crimes.

The practical effect of these "64 panels," as they came to be called, was to create a division of labor between local and international jurists. While the vast majority of court proceedings remained entirely in the hands of the local judiciary, the "64 panels" took responsibility for politically sensitive cases. Local judges indirectly manifested their acceptance of this arrangement by asking international judges to relieve them of cases in which external pressure and intimidation became too great for them to handle.

Close protection. In the same ad hoc fashion that the high-risk arrest team had been cobbled together, UNMIK police also had to create a Close Protection Unit to provide security for visiting international dignitaries and members of the Serb National Council who participated in the interim government. When international judges and prosecutors were added to their protection responsibilities, their limited capabilities were almost overwhelmed. Over the next several years, however, international judges and prosecutors were seldom threatened. Instead, intimidation was directed at witnesses and members of the local judiciary.

Incarceration. The first Kosovo Consolidated Budget did not recognize the need to fund prison management. KFOR had to fill the gap, managing all prisons and pretrial detention facilities until UNMIK police were able to begin assuming responsibility. The transfer of responsibility to UNMIK was constrained by the need to recruit international expertise in penal management and a delay in providing funds, especially to repair the main prison at Dubrava, severely damaged by NATO bombing. As UNMIK's Penal Management Division was able to recruit and train local corrections staff, the Kosovo Corrections Service began to take charge of the prisons in late 1999. International prison wardens provided supervision.

UNMIK was particularly ill prepared to provide maximum security for prisoners who constituted the gravest threats to public order. Most Serb suspects, including accused war criminals, were held in the predominantly Serb section of Mitrovica. UNMIK police were assigned to operate the facility there, even though management of prisons requires a distinctive set of skills and UNMIK police tended to regard prison duty as a form of punishment. In August 2000, fourteen Serb detainees, many of them indicted war criminals, escaped from the Mitrovica jail. Subsequently, the Penal Management Division took over supervision of the UNMIK police contingent there, providing training in basic prison skills and enforcing professional standards and procedures.

Although the U.S. military had initially considered the detention facility at Camp Bondsteel to be a stopgap measure, it continued to serve for years essentially as a maximum-security facility for Kosovo's most politically dangerous suspects. Cross-border subversion in southern Serbia and Macedonia in late 2000 and early 2001 demonstrated the continuing need for a facility secure enough to deal with the subversive and terrorist threat that menaced the peace, both inside and outside Kosovo. When the suspected ringleader of a February 2001 bus bombing in Nis was apprehended, UNMIK officials determined that the risk was too great to use a local detention center. His subsequent escape from Camp Bondsteel revealed that military detention facilities designed for handling prisoners of war also required modifications to preclude such breakouts.

It was not until 2002 that UNMIK developed the capacity to handle cases involving militant extremists in a reliable manner, largely by mobilizing international personnel and vital technical resources for surveillance and forensics analysis. Having such facilities enabled KFOR and UNMIK officials to begin jointly attacking the criminalized power structures responsible for obstructing implementation of Resolution 1244.

Continuing unrest. Several brazen murders of minorities in 2003, including Serb children machine-gunned while swimming, indicated that violence had not been wrung out of the interethnic equation. Assaults on leading Kosovo Albanian political figures early in 2004 suggested that it was creeping back into the intra-Albanian discourse as well. By 2004, however, both UNMIK police and KFOR were steadily reducing their personnel strength as if security conditions were becoming normalized. In March 2004, unfounded news accounts of Serb complicity in the drowning of three children from a Kosovo Albanian enclave created conditions for a popular reaction. Radical elements transformed this situation into a violent rampage against Serb communities and UNMIK facilities across the breadth of Kosovo. Two days of riots devastated Serb communities throughout Kosovo. The event was summarized in a report to the Security Council as follows:

> The onslaught led by Kosovo Albanian extremists against the Serb, Roma and Ashkali communities of Kosovo was an organized, widespread, and targeted campaign. . . . Properties were demolished, public facilities such as schools and health clinics were destroyed, communities were surrounded and threatened and residents were forced to leave their homes. . . . A total of 19 persons died in the violence, of whom 11 were Kosovo Albanians and 8 were Kosovo Serbs, and 954 persons were injured in the course of the clashes. . . . Approximately 730 houses belonging to minorities, mostly Kosovo Serbs, were damaged or destroyed. . . . 36 Orthodox churches, monasteries and other religious and cultural sites were damaged or destroyed.[85]

All UNMIK regional headquarters had to be evacuated, and several regional police headquarters were in danger of being overrun. No contingency plan existed to guide how UNMIK police and KFOR would coordinate their response to widespread civil disorder. Unaided by prior planning and exercises, the degree to which KFOR and UNMIK police integrated their efforts effectively to control mob violence varied. Material damage and loss of life were most effectively minimized in areas where commanders recognized that the situation had changed from peaceful conditions to an unsafe and insecure environment and understood their role to be providing military assistance to the civil authority. Coordination and communication were most effective in areas where KFOR soldiers, UNMIK police, and KPS had regularly coordinated their patrolling under normal conditions and where military police had permanent liaison teams within police stations equipped with communications capability. Ineffective results were obtained when KFOR commanders took the view that UNMIK police had primacy for policing and that this meant it was their sole responsibility to quell the riots. Requests to aid UNMIK police in reestablishing public order were viewed in some headquarters as detracting from KFOR's ability to perform its mission. Unity of effort was severely hampered as a result.

As of 2005, Kosovo remained well short of a postconflict situation. The lack of clarity about final status meant that Albanians and Serbs continued to view political interaction with each other as a zero-sum game, and violence remained the ultimate option. The process of dislodging extremist networks and bringing to justice those responsible for episodes of political violence still relied almost entirely on international resources, and especially on effective collaboration between KFOR and UNMIK.

UNMIK

In spite of UNMIK's sluggish deployment and UNHCR's faulty assumptions about the pace of resettlement, one early success story was the return of more than a million refugees and internally displaced persons and the effective delivery of assistance that they would require to survive the first winter. UNMIK was also expected to develop "provisional institutions for democratic and autonomous self-government" and to facilitate "a political process designed to determine Kosovo's future status."[86]

In April 2002, SRSG Michael Steiner linked the determination of Kosovo's final status to its ability to demonstrate responsible self-governance. Eight standards formed the centerpiece of this policy, which came to be known as "Standards before Status":

- functioning democratic institutions
- rule of law
- freedom of movement
- sustainable returns of refugees and displaced persons, and minority rights
- economy
- property rights
- dialogue with Belgrade
- Kosovo Protection Corps

According to Steiner, "Substantial progress toward these standards is also the prerequisite for resolving the status issue. . . . only the fulfillment of these standards will give the International Community confidence that Kosovo is ready for substantial self-government. The fulfillment of these standards is also necessary to remove the causes of future conflict and to make Kosovo a normal European society."[87]

The challenge was to effectively integrate the efforts of UNMIK's four pillars with those of their local counterparts in order to achieve the standards.

Pillar I: Humanitarian assistance. The international community had not anticipated the rapid and spontaneous return of more than a million refugees and internally displaced persons as soon as NATO bombing ended. The Kosovo Albanians generally proved to be less dependent on external support than anticipated, owing to long-practiced "coping mechanisms" and access to remittances from abroad.[88] Due to their resilience and the massive efforts undertaken by UN agencies and over 250 nongovernmental organizations, there was no humanitarian crisis. Tents, heating stoves, winter clothes, blankets and mattresses, and tons of food were provided to more than half the people of Kosovo.

Testifying to the success of this effort, the returning population survived the winter without further loss of life. By the summer of 2000, the vast majority of Kosovo Albanians had returned to their homes, allowing UNHCR to close Pillar I in June 2000. Pillar II absorbed the remaining humanitarian functions.

While its assistance to returning ethnic Albanians was successful, the international community was slow to recognize and respond to the unfolding plight of the Serbs of Kosovo. Roughly half that population eventually fled, and many who remained were confined to enclaves where they often lacked access to basic services. During UNMIK's emergency phase, when the Serb exodus was taking place, the mission was severely shorthanded: "consumed by the day-to-day challenge of setting up an administration, they 'had not been aware of the magnitude of the ethnic violence.'"[89] In November 1999, UNMIK prepared an "Agenda for Coexistence" that led to the creation of an Office for Community Affairs within Pillar II to work at the municipal level to address the availability of public utilities, health care, and other basic services.

Pillar II: Establishing an interim administration. One of UNMIK's top priorities was to establish institutions of democratic self-government. The KLA, however, had quickly filled the power vacuum created by the withdrawal of Serb authorities, proclaiming itself the "provisional government." The usurpation of power by the KLA created a crucial challenge for the mission. In the assessment of Jock Covey, UNMIK's principal deputy SRSG:

> They lacked the expertise and infrastructure to address the public's urgent humanitarian needs, and most Kosovar Albanians were inclined to look to the LDK for support and guidance. Over time, it became more and more apparent that this was not simply a heated political argument. KLA extremists would use any necessary means to displace Rugova and his LDK political apparatus.[90]

With a murderous power struggle unfolding between the KLA and the LDK, UNMIK could not simply choose one Albanian faction as its partner. It would first have to attenuate the inter-Albanian conflict before it could build a working coalition to serve as the basis for a functioning civil government.

First, the KLA had to be demilitarized. The political impact of the agreement to transform the KLA into the Kosovo Protection Corps was to liberate Kosovo Democratic Party (PDK) leader Hashim Thaci from the obligation to provide for the welfare of former KLA fighters. This gave him the political maneuvering room to take the risks associated with cooperating with UNMIK in establishing an interim administration. The next step required a dialogue between Thaci and the head of the LDK, Ibrahim Rugova. Not until December 1999 did Thaci and Rugova agree to establish the Joint Interim Administrative Structure (JIAS), which would be the UN-managed structure of local governance. There was nothing democratic about this bargain—both parties preserved their patronage and dealt the spoils to their followers. UNMIK provided policy direction and assistance to middle management, while LDK and PDK appointees performed day-to-day civil administrative functions.

The JIAS began administering Kosovo in February 2000. Its twenty administrative departments were jointly headed by a senior UNMIK staff member and a Kosovan who had been nominated by a designated political party or ethnic community and approved by the SRSG. Municipalities were run by UNMIK municipal administrators, advised by appointed municipal councils.

UNMIK used various other consultative bodies to incorporate the views of local leaders into its decision-making process. The Kosovo Transitional Council, established in July 1999, was drawn from all segments of society, including representatives from political parties and minority communities. An Interim Administrative Council, drawn from the leadership of the parties involved in the power-sharing agreement, acted as a quasi cabinet to advise the SRSG on proposed regulations, amendments to applicable law, and policies for the administrative departments. These provisional institutions sought to eliminate the parallel governing structures in both the ethnic Albanian and Serbian communities and integrate all ethnic communities into the political process.[91]

Although UNMIK kept the door open for Serb participation, continuing attacks against the Serb community undercut the few cooperative Serb leaders who agreed to become meaningful partners in the interim governing structure. As a result, the three Serb-dominated municipalities of Kosovo required special management by UNMIK. Only after the incidence of violence against the Serb population subsided and Slobodan Milosevic was removed from power in Belgrade did the Serbs join the peace process in a substantial manner.

The power-sharing arrangement between Thaci and Rugova led to municipal officials appointed on the basis of privilege, personal connections, and party loyalty. To begin replacing this ad hoc administration, UNMIK needed to hold municipal elections. Given that Rugova and the LDK had an extensive base of popular support, Thaci made it clear to UNMIK's political managers that he was not in any rush to hold an election.

By the summer of 2000 the political climate was tipping in favor of elections: the demobilization of the KLA continued to hold, and the temporary civil administration was functioning. Consequently, municipal elections were scheduled for October 2000. As the candidates kicked off their campaigns, however, a bout of politically motivated violence erupted. To stabilize the situation, UNMIK mobilized international police and KFOR troops to protect candidates at risk while it bore down hard on rival leaders thought to be responsible.

The voting to elect municipal councils in October 2000 proceeded in a generally calm fashion. Participation by Kosovo's Albanian electorate was massive, with roughly 700,000 out of 900,000 registered voters turning out. Kosovo Serbs, however, did not participate. Twenty-one municipalities were won by the LDK and six by the PDK. The three largely Serb municipalities remained under UNMIK supervision, as before.

Before a further transfer of executive and legislative functions could be made, the nature and powers of Kosovo-run institutions had to be defined. This was accomplished with the promulgation of a constitutional framework by SRSG Hans Haekkerup in May 2001. This document specified the areas of authority that would be transferred to the Provisional Institutions of Self-Government (PISG) and those that would be "reserved" for UNMIK pending resolution of Kosovo's final status. The latter included foreign policy, core functions relating to law enforcement, and the administration of socially owned enterprises.[92] Owing to Haekkerup's diplomatic efforts, the Constitution had been accepted by Belgrade, paving the way for election of a 120-member

Central Assembly, or parliament, in November 2001. Kosovo Serbs participated in the vote and gained twenty-two seats. Since none of the parties commanded a majority in the Assembly, protracted bargaining ensued until an acceptable division of powers could be hammered out. In March 2002, the PISG was established with LDK leader Ibrahim Rugova as president, Nexat Daci of the LDK as speaker of the Assembly, and Bajram Rexhepi of the PDK as prime minister. The process of transferring "nonreserved" governing competencies to the PISG was completed by the end of 2003.

A second round of municipal elections took place in October 2002. The leadership of all thirty of Kosovo's municipalities was at stake in this election, but Serb party leaders decided at the last minute to vote only in those municipalities where the Kosovo Serb population was in a majority and Serb "parallel structures" retained their influence. In spite of a subsequent agreement between UNMIK and authorities in Serbia in November 2002 to allow UNMIK to extend its writ over northern Mitrovica, de facto control of that area remained in the hands of Serb leaders who took their instructions from Belgrade.[93]

In October 2004, the second parliamentary election took place. A month later, the LDK and the Alliance for the Future of Kosovo (AAK) formed a coalition government, with AAK party leader and former KLA war hero Ramush Haradinaj replacing Bajram Rexhepi of the PDK as prime minister in a smooth transfer of power. An even stricter test of Kosovo's political maturity was passed when Haradinaj was indicted by the International Criminal Tribunal for the Former Yugoslavia in March 2005. He promptly resigned his position, turned himself in to The Hague, and appealed for all citizens of Kosovo to respect the rule of law, which they did.

Pillar III: Democracy and institution building. UNMIK was under pressure to begin training the new Kosovo Police Service (KPS) as quickly as possible. The first issue was to determine how recruitment should take place. The KLA regarded the police force as one of the spoils of war. As soon as Serb forces withdrew, "KLA police" quickly appeared. The UN advance team insisted that everyone joining the new police force would have to qualify individually. In the "Undertaking" between the KLA and KFOR, "KLA police" were not given any special status, although their members were allowed to be the first to be tested. Only a minority met the qualifications to enter police training.

The first class of 176 KPS cadets began a six-week training program in September 1999 at the Kosovo Police Service School. The program was later expanded to twelve weeks, with an additional three weeks devoted to field training. An important factor in the police school's success was the advance planning that had been performed by the OSCE. Within weeks of the start of UNMIK, the OSCE was recruiting experienced police trainers from its member states and organizing the curriculum for the police school.

By 2005, more than 6,282 KPS officers had been trained and deployed. They were performing general law enforcement and public safety tasks and had assumed full responsibility for twenty-six out of thirty-three police stations. UNMIK police had transitioned to a monitoring role in those locations.

UNMIK's democratization and governance activities concentrated on the institutions of government, political parties, and civil society. After the election of the first municipal assemblies in late 2000, institution-building programs focused on governance at the local level. Once the Kosovo Assembly was elected in November 2001, emphasis shifted to the legislative branch. With the formation of the Provisional Institutions of Self-Government, developing a professional and responsive civil administration also became a priority. Political party development programs aimed to strengthen the capacity of local politicians to identify popular concerns and articulate policy platforms. Efforts with civic groups placed particular emphasis on ethnic minority communities, the involvement of women, and participation at all levels.

The promotion of human rights entailed protecting vulnerable groups and individuals, assisting the development of institutions for this purpose, and monitoring law enforcement and the legal system. Protection included investigating cases of discrimination, ensuring individual property rights, and assistance to victims of trafficking.[94]

Pillar III's institution-building efforts initially emphasized developing the capacity of minority groups to participate in the electoral process. Subsequent initiatives promoted the development of nongovernmental organizations within minority communities and the creation of standing committees within each municipal assembly dedicated to protecting minority rights. Eventually a ministry was established to address minority concerns and facilitate the return process.[95] Ultimately, the standards established by UNMIK to determine whether Kosovo was prepared for talks to determine its political status heavily stressed respect for and assurance of the rights of minorities as top priorities.

Pillar III's mandate to monitor the law enforcement and legal system was an awkward one to carry out initially, since UNMIK itself was responsible for enforcing the law in Kosovo. As a result, the OSCE's Legal System Monitoring Section began to pass judgment on UNMIK's own performance. The use of lengthy extrajudicial detentions by both the KFOR commander (COMKFOR holds) and the SRSG ignited a sharp clash between elements of the mission responsible for establishing a safe and secure environment and those charged with upholding human rights standards. Given the institutional void that UNMIK and KFOR were initially faced with, it was impossible to strike a balance that was acceptable to both parties, especially initially, when the mission faced repeated threats from violent and subversive elements.[96]

In five years, the OSCE organized four free and fair elections: two at the municipal level and two for parliament. Pillar III also set in motion the process of transferring responsibility for organizing future elections to local institutions by developing an independent Central Election Commission and an accurate voter registry.

Pillar IV: Reconstruction and economic development.[97] The European Union sought to create conditions for the free market to function in Kosovo, with the slogan "construction not reconstruction" and an emphasis on "economic governance and development." Existing infrastructure and institutions were considered "incompatible with the goal of creating a sound economy."[98] Establishing a market-oriented macroeconomic framework would involve the creation of a banking system, convertible currency, a tax regime, a regulatory system, and legal codes conducive to free enterprise, private investment, and economic growth.

This was a strategy with a lengthy gestation period, hampered by lethargic implementation that failed to mobilize funding and human resources quickly enough. The U.S. Agency for International Development (AID) partially filled this gap with funding for the consultants who staffed the pillar initially. AID took responsibility for establishing the banking system, creating the Banking and Payments Authority of Kosovo (BPK) to serve as a central bank. It also set up the Central Fiscal Authority (CFA), which would take charge of the government budget, the treasury, and tax collection, including the customs service. Both the BPK and CFA began functioning in November 1999. By 2004 the banking industry consisted of seven banks with more than 210 branches. Revenue generation, primarily from excise and value-added taxes, was performing so well by 2004 that the Kosovo Consolidated Budget was entirely funded by domestically generated revenues.[99]

The extensive delay in staffing and funding Pillar IV's efforts delayed reconstitution of basic services that affected the daily lives of all Kosovo residents. During the winter of 1999–2000, Kosovans suffered from an acute gap in service by public utilities. The sporadic availability of electricity, water, and garbage collection was evidence that Pillar IV's exclusively macroeconomic focus had left a large gap between emergency relief and long-term development efforts. The repeated ensuing crises in public services severely undermined both the credibility of UNMIK and public support for it.

The most troubling manifestation of this "missing middle" between emergency relief and long-term development was UNMIK's chronic inability to establish a reliable system of power generation. The challenges confronted by UNMIK in this area were monumental. Kosovo's two power plants were aging and poorly maintained, with one nearing the end of its service life; the Serb engineers and technicians who had been operating the system had fled; and the power grid had been damaged during the bombing, hampering the ability to import electricity.

The EU managers of Pillar IV initially took a laissez-faire approach to such problems. This allowed competing local factions, including former KLA members, to vie for managerial control over the formerly Serb-run electric company, Komitet Elektroprivredne Korporacije Kosova (KEK),[100] and the coal mines associated with it. The result was a bloated, incompetent, and politicized workforce. During the first winter, hardliners inside KEK sought to use their control of the power grid as a tool to drive Serbs out by cutting off their power supply. The pretext used was that the Serbs had failed to pay their electricity bills, but this was also true for the vast majority of Kosovo Albanians. KEK was also a source of largesse (jobs, patronage, and kickbacks) for those who were in a position to exercise de facto control.

The task of assessing and funding essential repairs was left to international donors, which led to an uncoordinated and incomplete response. The result was a chronically unreliable supply of electricity and the refusal of many consumers to pay their bills. When combined with the widespread practice of pirating power, KEK was able to collect enough revenue to cover only 40 percent of its costs, even after more than four years under nominal international management. This was barely adequate to pay workers' salaries, meaning that fuel costs, import of electricity, and repairs were recurrently subsidized out of government coffers.

Since the top management positions were in UNMIK's hands, the United Nations became a convenient whipping boy for the power utility's inadequacies. Some of this was deserved, since one of KEK's early international managers had fled the mission after embezzling several million dollars.[101] The entire mission fell into disrepute with the local population as a result. The continued inability to rectify this problem created an adverse impression of UNMIK that became ever more pervasive over time.

Another chronic source of controversy and underperformance was the disposition of enterprises that were either owned by the *state* (Publicly Owned Enterprises, or POEs) or owned collectively by the *workers* (Socially Owned Enterprises, or SOEs). Although POEs and SOEs had accounted for the bulk of salaried employment prior to 1989, only about a third were considered to be capable of turning a profit in a competitive marketplace.[102] Attracting investment to viable enterprises required a formula for privatization, which proved elusive. One barrier was a division among key UN member states regarding the basic desirability of privatization. U.S. and European efforts to initiate the process were opposed by Russia and China. In addition to philosophical differences on this issue, opponents of privatization argued that the mandate to "administer" Kosovo did not permit altering property ownership rights. The United Nations' Office of Legal Affairs also persistently obstructed privatization efforts because of concerns that it would "expose the UN to unresolved ownership claims."[103] Little progress was made, therefore, until June 2002, when the Kosovo Trust

Agency, composed of both international and local representatives, was created. After two rounds of privatization, however, its work was brought to a halt by an opinion rendered by the UN Office of Legal Affairs in late 2003 that trust agency members did not have immunity from liability in lawsuits over awards they had made. This issue was eventually overcome in mid-2004, and efforts intensified to privatize the SOEs. By 2005, six rounds of privatization had been completed, generating some 42 million euros from asset sales.

Assessment

In assessing the unfinished international effort to bring a durable peace to Kosovo, measurements of progress must be taken against the conditions that prevailed when the mission began. The situation facing KFOR and UNMIK was especially daunting because this was not a case of postconflict reconstruction. It was the consequence of a coercive humanitarian intervention, and thus there was little peace to keep. NATO had not waited for Kosovo's internal conflict to become "ripe" for a diplomatic resolution. Such a course of action would have amounted to acquiescence in another of Slobodan Milosevic's campaigns of ethnic cleansing. When Serb security forces ultimately withdrew, a wave of violence ensued against Serbs who remained behind. The power vacuum created by the departure of Serbian authorities fueled another dimension of conflict: a vicious internal struggle for power among rival forces within the ethnic Albanian body politic. Entrenched in both the Serbian and Albanian communities were criminalized, war-hardened power structures that implacably opposed the UN mandate, relying on violence, intimidation, and illicit sources of revenue to sustain their obstructionism.

The Kosovo Force

KFOR's record in fostering safety and security was commendable, but powerful sources of conflict remained. Kosovo's political status continued to be an open issue and, hence, a casus belli, while the influence of radical and lawless elements remained an ominous threat on both sides of the ethnic divide.

During the first year of the mission, conditions were quickly established for the safe return of Kosovo Albanian refugees and displaced persons. KFOR initially failed, however, to protect Serb and other minority groups from intimidation, brutality, and murderous assaults. Roughly half the Serb population took flight. Although the situation gradually improved, enabling KFOR to remove most of its static security details from Serb enclaves, sporadic, high-profile killings continued to feed a perception of insecurity among Kosovo Serbs. In March 2004, two days of riots devastated Serb communities throughout Kosovo, revealing how vulnerable the peace process was to disruption by extremist elements.

The presence of KFOR helped to foster conditions that ultimately led to the demise of the Milosevic regime in October 2000 and his subsequent incarceration and trial at The Hague before the International Criminal Tribunal for the Former Yugoslavia. Subsequent attempts by ex-KLA extremists to export rebellion to southern Serbia and Macedonia were countered effectively by KFOR, leading to negotiated agreements that defused both crises. KFOR's presence provided an assurance that forceful alterations to national borders would not be tolerated. With the major exception of Mitrovica, UNMIK enjoyed a largely permissive operating environment as well as generally effective collaboration with KFOR on matters of mutual concern. By the spring of 2005 KFOR had reduced its original strength of 50,000 to 16,600.[104]

Kosovo's conflicts remained unresolved, however. Thus KFOR was ill prepared for the riots of March 2004, which left nineteen killed and hundreds of Serb homes and dozens of churches destroyed. The riots, and the loss of international credibility that resulted, dealt a severe setback to the peace process.

UNMIK

By 2005, the interim government of Kosovo was managing as many of its own affairs as the international mandate would permit. The Kosovo Police Service had assumed responsibility for running most police stations across Kosovo, although international judges and prosecutors were still required to deal with serious crimes involving interethnic violence, politically motivated murders, and organized crime. Key components of the macroeconomic framework were in place, including a well-regulated banking system and customs service. The Kosovo Consolidated Budget had demonstrated that it was capable of providing for the recurrent costs of governing Kosovo. After having been delayed for years, privatization was progressing. Reconstruction of the infrastructure was one of UNMIK's greatest shortcomings, as electricity generation remained unreliable, although the process of correcting financial irregularities in the publicly owned enterprises was advancing. UNMIK continued to have difficulty extending its writ over Serb-dominated areas, especially in northern Kosovo. In sum, much had been done to fulfill UNMIK's mandate of developing institutions capable of providing "substantial autonomy and meaningful self-administration for Kosovo."[105] The ultimate aim, however, was to facilitate a political process to determine Kosovo's political status.

The "Standards before Status" policy established by SRSG Michael Steiner in 2002 had provided a basis for relating the process of institutional development in Kosovo to the determination of its status. The absence of a plan to meet these standards, however, allowed a perception to grow among the Albanian population that UNMIK was standing in the way of status determination. The mission was stagnating. In November 2003, U.S. undersecretary of state Marc Grossman announced that the Contact Group had decided that progress toward attainment of the standards should be reviewed in mid-2005. If sufficient progress had been made at that point, the diplomatic process of resolving Kosovo's status was expected to commence. In December 2003, UNMIK produced a refinement of Steiner's eight standards that specified the thresholds that would have to be met and provided a set of indicators by which progress would be measured.[106] UNMIK and the PISG set about developing a joint implementation plan that would be reviewed on a quarterly basis by the Security Council and Contact Group in anticipation of the 2005 review date.

While the "review date" policy initially found solid support among the Kosovo Albanian political leadership, it was scarcely understood by the broader population and was resisted by Serb interlocutors. Belgrade's intransigent posture allowed fears to accumulate among Kosovo Albanians that their aspirations might be in jeopardy. This created an opening for extreme nationalist and violence-prone elements to assert themselves and seize the political initiative as soon as an opportunity presented itself. The dominant factor that produced an upheaval of violence in March 2004, therefore, was mounting frustration and apprehension caused by Kosovo's uncertain future status. UNMIK, however, was not empowered to resolve this source of conflict. It could attempt only to nurture conditions that would allow a process of negotiation to begin.

With the arrival of SRSG Søren Jessen-Petersen in August 2004 and the election of Ramush Haradinaj as prime minister in November 2004, the partnership envisioned under the "review date" policy began to be realized. UNMIK and the PISG managed to work constructively together toward attainment of the standards. In late May 2005, the UN secretary-general designated Ambassador Kai Eide, permanent representative of Norway to NATO, as special envoy to perform a comprehensive review to determine whether the conditions were suitable to begin addressing the status issue. On October 7, 2005, Eide delivered his conclusions: "While standards implementation in Kosovo has been uneven, the time had come to move to the next phase of the political process."

While the outcome remained to be determined, the Contact Group had already made it clear that certain options were off the table. These were "partition of Kosovo, union with any country after the determination of status, and return to the situation before March 1999."[107] Compared with mid-1999, prospects that Kosovo's future would be determined through peaceful means had advanced remarkably. Although the international community, increasingly in the form of the European Union, could expect to remain engaged indefinitely, the costs of doing so had become manageable.

Conclusions

The first question that the architect of any peace process should ask is "What kind of peace is this?" Kosovo was far from a case of post-conflict reconstruction. Before peace could reliably take hold, the fundamental conditions that served to perpetuate conflict would have to be transformed:

- *Political conflict* would have to be transformed from a zero-sum and polarizing process, which the parties sought to control through violent and coercive means, to a participatory political process in which conflicts could be resolved peacefully.
- The *security environment* would have to be transformed from a context dominated by armed groups, which were willing and able to use violence to pursue their unfulfilled war aims, to a context in which armed groups had been either dismantled or subordinated to legitimate governmental authority.
- The *institutions responsible for the rule of law* would have to be transformed from instruments of state repression that afforded impunity to political and criminal elites, to servants of all the people, capable of protecting basic rights and holding even the most powerful and dangerous elements in society accountable.
- The *political economy* would have to be transformed from a condition in which the gray and black markets predominated, and illicit wealth could determine who governed, to a functioning formal economy that preserved the revenues required for essential state services.

In addressing these challenges, UNMIK and KFOR confirmed certain lessons from recent experience and added a number of others about the process of transformation from violent internal conflict to a peace that can endure.

Transforming Political Conflict

Ensure the primacy of the peace process. In Resolution 1244, the Security Council explicitly directed that the UN civilian and the NATO military presence coordinate closely in a mutually supportive manner. One key to this was infusing the mission with a common sense of purpose—the primacy of the peace process—around which all efforts were to be unified.

The KFOR commander made it clear that any challenge to UNMIK's political managers was a challenge to him. If troublemakers created obstructions, UNMIK's political managers had the means to establish consequences. The managers conveyed to the entire international mission that neutrality and evenhandedness were wrongheaded when it came to the mandate. Their message: You are not to be neutral about Resolution 1244. Support those who support the peace process, and oppose those who obstruct it.

Identify and mediate the multiple layers of conflict. Political conflicts exist across multiple layers. The most obvious conflict may obscure other layers of violent internal struggle that must be dealt with before the peace process can make real progress. UNMIK discovered that before the violent struggle between Kosovo's ethnic Serb and Albanian communities could be addressed, the internal Albanian power struggle would have to be moderated.

Premature elections undermine the peace process. As a result of repeatedly supervising elections in the Balkans and elsewhere, the international community had become proficient at organizing the mechanics of the electoral process. These events had not always advanced the resolution of conflict, however. Elections in Kosovo became part of the process of transformation to shift the balance of political power from bullets to ballots. If elections had been held prematurely, the outcome could have been polarizing, and further hostilities would likely have erupted. Suitable conditions had to be set in place first.

Exit strategies prevent transformation. If an exit strategy is declared before the peace process has even begun, the international community will be deprived of its capacity to induce support for the peace process. Obstructionists will simply stonewall or go underground to avoid sanctions. Would-be supporters will be deterred from taking risks for peace because of the expectation that they will eventually be abandoned. Extremist power structures will remain intact in each rival community, polarizing the political process and obstructing any meaningful steps toward peace. Instead of striving for a self-defeating exit, strategists should plan for transitions and integration into regional and international structures.

Transforming the Security Environment
Peace enforcement benefits from an understanding of counterinsurgency doctrine. Securing the peace required that violent extremists who

persisted in undermining the peace process be defeated. This strategic challenge exposed the need to reinforce principles inherited from the peacekeeping tradition by drawing upon relevant aspects of the counterinsurgency model. The decisive component of the security strategy was to find, fix, and strike against the sources of violent obstructionism. This called for military commanders to construct a mutually supportive framework of operations with international civilian police so as to "fix," or constrain, the freedom of movement of subversive elements. Intelligence-led actions were mounted within this framework to strike at these targets, as directed by the political managers of the mission.

A robust capability to establish public order is a prerequisite. Peace enforcement, especially at the inception of a mission, is liable to entail responding to large-scale acts of retaliatory violence, civil disturbances, and extensive property crimes. Military combat forces, armed only with lethal force, are not equipped to deal effectively with these challenges. Even if international civilian police can be rapidly mobilized, this type of violence is of a far greater scale than individual police are equipped to handle. Extremists become proficient at exploiting this gap through the use of orchestrated "rent-a-mobs." Thus there will be a crucial gap in capabilities unless organized units of police with the capability to use nonlethal force are available to impose public order.

Planning in the absence of an end state. The military planning process begins by stating the objective. Clarity is essential. In Kosovo, however, the "final status" remained undetermined. Indeed, UNMIK found it necessary to cultivate ambiguity about the end state in order to move the peace process forward. It was possible, however, for UNMIK to identify the incremental steps that needed to be taken. This enabled UNMIK's civilian leadership to conduct "next-state" planning with KFOR. This entailed identifying an interim set of desired conditions and priorities for the near term.

Transforming Lawless Rule into Rule of Law

The mandate must provide adequate authority. The authority provided in the mandate must be commensurate with the magnitude of the task involved. UN Security Council Resolution 1244 endowed the special representative of the secretary-general with the equivalent of sovereign powers that included the right to legislate by issuing regulations, to appoint and remove officials, and to revise the existing legal code. UNMIK police had "executive authority" to enforce the law.

Capacity building must be holistic. It is necessary to develop capacity not merely for policing but also in relation to the judiciary, penal system, and legal code.

Sources of lawless rule must be dislodged. Institutionalizing the rule of law requires more than building local capacity. A prominent international role may be required to dislodge obstructionist power structures and begin erecting effective institutional safeguards in the state and society to maintain the rule of law. Merely building institutional capacity is insufficient when violence remains the dominant political resource and illicit sources of wealth are able to determine who governs. The timing of the evolution to local "ownership" for the rule of law therefore must not be governed exclusively by the development of local capacity. Establishing an environment capable of sustaining the rule of law is also a fundamental prerequisite.

The entire legal continuum must be in place if violent obstructionists linked to criminal power structures are to be dislodged successfully. The most crucial deficiencies are the legal code, the capacity to convert intelligence into evidence, and the difficulty in locating qualified international legal professionals. The Brahimi Report acknowledged that a rudimentary international legal code and code of criminal procedure should be developed. This would allow international authorities to avoid a legal vacuum at the inception of a mission. Structures and procedures need to be established for intelligence, to guide the collection of evidence and to avoid ritualistic classification of evidence gathered by military personnel, who may be the first to control a crime scene or contact witnesses. International personnel with relevant investigative skills and sophisticated technical means are required to gather evidence for critical security-related cases. Legal professionals with competencies spanning the entire spectrum of functions involved in the rule of law need to be identified in advance and prepared to serve in future international missions.

Transforming a Conflict Political Economy

The economic foundations of obstructionist power must be undercut.[108] The economic incentives for continued conflict must be removed, and criminally obtained wealth must be separated from the exercise of political power. External funding for subversive activities (e.g., from neighboring political entities) must also be curtailed.

Peace must pay so the coalition for peace can prevail. Peace is a political agenda, and as with any political agenda, local political leaders must be willing to carry it forward. Elites willing to take risks for peace, and their supporters, must benefit from the peace process if their backing is to be maintained. Ensuring tangible improvement in the quality of life by expeditiously restoring basic public services should be a top priority. Peace has to pay for *all* the parties to the conflict, moreover, if they are to develop a stake in sustaining peace.

The state must be fiscally autonomous and sustainable. Establishing the autonomy of the state from lawless forces that had held sway during the conflict is a primary concern. Essential to this end is the integrity of the revenue stream required to sustain essential state functions. If the political clout of "warlords" and similar obstructionists is to be contained, the state must have the ability to fund efforts to counter their subversive activities. If the coalition for peace is to be sustained, the state must also be able to deliver benefits to society based on need, not exclusively on the basis of connection to patronage structures.

The macroeconomic foundation for expanding the formal economy at the expense of the shadow economy must be established. The foundation for legitimate economic activity must be put in place, including restoring the banking system and creating the essential legal and regulatory framework. When sufficient alternatives exist to employment in the underground economy, citizens will have a broad interest in maintaining transparent and accountable political and economic structures. This is the foundation of a civil society.

When peace implementation began in Kosovo in June 1999, the process of making peace had scarcely progressed. Diplomats, military peace enforcers, international civilian police, civil administrators, and assistance providers were expected to discharge unprecedented responsibilities for governance over the territory. This required the simultaneous capacity to make peace, impose peace, and build peace. Owing to the added difficulty and complexity involved, Kosovo has been a dynamic source of innovation and adaptation. It has also been a harbinger of the central challenges that would typify subsequent interventions.

Notes

Nick Howenstein, Teuta Gashi, and Kirit Radia provided invaluable assistance researching often obscure bits of data required to complete this chapter, for which I am immensely grateful. Any errors that may have crept into this text remain my own doing.

1. Some 850,000 people were eventually registered as refugees in Macedonia, Albania, and elsewhere around the world. See UN High Commissioner for Refugees, "A Brief History of the Balkans," www.unhcr.ch/cgi-bin/texis/vtx/balkans. By the end of May 1999, some 580,000 persons were estimated to be displaced inside Kosovo. See "NATO's Role in Relation to the Conflict in Kosovo," North Atlantic Treaty Organization (NATO), www.nato.int/kosovo/history.htm.

2. In 2000, the ethnic breakdown was estimated to be 88 percent Albanian, 7 percent Serb, and 5 percent other. UN Interim Administration Mission in Kosovo (UNMIK), "Kosovo and Its Population: A Brief Description," Statistical Office of Kosovo, Provisional Institutions of Self-Government, June 5, 2003, 2–3, www.sok-kosovo.org.

3. Woodward put the unemployment rate (defined as a percentage of the working population) at 23.1 percent in 1985 and an estimated 22.2 percent by 1990. See Susan Woodward, *Socialist Unemployment: The Political Economy of Yugoslavia, 1945–1990* (Princeton: Princeton University Press, 1995), 205. Statistical surveys placed Kosovo unemployment at around 26 percent by the end of the 1980s.

4. Noel Malcolm, *Kosovo: A Short History* (New York: Harper Perennial, 1999), 340–41.

5. Louis Sell, *Slobodan Milosevic and the Destruction of Yugoslavia* (Durham and London: Duke University Press, 2002), 5.

6. UN Security Council Resolution 1160, S/RES/1160, March 31, 1998.

7. "Annan Warns against Kosovo Action without UN Mandate," *Agence France-Presse*, June 28, 1998. See also NATO, "Statement on Kosovo" (press release, May 28, 1998). For a detailed discussion of the interplay between force and diplomacy, see Ivo H. Daalder and Michael E. O'Hanlon, *Winning Ugly: NATO's War to Save Kosovo* (Washington, DC: Brookings Institution, 2000); and Wesley K. Clark, *Waging Modern War: Bosnia, Kosovo, and the Future of Combat* (New York: Public Affairs, 2001).

8. OSCE, "Kosovo/Kosova: As Seen, as Told," 5, www.osce.org/kosovo/documents/reports/hr/part1/ch1.htm.

9. UN Security Council Resolution 1199, S/RES/1199, September 23, 1998, para. 16.

10. Daalder and O'Hanlon, *Winning Ugly*, 42.

11. NATO, "Statement by the Secretary General" (press statement, Vilamoura, Portugal, September 24, 1998).

12. As Madeleine Albright relates in her memoir, "Early on the morning of October 13, NATO formally authorized the use of force, allowing four days for compliance. A few hours later, Holbrooke announced that he and Milosevic had a deal." See Madeleine Albright with Bill Woodward, *Madame Secretary: A Memoir* (New York: Miramax, 2003), 390.

13. The Kosovo Verification Mission was established on October 25, 1998, by Permanent Council Decision 263. Its tasks were to ensure compliance with the tenets of UN Security Council Resolution 1199. See OSCE, "Mission in Kosovo—Overview," www.osce.org/kosovo/overview.

14. See Interview with Ambassador William Walker, "War in Europe," *PBS Frontline*, February 22, 2000, www.pbs.org/wgbh/pages/frontline/shows/kosovo/interviews/walker.html.

15. Daalder and O'Hanlon, *Winning Ugly*, 75.

16. See *Interim Agreement for Peace and Self-Government in Kosovo* (Rambouillet Accords), February 23, 1999, www.kosovo.mod.uk/rambouillet_text.htm.

17. Daalder and O'Hanlon, *Winning Ugly*, 59.

18. President Clinton articulated three objectives: deter and punish Serb aggression against Kosovo's Albanian population; erode Serbia's military capabilities to wage war against Kosovo; and demonstrate NATO's commitment to oppose aggression. For a transcript, see "President Clinton's Address to the Nation," *PBS Online Newshour*, March 24, 1999, www.pbs.org/newshour/bb/europe/jan-june99/address_3-24.html.

19. Daalder and O'Hanlon, *Winning Ugly*, 156.

20. A G-8 presidency letter to the UN Security Council stated the conclusions of the meeting. United Nations, *Letter Dated 99/05/06 from the*

Permanent Representative of Germany to the United Nations Addressed to the President of the Security Council, S/1999/516, May 6, 1999.

21. NATO, "NATO's Role in Relation to Kosovo," www.nato.int/docu/facts/2000/kosovo.htm.

22. Daalder and O'Hanlon, *Winning Ugly,* 170.

23. NATO, *Military Technical Agreement between the International Security Force (KFOR) and the Governments of the Federal Republic of Yugoslavia and the Republic of Serbia,* June 9, 1999, www.nato.int/kosovo/docu/a990609a.htm.

24. Jock Covey provides an expanded treatment of these dynamics in "Making a Viable Peace: Moderating Political Conflict," in *The Quest for Viable Peace: International Intervention and Strategies for Conflict Transformation,* ed. Jock Covey, Michael J. Dziedzic, and Len Hawley (Washington, DC: United States Institute of Peace Press, 2005).

25. The Armed Forces of the Republic of Kosovo (FARK).

26. "Clinton: 'We Did the Right Thing,'" *Washington Post,* June 11, 1999, A31, www.washingtonpost.com/wp-srv/inatl/longterm/balkans/stories/clintontext061199.htm.

27. Jock Covey, "The Custodian of the Peace Process," in *Quest for Viable Peace,* ed. Covey, Dziedzic, and Hawley, 92.

28. Ibid., 93.

29. The 2002 census in Macedonia determined the total population to be 2,038,059, of which 440,000, or approximately 22 percent, are Albanian. See Republic of Macedonia State Statistical Office, www.stat.gov.mk.

30. Conflict, Security and Development Group, "Kosovo Report" (online report, part of *A Review of Peace Operations: A Case for Change* Web site, sponsored by the International Policy Institute, King's College London, February 28, 2003), para. 152, ipi.sspp.kcl.ac.uk/rep005/index.html.

31. UN Security Council Resolution 1244, S/RES/1244, June 10, 1999.

32. Ibid., para. 9.

33. UNMIK, Regulation 1999/8, January 21, 2000, www.unmikonline.org/regulations/index_reg_1999.htm.

34. UN Security Council Resolution 1244 (1999), para. 11.

35. The Kosovo Consolidated Budget was established by UNMIK Regulation 1999/17. It covered salaries of Kosovo employees (civil servants) and goods and services.

36. Data from the report of the conclusions of the First Donors' Conference for Kosovo, Brussels, July 28, 1999, www.seerecon.org/calendar/1999/events/kdc.

37. The Second Donors' Conference for Kosovo was held in Brussels on November 17, 1999, co-chaired by the European Commission and the World Bank. See "Second Donors' Conference for Kosovo Program for Reconstruction and Recovery," Economic Reconstruction and Development in South East Europe, European Commission and the World Bank. See www.seerecon.org/calendar/1999/events/k2dc/index.html.

38. Southeast Europe Country Unit, World Bank, "Memorandum to the President of the International Development Association to the Executive Directors on a Transitional Support Strategy of the World Bank Group for Kosovo," Report no. 28006-KOS, Annex IV (Washington, DC, April 13, 2004), www.seerecon.org/documents.cfm?ltype=bd&dr=on&c=ko. In addition to $81 million provided by the World Bank through 2003, in April 2004 a grant of $15 million was made for Kosovo through June 2005.

39. *First Interim Report of the European Agency for Reconstruction to the European Parliament, February-May 2000 (17/05/00),* www.ear.eu.int/kosovo/kosovo.htm.

40. Estimated KFOR costs are contained in the *Kosovo General Government 2003 Budget,* 13, www.esiweb.org/bridges/showkosovo.php?cat_ID=2, and can be extrapolated from the average per capita costs of NATO peacekeeping forces in neighboring Bosnia-Herzegovina, using data from International Institute for Strategic Studies, *The Military Balance* (London, 1996–99).

41. As described by Daalder and O'Hanlon, *Winning Ugly,* 34.

42. For a list of the G-8 Principles, adopted May 6, 1999, see news.bbc.co.uk/1/hi/world/europe/336979.stm.

43. Conflict, Security and Development Group, "Kosovo Report," para. 22.

44. Clark, *Waging Modern War,* 154–55, 162–63.

45. Linda Kozaryn, "NATO Planners Double Kosovo Peace Force Size to 50,000" (online report, American Forces Information Service, U.S. Department of Defense, May 20, 1999), www.defenselink.mil/news/May1999/n05201999_9905205.html.

46. "Transcript: Helsinki Press Briefing on Russia's KFOR Role, June 18," *USIS Washington File,* June 20, 1999, 8.

47. "Agreement on Russian Participation in KFOR," *DefenseLINK News,* no. 301-99, June 18, 1999.

48. See KFOR, "The International Security Presence in Kosovo," Backgrounder 99001, www.afsouth.nato.int/operations/kfor/backgrounder.html.

49. Ibid. See also U.S. Department of State, "Fact Sheet: KFOR Deployment," *USIS Washington File*, July 26, 1999, www.un.int/usa/99kos726c.htm.

50. Covey, "The Custodian of the Peace Process," in *Quest for Viable Peace*, ed. Covey, Dziedzic, and Hawley.

51. UN Security Council, *Report of the Secretary-General on the United Nations Interim Administration Mission in Kosovo (UNMIK)*, S/1999/779, July 12, 1999.

52. KFOR also included a similar capability with its Multinational Specialized Unit.

53. Covey, "The Custodian of the Peace Process," in *Quest for Viable Peace*, ed. Covey, Dziedzic, and Hawley.

54. See UN Security Council Resolution 1244 (1999).

55. UN Security Council, *S-G Report on UNMIK*, S/1999/779.

56. Ibid.

57. UN Security Council, *Report of the Secretary-General on the United Nations Interim Administration in Kosovo*, S/1999/779.

58. See UNMIK, "UNMIK Police Personnel," www.unmikonline.org/civpol/factsfigs.htm.

59. For online information on UNMIK Pillar I, see www.unmikonline.org/justice/index_pillar1.htm.

60. See UNMIK, "UNMIK Police Press Update," May 17, 2000, www.civpol.org/unmik/PressUpdateArchi/archive00.htm.

61. Conflict, Security and Development Group, "Kosovo Report," para. 29.

62. From May 2000 through August 2001, the number of consultants funded by the U.S. Agency for International Development varied between fifty-five and sixty. See U.S. Agency for International Development, www.usaid.gov/business/yellowbook/yellowbook01.xls.

63. Conflict, Security and Development Group, "Kosovo Report," para. 161.

64. *Kosovo Atlas*, 3rd ed. (Pristina, Kosovo: Humanitarian Information Center/Geographic Information Systems Map Center, 2002), ii.

65. Paul Currion, "Learning from Kosovo: The Humanitarian Community Information Center (HCIC), Year One," *Humanitarian Exchange* 18 (March 2001): 21, www.odihpn.org/documents/humanitarianexchange018.pdf.

66. Conflict, Security and Development Group, "Kosovo Report," para. 113.

67. See United Nations Office for the Coordination of Humanitarian Affairs, "Humanitarian Information Centres (HICs)," ochaonline.un.org/webpage.asp?Page=695.

68. There were 154 Serbs murdered between June and December 1999. The total did drop precipitously in 2000, though, to 55. For crime statistics compiled by UNMIK police, see UNMIK, "UNMIK Police Statistics," www.civpol.org/unmik/statistics.htm.

69. OSCE, "Parallel Structures in Kosovo," October 2003, 12, www.osce.org/documents/mik/2003/10/698_en.pdf. See also International Crisis Group, "UNMIK's Kosovo Albatross: Tackling Division in Mitrovica," Balkans Report no. 131, June 3, 2002, www.crisisgroup.org.

70. Rexhepi was prime minister of Kosovo's Provisional Institutions of Self-Government.

71. OSCE, "Parallel Structures in Kosovo," 14.

72. The Military Technical Agreement is available at NATO, www.nato.int/kosovo/docu/a990609a.htm.

73. Bob Churcher, "Kosovo Lindore/Presevo 1999–2002 and the FYROM Conflict," *Conflict Studies Research Centre*, March 2002, 6, 20, www.da.mod.uk/CSRC/documents/balkans/.

74. Ibid., 2.

75. Ibid., 5, 15.

76. See Deputy Prime Minister of the Republic of Serbia Nebojsa Covic's "Plan for the Resolution of the Crisis in the Territory of Southern Serbia."

77. Philip Gounev, "Stabilizing Macedonia: Conflict Prevention, Development and Organized Crime," *Journal of International Affairs* (Fall 2003): 232.

78. Churcher, "Kosovo Lindore/Presevo 1999–2002," 17.

79. Gounev, "Stabilizing Macedonia," 230.

80. For the text of the Ohrid Framework Agreement, see UK Defence Academy Conflict Studies Research Centre, www.da.mod.uk/CSRC/documents/ balkans/csrc_mpf.2004-07-22.4933876394/04(15)-Chap3-JP.pdf/file_view.

81. The issues discussed in this section are treated in detail by Halvor A. Hartz et al., "Safeguarding a Viable Peace: Institutionalizing the Rule of Law," in *Quest for Viable Peace,* ed. Covey, Dziedzic, and Hawley.

82. United Nations Regulation 1999/1, *On the Authority of the Interim Administration in Kosovo,* July 25, 1999, www.un.org/peace/kosovo/pages/regulations/reg1.html.

83. Ibid., 80.

84. UNMIK, Regulation 2000/34, UNMIK/REG/2000/34, May 27, 2000, www.unmikonline.org/regulations/index_reg_2000.htm.

85. UN Security Council, *Report of the Secretary-General on the United Nations Interim Administration in Kosovo,* S/2004/348, April 30, 2004, 1.

86. UN Security Council Resolution 1244 (1999).

87. See Michael Steiner, "Address to the UN Security Council," February 6, 2003, www.unmikonline.org/srsg/speeches/srsg060203.htm.

88. Conflict, Security and Development Group, "Kosovo Report," para. 119.

89. An unnamed senior UNMIK official cited in ibid., para. 123.

90. Covey, "Making a Viable Peace: Moderating Political Conflict," in *Quest for Viable Peace,* ed. Covey, Dziedzic, and Hawley, 101.

91. UNMIK, "UNMIK at 18 Months," www.unmikonline.org/1styear/unmikat18.htm.

92. UNMIK, Regulation 2001/9, UNMIK/REG/2001/9, May 15, 2001.

93. See UNMIK News Coverage Archives, "UN Assumes Administrative Control over Mitrovica," November 26, 2002, www.unmikonline.org/archives/news11_02full.htm#2611.

94. See OSCE, www.osce.org/kosovo/human_rights/ for a description of OSCE's pillar activities and mandates.

95. See Oliver Schmidt-Gutzat, "The Status of National Minorities: Minority Ethnic Communities in Kosovo and the Involvement of the OSCE Mission in Minority Rights Protection," *Details: A Newsletter of the OSCE Mission in Kosovo* 3, ed. 5 (August 2005), www.osce.org/kosovo/publications.html?lsi=true&limit=10&grp=258.

96. See Hartz et al., "Safeguarding a Viable Peace."

97. These issues are treated in greater detail by Stephanie A. Blair et al., "Forging a Viable Peace: Developing a Legitimate Political Economy," in *Quest for Viable Peace,* ed. Covey, Dziedzic, and Hawley.

98. Joly Dixon, "Kosovo: Economic Reconstruction and Development," Brussels, July 12, 1999.

99. See UNMIK, Regulation 2003/41, *On the Approval of the Kosovo Consolidated Budget and Authorizing Expenditures for the Period 1 January to 31 December 2004*, UNMIK/REG/2003/41, December 31, 2003. Annual Kosovo Consolidated Budgets available at UNMIK, www.unmikonline.org. The 2002 budget was in surplus €37 million. The budget forecasts for 2004 put revenues at €619 million and expenditures at €632 million, with the balance of €13 million drawing upon the 2003 budget surplus.

100. Also known as KEK (Korporata Energjetike e Kosoves) in Albanian.

101. See UNMIK Department of Public Information, Media Monitoring, "All Roads Lead to Joe Trutschler and His Servants in Kosovo," May 2, 2002, www.unmikonline.org/press/2002/mon/may/lmm020502.htm.

102. Conflict, Security and Development Group, "Kosovo Report," para. 170.

103. Ibid., para. 172.

104. United Nations, "Letter Dated 27 May 2005, from the Secretary-General addressed to the President of the Security Council," S/2005/348, May 27, 2005, www.un.org/Docs/sc/unsc_presandsg_letters05.htm.

105. UN Security Council Resolution 1244 (1999).

106. See UNMIK, "Standards for Kosovo," UNMIK/PR/1078 (press release, December 10, 2003), www.unmikonline.org/press/pressr03.htm.

107. UN Security Council, *Report of the Secretary-General on the United Nations Interim Administration Mission in Kosovo*, S/2005/335, May 23, 2005, 6, daccess-ods.un.org/TMP/2848030.html.

108. This section is derived from Blair et al., "Forging a Viable Peace," in *Quest for Viable Peace*, ed. Covey, Dziedzic, and Hawley.

6

East Timor

Michael G. Smith and Moreen Dee

Introduction

The Democratic Republic of Timor-Leste—more commonly known as East Timor—achieved its independence on May 20, 2002. On September 27, the new country became the 191st member of the United Nations. These occasions marked the end of a long and painful struggle for self-determination that began with Indonesia's occupation of the former Portuguese colony in 1975 and its incorporation the following year into Indonesia as its twenty-seventh province.

The international community mounted four peace operations in East Timor between June 1999 and May 2005. Collectively, these UN-mandated missions went well beyond traditional peacekeeping. In chronological order, they were as follows:

- The UN Mission in East Timor (UNAMET), June–October 1999, to conduct the Popular Consultation (or ballot), which enabled the people of East Timor to choose between autonomy within Indonesia or independence. UNAMET was a bold peacemaking initiative to resolve a long-standing dispute and prevent further conflict. Although the ballot was conducted successfully, peacemaking was thwarted by the failure of the Indonesian authorities to prevent the outbreak of violence.

- The International Force in East Timor (INTERFET), September 1999–February 2000, a multinational force assembled under UN mandate to undertake a peace enforcement operation to restore security in response to militia violence. INTERFET's operation was an example of modern peacekeeping, whereby security was imposed and measures taken to establish the conditions for a durable peace.

- The UN Transitional Administration in East Timor (UNTAET), October 1999–May 2002, which operated with and then replaced INTERFET, to administer East Timor and shepherd the country to independence. UNTAET's mandate required it to undertake peace enforcement, peacekeeping, and peacebuilding tasks designed to provide the conditions to sustain peace, based on democratization and national recovery.

- The follow-on UN Mission of Support in East Timor (UNMISET), May 2002–May 2005, which assisted the new nation with security and capacity building.[1] UNMISET was designed to make a further contribution to peacebuilding and provide the exit strategy for major UN involvement.

An examination of the United Nations' involvement in East Timor through these four missions provides an illustration of how complex peace operations could occur and evolve in the twenty-first century. This chapter analyzes the events leading to East Timor's independence and its first two years of nationhood, focusing on the four UN-mandated missions. The United Nations' role in peacebuilding, peacekeeping, and peacemaking is explained, with special attention given to the security dimension, covering in particular the role and effectiveness of the various military and police forces. Effective nation building, of course, requires much more than security: good governance and administration, the establishment of the rule of law, sustainable development, and the application of human rights are of equal importance. This chapter, however, concentrates on the internal and external security issues that underpinned East Timor's progress to independence and identifies the main security factors that shape the new nation's future.

Figure 6.1. Map of East Timor

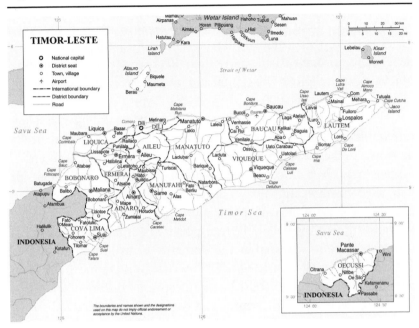

Source: UN Cartographic Section

Origins of the Operations

East Timor is a small, mountainous, largely infertile, and tropical country that shares an island and a border with Indonesia's West Timor (see figure 6.1). It also includes the small enclave of Oecusse, located on the northern coast of West Timor.[2] Much of its 15,000-square-kilometer territory is too rugged for habitation.[3] It is a poor country; its sandalwood resources have already been plundered, and coffee and potentially vanilla are the only economically viable agricultural crops. According to a World Bank analysis in 2003, two in every five East Timorese live below the poverty line.[4] But while its current agricultural and fishery resources are limited, East Timor does possess significant oil and gas reserves in the Timor Sea. Anticipated revenues from these reserves are expected to underwrite the country's economic viability.[5]

The population of around 925,000 is heterogeneous, with no common language (although use of Tetun as a lingua franca is widespread). The Roman Catholic Church is well established (a legacy of four centuries of Portuguese colonial rule) and influential (a legacy of the independence struggle), with more than 90 percent of the population practicing the religion. The capital and largest city is Dili, with a population of around 168,000.

East Timor has no manufacturing industries, and its infrastructure is underdeveloped and tenuous. The power supply, systematically destroyed in the postballot violence, is unreliable in the towns and non-existent in much of the countryside. The road network is fragile. Outside Dili, telecommunications coverage is poor in urban areas and non-existent for most of the rural population. The country has no rail services, government-owned public transportation, or internal air services (other than those provided by the United Nations). International air services are normally restricted to Dili,[6] which is also home to the main port facility. The north coast has a number of rudimentary ports, including Oecusse, but the south coast has none. The projected rate of development indicates that East Timor's infrastructure is likely to remain in an underdeveloped state for many years.

East Timor's twenty-four years of Indonesian occupation was contested militarily within the territory by the popularly supported nationalist guerrilla movement known as Falintil (the Armed Forces for the National Liberation of East Timor). Falintil operated with assistance from a large civilian network of clandestine supporters and from the clergy of the influential East Timorese Roman Catholic Church. Internationally, an active Timorese diaspora kept the quest for independence alive, aided principally by Portugal and an impressive array of international human rights organizations. The plight of the East Timorese was highlighted and additional credibility was given to their quest for self-determination in 1996, when the Nobel Peace Prize was awarded jointly to two Timorese, political activist Jose Ramos-Horta and Bishop Carlos Filipe Ximenes Belo.

As with all conflicts, the roots of the East Timor dispute are deep and transcend any single moment in history. Until Indonesian occupation in 1975, East Timor was known as Portuguese Timor, having been colonized and administered by Portugal for more than 400 years, with a brief Japanese interregnum during World War II.

It was the prospect of an unstable leftist government being established on its border, following Portugal's Carnation Revolution of April 25, 1974, that turned Indonesia's attention toward the isolated Portuguese colony. Indonesia had showed little interest in the territory when it acquired West Timor from the Dutch as part of its decolonization process in 1949. In 1974, however, the anticommunist Suharto regime was unwilling to accept self-determination for East Timor if it meant a neighboring government led by the left-wing Revolutionary Front for an Independent East Timor (Fretilin)—the major political party in the territory.[7] Later that year, a covert operation was launched involving East Timorese political groups opposed to Fretilin. It was designed to establish the conditions to justify the incorporation of East Timor into Indonesia. Initially, the Indonesian military worked closely with the small and relatively uninfluential Timorese Popular Democratic Association (Apodeti), which advocated integration with Indonesia. From early 1975, however, Indonesian authorities focused their efforts on winning over the leadership of the more popular right-wing Timorese Democratic Union (UDT), which was already on a collision course with Fretilin.

Preempting possible Fretilin action, and probably with the hope of averting an Indonesian invasion, the UDT orchestrated a coup on August 1975 that destabilized the weak Portuguese administration. Fretilin, however, was the victor in the subsequent fighting and assumed control of the country with the evacuation of the Portuguese military and the withdrawal of the Portuguese governor to Atauro Island. Fretilin reorganized its forces under the name of Falintil on August 20, and was soon under heavy attack in the border districts by Indonesian military forces (TNI[8]) supported by elements from the UDT and Apodeti. The intensity of hostilities increased and, failing to gain UN or international support, Fretilin declared independence on November 28. Independence was short-lived, however; on December 7, Indonesian forces assaulted Dili. Ignoring UN resolutions reaffirming the right of the East Timorese to self-determination,[9] Indonesia incorporated East Timor on July 17, 1976.

Negotiations and Peace Accord

The United Nations' involvement in East Timor began with Indonesia's occupation and the international body's refusal, together with most of the international community, to recognize Indonesian sovereignty. From December 1976, the General Assembly annually reaffirmed the right of the East Timorese to self-determination, but as the Cold War continued and President Suharto's power strengthened in Indonesia and internationally, the Security Council was unable and unwilling to take firm action. The question of East Timor thus remained unresolved in the United Nations for almost a quarter of a century.

In 1983, complying with the General Assembly's Resolution 37/30 of the previous year, the secretary-general instituted tripartite talks between Indonesia, Portugal, and the United Nations to review the prospects for settlement. Over the years these talks made little progress, and little was done to address either the political impasse or the plight of the East Timorese.

In March 1993, faced with evidence of a series of human rights abuses by TNI in East Timor, including video evidence of the indiscriminate killing of an estimated 150 to 270 unarmed civilians at the Santa Cruz cemetery in Dili on November 12, 1991, the UN Commission on Human Rights censured Indonesia for its poor human rights record in East Timor.[10] Although the number is difficult to verify, it has been reliably assessed that a third of the East Timorese population died as a direct result of Indonesia's administration—"the highest per capita death toll of any conflict in the 20th century."[11]

It was not until February 1997 that renewed vigor was applied to resolving the long-standing issue when Kofi Annan, as the newly elected UN secretary-general, appointed Ambassador Jamsheed Marker from Pakistan as his personal representative for East Timor.

The real turning point in the situation, however, came that same year with the Asian economic crisis. This crisis had a disastrous effect on the Indonesian economy and acted as a catalyst for the fall of the long-standing Suharto regime. Soon after his appointment as Indonesia's caretaker president, B. J. Habibie indicated that he intended to offer autonomy to East Timor. In May 1998, he announced that Indonesia was considering "special status" for the territory, which would entail autonomy in all areas of government except defense, foreign affairs, and monetary policy.

The subsequent presentation of this proposal to the secretary-general in New York in June provided the opportunity for Marker and the United Nations to become more closely involved, utilizing the tripartite talks already in place. Acting quickly, Marker visited Jakarta and East Timor for high-level discussions in July, and followed this up with a constructive tripartite session in August. In September, the United Nations presented a draft document on proposed autonomy for East Timor, and tripartite negotiations on this proposal began the following month.

In late January 1999, however, Habibie revealed that he had further plans of his own—a UN-monitored referendum in East Timor offering the choice between autonomy within Indonesia and independence. He obtained the Indonesian cabinet's agreement on January 27, 1999, and it was immediately announced that if the majority of the East Timorese rejected the offer of "autonomy plus" within Indonesia, "we will suggest to the People's Consultative Assembly (MPR), formed as a result of the next [Indonesian] elections, to release East Timor from Indonesia."[12] Habibie allowed limited time for discussion on this key decision, both within the cabinet and with the military, and this lack of consensus was later to prove crucial in the total breakdown of security following the ballot. The TNI, particularly its special forces (known as KOPASSUS), had masterminded the invasion in 1975 and, together with the Indonesian police (POLRI), had a deep psychological and economic attachment to retaining the province,[13] although both forces were strongly resented by the East Timorese.

No doubt Habibie's decision to hold a ballot was in part a reflection of his unpredictable and eccentric personality. But Indonesia was also under significant international pressure at the time, particularly from the Clinton administration, the World Bank, and the International Monetary Fund (IMF), to accelerate its democratization process, restrict the role of the military, reform its ailing financial sector, and reduce the level of corruption. The cost to Indonesia of maintaining its poorest province was difficult to justify domestically. East Timor received more support per capita than other provinces, but with little evident appreciation.

International condemnation of Indonesia's East Timor policy was also taking its toll. Increasingly at loggerheads with the UN Secretariat, Indonesia faced constant criticism from human rights activists over TNI actions in East Timor, Aceh, the Moluccas, and West Papua (Irian Jaya). East Timor's unique political status undercut TNI concerns that the loss of East Timor might lead to the "balkanization" of Indonesia. (The TNI's concern was further weakened by its initial assessment that the majority of East Timorese would probably support integration.) Habibie appears to have decided to allow the people of East Timor the option of self-determination in the hope that this gesture might also reduce international pressure on Indonesia on other fronts, particularly the Timor issues still outstanding between Indonesia, Portugal, and the United Nations.

In the March round of tripartite talks, Indonesia assented to the conduct of a UN-administered universal ballot. Given Indonesia's insistence that the results of the consultation be presented to the opening session of the new People's Consultative Assembly following the national elections due in June, planning for the consultation began immediately. A UN assessment mission traveled to Jakarta, East Timor, Australia, New Zealand, and Portugal to develop initial operational plans for the proposed consultation and to confirm logistic requirements.

Political Support for Peace—the May 5 Agreements

Despite the further deterioration in the situation on the ground in East Timor throughout April, the tripartite talks, held April 21–23, were productive. On May 5, 1999, agreements were signed between Indonesia, Portugal, and the United Nations for the conduct of a UN-supervised ballot and the maintenance of security by Indonesian authorities.[14] Article 5 stipulated that if the East Timorese accepted the offer of autonomy, then Indonesia would take steps to ensure this, and Portugal would agree to the removal of East Timor from the list of non-self-governing territories and accept its deletion from the agendas of the General Assembly and Security Council. Indonesia's twenty-seventh province would then become the Special Autonomous Region of East Timor. Article 6 stated that if the East Timorese rejected the offer of autonomy within the Indonesian republic, Indonesia would terminate its links with East Timor and, together with Portugal and the United Nations, "agree on arrangements for a peaceful and orderly transfer of authority in East Timor to the UN." The United Nations would then "begin a process of transition towards independence."

The question to be put before the voters was this:

Do you *accept* the proposed special autonomy for East Timor within the Unitary State of the Republic of Indonesia? **ACCEPT**

OR

Do you *reject* the proposed special autonomy for East Timor, leading to East Timor's separation from Indonesia?   **REJECT**

Based on an agreed timetable that included time for UN deployment, a public information campaign, voter registration, various appeals, and the voting itself, the ballot date was initially set as Sunday, August 8. (It would later be postponed to August 30.)

The agreements highlighted security concerns and authorized the UN secretary-general to assess whether the security situation would permit peaceful implementation of the consultation process. Article 3 stated clearly that Indonesia would "be responsible for maintaining peace and security in East Timor in order to ensure that the popular consultation is carried out in a fair and peaceful way in an atmosphere free of intimidation, violence or interference from any side."

The maintenance of law and order, including responsibility for the security of UN personnel, was, at Indonesia's insistence, made the sole responsibility of POLRI and TNI, although the United Nations was tasked to make available a number of police officers "to act as advisers to the Indonesian police in the discharge of their duties." The Indonesian security forces were required to maintain absolute neutrality throughout the process. Discussions between the United Nations and Xanana Gusmao, the commander in chief of Falintil, addressed the need to reinforce that neutrality with an entity that would reflect the wishes of all parties in the lead-up to the ballot. With support from the bishops, the Commission on Peace and Stability (Komisi Perdamaian dan Stabilitas, or KPS) was established in Dili on April 21. The May 5 agreements urged that the KPS become operational and cooperate with the United Nations in elaborating a code of conduct to be observed by all parties throughout the ballot process. On the day the KPS was set up, however, General Wiranto, the head of TNI, stepped in and presided over the formalities, effectively hijacking the commission as a TNI initiative. The KPS thus failed to have proper representation from the pro-independence factions and played little of its intended role.

The importance of the May 5 agreements to subsequent events should not be underestimated. The agreements provided legitimacy and international support for the UN ballot (and for subsequent missions in turn), all the more so because they had been promoted personally by the Indonesian president. The agreements did not constitute a peace accord in the traditional sense of warring factions agreeing to a cease-fire, however. The conflict in East Timor had been asymmetric in nature, with Falintil struggling for survival and the Indonesian administration far from threat of collapse. But the agreements influenced and shaped events in East Timor significantly, including the voluntary cantonment by Falintil as a confidence-building measure in the lead-up to the ballot.

The Situation on the Ground

A parallel and equally important political process had also commenced between the East Timorese factions. In the years following Indonesia's occupation, acrimony between Timorese political figures—particularly evident within the ranks of the large diaspora—continued to undermine efforts for self-determination. In April 1998, the National Council for Timorese Resistance (CNRT) was formed with representation from most parties. Most importantly, the CNRT brought together Fretilin and the UDT, and agreed upon a common strategy for the resistance movement. Its creation as a political umbrella group was thus a significant step in confirming solidarity for the independence cause, and as such, it would go on to play a defining role until well after the establishment of UNTAET. Another important move by the CNRT was its selection of Xanana Gusmao as its president despite his incarceration in Jakarta, thereby establishing him as the undisputed leader of the independence movement.

Although positive signs for peace were emerging on the political front with the tripartite talks and the formation of the CNRT, the security situation on the ground in East Timor was an altogether different story. Throughout 1998 and early 1999, as TNI sought to thwart prospects for independence, pro-independence activism gathered momentum. The Catholic Church, hoping to curb the volatility of some of these elements, organized a successful reconciliation meeting at Dare (near Dili) in September 1998, after which activists in the urban areas began showing more restraint. In the countryside, however, Falintil was less restrained as TNI strengthened pro-Indonesian militias and announced, on December 5, a policy of arming "civilian volunteers."

In early January, pro-integration and pro-independence elements clashed in the Ainaro and Suai districts, and fighting escalated over the next three months.[15] CNRT leaders were forced into hiding to avoid persecution, and "independence activists and presumed supporters [were] seized, tortured, and otherwise ill-treated; in some cases activists were killed. Many homes were destroyed and inhabitants displaced."[16] After Indonesia agreed to the consultation, militia activity increased again. On April 6, the militias attacked a church compound in Liquica, killing at least 30 of the estimated 2,000 local people who had sought sanctuary there. On April 17, the CNRT headquarters and the homes of pro-independence leaders and prominent East Timorese in Dili were attacked.[17] The TNI now sought to gain political as well as military advantage.

Against this deteriorating security background, final decisions on what would be the May 5 agreements were made on April 23 and were in respective capitals for approval by April 27.[18] Concerned, however, about the deteriorating security situation, the Australian prime minister John Howard met with Habibie that day in Bali. Indonesia had previously rebuffed suggestions that an international peacekeeping force be allowed into East Timor, and Howard's request that the matter be reconsidered was similarly firmly rejected by Habibie, as were later UN requests that TNI numbers in East Timor be substantially and verifiably reduced before voter registration commenced. In Bali, the Australian leader also raised the issue of an international police presence, arguing that the intended contingent of forty or fifty UN police (a number suggested by the Indonesians) would be insufficient to perform their advisory role during the ballot period. After prolonged discussion, Indonesia agreed to an expansion of UN police numbers to between 200 and 300.[19]

The May 5 agreements provided the conditions for the East Timorese to participate in a historic, internationally supervised ballot for self-determination. But relying on the Indonesian authorities to safeguard both UN personnel and the East Timorese people was a risky proposition, as subsequent events testified all too vividly.

The UN Mission in East Timor

On May 22, 1999, the secretary-general presented his *Report to the Security Council on the Question of East Timor.*[20] It drew on information from a UN assessment team that had visited East Timor from May 4 to 15 to evaluate the political and security situation and confirm arrangements with the Indonesians for the forthcoming UN mission. The secretary-general highlighted the challenges to be overcome in conducting the ballot in such a short period of time (by August 8) given the harsh physical environment, the isolation of many Timorese, and the rudimentary infrastructure available in the territory.

Given the prevailing climate of intimidation and violence, the question of security featured prominently in the secretary-general's report, which provided a disturbing assessment of the situation on the ground:

> Despite repeated assurances that measures would be taken by the Indonesian authorities to ensure security in East Timor and curtail the illegal activities of the armed militias, I regret to inform the Security Council that credible reports continue to be received of political violence, including intimidation and killings, by armed militias against unarmed pro-independence civilians. I am deeply concerned to learn from the assessment team that, as a result, the situation in East Timor remains extremely tense and volatile.[21]

The secretary-general emphasized the need for an effective KPS and welcomed the moderating role played by the bishops. In response to strong recommendations by assessment team members from the Department of Peacekeeping Operations (DPKO), he announced his intention "to assign a number of military liaison officers (MLOs) to maintain contact with their Indonesian counterparts."[22] Indonesia's foreign minister, Ali Alatas, acceded to the deployment of fifty unarmed MLOs in a lengthy and difficult telephone conversation with UN envoy Jamsheed Marker.

Mandate

The U.S. requirement to consult Congress resulted in the UN Security Council mandate for UNAMET being delayed until June 11, but this delay had little effect on administrative preparations, which were already under way. Security Council Resolution 1246 mandated UNAMET until August 31, 1999.[23] The resolution endorsed the secretary-general's report of May 22, authorizing the modalities, structure, responsibilities, and components of the mission as detailed in that report. Reinforcing the secretary-general's security assessment, the Security Council stressed that it was

> the responsibility of the Government of Indonesia to maintain peace and security in East Timor . . . in order to ensure that the popular consultation is carried out in a fair and peaceful way and in an atmosphere free of intimidation, violence or interference from any side and to ensure the safety and security of United Nations and other international staff and observers in East Timor.[24]

In being authorized "to organise and conduct a popular consultation on the basis of a direct, secret and universal ballot,"[25] UNAMET was responsible for preparing, conducting, and verifying the referendum.

Funding

Due to the tight time constraints in mounting the mission, the secretary-general established a voluntary Trust Fund for the Settlement of the Question of East Timor in May 1999, which enabled UNAMET's prompt deployment.[26] Contributions in cash to the trust fund eventually totaled $43.8 million, and contributions in kind totaled $7.1 million, for a total of $50.9 million.[27] The major contributors to the trust fund were Japan, Portugal, the United States, Australia, and the European Union, while Australia provided the bulk of the in-kind contributions.

On June 29, the General Assembly approved a budget of slightly more than $52.5 million for the period of May 5 to August 31.[28] (When the date of the popular consultation was postponed to August 30, the mission budget was increased by $1.9 million to carry it through September.) The substantial voluntary contributions received up to that point meant that just $7.2 million had to be assessed to UN member states (using the peacekeeping scale of assessment).[29] The secretary-general later received commitment authority of $38 million for "phase II" of UNAMET, which was originally intended to monitor a peaceful, postconsultation transitional period, for a total spending authority of

$92.5 million. The mission, whose remaining assets were largely folded into UNTAET, eventually cost $81.3 million. Voluntary contributions ($50.9 million) and the initial assessment ($7.2 million) left approximately $23.2 million to be assessed to member states.[30]

Planning, Preparation, and Deployment

In terms of planning, UNAMET was a success. An important factor was the preparation undertaken by the UN Department of Political Affairs (DPA), which had handled the earlier negotiations leading to the referendum, and which had become the Secretariat's authority on East Timor.[31] Australia had a special interest in the events taking place on its northern doorstep, and even before the May 5 agreements it had assembled a governmental team that liaised closely with the Secretariat through regular visits to New York, supplementing consultations through its UN permanent mission. Further, a core group of interested countries, increasingly appalled by the Indonesian government's apparent inability to curtail the human rights abuses taking place in the territory, cooperated closely with each other and the United Nations to optimize the chances for a successful ballot in the difficult circumstances.[32]

Capable field personnel were quickly selected, with Ian Martin (United Kingdom) confirmed as special representative of the secretary-general (SRSG), and the size and structure of the mission detailed. DPA's Electoral Assistance Division devised a workable plan that required registration of an unconfirmed number of eligible voters, believed to be around 350,000, widely spread within East Timor and around the world. Planning had already determined that 200 registration/polling stations would be required, with electoral offices in eight of the thirteen districts. The Australian Electoral Commission (AEC) and the International Organization for Migration (IOM) provided considerable additional assistance.[33] On polling day, UNAMET comprised 241 international mission staff, 420 UN volunteers, up to 280 UN police to advise the Indonesian police and supervise the escort of ballot papers on polling day, 50 MLOs, and around 4,000 local staff.[34]

UNAMET established a base in Darwin, Australia, where the electoral component, UN police, and MLOs underwent orientation and training before deployment to East Timor. UNAMET used Darwin for much of its planning and logistics and as a safe haven for rest and recreation. In time, it would also become a refuge for those escaping the violence.

Logistics support was a potential vulnerability. The United Nations normally takes time to arrange and assemble the requirements for such missions, but as Martin noted, "UNAMET was fortunate in being at the head of the surge of missions in 1999," and surplus stock was available from the United Nations' logistics base at Brindisi in Italy.[35] Additionally, the trust fund received immediate voluntary contributions, which, along with Australia's in-kind assistance in the form of helicopters, some vehicles, and other logistics support, ensured that potential difficulties in procurement were avoided.[36] The mission also benefited from the Asian economic downturn, resulting in readily available surplus stocks of four-wheel-drive vehicles from Japan.

Martin was appointed SRSG on May 21. After fruitful meetings in Jakarta with senior Indonesian officials and with Xanana Gusmao (who remained under house arrest), he arrived in Dili by June 1 and opened the UN office three days later—ten days before the mandate was officially authorized by the Security Council. By June 10, senior UNAMET personnel had visited every district within East Timor and had gained a good understanding of the challenges ahead. Nonetheless, it was increasingly obvious to Martin and the secretary-general that slippage on the ambitious timetable set out in the mandate was inevitable, as much for administrative as for security reasons.

Command and Control

Given the clear purpose of the mission and its manageable size, the command and control arrangements worked well overall (see figure 6.2). Marker remained the secretary-general's personal representative, but Martin assumed the key role once the mission deployed. A former secretary-general of Amnesty International and more recently the deputy high representative for human rights in Bosnia and Herzegovina, with previous operational experience in Rwanda and Haiti, Martin was well qualified to head UNAMET.

In New York, DPA retained lead responsibility and headed the interdepartmental task force to support the mission, and Martin reported to the secretary-general through DPA. As the various components of the mission became established, there was, by necessity, considerable

Figure 6.2. UNAMET Organizational Chart

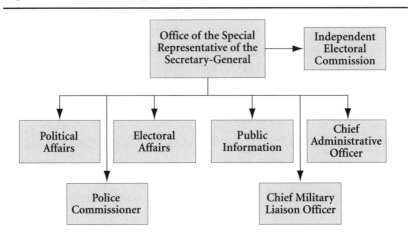

liaison with other offices of the Secretariat as well. UNAMET comprised six main components directly responsible to Martin (political, electoral, UN police, MLO, information, and administration) as well as an independent electoral commission (including three eminent international experts) to advise the secretary-general on the legitimacy of registration and voting and to adjudicate complaints, challenges, and disputes.

Field Operations—Implementation

Despite its excellent planning and logistic support and relatively rapid initial deployment, UNAMET was not complete on the ground until July 10. Thus voter registration did not begin as planned on June 22; instead, on that date, the secretary-general announced that the commencement of registration would be delayed three weeks, until July 13. The Indonesian government was prepared to accept this delay but was adamant that the ballot occur before the end of August.

Indonesia's demands, however, were not matched by actions to improve security on the ground. Annan noted in his announcement of June 22 that the delay would "give the Indonesian authorities time to address the pending security concerns."[37] Martin later wrote that it was "clear in mid-June that the security conditions deemed necessary for the consultation had not begun to exist," and that "the links between the local administration, the [pro-integration] Forum for Unity, Democracy and Justice, the militia, and the TNI were so close that they constituted a single operation to counter pro-independence activities and ensure a pro-autonomy vote."[38] On June 29, the UNAMET office in Maliana was stoned, and on July 4, a humanitarian convoy in Liquica was attacked. About 40,000 persons were confirmed to have been displaced as a direct result of the coercive pro-autonomy campaign, a figure that would rise to an estimated 60,000 by the end of July.

On June 21, the vice chief of the Australian Defence Force delivered a private message to key TNI leaders in Jakarta on the extent of Australia's knowledge of TNI activities and TNI-militia linkages, and of the potential consequences to Indonesia's reputation should the ballot fail because of these linkages.[39] The Australian initiative was strongly supported by the United States, but there was no indication that this or various American representations made around the same time had any effect on the TNI or the militias. Certainly, there was no suspension of the violence.

Registration

On July 14, the secretary-general advised the Security Council that voter registration had been authorized "based on positive assurances by the Indonesian authorities, on the condition that meaningful, visible improvements in the security situation will be observed in the immediate future."[40] Voter registration finally commenced on July 16. In his report to the Security Council on July 20, Annan noted that militia activities continued to pose a threat to the consultation process, particularly in the western districts.[41] On July 28, the secretary-general confirmed the date for the ballot as August 30, security permitting.[42]

The United Nations' information campaign for registration was well planned and proved effective, with high turnouts for registration. All but six of the planned 200 registration booths opened on July 16 (two for UN logistics reasons and four because of security concerns). The equivalent of twenty registration days were lost due to insecurity. The total number of valid registrations—more than 450,000—far exceeded UN expectations.[43] The high turnout could be attributed to a combination of good planning by DPA's Electoral Assistance Division (which enabled people to register at any center, thereby reducing the chance of intimidation in home locations), the hardworking electoral staff, and the thorough information campaign. Ultimately, however, the high turnout reflected the brave commitment of the East Timorese people to determine their own future in difficult circumstances.

After compilation, the registration lists were displayed in all registration centers and UNAMET offices from August 19 to 23 to allow for any challenges and appeals, which proved to be few. The independent electoral commission approved the registration process and on August 25 issued its formal determination confirming a sound basis for the conduct of the ballot.[44]

The Ballot and the Violence

From late July until the week prior to polling day, the security situation showed signs of improvement, and it was expected that the consultation would be conducted peacefully. Reports that postballot violence could be expected in the event of a pro-independence vote began to emerge in the final lead-up to the ballot.[45] The polling itself, on August 30, was not without incident, with seven polling stations forced to close temporarily during the day because of security concerns. The most serious incidents occurred in the Bobonaro and Ermera districts. Armed attacks took place in the latter, and resulted in the tragic deaths of three UN local staff at Atsabe.

Despite such militia intimidation, polling was conducted successfully. The rapid transportation of all ballot boxes to Dili for centralized and supervised counting reduced the possibility of missing or corrupted ballot papers, and at the same time improved the safety of the international staff and many of their local assistants. Counting was concluded on the evening of September 3, at which time the independent electoral commission determined that the popular consultation had been conducted fairly as a true reflection of the wishes of the East Timorese people.[46] On the morning of September 4 in Dili, and concurrently in New York, Ian Martin and Kofi Annan announced that 98.6 percent of eligible voters had participated, and that a clear majority of 78.5 percent had rejected autonomy and opted for independence.

Once the election results were announced in Dili, the militias unleashed a systematic campaign of terror with the complicity of

Indonesia's security forces. Extreme violence broke out on the afternoon of September 4, with gunfire, houses set alight, and thousands of East Timorese fleeing into the hills. By September 5, UNAMET staff had been forced to pull out of five towns, UN vehicles had been fired at in the streets in Dili, and several hundred East Timorese were seeking refuge in the UNAMET compound.

The exact number of deaths and human rights violations remains uncertain, but it has been estimated that the number killed was "greatly in excess of 1,000 persons."[47] Throughout the territory most of the buildings, utilities, and agricultural infrastructure were destroyed. Almost the entire population was displaced, and 250,000 people were transported to West Timor—mostly against their will—under TNI and militia control.[48] On September 6, the United Nations gave the Indonesian government twenty-four to forty-eight hours to prove the effectiveness of the martial law they had declared in the territory that day. From September 8 to 12, a UN Security Council mission visited Jakarta and Dili to press the Indonesian leadership to restore security.

Meanwhile, an Australian evacuation operation commenced.[49] In the period from September 6 to 14, nearly 2,600 people—Australians, UNAMET staff, media, and almost 1,900 East Timorese—were evacuated to Darwin.[50] A small UNAMET presence remained in Dili under the chief military liaison officer, but the perception of the East Timorese was that they had been abandoned by the United Nations in their hour of need. Later media commentary declared East Timor the most totally destroyed nation on earth, surpassing even the destruction of Kosovo.

Assessment of UNAMET

The level of postballot violence should not cloud the assessment of UNAMET's performance, which should be judged in relation to its mandate. At the operational level, the preparation and conduct of the ballot were an outstanding success, fulfilling the requirements of UNAMET's mandate. In a harsh climate and with rudimentary infrastructure, the ballot was extremely well planned and conducted. Even in the face of ongoing intimidation by pro-Indonesian militias, the impoverished people of East Timor were provided with an opportunity to express their democratic right of self-determination. And even knowing that violence might escalate after the ballot if the autonomy option were refused, the people courageously voted for their independence.

The main factors leading to operational success included the following:

- good planning and preparation by DPA, particularly for the process of registration and polling
- good leadership by Ian Martin and the UNAMET team
- an excellent public information campaign
- the timely allocation of adequate resources, largely through the establishment of a trust fund
- excellent support and goodwill from the international community, and the cooperation of the East Timorese population throughout the process
- the willingness of Falintil to voluntarily canton its troops and to honor its commitment not to engage in hostilities

At the strategic level, however, the success of the ballot is more contentious. At what price can freedom be judged, and to what extent do the ends justify the means? The systematic violence and destruction that escalated immediately after the ballot raise difficult questions about human rights and political morality. Knowing that security was unlikely to be guaranteed by Indonesia, was the United Nations justified in pursuing the ballot and then appearing to desert the East Timorese? In short, should the United Nations conduct such ballots without adequate security measures in place? In the case of East Timor in 1999, it is possible to criticize the United Nations on these counts and, by implication, apportion a share of responsibility for the killings and destruction.

Such questions and accusations, however, should be considered against the realities of the political situation prevailing at the time. First, the ballot was an Indonesian initiative, and could proceed only with the cooperation of the ruling power. President Habibie insisted that the ballot occur during his interregnum and was unwilling to accept more than a few weeks' delay. The United Nations and the CNRT both believed that delaying the ballot until security could be improved, or until Habibie's successor was confirmed, would lessen the chances of the ballot occurring at all. This view was supported by Security

Council members and other interested countries including Portugal, Japan, Australia, and New Zealand, all of whom considered this to be a restricted window of opportunity. Second, Indonesia had made it clear that it would not accept international peacekeepers under any circumstances—that it would take responsibility for guaranteeing security, and the peaceful and orderly transition of authority, should autonomy be rejected by the Timorese people. Third, although the United Nations, other nations involved, and the East Timorese themselves realized that security might not be guaranteed by Indonesia, none of the parties predicted the extent of the violence that ultimately ensued. As Kofi Annan put it on September 10, "We knew it was going to be difficult, we knew about the security problems, but not the carnage and chaos we have seen . . . if any of us had an inkling that it was going to be this chaotic I don't think anyone would have gone forward. We are no fools."[51] Finally, any suggestion that UNAMET should have remained active in East Timor during the postballot violence fails to consider the reality that the mission was neither mandated nor structured to conduct security operations. There was, however, a responsibility to protect the lives of UN personnel.

The International Force in East Timor

The violence and total breakdown in law and order following the ballot drew immediate international condemnation. Some of the effects of the militia rampage were telecast globally, as was the evacuation of UN personnel, media, and some East Timorese to Darwin. There was a clear need to respond rapidly, and a realization that a peace enforcement operation would be required to restore security. This force was known as the International Force in East Timor—INTERFET.

DPKO had begun contingency planning for a peacekeeping force should it be required in East Timor, but such a force could not be assembled and deployed in the short time required. The answer lay with the formation of a "coalition of the willing" of concerned nations that could be authorized by the United Nations to act quickly and decisively. Discussions among the core group at the United Nations quickly formulated preconditions for deploying this force. There was general agreement that the force required legitimacy in the form of a Security

Council mandate; that its deployment should be short-term until re-lieved by UN peacekeepers; that the force should stabilize the situation to enable a UN transitional administration to get established; that it should have a strong regional component; and that its deployment should be contingent on Indonesian consent.[52]

Intensive diplomatic activity was already under way. On Septem-ber 6, Kofi Annan asked for and received Australia's agreement to lead INTERFET, subject to Indonesia's consent. Keeping in contact with his counterparts in the United States, Portugal, Thailand, New Zealand, and Singapore, the Australian prime minister led an intensive diplo-matic effort, along with the secretary-general, to bring together a coali-tion of willing nations. A range of world leaders joined him in speaking continually with President Habibie and stressing the consequences for Indonesia's international standing should the country continue not to meet its obligations. Senior Australian military officers also worked with their international counterparts to confirm force contributions.[53]

A crucial element in Australia's planning was the attitude and support of the United States and the Association of Southeast Asian Nations (ASEAN) countries in ensuring the success of the operation, while at the same time recognizing and respecting Indonesia's posi-tion as the former governing power in East Timor as well as the major ASEAN power. Initially, the United States was undecided on how sub-stantially it should become involved in the East Timor crisis. This stance changed with the postballot violence. After discussions with Australian diplomats in Washington and video conferences between Washington and Canberra, the United States gave its support for an Australian-led force but indicated that the American contribution would be limited to specialist and logistic support capabilities, rather than ground troops. There can be little doubt, however, that the formation of the coalition was largely assisted by U.S. diplomatic support. More importantly, the Clinton administration (and the IMF) brought pressure to bear on the Indonesian government. When Indonesia remained obdurate, presi-dential demands were made for the admission of peacekeepers, further warnings were given of economic sanctions, and Pentagon contacts with TNI and arms sales were suspended.

Indonesia still did not acquiesce and so the Asia-Pacific Economic Cooperation (APEC) summit meeting, held in New Zealand from

September 10 to 13, came at an opportune time. Neither Habibie nor his foreign minister, Ali Alatas, attended, but the gathering provided an opportunity for APEC leaders to press the Indonesian representatives in attendance, particularly Habibie's senior economic minister, even warning of implications for Indonesia's future access to international financing. The meeting, which included four of the five permanent members of the Security Council, also afforded an opportunity to advance a coordinated response to the crisis.[54] In Jakarta, Habibie finally bowed to these pressures. On the evening of September 12, the Indonesian president informed the secretary-general that Indonesia would accept a multinational force.

Mandate

The UN Security Council now acted decisively. Stating its deep concern at "the deterioration in the security situation" and "the worsening humanitarian situation," it authorized a peace enforcement force in the early hours of September 15, through the unanimous adoption of Resolution 1264.[55] The mandate, under Chapter VII of the UN Charter, tasked INTERFET "to restore peace and security in East Timor, to protect and support UNAMET in carrying out its tasks and, within force capabilities, to facilitate humanitarian assistance operations."[56] It was tasked to deal forcefully with the militias and other threats. Based on a worst-case threat assessment, the mandate unambiguously allowed for security to be restored and maintained using all necessary and legitimate force, including deadly force. This was one of the most strongly worded mandates ever given by the Security Council, exceeding the mandate for the establishment of the international force in Kosovo led by the North Atlantic Treaty Organization (NATO), which had preceded it in June.

Linking this mandate to the May 5 agreements, Resolution 1264 called on the government of Indonesia to take INTERFET's mandate into account and underlined Indonesia's "continuing responsibility" under those agreements "to maintain peace and security in East Timor." The mandate was equally clear that the force was to be an interim measure, "replaced as soon as possible by a United Nations peacekeeping operation." The secretary-general was also invited "to plan and prepare for a United Nations transitional administration," which would incorporate the peacekeeping operation.

Funding

The speed with which INTERFET needed to act demanded stream-
lined funding arrangements. The lead elements of INTERFET deployed
to East Timor on September 20—only five days after the mandate had
been authorized. By this time, commitments from most of the nations
that would eventually constitute the force had been secured by Australia. Members of such coalitions, however, normally meet their own
participation costs, thus making it hard to secure forces, especially from
developing countries. To overcome this, Resolution 1264 authorized
the secretary-general "to establish a trust fund through which contributions could be channeled to the States or operations concerned." This
UN INTERFET Trust Fund (UNITF) was managed by Australia, which
as lead nation was responsible for the verification and consolidation of
all expenses and claims.[57] Nonetheless, the self-funding made it difficult to give the force a strong regional component, as many defense
budgets had been severely restricted as a result of the 1997–98 Asian
economic crisis.

The success of this fund was assured by Japan's contribution of
$100 million to an overall fund of $106.3 million. Other contributors
were Portugal, Brunei, Luxembourg, and Switzerland.[58] The process
faltered a little initially, as potential force contributors from developing
nations required trust fund reimbursement guarantees before commitment, and fund contributors wanted to know who and what they were
funding before handing over any funds. In order to gain immediate regional force participation, particularly from Thailand and the Philippines, Australia provided advance payment for costs incurred, to be re-
imbursed when trust fund finances were accessible. These procedures
ultimately worked well, but highlighted the immediate financial burden placed upon Australia as "lead nation." The success of INTERFET
required the willingness and capacity of Australia to pay up front, in
the hope that its actions would later qualify for reimbursement. The
developed nations that participated paid their own costs, which for
Australia, contributing more than 50 percent of the force and other
personnel, was more than $370 million.

A number of factors eventually combined to reduce demands on
the trust fund. First, the initial forces to deploy in strength were mainly
from self-funded countries, and their rapid success reduced the need

for subsequent non-self-funded forces. Second, INTERFET received considerable in-kind assistance from the United States, which provided strategic airlift and other support to coalition members at no charge, funded under a presidential authorization of $55 million.[59] Finally, the United Nations considerably reduced its fees for administering the trust fund, and thus the overall costs of the operation.

Planning, Preparation, and Deployment

INTERFET's structure was based on preparatory planning by DPKO in the lead-up to the ballot. The May 5 agreements had required the orderly handover of security from Indonesia to the United Nations if voters rejected autonomy. DPKO had, therefore, already derived a force structure and commenced discussions with member states for possible contributions, and it readily shared preparatory planning with Australia when it assumed leadership of the force. This became the start-state for INTERFET's planning and was a logical arrangement, given that the mission would subsequently transition to UN control. The task of modifying these existing plans to fit the requirement for rapid deployment was then undertaken by Australian Defence Force planners, and was effectively completed by September 7.[60]

As lead nation, Australia's first priority was to ensure that INTERFET comprised highly capable combat forces, at least some of which were Asian troops, and was based on a structure that could be replaced as quickly as possible by the United Nations. By September 16, a coalition had been assembled based on military contributions from Britain, Brazil, Canada, France, Ireland, Italy, New Zealand, and the United States to bolster Australia's major contribution. A number of the ASEAN states, plus the Republic of Korea, Germany, Denmark, Norway, Jordan, Egypt, Kenya, and Fiji, subsequently joined this group, bringing the total number of countries involved to twenty-two.[61] Among ASEAN countries, the traditional reluctance to interfere in the internal affairs of a member state compounded a natural caution about alienating the organization's most powerful member.[62] In the end, four out of the nine ASEAN states contributed forces—Malaysia, Singapore, Thailand, and the Philippines—with Thailand's contribution of 1,600 being the largest among these countries.

Considerable political tension had developed between Indonesia and Australia over the latter's involvement in East Timor.[63] Importantly, however, both countries were keen from the outset to ensure that INTERFET's deployment would not lead to conflict with TNI forces still deployed in East Timor. Accordingly, their representatives conducted high-level military negotiations at the UN Secretariat in New York from September 14 to 16, to ensure that the respective national capitals and field commanders were in full agreement. These discussions agreed on reception arrangements for INTERFET's arrival in Dili and the consultation procedures to be used by the force commanders in East Timor, Major General Peter Cosgrove from Australia and Major General Kiki Syahnakri of Indonesia.

Command and Control

Australia's maintenance of ready deployable forces for a range of short-notice contingencies throughout the region made it a logical choice to lead the stabilization force. As commander of Australia's Deployable Joint Force Headquarters for such contingencies, Major General Cosgrove was the obvious choice to command the force. Cosgrove's own working headquarters provided the operational core of INTERFET, to which international elements were added. Because Thailand was a member of ASEAN and deployed the next largest force after Australia, Major General Songkitti Jaggabattara was appointed as the deputy force commander.

Resolution 1264 granted the lead nation autonomy in exercising and fulfilling the mandate without undue interference. In practice, Cosgrove reported directly to Canberra, while consulting with the UN staff on the ground in East Timor. (Australia also assigned a military liaison team to New York to provide information to the United Nations and help bolster the capacity of the military attaché at its permanent mission.)[64] Throughout its deployment, INTERFET established and maintained close relations with UNAMET and the East Timorese leaders, and subsequently with UNTAET.

Within the coalition, the effective management of such a disparate group of nationalities with varying degrees of experience and capabilities was potentially a difficult task. The mandate required INTERFET to be immediately operational. Loyalty and support from all contingents was essential to fulfill the mission's objectives; to secure it, General Cosgrove respected the conditions imposed by each of the coalition partners, deploying each contingent to a location best suited to its capabilities, under command and control arrangements with which its government was comfortable.[65] With the buildup of forces and the maturing of the operation, Cosgrove reduced his span of operational control by appointing sector commanders for Dili and in the western border area. In the more peaceful central and eastern districts, however, Cosgrove retained centralized control of each of the national contingent commanders.

INTERFET's tough Chapter VII mandate made it easier for countries to agree on robust rules of engagement that enabled the force to be assertive in restoring security and nullifying militia elements. These rules, and their accompanying "orders for opening fire" and powers of detention, were consistent with international humanitarian law and the laws of armed conflict. There were some differences in interpretation (such as the unwillingness of some contingents to open fire when protecting property rather than people), but they were minor and not abnormal in coalition operations.

Cosgrove realized that cooperation with TNI was always going to be a determining factor on the speed and effectiveness of the INTERFET operation. Under instructions from their national governments, Cosgrove and Syahnakri worked to maintain professional military relations in a volatile situation. Until the final withdrawal of TNI forces on November 1, they maintained a joint committee to review operations. INTERFET shared high-level operational information with TNI, and strived to prevent inadvertent conflict between the two forces. Alan Ryan contends that in addition to the "reputation and obvious determination of the INTERFET forces," the preservation of good relations with TNI can be ascribed in part to the preexisting relationship between the Australian and Indonesian militaries, and to critical U.S. support in persuading TNI that East Timor was a lost cause.[66] The professional relationship between the two commanders proved its worth when Syahnakri was reassigned to command forces that included those in West Timor. On January 12, 2000, the commanders signed a memorandum of technical understanding aimed at maintaining peace and avoiding conflict between the TNI and INTERFET forces along the border.

Civil-military cooperation (CIMIC) is a critical factor in complex humanitarian interventions and peace enforcement operations, but initial arrangements for East Timor were weak.[67] There had been no joint preplanning between the UN Office for the Coordination of Humanitarian Affairs and Australia's Defence Headquarters. This lack of pre-mission coordination resulted in the establishment in Dili of both a UN Humanitarian Operations Centre (UNHOC) and an INTERFET Civil-Military Operations Center (CMOC). The UN humanitarian coordinator, Ross Mountain, had sought to forge better arrangements in Darwin before deployment, but these did not materialize until ten days after coalition operations commenced. Mountain had, meanwhile, drawn up a plan for humanitarian support that did not accord with either the geographic boundaries of the coalition force or with Cosgrove's priorities and therefore required adjustment.

Mountain and Cosgrove established excellent working relations, but the lack of pre-mission planning could have caused serious difficulties, particularly given the large number of humanitarian agencies and nongovernmental organizations (NGOs) operating within the country. Two key agencies were the World Food Programme (WFP) and the United Nations High Commissioner for Refugees (UNHCR), the former with major responsibility for food distribution and the latter in charge of the repatriation of more than 500,000 displaced people. The security implications of both sets of tasks required close collaboration with INTERFET. WFP required airspace clearance and landing rights to conduct operations, as well as to confirm requirements for convoy and warehouse protection and to set up secure areas where the organization could operate. UNHCR was particularly concerned with the potential mass return of refugees from West Timor. Although joint planning eventually proved successful, the overall experience was a sobering reminder of the lack of understanding by all concerned of the importance of CIMIC in pre-mission planning.

Overall, there was a lack of experience in CIMIC within INTERFET. Few of the contributing nations had CIMIC doctrine or appropriate capabilities embedded in their force structures. The relationship between UNHOC and the CMOC improved over time, with the agreement of common principles and the augmentation of the CMOC with a U.S. Army civil affairs detachment. Security situation permitting, Cosgrove was keen to give the humanitarian organizations as much latitude and independence as possible, wishing neither to overstretch INTERFET resources nor to create dependencies that could not be sustained after it departed. In any event, INTERFET's presence and the withdrawal of the militias enabled humanitarian operations to proceed without undue military interference, although some NGOs criticized the slowness with which they had been allowed to return to the Oecusse enclave, on the northern coast of West Timor.

Field Operations—Implementation

INTERFET commenced its deployment to Dili on September 20—only five days after passage of the UN mandate. Although coalition forces did not come under direct attack, the environment was far from permissive. In the initial days of operations, three journalists and eight nuns and religious workers were murdered by rampaging militia and TNI forces. The casualties included the Dutch journalist Sander Thoenes, killed in Dili on September 22. The nuns and religious workers were killed near Los Palos on September 25.[68]

Tension remained high in the first month as INTERFET established its presence. By the end of September, the force headquarters was fully operational in Dili, and more than 4,000 troops had been deployed. At TNI's final departure on November 1, a force of more than 8,200 operated throughout the country (including the Oecusse enclave). The coalition continued to strengthen, and at its zenith numbered almost 10,000 troops, with Australia providing around 5,400.[69]

General Cosgrove's strategy was to methodically and progressively restore security in all districts, using a step-by-step approach commensurate with force buildup.[70] Some criticized this approach as overly cautious, charging that it allowed the militia to withdraw unhindered to safe havens in West Timor. With the limited forces available, however, to have moved more quickly would have involved considerable risk not only to force safety but to the coherence of the still nascent coalition.[71] The coalition also assumed de facto responsibility for governance and the rule of law until the United Nations' administrative presence could be effectively established.

The speed with which INTERFET restored security, and the small number of casualties incurred, belied the dangerous situation on the ground.[72] Militia gangs, estimated to number around 10,000 and armed with homemade weapons and small arms, continued to wage their violent campaign until contested by coalition forces. Although militia leaders proclaimed their determination to thwart the multinational force, resistance quickly evaporated. Cosgrove insisted that a high tempo of coalition operations be maintained, particularly in the border region, thereby reassuring the civilian population while demonstrating to the militias that they were dealing with a well-trained, disciplined, and well-equipped international force rather than defenseless civilians.

INTERFET's first priority was to secure Dili, which was accomplished quickly in the face of sporadic shooting, arson, and looting. Vital installations such as the hospital, electricity station, and water supply facilities, as well as refugee centers, were secured. Following the successful occupation of Dili and the initial restoration of security in the capital, coalition forces progressively deployed to each of the districts in turn, with similar success. As INTERFET extended its presence, it found the towns and villages deserted and destroyed, with much of the population hiding in the countryside. By reoccupying the major nodes and patrolling aggressively, INTERFET reassured the people of East Timor, who gradually returned to start rebuilding their lives.

Cosgrove moved quickly to secure the border and thereby prevent major cross-border militia incursions from sanctuaries in West Timor. This strategy proved successful, resulting in only sporadic hit-and-run missions by militias, and enabling INTERFET and TNI commanders to exchange information at the border. The Oecusse enclave was the final district to be occupied, on October 22, 1999, after which INTERFET could claim to have achieved its mandate to restore security, although sporadic incidents involving the militias continued for some time in the western districts and in Oecusse. The last significant security incident took place on the border on October 16.[73]

With the security situation well under control by early November, INTERFET operations focused on supporting the establishment and activities of UNTAET and preparing for the transition to its peacekeeping force. Although combat patrolling continued, constabulary tasks became more common throughout the area of operations, with INTERFET engaged in national reconstruction, governance and administration, policing and law and order, and investigations into possible crimes against humanity.

In addition to the professionalism, discipline, and restraint exhibited by the INTERFET forces themselves and the cooperation of TNI, other factors contributing to success were the effective separation of the militias and Falintil as well as speedy logistical support. The effectiveness of relations between the TNI and the multinational force has already been discussed. In peace enforcement operations, success or failure often rests on effectively disarming and separating combatants. The main military threat in East Timor came from the two opposing sides at the time of the ballot: the pro-integration militias (created and supported by the TNI) and the Falintil fighters, with their twenty-four-year history of resistance. The coalition force's task of separating the combatants was made simple because Falintil had voluntarily cantoned prior to the ballot, and the militia had withdrawn to refugee camps in West Timor. Compared with many postconflict situations, the desired separation was quickly achieved and maintained, reducing the possibility of renewed conflict. Moreover, neither group possessed heavy weapons, nor were there any landmines to contend with. An invaluable factor in alleviating the burden on INTERFET was Falintil's disengagement from the postballot violence and its general cooperation with the multinational force.[74]

The isolation and harsh operating environment demanded that high priority be given to logistics. At the tactical level, the rapid deployment of air and maritime assets to East Timor was largely responsible for the speed and success of INTERFET's operations. Once fully established, INTERFET progressively replaced military support capabilities with civil contracts in preparation for the transition to UNTAET.

Just as important as removing the militia threat was INTERFET's restoration of public confidence and a sense of safety and security, particularly in the outlying areas. This was particularly important given that the violence following the ballot had dislocated roughly 70 percent of the population, proportionately higher than in most other postconflict situations.[75] As noted, UNHCR took the lead in repatriation, assisted by IOM and in close coordination with INTERFET. To help restore public confidence, particularly near the border, Cosgrove instructed his forces to maintain a visible and active presence while respecting the local population. As the people's trust in the multinational force grew, so did their willingness to return to their villages and commence rebuilding.

Important elements of CIMIC in complex peace operations include the contributions of military forces to reestablish and ensure the rule of law, particularly in the areas of policing, detention, collection of forensic evidence, and judicial affairs. Under instructions from Canberra, INTERFET took a minimalist role in these areas, and Cosgrove resisted suggestions from international commentators that the multinational force could or should do more. INTERFET established a detention center and assisted in the collection of evidence, but Cosgrove made it clear that his force would not become involved in civil policing or judicial proceedings. Relations between INTERFET and the UN police component, as it became established, were cordial; but planning and coordination were underdeveloped, with INTERFET eager to hand over as many responsibilities as soon as possible. Given the forces assigned and the temporary nature of the mandate, Australia was reluctant for a multinational force under its command to have such responsibilities, and the Australian government was keen for such authority to transition to UNTAET. The incomplete nature of UNTAET's planning, however, made this transition less effective than was required in a postconflict environment, with the result that weaknesses in these areas continued to cause problems for the interim administration and, ultimately, the new nation.

Assessment of INTERFET

Overall, INTERFET was an outstanding success as a peace enforcement operation. Under good leadership, it was mounted quickly, with strong regional and international support. Security was restored at the cost of few lives (and with no battle fatalities among the multinational force) and with exceptional cooperation from the host community. A major contributing factor to this success was the level of international commitment, which secured a swift and strong UN mandate and enabled the multinational force to be assembled and deployed quickly. The mandate itself was feasible and achievable, and provided the force commander with the authority required to restore security.

The main lesson of INTERFET seems clear enough: if coalitions of the willing are to be successful in enforcing the peace in nonpermissive environments, they must have a capable lead nation and comprise forces with professional warfighting skills. The security environment in East Timor was more benign than in many other postconflict situations, but when the coalition arrived it was far from permissive. Although INTERFET was not confronted militarily by the Indonesian government or by large-scale militia forces, this outcome could not be assured at the time of deployment.

A second lesson is that successful intervention relies on the degree of host-nation support. INTERFET was welcomed and supported warmly by the vast majority of East Timorese. Despite the low incidence of combat, the force conducted operations at high tempo to reassure the people of their safety, while abiding by international humanitarian law. Importantly, the speedy restoration of security by INTERFET resulted in large numbers of displaced people being able to resettle and commence rebuilding their shattered lives. INTERFET's presence provided security and gave confidence to the people, demonstrating that the visible presence of a professional military force can greatly assist in the rebuilding of civil society. (The return from West Timor of "hard-core" militia leaders and their supporters, on the other hand, was a more difficult task that became a major undertaking for UNTAET.)

A third and obvious lesson is that peace enforcement operations are costly, because they need to be mounted quickly and robustly. They require a sound funding base. In the case of INTERFET, Japan's pledge of $100 million to the operation's trust fund was invaluable, and encouraged Australia's willingness to accept the financial risk that reimbursement for its expenditure would have to be justified later against the conditions of the fund.

Fourth, although INTERFET demonstrated the value of prompt and effective peace enforcement, it also revealed several difficulties that can confront coalitions of the willing in restoring the rule of law. Such forces have to work efficiently with civilian agencies, often fulfilling a quasi-political role and assuming the responsibilities of governance until a civil administration can be reestablished. INTERFET successfully implemented border relations with the TNI but came under criticism for its lack of experience in CIMIC and its reluctance to engage in policing, correctional, and judicial tasks. INTERFET's experience suggests that good CIMIC capabilities can be as important to the mission as good warfighting skills—a major lesson for most of the coalition partners. To its credit, the force redressed many of its CIMIC shortcomings, particularly those related to humanitarian response. It remained intent, however, on a minimalist role in the application of the rule of law.

Despite this reluctance, a major lesson from East Timor (and other postconflict environments) is that military forces may have little option but to engage in this area, as it takes time to raise and deploy civilian personnel and assets capable of implementing the rule of law. To this end, military police units, civil affairs teams, and military judicial staff are likely to be required in greater numbers, both early in a mission and for longer time periods during transition than might be preferred by contributing nations. Not to provide for this contingency is to jeopardize the establishment and effectiveness of the rule of law, and place at risk the process of democratization.

Such issues notwithstanding, INTERFET was a very successful peace enforcement operation that provided a sound base for the transitional administration that succeeded it.

The UN Transitional Administration in East Timor

The Security Council authorized the establishment of UNTAET on October 25, 1999, under Resolution 1272.[76] UNTAET was far more than a peacekeeping or electoral mission and, in the history of the United Nations, represented the high-water mark in the application of the United Nations' authority. UNTAET's responsibilities surpassed those of all previous UN missions, including those for which the United Nations had gained experience in transitional and administrative duties in such places as Namibia, Cambodia, Eastern Slavonia, and Kosovo.[77] This reflected the specific circumstances peculiar to the history of East Timor following Indonesia's occupation in 1975 and the willingness of the international community to assign the United Nations leadership on this matter. These circumstances are rare in international politics, and the extent of the United Nations' responsibilities in East Timor should not be considered the norm for future peace operations.

This section of the chapter highlights the major developments during UNTAET's interregnum, concentrating on the security issues that underpinned its work—involving the military, the police, and the application of the rule of law. UNTAET's performance in other areas is mentioned only briefly because it has been examined more fully in other documents.[78]

Mandate

The secretary-general appointed Sergio Vieira de Mello of Brazil as SRSG and transitional administrator. As administrator, he had significant powers. UNTAET's mandate, under Chapter VII of the UN Charter, gave it "overall responsibility for the administration of East Timor" and authorized it "to exercise all legislative and executive authority, including the administration of justice," "to take all necessary measures to fulfil[l] its mandate," and "to perform its duties in close consultation and cooperation with the people of East Timor."[79] UNTAET was to provide security and maintain law and order; establish an effective administration; assist in the development of civil and social services; ensure the coordination and delivery of humanitarian and development assistance; support capacity building for self-government; and assist in the establishment of conditions for sustainable development. Table 6.1 lists the fourteen mission objectives specified in the secretary-general's report of October 4, 1999, which were endorsed by the Security Council in Resolution 1272.[80]

Funding

UNTAET was an expensive mission, with UN assessed contributions averaging more than $500 million per year. At independence, the assessed budget for UNTAET totaled around $1.28 billion, which represented "roughly 70 percent of total international funding to support East Timor during the transition."[81] Funding for UNTAET exceeded UN outlays for Sierra Leone and Kosovo, the next most expensive missions in the first years of the new millennium.[82] This cost per capita was particularly high, but the remoteness of East Timor, its harsh terrain,

Table 6.1. UNTAET's Fourteen Principal Mission Objectives

1. Assist and protect East Timorese displaced or otherwise affected by the conflict.

2. Facilitate emergency rehabilitation and reconstruction of services and infrastructure.

3. Administer the territory of East Timor and create the basis for good governance.

4. Develop mechanisms for dialogue at the national and local levels.

5. Assist the East Timorese in the development of a constitution.

6. Organize and conduct elections, and build the institutional capacity for electoral processes.

7. Undertake confidence-building measures and provide support to indigenous processes of reconciliation.

8. Create nondiscriminatory and impartial institutions, particularly those of judiciary and police, to ensure the establishment and maintenance of the rule of law and to promote and protect human rights.

9. Promote economic and social recovery and development, including in the fields of education and health.

10. Coordinate assistance to East Timor.

11. Develop administrative institutions that are accountable, transparent, and efficient.

12. Facilitate the strengthening and development of civil society, including the media.

13. Ensure that the development of any indigenous structures for security conform to the standards of civilian oversight, democratic accountability, and international human rights norms and standards.

14. Create conditions of stability through the maintenance of peace and security, including through programs for disarmament, demobilization, and reintegration, as may be necessary.

Sources: United Nations, *The United Nations Transitional Administration in East Timor, Report of the Secretary-General,* part IV, S/1999/1024, October 4, 1999, para. 29; and UN Security Council, Resolution 1272, S/RES/1272, October 22, 1999, paras. 1–2.

and its lack of infrastructure (made worse by the systematic destruction that followed the ballot) all drove up operating costs.

In addition to the assessed budget, the World Bank has calculated that reconstruction and development funding for East Timor, $209 per person, was the third highest in per capita terms of nine recent conflicts, exceeded only by Bosnia ($247) and the Palestinian Territories ($213).[83] Moreover, this assistance was provided from a wider section of the international community.

Funding arrangements for UN missions are often complicated, and East Timor proved no exception. In addition to the normal assessed contributions for UN peacekeeping operations, there were voluntary contributions intended to fund the new Timorese government, distributed through the United Nations' Consolidated Fund for East Timor, various UN agency reconstruction programs, and a trust fund for redevelopment purposes that was managed by the World Bank. As well, a number of countries provided bilateral donations for rehabilitation and development projects.

The existence of numerous funding streams for East Timor should not be taken to imply flexibility in expenditure procedures. As one analyst noted:

> In East Timor, despite the repeated assertions that this was a unique operation, the mission was subject to the same budgetary procedures as other peacekeeping operations—meaning a strict division between funds that could be used to support the peacekeeping mission and funds that could be used for humanitarian and development assistance. This might be reasonable in a country where the UN operation sits parallel to an existing government, but when the UN *was* the government it led to absurdity.[84]

The transitional administrator's ability to access and use these funds in the most efficient manner was constrained by poor planning in the Secretariat, and by UN fiduciary procedures that had been developed for more traditional peacekeeping missions. Although UNTAET had been authorized "to take all necessary measures to fulfil[l] its mandate," the adherence to extant UN financial regulations constrained Vieira de Mello's ability to allocate funds in a timely manner, eliciting criticism from the East Timorese and international observers. These financial constraints not only made it difficult for UNTAET to fulfill its mandate efficiently but also "created barriers to national ownership of the reconstruction planning process in the initial period, and prevented the integration of all funding sources into the national budget."[85]

Constraints on expenditures also impeded the efficient use of military assets and the prosecution of military operations. UN military engineers, for example, were underutilized because many potential reconstruction tasks could not be funded under the assessed budget, and the engineers were not allocated alternative funding. The inflexibility in UN funding caused other ridiculous situations; for example, "$27 million was spent annually on bottled water for the international staff," a sum equivalent to half the budget of the embryonic Timorese government, and which alternatively might have paid for water purification plants to serve both international staff and locals well beyond the life of the mission.[86]

Planning, Preparation, and Deployment

In the interval between the signing of the May 5 agreements—which confirmed a UN presence in East Timor regardless of the ballot outcome—and the mandate to establish UNTAET, relatively little planning was undertaken by the Secretariat for the establishment of a civil administration. This lack of planning proved a major weakness to UNTAET operations: first, causing the mission to have a slow start-up, with key personnel not arriving for some time, and second, necessitating fundamental changes in the mission's structure within its first year of operations.

Responsibility for the planning of UNAMET had rested with a small professional staff within DPA, supported by DPKO and other elements within the Secretariat. But despite the secretary-general's repeated concerns about security in the lead-up to the ballot, no worst-case planning was undertaken that anticipated a total breakdown of order. The overworked and underresourced staff in DPA had not wanted to preempt the ballot outcome and had assumed that after the ballot, a Phase II period of several months would enable such planning to be undertaken.[87] When a total breakdown in governance and security did occur following the ballot, the Secretariat's efforts were directed to authorizing the multinational force and reporting on the fluid situation within the ravaged territory.

Of more importance, however, was the internal division between DPA and DPKO as to which department would have prime responsibility for UNTAET—a demarcation dispute that was not resolved by the secretary-general in DPKO's favor until mid-September.[88] DPKO then hurriedly prepared its plan for the transitional administration, appointing a special project officer to coordinate within the Secretariat (and with the core group of countries) to devise UNTAET's structure and responsibilities. Given the lack of prior planning and the incredibly short time frame, the outcome was a remarkable achievement, but the planning suffered from several major weaknesses. Primary was the lack of close consultation with the East Timorese leaders who had indicated their desire to be involved and had then commented on the secretary-general's report of October 4 (most prominently represented by the CNRT). Another major stakeholder not closely consulted was the World Bank, which had been involved in social and economic planning for East Timor since early 1999.

The mandate authorized three components for the mission, all of which were to report to the SRSG: Governance and Public Administration (GPA), Humanitarian Assistance and Emergency Rehabilitation (HAER), and the military force. The lack of planning, however, meant that the SRSG and the key component heads had not been preselected. Although the secretary-general moved quickly to appoint the SRSG once the need for the mission was confirmed, there was insufficient time for the leadership team to be assembled and to conduct joint reconnaissance and planning. In fact, most component heads were not appointed until well after Resolution 1272; none of them could claim previous experience with East Timor or a full understanding of the complex circumstances in which they would find themselves; and they were given little opportunity to shape the structure and responsibilities of their own components. Generally speaking, component heads arrived in country ill-prepared and understaffed.[89]

Given its mandate, the United Nations' planning needed to reflect UNTAET's role as a de jure transitional government; instead, its structure more resembled a mixture of traditional peacekeeping and peacebuilding components. Emphasis was given to structure and staff tables rather than an explanation of the phases and processes required to steer East Timor to sustainable independence. As a result, the responsibilities and reporting lines of the legal, human rights, and public information offices; the judicial and detention services; and the district administrators were unclear. Of major concern was the lack of clarity as to how the administration would team with and develop the Timorese for independence (sometimes referred to as "Timorization"). Other critical aspects of government, such as customs, were not included in the administration at all, and no consideration was given to the future of the cantoned and armed Falintil resistance fighters. At best, the planning and preparation by the Secretariat provided a starting point for the mission, but many of the problems that were to beset UNTAET could have been minimized had more thorough and coordinated contingency planning occurred following the May 5 agreements.

Another major weakness in planning was the uncertainty of the legal basis under which UNTAET would operate. A decision to implement Indonesian law (except where it was in breach of international law) seemed logical given UNTAET's role as a caretaker administration. But this decision failed to recognize the practical implications, particularly within a mission that had limited experience in administering this law and that had not been preassigned any legal packages. The lack of a preexisting "legal tool kit" for UNTAET was also replicated in other areas. Although the application of the rule of law was seen as a major issue, no planning had been undertaken regarding how it could be effectively implemented. INTERFET had successfully enforced security, but it had refused to resolve judicial issues. Miscreants and criminals had been held under detention and evidence retained, but it was left to UNTAET to resolve these issues, and to do so without prior preparation and planning. Much of the criticism of UNTAET in relation to the ineffective judicial and detention system traces its origins to inadequate contingency planning.

DPKO also failed to plan and prepare an effective UN police component. In postconflict environments, police are essential for the maintenance of internal security. In East Timor, UN police were also responsible for the development of a local police force. DPKO failed to prepare a proper concept for police operations, and to indicate how UN police would cooperate with other components of the mission. In particular, the initial failure to integrate civil-military constabulary responsibilities with INTERFET made it more difficult for UN police to work closely with the UNTAET military component following INTERFET's withdrawal. Many of the police component's problems in East Timor, and much of the criticism it received, can be directly attributed to the lack of planning by DPKO, caused in itself by inadequate police resources within the Secretariat at that time.

In contrast to the inchoate planning conducted by the Secretariat for the civil administration, serious consideration was given to the requirements for the military component. Within DPKO, in the lead-up to the ballot, worst-case contingency planning was undertaken by the military adviser and his small Military Planning Staff (MPS) for a possible peacekeeping force following the ballot. Recognizing the MPS's severe lack of resources—caused mainly by the forced withdrawal of gratis officers from developed countries, and the military adviser's consequent overload in servicing a number of other important missions[90]—Australia provided assistance to the MPS to determine the structure and operational requirements for a military force to replace TNI in accordance with one of the options in the May 5 agreements. Had such planning been replicated for the civil administration, UNTAET would very likely have been better prepared for its challenging mission.

This military contingency planning, on which INTERFET was subsequently based, was then augmented by the deployment to New York of a small military team from Australia to assist the DPKO with the transition planning from INTERFET to UNTAET. Options for transition were developed, rules of engagement drafted, and the force structure and logistic arrangements confirmed. Key to this planning was the "transition in place" of 70 percent of the force and the coordinated deployment of the remaining troops. Much of this planning was based on the lessons learned from the United Nations' successful transition in Haiti in March 1995. Following the initial planning in New York, these Australian officers were deployed to Dili as the advance party of the military component of UNTAET, providing advice to the SRSG, maintaining liaison with INTERFET, and preparing for the handover.

A major weakness in military planning, however, resulted from the secretary-general's delay in appointing the force commander, who ultimately was not confirmed until December 30, 1999. The need to appoint a force commander as soon as possible had been a consistent lesson from previous UN missions, and had been applied successfully in Haiti. This seemed even more relevant for UNTAET given that INTERFET's mandate clearly stipulated its early replacement by UNTAET.

In the absence of a force commander, planning by the military adviser was incomplete, but due to time constraints the MPS was forced to make decisions over which the force commander could have little influence. The force commander (and other component heads) should have been appointed with the SRSG. He should have deployed to Dili to conduct reconnaissance, advise the SRSG, determine the concept of operations and rules of engagement, and generally work with the military adviser to confirm force composition and the transition arrangements from INTERFET. In reality, the force commander had only enough time to conduct brief liaison visits to New York and Dili before assuming his appointment on January 25, 2000, one week before the handover from INTERFET commenced. His influence in the planning process was minimal and, unlike the situation in Haiti, the United Nations became the receiver (rather than the architect) of a transition plan (in this case, one designed by INTERFET). Although the handover generally worked well, most of the problems encountered could be traced to the force commander's absence from the planning process.

Command and Control

The three components of the UNTAET mission all reported to Sergio Vieira de Mello, the SRSG (see figure 6.3). As its name implied, the Governance and Public Administration component was responsible for governing the country, reestablishing the rule of law, and rebuilding civil society. Its head also served as deputy SRSG.

GPA's responsibility was enormous. The UN mandate provided for an unspecified number of civil administrators and technical advisers as well as up to 1,640 police officers. What was lacking, however, was a detailed concept of how GPA decisions and priorities would be implemented with the support of the East Timorese. Noteworthy, also, was the subordination of the police commissioner to the deputy SRSG, and the police commissioner's absence from most high-level meetings.

Figure 6.3. Early Organization of UNTAET

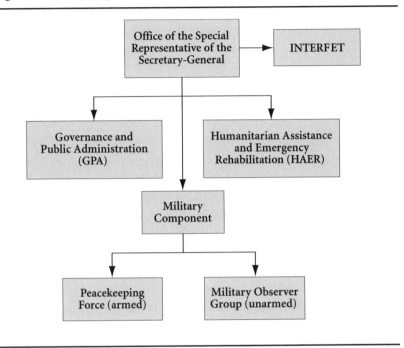

Given the fundamental importance of security, it would have been better to have elevated the stature of the police component by placing the police commissioner at the same level as the force commander, and insisting on joint planning for the maintenance of security.

The initial structure and responsibilities of GPA highlighted a fundamental problem in the mission, namely, a failure in many instances to distinguish functions that were components of peacekeeping from functions that were components of public administration and nation building. For example, the maintenance of internal security by UN police was a quintessential peacekeeping function pending the development of an indigenous police force that reported to a national executive government. As with most areas for which the GPA was responsible, the process for transition from UN police to local police authority was unclear, as were the reporting mechanisms and responsibilities to support this transition.

The mission's structure also provided for offices of political affairs, legal affairs, public information, human rights, and gender affairs, and for the appointment of district administrators, all posts filled by international staff and nominally attached to the office of the SRSG. For these elements, however, it was not always apparent to an observer whether decisions came from that office or from the GPA. Moreover, as with the three major mission components, the responsibilities and reporting arrangements for these elements lacked precision in distinguishing between internal mission requirements and tasks needed to prepare the new country for independence.

The second component, Humanitarian Assistance and Emergency Rehabilitation, was designed as a temporary measure to coordinate emergency relief and replace UNHOC, which had worked with INTERFET. Its staffing was not specified in the mandate. In the early days of UNTAET, when INTERFET still provided security, HAER was often the first UN element to establish contact with the people, and initial breakdowns in food distribution undermined public confidence in UNTAET.[91] HAER was dismantled in late 2000, long after the emergency phase had ended.

The third and largest component, and by far the most expensive, was the military force, mandated for up to 8,950 troops and up to 200 military observers.[92] Commanded by a three-star general, the force hovered at about 8,000 during 2000–2001, decreasing to around 5,000 at independence in May 2002 (see table 6.2).[93] Comprising more than thirty nations, with the main combat forces coming from eleven countries,[94] the military force continued the good work started by INTERFET and was generally judged by observers and the East Timorese as the most successful component of the mission.

Although UNTAET's structure was reasonably clear, it lacked a strategic plan to prepare the nation for independence. An attempt in early 2000 to match the mission structure to the fourteen objectives specified in the secretary-general's report of October 4 was stillborn, and for many months the mission lurched without clear long-term direction, preoccupied with the day-to-day problems of survival. The SRSG held daily meetings with component (and some office) heads, but these focused on immediate crises that were more fitting to an emergency relief mission than a transitional administration. Within his own office, the SRSG had difficulty managing the tasks and personalities of some of his senior staff, "which did little to advance mission harmony."[95]

During its first four months, UNTAET coexisted with INTERFET. Vieira de Mello and Cosgrove remained in close contact and established excellent personal relations, reporting on separate chains of command to New York and Canberra. While this arrangement worked well, INTERFET was an interim force not responsible to the transitional administration. A major adjustment occurred when UNTAET's peacekeepers replaced INTERFET, and military planning could be integrated within overall mission planning. By this time, however, the other UN elements (and particularly UN police) were already being established and showed little understanding of the need to coordinate civil-military affairs.

There were other uncertainties in command and control arrangements. Most significant was the lack of understanding as to how UNTAET was to work with the East Timorese to prepare them for independence. The prevalent view among the staff, who were predominantly non-Timorese, was that UNTAET would maintain security and govern the country until elections could be conducted in two or three years. In the absence of clear directives, mission staff generally expected that the East Timorese would mainly fill minor positions until after the elections—a type of neocolonialist arrangement. It was clear that UNTAET would have to prepare the way for a viable East Timor government, a proper judiciary, a small and efficient civil administration, and a professional police force. Less certain was how this could be achieved in consultation with the host population; how human rights could be interlaced into the process; how the rise of corruption and chronic unemployment could be prevented; how the destroyed infrastructure would be redeveloped; and how elections would be conducted. It was understood that UNTAET would maintain security against external threats, but less clear was the relationship it would have with Falintil and TNI, and how the security vacuum would be filled once the operation departed. In summary, there was no clear understanding of an "end state" and the benchmarks required to achieve the secretary-general's fourteen objectives.

These uncertainties within UNTAET, and with the East Timorese, were matched by loose coordination on reconstruction and

Table 6.2. UNTAET and UNMISET Troop and Police Contributions

Country	January 2001		February 2004	
	Troops and Observers	Civilian Police	Troops and Observers	Civilian Police
Argentina	—	5	—	1
Australia	1,600	102	316	21
Austria	—	10	—	—
Bangladesh	551	45	39	9
Bolivia	2	—	2	—
Bosnia and Herzegovina	—	12	—	5
Brazil	83	10	70	5
Canada	3	20	—	7
Cape Verde	—	2	—	—
Chile	32	—	—	—
China	—	55	—	16
Denmark	4	—	2	—
Egypt	75	15	—	—
Fiji	191	—	180	—
France	3	—	—	—
Ghana	—	86	—	5
Ireland	44	—	1	—
Japan	—	—	377	—
Jordan	723	222[a]	4	—
Kenya	264	26	2	—
Korea, Rep. of	440	—	3	—
Malaysia	35	41	16	140
Mozambique	12	3	2	—
Nepal	162	47	7	3
New Zealand	682	27	7	—
Niger	—	—	1	—
Nigeria	—	51	—	—

Table 6.2. *(cont.)*

Country	January 2001		February 2004	
	Troops and Observers	Civilian Police	Troops and Observers	Civilian Police
Norway	6	2	—	2
Pakistan	788	7	77	9
Peru	23	—	—	—
Philippines	640	105	48	16
Portugal	768	165a	522	20
Russia	2	4	2	1
Samoa	—	—	4	—
Senegal	—	25	—	—
Serbia and Montenegro	—	—	2	—
Singapore	24	40	3	—
Slovenia	—	2	—	—
Spain	—	18	—	5
Sri Lanka	—	29	—	6
Sweden	2	10	2	1
Thailand	714	37	57	8
Turkey	2	18	1	1
Ukraine	—	8	—	3
United Kingdom	4	15	—	4
United States	2	80	—	18
Uruguay	5	—	2	—
Vanuatu	—	24	—	—
Zambia	—	5	—	3
Zimbabwe	—	20	—	5
Total	7,886	1,393	1,744	319

[a]Included in totals are police rapid-response units of 120 officers each.

Sources: United Nations, *Report of the Secretary-General on the United Nations Transitional Administration in East Timor (for the period 27 July 2000 to 16 January 2001),* S/2001/42, January 16, 2001, 8; and *Special Report of the Secretary-General on the United Nations Mission of Support in East Timor,* S/2004/117, February 13, 2004, 19–21.

development priorities between the mission, the UN Development Programme, the World Bank group, and bilateral donors. The World Bank had insisted on a joint assessment mission, which was conducted in late October and early November 1999, but "there was a lack of continuity and ownership of some recommendations . . . especially those relating to the civil service and judiciary. Better continuity planning could have avoided this."[96] In the absence of an East Timor government, the World Bank was required to work closely with UNTAET to ascertain priorities and prepare for donor meetings every six months, but it took most of the first year before these arrangements started to work efficiently.

Within the military component, command and control arrangements sometimes reflected national priorities rather than the interests of the SRSG and force commander, illustrating the fact that in multinational forces, authority is ultimately retained by each of the national contingent commanders (see figure 6.4). This was vividly demonstrated during UNMISET, for example, when on December 4, 2002, a visiting Portuguese minister gave directions to the Portuguese battalion regarding their deployment during the rioting in Dili. A couple of months earlier, Canberra had unilaterally commanded the Australian battalion to deploy troops from the border to provide security to the Australian embassy.

The difficulty of command and control was most evident in the relationship between Canberra and UNTAET over the use of the Australian contingent—perhaps a legacy of Canberra's much closer direction of INTERFET during the period when the Australian forces were in the lead and there was no SRSG to contend with. The differences of opinion partly reflected Australia's continuing concern about its longer-term relationship with Indonesia, but these differences were compounded by a convoluted command and control system. During INTERFET, General Cosgrove had benefited from having direct access to defense headquarters in Canberra, but such access was not available to senior Australian commanders in UNTAET.

Australia provided the largest national contingent to UNTAET, including the critical positions of deputy force commander and commander of Sector West. Australian forces occupied the difficult border district of Bobonaro and provided essential logistic support to UNTAET.

Figure 6.4. UNTAET Peacekeeping Force Organization, December 2000

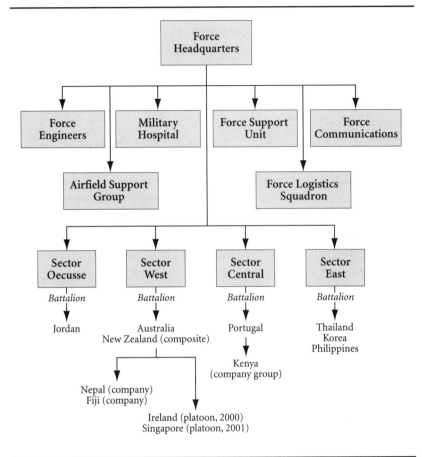

It was evident that without Australia's continued involvement the mission's success would be in jeopardy, but differences emerged between UNTAET and Australia regarding the conduct of operations. Key among these was Australia's refusal to allow the force commander to deploy Australian forces outside their tactical area of operations—even to reinforce other contingents subjected to militia attack, including their sister New Zealand battalion, which formed part of the same sector. This stance was particularly contentious given that Australia insisted that provision be made for its own battalion to be reinforced (with contingency plans made and rehearsals conducted) in the event of major militia infiltration in its area.

Another point of disagreement related to Australia's tight control of its Black Hawk helicopters, including the fact that they were not made available to evacuate UNHCR staff from Atambua following the terrible murders in September 2000. Less capable helicopters from another contingent were used instead, increasing the time and number of lifts required.

Yet another point of difference concerned the overt carriage of weapons by Australian troops in public places in Dili, at a time when a policy of demilitarization was being actively pursued by the SRSG to return the capital to normalcy. Such issues brought Australia's reputation with other troop contingents into question, causing some senior UNTAET commanders to doubt the country's willingness to be a team player. The SRSG's repeated requests that Australia review its policies on these matters received no response from Canberra.

These weaknesses in mission planning, structure, and command and control had a lasting impact on the conduct of field operations.

Field Operations—Implementation

On November 16, 1999, Sergio Vieira de Mello took office in Dili, inheriting a small number of experienced UNAMET personnel and what remained of its vehicles and equipment, much of which had been destroyed by the militias. Additional personnel and resources were slow to materialize, reflecting the lack of detailed planning by the Secretariat, compounded by the total devastation and the enormity of the reconstruction task.

It is not possible to cover all aspects of UNTAET's field operations in this chapter. Accordingly, priority is given to the political transition to independence, and the major security issues that accompanied that process.

Political Transition to Independence

UNTAET successfully managed East Timor's political transition to independence, but the process was far from smooth. On arrival in East Timor, the transitional administrator acted quickly to establish close personal relations with the East Timorese leadership, particularly the president of the CNRT, Xanana Gusmao. On December 2, 1999, a National Consultative Council (NCC) was established with representation from most political parties, the Catholic Church, and special-interest groups. Being unelected, the NCC had limited powers of review; real decision-making authority remained within UNTAET, and particularly within the offices of the SRSG and deputy SRSG, neither of which included senior East Timorese representation.

Within six months, however, it was evident that UNTAET had failed to satisfy the aspirations of the East Timorese and was attracting international criticism. Security had been maintained but militia infiltration from West Timor was increasing, coupled with heightened internal unrest and criminal activity. The pace of reconstruction in the two major centers of Dili and Baucau had been slower than expected, and there was little evidence of restoration in the rural areas beyond basic shelter and some NGO activities. District administrations were inadequately resourced, UN police were reluctant to establish police stations outside the main centers, and health and education services were far worse than under the Indonesians. The fragile road system had continued to deteriorate (partly due to heavy military traffic), thereby increasing the isolation of settlements in outlying areas. The reactivation of telephone services, radio and television, and power stations was slow. Unemployment rose steadily as the population of Dili grew beyond its preballot number and brought with it rising law and order problems. The Falintil resistance fighters remained under voluntary cantonment at Aileu but were increasingly restless, living in deplorable conditions with no certainty as to their future. Amid this unsatisfactory environment, the East Timorese people could see numerous UN four-wheel-drive vehicles and many well-paid international UN staff. Understandably, the euphoria that had greeted the United Nations' arrival abated, and criticism of UNTAET's performance began to grow.[97]

Aware of these problems and of the need for UNTAET and the East Timorese leadership to work more closely, Vieira de Mello progressively implemented changes to accelerate the handover of authority to the East Timorese. In July 2000, the GPA was totally remodeled and replaced by the East Timor Transitional Administration. A transitional cabinet of nine ministers, five of whom were East Timorese, reported to Vieira de Mello. The NCC was reformed and renamed the National

Council under the presidency of Gusmao. International district administrators were progressively replaced by East Timorese. Coordination
between UNTAET and the World Bank Group improved. An international and independent study by King's College London paved the way
for the transition of Falintil into a national defense force.[98]

Once the process of "Timorization" developed momentum, the
East Timorese leadership became worried that they might be handed the
reins of power without adequate preparation or continuing support,
and were keen for the United Nations to continue to have a major role
in a process stressing teamwork and cooperation. In June 2001, the
CNRT was formally disbanded in preparation for Constituent Assembly elections in August, which were conducted successfully under UN
control. Fretilin emerged as the most popular party, from which Mari
Alkatiri was appointed chief minister.

The assembly's principal function was the development of a constitution establishing the institutions and powers of government. This
task was completed in March 2002, facilitating the democratic election
of Xanana Gusmao as president in April. The powers of the president
were mainly ceremonial, except in matters of defense, for which he was
designated commander in chief of the defense forces. With the granting of independence on May 20, Mari Alkatiri became the first prime
minister, and Xanana Gusmao the first president, of the world's newest
nation and the poorest state in Southeast Asia.

The process of political transition had been far from perfect, characterized by mistakes and strained relations between UNTAET and the
East Timorese political factions. Nevertheless, UNTAET learned as it
went, and with the commitment and cooperation of the SRSG and
East Timorese leaders, the outcome was generally judged a success by
the United Nations and the international community.

The Military Component and External Security

The military transition from INTERFET to UNTAET was conducted
progressively during February 2000, with the official handover occurring on February 23.[99] For the East Timorese the transition appeared
seamless, but some risks and gaps appeared in force capability. The
incoming force headquarters was not assembled and rehearsed prior
to transition. Billets were slow to be filled, and the headquarters lacked

basic resources for many weeks. There were shortages in logistic support, engineer capacity, and combat aviation, all of which took some months to rectify. The force structure was similar to INTERFET, comprising seven maneuver battalions deployed throughout the thirteen districts, but with four sector commanders and a chief military observer. Sector East, commanded by a Thai senior colonel from the air base at Baucau, occupied the four eastern districts, with battalions from the Philippines (Manatuto), the Republic of Korea (Lautem), and Thailand (Baucau and Viqueque). Sector Central, commanded by a Portuguese colonel based in Dili, covered the six districts of Dili, Aileu (less the Falintil cantonment), Manufahi, Ainaro, Liquica, and Ermera. A Portuguese battalion was thinly stretched throughout this area, assisted by a company group from Kenya in the difficult district of Ermera. Sector West, commanded by an Australian brigadier based in the remote town of Suai in the southwest, controlled the two difficult border districts of Cova Lima (with a New Zealand composite battalion group) and Bobonaro (with an Australian battalion group). Sector Oecusse was commanded by a Jordanian colonel and secured by a battalion from Jordan (the only country willing to deploy to the remote enclave). Force aviation, engineers, medical, communications, and logistic elements were commanded directly by the force headquarters.

Under INTERFET, the UN military observer group (UNAMET's former MLOs) had monitored the security situation in East Timor and reported to the SRSG and DPKO in New York. After the arrival of UNTAET, the observers reported directly to the force commander. These revised command and control arrangements worked well, unifying military command arrangements and providing a model for future UN operations. The military observers continued to assist the civil administrators and UN police within each district, but were given two new and important priorities. The first was to establish liaison with the Falintil fighters cantoned in Aileu, to maintain professional relations and monitor their progress while assisting the district administrator on this sensitive issue; the second was to deploy greater numbers of observers to the border districts (including Oecusse) to report on activities there. As Falintil transitioned to a national defense force, the number of UN military observers was reduced and they were concentrated along the border.

In the month following transition from INTERFET, the security environment remained benign in the Oecusse enclave and in the central and eastern districts. Along the western border, however, militia infiltration and attacks increased, and the peacekeepers had to intensify their operations and pay greater attention to force protection. These incursions were initially contained, but from July to September militia activity intensified. Well-armed and highly trained militias, infiltrating in small groups of around 150, tried hard to avoid peacekeeping forces, but two UNTAET soldiers and a larger number of militia were killed in separate incidents. The militia failed to reestablish a viable presence or gain the support of the people, and by September had been forced to return to sanctuaries in West Timor.

In countering the militia threat, UNTAET revised its concept of operations, shifting its focus from directly contesting the militia to protecting the people and maintaining their confidence. More emphasis was given to CIMIC activities so as to reassure the population and gain better information on militia activities. Falintil members were integrated into peacekeeping units to improve tactical intelligence, and the secretary-general sought and won approval for additional troops. The rules of engagement were modified to enable the peacekeepers to initiate fire against suspected militia.

In managing the border, UNTAET peacekeepers maintained professional relations with the TNI. The memorandum of technical understanding signed by INTERFET in January 2000 was updated in April 2000 and again in August 2001, and procedures were put in place to prevent and report overflights. Nevertheless, there were differences in emphasis: Indonesia wished to prevent border clashes with UN forces, but TNI was unwilling to accept responsibility for any militia activity on either side of the border. UNTAET was similarly intent on avoiding conflict with Indonesian forces but primarily wanted TNI to prevent the militia from operating with impunity in West Timor. Sadly, it took the murder of three UNHCR workers at Atambua in West Timor on September 6, 2000, followed by a stern Security Council resolution on September 8 demanding that Indonesia restore security and prevent militia activity and cross-border incursions into East Timor, before militia activity was brought under control.[100]

A corollary of militia activity in West Timor was the continued presence of large numbers of East Timorese in refugee camps, many of whom experienced militia intimidation. Considerable effort was expended by UNHCR, UNTAET, the bishops, and Xanana Gusmao to encourage the return of refugees before independence, by which time only about 10 percent of the original 250,000 remained in West Timor. Under UNHCR leadership and with the assistance of the IOM and UNTAET, coordinated efforts were made to facilitate the return and processing of refugees. The partnership established between UNHCR and the military component, in particular, provides a useful model for civil-military cooperation and joint planning in future missions.

With a diminished external threat, increased development by the civil sector, and commencement of Falintil's transition from a guerrilla force into a professional defense force (Falintil–FDTL), the military component was progressively decreased to around 5,000 troops at independence, with most of the force deployed in Dili, in Oecusse, and along the western border. Australia and Portugal provided the major assistance for the new defense force, including new facilities, weapons, and other equipment. This force comprised around 2,500 troops, a headquarters, two light infantry battalions, and a small maritime element. A civilian-led office of defense force development was created to ensure the subordination of the military to civilian authorities, but at independence the mechanisms to achieve this remained underdeveloped.

The military component of UNTAET performed to a high standard. It was respected by the East Timorese and was the least criticized element of the transitional administration. Its warfighting skills were commensurate to the threat, but its expertise in CIMIC and constabulary functions was initially lacking and required continuous upgrading with subsequent force rotations. Unfortunately, the military's professionalism was not matched by UN police, whose performance in the maintenance of internal security was continuously criticized within UNTAET itself as well as by the East Timorese.

UN Police, Internal Security, and the Rule of Law

As already stated, most of the difficulties that confronted the police component stemmed from the inchoate planning conducted by the

Secretariat in the lead-up to the mission. The UNTAET mandate required UN police to undertake monitoring, train and develop a police force from scratch, and implement law enforcement using a combination of community policing and riot control. The United Nations had little experience in the latter two areas, and DPKO was inadequately staffed to plan such an intricate operation.

Police personnel were slow to arrive in the mission area, and many had not been properly briefed and prepared for their tasks. Heated debates occurred as to whether the force should be armed, and the various nationalities addressed this issue based on their own experience and practice. With violence on the increase, the SRSG decreed in 2000 that police could be armed, but most nationalities continued to operate in accordance with their national policies.

Few of the international police had a sound understanding of the Indonesian criminal code that applied in East Timor, and fewer still had language skills or understood the local customs and traditional laws—deficiencies made more difficult to overcome by the rapid turnover in police and their lack of accountability. Initially, no specialist "trainers" were included in the contingent, and UN police lacked expertise in other specialist areas of policing.

Stations were opened in most district capitals, but they were inadequately staffed and resourced, and operations were not conducted with uniformity throughout the mission. Due to the shortage of vehicles and equipment, the first police commissioner was reluctant to establish police posts in the subdistricts. This feat was not achieved by his successor until late 2000, and then only after militia infiltration had been cut off by the military component, and on specific direction from the SRSG. The planned maritime police unit failed to arrive, creating an important capability gap in coastal surveillance, and one that could not be covered effectively by the military component or the nascent customs and immigration office.

Vieira de Mello was dissatisfied with the overall standard of policing and repeatedly called for improvement in the selection and preparation of police personnel. On his insistence, in an effort to improve standards, a trial was conducted that assigned single nationalities to specific districts, in contrast to the normal practice of having mixed nationalities (as similarly applied to military observers). The trial proved inconclusive and would have been impracticable to replicate through the thirteen districts, given that the force of more than 1,500 police derived from forty-one different countries. The disparity in UN police nationalities and standards was a major problem, but a related concern was the variability in the implementation of community policing. As one analyst noted from his examination of UNTAET community policing, there was an "absence of a coherent definition of the concept" and the skills required to be effective on the ground.[101]

One positive aspect of the performance of UN police was their initial training of police cadets to establish the East Timor Police Service (PNTL), which commenced in early 2000. Given the police component's resource shortfalls, this was a remarkable achievement, although it was not backed by a coherent plan for the creation of the PNTL as a national asset. A comparison with the creation of the local defense force, Falintil–FDTL, illustrates this point. Starting much later than PNTL, Falintil–FDTL grew from a coherent strategic plan, with each of the elements clearly identified. PNTL, however, commenced training cadets without a clear understanding of force composition, and without consideration of the specialists that would be required for an effective police force following independence. Again, this reflected the lack of strategic oversight from the Secretariat in New York.

Overall, UN police did not perform to an acceptable standard in East Timor. Given the shortage of trained police even in developed countries, and the difficulties of transcending cultural and language differences, it is not surprising that policing has remained a problem for peace operations. Supporting the findings of the Brahimi Report, one analysis of international policing has noted that "international order will require greater priority to be given to the requirements and delivery of [police-based] peace operations in broken states so that states can be rebuilt ... without having to rely on military or other coercive means to survive."[102] The lesson from East Timor, and other missions, is that the United Nations must improve its selection and training of UN police contingents, either with the cooperation of member states or through a more radical approach of outsourcing to commercial enterprises.[103]

Inadequacies in implementing the rule of law went beyond UN police. Requirements for the judicial and penal (correctional) sectors were poorly planned by the Secretariat and slow to materialize on the ground in East Timor. The United Nations had experienced similar problems in implementing the rule of law in Cambodia in the early 1990s. These lessons were now relearned by UNTAET.

Assessment of UNTAET

Overall, UNTAET was judged a success by the international community, but its interregnum revealed many lessons and disappointments. A King's College study tasked to assess the United Nations' role in East Timor "found much to admire about UNTAET, which was required to carry out a uniquely broad mandate in extraordinary difficult circumstances."[104] A World Bank assessment judged UNTAET to be an "exemplary peacekeeping operation," although its role "was fundamentally different from the UN missions' role in other post-conflict situations."[105] James Dunn, an independent and highly respected East Timor analyst since 1975, judged UNTAET to be a success, but still "the imperfect product of an imperfect world."[106]

The unprecedented powers bestowed on UNTAET need to be balanced against the United Nations' lack of practical experience in the application of governance, civil administration, justice, and nation building—difficulties further compounded by the total destruction and devastation in the wake of the militia rampage. An inexperienced and multinational UN mission was tasked to govern and reconstruct a country from ground zero. Not surprisingly, the effort encountered significant challenges.

The UNTAET interregnum in East Timor provides an excellent case study in analyzing the requirements for conducting complex peace operations. On the one hand, the responsibilities given to UNTAET, and the physical destruction in which it had to operate, were greater than for other peace operations. On the other hand, UNTAET enjoyed a climate of political goodwill rarely experienced in international politics. Despite the complexity of UNTAET's task, it operated with enormous international support, compliance from Indonesia, and the support—though at times fractious—of the East Timorese people. Overall, UNTAET fulfilled its mandate and can be assessed as one of the United Nations' most successful peace operations.

Underlying this success, however, were a number of lessons (mostly relearned). A report card for the operation might read as shown in table 6.3.

Table 6.3. UNTAET's Performance: A Hypothetical Report Card

Good	Satisfactory	Poor
• Strong and achievable mandate	• UNTAET partnership with host population	• Pre-mission planning for transitional phases and civil administration
• Peacekeeping force planning and military operations	• Cooperation between UN components and elements	• Development of an UNTAET strategic plan
• Maintenance of security from militia attacks	• Transition from INTERFET to peacekeeping force	• Pace of reconstruction
• Peacekeeping force relations with Falintil and TNI	• Maintenance of internal security	• Implementation of governance from village to national level
• Tactical management of border issues	• Donor relationships: UN, World Bank Group, others	• Planning and resources to implement the rule of law
• Resettlement of displaced people and returnees	• Falintil demobilization and reintegration	• Financial arrangements for prosecution of mandate
	• Development of an indigenous defense force	• UN police planning with peacekeeping force
	• Implementation of human rights	• Legal and judicial planning
		• Role of and resource attribution to district administrators
		• Development of a viable civil service
		• UN police planning, preparation, selection, and operations
		• Development of an indigenous police force
		• Political resolution of border issues
		• Peacekeeping force expertise in CIMIC and constabulary tasks

The UN Mission of Support and an Independent Timor-Leste

The East Timor leadership and Vieira de Mello recognized early on that a number of critical elements would remain fragile in East Timor after independence, so they sought and gained early support from the secretary-general and a large number of donor countries for a continuing UN presence. The stability and development of the new nation would require ongoing assistance from the international community, they realized, particularly to guarantee security and to build capacity in the critical areas of governance, public administration, and the rule of law.

While UNTAET had fully administered the territory, the purpose of UNMISET was to support the government and people of East Timor as they assumed control of their new country. In line with the recommendations of the Brahimi Report—and implementing the lessons from UNTAET, Kosovo, and Bosnia—the planning for UNMISET began more than twelve months before the proposed date for East Timorese independence. This planning included the development of a strategic framework that set out the parameters of the mission and confirmed two separate, albeit complementary, implementation processes —the UN development assistance framework and the national development plan of East Timor.

As proposed in the Brahimi Report, an integrated mission task force was established in New York that consulted with working groups in Dili comprising civilian, police, and military planners. This was very different from what had occurred in the rushed formation of UNTAET. Based on this planning, Kofi Annan presented a number of proposals for a successor mission in his reports to the Security Council in late 2001 and early 2002.[107] These were consolidated in detailed proposals for UNMISET, presented in the secretary-general's report of April 17, 2002. The proposed implementation plan for UNMISET was comprehensive, consisting of three key programs: stability, democracy, and justice; internal security and law enforcement; and external security and border control. Principally, the plan provided for the following:

- the presence of a "continued and appropriately reduced" military component following independence "to ensure the security and stability of the nascent state"

- the development and implementation of a "milestone-based approach" to achieve the mission's gradual withdrawal over a two-year period
- the introduction of coordination mechanisms to dovetail UNMISET's work with that of the "wider UN system, bilateral donors, civil society and the structure and national development plan" of the government of East Timor[108]

UNMISET was established under Resolution 1410 of May 17, 2002, which provided it with a comprehensive, practical, and responsible mandate. Importantly, it also set out a clear exit strategy for the United Nations from East Timor. Over a two-year period, the mission was to "fully devolve all operational responsibilities to the East Timorese authorities as soon as feasible, without jeopardizing stability," while downsizing of the mission was to "proceed as quickly as possible, after careful assessment of the situation on the ground."[109] In essence, the mission "would provide assistance to the core administrative structures critical to the viability and political stability of East Timor." It would also "provide interim law enforcement and public security, assist in the development of the East Timor Police Service and contribute to the maintenance of the new country's external and internal security."[110] Kamalesh Sharma, a senior Indian foreign service officer, was appointed SRSG and took over from Vieira de Mello on May 21, 2002. Sharma had held several ambassadorial appointments and most recently had been India's permanent representative to the United Nations in New York.

Progress in building Timorese institutions and establishing internal and external security in the country did not go as quickly as hoped, however. In May 2004 the mission was extended for six months by Resolution 1543, and it was later extended for another six months, until May 2005. During this final consolidation phase the mission was significantly downsized, and it eventually transitioned to a UN political mission, the United Nations Office in Timor-Leste (UNOTIL), in May 2005.

Funding

UNMISET was funded through a special account and assessed contributions, with total expenditures of $287.9 million for July 2002–June 2003.

(The first two months of UNMISET were funded from the unexpended funds in the UNTAET budget.) Spending declined to $196.1 million for July 2003–June 2004, and $85.2 million was budgeted for 2004–5.[111] Resolution 1410, however, emphasized that "further UN assistance to East Timor should be coordinated with bilateral and multilateral donors, regional mechanisms, non-governmental, as well as private sector organizations and other actors in the international community."[112]

With very limited resources, East Timor faced considerable difficulties in implementing its programs without continued financial support and appropriate expertise from the international community, particularly in regard to funding police and military institutions. Such considerations were evident in UNMISET's planning, which put training and governance mechanisms in place with UNMISET funding, but left to bilateral donors the task of providing material and financial support to fully establish the East Timorese police and military.

Priorities identified in this area for the PNTL included funds for capital investments, a reliable communications system, weapons, basic equipment for special police units, and rehabilitation services for returnees and former militia, as well as the maintenance of police buildings. With the planned downsizing of the military component over the mission's expected two-year and eventual three-year duration, critical funding was identified for the fledgling Ministry of Defense and defense force, including $5.5 million for vehicles and a permanent base for the first Falintil–FDTL battalion.[113]

Planning, Preparation, and Deployment

Although the planning process for the transition to UNMISET was far more organized than that for UNTAET, it still encountered difficulties. Final consolidation of planning (begun in March 2001) was achieved only when the planning teams from both Dili and New York met in East Timor from March 17 to 24, 2002, two months before independence. The security component of the mission, drawn from the police and military components of UNTAET, was already on the ground in East Timor, but key civilian players for the new mission had not yet deployed there. Consequently, and despite the long period of planning, difficulties emerged in managing a smooth transition between the missions and in arranging recruitment of the specialists required by UNMISET.

Mission planning had identified some 100 core functions in the areas of government administration in which assistance was required post-independence, but six months after UNMISET's establishment, fourteen of the envisaged 100 advisers were still in various stages of recruitment.[114] Thus, while the integrated task force planning for UNMISET demonstrated the benefits of implementing the recommendations of the Brahimi Report, such planning failed to ensure the timely selection and deployment of civilian staff. This result—commonly repeated in many UN missions—raises serious questions as to the adequacy of UN personnel practices and whether "outsourcing" alternatives could be any less efficient.

UN-Timorese coordination posed an even greater difficulty for planning, however. Not only was the United Nations transitioning from one mission to another, but the role of the incoming mission was much more focused on supporting the new government, which required close collaboration in planning between UN and East Timorese staff. On this issue the King's College assessment noted that the transition initially included no senior Timorese representation. Once it did,

> Communication between East Timorese and international members of the team was poor and the decision-making process was slow. Many of the tasks the team set itself were not accomplished, in particular regarding the transfer of residual government functions from UNTAET, the establishment of offices to handle areas, such as defense and police policy development and management, where none had hitherto existed, and civil service recruitment.[115]

Given the ample time available for this planning and the inadequate result, the findings of the King's College study suggest a weakness in the ability of the United Nations to integrate local representation in its planning processes. Since capacity building is an essential element of poverty reduction and postconflict reconstruction, this weakness in UN processes warrants closer attention.

Field Operations—Implementation

The civilian component of UNMISET continued to support core administrative structures, particularly in the areas of finance, governance, infrastructure, and judicial and legal services. International experts provided guidance and critical assistance to the emergent government. Other civilian personnel focused on such key issues as gender affairs (with high priority given to the prevention of domestic violence) and HIV/AIDS. A Serious Crimes Unit assisted in the conduct of criminal investigations and proceedings, and a Human Rights Unit maintained liaison with the Commission on Reception, Truth and Reconciliation and helped facilitate human rights training for UN and East Timorese officials, in particular police and defense personnel.

UNMISET's authorized strength of 1,250 UN police—renamed UNPOL on transition from UNTAET to UNMISET—and 5,000 peacekeeping troops was progressively reduced. Peacekeeping troops were initially scheduled to be withdrawn by July 2004, but withdrawal was delayed first to December 2004 and finally to May 2005. UNPOL was tasked to undertake executive policing and to continue the development of PNTL.

In terms of external security, much depended on developments within Indonesia, which remained unpredictable. Indonesian-supported militia groups dormant in West Timor required monitoring as UN peacekeepers withdrew. The small indigenous border police unit would be unable to counter a resurgence of militia activity, and any deployment of Falintil–FDTL to the border could have acted as a catalyst to reignite militia operations. As with the PNTL, Falintil–FDTL formally assumed full responsibility for external security by May 2004. UNMISET maintained an infantry company and a gendarmerie unit until May 2005, to assist the Timorese and provide excess capacity in case of emergency, with the option of taking temporary security responsibility for specific areas if the need arose.[116]

In terms of security, however, the main attention remained centered on the internal issue of law enforcement. Here the expectations of many East Timorese were not met in the initial years following independence, leading to fears of a rise in political unrest and criminal activity in a climate of long-term unemployment and slow economic recovery. Disaffected former Falintil members and their clandestine supporters also remained a potentially disturbing influence, and their aspirations needed to be met given their influence within the community. Rumors of a rift between the nascent police and defense forces were also of concern for the future stability of the country. Members of the two forces clashed a number of times in early 2005, even as UN forces were preparing to withdraw.[117]

On December 4, 2002, internal security concerns came to a head when a peaceful student protest in Dili ended in the largest violent conflict since independence.[118] The incident highlighted the need to strengthen the PNTL and was, in essence, a reflection of the inadequacies identified within UN police during the UNTAET period. In response to UNPOL and PNTL's inability to handle security-related incidents, the Security Council, under Resolution 1473 of April 4, 2003, authorized a revised schedule for downsizing international police personnel and adjusted the planning for the gradual transfer of authority to the PNTL. The resolution also allowed for the inclusion, initially for a period of one year but eventually extended to May 2005, of an internationally formed unit to respond to civil disturbance.[119]

UNMISET subsequently adjusted its capacity for police training in key areas, placed greater emphasis on human rights and the rule of law, and retained a greater monitoring and advisory presence in the districts where the PNTL had taken over the policing authority. Notably, the secretary-general requested that a 144-strong backup UN security force remain in Timor-Leste after May 2005 to ensure overall security in the country and deter criminal activities, particularly in border areas, but the Security Council denied this request in mandating the deployment of UNOTIL, the follow-on political mission.[120]

Policing in East Timor, including the building of PNTL, was always going to be a long-term endeavor, as was the development of the national defense force. The UNMISET mandate did not take the prospect of deterioration in the security environment into consideration. If the United Nations' efforts to create a stable and viable nation were to be fulfilled, it was important that the development of both the PNTL and Falintil– FDTL progress as thoroughly and as quickly as possible.

As for all UN missions, adequate funding for UNMISET was crucial. There was a need not to waste the substantial investment the international community had already made in East Timor. UNMISET could not operate in isolation from the broader international effort to assist. The mission had to foster the relationship between the mission and the wider UN system of agencies, funds, and programs, as well as the national development plan of the East Timor government.

Gleaning what it can from the competitive world of bilateral and multilateral funding, East Timor has made considerable progress, but its government structures are unlikely to become fully functional or financially sustainable until significant benefits flow into the economy from the Timor Sea oil and gas reserves. Until then, budgetary support from the international community will remain imperative. Moreover, in order to attract foreign investment and avoid corruption, the East Timor government will need to enact laws regarding taxation, property rights, and political risk insurance. Unless and until these conditions are met, and the internal security situation is judged to be stable, foreign investment and economic growth is likely to remain constrained.

Conclusion

East Timor represents a significant chapter in the history of UN peace operations, but one that is likely more the exception than the rule. While the probability of complex peace operations is high, the United Nations' involvement in future missions is likely to be less grand than that represented by UNTAET, and more akin to its experience in other missions. Regardless of the responsibilities assigned to governments and international organizations in the future, however, the lessons of East Timor are largely the same as those of earlier peace operations. In such operations the challenge is not so much to stop the fighting as it is to build peace, enhance stability, develop the capacity of new or renewed states, and promote the human rights of the people. This case study provides a useful illustration of the spectrum of peacemaking, peace enforcement, peacekeeping, and peacebuilding activities that are required to rebuild states and create conditions for sustainable peace (see figure 6.5). One analysis of the United Nations' involvement in East Timor has highlighted thirteen factors that were relevant to success.[121] While each of these factors was important, "strategic success" was mainly due to the legitimacy of UN intervention and the feasibility of successive mandates to achieve a clear political end state. In such circumstances the continuing commitment of the international community and the unambiguous support of the polity within the host country facilitated progress. Seldom in international politics do these circumstances coalesce to the extent that was the case in East Timor.

Figure 6.5. Timelines of Violence and Intervention in East Timor, 1999–2005

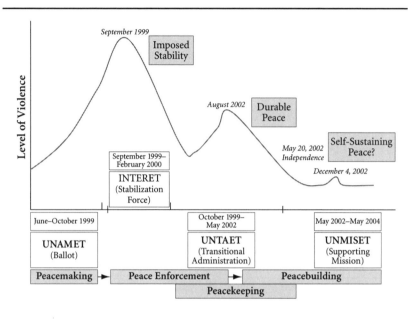

Regardless of such strategic issues, the overwhelming lesson for the UN Secretariat is that East Timor demonstrates the essential need for detailed and integrated operational planning. Such planning occurred for the more simple UNAMET and UNMISET missions, but the success of UNTAET's more complex task was jeopardized by the weakness of mission planning.

The question is not so much whether the United Nations was successful in East Timor, but rather how much more successful UNTAET might have been had many of the lessons from earlier peace missions been acted upon more fully. The lessons learned from East Timor support and, indeed, helped shape the recommendations of the Brahimi Report. The success of future UN peace operations is likely to depend, therefore, on the implementation of the Brahimi reforms and the full support of member states.

For financial reasons, the developed nations will need to do most of the heavy lifting to make these reforms a reality. Some countries need to do more to support the development of doctrine and expertise for peace operations. More work is required to develop regional centers of excellence that better coordinate training for good governance, the rule of law, security, human rights, and sustainable development. In particular, better bridges need to be built between civil administrators, police, and military establishments, and greater understanding of local customs is required. This is a hard task even within developed nations, but if world peace based on the system of states is to be preserved and enhanced, then this training must be extended within the international community. Finally, the early involvement of local leaders in mission planning and implementation stands out as an important lesson if capacity building is to be effective in postconflict environments.

Notes

1. UNMISET was scheduled to conclude in May 2004, but was extended at reduced strength for one year. In May 2005, UNMISET was replaced by a smaller UN Mission, the United Nations Office in Timor-Leste (UNOTIL).

2. The geographic peculiarity of the enclave is the result of Portuguese and Dutch colonial conquests and rivalry in Timor and the adjacent islands. The capital was originally Lifau, established in Oecusse in 1701, but it was moved to Dili in 1769. See James Dunn, *Timor: A People Betrayed* (Sydney: ABC, 1996), 13–16.

3. East Timor, excluding the Oecusse enclave located on the north coast of West Timor, is approximately 164 miles long and 57 miles wide.

4. See World Bank, "Timor-Leste: Poverty in a New Nation: Analysis for Action" (Washington, DC, 2003), 25.

5. It has been estimated that East Timor's revenue from the Bayu-Udun gas field in the Timor Sea will be $2.5–3 billion. Additional revenue is anticipated from the Greater Sunrise field.

6. An alternative and more capable airport is at Baucau, but it is not permanently in operation.

7. The Carnation Revolution saw the overthrow of the authoritarian regime of Marcello Caetano (the successor to Oliveira Salazar). Suharto and

the military came to power in 1966, following the 1965 abortive coup and its bloody aftermath, which nullified the communists.

8. The Indonesian military is known as Tentara Nasional Indonesia (TNI), and the police are referred to as Polisi Republik Indonesia (POLRI).

9. The first resolution was from the General Assembly on December 12, 1975, followed by the Security Council ten days later, and again on April 22, 1976.

10. William Maley, "The UN and East Timor," *Pacific Review* 12, no. 1 (February 2000): 66.

11. John Martinkus, *A Dirty Little War* (Sydney: Random House Australia, 2001), xv. This figure is supported by Amnesty International.

12. Department of Foreign Affairs and Trade (DFAT), *East Timor in Transition 1998–2000: An Australian Policy Challenge* (Canberra: Brown and Wilton, 2001), 38.

13. This attachment was cemented further by the significant number of casualties sustained by TNI during the occupation. Indonesian casualty figures are difficult to verify; Adam Schwarz has claimed that between 1976 and 1980, they may have been as high as 10,000. See his *A Nation in Waiting: Indonesia in the 1990s* (Sydney: Allen and Unwin, 1994). Harold Crouch has offered a figure of several thousand for the whole period: "The TNI and East Timor Policy," in *Out of the Ashes: Destruction and Reconstruction of East Timor*, ed. James Fox and Dionisio Babo Soares (Adelaide: Crawford House, 2000), 152. General Wiranto has claimed a figure of 1,500 killed and 2,400 wounded. See *Kompas*, September 13, 1999.

14. The full May 5 agreements are contained in DFAT, *East Timor in Transition,* 191–209. A condensed version is in Ian Martin, *Self-Determination in East Timor: The United Nations, the Ballot and International Intervention*, International Peace Academy Occasional Paper (Boulder, CO: Lynne Rienner, 2001), 141–48. Signatories were Ali Alatas, foreign minister of Indonesia; Jaime Gama, foreign minister of Portugal; and Kofi Annan, UN secretary-general.

15. For a full account, see Martinkus, *Dirty Little War,* chap. 5.

16. Martin, *Self-Determination in East Timor,* 25. Martin cites evidence from Amnesty International and a number of observers.

17. Komnas HAM (Indonesian Human Rights Commission), *Report on the Investigation of Human Rights Violations in East Timor, Executive Summary,* Jakarta, January 31, 2000.

18. Agreement on the final text was reached on April 23, 1999.

19. For an account of the Bali summit, see DFAT, *East Timor in Transition,* 78–81.

20. United Nations, *Question of East Timor: Report of the Secretary-General,* S/1999/595, May 22, 1999.

21. Ibid., para. 23.

22. Ibid., para. 27.

23. UN Security Council Resolution, *The Situation in East Timor,* S/RES/1246, June 11, 1999.

24. Ibid., para. 9.

25. See UNAMET home page, www.un.org/Depts/dpa/prev_dip/fst_prev_dip.htm.

26. United Nations, *Question of East Timor,* S/1999/595, para. 29.

27. UN General Assembly, *Financing of the United Nations Mission in East Timor: Report of the Secretary-General,* A/54/775, March 1, 2000.

28. UN General Assembly Resolution, *Financing of UN Mission in East Timor,* A/RES/53/240, June 29, 1999.

29. Assessed contributions for peacekeeping operations are calculated roughly on the basis of gross national product and range from 0.001 percent of the budget to about 27 percent (for the United States). For the complete peacekeeping scale of assessment, see United Nations, *Scale of Assessments for the Apportionment of the Expenses of United Nations Peacekeeping Missions. Report of the Secretary-General,* A/58/157, July 15, 2003.

30. UN General Assembly Resolutions, *Financing of UN Mission in East Timor* (A/RES/54/20A, November 22, 1999; and A/RES/54/20B, April 7, 2000). Further details of UNAMET's budget are contained in UN General Assembly, *Financing of the United Nations Mission in East Timor: Report of the Advisory Committee on Administrative and Budgetary Questions* (A/54/406, September 28, 1999; and A/54/802, March 17, 2000).

31. Considerable credit rested with Francesc Vendrell (Spain), DPA's director of Asia and the Pacific, who had a thorough understanding of the East Timor situation and was able to advise and support Marker, and the DPA undersecretary-general, Sir Kieran Prendergast (United Kingdom). Vendrell was subsequently appointed Marker's deputy.

32. The core group included Australia, Japan, New Zealand, the United Kingdom, and the United States. (Portugal joined this group during UNTAET.)

33. The AEC initially provided advice and personnel support to the Electoral Assistance Division in New York. Later, at the United Nations' request, the AEC assisted with the compilation of registration and ballot data in Australia, but did not deploy personnel to East Timor. The IOM and the AEC were engaged by the United Nations to assist in the registration and voting of the East Timorese diaspora.

34. Martin, *Self-Determination in East Timor,* 39. The UN volunteers came from more than seventy countries, UN police from twenty-seven countries, and MLOs from seventeen countries.

35. These stocks were rapidly depleted by subsequent missions.

36. DFAT, *East Timor in Transition,* 94–95.

37. United Nations, *Question of East Timor: Report of the Secretary-General,* S/1999/705, June 22, 1999.

38. Martin, *Self-Determination in East Timor,* 43, 45.

39. See DFAT, *East Timor in Transition,* 98–99.

40. UN Security Council, *Letter from the Secretary-General Addressed to the President of the Security Council,* S/1999/786, July 14, 1999.

41. United Nations, *Question of East Timor: Report of the Secretary-General,* S/1999/803, July 20, 1999.

42. United Nations, *Letter from the Secretary-General Addressed to the President of the Security Council,* S/1999/830, July 28, 1999.

43. The final figure was 451,792, including around 13,000 East Timorese living abroad.

44. Electoral Commission, East Timor Popular Consultation, *Determination: Registration of Voters,* August 25, 1999.

45. See David Goldsworthy, "East Timor," in *Facing North: A Century of Australia's Engagement with Asia, Volume 2: 1970s–2000,* ed. Peter Edwards and David Goldsworthy (Melbourne: Melbourne University Publishing, 2003), 242–43; Martin, *Self-Determination in East Timor,* 81–82; Martinkus, *Dirty Little War,* 229; and John B. Haseman, "East Timor: The Misuse of Military Power and Misplaced Military Pride," in *Out of the Ashes,* ed. Fox and Babo Soares, 184–85.

46. Martin, *Self-Determination in East Timor,* Appendix 6, 157.

47. James Dunn, "Crimes against Humanity in East Timor, January to October 1999: Their Nature and Causes" (unpublished UN report, 2001), 20.

48. Ibid., 91–94. For further accounts of the violence and destruction, including complicity by the Indonesian authorities, see Parliament of the Commonwealth of Australia, *Final Report of the Senate Foreign Affairs, Defence and Trade References Committee: East Timor* (Canberra: Government of Australia, December 2000), 92–95; Martinkus, *Dirty Little War;* Peter Bartu, "The Militia, the Military, and the People of Bobonaro District," *Bulletin of*

Concerned Asian Scholars 32, nos. 1–2 (2000): 35–42; and Dunn, "Crimes against Humanity in East Timor."

49. The evacuation by the Royal Australian Air Force (RAAF) was code-named Operation Spitfire. With the cooperation of Indonesian authorities, nine RAAF Hercules flights and one UN flight carried 539 evacuees, including 76 Australians, members of the media, and a large number of UNAMET personnel. Over the following days, ten RAAF flights and one Royal New Zealand Air Force flight ferried to Darwin the East Timorese who had taken refuge in the UNAMET compound and most of the remaining UNAMET staff.

50. Martin, *Self-Determination in East Timor,* 100–1.

51. Quoted in Martin, *Self-Determination in East Timor,* 121.

52. DFAT, *East Timor in Transition,* 133.

53. Ibid., 133–34.

54. For discussion of the Auckland APEC meeting, see Martin, *Self-Determination in East Timor,* 107; and DFAT, *East Timor in Transition,* 135–37.

55. See UN Security Council Resolution, *The Situation in East Timor,* S/RES/1264, September 15, 1999. The unanimous vote was achieved despite earlier objections from two members of the council—Malaysia and Bahrain—to the proposals for Australian leadership of the force.

56. The protection provided for UNAMET was extended to UNTAET when it took over on October 25, 1999, until the handover to UNTAET peacekeepers on February 23, 2000.

57. UNITF was structured to help developing nations participate in INTERFET by meeting costs that would have been met by the United Nations if the operation had been a UN-funded peacekeeping operation. UN financial regulations and rules were to be observed in the establishment and management of UNITF. Claims certification and payment remained the responsibility of DPKO, as the program manager of the trust fund.

58. Portugal $5 million, Brunei $598,000, Luxembourg $366,000, and Switzerland $314,000. There were several other minor donors, including China, which did not commit any troops to the operation.

59. This was facilitated as a U.S. "drawdown" facility that, with U.S. agreement, could draw against the authorization to meet the costs of U.S.-provided support, up to a total of $55 million. The final cost to the United States of support provided against the drawdown facility was approximately $50 million.

60. When Annan asked Australia to lead the MNF on September 6, Australia was in a position to deploy some 2,000 troops with forty-eight to seventy-two hours' notice. See DFAT, *East Timor in Transition*, 133.

61. For political reasons, Portugal agreed not to deploy ground forces to East Timor until transition to the military component, but assisted INTERFET with the positioning of a Hercules C130 aircraft and a naval surface combatant in Darwin.

62. See Moreen Dee, "'Coalitions of the Willing' and Humanitarian Intervention," *International Peacekeeping* 8, no. 3 (2001): 9. For details on the raising of the force, see Alan Ryan, *Primary Responsibilities and Primary Risks: Australian Defence Force Participation in the International Force East Timor*, Study Paper no. 304 (Duntroon, Australian Capital Territory: Land Warfare Studies Centre, 2000), 45–60.

63. Goldsworthy, "East Timor," 253.

64. Known as the INTERFET Liaison Team, the officers were fully funded by Australia. Although it exchanged information on INTERFET operations, the team's main purpose was to assist DPKO in planning the transition from INTERFET to the military component of UNTAET.

65. For political reasons, initially a number of countries did not wish to deploy forces to high-risk areas, while others asked that their contribution be deployed for humanitarian tasks only. General Cosgrove and subsequent UNTAET force commanders sought adjustments to force composition in later force rotations.

66. Ryan, *Primary Responsibilities and Primary Risks*, 71–72, 75.

67. For an analysis of CIMIC and lessons learned during the INTERFET period, see Michael H. Elmquist, "CIMIC in East Timor" (paper delivered at the conference "Challenges of International Cooperation in Complex Humanitarian Emergencies," Asia-Pacific Center for Security Studies, Honolulu, HI, November 4–6, 2003).

68. DFAT, *East Timor in Transition*, 146.

69. Bob Breen, *Mission Accomplished: East Timor, The Australian Defence Force Participation in International Force in East Timor (INTERFET)* (Sydney: Allen and Unwin, 2001), 5. For a breakdown of the force composition, see Ryan, *Primary Responsibilities and Primary Risks*, Annex A.

70. This was referred to as an "oil spot" strategy, whereby the force established its authority at key locations, from which it expanded (like oil spots) until the entire territory was under its control.

71. Ryan, *Primary Responsibilities and Primary Risks*, 73.

72. INTERFET suffered no combat fatalities and only two noncombat fatalities in its five months of operations. Two Australian soldiers were wounded in combat, two soldiers died from accident or illness (one New Zealand and one Australian, respectively), and 1,080 noncombat injuries were reported. See Breen, *Mission Accomplished,* 5.

73. Between October 6 and 16, there were five exchanges of fire: four between INTERFET forces and militia, and one between INTERFET and TNI troops. Three militia were killed, and three wounded, in the October 16 incident.

74. For Falintil's contribution to security restoration and maintenance, see Michael G. Smith with Moreen Dee, *Peacekeeping in East Timor: The Path to Independence* (Boulder, CO: Lynne Reinner, 2003), 48–50. Falintil did not always adhere to INTERFET's demands, but there were few disputes and none that included combat or violence.

75. By mid-October, some 64,000 East Timorese had returned to Dili, restoring the capital to more than half of its preballot population.

76. UN Security Council Resolution, *The Situation in East Timor,* S/RES/1272, October 22, 1999. UNTAET's mandate was extended successively under S/RES/1338, January 31, 2001, and S/RES/1392, January 31, 2002.

77. United Nations, *Report of the Secretary-General on the United Nations Transitional Administration in East Timor,* S/2001/983, October 18, 2001, 11.

78. For a detailed assessment of UNTAET's performance and lessons learned, see Conflict, Security and Development Group, "East Timor Report" (online report, part of *A Review of Peace Operations: A Case for Change* Web site, sponsored by the International Policy Institute, King's College London, 2003), ipi.sspp.kcl.ac.uk/rep006/index.html. A more general assessment of UNTAET is contained in James Dunn, *East Timor: A Rough Passage to Independence* (Sydney: Longueville, 2003), chap. 14. For a comprehensive assessment of economic, social, and development issues during the UNTAET period, see Klaus Rohland and Sarah Cliffe, "The East Timor Reconstruction Program: Successes, Problems and Tradeoffs," *World Bank CPR Working Papers,* Social Development Department, Paper no. 2 (November 2002). For an economic and social assessment of East Timor at the end of UNTAET's mandate, see World Bank, "Timor Leste, Poverty in a New Nation: Analysis for Action" (Washington, DC, 2003). For an assessment of the legal constraints on UNTAET's success, see Jonathan Morrow and Rachel White, "The United Nations in Transitional East Timor: International Standards and the Reality of Governance," *Australian Year Book of International Law* 22 (2003).

For an assessment of the difficulties of implementing human rights under UNTAET, see Sidney Jones, "East Timor: The Troubled Path to Independence," in *Honoring Human Rights under International Mandates: Lessons from Bosnia, Kosovo and East Timor: Recommendations to the United Nations,* ed. Alice H. Henkin (Washington, DC: Aspen Institute, Justice and Society Program, 2003), 115–46. For an assessment of UNTAET's executive decision making and problems in building an effective public administration, see Sue Ingram, "Mission Implementation: Developing Institutional Capacities," in *The United Nations Transitional Administration in East Timor: Debriefing and Lessons,* Report of the 2002 Tokyo Conference cosponsored by United Nations Institute for Training and Research, the Singapore Institute of Policy Studies, and the Japan Institute of International Affairs (United Kingdom: Martinus Nijhoff, 2003), 85–93. For an assessment of UNTAET's difficulties in melding international standards of governance with East Timor's traditional social practices, see Tanja Hohe, "The Clash of Paradigms: International Administration and Local Political Legitimacy in East Timor," *Contemporary Southeast Asia* 24, no. 3 (December 2002): 569–89; and Hohe, "Totem Polls: Indigenous Concepts and 'Free and Fair' Elections in East Timor," *International Peacekeeping* 9, no. 4 (Winter 2002): 69–88.

79. UN Security Council Resolution, *The Situation in East Timor,* S/RES/1272 (1999), para. 1.

80. Ibid., Art. 2. See also United Nations, *The United Nations Transitional Administration in East Timor, Report of the Secretary-General,* part IV, S/1999/1024, October 4, 1999, paras. 25–31, 7–9.

81. Rohland and Cliffe, "The East Timor Reconstruction Program," 7.

82. For the period of July 1, 2000–June 20, 2001, respective expenditures were UNTAET, $528.6 million; UNAMSIL, $493 million; and UNMIK, $383.5 million. The next most expensive mission was the UN Organization Mission in the Democratic Republic of the Congo, at $246.5 million. See United Nations, *Administrative and Budgetary Aspects of the Financing of the United Nations Peacekeeping Operations, Report of the Advisory Committee on Administrative and Budgetary Questions,* A/56/887, April 5, 2002, 23.

83. Rohland and Cliffe, "The East Timor Reconstruction Program," 7.

84. Simon Chesterman, *You, the People: The United Nations, Transitional Administrations, and State Building* (New York: Oxford University Press, 2004), 195.

85. Rohland and Cliffe, "The East Timor Reconstruction Program," ii.

86. Chesterman, *You, the People,* chap. 6.

87. For an assessment of the United Nations' anticipated phases for planning and preparation, see Conflict, Security and Development Group, "East Timor Report," 222–28.

88. On the bureaucratic infighting, see Astri Suhrke, "Peacekeepers as Nation-Builders," *International Peacekeeping* 8, no. 4 (2001): 6; and Martin, *Self-Determination in East Timor*, 126.

89. The scale of civilian recruitment necessitated by UNTAET (and by UNMIK, in Kosovo), together with the unaccustomed breadth of skills required by these missions, completely overloaded DPKO recruiters and led, according to the United Nations' Joint Inspection Unit, "especially during the early critical phase of UNTAET operations, to a flow of generalists [into the mission] whose background, skills and competencies rarely matched their required tasks . . . especially under its governance and public administration pillar." See United Nations, *Report of the Joint Inspection Unit Entitled 'Evaluation of United Nations System Response in East Timor: Coordination and Effectiveness,'* A/58/85–E/2003/80, May 28, 2003, 19–20.

90. "Gratis" officers (unfunded by the United Nations), who had been provided by developed countries to enhance the capability of the MPS and other elements of DPKO, had been withdrawn at the insistence of some developing nations. The small staff in the MPS were fully occupied with a number of new or emerging missions, including Kosovo, Eritrea/Ethiopia, Sierra Leone, and the Democratic Republic of the Congo.

91. Cedric de Coning, "The UN Transitional Administration in East Timor: Lessons Learned from the First 100 Days," *International Peacekeeping* 6, no. 2 (2000): 85.

92. UN Security Council Resolution, *The Situation in East Timor*, S/RES/1272, para. 3.

93. The first force commander was Lieutenant General Jaime de los Santos (Philippines). He was replaced in July 2000 by Lieutenant General Boonsrang Niumpradit (Thailand), and then by Lieutenant General Winai Phattiyakul (Thailand) on August 31, 2001.

94. Smith with Dee, *Peacekeeping in East Timor*, Annex C, 173–78.

95. Dunn, *East Timor: A Rough Passage to Independence*, 369.

96. Rohland and Cliffe, "The East Timor Reconstruction Program," ii.

97. For example, see Jarat Chopra, "The UN's Kingdom of East Timor," *Survival* 42, no. 3 (2000): 27–39.

98. Centre for Defence Studies, "Independent Study on Security Force Options and Security Sector Reform for East Timor" (King's College London, August 8, 2000).

99. For a fuller account of the UN military forces and lessons learned, see Smith with Dee, *Peacekeeping in East Timor,* chaps. 3 and 5.

100. UN Security Council Resolution, *Measures for the Security of Refugees and UNHCR Staff in East and West Timor,* S/RES/1319, September 8, 2000.

101. Erin Mobekk, *Policing Peace Operations: United Nations Civilian Police in East Timor* (Department of War Studies, King's College London, October 2001), 58–60.

102. John McFarlane and William Maley, "Civilian Police in United Nations Peace Operations," Australian Defence Studies Centre Working Paper no. 64 (Canberra, 2001), 4.

103. See, for example, Graham Day, "After War, Send Blue Force," *Christian Science Monitor,* May 30, 2001.

104. Conflict, Security and Development Group, "East Timor Report," 215.

105. Rohland and Cliffe, "The East Timor Reconstruction Program," i.

106. Dunn, *East Timor: A Rough Passage to Independence,* 375.

107. See United Nations, *Progress Report of the Secretary-General on the United Nations Transitional Administration in East Timor* (S/2001/719, July 24, 2001, paras. 52–60; S/2001/983, October 18, 2001, paras. 59–80; and S/2002/80, January 17, 2002, paras. 76–94).

108. United Nations, *Report of the Secretary-General on the United Nations Transitional Administration in East Timor,* S/2002/432, April 17, 2002, para. 63.

109. Ibid., paras. 7 and 8. The initial twelve-month period under Resolution 1410 was extended until May 20, 2004, by Resolution 1480 of May 19, 2003.

110. UN Security Council, *The Situation in East Timor,* S/RES/1410, May 17, 2002, para. 2.

111. UN General Assembly, *Financial Performance Report for the Period from 1 July 2003 to 30 June 2004 and Proposed Budget for the Period from 1 July 2005 to 30 June 2006 of UNMISET: Report of the Advisory Committee on Administrative and Budgetary Questions,* A/59/736/Add.17, May 23, 2005; UN General Assembly, *Performance Report on the Budget of the UNMISET for the Period from 1 July 2003 to 30 June 2004,* A/59/655, December 21, 2004; UN General Assembly, *Performance Report on the Budget of the UNMISET for the Period from 1 July 2002 to 30 June 2003,* A/58/636, December 18, 2003; and UN General Assembly, *Performance Report on the Budget of UNTAET and UNMISET for the Period from 1 July 2001 to 30 June 2002,* A/57/666, December 18, 2002.

112. UN Security Council, *The Situation in East Timor,* S/RES/1410 (2002), May 17, 2002, para. 10.

113. United Nations, *Report of the Secretary-General on the United Nations Transitional Administration in East Timor,* S/2002/432, April 17, 2002, para. 112.

114. United Nations, *Report of the Secretary-General on the United Nations Mission of Support in East Timor,* S/2002/1223, November 6, 2002, para. 12.

115. Conflict, Security and Development Group, "East Timor Report," 217, para. xii.

116. United Nations, *Report of the Secretary-General on the United Nations Mission of Support in East Timor,* S/2004/333, April 29, 2004, para. 53.

117. Sukehiro Hasegawa, in UN Security Council, 5132nd meeting, February 28, 2005, S/PV.5132, 4.

118. On this occasion, a group of local high school students and teachers were continuing their protest in front of the National Parliament about the arbitrary arrest of a fellow student. Others joined in and, allegedly manipulated by dissident political leaders, were incited to violence, which escalated when the crowd moved on to the police headquarters. Two students were shot and killed, and twenty-six people were injured. A state of emergency was declared and the city placed on curfew when the rampage continued with the looting and attacking of foreign-owned stores, and the burning of vehicles and houses, including those of Prime Minister Mari Alkatiri and some relatives, and a number of informal structures around the mosque in the Muslim area. The UN peacekeeping force, UNPOL, and PNTL secured the city the following morning.

119. UN Security Council Resolution, *The Situation in Timor-Leste,* S/RES/1473, April 4, 2003. On April 29, 2004, the secretary-general advised the Security Council that in addition to PNTL, UNMISET's police component comprised 200 police advisers and an anti-riot unit of 125 police officers.

120. UN Security Council, *End of Mandate Report of the Secretary-General on the United Nations Mission of Support in East Timor (for the Period from 17 February to 11 May 2005),* S/2005/310, May 12, 2005, para. 31.

121. Smith with Dee, *Peacekeeping in East Timor,* chap. 4. The authors call these thirteen lessons "The Peacekeeping Baker's Dozen."

7

Afghanistan

J Alexander Thier

Introduction

Afghanistan was one of the world's most dramatic warscapes for more than two decades. A coup in 1978 touched off a descent into conflict and destruction that involved more than one million deaths, a Soviet invasion and covert military intervention by dozens of countries, the fracturing of the state, and massive refugee and landmine crises. These decades of devastation razed Afghanistan's physical, political, and social infrastructure, creating fertile ground for the virulent combination of fascist-utopian ideology, terror, and narcotics that took hold there in the late 1990s. By early 2001, the Taliban controlled most of the country and were in the financial and ideological thrall of Osama bin Ladin and his al Qaeda terrorist network.

In October 2001, an international military coalition led by the United States invaded Afghanistan to topple the Taliban and al Qaeda. Quick battlefield success left the Coalition and the United Nations to guide a complex political transition. Several Afghan factions that had waged a brutal civil war against one another in the 1990s moved quickly to fill the post-Taliban power vacuum. A hasty peace agreement between faction leaders and other Afghan politicians meeting under UN auspices in Bonn, Germany, concluded on December 5, 2001, provided a roadmap for how to put the state back together, punctuated by milestones such as the selection of an Afghan transitional administration, ratification of a new constitution, and "free and fair" elections by June 2004.[1] The UN Assistance Mission in Afghanistan was created to help Afghans reconstitute and consolidate a legitimate governing authority. A multinational International Security Assistance Force deployed to Kabul to assist the government in securing the capital.

Nearly four years after the initial U.S. intervention, a basic lack of security continued to pervade all aspects of life in Afghanistan, hampering both political and physical reconstruction efforts. Tensions between the two primary objectives of the international engagement in Afghanistan—to root out and destroy terrorist networks and those who harbor them, and to create a viable, peaceful, and prosperous Afghanistan—were evident from the earliest days of that engagement. Although not inherently contradictory, the goals of the war on terror and the chosen means of achieving them often seemed at odds with longer-term aims of national reconstruction. Assessments of progress depended on which set of goals the speaker valued most highly.

On May 1, 2003, for example, U.S. Secretary of Defense Donald Rumsfeld announced from Kabul that U.S. forces in Afghanistan had officially ended major combat operations. The forces were to move into "Phase Four"—stabilization and reconstruction of the country.[2] On May 6, 2003, however, the UN Security Council issued a statement expressing "serious concern at the deterioration of security in many areas of Afghanistan, and at the recent attacks on United Nations and other personnel of aid organizations."[3] After a briefing to the council that same day, Special Representative of the Secretary-General (SRSG) Lakhdar Brahimi said, "Although specific aspects of the Bonn Agreement are proceeding, the progress as a whole is challenged by the deterioration in the security environment."[4] Two years later, that environment remained a serious challenge to legitimate, democratic government.[5]

Origins of the Operations

Afghanistan is a landlocked country dominated by stark mountain ranges and barren desert (see figure 7.1). The Hindu Kush mountains

Figure 7.1. Map of Afghanistan

Source: UN Cartographic Section

create a spine from southwest to northeast, where they meet with the formidable Pamir, Karakoram, and Himalaya ranges. Narrow river valleys and mountain passes have served as trade and transport routes for thousands of years, threading through the otherwise impenetrable terrain. A physical and cultural crossroads for thousands of years, Afghanistan has served as both bridge and buffer between Eurasia and the subcontinent—and as a sand trap for the armies of the British Empire in the latter half of the nineteenth century and the Soviet Union in the 1980s.

Afghanistan is an ethnically and linguistically diverse country, with no majority group.[6] The stark landscape, limited infrastructure, and lack of water constrain the growth potential of the country's mostly remote, atomized communities. Throughout history, the population has proven difficult to subjugate and even more difficult to rule. Physical barriers reinforce internal ethnic and cultural divisions, while each international border divides coethnic populations, most significantly along the 1,520-mile border with Pakistan that splits the largely independent, tribalized Pushtun population. Afghanistan also shares borders with Iran, Turkmenistan, Uzbekistan, Tajikistan, and a remote corner of China.

The population is far less religiously diverse, with approximately 80 percent Sunni Muslims and 19 percent Shi'a Muslims. Afghanistan has never undergone a full census, but its population is estimated to be 20 to 25 million, with well under 30 percent of the population urbanized.[7] The majority of Afghans live as subsistence farmers. The main sources of government revenues historically were duties from transit trade and exports of agricultural production, such as dried fruits and nuts. The production and trade of opium, however, currently accounts for about 40 percent of Afghanistan's overall gross domestic product, none of it generating licit revenue.[8]

Afghanistan has been in a state of political upheaval since 1973, when a former prime minister ousted the long-ruling king in a bloodless coup. Since 1978, when a Communist clique in Kabul engineered another coup, the country has been engaged in ongoing iterations of a devastating war fueled by local, regional, and global rivalries. Two interrelated factors stand at the center of Afghanistan's conflicts of the past three decades: the impact of modernization on a traditional, isolated society; and foreign-power competition and interference.

The Impact and Collapse of Modernization

For more than three decades Afghanistan had been peaceful, pursuing a slow course of modernization combined with a nonaligned foreign policy. In 1963, however, King Mohammad Zahir, who had previously ruled indirectly, took control of his government and his nation's destiny. The king pressured his first cousin, Prime Minister Sardar Daoud, to step down. Daoud had begun to modernize the Afghan military and undertake massive infrastructural projects, both of which sank Afghanistan into debt. He had also provoked a costly political and trade conflict with Pakistan over the issue of "Pushtunistan"—the push for reunification of the Pushtun regions of Afghanistan and Pakistan. Daoud peacefully relinquished power.

In 1964, a new constitution initiated what came to be known as the "New Democracy" period. This constitution, drafted over an eighteen-month period after wide-ranging consultations with all sectors of society, provided for a popularly elected parliament, elected city councils, provincial advisory councils, and an independent judiciary. It also excluded members of the king's family from positions of power. Two parliamentary elections were held, and the country briefly experienced a democratic government. Control of the state apparatus remained largely in the hands of an unrepresentative elite, however. The tension between that elite and Afghanistan's traditional, rural majority was a critical cleavage in Afghan society.

In 1973, former Prime Minister Daoud launched a coup to regain power and speed Afghanistan's modernization. Daoud declared Afghanistan a republic and himself president with extensive powers. His efforts to spur modernization led Daoud to seek out increased foreign assistance. By attracting funds from both the United States and the Soviet Union, Daoud stoked an intense Cold War rivalry between the superpowers in Afghanistan.

This competition also fueled growing political activism in Kabul, especially within the two factions of the Communist Party, here known as the People's Democratic Party of Afghanistan (PDPA). In 1978 the PDPA seized power, but the new leadership was far out of touch with the traditional Afghan society that dominated outside Kabul, and quickly alienated it. An Islamic resistance movement sprang up in the countryside, and political infighting between two factions of the PDPA made the new Kabul government unstable.

Foreign Intervention and Interference

Seeking to avert a complete collapse of the Communist victory, the Soviet Union invaded Afghanistan in 1979. This invasion galvanized the resistance movement, and with the assistance of foreign military support, it morphed into a series of guerrilla militias, or mujahideen parties, that fought a devastating and ultimately successful ten-year war of attrition against the Soviets.

The mujahideen parties were led by a mixture of traditional and Islamist leaders. The traditional leaders emerged from tribal or religious contexts, while the Islamist leaders emerged from party structures dedicated to the promotion of Islam as a political organizing principle. The war came to be seen as an effort not only to oust a foreign invader but to fight anti-Islamic, infidel leadership abroad and at home. Many of the mujahideen leaders spoke of creating a state based on Islam as a political and legal organizing principle. While the United States provided the bulk of military aid, Saudi Arabia, Pakistan, and Iran provided the theological guidance for these groups.

For its own part, the United States made no effort to regulate the distribution of arms and funding based on ideology, leaving the decision making to Pakistan. Indeed, the Hezb-i-Islami party, led by Gulbuddin Hekmatyar, which received the most materiel of any party, was among the most radical and anti-Western of the major parties. Its Islamist ideology was spread to hundreds of thousands of Afghans through recruitment of mujahideen and through education programs run by them in the refugee camps of Pakistan. With the Soviets in the cities and the mujahideen in the countryside and refugee camps, a new ideological facet of the old urban-rural conflict emerged between radicalized cadres. Rifts also grew between the traditional promonarchy mujahideen and the more radical devotees of political Islam.

More than six million refugees fled to Iran and Pakistan.[9] Both countries, sympathetic to the struggle against Communism and for Islam, became primary bases for the mujahideen parties, who organized, raised money, and received arms there. For its part, the United States saw an opportunity to fight Soviet expansion and the spread of communism while giving the Soviet Union "its Vietnam."[10] U.S. and Saudi financing poured into the coffers of Pakistan's military intelligence agency, Inter-Services Intelligence (ISI), which "ran" the mujahideen groups from the border areas.[11] After years of fighting and arms shipments, the war economy expanded and its network of illegal trade in drugs and arms took root. Regional and great-power rivalry, and the dependence of Afghan antagonists on foreign support, have made foreign intervention a mainstay of conflict perpetuation in Afghanistan.

Soviet Withdrawal and the Start of Civil War

Failure on the battlefield and political and economic upheaval at home made the continuing intervention in Afghanistan costly and unpopular in the Soviet Union. Although the withdrawal of troops was not completed until 1989, the beginnings of a withdrawal policy began in 1985, and negotiations ongoing since 1982 resulted in the *Agreements on the*

Settlement of the Situation Relating to Afghanistan in 1988, commonly known as the Geneva Accords.[12] The essence of these accords was non-interference: the Soviet Union would withdraw its forces under United Nations observation, and the United States would halt its aid to the mujahideen. The Soviets withdrew, but both sides continued support to their clients, and the fight between the mujahideen and the Soviet-backed government in Kabul continued. During this period, as their control of territory grew, battles for control between mujahideen groups also intensified. In 1986 the Soviet Union engineered an internal coup in the Kabul government, replacing the intransigent Babrak Karmal with the brutal yet more forward-looking head of the Afghan secret police, Mohammad Najibullah.[13]

The collapse of the Soviet Union cut off support to the Najibullah government, and it soon collapsed. A UN-brokered peace deal for a transition to an interim government imploded as a series of defections and preemptive moves for power in Kabul led to Najibullah's ouster in April 1992.[14] A mixture of mujahideen groups and government militia moved quickly to take different sectors of Kabul. Long-standing rivalries between these parties—exacerbated by ideology, hunger for power, foreign designs, and the limited attention of the international community—delivered a country already devastated by thirteen years of brutal conflict into the hands of radicals and opportunists. Fighting erupted in divided Kabul, destroying the capital, the country's remaining infrastructure, and the hopes of the Afghan people.

The mujahideen parties had largely formed along regional, and therefore ethnic, lines in the Soviet era. After the outbreak of civil war among these groups, the country effectively divided into six or seven semiautonomous regions, with fighting within and between each region. As the conflict dragged on, becoming more brutal and intractable, it began to take on a more explicitly ethnic character. While ethnic tensions were not new to this diverse country, ethnicity began to be associated with factions and the atrocities committed by those factions, further deepening mutual animosities.

The focus of the international community shifted toward the emerging democracies in eastern Europe and the war in Yugoslavia. Other crises emerged as well, and Afghanistan was largely ignored as the civil war continued. Between 1992 and 1996, the UN Security Council had only one open debate on Afghanistan.[15] Several politically weak UN missions, the Office of the Secretary-General in Afghanistan and Pakistan and its successor, the United Nations Special Mission to Afghanistan (UNSMA), shuttled occasionally between the parties, but were unable to broker meaningful settlements. The United Nations engaged in humanitarian efforts, coordinated by the UN Office for the Coordination of Humanitarian Assistance (UNOCHA), including a successful demining program.[16] Other international and local organizations worked throughout the country on a variety of humanitarian and small-scale development programs, but prospects for serious reconstruction work were dim.

Rise of the Taliban and al Qaeda

In 1994, the civil war was raging with little prospect of either short- or long-term solution. Each major group had powerful supporters in the neighboring countries and others interested in the region, including Pakistan, Russia, Iran, and Saudi Arabia.[17] Despite the deleterious impact on legal trade, the growth of the opium trade and regional instability, and continuing refugee crises, the outside powers were unable to come to a mutually acceptable arrangement, and consistently worked to undermine each other.

Many of the factions worked to consolidate regional power bases. When they were successful, these regional centers often remained relatively peaceful, and the factions established quasi-functioning mini-states. Some areas of the country, however, continued to suffer from splintering factions, roadblocks, and looting, especially the Pushtun-dominated south. In 1994 the Taliban were formed, funded by Pakistan, and manned by thousands of willing recruits from fundamentalist madrassas in the border region.[18] The Taliban were created in an attempt to resolve the chaos in southern Afghanistan. Internecine warfare and warlordism were preventing Pushtuns from regaining control of the country, and were preventing Pakistan from opening a secure trade link to central Asia.[19]

The Taliban won early admiration by moving quickly to establish law and order—and open trade routes—in areas under their control. Meeting little or no armed resistance, within two years they were able to take over much of the country, including the Pushtun regions, Herat, and Kabul.[20] At first regarded as simply another faction in the civil war, the Taliban soon came to dominate the country, and their extreme ideology led to a series of renowned excesses, such as the banning of girls' education and most employment for women, imprisonment for shaving one's beard, massacres of ethnic minorities in the center and north of the country, and the destruction of the ancient stone Buddhas of Bamiyan.[21]

As the Taliban grew, another problem that would prove their undoing grew with them. Since the early days of the mujahideen war against the Soviets, radical recruits from across the Arab and Muslim worlds came to Afghanistan to learn jihad.[22] Massive sums of private Arab money were channeled into Pakistan for these purposes, and a substantial population of radicalized young men, "Afghan-Arabs," was created. A key player in funding circles through the 1980s was Osama bin Ladin, the scion of the billionaire Saudi construction family. Following the Soviet withdrawal and the Gulf War, during which Saudi Arabia allowed U.S. troops to be stationed in Islam's holy land, bin Ladin and others became disaffected and began to agitate against the United States and the Saudis. Bin Ladin's efforts became pronounced enough that the government of Sudan, where he had sought refuge in 1991, was pressured to kick him out. In May 1996 bin Ladin made his way back to Afghanistan, and soon thereafter came under the protection of the Taliban.[23]

Bin Ladin provided the Taliban with funding and ideology; in return, the Taliban gave him a free hand in Afghanistan, a place to build his fledging al Qaeda network into a full-scale organization. Bin Ladin beefed up training camps and communications facilities, built a military brigade to support the Taliban, and laid in significant supplies of weaponry and food.[24] In August 1998, when two U.S. embassies were simultaneously bombed in Kenya and Tanzania, al Qaeda was blamed. The United States responded with a cruise-missile attack on al Qaeda bases in Afghanistan and engineered a sanctions regime against the Taliban, who refused to hand over bin Ladin. Rather than becoming alienated from bin Ladin, the Taliban leadership became more alienated from the world as they continued to conquer the remainder of Afghanistan. Through this period, bin Ladin and the al Qaeda leadership became increasingly intertwined with the Taliban.[25]

The outside world remained mostly disengaged throughout this period. Although the UN secretary-general appointed Lakhdar Brahimi —a far more eminent diplomat than the previous two officeholders— as his special representative to Afghanistan, there was little political support for real change in the country. Brahimi convened an innovative "six-plus-two" process in 1999, shortly before his resignation as SRSG.[26] The process was an attempt to bring together Afghanistan's six neighbors (Pakistan, Iran, Turkmenistan, Uzbekistan, Tajikistan, and China) with the United States and Russia to craft an agreement that would pressure their various clients to negotiate an end to hostilities. The Taliban's unwillingness to negotiate and Pakistan's deep ties with them made meaningful dialogue impossible, however. In 2001, despite a payment of some $43 million by the U.S. government to the Taliban for drug control measures, Washington had already begun channeling support to their opponents.[27]

Operation Enduring Freedom and the Afghan Allies

The Taliban's chief opponent was Ahmad Shah Mahsood. On September 9, 2001, al Qaeda operatives posing as journalists assassinated him. We cannot know for certain whether the timing of these events was coordinated, but there could have been little doubt that the events of September 11 would trigger a response against al Qaeda in Afghanistan, and killing Mahsood may have been meant to undercut a military response. The result of these attacks was so spectacularly devastating, however, that the force, fury, and rapidity of the reprisals were likely not anticipated, at least not by the Taliban: the United States officially commenced Operation Enduring Freedom on October 7, 2001, only twenty-six days later.[28]

At that point, the Taliban controlled approximately 90 percent of Afghanistan's territory but had been unable to dislodge the remaining resistance from their redoubts in the mountainous northeast of the country. Officially known as the United National Islamic Front for the Salvation of Afghanistan, the "Northern Alliance" was composed of the remainder of several once-powerful military/political parties who were brought together by the common struggle against Taliban rule.[29] Most of the territory and soldiers in the Northern Alliance belonged to the Shura-i-Nizar, the wing of the Jamiat-i-Islami party controlled by

Ahmad Shah Mahsood.[30] Other groups held small pockets of land, and there was very little practical coordination between these parties, all of which had faced one another on the battlefield during the civil war period between 1992 and 1996.

The initial military campaign against the Taliban and al Qaeda was rapid and decisive. First, Taliban and al Qaeda air defenses, air bases, command and control facilities, and training camps were targeted by American air power. Then "targets of opportunity" such as military vehicles were hit, along with defense emplacements around the major cities.[31] There was basic disagreement between the U.S. State Department and the Pentagon about what to do next. The State Department, led by Colin Powell, a former general and former chairman of the Joint Chiefs of Staff, wanted to consider longer-term political consequences and adjust the campaign accordingly. The Defense Department, led by Donald Rumsfeld, wanted to dislodge the Taliban as quickly as possible, regardless of such consequences. The Defense Department prevailed.[32]

U.S. Special Forces and Central Intelligence Agency (CIA) paramilitary teams attached themselves to Northern Alliance militias to advise, coordinate attacks, retrieve intelligence, and eventually call in air strikes.[33] Cash, arms, and communications equipment were provided to the Northern Alliance forces directly by U.S. military intelligence personnel. After three weeks of bombing, the Northern Alliance had gained little ground, despite reportedly high Afghan civilian casualties. In late October, the decision was made to "unleash the Northern Alliance," and the beginning of November saw a dramatic rise in bombing, particularly of the Taliban front lines. On November 9, Northern Alliance forces captured Mazar-i-Sharif in the north, and the rest of the country began to crumble.

From a short-term military perspective, the collaboration was a remarkable success, leading to the collapse of the Taliban within five weeks.[34] From a longer-term political and military perspective, the choices made at the start of Operation Enduring Freedom proved extremely costly. Although the Taliban were decisively overthrown, the efforts to destroy al Qaeda and their support network were not as successful. Most of the top leadership, including Osama bin Ladin, his top deputies, and Taliban leader Mullah Omar, escaped. Hundreds of al

Qaeda hiding in the mountains of Tora Bora in eastern Afghanistan were able to escape into Pakistan during Coalition operations there. The botched operation was blamed on U.S. unwillingness to use its own troops on the ground, and on the incompetence or corruption of Afghan commanders.

In October 2001, a group of Pushtun leaders warned that "the fall of the Taliban regime . . . will create a political vacuum" that could ignite "a new phase of bloodshed and disorder."[35] The United States, its Coalition partners, and the United Nations were aware of these concerns, and began a dialogue in Afghanistan, in Pakistan, and with the supporters of the former Afghan king in Rome to create a broader-based Afghan political coalition. Many were specifically calling for Kabul to be protected as "neutral political space," a demilitarized zone in which politics could flourish away from the threat of armed conflict.[36] While Western leaders' public statements warned the Northern Alliance to stay out of Kabul, U.S. political leadership at the highest levels encouraged the Northern Alliance to march to the outskirts of the city as the Taliban started to abandon it. On November 13, despite repeated assurances that they would respect international calls to stay out, the Northern Alliance took Kabul.[37]

As Taliban influence receded around the country, the newly reinvigorated factional armies rolled into their old domains, one after the other. Operation Enduring Freedom effectively turned control of Afghanistan back to an array of regional commanders who had spent the early 1990s in a vicious civil war. With the Northern Alliance in control of Kabul, and various groups in control of the countryside, the post-Taliban political environment looked eerily like the pre-Taliban environment, with a few significant differences. First, the security environment was dominated by the U.S. military, willing to knock over any obstacle between it and al Qaeda. Second, the dominance of the main factions in their areas of operation, especially the Shura-i-Nizar, was greater than it had ever been before.

The subsequent, unstable security situation in Afghanistan left the success of the entire operation in question. Indeed, the planning and conduct of U.S. operations evidenced a cavalier disregard for political and economic consequences—not only to Afghanistan but also to the United States. The U.S. presence in Afghanistan is estimated to have cost approximately $2 billion per month for the first several months, and up to $1 billion per month for the duration of the operation.[38] More importantly, the long-term security problems that could keep U.S. forces in Afghanistan for years to come resulted in part from how the war itself was fought.

U.S. use of proxy Afghan forces meant that those forces had to be funded, armed, and trained. This assistance gave factions the opportunity to put their hands back on the levers of power, and they were therefore able to extract far more funding and support from other sources as well. Indeed, the fact that the United States kept a lid on interfactional fighting meant that factions did not have to expend resources as they had during the civil war, arguably allowing them to further consolidate their power locally.

As of early 2003, approximately 11,500 Coalition soldiers were in Afghanistan, 8,500 of them U.S. forces. The U.S. military indicated that it planned to scale back its forces in the country by June 2004. According to the then commander of Coalition forces, Lieutenant General Dan McNeill, the Afghans would by that time "have the ability to take on a large share of their own security."[39] This assessment was largely predicated on dealing with the threat posed by remnants of al Qaeda and the Taliban, not on any ability to provide security countrywide.

By December 2004, however, the Coalition had actually grown to roughly 19,600 troops, of which roughly 1,600 remained non-U.S. forces. It showed no signs of drawing down, even as training of Afghan military and police forces (discussed in later sections) continued at an accelerated rate.[40]

The Bonn Process

A diplomatic scramble to organize Afghanistan's non-Taliban political leadership accompanied the fast-moving military campaign. There was widespread insistence, given the civil war of the 1990s, that representation at the table should be broad. UN secretary-general Kofi Annan reappointed Lakhdar Brahimi as his special representative to Afghanistan on October 3, 2001. Brahimi had served as SRSG to Afghanistan from 1997 to 1999 and was intimately familiar with the politics and the players. Although the Northern Alliance and its nominal political head, Burhanuddin Rabbani, continued to hold Afghanistan's seat at the United Nations, a wide variety of Afghan political groups were engaged in discussions with the United States and the United Nations.

Getting to Bonn

Representatives of the Northern Alliance and the former Afghan king held talks in Rome, and on October 1, 2001, they agreed to form a Supreme Council of National Unity of Afghanistan. This council was supposed to meet to agree on convening a *loya jirga,* or grand assembly,[41] although others felt that they should first select an interim government. One critical factional element, the non-Taliban Pushtun mujahideen, felt excluded from this agreement and by heavy Coalition use of the Northern Alliance. In response, some 1,500 Pushtun tribal and religious leaders met in Peshawar, Pakistan, on October 24–25 to formulate a role for themselves. The meeting was led by the head of the National Islamic Front of Afghanistan, Pir Syeed Gailani, a former mujahideen leader and religious figure. This meeting reiterated the call for a loya jirga to establish the next government.

Events on the ground quickly overtook these negotiations. The day after Kabul fell into the hands of the Northern Alliance, the UN Security Council passed Resolution 1378, affirming the United Nations' central role in supporting political transition efforts and calling for a new government that would be "broad-based, multi-ethnic and fully representative of all the Afghan people."[42] The resolution also encouraged member states to ensure the safety and security of the capital and an eventual transitional authority. This final appeal appeared to be a call to create an international security force that could provide the essential "political space" needed in Kabul to create a broad-based government.[43] The Northern Alliance quickly rejected proposals for a security force, however, arguing that they would provide security themselves.

As the noose began to close on the Taliban in their home base of Kandahar, the intense diplomacy of the United Nations and the United States persuaded key Afghan parties to meet to name an interim administration and chart the future political transition. The meeting began in Bonn on November 27 and included representatives from four main Afghan groupings: the Northern Alliance; the Rome Group, composed of family and supporters of the former king; the Peshawar

Group, comprising Pushtun mujahideen, tribal, and religious leaders based in Pakistan; and the Cyprus Group, a mixture of factions with close ties to Iran. Numerous Afghan civil society groups from inside and outside the country felt that these factions did not represent the Afghan people. Indeed, the Bonn Agreement itself acknowledges in its preamble that many groups were not "adequately represented" at the talks. Concerned Afghans outside the process organized a civil society forum to take place near Bonn, in tandem with the political negotiations, to inject alternative voices into the process.

This meeting initially evoked the failed peace talks held from 1992 to 1994 in places like Islamabad and Ashkabad. Many of the same representatives had come together before with UN mediation and inked flowery agreements and swore on Korans to abide by them. Each of these efforts had dissolved almost instantly. In his opening remarks Lakhdar Brahimi, the conference chairman and UN special representative for Afghanistan, warned the delegates, "You must not allow the mistakes of the past to be repeated, particularly those of 1992."[44] The situation in Afghanistan was quite different in 2001, however, and those with the power to twist arms to make agreements and keep them on track were again interested.

In the end, the Bonn talks were dominated by the Panjshiri Tajik faction of the Northern Alliance, the Shura-i-Nizar. With undisputed control of the capital, the strongest military, and a strong battlefield alliance with the United States, they could successfully insist on key positions in the new government. In exchange, they agreed to a relatively unaffiliated Pushtun tribal leader, Hamid Karzai, as head of the interim administration; to a limited international security force in Kabul; and to a transition process that would lead to the creation of a new constitution and elections in just thirty months.

The Bonn Agreement

The Bonn Agreement provided a framework for transformation of the Afghan political system. It was extraordinarily ambitious in scope but provided little detail on how its most essential objectives can or should be accomplished. Despite its weaknesses, the completion of the agreement was a cause for rejoicing in Afghanistan. A unique and unexpected moment had arrived that created a new chance for peace. It was widely perceived, moreover, that to squander this chance could mean many more years of darkness and repression.

The agreement laid out the powers of an interim authority, to be replaced by a transitional government authority after six months. These two administrations were to be responsible for shepherding the reconstruction process and unifying Afghanistan's political and military institutions. The agreement provided guidance as to the laws and institutions that should control these decisions. It did not provide details such as how and when disarmament and integration of military forces must occur, or what the powers of the emergency and constitutional loya jirgas should be. Nor did it clearly lay out, or guarantee, penalties for transgressions.

The lack of detail was understandable in an agreement produced in a short time under intense pressure. The agreement represented a decision to push difficult questions into the transition process, rather than resolve them up front. Instead, the agreement established a series of milestones to which the parties could eventually be held when the time was ripe. Thus the Bonn Agreement set two simultaneous processes in motion, a state-building process and a peace process. The state-building process would be the engine for reconstruction, for the formation of long-term security arrangements, and for a return to national unity. The peace process would maintain order among factions, allowing them to lessen their enmity while acknowledging, if implicitly, their de facto control of the country. The Bonn Agreement envisioned that the state and political institutions, such as a constitutional process and elections, would slowly draw sovereign authority back to the government and people, and away from the rule of the gun.

The Bonn Agreement provided for the drafting of a new constitution, to be approved by a constitutional loya jirga, which would convene just two years after Bonn.[45] Until the adoption of a new constitution, the 1964 constitution would be in force, but without a king or legislature, thus excluding a substantial portion of the meaningful provisions of that instrument.[46] Bonn also allowed for the operation of existing laws that did not contradict the provisions of the agreement or the 1964 constitution. While sensible, this provision has been unenforceable due to the enormous number of laws created by multiple, mutually antithetical regimes over thirty years, and due to a general inability to enforce laws throughout the country. The chairman of the interim and transitional administrations was given the power to make law by decree with the agreement of his cabinet, which simplified pressing legal issues.[47]

The agreement called for the creation of an independent human rights commission, a judicial commission, and a civil service commission. These commissions were given expansive mandates by decree. The human rights commission was to be responsible for deciding how to address past abuses, for conducting investigations, and for human rights education. With nearly twenty-five years of atrocities to address, some of which were committed by still powerful faction leaders, and with new abuses being committed, the commission was given an enormous and somewhat untenable mandate. The judicial commission was similarly saddled with an unfathomably large mandate—to reform and reconstruct the country's laws and judiciary. The civil service commission was charged with the overhaul of civil service employment, including the establishment of transparent and fair appointment processes and a new employee pay scale.

The Bonn Agreement also attempted to address the fractious security situation in four ways. First, the agreement required that "upon the official transfer of power, all mujahideen, Afghan armed forces and armed groups in the country shall come under the command and control of the Interim Authority, and be reorganized according to the requirements of the new Afghan security and armed forces."[48] Second, the agreement asked the international community for its assistance in establishing and training a new Afghan army. Third, the agreement requested that the UN Security Council establish a force to "assist in the maintenance of security for Kabul and its surrounding areas," and possibly in other areas. Fourth, the Bonn participants pledged to remove all military units from Kabul and other areas where the UN-mandated force was deployed.[49]

In comparison with the process of political transition established by the agreement, the security provisions were demonstrably weak, and critical aspects of the agreement went unenforced as a result. For example, the provision putting all armed forces under the control of the Afghan interim administration established an important principle but was unenforceable. The most specific security requirement, that all military units withdraw from Kabul, also was not enforced. The International Security Assistance Force (ISAF) deployed to Kabul and successfully infused a sense of security among citizens there (discussed further, below), but the lengthy refusal of key Western military powers to expand the force to other areas left the rest of the country considerably less secure than it might have been.

The final critical aspect of the Bonn Agreement was the selection of the interim cabinet. In Afghanistan, confidence in peaceful transitions of power was understandably low, and thus the composition of the interim administration also defined, to many, the future composition of the Afghan government. The division of posts was widely viewed to be extremely lopsided, with the Panjshiri faction of the Shura-i-Nizar claiming the three most powerful ministerial posts: defense, interior, and foreign affairs. The selection of Hamid Karzai, head of the Pushtun Popalzai tribe, as chairman and the agreement to allow the return of the former king were attempts to reduce Pushtun alienation from the interim administration. The potential power of the chairman and that of the former king were far less concrete, however, than the very real power that the Shura-i-Nizar triumvirate exerted over Kabul and Afghanistan's foreign relations. It was not only the less well represented non–Northern Alliance groups who complained that "injustices have been committed in the distribution of ministries."[50] Powerful members of the Northern Alliance, such as Rashid Dostum and Ismael Khan, decried the outcome as unfair and even humiliating.[51]

Political Support for Peace

Transforming the broad framework of Bonn into a multiyear effort to quell a restive country would require sustained efforts on the part of Afghans, the international coalition, major donors, and the countries of the region. Afghanistan in 2001 was the product of decades of international intervention: from outright invasion by the Soviets to the not-so-covert arms pipeline funded by the United States and Saudi Arabia, from Pakistani military officers working with the Taliban to al Qaeda battalions fighting the Northern Alliance to the dozens of nations that participated in Operation Enduring Freedom. Transforming Afghanistan from a black hole of suffering, extremism, and criminality into a functioning country would require concerted political support from many quarters.

International Actors

Holding the coalition of actors assembled through the Bonn process together in a peaceful transition process has been the primary occupation of the political arms of both the United Nations and the Western powers engaged in Afghanistan. Among those working toward peace in Afghanistan, there has been nearly universal support for the Bonn Agreement as the overall framework for this process. Standing at the head of this effort on the behalf of the United Nations was SRSG Brahimi, a diplomat with unusually high international standing and considerable prior experience with Afghanistan. Brahimi maintained a direct relationship with most of country's political-military leadership and worked steadfastly, with the full support of the Security Council, to ensure that the framework of the Bonn Agreement did not collapse. From March 2002 until January 2004, he did so as head of the UN Assistance Mission in Afghanistan (UNAMA), a nonmilitary operation whose job it was to provide political advice to the emerging Afghan government as well as to coordinate UN assistance to the country. Succeeded as head of mission by Jean Arnault, his political deputy from UNAMA's inception, Brahimi went on to serve as the secretary-general's special adviser on Iraq.[52]

The United States, and to a lesser extent the United Nations, treated peace and security as its foremost concerns in Afghanistan, subordinating, at least in the short term, other principles such as broad representativeness in government and human rights accountability. Its approach rested on the premise that a lasting peace could be forged only if the country's regional faction leaders—all armed, many dangerous—could be kept inside Bonn's political tent.

Heading the U.S. effort in the country for more than three years was the U.S. special envoy (later ambassador) to Afghanistan, Zalmay Khalilzad. Ambassador Khalilzad, an Afghan by birth, found himself in charge of the U.S. National Security Council office responsible for Afghanistan on September 11, 2001. Indeed, he was actively working on a change of U.S. policy toward Afghanistan prior to the terrorist attacks on that day. Subsequently, Khalilzad was the most visible nonmilitary U.S. figure in Afghanistan, appearing at critical moments to apply political pressure to Afghan decision makers. He remained U.S. ambassador from November 2003 to June 2005, when he took up his new post as ambassador to Iraq.

The United States focused on stability first, because instability could provide an opening for the return of the Taliban and al Qaeda, the bulk of whose forces were not captured or killed in the early fighting but escaped into Pakistan or, in the case of the Taliban, melted back into their villages. Al Qaeda in particular had no stake in the peace process and would continue seeking to derail it at all costs. Security and stability would also give the United States an exit strategy from Afghanistan.

In late 2002, a fear emerged in Kabul that the United States' focus on Iraq would draw the country's attention away from Afghanistan. Khalilzad, also responsible for aspects of Iraq policy, was seen less frequently in Kabul, and the security situation and disarmament of factional leaders did not appear to be progressing. Deteriorating security in Afghanistan in the fall of 2002 and spring of 2003, coupled with the unexpected instability in Iraq, caused the U.S. administration to rethink its level of commitment to Afghanistan. That fall, Washington adopted an "accelerating success strategy," significantly increasing funding for Afghanistan and moving Khalilzad to Kabul as ambassador. Despite this renewed commitment, along with accelerated training for Afghan security forces, Karzai still found himself forced to accommodate, rather than disarm, factional leaders for nearly another full year.[53]

The United Kingdom, Germany, and Japan played important supporting roles, stepping in to assist at critical moments; Germany hosted the Bonn process, for instance, and gave considerable support to the emergency loya jirga. Germany was also the lead donor for the police sector, which will play a long-term role in the stabilization process. The British, who led the first ISAF, continued to push the Bonn process and had the lead international role in controlling narcotics—among the most important issues for long-term stability. Japan hosted the initial reconstruction pledging conference in Tokyo in January 2002 and acted as lead donor for the disarmament, demobilization, and reintegration (DDR) process for Afghan militia forces.

Afghanistan's neighbors, particularly Pakistan, Iran, and Uzbekistan, along with Russia and India, publicly supported the Bonn process, but after decades of intensive power competition it has been difficult for these states to align their interests with their competitor-neighbors and to cut off support to their clients in Afghanistan. These actors see themselves in a long-term game, and their influence has been deeply deleterious to peace over the last twenty-plus years. The Soviet invasion, Pakistani-Indian power competition, and the fact that each of Afghanistan's neighbors was supporting one or more favored factions all fueled conflict within Afghanistan. When SRSG Brahimi briefed the Security Council on November 13, 2001, he argued that it would be impossible to achieve a durable solution without the consensus of Afghanistan's neighbors.[54]

The neighbors in turn faced pressures from Afghanistan, including substantial insecurity on their borders, massive narcotics and arms trafficking, and the special interests of ethnic and sectarian populations that straddled national borders. Pakistan and Iran also struggled with enormous refugee populations. All were hobbled by internal political crises pitting conservative Islamic movements against more moderate executives—crises made more volatile by the presence of U.S. forces in the region or on national soil.

The neighbors' years of support to various movements inside Afghanistan likely continued, post-Bonn. The Pakistani military intelligence agency, the ISI, was accused of activity in southern Afghanistan —perhaps even in support of its old customers, Gulbuddin Hekmatyar and the Taliban. The Iranians were similarly accused of supporting their neighbor in western Afghanistan, the strongman Ismael Khan, and the Shi'a Hazara parties.[55]

Russia continues to play a role in Central Asian security issues, and its experiences in Afghanistan and Chechnya still weigh on the Russian political consciousness. Russia nonetheless made deals with minister of defense Mohammad Fahim to provide helicopters and gunships to his ministry rather than to the national army, and for a time reinforced its troop presence in Tajikistan, avowedly due to concerns about drugs, Taliban, and al Qaeda.[56]

India supported the Northern Alliance during the period of Taliban rule, that being the antithesis of Pakistani policy. In the post-Bonn period, India has offered substantial amounts of reconstruction aid, pledging $400 million through 2008, having decided that being on good terms with Afghanistan and working to ensure its stability could pay both strategic and economic dividends. Projects supported include road links from the Iranian port of Chahbahar through Afghanistan to Central Asia; the Salma Dam hydroelectric power project in Herat; other power transmission projects in Kabul; and training for Afghanistan's civil service.[57] India has also taken on a project with significant political symbolism, constructing Afghanistan's new parliament building.

The neighbors are also going along with many other efforts to support Afghanistan's transition to stability, including the December 2002 "Kabul Declaration on Good Neighborly Relations," in which they proclaim a common desire for peace and stability, support for the Bonn process and the transitional government, and determination to fight "terrorism, extremism, and narco-trafficking."[58] It remains to be seen, however, whether these impulses will overwhelm the neighbors' more traditional impulses to support their own Afghan clients.

The Afghans

Ultimately, the longevity and sustainability of the ongoing peace process will depend on the Afghans themselves. The Afghan people are weary from years of conflict and migration. The physical, economic, and cultural devastation of multiple wars has left the population desperate for basic security, that is, freedom from war and predation. It has also left many aspects of society weak, and the ability of traditional institutions to enforce norms on social and political actors has broken down. In this vacuum the *tofangdar*, or gun-holders, flourish. Many Afghans believe that international attention and resources will not last, especially if the country reverts to war.

For many ordinary Afghans, the regime change in 2001 heralded a return to warlordism, evoking the chaotic pre-Taliban years. Yet many commanders in the often loose hierarchy of armed factions were not mere predators but evolved as local leaders through the years of war. Some came from positions of traditional leadership, or earned the respect and loyalty of the population. Others, however, did rise to prominence through acts of brutality, attracting disaffected recruits through religious radicalism and the lure of money provided by foreign sponsors. Many were revered by some elements of their communities and hated by others.

By 2002, these leaders—the commanders, warlords, and regional power brokers—stood at a crossroads. In one direction lay the Bonn vision of a more harmonious, peaceful future. Regional leaders had much to lose in this transition. The process of building a national army and demobilizing local militias would diminish their military power. The reconstruction of the central government, which meant central appointments to positions of authority and pressure to turn over customs revenues, would reduce their resources and ability to dispense largesse. Eventually, they would have to harness electoral power or face being phased out, powerless, and possibly at risk of prosecution or humiliation by a truth commission in the future. Even if a reckoning for past abuses seemed unlikely for some while, the major leaders were all made aware of this possibility by the work of human rights nongovernmental organizations (NGOs), activists, and the establishment of the Afghan Independent Human Rights Commission, as mandated by the Bonn Agreement.

What lay in the other direction was unclear. It seemed unlikely that the status quo ante of the civil war years could hold—with independent fiefdoms throughout the country and battles for Kabul and areas of overlap. This status quo ante was economically attractive only to the very few who envisioned being able to capture the limited resources of cross-border trade, because investment in agriculture and industry would be hobbled and reconstruction funds would dry up. Those seen as spoilers would come under significant pressure, drawing the ire of the government and the international community.

The U.S. military possessed the capability in Afghanistan to overwhelm any domestic force arrayed against it within days. If the United States decided that one of the established regional leaders had fallen afoul of its goals in the country, he very likely could be driven from power just by the threat of force. The power of the B-52 has become legend in Afghanistan; faction leaders fear and admire its potential for immediate and devastating consequences. At the same time, the United States has shown no stomach for challenging the most recalcitrant of the regional leaders, and may be perceived as being even less likely to do so as time goes on.

Most regional leaders hedged their bets. The leaders of the Shura-i-Nizar, Hezb-i-Wahadat, and Junbesh-i-Milli factions, as well as Ismael

Khan, all maintained their armies, their independent sources of revenue, and their links with foreign sponsors. At the same time they cooperated to some degree with the central government, signing agreements to support the national army and the DDR process, and to provide revenues to the central government.[59] But most needed incentives to stay on the cooperative path, and sustaining such incentives looked to be very difficult, as the legal system was neither independent nor powerful enough to enforce power- and revenue-sharing agreements.

Of the independent revenue sources available to these leaders, the most significant was opium. Afghanistan's post-Taliban opium production boomed, to 3,600 metric tons in 2003, or 75 percent of global opium production. The phenomenal amount of illicit, untraced wealth that the opium trade produces can be employed in turn to defend the trade and provide a nearly unlimited budget for arms, soldiers, and terrorist operations. Recent estimates put profits within Afghanistan at $2.8 billion per year—a sum greater than all aid to Afghanistan and the country's entire national budget combined, including support to the national army and police.[60] Any long-term plan for stability must address the poppy problem in a meaningful and effective way, or prospects for peace will be dim. The bulk of the opium is produced in Pushtun areas, increasing both the risk of instability and the likelihood that antipoppy campaigns will be seen as a further attack on Pushtun interests.

Many Pushtuns are increasingly alienated from a process seen to have simultaneously stripped power from them, awarded it to those they perceive to be hostile to their interests, and criminalized their homelands. Geography, politics, and ethnicity have made the Pushtun areas ground zero for the campaign against al Qaeda, the Taliban, and Hekmatyar. As Coalition forces systematically armed and empowered the Northern Alliance (which lacks significant Pushtun representation), they disarmed and humiliated the largely Pushtun southern and eastern parts of the country, hunting weapons caches, kicking in doors, and arresting people. As a result, Pushtun disenfranchisement and resentment grew. Although no single Pushtun force is capable of undoing the Bonn process, weak Pushtun support for the process or for the future government would make those arrangements untenable in the long term.

The constitutional convention in late 2003 marked a distinct turnaround in Pushtun politics, however, as Karzai and his supporters secured a presidential system for Afghanistan. Pushtuns saw this as a victory due to their status as the nation's largest ethnic group, and therefore the likely political beneficiaries of that system. Strong Pushtun turnout in the October 2004 presidential elections indicated continued support for Karzai and his government. His 85 percent win in the southern provinces helped keep his national total above the 50 percent threshold needed to avoid a runoff.[61]

Many former Taliban have gone back to their villages and will remain peaceful if left undisturbed by government and international forces, but others have rejected the Western-influenced government in Kabul and the continued presence of foreign troops in Afghanistan. If Pushtun disaffection with the government or foreign military forces were to grow, this latter group would find a sympathetic recruiting ground throughout the south and east. Attacks on government and international military forces and on aid workers increased through mid-2003. After tailing off during the long winter, attacks resumed at an equally high rate in the spring of 2004 and again in 2005.[62] In Pushtun areas, these attacks have been preceded or accompanied by antigovernment and anti-Coalition propaganda leaflets known as *shab-nama,* or "night letters." The leaflets, which decry Western imperialism and threaten retaliation for collaborators, are a familiar tactic of the mujahideen rebels.

On the brighter side, Afghan NGOs and civil society have emerged to support the stabilization effort. Due to the breakdown of the state and the policies of aid agencies in the 1980s and 1990s, a large number of Afghan NGOs were formed to carry out humanitarian aid and development work. Generally working on a fairly small scale with local communities, many of these organizations promoted basic aspects of social organization, including requiring local committees to develop, approve, and contribute to priorities, printing newsletters, and sometimes promoting cultural practices such as music and crafts. Today Afghanistan has hundreds of NGOs and associations, many of which are branching out into more political activities—publishing newspapers, making films, teaching human rights and conflict resolution, and forming nascent political parties. These organizations, while largely urban based, are helping to create a popular basis for peace, civil society, and an end to the impunity of the warlords.

Operation Enduring Freedom after Bonn

In June 2002, Combined/Joint Task Force 180 (CJTF-180, the name for the combined Coalition forces deployed in and around Afghanistan) took command responsibility for all operations in Afghanistan, which had previously been dispersed through branches of the U.S. Central Command, half of which were outside Afghanistan. Bagram Air Base, north of Kabul, housed from several hundred to more than a thousand U.S. troops at a time, many of whom provided force protection for the base itself. The largest concentration of U.S. troops, however, was at the Kandahar airport in southern Afghanistan.[63]

CJTF-180 was commanded by Lieutenant General Dan McNeill until June 2003. In late 2003, it became Combined Forces Command–Afghanistan (CFC-A); its new commander, Lieutenant General David Barno, relocated his offices from Bagram to space near the U.S. embassy in Kabul, to better coordinate with the ambassador and with other U.S. policy initiatives in the country.

Non-U.S. Coalition forces in theater operated under the control of CFC-A. At times, a substantial fraction of Coalition forces (air, ground, and naval) in and around Afghanistan were non-American, primarily British, Australian, French, German, Canadian, Danish, and Italian, and including special forces.[64] The Coalition has also been involved in efforts to stabilize the security situation and to aid in the reconstruction of the country, tasks that are considered to be part of the overall mission of Operation Enduring Freedom. They are detailed below.

Mandate

Operation Enduring Freedom derived its mandate from a variety of sources, both specific and implied. Fundamentally, the operation relied on the justification of self-defense in response to terrorist acts against the citizens and property of the United States, especially the attacks of September 11, 2001. Use of force in self-defense is a right recognized by Article 51 of the UN Charter. This justification underlay the subsequent expressions of support for U.S. actions in Afghanistan, whether based in U.S. or international law.[65]

In Afghanistan itself, however, there was a notable lack of official legal sanction for the ongoing presence of Coalition troops. The Bonn Agreement did not acknowledge the presence of, or ongoing operations performed by, the Coalition. Unlike ISAF, these forces had no basing or access agreement with the Afghan interim or transitional authorities. Although negotiations were reportedly ongoing at one point, as of 2005 the United States had yet to complete a status-of-forces agreement with the government that would define the legal status of U.S. personnel in Afghanistan.[66] Coalition forces were not subject to the will of the interim, transitional, or elected governments of Afghanistan, and there were no formal requirements for authorization or reporting of actions taken by the Coalition. Although there was often close cooperation and consultation on the ground between Coalition forces and the central government, it would be difficult to find any more specific mandate for Coalition presence than the general language of the Bonn Agreement and Security Council resolutions exhorting the international community to aid Afghanistan in its bid for stability and reconstruction.

Planning, Deployment, and Implementation

The planning and initial deployment of Operation Enduring Freedom into the Afghan theater of operations faced several serious hurdles. First, the very objectives of the campaign were initially unclear regarding the Taliban. Second, the Coalition needed bases and overflight rights in the region that did not exist as of September 12, 2001. Third, Afghanistan was, in the minds of many, a quagmire waiting to happen. Conventional wisdom on Afghanistan was that it was a country of fiercely independent, extremely resilient people mired in tribalism who stopped fighting each other only long enough to destroy invading armies.

It was from these circumstances that the United States devised its initial strategy: to partner with the anti-Taliban Afghan forces, using massive airpower and a small but forceful presence of U.S. Special Forces soldiers and CIA paramilitary operatives. The United States was looking for a means of fighting a war without making itself vulnerable or appearing to be an invading and occupying force. The introduction of ground forces would come as the war progressed. Allied combat support was also limited in the beginning, with only Great Britain participating in initial combat missions.

The Coalition's initial military campaign having been recounted earlier in this chapter, the following section focuses on its subsidiary mission: promoting security by deploying civil affairs teams, training the Afghan National Army, and creating Provincial Reconstruction Teams.

Managing (In)Security

Early in the war, U.S. Special Forces teams fanned out to accompany the factional forces that the United States was supporting with funds, advice, intelligence, and air support. The Special Forces teams, or A-teams, consisted of twelve soldiers with specialties in weapons, engineering, medical care, communications, and operations and intelligence. These teams have remained throughout the country, gathering intelligence and working with factional leaders. While much of their mission has been focused around the war on terrorism, they have also come to play a complex role as mediators and messengers, even attempting to mediate "green-on-green" disputes. (The U.S. Army refers to all military forces in Afghanistan that are not Taliban, al Qaeda, or Hekmatyar, or that are nominally "progovernment" or "pro-Bonn," as "green" forces.) With the capability to call in massive airpower within hours, these forces are the ambassadors of B-52 diplomacy. The teams have some funds to disperse as they see fit, "to influence people and do favors."[67]

Coalition policy was not to intervene in "green-on-green" fighting, but its rules of engagement in such circumstances remain classified. Through 2004 a number of "green-on-green" flare-ups occurred throughout the country, most notably in the north and west, and the Coalition intervened directly with military force on numerous occasions. For instance, in December 2002, B-52 bombers struck the front lines of an ongoing conflict between "green" forces in western Afghanistan. The fighting quickly stopped. While the U.S. military claimed that the attack was to protect U.S. forces caught in the cross-fire, Afghan factional leaders claimed that the U.S. intervention was to stop the fighting. U.S. officials encouraged this perception, however, hoping it would prevent similar violence in the future.

When factional fighting did erupt once again near Herat in August 2004, the United States airlifted a battalion of the new Afghan National Army (ANA) to the trouble spot, along with its embedded

Coalition advisers, and provided air cover while the ANA troops positioned themselves between the two factions. The ANA thereafter established, with U.S. assistance, a permanent garrison in Herat that helped cement central government authority and facilitate the replacement, one month later, of Herat's previously untouchable strongman, Ismael Khan.[68]

Coalition policy appeared calibrated to maintain an ambiguous yet credible threat of force against factional elements that went too far in their own use of force, so as to affect the choices of factional leaders without actually making a commitment to intervene. The classified nature of U.S. rules of engagement keeps those leaders from knowing how far they can go before incurring the wrath of the U.S. armed forces. Not knowing where the line is may ensure even greater caution, for fear of miscalculation.

Civil Affairs

Coalition civil affairs efforts mostly involved mobile teams conducting "hearts-and-minds" work in conjunction with more security-oriented missions. These were guided by the Coalition Joint Civil-Military Operations Task Force (CJCMOTF, or "Chick Motif"), which was established in October 2001. CJCMOTF was responsible for planning, coordinating, and executing Coalition humanitarian and reconstruction operations. In the early phases of the war, a Humanitarian Affairs Coordination Center was also established at the U.S. Central Command headquarters in Tampa. UN agencies and Coalition partners sent representatives to the center to coordinate activities.

At first the Coalition engaged in emergency humanitarian assistance, dropping food rations from aircraft and providing logistics and security support for international organizations bringing food into the country. CJCMOTF sent Coalition Humanitarian Liaison Cells (known as "Chicklets") to accompany the U.S. Special Forces A-teams. The Chicklets were usually six soldiers from civil affairs battalions who engaged in small-scale humanitarian or reconstruction activities, paid for by the U.S. Defense Department's Overseas Humanitarian, Disaster, and Civic Aid (OHDACA) fund. In early November 2002, these teams were renamed CAT-A's (Civil Affairs Team–Alphas). They became roving teams operating out of a permanent Civil-Military Operations

Center and more focused on projects, undertaking needs assessments, sharing information, and vetting projects with NGOs, the United Nations, and the transitional government.

CJCMOTF reported an expenditure of $3.5 million on such activities through November 2002.[69] Most were undertaken in consultation with local leadership only, and were not coordinated with the central government or with international organizations or local NGOs.

The third phase transitioned to larger projects that were more targeted at the reconstruction of the state apparatus. CJCMOTF had $12 million in OHDACA funds to disburse through this program in 2003. It made an effort to conform these expenditures to the priorities of the central government as well as local authorities, and made increased efforts to consult with international and Afghan organizations working in each team's area. CJCMOTF planned, in early 2003, to target its funds increasingly at infrastructure projects such as roads and bridges, government buildings (including courthouses), and possibly border posts, but this approach was rejected by OHDACA in favor of "humanitarian" projects.[70] Still, by April 2004, CJCMOTF projects had helped to build 400 schools, dig 600 wells, and construct 170 health clinics. Most of these projects were subcontracted to NGOs and other contractors, who employed up to 30,000 Afghan laborers for at least short stints.[71] By this time, moreover, CJCMOTF had a growing network of more or less permanent outposts in the provinces.

Provincial Reconstruction Teams

In November 2002, the Coalition began to evolve a new model for its noncombat military operations in the field. This concept, the Provincial Reconstruction Team (PRT),[72] evolved from the work of the earlier civil affairs teams. Devised in response to the need for a more significant foreign military presence in the field, the PRTs operated from protected bases housing, initially, from forty to a hundred military and affiliated personnel. The first three U.S.-led teams deployed to Gardez, Bamiyan, and Kunduz, and the fourth, led by the United Kingdom, deployed to Mazar-i-Sharif in late July 2003.[73]

The PRT network began to expand rapidly in 2004, and the ISAF, under North Atlantic Treaty Organization (NATO) command, assumed control of some of the teams in the fall. By mid-2005, two networks of

PRTs existed—those reporting to CJCMOTF and the Coalition, and those reporting to ISAF. Ownership of the PRTs evolved equally rapidly: New Zealand assumed responsibility for Bamiyan in September 2003; Germany took over Kunduz in October, which then switched from Coalition to ISAF command the following January. In November 2003, South Korea assumed joint responsibility (with the United States) for the PRT in Charikar, north of Kabul; in August 2005, Canada took over the PRT in Kandahar with 250 troops. (There is also a 2,000-strong Canadian battle group at the head of Coalition forces that replaced U.S. troops in Kandahar—one of Afghanistan's most dangerous and violent locales.)[74] Table 7.1 shows the PRT structure as of mid-2005 (plans called for at least one PRT in each province).[75]

There was early controversy and confusion over whether PRTs were intended to act primarily as security-producing operations or as reconstruction operations. This confusion emanated from a variety of sources, including official statements, the observed structure of the teams, and past practices. According to CJCMOTF, the purpose of the PRTs was

(1) to help strengthen the Afghan central government's influence, credibility, and ability to operate in the countryside; and

(2) to assist in the removal of regional causes of instability (including residual terrorist threat; poor infrastructure; economy and education; and competition [sometimes deadly] among regional power brokers, and between regional power brokers and the central government)[76]

However, U.S. military and government officials variously described the purpose of the PRTs as to "extend the ISAF effect," to undertake "peacekeeping-like operations," and to "coordinate assistance."[77] The PRTs were also tasked to facilitate information sharing between NGOs, the United Nations, and the Afghan government and to monitor the security situation. They were expected to report on a wide variety of issues, including government operations, infrastructure improvements, commerce, health care and basic human needs, security operations, economic improvement, Afghan acceptance of the rule of law, and local and provincial leaders' acceptance of the Afghan central government.[78]

The contrast between these grand goals and the limited resources of the PRTs was striking. One military official dismissed the notion

Table 7.1. Provincial Reconstruction Teams in Afghanistan

Area	Province	City	2003	2004	2005
Center	Bamiyan	Bamiyan	U.S. (Mar) >>N.Z. (Sep)		
Center	Parwan	Charikar	U.S./ROK (Nov)		
North East	Kunduz	Kunduz	U.S. (Mar) >> FRG (Oct) >>	FRG (Jan)	
North East	Badakhshan	Faizabad		*FRG (Jul)*	
North	Balkh	Mazar-i-Sharif	U.K. (Jul)	*>> U.K. (Jul)*	*>> Italy (Jun)*
North	Faryab	Maimana		*U.K. (Jul)*	*>> U.S. (Jun)*
North	Baghlan	Pul-i-Khumri		*Neth (Oct)*	*Spain (Sum.)*
					Lithuania (Sum.)
West	Herat	Herat	U.S. (Dec)		
West	Farah	Farah		U.S. (Sep)	
West	Badghis	Qala-i-Now			
West	Ghor	Chaghcharan			
South	Kandahar	Kandahar	U.S. (Dec)		*>> Canada (Aug)*
South	Zabul	Qalat		U.S. (Apr)	
South	Helmand	Lashkar Gah		U.S. (Sep)	
South	Uruzgan	Tarin Kot		U.S. (Sep)	

South East	Ghazni	Ghazni	U.S. (Feb)		U.S. (Mar)
South East	Paktiya	Gardez			U.S. (Mar)
South East	Khost	Khost			
South East	Paktika	Sharana		U.S. (Sep)	
East	Nangrahar	Jalalabad		U.S. (Jan)	
East	Kunar	Asadabad		U.S. (Feb)	

Note: Dates refer to official openings, often taking place after a few months of operations. Coalition PRTs are in **bold**. NATO PRTs are in *italic*.
FRG = Federal Republic of Germany. Neth = Netherlands. N.Z. = New Zealand. ROK = Rep. of Korea. U.K. = United Kingdom. U.S. = United States

Sources: Peter Viggo Jakobsen, "PRTs in Afghanistan: Successful but Not Sufficient," Danish Institute for International Studies, DIIS Report 2005:6 (Copenhagen, 2005). NATO Multimedia, "Afghanistan: International Security Assistance Force (ISAF)—Provincial Reconstruction Teams (PRTs)," updated June 9, 2005, www.nato.int/multi/map-afghanistan.htm. Kenneth Katzman, "Afghanistan: Post-war Governance, Security, and U.S. Policy," Congressional Research Service, The Library of Congress, CRS RL30588, updated June 15, 2005. American Forces Press Service, "Canadian Military Assumes Command of Afghanistan PRT," August 17, 2005. NATO, "NATO in Afghanistan: How Did This Operation Evolve?" updated June 9, 2005, www.nato.int/issues/afghanistan/evolution.htm. UN Security Council, "Letter dated 1 July 2005 from the Secretary-General addressed to the President of the Security Council," S/2005/431, July 5, 2005.

that the limited PRTs could have an impact anything like that of ISAF on the security front. For example, the Bamiyan PRT had forty soldiers, nearly half of whom were there simply to protect the base and thus could not leave the facility. That left two to three teams available for patrolling in a region that would take days to drive across. The PRTs were certainly ineffective at controlling small-scale criminality but may have had a broader effect on the decision making of factional leaders. The U.S. forces, albeit small in number, carried tremendous "reach-back" capabilities—the power to call in overwhelming military force with great speed—and the PRTs shared at least some of those capabilities. In other words, a show of force for the Coalition in Afghanistan does not have to be a large on-the-ground presence, just a visible presence.

Despite the use of "reconstruction" in the name of the PRTs, this activity was relatively low on their list of priorities, so in their first year the PRTs and the remaining CAT-A teams had relatively little to spend. NGOs nonetheless argued that these teams were engaging in basic reconstruction activities that could be undertaken more cheaply and effectively by others, without the associated dangers of confusion between military and civilian actors. In response to this criticism, the PRT concept evolved to emphasize the teams' contribution to the security environment over the impact of limited direct reconstruction programs. The PRTs gained "embedded" officers from the U.S. Agency for International Development and the Afghan government's Interior Ministry, indicating their connection to the larger U.S. assistance program and to efforts to extend the writ of the central government.

The fundamental question after the first year of this program was whether the presence of Coalition military units throughout the country extended Kabul's authority more than it highlighted the weakness of the transitional government. This concern related not only to local perceptions but also to the way in which the PRTs interacted with and supported local and regional leadership. Over time, a formal consultative arrangement with mixed international and Afghan membership evolved to govern the activities of the PRTs—both Coalition- and NATO-managed. A PRT executive committee, meeting monthly, has provided overall policy guidance. Cochaired by the minister of the interior and the commanders of ISAF and CFC-A, it also included the ministers of finance and of reconstruction and development, the NATO senior civilian representative in Afghanistan, the SRSG of UNAMA, and the ambassadors of PRT troop contributors and "potential contributors."

The committee devised standard terms of reference for all PRTs and policies to govern transitions from PRT-supported to full Afghan government authority. A PRT working group, meeting weekly, served as "a civil-military discussion and coordination forum on operational issues," and reported to the executive committee. An NGO civil-military working group, chaired by UNAMA, met monthly to "facilitate communication among NGOs, international military forces, and the Afghan government, and address NGO concerns."[79]

In January 2005, reflecting the evolution of PRT activities from humanitarian action to reconstruction to support for the central government, the PRT executive committee promulgated the following mission statement, accepted by both ISAF and CFC-A:

> Provincial Reconstruction Teams will assist the Islamic Republic of Afghanistan to extend its authority, in order to facilitate the development of a stable and secure environment in the identified area of operations, and enable SSR [security sector reform] and reconstruction efforts.[80]

Common terms of reference notwithstanding, the structures and operational styles of the PRTs continued to vary by owner and operating environment. In U.S. PRTs, located mostly in less stable parts of the country, both the civilian and military components of the team worked under military command, with emphasis on "quick-impact" infrastructure projects, the budget for which increased to $52 million in 2004. In the UK model, on the other hand, used in Mazar-i-Sharif, in Maimana, and by the New Zealand contingent in Bamiyan, the military, political, and development components led "jointly." The military component promoted local security with small, lightly armed mobile observation teams whose members lived among villagers while on extended patrols and supported disarmament and demobilization of local fighters. The political component stressed local institution building, and the development component selected projects with priority on "support for local authorities and courts." Finally, in the German model, the civilian and military components were completely

separate. Germany provided a comparatively large military component (270 troops for the Kunduz PRT) with primary emphasis on force
protection and on security for the civilian component. German patrols
were heavily armed and returned to base at night. Although "seen as
less effective than the British," the German security presence nonetheless seemed to contribute to the "relocation of dozens of NGOs . . . to
the area since the German PRT was established." Definitive conclusions
about the three models' effectiveness were difficult to draw because
there was "no systematic monitoring" of PRT performance against pre-
set strategic objectives, and each operated under somewhat different
physical, political, and ethnological circumstances. Separate third-party
analyses suggested that the British model seemed to find most favor
with the aid community and with Afghans, although it was used in areas
less directly exposed to threat from hostile forces than were Coalition
operating areas.[81]

A mid-2004 opinion survey of 700 Afghans living in six cities
around the country, conducted by the Human Rights Research and
Advocacy Consortium, found that very few (about 3 percent) wanted
their security to be provided by international forces alone. One-third preferred that it be provided by Afghan security forces exclusively. Nearly
60 percent, however, preferred to see responsibility for security shared
between international and national forces, expressing hope that the new
Afghan National Army would prove an effective counterweight to local
"commanders" but seeing international forces as added insurance.[82]

Creation of the National Army

The keystone of the Coalition security plan in Afghanistan was the
effort to create the Afghan National Army. The army was expected to
grow slowly, establishing itself as the lone authorized military force in
the country. As the ANA developed, a simultaneous DDR process was
intended to shrink the remaining factional militias. Gradually, the balance of military power would shift in favor of the central government,
allowing it to maintain peace and security.

Chairman Karzai signed a decree in Bonn on December 1, 2002,
establishing the ANA and setting out its parameters. According to this
decree, the entire military, including civilian personnel, was not to exceed 70,000. There was to be a central command in Kabul, with three

other commands deployed "on the basis of strategic and geographical factors."[83] The military would be subordinate to civilian authority, and the head of state would be the commander in chief. A military commission, which included a number of Afghanistan's key factional leaders, was formed within the transitional administration to oversee the process. Two subcommissions were also established—on recruitment of soldiers and selection of officers—to ensure ethnic diversity and merit-based appointments.

The United States took the lead for this project and through 2002 committed $50 million to it.[84] The training program, which included officers from France, Hungary, Romania, and Germany, planned to train, by June 2004, three full brigades (two light infantry brigades and one quick-reaction brigade) that would constitute the central corps command of the ANA. Each brigade would consist of five battalions, and each battalion would have about 600 soldiers, for a total of approximately 9,000 soldiers trained. This process also entailed the rehabilitation and reorganization of the Kabul Military Training Center and substantial reform of the Ministry of Defense. Having started slowly, the program was basically on track by spring 2004. A $500 million investment had produced, to that point, an army of roughly 8,000 soldiers and four new battalions in training at any one time. In March 2005, that training capacity was expanded to six battalions at a time, intended to further bolster ANA ranks in time for parliamentary elections scheduled for September 2005 and raise the force level to 43,000 by the end of 2006. By spring 2005, the ANA had grown to 20,000 troops, and battalions had been deployed to four garrisons outside of Kabul, in Mazar-i-Sharif, Herat, Gardez, and Kandahar. U.S. engineers were at work building ANA regional command headquarters in each location; the $63 million base at Herat was designed to accommodate 4,000 troops (a brigade with five battalions—the standard model for each regional command).[85]

The national army had to be created essentially from scratch. Initially led by U.S. Special Forces personnel working in parallel with French army instructors, ANA training transitioned, after the start of the war in Iraq, to the control of a sequence of U.S. National Guard command headquarters. As Task Force Phoenix, the guard units managed a multinational training group of 1,200 personnel that ran recruits through ten weeks of basic training and twenty weeks of unit training, and then continued to advise them in the field. The roughly 300 (later 600) members of these embedded training teams operated at several levels: A Training Assistance Group advised the Afghan officers and noncommissioned officers who, after roughly the first year of the training program, conducted the basic training courses. The Central Corps Assistance Team worked with the ANA's central corps command staff at Pol-e-Charki garrison outside Kabul. The Brigade Training Teams advised command staff at the brigade and battalion levels and accompanied ANA units into the field. Finally, Mobile Training Teams promoted correct equipment use and maintenance by operational units.[86]

The financial difficulties of sustaining the army were foremost in the minds of planners. Future development aid commitments will not go to the army, and the state can easily be hobbled if all its discretionary revenue is eaten up by the military. Pressure was exerted at one point to create an even larger army (up to 100,000 troops), mostly to accommodate members of militia forces that were claimed to number that many men. These pressures were strongly countered, however, by the twin realities of financing and the need to train professional soldiers rather than to make the new army a jobs program for the militias.

Two issues proved particularly difficult: the factional tendencies of the Ministry of Defense and retaining trained soldiers. The Ministry of Defense was controlled by Mohammad Fahim, the military leader of the Shura-i-Nizar. With his own substantial armed forces already in or near Kabul, Fahim tried to make the ANA an extension of those forces. About ninety of the one hundred generals appointed to the ANA during the interim administration reportedly were Panjshiri, and most of the initial wave of recruits sent by commanders for ANA training were Tajik.[87] Attempts to reform the Defense Ministry were repeatedly rebuffed and seen as hostile to the Northern Alliance. One alliance official described a July 2003 conference on defense reforms as a "U.S.-led effort to undercut the power of the alliance." Karzai and his U.S. backers took the first major step toward addressing this problem in September 2003 when twenty-three senior leaders in the Defense Ministry— though not the defense minister—were replaced. When Karzai selected a running mate for the October presidential elections, however, he did not select Fahim. Further, when the newly elected Karzai selected his cabinet that December, he dropped Fahim in favor of the army's first deputy chief of staff, Abdur Rahim Wardak, a Pushtun and a professional soldier of the old royalist army. These successive moves were made possible in part because the heavy weapons held by Kabul-based militia forces largely loyal to Fahim were removed from the city between January and September 2004 by ISAF and cantoned under international observation in four locations, with ammunition removed.[88] By mid-2004, moreover, the Central Corps of the ANA had been trained and equipped and was a potential counterweight to Fahim's militia.

For other factional leaders to be persuaded that the ANA would not be used as a tool of one faction against another, the rest of the political process also had to be seen as moving toward fair and broad representation. This was a necessary precursor to factional leaders' willingness to give up their own insurance policies against narrow central government control. Thus the outcome of the electoral process was expected to have substantial impact on the plan to shift the balance of military power in favor of the ANA (see the "Supporting elections" section under UNAMA, below).

This situation was further complicated by the establishment of regional corps commands, which legitimated the various warlord armies as the Afghan Militia Forces (AMF) and provided funds from the Ministry of Defense to each AMF corps commander to pay his troops. As would subsequently be determined in the process of implementing DDR, the numbers of AMF troops were inflated successively as they passed up the chain of command, creating multiple opportunities for skimming funds. Thus, for example, the ministry listed 1,700 troops in AMF Division 25, while its commander claimed to have 1,200 and the local PRT estimated just 770, which the DDR program and the ministry later accepted as the target for purposes of DDR. So the DDR program's declared goal of disarming 40 percent of a claimed 100,000 AMF fighters was sufficient to disarm nearly every fighter who was not a ghost soldier, a name listed by a commander to pad his payroll.[89]

The second problem was retaining trained soldiers. About half of the first battalion trained left the army, owing variously to low pay, factional allegiances, and a dislike of military service, and the loss rate remained 10 to 15 percent per month through 2003. Training for the ANA under the Coalition was quite different from being a militia member. The restrictions and discipline of modern military life—and the alienation from home and tribe—were difficult for many Afghans, especially when the draw of home included greater economic opportunities. Soldiers in training were receiving $30 per month during training and $50 per month on completion, whereas the anti–al Qaeda units that were formed to fight the war received training and salaries per soldier of up to $150 per month from the Coalition. In 2004 basic soldier salaries were increased to $70 per month upon completing training, and to an average of $110 per month for deployed troops. ANA recruiting centers independent of local commanders had been established in each province—increasing the likelihood that volunteers would be motivated to complete their enlistments—and by midyear the loss rate had dropped to between 1 and 2 percent per month.[90]

Challenges aside, the creation of the ANA moved forward more quickly than most international programs in Afghanistan. The U.S. military has an enormous amount of political authority in the country, due to the success of the anti-Taliban campaign and their support for key Afghan factions. Massive resources, including significant personnel, were brought to bear on issues that CJTF-180/CFC-A was authorized to address. The capacity of the Afghan government to absorb assistance was so limited that simply funding programs that required substantial technical means and know-how was not sufficient. Rather than rely on the Afghan government for implementation, the U.S. military implemented its programs directly. The United States did support creation of effective Afghan decision-making bodies for the long term, however, such as a National Security Council and a reorganized Defense Ministry—both crucial to establishing a national security apparatus.

The U.S. military also leaned on the factional leaders to participate in this new setup, hoping to narrow the alternatives to cooperation so significantly that factional leaders would feel they had no choice but to go along. For this strategy to work, the Coalition needed to inspire confidence that it would see the process through and that it had the will to disarm the spoilers. The growing size of the Coalition itself and the growing resources devoted to the accelerated training of the ANA, as well as its use both in Coalition operations and as the primary force for dealing with disorder—as in Herat—were welcome indicators to that effect.

Assessment of Operation Enduring Freedom

Widespread insecurity and factional competition following the collapse of the Taliban hindered efforts to create a broadly representative and legitimate government as well as to accomplish the physical reconstruction of the country. The Coalition engaged in a series of efforts to address the security situation, including mediation, coercion, payoffs, and security sector reform, but lacked a consistent, coherent public policy that would promote peace. The ultimate Coalition mission in Afghanistan was twofold: first to rid Afghanistan of al Qaeda and its supporters, and second to create a peaceful and secure Afghanistan that would no longer serve as a terrorist breeding ground. These goals were not contradictory but interdependent. The implementation strategy to achieve the first goal, however, made the second goal far more difficult to achieve.

From the onset of the military campaign, the overwhelming focus of Coalition forces in Afghanistan was on fighting the remnants of al Qaeda, the Taliban, and those troops loyal to renegade warlord Gulbuddin Hekmatyar. The Coalition arrayed its military and financial resources to achieve this goal as quickly as possible, funding, arming, and training many militias that had fought against one another in the earlier civil war period. When the war against the Taliban and al Qaeda created a power vacuum, these militias and their warlords or regional commanders filled it, creating security problems whose resolution would take years or, at the district and village level, possibly decades.

Indeed, the greatest ongoing threat to peace through 2003 did not appear to be al Qaeda or Taliban forces but interfactional rivalries and various faction leaders' discontent with the post-Bonn division of power. The Coalition thus found itself unhappily thrust into the role of unofficial peacekeeper between the Frankenstein factions it had reanimated. For the first nineteen months of operations, the Coalition was extremely circumspect about this role, downplaying both the extent of the threat and its role in preventing it, but also weathering considerable criticism of its apparent lack of commitment to security and stability in Afghanistan.[91]

Despite the United States' ample knowledge of the risks of returning Afghanistan to its pre-Taliban warlords, there is no evidence that the U.S. military made any advance plans to provide security in

Afghanistan once it had toppled the Taliban. Despite ample security problems throughout the country subsequently, the United States repeatedly blocked alternative solutions such as the expansion of ISAF beyond Kabul, and refused to allow its own forces to take on a formal peacekeeping role. Initially, U.S. officials argued that an expanded peacekeeping force could get in the way of combat operations, and could require backup that would divert Coalition forces from those operations. Later on, U.S. officials relaxed their active opposition to ISAF expansion but did nothing to encourage it.

The U.S. administration finally awakened to the need to change course in the latter half of 2003, realizing that the crumbling security situation threatened the crafting of a new constitution and the holding of elections considered sufficiently free and fair to bestow nationwide legitimacy on the new government—whose increasing power and competence was a critical component of the U.S. exit strategy. The upgrading of the military command structure, the acceleration of both ANA training and PRT deployments, and the waiving of U.S. objections to the expansion of ISAF all were welcome developments.

The ultimate sustainability of these new creations depended critically, however, on the construction of a government that was capable of governing, including generating the revenues that would be needed to sustain the infrastructure and institutions, such as the army, that were being built with (sometimes halting) international assistance. The job of coordinating the international effort to support the new government fell to the United Nations.

UN Assistance Mission in Afghanistan (UNAMA)

Understanding the work of the United Nations, in situ, can be a complicated task. Although its legions of white vehicles all have the same two letters on the sides, the United Nations is a complex mixture of organizations and identities: a political organization of member states; an administrative entity responsible for policy and management of UN missions around the world; and a collection of operational UN programs and specialized agencies—such as the World Food Programme, the UN Children's Fund (UNICEF), the World Health Organization, and the High Commissioner for Refugees (UNHCR)—that implement assistance programs around the world.

The structure and role of UNAMA reflected this complexity. The mission was at once a support mechanism to the Afghan authorities; an independent monitor of the implementation of the Bonn process; a standard-bearer and enforcer for human rights and gender issues; a fund-raiser; and the coordinator of a massive humanitarian aid, relief, and reconstruction effort undertaken by more than twenty UN agencies and programs. Each of these functions was part of supporting the ongoing peace process in Afghanistan.

Mandate

The Bonn Agreement laid out a strong implementation role for the United Nations. Annex II of the agreement first made the SRSG "responsible for all aspects" of the United Nations' activities in Afghanistan, then gave the United Nations responsibility for monitoring and assisting the implementation of the agreement, and advising on the establishment of "a politically neutral environment conducive to" holding the emergency loya jirga and resolving disputes related thereto. Annex II gave the United Nations "the right to investigate human rights violations and, where necessary, recommend corrective action," and the job of developing and implementing a "program of human rights education to promote respect for and understanding of human rights."[92]

The agreement also asked the United Nations to register voters and conduct a census, and asked the Security Council to mandate an international security force. The council endorsed the Bonn Agreement, and specifically the UN role established in Resolution 1383, which passed only one day after the agreement was signed.[93]

On March 18, 2002, the secretary-general presented a report jointly to the General Assembly and Security Council, outlining a proposed structure for a unified UN mission in Afghanistan. The goal of the mission would be to "integrate all the existing United Nations elements in Afghanistan into a single mission," responsible for fulfilling the duties assigned to the United Nations under Bonn, promoting "national reconciliation and rapprochement," and managing all UN humanitarian and reconstruction assistance.[94]

On March 28, 2002, Security Council Resolution 1401 established UNAMA with the mandate and structure requested by the secretary-general. With respect to other UN agencies and activities in Afghanistan, the Security Council declared that it

> *reaffirms* its strong support for the Special Representative of the Secretary-General and *endorses* his full authority, in accordance with its relevant resolutions, over the planning and conduct of all United Nations activities in Afghanistan. . . .

This was a potentially pathbreaking approach to UN operations in postconflict settings, except that the Security Council has at best arguable authority to direct such independent UN agencies as the UN High Commissioner for Refugees or the World Food Programme, which answer to their own executive boards and their own funders (ministries of development or agriculture rather than ministries of defense). UNAMA could either insist on coordinated action or provide some added value that made everyone's work a little easier and made coordination a boon rather than a chore. The UN Operations Center in Afghanistan (see "Planning and Deployment," below) provided that added value.

The Security Council also introduced a note of conditionality, suggesting that assistance ought to be provided "where local authorities contribute to the maintenance of a secure environment and demonstrate respect for human rights."[95] These duties made the United Nations an adviser to the state of Afghanistan but transferred no governing authority at all to the organization.

Funding

UNAMA was funded by assessed contributions, which UN member states are obligated to pay, but its budgets were allocated through the section of the UN regular budget for "special political missions." Member states were therefore billed for UNAMA according to the regular UN scale of assessment rather than the peacekeeping scale (under which the permanent members of the Security Council pay a roughly 22 percent larger share of the costs, and developing countries pay a 40 to 90 percent smaller share). UNAMA's budget was also separate from voluntary trust funds established to support relief, development, DDR, and other objectives. The mission spent about $41 million in its first twelve months (mid-March 2002 to mid-March 2003) and $39 million in the remainder of calendar year 2003. Thereafter it ran on a calendar-year budget, matching the United Nations' regular budget year. UNAMA spent about $57.6 million in 2004 and was authorized to spend $63.6 million in 2005. Of that budget, 10 percent went toward security-related equipment and personnel.[96]

Planning and Deployment

As Operation Enduring Freedom began, it was clear that the UN posture in Afghanistan was about to undergo a radical change. For years it had been divided into a political mission (UNSMA) and humanitarian and development missions led by UNOCHA and the UN Development Programme (UNDP), respectively. Few international staff were working inside Afghanistan and assistance budgets were small, with annual UN appeals routinely garnering only a fraction of the funds requested. The likely presence of international military forces and a UN-approved government greatly increased Afghanistan's prospects for receiving significant donor funding and possibly peacekeeping forces. Still reluctant to commit U.S. military forces to "nation building," President Bush encouraged a strong role for the United Nations in Afghanistan.[97]

Upon his reappointment as SRSG, Lakhdar Brahimi had before him the potential for an expansive mandate for the UN operation in Afghanistan. In August 2000, a UN panel he chaired had issued the *Report of the Panel on United Nations Peace Operations*.[98] Known as the Brahimi Report, it made sweeping recommendations for alterations to the mission, planning, and structure of UN peace operations. One year later, Brahimi found himself leading the first effort to implement the sort of mission planning process called for in his panel's report: an Integrated Mission Task Force (IMTF). The IMTF was a planning body to be assembled from the UN departments and agencies that would be involved in implementing the mission, and was intended to have decision-making authority during the planning stages of an operation. The IMTF established for Afghanistan in October 2001 proved crucial to the eventual mission design but served as more of an information clearinghouse than a decision-making mechanism.[99]

Through the IMTF, Bonn, and consultations on the ground, the role and structure for UNAMA were hammered out. UNAMA would operate according to several basic principles: First, the Afghan authorities should be in the driver's seat. This required "close coordination and consultation" to ensure that Afghans and their priorities guided the work of the United Nations. Second, in order to ensure that Afghans developed and utilized their capacity, the mission was to have a "light expatriate footprint." As many jobs as possible should be in the hands of Afghans, both to build their capacity and to avoid crowding them out with international staff. Third, UNAMA should have a "unified presence and coordination capacity" in major regional and provincial centers. Fourth, human rights and gender issues should be "mainstreamed" in UN efforts. In other words, these issues should be a part of all work, not separate programs. Fifth, reconstruction must begin immediately in order to bolster the peace process, rather than awaiting completion of a political settlement. Significantly, UNAMA's roles also included monitoring Afghan authorities' compliance with the Bonn Agreement.[100]

UNAMA was headquartered in Kabul, with regional offices in Herat, Jalalabad, Kandahar, Mazar-i-Sharif, Bamiyan, Gardez, and Kunduz. UNAMA also maintained liaison offices in Islamabad and Tehran. Although not a peacekeeping operation, UNAMA was viewed by the United Nations as a "complex" (multicomponent) operation with significant logistical, communications, and security requirements. Therefore, from November 2002 onward, the mission was directed and supported by the UN Department of Peacekeeping Operations. Consistent with the concept of the light international footprint, a majority of its personnel were national hires; however, almost as many of its professional-level staff were Afghan as were international two years into the mission—unusual for any UN peace operation.

Table 7.2 shows the staff breakdown for 2002 through 2005. UNAMA's predecessor mission had 30 international personnel and 49 Afghan national staff. Within nine months, the mission had built up to 232 internationals, of whom up to a third were security personnel. National staff grew even faster, to 343 by the end of 2002, rising thereafter to more than 850, of whom 150 were national professional officers. In 2004 and 2005, nearly three-quarters of UNAMA's staff were Afghan.

Table 7.2. UNAMA Staffing, 2002–5

	2002	2003	2004	2005
International Staff				
Professional and Higher Level	139	173	170	146
Field Service and Security Service	74	110	96	83
General Service	19	23	23	22
Subtotal	232	306	289	251
National Staff				
National Officer	40	164	143	138
Local Level	343	677	737	739
Subtotal	383	841	880	877
UN Volunteers	N/A	N/A	43	43
Total	615	1,147	1,212	1,171

Sources: United Nations, *Estimates in respect of matters of which the Security Council is seized, Report of the Secretary-General,* A/C.5/57/23, November 15, 2002, 11; and *Estimates in respect of special political missions, good offices and other political initiatives authorized by the General Assembly and/or the Security Council, Report of the Secretary-General,* A/C.5/58/20, December 1, 2003, 15; A/59/534/Add.1, November 23, 2004, 21; and A/60/585, December 12, 2005, 14.

UNAMA was functionally divided into Pillar I (Political Affairs) and Pillar II (Relief, Recovery, and Reconstruction). Each of these was headed by a deputy SRSG. The SRSG also had a number of special advisers on cross-cutting issues, such as human rights, gender, drugs, rule of law, police, military, and DDR. Pillar I was largely responsible for aiding progress toward a political settlement and supporting the commissions established through the Bonn process. Pillar II focused on humanitarian aid and the overall plan for rebuilding the government and infrastructure of the country. UNAMA viewed the relationship between these functions as symbiotic—without political progress, recovery would lag, and without recovery, political transformation would be difficult. Many issues, as indicated by the number of special advisers, did not align well with either pillar. For instance, security sector reform and DDR were considered essential to the political transition but had significant implications for recovery and development as well.

Pillar I: The Political Process

The primary functions of Pillar I were concentrated on the Bonn process, conflict management, and human rights issues. The Bonn Agreement required a series of steps leading up to elections in June 2004. First, the emergency loya jirga required a massive political and logistical effort to elect delegates and organize the event. Second, the commissions established by Bonn, including the loya jirga commission, the constitutional commission, the judicial reform commission, and the human rights commission, all required various forms of support, including office staff and expert technical assistance. Third, a constitutional loya jirga was to be convened by December 2003 in order to ratify a new constitution. The final step, "free and fair" elections, posed enormous challenges, including nationwide voter registration, political party formation, the creation of an elections infrastructure, and the task of paying for it all.

Conflict management and prevention were also key tasks of Pillar I. Political affairs officers in each regional office were responsible for monitoring and reporting on political and military developments in the region. These officers were also expected to liaise with the local authorities to address political issues as they arose.

Pillar I also had responsibility for human rights issues. The location of human rights within the political pillar was the subject of intensive discussions in the planning phase of the operation. Some had wanted to separate human rights from the other pillars, or from the mission entirely, to safeguard the integrity and impartiality of the human rights office.[101] In the end, however, human rights remained within Pillar I, with human rights officers in Kabul and field officers with human rights responsibilities.

Pillar II: Aid Coordination

Pillar II had the task of coordinating the work of up to twenty UN agencies and offices whose programs accounted for more than half of the entire donor assistance budget to Afghanistan. This pillar was supposed to ensure that the United Nations worked in cooperation with the Afghan government and local authorities, and international and local NGOs. A critical part of this role was to support the government, providing capacity where needed while building the government's ability to carry out the aid coordination role itself. The Afghan interim administration established its own aid coordination mechanism, the Afghan Assistance Coordination Authority (AACA), early in its tenure. The AACA, headed by former World Bank official Ashraf Ghani, quickly became the focus of aid coordination for the government.

Pillar II had to transform the existing UN operation and build itself while attending to the pressure of initial funding conferences and needs assessments. With UN support, the interim administration went to the world in January 2002 with a plan for recovery and reconstruction requiring $10 billion over ten years. At the same time, the United Nations was engaged in a series of massive relief programs within the country. The United Nations needed to raise funds to meet both these immediate needs and the government's long-term requirements. Pillar II was also responsible for dismantling and absorbing UNOCHA, the previous UN aid coordination body, which had operated in some form in Afghanistan and neighboring countries for twelve years.

UN Operations Center

When UNAMA was set up in March 2002, other UN agencies and programs were already at work in Afghanistan, including UNICEF, UNHCR, UNDP, and the Mine Action Center. As indicated earlier, merely trying to exercise "authority" over the "planning and conduct" of their work would have been an exercise in frustration. The key to better coordination turned out to be colocation, not just of administrative offices but of fuel dumps and warehouses, motor pools, medical facilities, and at least some residential facilities. In 2003, in collaboration with UNICEF and the UN Office for Project Services (UNOPS),[102] UNAMA leased a forty-four acre compound on the outskirts of Kabul from a bankrupt parastatal road-building and rehabilitation company for what became the UN Operations Center in Afghanistan. At a cost of $16,000 per month, the United Nations acquired enough space to house many UN agencies' offices and Kabul-area operational equipment and supplies. One agency joining the center reduced its office rental expenditures from $50,000 to $3,000 per month (its share of the monthly lease). The parastatal company, in turn, received enough hard currency over time to replace operating assets destroyed in the civil war and get back in business.[103] UNAMA used primarily local day labor to construct and refurbish buildings on the site for administration, security, and training staff; offices for the Afghan New Beginnings Program (the DDR effort); and a UN medical clinic. UNICEF warehouses on the compound were used to compile and store 40,000 polling kits for the presidential election.

By March 2004, UNAMA had a common services agreement for use of the center with UNHCR as well, and a residential building was under construction to house UN volunteers. The compound's perimeter walls and gated entry provided some protection against unwanted entry. By November, the World Health Organization and the UN Population Fund were building offices within the center compound and an international commercial bank had opened for business, allowing UN agencies to reduce at least some of their need for large amounts of cash on hand. Based on the recommendations of a multiagency team that spent much of July 2004 assessing UN security needs, a Joint Security Information and Operations Center was established inside the compound, with representatives from UN agencies, the Afghan government, ISAF, the Coalition, and NGOs, to, in UNAMA's words, "coordinate responses to complex developments." By late 2004, UNOPS had assumed responsibility for common services within the compound and UNAMA had, in turn, sent people to work with the UNOPS regional operational center in Dubai, which would also be used as a "storage site for disaster-recovery services."[104] UNAMA has, in short, built the sort of close cooperation that its original mandate called for by providing or facilitating common services that reduce the cost and raise the efficiency and security of headquarters operations for all of the agencies involved.

Implementation

UNAMA supported the transitional Afghan government's efforts to rebuild shattered infrastructure and reconnect Kabul with the provinces, worked to keep the Bonn process on track, and strove to coordinate the provision of international relief and development assistance. Some of these efforts were more successful than others.

Supporting the Government

One of UNAMA's fundamental tasks was to coordinate support to the Afghan government as it set out to reestablish its capacity and legitimacy. Central government institutions were almost completely moribund by the time the Afghan interim administration came to power in December 2001. Many government buildings had been destroyed, and those standing were barren of trained staff, furniture, even pens and paper. Once installed, the new ministers of the interim administration were each given a vehicle and an "instant office" including a desk, chair, computer, and stationery. When the new government resumed accounting, the central bank had the equivalent of seventeen U.S. dollars on its books.

The conditions of provincial and local institutions were more varied. Although disconnected from Kabul, some of the local institutions had continued to work, but the change of guard had left them without supplies or budget. Most significantly, provincial and local administrations quickly fell under the control of local power holders and thus remained outside the control of Kabul.

The effort to reestablish government institutions included physical rehabilitation of buildings, provision of trained Afghan expatriate and international staff, training for local staff, and budgetary support. Some of this support was coordinated through the United Nations, but much of it was provided directly by donors and implementers. Most of the support went to Kabul and was concentrated in just a few of the more than thirty ministries and commissions in the new governmental framework. Two ministries in particular garnered significant international support, the Ministry of Finance and the Ministry of Rural Rehabilitation and Development. Both ministries were headed by articulate, Western-educated Afghans deeply familiar with the international aid system, and in both cases these ministers sought to downplay any coordination role by the United Nations or other entities outside the government.

The United Nations' most significant roles may in fact have been fund-raising and helping Kabul to coordinate with the provinces. UNAMA, with its regional offices, had greater presence in and communications with the provinces than did the government, early on. As a result, those offices helped to establish, where feasible, provincial coordination bodies chaired by the provincial governors. Many of the governors, though approved by Kabul, had been appointed mainly at the insistence of warlords and were corrupt and weak, with little authority over the ministry departments at the provincial level. Nevertheless, UNAMA worked on improving coordination with the technical departments. In several cases, when challenged to administer, governors rose to the occasion, which drew them closer to Kabul and away from their regional sponsors.

Ultimately, the process of establishing significant UN offices in an environment such as Afghanistan required substantial inwardly focused expenditure of physical and human resources. Because of UNAMA's access to international funding and procurement, basic UN offices were almost always better equipped than those of even the highest-level government officials. To complicate matters further, international salaries dwarfed those of local UN staff, and those of local UN staff in turn dwarfed salaries of people in the government. This was not a problem unique to Afghanistan; every international organization operating in war-torn settings faces this conundrum. These economic disparities often created other disparities in power dynamics, in which even the lowest-level international staff members see themselves as senior to Afghan staff regardless of official rank, and feel superior to government staff as well. UNAMA's start-up phase, even with its light-footprint ethic, did not escape these disparities.

Shepherding the Peace Process

Keeping the Bonn process on track was UNAMA's overriding focus. Aid and reconstruction included a universe of actors, but the political process was mostly in the hands of a few players, with whom Brahimi worked well.[105] Producing the Bonn Agreement itself was a major accomplishment, in which Brahimi played a key role. As the visible architect of the agreement, he continued to be central to its implementation as partner, mediator, and monitor throughout his tenure as SRSG.

The Bonn Agreement established an aggressive set of goals, albeit somewhat out of touch with the realities plaguing Afghanistan's political and security environment. While establishing tight timelines for choosing a transitional administration, ratifying a new constitution, and holding elections, the Bonn Agreement did not establish the modalities for disarmament, for creation of a national army and police force, or for the centralization of authority and revenue collection. The government's lack of control over security and resources—the keys to establishing the rule of law—consequently hobbled the process of political consolidation.

Emergency loya jirga. The emergency loya jirga was the first major test of the Bonn process. This assembly, held in Kabul June 10–21, 2002, was an opportunity to accord national legitimacy to the peace process begun in Bonn. From one perspective, it was a success: representatives from across Afghanistan came together to elect, or rather anoint, a head of state, and the major armed factions kept their hats in the political ring rather than returning to violence. Given the past three decades of war and turmoil, this was a significant step. Its greatest success may have been the selection process for the delegates. Although participants were subject to significant intimidation in certain areas, the process brought together communities to discuss issues and to peacefully choose representatives. A two-phase local indirect election system, combining consensus-based selection of local leaders with a secret ballot in the second round, chose 1,051 representatives from up to 390 electoral districts in thirty-two provinces. Another 500 delegates were appointed by the independent loya jirga commission in consultation with various organizations, civil society groups, nomads, and refugees.

The overall delegate selection process was intended to create balance: on a regional and rural/urban basis, by allowing at least one representative for each administrative district *(uluswali);* on an ethnic basis, primarily by relying on geographic concentrations; on a gender basis, by reserving 160 appointed seats for women; and on a sociocultural basis, by providing seats for religious figures, refugees, nomads, and traders. The geographical, ethnic, and ideological diversity under the tent was a testament to the success of the system and, critically, to the ability of Afghans to choose representatives.

UNAMA supported this process by placing a coterie of experienced political affairs officers with in-depth knowledge of Afghanistan on the loya jirga commission and in its regional offices. The United Nations and the Asia Foundation also quickly mobilized a team of election observers, many with appropriate language skills, that added an essential element of "witnessing" to the process.

In the last days before the loya jirga, however, the fair selection process was undermined when up to a hundred extra "political" delegates were summarily added to the rolls. These delegates, mostly provincial governors and other political-military figures unwilling or unable to stand for election, laid a blanket of intimidation over the delegates. While delegates may have been physically safe under the watchful eyes of ISAF and the international media, they knew they would eventually have to deal with local authorities back home.[106]

The key expectation for the loya jirga on the part of the assembled delegates, most Afghans, and the international community was that it would correct the ethnic/factional imbalance that was produced at the Bonn conference and that favored the Panjshiri Tajiks of the Shura-i-Nizar. No matter how fair the selection process for delegates, the legitimacy of the loya jirga would ultimately be determined by who came away with what governmental positions and how those positions were allocated. In the end, an opportunity for real participation and reconciliation was missed, as was the opportunity to assert civilian leadership, promote democratic expression, and draw authority away from the warlords.

The loya jirga's task was to choose the head of state, the structure of the transitional administration, and its key personnel.[107] Many delegates came armed with plans and speeches outlining the powers and functions of a new parliament, cabinet ministries, and independent commissions. Ultimately, delegates were given little opportunity to address any of these tasks seriously due to behind-the-scenes deal making, procedural confusion, and poor chairmanship. The exact substance of decisions to be made had been vague since Bonn, most likely because many of the power struggles evident at that conference were still unresolved when the emergency loya jirga convened. This lack of clarity was exploited by those wanting to expand or contract the agenda to suit their needs. The results were several agendaless days, chaotic speakers' lists, and delegates frustrated by not knowing what issues they were to decide, when, or how.

One day before the loya jirga began, the former king, Zahir Shah, withdrew himself from consideration for the position of head of state, apparently under significant pressure from the Shura-i-Nizar and the United States. U.S. envoy Khalilzad played a direct, visible role as king-unmaker. On the eve of the loya jirga, Khalilzad called a press conference at the U.S. embassy to announce, before the king himself, that the king would not seek office at the loya jirga. In a staged press conference two hours later, the king sat impassively, flanked by Khalilzad and Foreign Minister Abdullah Abdullah, as a statement to the same effect was read on his behalf. This overt orchestration set a cynical tone for the gathering, and significant Pushtun discontent erupted at the outright exclusion of Zahir Shah. U.S. embassy officials confided that the strong-arming of the former king was lamentable, but they felt it was the only way to keep the delicate process on track.

Once the loya jirga began, another crucial error was made in allowing the National Security Directorate, Kabul's Panjshiri-controlled secret police, onto the loya jirga grounds. What with warlords and governors occupying the front rows while directorate agents scurried around the side consultation tents, an air of repression and intimidation filled the main tent. Many delegates complained of threatening phone calls, and the minister of defense threatened the husband of Mahsood Jalap, the female candidate for president, in front of a large group. The discontent among delegates was compounded by the assembly's failure to redistribute the power of the key security ministries of Defense, Interior, and Foreign Affairs away from the Shura-i-Nizar.

To many delegates, who had come great distances from inside and outside the country to participate in the selection of their government for the first time in decades, the last-minute deal-making outside the tent was dispiriting. Inside the tent, delegates had no illusions that this was to be a fully democratic process. Compromise among and with those still prepared to use force to achieve their political ends remains unavoidable in today's Afghanistan. The orchestration of outcomes throughout the process, however, set a heavy-handed and disappointing tone.

Constitutional loya jirga. The Bonn Agreement called for the drafting of a new constitution for Afghanistan and a second loya jirga to debate and to ratify its work. The constitution's drafting commission was appointed in October 2002 and gave a preliminary draft to the thirty-five-member constitutional commission in late April 2003. UNAMA and UNDP helped the commission set up a secretariat whose job it was to educate the public about the constitution and to "facilitate . . . nationwide consultations."

The latter found strong support for a constitution that adhered to Islamic principles; for a government strong enough to enforce the rule of law and uphold human rights; and for free, mandatory education through at least the sixth grade for both sexes—a notable sentiment in a country where ideas about women's rights were just beginning to take hold and female literacy was estimated to be just 12 percent. UN observers and Interior Ministry security officers accompanied the commission's teams on their journeys, but deteriorating security conditions limited meetings to provincial capitals.[108] The draft constitution was made public on November 3, 2003.

The 502 members of the constitutional loya jirga were either provincial delegates (340), representatives of "special constituencies" such as women, nomadic tribes, and religious minorities (110), or presidential appointees (52). The provincial delegates were selected in meetings held in eight regional centers more readily protected than provincial capitals, as well as in Iran and Pakistan to represent refugee populations. The selection process ended only six days before the loya jirga convened on December 14.

In response to allegations that regional faction leaders unduly influenced the selection process or intimidated electors, the secretary-general could say only that UNAMA and the constitutional commission did the best that they could under prevailing security conditions. Scheduled for ten days, the loya jirga needed twenty-one to reach consensus, and did so only after minority delegations rebelled and both U.S. ambassador Khalilzad and UN SRSG Brahimi intervened, working behind closed doors with rival delegates in the loya jirga's final twenty-four hours.[109]

The resulting constitution established a unity state with a strong presidential system including a directly elected president, two vice presidents, and a bicameral legislature. The president is limited to two five-year terms. If no presidential candidate wins a majority of the vote, a runoff election is to be held within two weeks. The 249 members of the lower house *(wolesi jirga)* are to be elected by popular vote. Of the 102 members of the upper house *(meshrano jirga)*, one-third are to be appointed by the president, one-third are to be selected by provincial councils, and one-third are to be selected by vote of nearly 400 district councils (one administrative level down from provincial councils). The constitution specifies the legal equality of men and women, that at least sixty-eight members (25 percent) of the lower house should be women, and that half of the president's appointees to the upper house are to be women. The constitution also guarantees minorities the right to use their language for official purposes in regions where they dominate. Although the constitution says that laws may not contradict the beliefs and provisions of Islam, it does not make sharia the law of the land. It does, however, place the power of judicial review in the hands of the Supreme Court—effectively making the high court the arbiter of whether laws and government policies are sufficiently "Islamic."[110]

Containing factional fighting. The prevailing factional environment outside of Kabul created not only a need for sustained dialogue on the political transition, but also tensions between regional power holders that occasionally devolved into hostilities. UNAMA played a more traditional diplomatic role on such occasions, shuttling between factions to quell outbreaks of fighting, especially in the north, center, and west of the country, which lacked a significant Coalition presence. Without a peacekeeping force, the United Nations was left to play a minimally effective good offices role.

The most troublesome recurrent tensions were in the north, where rival warlords battled for control of revenue sources and the regional seat, Mazar. These tensions dated from the civil war period, and the leaderships of the loose warlord militias were often not strong enough to compel their own commanders to stop fighting. A Security Commission of the North was established with UN assistance to mediate disputes. With such help, the commission was able to stop some individual outbreaks of fighting. Not until 2004, however, when mediation by the British PRT and ANA deployments induced the cantonment of heavy weapons and encouraged demobilization of militia forces, did fighting subside in both the north and west.

Promoting human rights. The Afghan people have suffered a horrific, virtually uninterrupted torrent of abuse on a mass scale for twenty-five years. No community escaped unscathed, and a litany of accusations have been brought against many prominent power holders.[111] There were, moreover, substantial indications that abuse of human rights through torture, wrongful imprisonment, and unlawful execution continued into the interim/transitional government period.[112] Efforts to promote human rights needed to address both past and present abuses.

A familiar debate emerged in Afghanistan concerning the sequencing of "peace" and "justice." On one side was the current "establishment," the transitional administration and UNAMA, more concerned about not upsetting a fragile peace process than about reckoning with the past. This was not simply a matter of priority, because as with most complex political situations, the past is not only prologue, it is present. Many of those in the peace process could be called to answer for past abuses they had committed, while some have remained actively engaged in the systematic deprivation of human rights. Since these were powerful players, dealing with the past could undermine the peace process, meaning that peace had to come before justice.

On the other side of this debate sat the Afghan Independent Human Rights Commission, the human rights community, and Afghan civil society. They believed that human rights abuses were not symptoms of larger problems but were themselves a source of the conflict and enabled it to continue. They argued that a peace process that counted serial abusers among its key players was abhorrent to UN principles and the community of nations, and would crumble. In other words, without justice there could be no peace.

The UN family found itself divided between these perspectives. UNAMA chose early on to mainstream human rights, meaning that its political officers would also carry a human rights portfolio but there would be no cadre of human rights officers in the mission. The idea behind mainstreaming was that all personnel should be attentive to the human rights issues raised by their work rather than leaving these concerns to a separate, ghettoized section. In an operation struggling with heavy workloads and insufficient training, however, mainstreaming often means that human rights is handled erratically.

UNAMA officials through the highest level admitted that attention to human rights concerns, and to the human rights commission, was minimal and slow, and many in the international community called for UNAMA to increase its human rights field presence and monitoring capacity.[113] Beginning in June 2004, UNAMA and the commission did begin to track reported violations of freedom of expression, assembly, association, and movement connected to the election campaign. Their first report, issued a month later, painted a picture of self-censorship based on well-founded fear of reprisals by local authorities for speaking out, and of active censorship of mass media outside Kabul by various factions.[114]

Other elements of the UN system, such as the High Commissioner for Human Rights, the Special Rapporteur for Extrajudicial Killings, and the Independent Expert on the Situation of Human Rights in Afghanistan, pushed harder for accountability mechanisms. The Special Rapporteur recommended in early 2003 that an international, UN-backed independent commission of inquiry be created to begin investigating the "grave human rights violations of the past, which could well constitute a catalogue of crimes against humanity."[115]

The Independent Expert reported in 2004 and 2005 on both progress made by the government toward respecting human rights and on continuing widespread violations of human rights, laying responsibility at the feet of many different actors: factional commanders and drug traffickers (often, in his view, one and the same); members of the Afghan military, intelligence services, and police; and members of the U.S. Coalition. He concluded that Afghanistan continued to suffer from a "justice deficit at almost every level of society" and that "if corruption continues to intensify . . . it will become virtually impossible to establish and sustain a meaningful commitment to rule of law in Afghanistan."[116] The United Nations also undertook an extensive exercise to catalog major abuses in the 1980s and 1990s, but the report, which named several figures prominent in post-Taliban Afghanistan, was shelved by UNAMA and never released.

Supporting elections. In July 2003, the transitional government established the Joint Electoral Management Board (JEMB), with six Afghan commissioners and five international elections experts, including UNAMA's chief electoral officer. The JEMB issued rules and regulations for the elections, registered parties, certified the voter rolls, and hired and trained 5,000 Afghan voter registrars. The start of registration was pushed back from October to December 2003 when donations to fund it were slow to arrive.[117] Security conditions also slowed the registration process, much as they slowed the formal census needed to apportion representatives and draw voting boundaries at the district level.[118]

In February 2004, the administrative secretariat that had planned and carried out the nationwide consultations for the constitutional commission was transformed, by presidential decree, into an electoral secretariat for the JEMB in which UN and Afghan personnel worked together on registration and on election planning and logistics.[119] By March, only 10 percent of an estimated 10.5 million potential eligible voters (including refugee populations in Iran and Pakistan) had been registered.[120] In the spring, registrars fanned out into rural areas so that, by May, UNAMA was running 1,600 registration centers and registering up to 120,000 voters a day. There were widespread charges of fraud in the registration process, with some provinces registering 140 percent of the expected eligible population. The registration surge came too late to support June elections, however. The JEMB postponed presidential and lower house parliamentary elections until the fall and pushed back district-level elections to April 2005. Ultimately, the parliamentary votes would be pushed back further, the lower house elections to September 2005 and the district-level voting until 2006.

On May 27, 2004, the cabinet passed the electoral law, which codified the election rules and specified that the process would use "single, non-transferable votes with multiple-seat constituencies." Voters would cast ballots for individuals rather than party lists, and the number of seats per constituency (that is, per province) would be determined by provincial population. This is a highly unpredictable system for parliamentary elections, and as such is used only in Vanuatu, the Pitcairn Islands, and Jordan. For purposes of the initial lower house vote, the government opted to use the census of 1979. On June 5, the government delineated provincial boundaries for electoral purposes, in the process establishing two new provinces, Panjshir and Daikundi, for a total of thirty-four.[121]

The elections went ahead despite growing Taliban attacks against elections workers. In June and July, four female Afghan elections workers were killed in separate bomb attacks in Nangrahar province; a JEMB team leader was gunned down in Uruzgan; a bomb detonated at a voter registration site in Ghazni, killing two; and a police-escorted

UN electoral convoy in the southeast was attacked with roadside bombs, rocket-propelled grenades, and automatic weapons.[122]

On October 9, despite threats of violence, 70 percent of registered voters turned out at the polls. Many observers credited the deterrent effect of a temporarily expanded ISAF presence, together with Coalition forces, the ANA, and the national police, all providing security for the elections. There was political turmoil on election day, however, due to a faulty system of applying indelible ink to voters' fingers to prevent multiple voting. In the middle of the day Karzai's opponents banded together to call for a boycott of the vote, but the vast majority of the population did not respond.

Hamid Karzai was elected president of Afghanistan with 55.4 percent of the vote in a field of sixteen candidates, thereby avoiding a runoff. His nearest competitor, Younus Qanooni, a leader in Jamiat-i-Islami and Karzai's former minister of interior and education, drew 16.3 percent. Qanooni drew 85 percent in Panjshir, however, and was the leading candidate in six other, mostly Tajik-majority provinces. Karzai did equally well in Pushtun-majority provinces, winning up to 85 percent of the vote in most of the south and southeast, plus 80 percent of the vote among Afghan refugees in Pakistan. But he also polled 57 percent of the vote in Tajik-majority Herat, where he had recently sacked governor Ismael Khan, which analysts considered a favorable omen for national unity. Complaints about election-related fraud were investigated by an international panel of electoral experts convened by UNAMA at the request of the JEMB. The panel found that, while some irregularities had occurred, they were not sufficient to have changed the results of the election.[123]

Within a few months, the electoral support system spun up again, for elections to the wolesi jirga. In January 2005 an independent election commission, assisted by UN-appointed international experts, replaced the JEMB. UNAMA cut back its electoral support staff, and UNDP stepped into the mission's former primary supporting role, recast as development rather than transitional assistance. As Barnett Rubin et al. noted, however, in an April 2005 report for the Netherlands' Clingendael Institute, the number of elections currently called for in the new constitution (8 to 10 every decade for the presidency, wolesi jirga, and district councils) could impose a financial burden that may be difficult to sustain and may cut into the government's ability to rebuild, educate its people, and maintain public health. The initial voter registration and presidential elections alone cost roughly $100 million.[124]

More than 5,000 candidates ran for seats in the first elections for the lower house of parliament and provincial assemblies in September 2005. In the run-up to the elections, the government and UNAMA also formed an electoral complaints commission to investigate violations of the elections law, which requires candidates to resign from government positions and to sever all ties to armed groups. Initially, the commission investigated hundreds of complaints, but was able to find sufficient evidence to exclude only a dozen candidates. Days before the elections, however, the commission removed another twenty-one military figures from the ballot.

Relief, Recovery, and Reconstruction

Promoting the "three R's"—relief, recovery, and reconstruction—was an essential part of the UN mission in Afghanistan, including not only support to the government in coordinating overall donor assistance but critical aspects of the peace process, including security sector reform, DDR, and drug control efforts. These efforts involved the government, militias, international military, numerous donors, and hundreds of implementers, including the full array of the UN family.

UNAMA was given a clear mandate to coordinate all UN activities in Afghanistan—a difficult task at best, and one made harder without the authority to control the moving parts or the ready ability to acquire such authority. The situation highlighted one of the United Nations' most significant, intractable problems: while agreements like Bonn and Security Council Resolution 1401 may give UN missions like UNAMA large, strongly worded mandates, the reality of coordination on the ground is far more complex. As Nigel Fisher, deputy SRSG for Pillar II, has said, "Despite talk, [the UN] agencies poured in the traditional way, heavy and non-consultative."[125] Some of the UN agencies even argued that, because they were not creatures of the Security Council and had separate boards of member states, Resolution 1401 did not apply to them.

Securing funds and coordinating aid. It was clear, after the fall of the Taliban, that the international community would dedicate resources to

Afghanistan in a way it had never done before. Typically, military intervention has meant a windfall of support, and responding to Afghanistan's physical and economic devastation was seen as not only a moral but also a security imperative. The UN missions to Afghanistan were heavily involved in defining both humanitarian and reconstruction priorities and raising funds for these programs, even prior to the creation of UNAMA.[126]

The United Nations was able to support the new Afghan interim authority in putting together a hasty but fairly comprehensive aid and reconstruction program for the donors. Various donors responded with a total of $5.2 billion, pledged over five years in Tokyo in January 2002 ($3.8 billion in grants and $1.4 billion in loans).[127] Donors pledged an additional $700 million in grants over the next year, lifting the five-year grant total to $4.47 billion.[128] Of the $1.84 billion actually disbursed during the first fifteen months of the grant period, only $296 million (16 percent) went directly to the transitional administration. About half was channeled through the United Nations.[129]

While disbursement rates were high, the amount disbursed per capita was relatively low in comparison to other recent crises. Afghanistan received $62 per capita in the first year of its crisis, versus $326 per capita for Bosnia, $288 for Kosovo, and $195 for East Timor.[130] Moreover, the biggest chunk of funds disbursed in the first year ($836 million) was humanitarian aid, which has low long-term visibility and is less likely to fulfill the high expectations for "results" that Tokyo and the arrival of the international community and new government provoked.

The Afghan government pressed for more direct support, pointing out that its modest 2003 budget already had a $242 million gap in pledges. A reassessment of revenues and needs through March 2011 led the government to conclude that it would need a total of $27.6 billion in external aid over that period.[131] A second donors' conference in Berlin, March 31–April 1, 2004, produced pledges of $8.2 billion toward the transitional administration's 2004–6 funding goal of $12 billion. The United States and the European Union pledged more than half of the total ($2.9 and $2.2 billion, respectively).[132]

In November 2002 the U.S. Congress passed the Afghanistan Freedom Support Act, which authorized $3.3 billion for economic, political, humanitarian, and security assistance to the country over four years.

Of these funds, $2 billion was for development assistance and $1 billion for the expansion of ISAF. For FY 2003, Congress earmarked $372 million for Afghanistan in the foreign aid appropriation bill and another $737 million in the FY 2003 supplemental appropriation.

The Bush administration did not include any funds for reconstruction in Afghanistan in its budget proposal for FY 2004—a glaring oversight rectified by Congress's addition of $403 million to the budget. This oversight might have suggested that the Bush administration's attention had drifted dangerously elsewhere, except that its penchant for funding war-related expenses outside the regular U.S. budget cycle was evident as well with the war in Iraq. In the fall of 2003, Congress passed a supplemental appropriation bill containing $1.3 billion for relief, reconstruction, and security assistance to Afghanistan, including $220 million for counternarcotics and accelerated training of Afghan police. The regular appropriation for foreign assistance in fiscal year 2005 (passed in 2004) provided $985 million for Afghanistan, including $400 million to train and equip the ANA, $220 million for the Afghan national police, and $2 million for the human rights commission. In February 2005, Congress passed a further supplemental appropriation of $3.35 billion, of which about one-third ($1.285 billion) was for the ANA and $360 million for police training.[133]

In the hurly-burly of the ongoing conflict, and with hundreds of UN offices, NGOs, and embassies all setting up shop in the country, coordination was tremendously difficult. An early internal joint assessment by the United Nations and the interim administration reached five telling conclusions about the state of coordination and capacity in Kabul:

1. Assistance agencies (both international and Afghan) are most often "doing their own thing," with very little advance consultation with local authorities or even with each other.

2. Local authorities, lacking tools and in some cases qualified personnel, are not currently in a position to lead project planning and implementation.

3. Trust/confidence among the various stakeholders needs to be built from a very low starting point.

4. Local authorities feel isolated from Kabul, and generally the information flow between Kabul and the provinces needs improvement.

5. There are uneven relations between regional and provincial centers on the one hand and districts or local communities on the other.[134]

Security sector reform and the rule of law. Establishing a secure environment for physical and political reconstruction has been a top priority of UNAMA and the donor community since Bonn. It was decided early on that efforts in these sectors would be co-coordinated by the transitional administration (with UNAMA supporting) and by a lead donor. The job of the lead donor is to provide and coordinate support to the sector. The lead donors in the security sector were as follows: national army, United States; police, Germany; DDR, Japan; drug control, United Kingdom; and justice, Italy. The concept of lead donor helped to create donor accountability and concentration. If a particular sector faltered, pressure could be placed clearly on one donor. It could also cause serious delays, however, if the lead donor did not respond aggressively to the mission or did not cooperate well with the government or UNAMA.

Disarmament, demobilization, and reintegration. DDR was conducted under the aegis of the Afghan New Beginnings Program, funded by Japan and run by UNDP. The program was particularly challenged and very slow to start, inaugurated in February 2003 but not operational until the following October.[135] Its fundamental problem was the lack of clear agreement or common understanding of what the DDR process should be. With initial estimates of 100,000 men under arms in factional militias and an equal number of reservists, DDR was accorded high priority. Some militia were to be recruited into the national army, but there was significant ambiguity as to what constituted the national army. In Kabul, the ANA is typically referred to as consisting of the new units trained under Coalition supervision. In the Ministry of Defense and the provinces, however, it was unclear whether or not the soldiers serving in the so-called Afghan Militia Forces (AMF) of recognized corps commands were part of the national army. When asked about disarmament, the spokesman for Ismael Khan, the self-proclaimed emir of western Afghanistan, first said that the government was going to retain a 100,000-man "resistance militia" above and beyond the 70,000-person ANA. Failure to tackle these difficult issues in the

Bonn Agreement left them ambiguous and made the agreement more difficult to implement and even to negotiate as regional powers became increasingly entrenched.

Spurred by the DDR special adviser's office in UNAMA, the transitional administration formed a disarmament commission and the Japanese government pledged more than $50 million to the initial phase of the process. The UN-devised plan totaled $130 million over three years and planned to pay 95,000 soldiers up to $250 each for their weapons and then provide employment for the demobilized soldiers. Implementation of the program was delayed by a lack of jobs but, more significantly, by lack of cooperation from militia leaders outside Kabul, who saw that the bulk of forces in the capital still belonged to the minister of defense. His forces were viewed as simply another faction. UNAMA acknowledged that DDR could not proceed until the necessary reforms in the ministry, such as merit-based recruitment and promotion, had been implemented.[136] A powerful northern corps commander closely associated with the Shura-i-Nizar put it bluntly: "Since a broad-based national army has not been formed and there is no powerful government [in Kabul], putting guns away would be nonsense."[137]

Pilot DDR programs in Mazar-i-Sharif and elsewhere resulted in a few thousand fighters being nominally disarmed, but some entrepreneurial militia commanders were found to be offering their reservists for demobilization, rather than their full-time fighters, and to be extorting the program's severance payments from those who were demobilized. Thus, in some instances at least, DDR appeared to be adding more militia resources than it was taking away.[138] Moreover, close inspection of AMF rolls revealed that the majority were "ghost soldiers," simply names listed to pad payrolls. As a result, estimates of AMF strength were revised downward from 100,000 fighters to between 60,000 and 80,000. Some 40,000 of these soldiers were to be demobilized by June 2004 and an additional 20,000 by September 2004, a month before the presidential election. About 15,400 had been disarmed by July 2004 and another 5,500 by September.

By summer 2005, the program had disarmed 63,380 AMF troops, demobilized 59,290, and started 57,590 on some type of reintegration program (agriculture, 43 percent; vocational training, 25 percent; ANA or demining, 5 percent). Only 12 percent of the total (about 6,900) had actually completed the reintegration program, however, and New Beginnings estimated that another $21 million was needed to complete reintegration, carry out an ammunition survey (thousands of tons of ammunition were estimated to remain in arms caches throughout the countryside), and "disband illegal armed groups."[139] One analysis maintained, however, that New Beginnings was essentially superficial in nature, did not address "the informal structures that sustained the façade" of the AMF, and had no qualitative measures of its own effectiveness. It also charged that between 2 and 20 percent of groups nominally disarmed had already rearmed by mid-2005, using caches of weapons hidden by their commanders.[140]

New Beginnings, of course, had focused only on AMF forces: quasipublic militias paid by the Ministry of Defense. Dismantling those forces saved the new government $120 million a year in what amounted to payoffs, but left untouched upwards of 80,000 fighters in some 1,800 private militias involved in drug trafficking and political intimidation. So, in January 2005, the government launched the Disarmament of Illegal Armed Groups program. Whereas troops with AMF units had been offered cash payments to enter DDR, the new program offered incentive payments to local communities and threatened to punish members of armed groups found in violation of the decree banning them. Arms analyst Christian Dennys noted that fighters hired by the Coalition for anti-Taliban operations or to guard the Jalalabad PRT would fall outside the definition of illegal armed groups, as would the veritable army of guards (around 25,000) hired through local commanders by the private security firm supporting a major Western roadbuilding contractor in the south. If so many armed elements were to be left at large, then the focus, he suggested, should be on building secure local communities rather than rooting out armed groups per se.[141]

Coalition leaders, meanwhile, put greater weight on the cantonment of militias' heavy weapons.[142] ISAF managed to canton about two-thirds of the heavy weapons in and around Kabul by July 2004; all "declared" heavy weapons in Kabul by the end of the year; and all "known" heavy weapons in the Panjshir valley by March 2005, after former defense minister Fahim consented to the program. Countrywide, ISAF reported that 94 percent of heavy weapons had been cantoned by March 2005. UNAMA claimed that 8,600 serviceable heavy weapons had been cantoned by that time, and nearly 10,900 by the following July.[143]

Rebuilding the national police. The formation and training of a national police force faced multiple challenges, as UNAMA repeatedly noted when reporting on the international community's modest progress in developing a modern police force for Afghanistan. Initially, the Ministry of the Interior, which is responsible for the police, was dominated, as was the Defense Ministry, by commanders and members of the Shura-i-Nizar.[144] Although the powerful minister Younus Qanooni was replaced by Ali Ahmad Jalali in June 2002, Qanooni's informal influence within the ministry continued for some time.

Jalali was a former royalist army officer and professor of military history who had spent years working for Voice of America, the U.S. government's international broadcasting service, in Washington, D.C. His appointment as minister, along with the partial removal of the high-level factional elements, a comprehensive reform program that established the number and distribution of police as well as a training and recruitment policy, and a watchdog human rights agency appeared to set the process back on track. Still, the ministry had not built an effective police command and control system by late 2004.[145] Analysts noted, moreover, that a high percentage of new police officers appeared to be demobilized AMF troops, which risked the replication of old militia loyalties and impulses within the police force.[146]

The police training program envisioned 50,000 police and 12,000 border guards, all under central government control, who were to be fully deployed and trained by 2007. The German government, as lead donor, focused heavily on establishing a national training academy in Kabul, which graduated its first class in 2003. By October 2004, the Kabul academy had roughly 2,600 graduates, 70 percent of them noncommissioned officers, of whom about 750 were border police. In two and a half years, the academy graduated fifty-five female officers.

Because police training was slow in moving out to the provinces, the U.S. government stepped in to speed up the program. The pace of training increased dramatically in 2004, after the U.S. Congress passed the supplemental funding legislation noted above. Five regional training centers began to run police recruits through an eight-week basic training course and devised a two-week course for "veteran officers who lacked formal training." By mid-2004, 19,500 officers had received at least some training through the expanded program, but provincial and district-level facilities and equipment remained meager, and there was no follow-on mentoring or on-the-job training program akin to the one developed for the ANA.

Although the numbers of police finishing the accelerated training programs continued to grow, with 40,000 of a nominal 58,000 police nationwide having finished one or more programs, the quality of that force remained questionable.[147] Only a fraction of the nominal force was available for election security in October 2004, and in May 2005 police in several cities badly mishandled the worst rioting to hit the country since the fall of the Taliban, firing on crowds, killing a dozen protesters, and wounding several dozen more in Jalalabad, Badakhshan, Kabul, and elsewhere.[148]

Once trained, police had to be paid, regularly. A law and order trust fund, established by UNDP in May 2002 in cooperation with the transitional administration for payment of police salaries, acquisition of nonlethal equipment, and rehabilitation of police facilities, attracted only a fraction of the funds needed to sustain Afghan law enforcement. Indeed, implementation did not start until November 2003, eighteen months after inception. The first two phases of the fund, timed to coincide with the government's fiscal year, were budgeted at $275.8 million through March 2005, whereas money received totaled $120 million, according to UNDP-Afghanistan. Donors pledged another $350 million at a conference on police reconstruction in Doha in May 2004, although some may have preferred to distribute funds bilaterally.[149]

By June 2005, the principal police trainers, Germany and the United States, had realized that they could not just train and release their police recruits and expect them to form an effective police force in a hostile environment with minimal equipment and irregular pay. They proposed a billion-dollar police reform and mentoring program, drawing heavily on the embedded training team concept used in the ANA. Pay and rank reform, looking toward pay parity with the ANA, were also among the program's objectives.[150]

Counternarcotics programs. Drug control efforts also figured prominently in security and law and order planning. The opium production base and the networks that support it would have a significant impact on security in any country. The combination of this massive drug trade with warlordism and terrorism, all of which thrive on insecurity, could make an intractably dangerous alliance.

The transitional administration and the United Kingdom, as lead donor, undertook a series of initiatives, including the establishment of a directorate for counternarcotics within the office of the presidency, a poppy-eradication campaign targeting farmers, and coordination of drug interdiction efforts with regional countries. These programs, however, yielded relatively few results over two years; poppy acreage and heroin production both continued to climb. The eradication campaign met with armed resistance from farmers, causing the transitional administration to back off its plans in several areas.

In late 2004, President Karzai convened a national counternarcotics jirga to communicate to provincial political and tribal leaders that unless poppy cultivation and heroin production were cut substantially, they would "shame him and the nation." Karzai pledged to destroy all of the country's opium poppy fields within two years. In late 2004, the U.S. government announced Plan Afghanistan, a multiyear, multibillion-dollar eradication and interdiction program modeled on the controversial Plan Colombia, which had militarized the drug war in that embattled nation. In January 2005, the counternarcotics directorate of the National Security Council became a ministry in its own right. Karzai also appointed General Mohammad Daud, a Northern Alliance commander in Kunduz, as deputy minister of the interior for counternarcotics. While seen as a young and effective commander by some, he was also heavily implicated in opium smuggling in Kunduz, a key transit province.[151]

In February, the government announced a broad-scope counternarcotics implementation plan, and in June donors established a counternarcotics trust fund. Crop eradication efforts initiated and run at the provincial level appeared to hold promise in five key poppy-producing provinces, but farmers in many areas had "presold" their 2005 crops to cover current debts, and so while efforts to suppress plantings seemed to make some headway, farmers needed both security and immediate alternative livelihood aid to avoid financial disaster and reprisals from the traffickers to whom they had promised their crops. Finally, having steered clear of the narcotics issue for several years, the Coalition began to get involved. U.S. Defense Department funding for counternarcotics efforts in Afghanistan ($242 million) was included in the second supplemental appropriation bill for fiscal year 2005 and signed into law in May 2005.[152] Kabul and Washington butted heads over the program because Washington insisted on aerial spraying, which Karzai adamantly opposed as likely to lead to a serious anti–United States backlash.

Reform of the judicial system. Ultimately, an indigenous system of law enforcement hinges on a functioning judicial system. Establishing the rule of law requires more than armed, trained police and soldiers. It requires building institutions that can enforce and moderate the system with fairness, legitimacy, and stability. In post-Bonn Afghanistan, the Supreme Court, the Ministry of Justice, and the prosecutor general's office were headed by individuals associated with different factions, each competing for power in an environment with no neutral referees.

The work of reestablishing the judicial system will take many years under the best of circumstances, given the almost complete destruction of the physical infrastructure and human resources in this sector, and the near-total absence of the citizen confidence that is crucial for the courts to function as a dispute resolution mechanism. Indeed, the vast majority of disputes—both civil and criminal—are resolved by traditional or informal mechanisms. The absence of effective, legitimate government courts has caused the informal system to bloom. Few judges or tribal elders are familiar with Afghanistan's laws. Madrassa-trained judges rely instead on individual interpretations of Islamic law, and tribal elders on customary law—both of which may require or condone practices deemed contrary to human rights by the international community. The inaccessibility of these practices, and their Islamic content, makes engagement complicated for the largely non-Muslim international community.

In order to ease the transition and spur progress in critical areas, the transitional administration established a Bonn-mandated judicial commission. The first commission had to be disbanded due to intense rivalries and the perception of a lack of independence. The second attempt, the Judicial Reform Commission, was widely respected as neutral and populated with qualified, motivated individuals. Saddled with an enormous mandate—to reform the law, and rebuild and train the judiciary—but given limited resources, the commission struggled to establish itself and to coordinate competing donors and competing Afghan government institutions. By 2005, the government was shifting responsibility for judicial reform to a Consultative Group for Justice, led by the Ministry of Justice and including the attorney-general's office and the Supreme Court. Indicative of just how far reform and reconstruction of the judicial system had lagged, UNDP and UNAMA, in August 2005, reported that they were helping the Consultative Group conduct "a comprehensive needs assessment" as the basis for "future justice sector reform efforts," fully two and a half years after the Judicial Reform Commission produced a "master plan" for the justice sector with the help of the very same actors.[153]

The Supreme Court was controlled at this time by a conservative Islamist who has proclaimed on more than one occasion that the Koran is the constitution of Afghanistan. Chief Justice Shinwari used his powers of appointment to consolidate the hold of the conservative ulema, or clergy, on the courts. The Supreme Court nominates all judges to the president for appointment to the bench and thereafter "controls their careers, salary, and discipline, while also hearing their cases," a relationship that invites corruption. The new constitution does not reform the judiciary, which therefore remains a "self-perpetuating caste."[154] Since the new constitution was put into place, the chief justice has used his position to denounce "un-Islamic" practices, television broadcasts, and even a presidential candidate. In each of these instances, the court had no case before it concerning the matter, as was required by law in order for the chief justice to make a ruling. Ultimately, given the fundamental importance of a functioning judicial system for establishing the rule of law, the inattention paid to this sector endangered the overall state-building process in Afghanistan.

Assessment of UNAMA

UNAMA was given enormous responsibility in a complex and difficult environment. The Bonn process merely supplied a roadmap for a peace process between longtime opponents in a nation ravaged by war, poverty, and terrorism. One of the key recommendations of the Brahimi Report was that peace operations should have clear, credible, and achievable mandates. One could argue, in the case of Afghanistan, that a clearly achievable mandate would have been too far below the desires and expectations of both the Afghans and the international system. Instead, UNAMA was given an inspirational mandate—in line with the nature of the Bonn Agreement itself. Thus, despite its many successes, it also experienced important failures.

The most critical success—and simultaneous failure—was the maintenance of the Bonn Agreement status quo. UNAMA worked assiduously to keep the key faction leaders on the path to peace, frequently shuttling among factions, and between factions and the central government, to resolve disputes. SRSG Brahimi used his personal status and relationships with the factions to keep them within the Bonn tent. As a result, long-term outbreaks of factional fighting were avoided for the most part.

The pursuit of this approach above all others, however, meant that other key Bonn Agreement goals—for example, the mission of creating a broadly representative government and ensuring human rights accountability—lagged badly. This ultimately delayed some of the hard work of the peace process, in which factional leaders must accept sacrifices. Such delays may be important, warranted by the need to go slowly, build trust, and acclimatize. But they can also be a recipe for disaster, as these leaders consolidate power while international support for the peace process wanes.

Few factional leaders have rejected the Bonn process outright, and so the goal of keeping these leaders in the tent, and off the battlefield, has been accomplished. But the transition to "peace" has not been accompanied by a transition to the rule of law. Even as these leaders have participated in political processes and disarmament, they have entrenched themselves in opium trafficking, politics, and government, which will have long-term ill effects.

On the assistance side, UNAMA faced a similar conundrum. Pressure to deliver assistance to a needy population with very high expectations directly challenged the ability of the United Nations to fully support the capacity development of the government, because to do so would inevitably delay delivery of aid. Lack of government capacity and an emphasis on relief stalled visible reconstruction, and both the interim authorities and the international community risked loss of legitimacy. Moreover, the operational habits that UN agencies and NGOs have developed over the last decade in Afghanistan—and in other states where central government actors may be ineffectual or repugnant (as under the Taliban)—led them to make every effort to avoid local government control. As a result, UN agencies and the NGO community beefed up or rushed very rapidly into post-Taliban Afghanistan, before UNAMA received its mandate, and began their work with little reference to the new central authorities. Unfortunately, the central government simply did not have the initial capacity to step up and deliver coordination or control.

Was UNAMA to blame for these problems? Although the political mission had an important presence, it stood deep in the shadow of the Coalition. The U.S. military dominated U.S. security and policy decision making inside Afghanistan. Although influencing a U.S. embassy can be difficult, influencing the U.S. military, stationed outside Kabul in Bagram with an admittedly narrow view of the Afghan context, was even more difficult. Thus, in reality, the United Nations had very little latitude for decision. How could the United Nations effect the dismantlement of regional power brokers as the Coalition built them up? Coalition refusal to expand ISAF was also a key indicator of the relative powerlessness of UNAMA and the transitional administration in the realm of Afghan national security.

UNAMA was responsible for the effects of its light-footprint policy, however. The principle of Afghan ownership and decision making was crucial for UNAMA's mission, but the means used to support this principle were questionable. Limiting UNAMA's professional capacity served only to weaken its ability to act in many places on many issues at once. Required instead was a strong but subordinate footprint—that is, substantial international staff, subordinated to Afghan decision makers.

One of the best examples of this approach was in the standing up of the AACA. There were significant UN secondments to the process. Expert policy planners and analysts with laptops churned out presentable material under Afghan direction. They contributed valuable skills in short supply but did not drive the process. Having fewer of them would not have made the effort more effective. At the same time, the other operating principle of the light footprint, that jobs should go to Afghans where possible, was not put into effect in 2002 and 2003. Many UN support jobs that were filled initially by internationals could easily have gone to Afghans. Also, numerous Afghan national officers in the United Nations, many of whom had, in effect, been running UN offices in Afghanistan in the previous decade, suddenly found themselves with little to do as expatriate staff poured in and took over their responsibilities. UNAMA increasingly brought Afghans into professional roles, but eventually many of the best professionals left to start NGOs or took highly paid, high-level government positions funded by donors.

International Security Assistance Force

The story of the International Security Assistance Force, from an implementation perspective, is the most straightforward, most popular, and most successful aspect of the international intervention in Afghanistan. From a political perspective, however, the ISAF story is endemic of the failures of the international intervention, limited by forces working at cross-purposes and by exogenous policy considerations. Deployed to Kabul and its environs since early 2002, the multinational force was the only international military support explicitly dedicated to the maintenance of peace and security. As such, the Afghan government, the United Nations, and international and domestic civil society repeatedly called for its expansion beyond Kabul. Two years would go by, however, before the first ISAF-controlled troops set foot outside the Kabul area.

Mandate

One of the hardest-fought aspects of the Bonn Agreement was Annex I, which called for an international security force to be deployed to Kabul. The triumphant Northern Alliance forces were, by that time, firmly in control of Kabul, and they attempted to prevent the deployment of the force. In the end, however, many Afghans and international participants already felt that too much had been given away to the alliance during their unimpeded land grab, and the force was mandated in the agreement:

> Conscious that some time may be required for the new Afghan security and armed forces to be fully constituted and functioning,

the participants in the UN Talks on Afghanistan request the United Nations Security Council to consider authorizing the early deployment to Afghanistan of a United Nations mandated force. This force will assist in the maintenance of security for Kabul and its surrounding areas. Such a force could, as appropriate, be progressively expanded to other urban centers and other areas.[155]

The Security Council, for its part, rapidly took up the call and unanimously passed Security Council Resolution 1386 on December 20, 2001, authorizing deployment of the force. Invoking its powers under Chapter VII of the UN Charter, the Security Council charged the force to "assist the Afghan Interim Authority in the maintenance of security in Kabul and its surrounding areas, so that the Afghan Interim Authority as well as the personnel of the United Nations can operate in a secure environment." The resolution also gave ISAF the power to take "all necessary measures" to fulfill its mandate.[156] Notably, however, the resolution limited the force to Kabul and its surrounding areas, whereas the Bonn Agreement entertained the possibility of expanding the force beyond Kabul. ISAF's initial six-month mandate was extended repeatedly.[157]

Upon deployment, ISAF completed a military technical agreement with the Afghan interim authority to outline ISAF's mission, area of responsibility (AOR), and relationship to the interim administration and Afghan military forces. This agreement authorized ISAF to use force only "to protect ISAF and its Mission."[158] This grant of authority might be broad or narrow, depending on how the ISAF commander interpreted the mission should any tension arise between assisting the Afghan government and maintaining security. Still, the ISAF commander (COMISAF) retained authority to use force "without interference or permission" and had "complete and unimpeded freedom of movement throughout the territory and airspace of Afghanistan." The agreement explicitly contradicted Resolution 1386, however, by allowing the interim administration to return all Afghan military units, including factional armies, mujahideen, and armed groups, to designated barracks in Kabul.[159] The agreement listed some ninety locations within the Kabul AOR where these forces could be located. This provision essentially ensured that certain factional forces would be able to deploy throughout Kabul without effective monitoring.

ISAF's rules of engagement were primarily defensive in nature. It could intervene in active crime situations, or in other security situations if explicitly requested by the government, but the rules explicitly excluded both interposition between warring factions and seizing or holding ground.[160]

ISAF was the only international force in Afghanistan with an explicit mandate to maintain peace and security. Its area of operations covered a minute, if critical, portion of the country's territory, despite substantial insecurity elsewhere. Virtually every significant organization, personality, and commentator dealing with Afghanistan called for the expansion of the force, including Chairman Karzai, SRSG Brahimi, the Republican-controlled U.S. Congress, consortiums of aid NGOs, the International Crisis Group, the Stimson Center, and the Council on Foreign Relations.[161] The views of ordinary people, collected over months by NGOs and the media, were also almost exclusively proexpansion.[162]

ISAF was initially authorized, however, amid intense and rapidly changing Coalition military engagement, and U.S. military commanders were concerned about a peacekeeping force getting in their way, needing airlift support, or perhaps needing rescue. With the possibility of action in other theaters as well, the United States was not willing to commit troops or resources of its own to the potential quagmire of Afghan peacekeeping. In the fall of 2002, the U.S. administration publicly dropped its outright opposition to the expansion of ISAF,[163] but in reality, nothing could happen without strong U.S. support. NATO expressed interest in expanding ISAF's area of operations when it took over management of the force in August 2003. Thus Afghanistan became a critical new area of focus for the alliance—on the front lines of the war on terrorism, but not Iraq. That October the Security Council passed Resolution 1510, authorizing operations outside Kabul in support of efforts by the transitional authority and its successors to create a secure environment for peacebuilding.[164]

Funding

ISAF is a UN-mandated force, but participation in and funding of the force is purely voluntary. Resolution 1386 "*stresses* that the expenses of the International Security Assistance Force will be borne by the participating Member States concerned."[165] The resolution also required the United Nations to establish a trust fund to channel contributions to participating member states, but by May 2002, when Resolution 1413 extending ISAF was approved, the force's trust fund had still not been established, and it thereafter slipped into obscurity as other means were found to fund the contributions of some of ISAF's less wealthy troop contributors.[166] The United States, for example, gave Turkey $228 million (including $200 million in debt relief) to facilitate its assumption of the lead nation role in ISAF from June to December 2002.[167]

Because most of ISAF's troop contributors pay costs nationally, actual costs for the mission are almost impossible to determine. Estimates of ISAF's annual costs have ranged from about $600 million to $2 billion a year for a force of 5,000. It was likely that ISAF would reach or exceed 10,000 troops as it continued to expand geographically, with an associated annual cost of $1.2–$4 billion.[168]

Planning and Deployment

ISAF was envisioned as a multinational "coalition of the willing"; it grew over time from sixteen to thirty-seven contributing nations.[169] The force was first fully deployed on February 18, 2002, with about 5,000 troops.[170] Components under COMISAF included force headquarters (with a substantial force protection component), brigade headquarters for the Kabul multinational brigade, two infantry battle groups, other infantry units, a reconnaissance squadron, an engineer group, explosive ordnance disposal teams, a hospital and mobile medical teams, a civil-military cooperation center, a logistics unit, an intelligence unit, a liaison unit, helicopter support, military police, and air transport support.

ISAF has articulated five tasks that define its mission goals:

1. Assist the Transitional Administration (now the government) in providing a security framework around political institutions and other key sites in Kabul.
2. Conduct presence patrolling in AOR.
3. Assist with the establishment of new Afghan security institutions/ structures including new Afghan armed forces.
4. Provide assistance to the Transitional Administration/government in reconstruction.

5. Identify and arrange training and assistance tasks for future Afghan security forces.[171]

The original sixteen contributors signed a memorandum of understanding to formally establish the force under British command on January 10, 2002. After six months the force was turned over to Turkish command, and it passed to joint Dutch-German command in early 2003. These frequent changes of command disrupted the effectiveness and continuity of operations, and the main force components pushed for a solution that would not require any one nation to assume long-term command, but that would also maintain continuity. Given the force composition, NATO was an obvious solution; in August 2003 it assumed overall command of the force, its first mission outside of the European theater, which it planned to continue as long as necessary.[172] By spring 2005, the total force had grown to thirty-seven contributors (twenty-six NATO and eleven non-NATO) and about 8,200 troops (see table 7.3). COMISAF continued to rotate among NATO members. Canada took the lead from February to August 2004, Eurocorps (with a French force commander) from August through February 2005, and Turkey once again for the next round.

In late 2003, Germany established a PRT in and around the northeastern city of Kunduz; in December, it became the first ISAF-linked PRT. By March 2004, it included 226 German troops. NATO's Istanbul summit approved the establishment or Coalition handover of four more PRTs—Mazar-i-Sharif, Maimana, Faizabad, and Baghlan—which was done by October, completing Phase I of ISAF expansion. Phase II, announced in February 2005 and initiated in May, moved the operation further west, assuming command of two PRTs in Herat (Italy) and Farah (still U.S. led but now working for ISAF) and new PRTs to be set up in Chaghcharan (Ghor province) and Qal'eh-ye (Badghis). ISAF set up a forward support base in Herat to serve all four western PRTs, and another in the north.[173]

Structuring the relationship between the Coalition and ISAF caused some initial concern. The United States insisted that ISAF could not be independent of the Coalition chain of command, in case ISAF operations should come into contact with Coalition forces. Several ISAF contributors insisted on operational independence from the

Table 7.3. Troop Contributions to the International Security Assistance Force, 2002–5

Troop Contributor	July 2002	March 2004	May 2005
Afghanistan	—	80	—
Albania	—	22	22
Austria	71	—	3
Azerbaijan	—	22	22
Belgium	19	280	600
Bulgaria	32	38	35
Canada	—	1,756	1,250
Croatia	—	47	47
Czech Republic	132	17	17
Denmark	36	96	55
Estonia	—	6	9
Finland	31	42	82
France	520	536	800
FYROM (Macedonia)	—	11	20
Germany	1,121	1,833	1,000
Greece	163	167	151
Hungary	—	13	140
Iceland	—	1	14
Ireland	7	7	10
Italy	403	481	500
Latvia	—	11	11
Lithuania	—	2	10
Luxembourg	—	—	10
Netherlands	232	24	400
New Zealand	8	3	—
Norway	17	241	250
Poland	—	18	20
Portugal	—	1	47
Romania	55	27	73
Slovakia	—	—	17
Slovenia	—	21	22
Spain	349	118	500
Sweden	38	46	85
Switzerland	—	4	4
Turkey	1,322	151	1,800
United Kingdom	426	354	—
United States	—	60	194
Total	4,982	6,536	8,220

Sources: UN Security Council, *Monthly Report on the Operations of the ISAF,* August 16, 2002. NATO, "NATO in Afghanistan, Fact Sheet," updated April 22, 2004. Kenneth Katzman, "Afghanistan: Post-war Governance, Security, and U.S. Policy," no. RL30588 (Washington, DC: Congressional Research Service, updated June 15, 2005).

Coalition, however. Ultimately, it was agreed that operational command would belong to the ISAF commander, but the United States would exercise ultimate authority.[174] In order to liaise with the Afghan government and the United Nations, ISAF participated in a Joint Coordination Body that brought together the ministries of defense and interior, ISAF, and UNAMA.

Implementation

Starting in January 2002, ISAF carried out an extensive patrolling regime throughout its area of operations. Although unlawful activities, especially by armed gangs, remained a problem in Kabul, ISAF reported a 70 percent drop in crime in the operation's first six months, according to incident reports collected by ISAF and the Afghan police.[175] More significantly, the nighttime curfew in Kabul was lifted in November 2002 for the first time in twenty-three years. The impact of this change on ordinary Kabulis was significant. No government had been able to control security in Kabul for more than two decades, and many feared that the as-yet-unreformed forces of the Ministry of Defense and police would not be capable or trustworthy enough to maintain security on their own. ISAF allayed those fears. Patrolling also allowed for intensive on-the-job training of the police forces in Kabul.

ISAF's relationship to the Afghan government remained somewhat ambiguous. From a practical perspective, coordination was intensive. Given the divided nature of the government and its various security apparatuses, however, the relationship was not entirely cooperative. Several confrontations occurred between ISAF and the heavily armed men of prominent militia commanders. Following the murder of transport minister Abdul Rahman in February 2002, government security officials claimed that an angry mob was responsible, whereas President Karzai called the killing an assassination. Individuals connected to the Ministries of Defense and Interior were suspected of involvement in the killing. When Vice President Haji Qadir was killed, President Karzai immediately requested ISAF's assistance with the investigation, due to similar suspicions that Afghan "government" security forces were involved in the attack. Although the results of the investigation were inconclusive as to parties responsible, ISAF's report cleared the individuals whom Afghan security forces had arrested. ISAF's participation in the investigation was seen as highly political, given the tensions and suspicions within the government.

ISAF did not escape the ongoing security problems in Kabul and Afghanistan. Numerous direct attacks against the force occurred, including shooting and grenade attacks against patrols, and several rocket and bomb attacks at ISAF troops and facilities. On June 7, 2003, a vehicle packed with explosives drove up next to an ISAF bus transporting German soldiers and detonated, killing four soldiers aboard the bus and wounding thirty-one soldiers and bystanders. The following October, a mine killed two Canadian ISAF troops and wounded three others. In May 2004, a Norwegian peacekeeper was killed in an attack on an ISAF convoy, and in June a German ISAF vehicle was hit by a roadside bomb, which killed bystanders. In September, rocket attacks injured German ISAF troops in Kunduz; in October, a suicide attacker detonated grenades as an ISAF vehicle passed near the Kabul airport; and in November a German patrol was hit by a roadside bomb. In late May 2005, rockets hit the ISAF compound in Kabul. None of the latter attacks caused fatalities, however. These attacks were, moreover, relatively few in comparison to the lethal assaults against aid workers, election workers and, increasingly, active local supporters of Afghanistan's attempt to transition to democracy.[176]

Security Sector Training

ISAF quickly undertook to train the first battalion of the Afghan national guard, a force intended both to protect the president and to serve as a model battalion for the new Afghan army. Regiment instructors from six troop-contributing nations designed a seven-week course that emphasized communications, patrolling, and crowd control. The recruitment process was intended to create a multiethnic force of up to 600 young soldiers with limited affiliation to existing militias. In addition to training, ISAF provided uniforms, accommodations, transportation, communications, and weaponry.

ISAF's role in underpinning the security arrangements for the constitutional loya jirga provides perhaps the best example of the international community working in tandem to support and promote both peace and security and an Afghan-led process. ISAF's national guard unit training program produced a battalion of well-dressed, well-behaved Afghan soldiers that made a powerful, visible impression at the constitutional loya jirga. The sight of Afghanistan's warlords parading by a phalanx of armed and disciplined Afghan central government soldiers struck a hopeful chord. ISAF worked closely with UNAMA in planning security aspects of the assembly, and with Kabul military and police units to provide security during the event.

Following the multidonor security sector conference in Geneva in April 2002, it was apparent that the United States was going to take the key role in creating the new national army. While continuing to train national guard units through the summer of 2002, ISAF took on a significant training project for bodyguards in direct response to the assassination of Vice President Qadir in July. Following the assassination attempt against President Karzai in September, however, an additional team of bodyguards consisting of former U.S. Special Forces personnel working for the U.S. security contractor DynCorp assumed responsibility for security of the president and the presidential palace.[177]

Civil-Military Cooperation

Conducting small-scale reconstruction projects throughout its area of operations was an important component of ISAF's mission in Kabul. Projects focused on community needs, including schools, hospitals and clinics, water supply, fire and police stations, and various other public works. These projects were intended to improve force protection and projection by building trust and cooperation with the local community. By conducting small-scale rehabilitation projects that were quickly completed and highly visible, ISAF managed to establish itself as a rapid and effective implementer. Projects were funded by various sources, including the European Union and other donors, most of which were members of the force.

Initially the Kabul multinational brigade managed these projects, but they were shifted to ISAF headquarters in 2002 to improve coordination and capacity. A civil-military cooperation center was established to liaise with government, donors, and NGOs in the crowded Kabul environment, and to prioritize and approve reconstruction projects. ISAF managed to attract donor funds to implement such projects throughout its area of operations. European donors, such as the European Union, were especially keen to demonstrate that ISAF's presence in Kabul supported both security and reconstruction, which also made a more effective argument for ISAF expansion.

To help secure the presidential elections in October 2004, NATO temporarily increased ISAF's troop strength by two battalions (about 2,000 troops). It did so again for the September 2005 parliamentary elections.

Assessment of ISAF

But for the failure to demilitarize Kabul for nearly three years, and the fact that it patrolled only Kabul for much of that time, ISAF's mission was a resounding success. The most significant change in its operation came when it did finally expand to other parts of Afghanistan.

Once the UN Security Council and NATO's North Atlantic Council formally approved ISAF expansion, the issue became one of troop availability. Although NATO members contributed a few hundred troops here and there, the 10,000 to 15,000 needed to effectively expand the force proved hard to find. PRTs were a compromise solution to expansion at low force levels. They were intended to have ISAF-like effects in their areas of operation, but the difference between a 50- to 100-strong force, mostly dedicated to force protection, and a 5,000-strong multinational force with patrolling, law enforcement, training, medical, and reconstruction capacity is substantial. Most important, perhaps, is attention to civilian relations and basic law enforcement functions. ISAF's principal achievement in Kabul was not deterring factional fighting but deterring crime and boosting the population's confidence. The PRT model is unlikely to have similar effects unless the numbers of troops assigned to each PRT increase substantially. As ANA units with embedded Western training teams began to deploy in many of the same areas from about mid-2004 onward, however, they and the PRTs could reinforce one another in ways that may lessen the need for larger foreign forces.

The single significant failure of ISAF was its longstanding inability or unwillingness to enforce a key provision of the Bonn Agreement and Resolution 1386, the withdrawal of all Afghan military units from Kabul.[178] ISAF's mandate in this regard seemed clear from a straightforward reading of Resolution 1386, which called upon the Afghan parties to the Bonn Agreement to implement their pledge to withdraw, *"in cooperation with*" ISAF.[179] Given ISAF's power to take "all necessary measures to fulfill its mandate" under this Chapter VII resolution, ISAF seemed remiss in failing to enforce the provision.

Rather than undertake this dangerous and difficult mission while underresourced, however, ISAF chose to downplay its enforcement role, implicitly leaving such decisions to the transitional administration. Like UNAMA, ISAF's command chose to position itself to assist the government, advising certain courses of action but leaving the decisions, even if in violation of international agreements, to the government. The ISAF mandate was the more difficult of the two to construe as primarily assistance focused, however. While the decision not to stand up for certain principles was lamentable in UNAMA's case, ISAF's failure to act more forcefully seemed directly contrary to the will of Resolution 1386. In any event, that failure was gradually corrected as a combination of ANA growth, heavy weapons cantonment, DDR, and the increased legitimacy of the Karzai government after the presidential elections conspired to reduce—but not eliminate—the militia threat in Kabul.

Overall Assessment and Conclusions

The situation in Afghanistan, and the approach of the international community there, remained fluid in mid-2005. Afghanistan was not forgotten or abandoned by the world, as in 1993, but its long-term problems—warlordism, terrorism, the Taliban, the narcotics trade, and an uneducated and underemployed population—require greater and sustained focus if peace and stability are to prevail. The United Nations and key donors hoped to establish a highly centralized Afghan state with a monopoly on the use of force, run by a popularly elected, broadly representative government that would enforce the rule of law instead of the rule of the gun. Given Afghanistan's own history and the litany of postconflict failures (many chronicled here), were these hopes misplaced?

Nation building is largely about building stable, legitimate institutions, which requires a conducive environment and substantial, sustained investment over many years. Afghanistan did not provide especially fertile ground for stable, centralized, legitimate government.

Although peaceful for decades before the upheaval of the late 1970s, Afghanistan was never completely consolidated as a state. Nearly three decades of turmoil broke down many of the institutions and much of the infrastructure built over the previous century—and created dramatic obstacles to stability.

Yet while central control was cut off, the bureaucratic structure of the state proved somewhat resilient.[180] With time, Afghanistan could establish a competent government with the power to regulate certain aspects of life in its highly traditional and diverse society. Afghanistan's history, however, suggests that attempts by government to impose central control not backed by broad social consensus will likely end in disaster. Indeed, the current political and military divisions in the country partially reflect reactions to previous government oppression.

Did the international community implement a consistent, tenable policy to achieve its ends? The main goal of the countries supporting the process was to rid Afghanistan of terrorist elements and help (re)construct basic infrastructure. Foreign contributions to this effort were substantial. More than 17,000 foreign troops deployed to Afghanistan to combat terrorism and maintain security in the capital. The United Nations and donors coordinated more than $5 billion in aid over five years and pledged another $8 billion on top of that.

Yet several glaring failures in combination greatly hampered the potential for a successful transition to peace and stable governance. First, the Pentagon demonstrated dangerous shortsightedness in funding and arming Afghanistan's warlords, then clearing the way for them to seize control of large chunks of the country. The return of warlord militias brought internecine fighting, ethnic tensions, clients for outside interference, and a booming narcotics trade. These regional power brokers were able to consolidate their power faster than the internationally supported Bonn process could consolidate the state. Ironically, Coalition actions intended to benefit the government consolidation may in fact have helped the warlords more. In some cases, security improved just enough to minimize inter-warlord feuding, allowing the militias to collect taxes and conserve resources that they would have previously spent on fighting their competitors.

Second, in the face of insecurity throughout post-Taliban Afghanistan, the United States and its Coalition allies simultaneously refused to undertake peacekeeping duties and blocked the expansion of Afghanistan's lone peacekeeping force, ISAF. The Coalition got around to formulating a security policy for Afghanistan beyond the war on terror only about a year after its invasion, and implementation even then was halting. The PRTs were, at best, a crude peace enforcement mechanism, capable of preventing severe backsliding but lacking the resources and stature to make serious improvements in security or undertake substantial reconstruction.

The lack of a broadly deployed international force allowed general insecurity to prevail in most regions, delaying reconstruction and reassertion of central government control. As of this writing it remains to be seen whether the belated expansion of ISAF, using the PRT model, will have a serious, positive impact on the security situation, which in the view of many observers continued to deteriorate well into 2005, with terrorist violence directed specifically at those, both Afghan and non-Afghan, who were trying to build a better future for the country.

Third, funding and human resources dedicated to reinvigorating Afghanistan's economy and government were less than the demonstrated need and less than the amount supplied in similar situations elsewhere. UNAMA's light-footprint policy, while intended to avoid crowding Kabul with too many expatriate managers, led not to a blossoming of Afghan-run government institutions (with a few notable exceptions) but to a critical lack of qualified personnel. As a result, neither the transitional administration nor the United Nations had the capacity to spend resources quickly and efficiently—let alone to increase programming. The light-footprint principle is valuable—that the Afghans should be in charge. Implementing such a policy effectively in the future, however, would require limiting not the number but the decision-making authority of international personnel while increasing the authority of competent Afghan personnel and giving them sufficient resources.

In this case, government salaries were so low that most competent Afghans took jobs with international organizations and were made subordinate to those organizations' expatriate staff. Thousands of Afghans living abroad were not offered reasonable salaries to return, while international staff who had never been to the country before and would remain there for only twelve to twenty-four months were highly paid. Far more should be invested in government employees and offices, and less in international offices. Clean, furnished UN and NGO offices with high-speed Internet access, massive generators, and satellite communication were created from scratch, while government offices remained dank and unequipped. Other donors similarly married grand commitments with limited resources. Creation of a national police force, a drug enforcement entity, and a judicial system—all virtually from scratch—required massive infusions of funding and expertise. In each case, implementation was slow and underresourced.

Keeping and expanding the peace in Afghanistan will require dramatic improvement on all fronts. For several more years, foreign military forces will need to do more to make Afghanistan secure, from police training and law enforcement to engaging in the disarmament process. Long-term donor coordination and commitment will also be needed. UNAMA reorganization and greater U.S. technical assistance for government ministries were good signs that lessons were being learned and corrective action was being taken. By mid-2005, however, Afghanistan's political and security situation had evolved only part of the way to where it needed to be to sustain a stable state. Initial national elections were a milestone, not a stop sign, for international involvement in Afghanistan.

The experience in Afghanistan offers several important lessons for future interventions in failing or unstable states. The first lesson—already confirmed, painfully, in Iraq—is to plan for the peace as well as the war. In order to achieve a long-term positive outcome, regime change must include *both* the removal of a bad regime and good-faith efforts to introduce a representative and rights-respecting one in its stead. Replacing a bad regime with warlordism or chaos reflects either failure or unwillingness to plan. War, or regime removal, is not a policy in itself but a means of achieving a policy, which must be to create secure, stable environments in which the local population can (re)develop self-governance.

The second lesson is that insecurity interferes with state consolidation at all levels. Insecurity is extremely costly, simultaneously engaging troops and forestalling serious reconstruction efforts. Insecurity on the microlevel—predation, restrictions on travel, criminality, intimidation—also prevents progress by preventing communication, travel, development of government legitimacy, local and international personnel recruitment, and investment. Institutions created in insecure environments will tend to reflect that insecurity through lack of resources, and through incompetence and corruption, as behavior conducive to personal survival takes precedence over job performance and institutional loyalty.

The third lesson is that local capacity building and local decision making must be bedrock principles of donors and implementers. Both relief and infrastructure are important, but resolving poverty and economic stagnation are long-term, not short-term, projects. Some degree of efficiency in delivery should be sacrificed early on in exchange for developing local capacity to deliver in the long run. Donor funding must be subject to longer-term planning. Often there is a glut of money early on in crises, when the capacity to absorb these funds is low, and a dearth of money once institutions get up and running. Rather than flood postconflict environments with a UN/NGO economy that often collapses after a few years, leaving few sustainable institutions in its wake, funding levels should rise gradually, creating permanent institutions and then providing them with sufficient resources. Such an approach is not only principled but utilitarian, lessening dependence and the possibility of failure.

A fourth lesson is that timetables, such as those found in the Bonn Agreement, can be critical to maintain momentum in a peace process but often entail sacrifices in the quality of the outcome. Having a written date by which significant milestones must be met—the writing of a constitution, the holding of an election—kept pressure on the Afghans, the Coalition, and donors to make progress. As a result, an overall sense of momentum has characterized the first four years of the intervention.

Having deadlines without substantive benchmarks, however— for instance, requiring certain disarmament goals to be met before elections can be held—has had the effect of undermining key achievements. Thus Afghanistan has a new constitution and many new laws, but it does not enjoy the rule of law. It is also far more difficult to set timetables with the requisite political backing for long-term goals such as reconstruction and improvements in life expectancy and education.

Afghanistan also offers several important operational lessons for peacekeeping per se. The first is that peacekeeping and war-fighting may have to coexist in one theater. The prevention of ISAF expansion, coupled with the Coalition's refusal to engage in peacekeeping, meant that an important opportunity was missed for stability to take root immediately after the Taliban were pushed out of each part of the country. ISAFs, beefed-up PRTs, or even international police forces could have deployed to numerous areas throughout the country where militia commanders were fortifying their bases of control. Although more aggressive deployment would potentially have invited confrontation with Afghan militia forces, the risks of confrontation only became greater as their forces accumulated resources. ISAF has had a critical symbolic effect on Afghans, demonstrating that the international community is interested not just in al Qaeda but in peace. No foreign military force would seek to challenge all of Afghanistan's militia forces, but an expanded ISAF could have played an important policing role in the first year of the intervention, constraining the freedom of warlord militias.

The second lesson is that operational design and planning should be based on a realistic assessment of the length of deployment. The shift of ISAF leadership every six months for the first several authorizations had undercut the effectiveness of the operation. Rapid changes in personnel and politics should be avoided in unstable situations like post-Bonn Kabul. Unified NATO command has integrated the mission much more effectively, leading to advances on important political issues such as the removal of heavy weapons from Kabul as required by the Bonn Agreement. NATO assumption of command, combined with the move of the American military command from Bagram to Kabul, aided coordination between the Coalition and ISAF. Such colocation of command elements would be advisable in future situations as well.

Finally, a critical lesson is that local security is a priority in factionalized environments. The breakdown of authority in conflicts virtually ensures that power vacuums will be created at the local level. As the conflict abates, the forces that have filled the security vacuum will easily become entrenched if they are not brought into the fold of national security arrangements. This was painfully evident as Afghan militia commanders defied central government will. Overcoming this trend entails active engagement of international military forces, either to police the transition themselves or to provide training, resources, and ongoing mentoring with the goal of creating security organizations both loyal to the state and dedicated to the public welfare.

Notes

1. The *Agreement on Provisional Arrangements in Afghanistan Pending the Re-establishment of Permanent Government Institutions* (Bonn Agreement) was concluded on December 5, 2001.

2. Vernon Loeb, "Rumsfeld Announces End of Afghan Combat," *Washington Post,* May 2, 2003, A16.

3. UN Security Council, "Press Statement by President of Security Council on Afghanistan," SC/7753, May 6, 2003.

4. UN Security Council, "Unstable, Insufficient Security in Afghanistan Casts Long Shadow over Peace Process, Special Representative Tells Security Council," SC/7751 (press release, May 6, 2003).

5. Swisspeace, "FAST Update—Afghanistan: Semi-annual Risk Assessment, December 2004 to May 2005," www.swisspeace.org/fast.

6. The ethnic composition of the Afghani populace is estimated, albeit based on limited data, as 38 percent Pushtun, 25 percent Tajik, 19 percent Hazara, and 6 percent Uzbek; various other ethnic groups (Amok, Turkmen, Bloch, and others) make up the remaining 12 percent. See *CIA World Factbook,* 2000, www.cia.gov/cia/publications/factbook/geos/af.html.

7. A partial census was conducted in the 1970s, and all population figures have been extrapolated from this data. The UN Population Fund (UNFPA) began work on a new census in October 2002 with a "household listing phase." Approximately two years later, "work for 30 out of the 34 provinces is complete and the results ready for publication. Fieldwork in the provinces of Paktika, Helmand and Daikondi is ongoing, and will start in Zabul, as soon as the Ministry of Interior will give the security clearance." The household listing "prepares the way for the Census Proper, which is proposed to take place sometime in mid-2006," and which will seek more personal data, including "the relationships in the household; age and sex of all persons in the household; the language spoken of all persons in the household; and [other] educational, economic and social data." UNFPA Afghanistan, "Latest News," afghanistan.unfpa.org/latestnews.html (accessed August 17, 2005).

8. UN Office on Drugs and Crime and Government of Afghanistan Counter Narcotics Directorate, "Fact Sheet," *Afghanistan Opium Survey 2004* (Vienna, November 2004), 1.

9. UN High Commissioner for Refugees (UNHCR), *The State of the World's Refugees* (Oxford: UNHCR; Oxford University Press, 2000).

10. Former national security advisor Zbigniew Brzezinski claimed in an interview in 1998, "The day that the Soviets officially crossed the border, I wrote to President Carter: We now have the opportunity of giving to the USSR its Vietnam war." "Interview of Zbigniew Brzezinski," *Le Nouvel Observateur* (France), January 15–21, 1998, 76.

11. William Maley, *The Afghanistan Wars* (New York: Palgrave Macmillan, 2002), 72–76. U.S. aid to the mujahideen is believed to have been about $100 million per year until 1985, an amount matched by other backers led by Saudi Arabia and China. This amount climbed to a combined $500 million per year in 1985, with the signing of U.S. National Security Decision Directive 166 and the provision of advanced weaponry, including Stinger missiles. See Mark Urban, *War in Afghanistan,* 2nd ed. (London: Macmillan, 1990), 162–63.

12. John K. Cooley, *Unholy Wars* (London: Pluto, 2002), 162–65. The death of Soviet premier Konstantin Chernenko and the rise of Mikhail Gorbachev instigated new thinking about Afghanistan within the Soviet leadership. For an in-depth discussion of the negotiations and process leading to the Geneva Accords, see Barnett Rubin, *The Search for Peace in Afghanistan* (New Haven: Yale University Press, 1995).

13. Maley, *Afghanistan Wars,* 106–7.

14. Rubin, *Search for Peace in Afghanistan,* 128–33.

15. Alexander Thier, "Afghanistan: Minority Rights and Autonomy in a Multi-ethnic Failed State," *Stanford Journal of International Law* 35, no. 2 (1999).

16. For assessments of the demining program, see U.S. Department of State, *Hidden Killers: The Global Landmine Crisis:* 1994 ed., chap. 7, www.state.gov/www/global /arms/rpt_9401_demine_ch7.html; and 1998 ed., chap. 3, "Mine-Affected Countries," www.state.gov/www/global /arms/rpt_9809_ch3g.html.

17. Maley, *Afghanistan Wars,* 216–17.

18. Ahmed Rashid, *Taliban: Islam, Oil and the New Great Game in Central Asia* (New Haven: Yale University Press, 2000), 17–30.

19. Maley, *Afghanistan Wars,* 218–22.

20. Herat, the first significant non-Pushtun area to fall to the Taliban, was taken over in blitzkrieg fashion in September 1995, and Kabul fell almost exactly one year later.

21. See excerpts from Taliban religious decrees in Rashid, *Taliban,* 217–19.

22. Cooley, *Unholy Wars,* 81–106.

23. Rashid, *Taliban,* 128–40.

24. Ibid., 139.

25. Maley, *Afghanistan Wars,* 256–57.

26. Mark Duffield, Patricia Gossman, and Nicholas Leader, "Review of the Strategic Framework for Afghanistan," Afghanistan Research and Evaluation Unit (AREU), 2001, 18–19, www.areu.org.af/publications.html.

27. Steve Coll, *Ghost Wars* (New York: Penguin, 2004), 466–69, 554–58.

28. Its original name, Operation Infinite Justice, was changed after objections from Muslims that only Allah can mete out infinite justice. Bob Woodward, *Bush at War* (New York: Simon & Schuster, 2002), 134–35.

29. The Northern Alliance primarily consisted of Jamiat-i-Islami, Junbesh-i-Milli, Hezb-i-Wahadat, and Harakat-i-Islami. It also includes other, more marginal participants such as Haji Qadir's eastern Shura, and Ittihad-i-Islami. It is noteworthy that the Northern Alliance was mostly devoid of significant Pushtun representation.

30. The late Ahmad Shah Masood formed the Shura-i-Nizar (supervisory council) within the predominantly Tajik Jamiat-i-Islami party, which was nominally headed by former president Burhanuddin Rabbani. Much of their strength was located in the Panjshir Valley, Mahsood's redoubt. This wing of Jamiat, in which the military and administrative power of the party became concentrated, was controlled by defense minister Mohammad Qassem Fahim, by former interior minister and now education minister Younus Qanooni, and by foreign minister Abdullah Abdullah.

31. United Kingdom, House of Commons Library, "The Campaign against International Terrorism: Prospects after the Fall of the Taliban," Research Paper 01/112, December 11, 2001, 11.

32. Robert Kagan and William Kristol, "A Winning Strategy: How the Bush Administration Changed Course and Won the War in Afghanistan," *Weekly Standard,* November 26, 2001.

33. Christian Caryl and John Barry, "Facing a Long, Cold War, the White House Is Casting Its Lot with the Northern Alliance," *Newsweek,* November 12, 2001.

34. In addition to the U.S. and UK forces, as of October 31, 2001, the Coalition included direct military support from seventeen nations. See David J. Gerleman, Jennifer Stevens, and Stephen Hildreth, "Operation Enduring

Freedom: Foreign Pledges of Military and Intelligence Support," no. RL31152 (Washington, DC: U.S. Congressional Research Service, updated October 17, 2001), fpc.state.gov/documents/organization/6207.pdf.

35. "Final Resolution, Conference for Peace and National Unity, Peshawar, Pakistan, October 25, 2001," *Afghan Islamic Press,* October 25, 2001, cited in *SWB [Summary of World Broadcasts] Asia-Pacific,* October 27, 2001. This conference was a meeting of mainly Pushtun former mujahideen, tribal, and religious leaders.

36. Jarat Chopra, Jim McCallum, and Alexander Thier, "Planning Considerations for International Involvement in Post-Taliban Afghanistan," *Brown Journal of World Affairs* 8, no. 2 (Winter 2002): 47. This paper was produced from the proceedings of a conference at the U.S. Army War College that brought together high-level officials from the U.S. military, the North Atlantic Treaty Organization (NATO), the U.S. State Department, and the United Nations as well as several prominent academics. The conference unanimously agreed that Kabul should be protected as a neutral political environment.

37. United Kingdom, House of Commons Library, "Operation Enduring Freedom and the Conflict in Afghanistan: An Update," Research Paper 01/81, October 31, 2001, 34–35; Woodward, *Bush at War,* 308–9; and United Kingdom, House of Commons Library, "Campaign against International Terrorism," 13.

38. Anthony H. Cordesman, *The Lessons of Afghanistan* (Washington, DC: Center for Strategic and International Studies, 2002), 11; Steven M. Kosiak, "Estimated Cost of Operation Enduring Freedom" (Washington, DC: Center for Strategic and Budgetary Assessments, November 2001), www.csba.org/ (click "publications," then "military operations").

39. Olivier Fabre, "Afghan Scale-Down Possible Next Year—U.S. General," *Reuters,* May 23, 2003.

40. Kenneth Katzman, "Afghanistan: Post-war Governance, Security, and U.S. Policy," no. RL30588 (Washington, DC: Congressional Research Service, updated December 28, 2004), 22.

41. The loya jirga is an Afghan tradition with an august but vague history. The concept was extrapolated from the model of the tribal *jirga* or *shura,* an ad hoc, village-based institution that allows broad representation and, nominally, consensual decision making. The loya jirga is intended to be a national manifestation of community decision making. It has been used on average every twenty years to confirm the succession of monarchs, to pass constitutions, and to approve government policy. The last loya jirga deemed broadly legitimate was held in 1964 to approve a new reformist constitution.

42. UN Security Council Resolution 1378, S/RES/2001/1378, November 14, 2001.

43. Chopra, McCallum, and Thier, "Planning Considerations," 2–4.

44. Ahmed Rashid, "Breaking the Cycle," *Far Eastern Economic Review,* December 6, 2001, 16.

45. *Agreement on Provisional Arrangements in Afghanistan Pending the Re-Establishment of Permanent Government Institutions* (hereafter cited as Bonn Agreement), Art. I, para. 6 (Art. I(6)), www.uno.de/frieden/afghanistan/talks/agreement.htm.

46. Bonn Agreement, Art. II(1).

47. The power of decree was granted to the interim administration in the Bonn Agreement, Art. III.C(1), but was never explicitly granted to the transitional administration through the Bonn Agreement or the emergency loya jirga. The transitional administration has, however, continued to exercise this power. As of December 2002, Chairman Karzai had issued more than 150 decrees.

48. Bonn Agreement, Art. V(1).

49. Bonn Agreement, Annex I(2–4).

50. "Uzbek Warlord Rejects Afghan Accord," quoting Pir Sayeed Gailani, *Reuters,* December 6, 2001.

51. Ibid.

52. UN Assistance Mission in Afghanistan, "Biography of Jean Arnault," www.unama-afg.org/about/SRSG.htm; Ahmed Rashid, "UN Troubleshooter Ready to Tackle Daunting Challenges in Iraq," May 25, 2004, www.eurasianet.org.

53. Pamela Constable, "Afghan Denies Power-Sharing Deal: Karzai Promises Not to Form Political Coalition with Former Militia Leaders," *Washington Post,* June 4, 2004, A16.

54. Carl Conetta, "Strange Victory: A Critical Appraisal of Operation Enduring Freedom and the Afghanistan War," Research Monograph no. 6 (Cambridge, MA: Project on Defense Alternatives, January 30, 2002).

55. See, for example, "U.S. General: Groups Supply Afghan Rebels," *Associated Press,* April 30, 2003; Ron Synovitz, "Afghanistan: Analysts Say Some Neighbors Interfering in Kabul's Internal Affairs," *Radio Free Europe/Radio Liberty (RFE/RL),* February 9, 2003.

56. "Putin Sending Troops to Tajikistan," *BBC News,* April 28, 2003. As many as 8,000 troops from Russia's 201st Motorized Rifle Division had been based in Tajikistan since the end of the Cold War, along with an unspecified number of Russian border troops who served as the officer corps of a Tajik-manned border guard force. In 2004, the two countries ratified a status-of-forces agreement giving long-term base rights for about 5,000 Russian troops, and the border force became all-Tajik, with Russian training advisers. See "Tajikistan: First Permanent Russian Military Base Opened," *RFE/RL,* October 17, 2004, www.rferl.org; Vladimir Socor, "Russian Army Base in Tajikistan Legalized; Border Troops to Withdraw," *Eurasia Daily Monitor* 1, no. 108 (October 19, 2004), www.jamestown.org.

57. Sudha Ramachandran, "Delhi Puts a Dent in Karzai's Dreams," *Asia Times Online,* March 2, 2005, www.atimes.com/atimes/South_Asia/ GC02Df06.html.

58. UN Security Council, *Letter Dated 24 December 2002 from the Permanent Representative of Afghanistan to the United Nations Addressed to the President of the Security Council,* S/2002/1416, December 24, 2002.

59. Transitional Islamic Government of Afghanistan, Security Council Instruction 1213, May 20, 2003.

60. UN Office on Drugs and Crime and Government of Afghanistan Counter Narcotics Directorate, "Fact Sheet."

61. British Agencies Afghanistan Group (BAAG), "Afghanistan: Monthly Review," October 2004, www.baag.org.uk/publications/monthlyreview.htm.

62. "Wave of Attacks Alarms International Forces," *UN Integrated Regional Information Network (IRIN),* June 16, 2004. See also the monthly BAAG reviews and Swisspeace, "FAST Update."

63. Johann Price, "Operation Enduring Freedom: Commands and HQs June 1, 2002," orbat.com/site/agtwopen/oef.html.

64. Global Security.org, "Operation Enduring Freedom—Order of Battle," www.globalsecurity.org/military/ops/enduring-freedom_orbat-01.htm.

65. U.S. Congress, Senate, *Authorization for Use of Military Force,* S.J. Res. 23, 107th Cong., 1st sess., September 14, 2001; UN Security Council Resolution 1373, S/RES/1373, September 28, 2001.

66. UN Economic and Social Council, *Report of the Independent Expert on the Situation of Human Rights in Afghanistan, M. Cherif Bassiouni* (hereafter cited as Bassiouni Report), E/CN.4/2005/122, March 11, 2005, 6. See also Center for Law and Military Operations, *Legal Lessons Learned from Afghanistan and Iraq: Volume I, Major Combat Operations (11 September 2001 to 1 May 2003),* August 2004.

67. Author interview with Colonel Lindsay Gudridge, U.S. Army Civil Affairs, CJCMOTF Afghanistan, April 20, 2003.

68. Gretchen Peters, "As Afghan Fighting Drags On, U.S. Turns to Rebuilding," *Christian Science Monitor,* December 6, 2002; Marc Kaufman, "U.S. Lands in the Middle of Afghan Feuding; Despite Stated Policy, Force Reluctantly Being Used to Subdue Local Conflicts," *Washington Post,* March 28, 2003; and BAAG, "Afghanistan: Monthly Review," August 2004, 1, www.baag.org.uk/publications/monthlyreview.htm.

69. U.S. Central Command, "Operation Enduring Freedom," www.centcom.mil/Operations/Coalition/joint.htm.

70. The author worked with representatives of the CJCMOTF on a courthouse rehabilitation proposal in his capacity as legal adviser to the Afghan Judicial Reform Commission. The proposal was rejected by OHDACA for the reasons cited.

71. Peter Viggo Jakobsen, "PRTs in Afghanistan: Successful but Not Sufficient," DIIS Report 2005–6 (Copenhagen: Danish Institute for International Studies, 2005), 16.

72. These were originally to be called Joint Regional Teams, but Afghan government officials objected that Afghanistan had no "regional" governing units. The name was changed, but CJCMOTF literature still presented the initial eight PRT locations as "regional bases of operation."

73. Ahmed Rashid, "Team Approach Spreads in Afghanistan, but Security Worries Remain," *Eurasia Insight,* August 8, 2003; and "British Military to Launch Civil-Military Project in Afghan North," *Agence France-Presse,* May 12, 2003.

74. "Canadian Military Assumes Command of Afghanistan PRT," *American Forces Information Service,* August 17, 2005, www.defenselink.mil/news/Aug2005/20050817_2466.html; and Canadian Broadcasting Company, "Canada in Afghanistan," *CBC News Online,* May 18, 2006, http://www.cbc.ca/news/background/afghanistan/canada.html.

75. Katzman, "Afghanistan: Post-war Governance," 26; and Jakobsen, *PRTs in Afghanistan,* 13.

76. CJCMOTF, "Provincial Reconstruction Teams: First Lessons Learned in Initial Implementation; A Summary Discussion of CJCMOTF's Lessons Learned of Particular Relevance to UN Agencies and the Civilian Assistance Community," unpublished draft, April 27, 2003.

77. See Barbara J. Stapleton, "Briefing Paper on the Development of Joint Regional Teams in Afghanistan," BAAG, January 2003; and Agency Coordinating Body for Afghan Relief (ACBAR) Policy Brief, "NGO Position Paper Concerning the Provisional Reconstruction Teams," January 2003.

78. CJCMOTF presentation on the PRT concept, Kabul, April 24, 2003.

79. Jakobsen, *PRTs in Afghanistan,* 15–16.

80. PRT Executive Committee, "Terms of Reference for CFC and ISAF PRTs in Afghanistan," in *Afghanistan 2005 and Beyond: Prospects for Improved Stability Reference Document,* ed. Barnett R. Rubin, Humayun Hamidzada, and Abby Stoddard (Clingendael: Netherlands Institute of International Relations, April 2005), Appendix 1, Art. 1, www.clingendael.nl/cscp/publications/occasional%2Dpapers/.

81. Jakobsen, *PRTs in Afghanistan,* 17–27, 30; and Rubin, Hamidzada, and Stoddard, *Afghanistan 2005 and Beyond,* 58.

82. Human Rights Research and Advocacy Consortium, "Take the Guns Away: Afghan Voices on Security and Elections," September 2004, www.afghanadvocacy.org.

83. Islamic Transitional State of Afghanistan, *Decree of the President of the Islamic Transitional State of Afghanistan on the Afghan National Army,* December 1, 2002, www.unama-afg.org/docs/_nonUN%20Docs/_Internation-Conferences&Forums/Bonn-Talks/decree%20on%20army.pdf.

84. Mark Sedra, "Challenging the Warlord Culture," Paper 25, 2002, Bonn International Center for Conversion, 28, www.bicc.de/publications/papers/papers.html.

85. Global Security, "Afghanistan: Army," www.globalsecurity.org/military/world/afghanistan/army.htm.

86. Global Security, "Coalition Joint Task Force Phoenix," www.globalsecurity.org/military/agency/dod/cjtf-phoenix.htm. About 1,000 ANA soldiers participated in combat operations against "anti-Coalition forces" for the first time in Afghanistan's troubled Paktiya province in late July 2003. See "Afghanistan Report," *RFE/RL,* July 24, 2003.

87. Anja Manuel and P. W. Singer, "A New Model Afghan Army," *Foreign Affairs* 81, no. 4 (July/August 2002): 57.

88. "Afghanistan's Karzai Appoints Reformist Cabinet," *Agence France-Presse,* December 23, 2004; Rubin, Hamidzada, and Stoddard, *Afghanistan 2005 and Beyond,* 39. The International Crisis Group (hereafter cited as Crisis Group) noted that ISAF pressed for removal of heavy weaponry from Kabul at about the time the Defense Ministry was reorganized, helped to implement their removal, and monitored the cantonments, most of which were guarded by AMF troops. Crisis Group, "Afghanistan: Getting Disarmament Back on Track," Asia Briefing no. 35, February 23, 2005, 10.

89. Ibid., 5.

90. Sedra, "Challenging the Warlord Culture." Roughly 2,500 other recruits had left the army by spring 2004, citing low pay, ill health, or family reasons. Some trekked home monthly to hand their cash salary payments (which U.S. advisers disburse) to their dependents, then trekked back to rejoin their units. A Defense Ministry spokesman estimated that as few as 300 were "officially considered deserters." See Hafizullah Gardesh, "Army Loses a Quarter of Recruits," *Institute for War and Peace Reporting*, ARR no. 107, February 25, 2004, www.iwpr.net/index.pl?archive/arr/arr_200402_107_2_eng.txt. See also Crisis Group, "Afghanistan: Getting Disarmament Back on Track," 4; and United Nations, *The Situation in Afghanistan . . . , Report of the Secretary-General*, A/58/868-S/2004/634, August 12, 2004, 9.

91. Crisis Group, "Afghanistan Briefing: The Afghan Transitional Administration: Prospects and Perils," July 30, 2002, www.crisisweb.org. See also Chris Johnson et al., "Afghanistan's Political and Constitutional Development" (London: Overseas Development Institute, January 2003); United States Institute of Peace, "Unfinished Business in Afghanistan," Special Report 105, April 2003; Mahmood Karzai, Hamed Wardak, and Jack Kemp, "Winning the Other War," *Washington Post*, April 7, 2003, A15; and Carlotta Gall, "In Afghanistan, Violence Stalls Renewal Effort," *New York Times*, April 26, 2003, 7.

92. Bonn Agreement, Annex II(1, 2–6).

93. UN Security Council Resolution 1383, S/RES/1383, December 6, 2001.

94. United Nations, *The Situation in Afghanistan . . . , Report of the Secretary-General*, A/56/875-S/2002/278, March 18, 2002, paras. 94–97.

95. UN Security Council Resolution 1401, S/RES/1401, March 28, 2002.

96. United Nations, *Estimates in Respect of Special Political Missions, Good Offices, and Other Political Initiatives Authorized by the General Assembly and/or the Security Council, Report of the Advisory Committee on Administrative and Budgetary Questions*, A/59/569/Add.1, December 8, 2004, 7. The reduced budget request for 2005 reflected a substantial shift of responsibility for program administration from UNAMA to the UN Development Programme. Ibid., 8.

97. "It would be a useful function for the United Nations to take over the so-called 'nation building,'" President George W. Bush, White House press conference, October 11, 2001, www.whitehouse.gov/news/releases/2001/10/20011011-7.html.

98. United Nations, *Report of the Panel on United Nations Peace Operations*, A/55/305-2000/809, August 21, 2000.

99. For an account of the workings of the United Nations' post-9/11 planning process for Afghanistan, see Michele Griffin, "The Helmet and the Hoe," *Global Governance* 9 (2003), 199–217.

100. United Nations, *SG Report on Situation in Afghanistan*, A/56/875, para. 98.

101. Conflict, Security and Development Group, "Afghanistan Report" (online report, part of *A Review of Peace Operations: A Case for Change* Web site, sponsored by the International Policy Institute, King's College London), para. 73.

102. The UN Office for Project Services is a ten-year-old, self-financing spin-off from UNDP that markets its management and procurement services to UN operating agencies, for a fee that is "determined on a case-by-case basis and take[s] into account level of effort, complexity and risk." See UN Office for Project Services, www.unops.org/UNOPS/Services/Overview.

103. United Nations, *The Situation in Afghanistan and Its Implications for International Peace and Security: Report of the Secretary-General*, A/57/762-S/2003/333, March 18, 2003, para. 57; and Stimson Center interview, Freetown, Sierra Leone, July 2005.

104. United Nations, *The Situation in Afghanistan . . .*, *Report of the Secretary-General* (A/58/742-S/2004/230, March 19, 2004, para. 51; and A/59/581-S/2004/925, November 26, 2004, paras. 70–73).

105. Author's observations and interviews. The diplomatic side was not stress-free, however: Brahimi was appointed SRSG over his immediate predecessor, UNSMA head Francesc Vendrell, causing a public rift that deepened when Vendrell resigned and was then appointed as the European Union's special representative to Afghanistan.

106. For further information on delegate intimidation before and after the loya jirga, see Human Rights Watch, "Killing You Is a Very Easy Thing for Us: Human Rights Abuses in Southeast Afghanistan," July 2003.

107. The emergency loya jirga was to choose a "Head of the State for the Transitional Administration and . . . approve proposals for the structure and key personnel of the Transitional Administration." Bonn Agreement, Art. IV(5).

108. United Nations, *The Situation in Afghanistan. . .*, *Report of the Secretary-General*, A/57/850-S/2003/754, July 23, 2003, paras. 11–12.

109. United Nations, *The Situation in Afghanistan . . .*, *Report of the Secretary-General*, S/2003/1212, December 30, 2003, paras. 34–37; and Golnaz Esfandiari, "Afghanistan: Loya Jirga Approves Constitution," RFE/RL, January 5, 2004.

110. Katzman, "Afghanistan: Post-war Governance," 11–12; and United Nations, *SG Report on Situation in Afghanistan*, A/58/742-S/2004/230, para. 3.

111. See Human Rights Watch, "Blood-Stained Hands: Past Atrocities in Kabul and Afghanistan's Legacy of Impunity," July 2005; and Afghan Justice Project, "Casting Shadows: War Crimes and Crimes against Humanity: 1978–2001," July 2005.

112. See Amnesty International, "Afghanistan: Out of Sight, Out of Mind: The Fate of the Afghan Returnees," ASA 11/014/2003, June 23, 2003; Amnesty International, "Afghanistan: Crumbling Prison System Desperately in Need of Repair," ASA 11/017/2003, July 8, 2003; Human Rights Watch, "We Want to Live as Humans: Repression of Women and Girls in Western Afghanistan," December 2002; Human Rights Watch, "All Our Hopes Are Crushed: Violence and Repression in Western Afghanistan," October 2002; Human Rights Watch, "Paying for the Taliban's Crimes: Abuses against Ethnic Pushtuns in Northern Afghanistan," April 2002. U.S. State Department, "Country Reports on Human Rights Practices, 2002: Afghanistan," March 31, 2003, www.state.gov/g/drl/rls/hrrpt/2002/18308.htm; United Nations, *Interim Report of the Special Rapporteur of the Commission on Human Rights on the Situation of Human Rights in Afghanistan*, A/57/309, August 13, 2002; and United Nations, *Report by Ms. Asma Jahangir, Special Rapporteur on Extrajudicial, Summary, or Arbitrary Executions, on Her Mission to Afghanistan (13 to 23 October 2002)*, E/CN.4/2003/3/Add.4, February 3, 2003.

113. Human Rights Watch, "Killing You Is a Very Easy Thing for Us," 93; United Nations, *Report by Ms. Asma Jahangir*, E/CN.4/2003/3/Add.4, 3.

114. Ibid., paras. 15–16.

115. Ibid.

116. United Nations, Bassiouni Report, E/CN.4/2005,122, 5–8. Six weeks after his report was released, Bassiouni was himself let go by the United Nations Commission on Human Rights, allegedly at U.S. urging and owing to his reports' severe criticism of Coalition practices regarding detainees. See Pam O'Toole, "Ex-Afghan Rights Chief Attacks U.S.," *BBC News*, April 27, 2004.

117. United Nations, *SG Report on Situation in Afghanistan*, S/2003/1212, para. 41. Only $40 million of the $78 million estimated to be needed for voter registration had been received by December 2003.

118. "Security conditions" in this case included the refusal of "district administrators" of de facto districts created during the war years to relinquish control of those districts in favor of prewar administrative boundaries. The cabinet decided to hand the problem of defining district boundaries to the new National Assembly. See United Nations, *The Situation in Afghanistan . . . , Report of the Secretary-General,* A/59/744-S/2005/183, March 18, 2005, para. 8.

119. Ibid., para. 13.

120. United Nations, *SG Report on Situation in Afghanistan,* A/58/742-S/2004/230, para. 11.

121. United Nations, *SG Report on Situation in Afghanistan,* A/58/868-S/2004/634, paras. 8–10.

122. Ibid., paras. 18–19.

123. Kenneth Katzman, "Afghanistan: Presidential and Parliamentary Elections," no. RS21922 (Washington, DC: Congressional Research Service, updated July 7, 2005), 3; BAAG, "Afghanistan: Monthly Review," October 2004, 2–4, www.baag.org.uk/publications/monthlyreview.htm; and United Nations, *SG Report on Situation in Afghanistan,* A/58/868-S/2004/634, para. 8.

124. Rubin, Hamidzada, and Stoddard, *Afghanistan 2005 and Beyond,* 2.

125. Author interview with Nigel Fisher, deputy SRSG, Kabul, April 27, 2003.

126. The Afghanistan Reconstruction Support Group, a forum for donor assistance that grew out of long-standing arrangements on Afghanistan, met for the first time in Washington, D.C., in November 2001. This group continued to meet through 2002, but was disbanded at the end of the year as the Transitional Administration assumed full responsibility for donor coordination.

127. Transitional Government of Afghanistan, "Analysis of Aid Flows to Afghanistan," March 30, 2003, www.af/resources/mof/adf-ahsf-artf/Aid_Analysis-with_graphs.pdf.

128. It should be noted that while several donors made multiyear commitments over the five-year period, others did not. Most notably, the United States, France, and the Netherlands made pledges for only one year, and Japan for three. The United States has committed approximately $300 million for the second year as well.

129. Transitional Government of Afghanistan, "Analysis of Aid Flows to Afghanistan."

130. Care International, "Rebuilding Afghanistan: A Little Less Talk, a Lot More Action," October 1, 2002, www.careusa.org/newsroom/special reports/afghanistan/09302002_policybrief.pdf.

131. Islamic Transitional Government of Afghanistan (ITGA), Asian Development Bank, UNAMA, UN Development Programme, and World Bank

Group, "Securing Afghanistan's Future: Accomplishments and the Strategic Path Forward" (Kabul, March 17, 2004), executive summary, 11, www.af/resources/mof/recosting/SECURING%20AFGHNAISTANS%20FUTURE.pdf.

132. Katzman, "Afghanistan: Post-war Governance," 44.

133. Michael Buchanan, "Afghanistan Omitted from U.S. Aid Budget," *BBC News,* February 13, 2003; and Katzman, "Afghanistan: Post-war Governance," 50.

134. UNAMA, "Local Coordination and Capacity Building: Conclusions from Five AACA-UNAMA-Donor Joint Missions," May–July 2002.

135. United Nations, *The Situation in Afghanistan . . . , Report of the Secretary-General,* A/60/224-S/2005/525, August 12, 2005, para. 26.

136. United Nations, *SG Report on Situation in Afghanistan,* A/57/850-S/2003/754, paras. 26–27.

137. "Afghanistan Report," *RFE/RL,* May 23, 2003 (quoting General Ata Mohammad, commander of the 7th Army Corps).

138. Ron Synovitz, "Afghanistan: Disarming Militias Seen as Critical to Success of Peace Process," *RFE/RL,* March 29, 2004.

139. Michael Bhatia, Kevin Lanigan, and Phillip Wilkinson, "Minimal Investments, Minimal Results: The Failure of Security Policy in Afghanistan," AREU Briefing Paper, June 2004, 16. See also United Nations, *SG Report on Situation in Afghanistan,* A/58/868-S/2004/634, 30.

140. Christian Dennys, "Disarmament, Demobilization, and Rearmament?" (Kabul: Japan Afghan NGO Network, June 2005), 8, www.jca.apc.org/~jann/Documents/Disarmament%20demobilization%20rearmament.pdf.

141. Dennys, "Disarmament," 9.

142. Lieutenant General David W. Barno, "Afghanistan: The Security Outlook," transcript of remarks made at the Center for Strategic and International Studies, Washington, D.C., May 14, 2004, 25, www.csis.org/isp/pcr/040514_barno.pdf. Lieutenant General Barno assumed command of Combined Forces Command–Afghanistan in late 2003.

143. United Nations, *Quarterly Report to the United Nations on the Operations of the International Security Assistance Force,* S/2005/230, April 7, 2005, Annex/Enclosure; and United Nations, *SG Report on Situation in Afghanistan,* A/59/744-S/2005/183, para. 23. Reporting on heavy weapons is somewhat slippery, and numbers may vary depending on whether the reporting organization counts only fully operational weapons or also includes serviceable weapons (which may mean reparable, or just useful for spare parts). Heavy weapons also mean more than tanks and artillery and may include any weapon with a barrel exceeding a certain diameter, even rocket-propelled grenade launchers. So the weapon count alone is but a crude gauge of how much firepower is being rounded up.

144. Antonio Giustozzi, "Re-building the Afghan Army" (draft paper for the Crisis States Program, Development Research Centre, London School of Economics, April 2003).

145. United Nations, *SG Report on Situation in Afghanistan,* A/59/581-S/2004/925, November 26, 2004, paras. 23–25.

146. Rubin, Hamidzada, and Stoddard, *Afghanistan 2005 and Beyond,* 37; Crisis Group, "Afghanistan: Getting Disarmament Back on Track," 6–8.

147. United Nations, *SG Report on Situation in Afghanistan* (A/59/581-S/2004/925, paras. 23–25; and A/60/224-S/2005/525, para. 33).

148. Rubin, Hamidzada, and Stoddard, *Afghanistan 2005 and Beyond,* 40; "Afghan Anti-U.S. Violence Escalates," *BBC News—South Asia,* May 12, 2005, newsvote.bbc.co.uk.

149. UNDP Afghanistan, "Law and Order Trust Fund for Afghanistan," www.undp.org.af.

150. United Nations, *SG Report on Situation in Afghanistan,* A/60/224-S/2005/525, para. 34.

151. Author interview with UN official, December 2004.

152. United Nations, *SG Report on Situation in Afghanistan,* paras. 36–39; and Katzman, "Afghanistan: Post-war Governance," 16–17.

153. United Nations, *SG Report on Situation in Afghanistan,* para. 43.

154. Rubin, Hamidzada, and Stoddard, *Afghanistan 2005 and Beyond,* 42.

155. Bonn Agreement, Annex I.

156. UN Security Council Resolution 1386, S/RES/2001/1386, December 20, 2001.

157. Ibid.; S/RES/2002/1413, May 23, 2002 (extending ISAF for six months); S/RES/2002/1444, November 27, 2002; S/RES/2003/1510, October 13, 2003; and S/RES/2004/1563, September 17, 2004 (each extending for another year).

158. UK Ministry of Defence, *Military Technical Agreement between the International Security Assistance Force and the Interim Administration of Afghanistan,* www.operations.mod.uk/isafmta.doc.

159. Military units are defined in the agreement as including "all Afghan factions, armed representatives or personnel with a military capability, to include all mujahideen, armed forces, and armed groups, other than the

'Police Force' defined at paragraph 4e. The definition of 'Military Units' in this context does not include the ISAF, Coalition Forces or other recognized national military forces." See ibid.

160. Author correspondence with Terry Hay, Media Operations, ISAF headquarters, November 2002.

161. See, for example, U.S. Congress, "Afghanistan Freedom Support Act," S. 2712, November 14, 2002 (funding an expansion of ISAF); Crisis Group, "Securing Afghanistan: The Need for More International Action," March 15, 2002; ACBAR, "To the Members of the UN Security Council," June 20, 2002 (letter signed by sixty-six Afghan and international NGOs calling for ISAF expansion); William J. Durch, "Security and Peace Support in Afghanistan: Analysis and Short- to Medium-Term Options," Henry L. Stimson Center, June 28, 2003; and Council on Foreign Relations and the Asia Society, "Afghanistan: Are We Losing the Peace?" June 2003, www.asiasociety.org/policy_business/afghanistan061703.pdf.

162. Human Rights Research and Advocacy Consortium, "Speaking Out: Afghan Opinions on Rights and Responsibilities," November 2003, www.afghanadvocacy.org.

163. U.S. undersecretary of defense Douglas Feith said the United States stated that its government would be "perfectly delighted" if ISAF were expanded. See "Afghan About-Face: U.S. Military Takes a Softer Tack," *Washington Post*, October 1, 2002, A1.

164. UN Security Council Resolution 1510, S/RES/2003/1510, October 13, 2003.

165. UN Security Council Resolution 1386, S/RES/2001/1386.

166. UN Security Council, *Security Council Extends Afghanistan Security Force for Six Months, Unanimously Adopting Resolution 1413 (2002)*, SC/7410/4541, May 23, 2002.

167. Henry L. Stimson Center, "The Second Supplemental: The Administration's March FY02 Supplemental Budget Request," 2002, www.stimson.org/fopo.

168. The lower estimate is by Durch, "Security and Peace Support in Afghanistan" (online at www.stimson.org/fopo/pubs.cfm?ID=58), based on the average annual per capita cost of non-U.S. troops sent to Kosovo ($120,000). Given Afghanistan's more demanding logistics and need for airlift, annual per capita troop costs in Afghanistan could be $10,000 to $20,000 higher than in Kosovo. The higher estimate is contained in ITGA et al., *Securing Afghanistan's Future*, 78, without corroborating details.

169. Contributing nations included Albania, Austria, Belgium, Bulgaria, Canada, the Czech Republic, Denmark, Finland, France, Germany, Greece, Ireland, Italy, the Netherlands, New Zealand, Norway, Romania, Spain, Sweden, Turkey, and the United Kingdom.

170. UN Security Council, *Report on the Activities of the International Security Assistance Force in Afghanistan,* S/2002/274, March 15, 2002.

171. Information provided by Terry Hay, Media Operations, HQ ISAF, November 2002.

172. NATO secretary-general George Robertson said in Brussels on July 16, 2003, that NATO would remain in Afghanistan "until the job doesn't need to be done." "Afghanistan Report," *RFE/RL,* July 24, 2003.

173. NATO, "NATO in Afghanistan: How Did This Operation Evolve?" updated June 9, 2005, www.nato.int/issues/afghanistan/evolution.htm.

174. UN Security Council, *Letter from the Permanent Representative of the U.K. to the President of the Security Council,* S/2001/1217, December 19, 2001.

175. UN Security Council, *Second Report on the Activities of the International Security Assistance Force in Afghanistan,* S/2002/479, April 25, 2002.

176. "Afghanistan: Government Acts to Strengthen Security after Suicide Attack," *IRIN,* June 9, 2003; "ISAF Treating Deadly Kabul Mine Blast as Deliberate Attack," *Agence France-Presse,* October 8, 2003; and BAAG, "Afghanistan: Monthly Review," May and June 2004, www.baag.org.uk/publications/monthlyreview.htm.

177. Peter Beaumont, "U.S. Pulls Out Karzai's Military Bodyguards," *Observer,* November 24, 2002, observer.guardian.co.uk/afghanistan/story/0,1501,846595,00.html.

178. "The participants in the UN Talks on Afghanistan pledge to withdraw all military units from Kabul and other urban centers or other areas in which the UN mandated force is deployed." See Bonn Agreement, Annex I.

179. UN Security Council Resolution 1386, S/RES/2001/1386, emphasis added.

180. Detail about the state of the civil service in several provinces throughout Afghanistan is available in AREU and World Bank, "Assessing Sub-national Administration in Afghanistan: Early Observations and Recommendations for Action," March 2003, lnweb18.worldbank.org/sar/sa.nsf/Attachments/assess/$File/Afgh+Assess+Report.pdf.

8

Are We Learning Yet?
The Long Road to Applying Best Practices

William J. Durch

I t is risky to attempt to summarize the lessons from as complex a set of transitional conflict environments as the six cases addressed in this volume, especially because most of these operations continue at the time of writing. But the international system, its members, and its institutions continue to undertake new operations in other conflict zones. The United Nations alone has launched five new operations fielding 40,000 new troops since the case studies in this volume were commissioned. The implementation of these missions has in many respects shown the value of UN reforms undertaken since 2002, as do the later experiences of the operations in this volume, but some of the old mistakes are still made.

The obligation of medicine and international assistance alike is to "first, do no harm," but the widely varying norms of human interaction and the details of each conflict make it difficult to know just which sorts of activities meet the no-harm test for most, let alone all, of the intended beneficiaries in a given situation.[1] Every complex peace operation is a risk-prone venture of uncertain outcome, even with detailed advance planning, a generous allocation of resources, and the greatest willingness on the part of the international community to take risks in the interests of peace—none of which obtained consistently for any of the cases examined in this volume.

Complex peace operations and the conflict zones where they take place in fact present serious dilemmas to outsiders. The urge to help, deriving partly from moral and ethical considerations and partly from the national and institutional interests of the assistance providers, is at some point constrained not only by the direct costs of providing that help but by the opportunity costs: doing A may preclude B, and maybe C and D as well, in other locales.[2] Would-be aid providers also may face choices between helping the hardest cases and helping others where feasible levels of intervention seem more likely to produce durable positive results. These are not, of course, choices unique to peace implementation, but they are all the more difficult for potentially involving millions of people who did nothing worse than live in the wrong place at the wrong time. Thus, while the United Nations' High-Level Panel on Threats, Challenges and Change endorsed the principles of the "responsibility to protect," and while those principles speak potentially to the highest order of ethical behavior,[3] a government's first responsibility is still to its own people. Extending this responsibility to others requires justification of the ensuing costs and risks. Part of that justification is a reasonable prospect of success, and success is a function of not only good local knowledge but a sense of what has worked and how well, and what has not worked and how badly, among those things that every mission needs to do: gather political support; find funding; recruit, train, deploy, lead, and support military and nonmilitary personnel; and execute the mandate in the face of varying degrees of motivated opposition.

Building on the Literature: Six Cases, Plus

This section builds on the literature reviewed in chapter 1, leaning most heavily on the findings of the six cases in this volume but also drawing selectively from key earlier missions and from the new missions launched in the UN's "fourth surge," from 2003 to 2005. In structure, it parallels the case chapters.

Political Support and the Character of the Peace

"Consent of the local parties," a UN mantra for decades, is no less important for having been reduced over time to a kind of cliché. If local political and combatant leaders do not actively support a peace settlement, will not tolerate electoral loss, think they might not survive it, or use a period of peace mostly to rearm and retrain their forces, then peace will not likely endure for long after outside forces leave.

Much depends, therefore, on the way peace has been achieved. When outsiders implement a locally agreed-on accord, the elements of consent are theoretically in place before they deploy, although several cases in this volume show how theory and reality can clash. A party may sign in bad faith, as did Sierra Leone's Revolutionary United Front (RUF). Credulous or cynical negotiators may shunt the most difficult implementation issues to a third party, such as the United Nations, as did negotiators of the 1999 Lusaka Agreement to end the war in the Democratic Republic of the Congo. Governments may sign a peace but use surrogate forces to wreak vengeance when their side loses an election or referendum, as did Indonesia after the East Timorese voted in August 1999. And participants in power-sharing arrangements may use their new positions primarily to buttress the power of their faction, as occurred in Afghanistan.

Especially when consent is uncertain, a peacekeeping force must implement provisions of a peace accord fairly and treat comparable transgressions of the peace with comparable firmness, regardless of the source of transgression. That is the definition of impartiality in the new era of peace operations, and it applies regardless of the level of force that may be authorized or that may be needed to maintain or implement peace. An invited international force will not long maintain its authority or its legitimacy in the eyes of the local population if it is not seen to carry out its duties in such a manner.

When outsiders impose a peace, as in Kosovo, local consent must be engineered after the fact, even among the parties on whose behalf the internationals acted. Those parties, having been delivered from whatever forces assailed them, will likely try to implement their own preferred outcomes using all means at their disposal unless they are controlled in turn. They will not await outsiders' permission to act, as Michael Dziedzic notes in the Kosovo chapter in this volume.

An accord might also be inked by only some of the belligerent parties. Peace implementation may then occur in parallel with continuing counterinsurgency operations, as was the case in Afghanistan.

Quality, Clarity, and Feasibility of Mandates

When the Brahimi Report enjoined the Security Council to create "clear, credible, and achievable mandates," it was voicing a long-standing sentiment in the peacekeeping community, where muddled instructions and underresourcing relative to assigned tasks have long been viewed as sources of risk for complex peace operations. Muddled language may reflect either compromise among conflicting interests on the council or aversion to taking risks where no member's interests are especially deep, but pressure of one sort or another nonetheless requires the dispatch of a UN mission.

Matching Resources to Tasks

Underresourcing has been a chronic problem for UN operations, either because the Secretariat reduces its resource requests to what the political traffic will bear, or because powerful Security Council members refuse to support more than a fraction of what objective analysis suggests is needed to achieve a mission's objectives. The Brahimi Report argued that the Secretariat was not doing anyone, especially troop contributors, any favors by underestimating the costs of operations and that it must, instead, tell the council "what it needs to know, not what it wants to hear."[4] For a time, both Secretariat and Security Council seemed to take this admonition to heart although, as Philip Roessler and John Prendergast argue, it took a series of massacres in the northeastern Congo to energize the council to substantially strengthen the UN Mission in the Democratic Republic of the Congo (MONUC) and to authorize, ad interim, the deployment of a French-led security force. Two months later, the council backed deployment of troops from the Economic Community of West African States (ECOWAS) to maintain order in Monrovia, Liberia, until a large UN operation with a forceful mandate could be deployed to absorb those troops and implement a shaky peace agreement. The following spring, the council took similar action with regard to troubled Côte d'Ivoire. There, ECOWAS and French troops, operating separately, had maintained an uneasy cease-fire since late 2002 between the government and the rebel "Forces Nouvelles," which loosely controlled the northern half of the country. The ECOWAS force blended into a larger UN operation begun in April 2004, which gave West African troop contributors access to UN logistics support and UN reimbursements.

Establishing the UN Operation in Côte d'Ivoire (UNOCI) entailed serious opportunity costs, however. Global UN troop deployments were approaching historical peaks, but with very few troops from developed states. UNOCI was authorized to deploy 6,000 troops, four times as many as it rehatted from ECOWAS. Money and troops needed by other UN missions (especially the Francophone venues of the Congo, Burundi, and Haiti) were channeled instead into Côte d'Ivoire. A well-structured mid-2004 request from the secretary-general for additional troops to shore up a crumbling peace in the eastern Congo was cut in half by the Security Council, in a move reminiscent of the cuts in requests for forces to protect Srebrenica in Bosnia a decade earlier.[5]

The French force in Côte d'Ivoire continued to function with its own rules of engagement, and its potential to be a lightning rod for local unhappiness with French policies became clear when Ivoirian government forces attacked a French outpost. French forces immediately retaliated, destroying the small Ivoirian air force—consistent with French doctrine but potentially posing great risks to other international forces and personnel in the country. It would have been better, perhaps, had France been encouraged to shoulder this burden as the lead or "framework" nation (a NATO term) of a coalition force, leaving the United Nations out of the picture except as a peacemaker/observer.

Transitional Authority: Heavy versus Light

If the international community decides to provide assistance to a state or territory transitioning from internal conflict, colonial control, or both, how much authority should a transitional assistance mission possess, and in what issue areas? In 1999, the Security Council gave the UN special representatives of the secretary-general (SRSGs) in Kosovo and East Timor essentially unlimited legislative and executive powers over these territories. Their mandates (Resolutions 1244 and 1272, respectively) were remarkably broad, and their accountability was not at all clear. There is at least irony in a mission supporting political independence and democratic governance through rule making by unelected foreigners. That, however, is the position in which transitional administration mandates place the United Nations (or the Coalition Provisional Authority, or whatever organization assumes responsibility for a failed state, would-be state, or forcefully disestablished government).

The United Nations' chief diplomatic troubleshooter for Afghanistan, Lakhdar Brahimi, was determined to take a different approach. Six weeks after the United States intervened militarily to oust the Taliban and their al Qaeda "guests," Brahimi gathered most of the rest of the country's factions around a table in Bonn, Germany, to design not a peace agreement but a peace process. To support that process, he proposed a "light footprint" for the UN Assistance Mission in Afghanistan (UNAMA), and the UN Secretariat crafted such a mission in line with his wishes. UNAMA's job would be not to run Afghanistan but to coordinate international aid and advice to the interim governing structures created at Bonn, while leaving leadership in Afghan hands from the start.

UNAMA could afford a light political footprint in part because U.S. coalition forces continued to push back the Taliban and al Qaeda and to provide security in the least stable parts of the country, albeit in league with local warlords. In addition, the International Security Assistance Force (ISAF), a coalition of the willing mandated by the UN Security Council, provided welcome stability in the environs of Kabul, the capital city. ISAF proved to be a durable operation, and since August 2003 has functioned under NATO management. In other places, however, UN forces have arrived to replace relatively brief coalitions of the willing (as in East Timor, Haiti, or the Ituri district of the Congo). UN forces have also replaced or rehatted (absorbed) troops from regional organizations' operations, as noted above. In all of these cases, the international security footprint was substantial even if the political footprint remained relatively light and largely advisory. Alexander Thier argues that, in Afghanistan, the level of authority given UNAMA may have been appropriate, but that much more assistance could have been supplied by the mission—in the form of expatriate Afghan professionals on short-term contracts, to help meet Afghan ministers' critical need for people to help them rebuild their ministries and reinstitute capable central government in the country. In other words, on the civilian side, "light" need not and perhaps should not be "thin," if political competence is to be restored.

In all cases of major international presence, the economic footprint of a PSO is difficult to minimize and can have unintended consequences, especially in the labor market. Most of that impact derives, however, from the civilian component spending its "mission subsistence allowance," from local procurement of goods and services by the mission, and from the hiring of local people by the mission.[6] Military units may have indirect economic impact when such activities as clearing bridges and roads of mines to further their own movements also facilitate local commerce. They may also undertake voluntary infrastructure repairs "off budget," as did the Pakistani, Bangladeshi, and other contingents in Sierra Leone.

Issues in the Pace and Scale of Deployments

Gradual withdrawal of a PSO is desirable, if only to cushion the impact on the local economy, but gradual deployment is not. When NATO went into Bosnia in late 1995, it deployed a force fully equipped for combat that was two and a half times larger than the UN force it replaced; when NATO went into Kosovo, it had 45,000 troops, also combat equipped. Both of these forces functioned under Security Council mandates. Although both fell short in the public security realm, neither experienced any trouble from the organized combatants that they were supposed to disarm, demobilize, or escort out of the area.

In Africa, on the other hand, until roughly mid-2003 and the buildup in the northeastern Congo, the Security Council still seemed to see peacekeeper deployments as rewards for, rather than guarantors of, the good behavior of local factions. That is, parties structurally incapable of keeping the peace unaided were asked to prove they could keep the peace unaided in order to get outside help. Since many of the parties to the conflict in the DRC were also madly digging up the country's mineral riches, the last thing they actually wanted within view was a UN observer taking notes, and all they had to do to avoid that was to behave irresponsibly. The council's incremental strategy for the DRC also reflected the cost and risk aversion of the United States and other council members, who seemed equally uninterested in imposing sanctions or aid conditionality on the countries and governments most busy stripping the Congo of its resources. Meanwhile, roving bands of fighters continued their wholesale predation of Congolese civilians, and millions of persons displaced by the violence slowly starved in the bush.

As Roessler and Prendergast relate in the Congo chapter in this volume, for several years there was no coherent international strategy for either halting the war or enforcing the peace in the DRC. Such a strategy modeled on NATO's Balkan operations, however, would have needed nearly a million troops. Cut the requirement in half and it would still be an unachievable number.

Did NATO therefore over-deploy in the Balkans? It may have; it certainly could afford to, as these were small places close to home. Can lower-density deployments make a difference, without posing undue risks to peacekeepers? Recent UN operations in the eastern Congo and the Ituri district—those parts of the country bordering Uganda, Rwanda, and Burundi—resulted in just nineteen UN fatalities due to hostile action in two years, through mid-2005. Half of those occurred in a single militia ambush in Ituri, which triggered a retaliatory response by MONUC. That operation has concentrated its troops, about 16,000 at this writing, in the one-fifth of the country that is most troubled. Although it remains technically outnumbered in the eastern DRC, MONUC functions in concert with the nascent (if still wobbly) Congolese army. The opposition groups it faces are, in Doyle's terminology, "many and incoherent," with little or no ability to stand their ground against capable modern fighting units and with but fleeting ability to combine against the United Nations. And, despite being heavily outnumbered, the 7,000 UN troops from India, Pakistan, and South Africa deployed in the Kivus have been able to advance their mandate because they have been willing to engage. Sustainability of results requires, of course, that the Congo's fitfully evolving army continues to support both the peace process and the still-weak central government.

Had the armed groups operating outside the Congo's peace process been either stronger or more coherent, then the forces supporting that process would have had to be stronger as well. In fairness to the original planners of MONUC, there was concern at the outset that a country so large and anarchic would in fact be a bottomless pit for peacekeeping resources. Had the United Nations gone in stronger, sooner, many lives might have been saved, but UN forces would have encountered not only ragtag militias but the armies of neighboring states like Rwanda and Uganda, as well as their proxy fighters. It is highly unlikely that the distant capitals of UN troop contributors, upon calculating national interests, would have let their troops fight under those conditions, no matter where those capitals were.

Issues in Planning and Implementation

Few countries, besides a handful of major powers, have the capability to plan and implement military operations outside their home territory. In Europe, only Britain and France "possess strategic headquarters staffed by experienced officers that could plan and command operations" up to and including limited expeditionary warfare beyond Europe's borders. Analysts Julian Lindley-French and Franco Algieri estimate, moreover, that of the 1.7 million "uniforms" maintained by European states, only about 10 percent could be used in medium- to high-intensity military tasks.[7] In Africa, plans for an African Standby Force for the African Union are ambitious but limited by cost and available resources. The African Union at present "has neither its own forces nor forces on call prepared to deploy rapidly and effectively . . . [and] lacks a robust headquarters management and planning capacity (there are few military personnel on . . . staff), logistics and enabling units, airlift, ground transportation, [or] mobile communications systems."[8] The development of the regional standby brigades called for in current AU plans will be aided by American and European bilateral and multilateral assistance programs but the cost of actually mounting and sustaining operations will also need to be met, somehow. The African Union plans to establish a "small headquarters planning element" by 2010, but it will still need all of above-noted resources in order to launch an operation and keep it going.[9]

In contrast, NATO has both a largely civilian international staff of several thousand people and a 380-strong international military staff, both with operations divisions that have planning responsibilities related to peace support operations. NATO also has a strategic-level military headquarters (Allied Command Operations) with two operational-level regional headquarters (Allied Forces North and South) akin to U.S. Regional Combatant Commands.[10] Although NATO is geared toward combat operations as well as peacekeeping, in late 2004 the organization was primarily in the peacekeeping business, with about 20,000 peacekeeping troops deployed in Kosovo and Kabul. NATO also gave planning support to the European Union's 7,000 peacekeepers in Bosnia, and the EU is to have an "embedded" planning cell within NATO military headquarters to facilitate future NATO support to EU field operations.

UN Planning and Support Capacity

The post–Brahimi Report UN Department of Peacekeeping Operations (DPKO) had substantially more planning capacity in late 2005 than it did in 1999, but its capacity was still far short of NATO or the three major powers. Although DPKO does not plan for expeditionary warfare, it does manage substantial forces at great distances (62,500 troops and observers and 7,200 police at the end of 2005). Some of them periodically find themselves in low-intensity combat against "spoiler" forces or organized criminal syndicates. To support these forces, DPKO has just sixty military officers in its military division, of whom roughly two dozen are planners.

During the last UN mission bulge, in the early to mid-1990s, states that could afford to do so seconded military officers to the United Nations while continuing to pay their salaries and related costs. (The United Nations paid for office overhead and equipment.)[11] The resulting national imbalance (few members of the "Global South" could afford to second such officers) eventually led the General Assembly to demand that these "gratis military personnel" be replaced with paid staff.[12] By early 1999, the departure of gratis personnel had cut the staff of DPKO by one-third just a few months before the Security Council launched missions in Kosovo, Timor, Sierra Leone, and the Congo. Although DPKO substantially expanded both its military and its logistics staffs between 2001 and 2003 along the lines recommended in the Brahimi Report, the doubling in size of UN operations between 2003 and 2005 all but erased the relative gains made in UN capacity to plan, recruit, and manage these operations.[13]

Civilian mission elements, from human rights to police to elections, are often critical to complex peace operations, but as of late 2005 there was still no full-time cadre of substantive civilian mission planners within DPKO or anywhere else in the UN system. There were many competent logistics, transport, and information technology specialists prepared to recruit, set up, house, and Web-enable a new mission, but there was no team responsible for planning *how to implement the mandate.*[14] To its credit, DPKO was chairing a working group mandated to devise a true "integrated mission planning process." Although it remained a work in progress as of this writing, it incorporated recommendations from the Brahimi Report that each new complex peace operation undertaken by the United Nations be planned by an Integrated Mission Task Force (IMTF) with decision-making authority over most aspects of the mission. According to the report, the ideal IMTF would be

> an entity that includes all of the backstopping people and expertise for [a] mission, drawn from an array of Headquarters elements that mirrors the functions of the mission itself. . . . The leader of the IMTF . . . [should have] line authority over his or her Task Force members for the period of their secondment, and should serve as the first level of contact for the peace operation for all aspects of their work.[15]

An IMTF was attempted for Afghanistan, and, as Alexander Thier notes in that chapter in this volume, the task force was crucial to mission design. It served more as an information clearinghouse than as a decision-making body, however, and subsequent IMTFs have done little better.

As rank conscious as any military organization and as turf conscious as any other bureaucracy, but much less in control of its destiny, the UN Secretariat may never be able to sustain the sort of decision making that a good interagency process requires. It has never had an organizational entity—an office or division[16]—charged with creating and supporting IMTFs, developing agreed-upon protocols for their functions, and finding physical space for their members to use during the crucial early weeks of mission planning and preparation. (This may seem trivial, but it is not; the UN headquarters building in New

York is cramped, and every square foot of leasable office space nearby is exorbitantly expensive.)[17]

Collaboration among UN agencies and headquarters departments is not all that is needed for effective mission planning, however. The Brahimi Report argued that the leaders of a new operation—its civilian head of mission (the SRSG) and its top military appointee (the force commander)—should be involved as early as possible in planning, to ensure their contribution to and support for the resulting plans and strategies. Unless the mission leadership team is closely connected to the headquarters mission planning process and sees it as valuable, however, a strong-willed SRSG may seek to do mission planning with his or her own hand-picked team and view headquarters in New York as a cross between Temps Inc. and Home Depot—that is, as a place that supplies warm bodies and building supplies only, rather than as a source of strategic direction as well.[18]

Finding Mission Leadership and Managing Missions

Once headquarters is doing its part of the job right, the key to effective collaboration with the field lies in selection of the right people and personalities to lead operations, which is critical to mission success. Incompetent, indecisive, or mutually antagonistic personalities at the apex of an operation, especially one with a difficult mandate and treacherous political waters to navigate, can destroy its effectiveness. As Eric Berman and Melissa Labonte relate in the Sierra Leone chapter in this volume, a nearly complete breakdown in communications and a complete lack of respect between the operation's original force commander (from India) and the SRSG and deputy force commander (both from Nigeria) led to mission paralysis and vulnerability to an embarrassing sequence of attacks by the thuggish RUF.

The Brahimi Report argued that managerial competence should be as important as national origin and other political considerations in the selection of mission leaders. The Secretariat subsequently started building lists of competent potential leaders, but UN member states urged the secretary-general to leave such lists open to other (i.e., politically favored) nominees. In practice, SRSGs must be acceptable to the region where a new mission deploys and the country that contributes the most troops to an operation expects to nominate the force commander.

In 2003, however, the United Nations did make exceptions to the regional rule for SRSGs, appointing Americans in Liberia, when civil disorder led to the dispatch of a large UN peace operation, and the Congo, when the UN mission and the country both reached a critical political and military turning point. Both gave their missions much better access to and visibility in Washington, but regional politics in Africa and other regions will limit the extent to which the United Nations can look for SRSGs from among the Security Council's permanent members, and nationality is in any case no guarantee of managerial skills.

Indeed, the sorts of gifted political leaders who might make the best SRSGs at the political level—able to jawbone local political leaders into living up to the bargains they have signed, or able to inspire their own staff to do their jobs well—may be exceedingly poor administrators. The United Nations has addressed this problem by pushing mission management and other tasks one level down, as needed, to one or more deputy SRSGs, who tend to be career UN officials, increasingly ones with previous field experience. Their knowledge of the UN system and its policies and procedures can make up for an SRSG's lack of experience and free him or her from the daily demands of mission management.

In many countries, a UN country team, consisting of development and humanitarian agencies, may have remained in a country through its times of trouble or may have returned there prior to the Security Council's mandating a peace operation, to provide humanitarian relief or to initiate reconstruction. In such cases, the UN resident coordinator who heads the country team may be appointed deputy SRSG of a new peace operation. Sometimes the resident coordinator is the appropriate fit for this role, and sometimes not. Sometimes the rest of the country team is integrated into the new mission but often it is not, reflecting the UN system's decentralized structure, management, and funding.[19]

Mission Structure: Integration or Coordination?

Each PSO is assembled from a mix of national and international parts, and its management structure can vary from a fully integrated hierarchy to a loosely guided swarm. "Integrated mission" is the UN term of art for a complex peace operation mandated by the Security Council that is given authority over all UN agencies and activities within its area of responsibility. Such a mandate makes the SRSG the chief UN officer in that country, outranking the head of the prior UN country team.[20] DPKO argues that integrated missions should be the norm wherever there is a Security Council peacekeeping mandate, in order to focus the United Nations' effort on rebuilding the state. During their many years of directly aiding a population displaced and terrorized by civil war, UN and other humanitarian agencies may have needed to do an end run around government, but that approach may not well serve the international community's postwar objective of building up the credibility and capability of the new national government and the public's confidence in it. Unless there is a stable and responsive state, runs this argument, humanitarian assistance cannot be effective and is likely to be needed for a much longer period. Therefore, once the United Nations has been tasked to help create a stable state, all components of the UN system should pitch in to support that objective or at least not work visibly at cross-purposes with it.[21]

Humanitarian agencies bridle at being made to appear supporters of visibly political objectives by being brought into the management structure of a peace operation, especially if the operation's mandate is based on Chapter VII of the UN Charter—the enforcement chapter. With such a mandate, which is increasingly common for new UN operations, the military component may, for example, use force against a violent local group whose actions are impeding implementation of a peace agreement. From a political point of view, such use of force may be necessary to keep the peace from coming apart. From the perspective of humanitarian agencies, however, close association with an operation that uses force in such a manner may make their staff targets of one faction or another. It may also wreck the agencies' reputation for neutrality—that is, for equidistant relations with all groups and a hands-off attitude toward local politics—in the next crisis, where they may lack any military security support and a reputation for neutrality may be their best available protection.[22]

In the chapter on Bosnia in this volume, Elizabeth Cousens and David Harland concluded that the disorganized international civilian effort produced meager and even counterproductive results, giving the worst local political elements an opportunity to strengthen their hold on wealth and power and to build ties to (or to become) criminal syndicates. A stronger and more integrated civilian component, they argued, with a security component more engaged in breaking up those syndicates or preventing them from forming at the outset, might have set Bosnia on the road to political and economic recovery much more quickly.

The United Nations and its European institutional partners tried a more consolidated approach for the UN Interim Administration Mission in Kosovo (UNMIK), where the SRSG became the manager of a multi-"pillar" arrangement of collaborating agencies. NATO's Kosovo Force (KFOR) coordinated closely with UNMIK, although this coordination proved too weak at the town and village level to contain orchestrated social violence even five years after deployment.

East Timor did not need a pillarlike structure because there were no regional operating agencies in Southeast Asia comparable to those in Europe clamoring for a role in Kosovo. An Australian-led coalition of the willing kept order for five months while the United Nations pulled together an integrated successor operation with very little strategic guidance. Australia remained the top troop contributor to UNTAET, and a number of other troop contingents transferred as well, applying their on-the-job training to the successor operation.[23]

MONUC is not a fully integrated mission but has had an integrative effect in other ways. Its extensive air transport system allows UN agencies and NGOs working in the DRC to book passage across country free of charge, on a space-available basis. MONUC has thereby eased, for those agencies and organizations, what otherwise would have been a difficult and expensive transport problem. MONUC also set up Radio Okapi, a network of shortwave and FM stations with carefully structured programming whose news, entertainment, and public service programming reach an estimated 70 percent of the population. Okapi was established and operates with partial support from Fondation Hirondelle, a Geneva-based nonprofit whose main mission is to set up radio broadcast networks in postconflict environments. MONUC thus reflects integration between the United Nations and the nonprofit private sector, which promoted national integration by giving the Congolese access to a nationwide radio network not controlled by any political party or group.[24]

Afghanistan's two decades of conflict produced a patchwork of foreign relief and development efforts, UN and non-UN, public and private, more or less adapted to operating outside the writ of those claiming to govern the country, whether Soviet proxies or ethnic militias or the holy warriors of the Taliban. UNAMA's job was to help re-channel aid through the new post-Bonn Afghan authorities while helping to build their capacity to govern the rest of the country.

A decade of experience in Europe, Africa, and Asia suggests strongly that complex international efforts in potentially dangerous situations work better if actively and authoritatively managed, rather than coordinated. The ability to develop coherent contingency plans, move resources reliably and in a timely manner, and respond to unexpected crises may all be greater if the mission components involved are accountable to the same authority structure. This is how the command structures of good military organizations work and why civilian planners tend to turn to military organizations for disaster response as well as security.

Achieving Unity of Effort

The effectiveness of any peace operation depends in part on its unity of effort. Even in the most highly integrated operations, military forces will respond first and foremost to their national chains of command and act within the limits of their national doctrines and rules of engagement. Retaining ultimate command is a fundamental issue with most national capitals and will therefore always be a fundamental constraint on how well, and how reliably, multinational peacekeeping forces deal with violent challenges to peace implementation.

Military forces must also work well with and on occasion assist the police. The police in turn must work well with other criminal justice mission elements, the other civilian elements of the mission, and the local population. Generating consistent and desired behavior from such polyglot forces is never easy. Indeed, the only way to do so may be via upstream, high-level political agreement on mission objectives among police and troop contributors. Troops and police who are sent into the field need to hear a message from their government that is consistent with the objectives of the operation they are joining.

Civil-military accord on mission objectives also can be key to effective peace implementation. Anytime the military is disengaged from or potentially working at cross-purposes with civilian efforts, implementation may be frustrated. During its first year in post-Dayton in Bosnia, for example, IFOR supervised the separation of national forces while civilian implementers were trying to promote returns of national minorities to those same zones. NATO's deep reluctance to get involved in more than force separation for nearly two years helped to strengthen ethnic nationalists' grip on Bosnian politics.

Troop Contingents: Timeliness of Deployment

Throughout the 1990s, UN peacekeepers required four to six months to deploy following adoption of a mission mandate by the Security Council. The United Nations assembles its peacekeeping forces from the farthest reaches of the globe, leasing the strategic lift needed to transport them to locales far removed from troop contributors' home bases. Some participating forces may lack basic equipment, and most cannot be sustained in the field without UN support and UN cost reimbursement.

Expert observers of conflicts and conflict resolution have argued, however, that if there is no visible and effective peacekeeper presence within six to twelve *weeks* of the signing of a peace accord, where an accord calls for such a force, then the peace may begin to unravel.[25] The peace process stalls because the tool intended to implement it has not appeared. Would-be spoilers perceive a free lunch, while serious supporters of peace may lose heart. The security dilemma that peacekeepers are supposed to disrupt instead remains all parties' dominant problem.

The Brahimi Report set the United Nations' first deployment benchmarks: thirty days for traditional peacekeeping and ninety days for complex operations. The secretary-general subsequently defined these benchmarks to mean that 5,000 troops, half of them self-supporting, should be deployed to a traditional operation within thirty days of the issuance of a Security Council mandate, or that 5,000 troops should be deployed to a complex operation within ninety days.[26]

On the whole, NATO and its member states have done better at deploying forces quickly into postconflict settings, and there are many structural reasons for this. In the case of Bosnia, what became IFOR had been positioned to extract UN peacekeepers and aid providers in the face of a crumbling security situation. Eight weeks of peace talks gave NATO the opportunity to alter its operational plans. Three years later, the crisis and confrontation over Kosovo evolved over several months and permitted the prepositioning of initial elements of what would be KFOR in Macedonia and Albania. Both crises were contiguous to NATO territory. Participating forces were highly mechanized, and participating countries could afford to support them.

UN DPKO has, however, risen to the challenge on several occasions. Its upgraded military planning service, in collaboration with military staff already in the field, pulled together a workable plan for the forceful expansion of MONUC in the late spring and summer of 2003 and for a large operation in Liberia several weeks later. In the spring and summer of 2004, DPKO had to implement four more deployments of roughly 6,000 troops each, in Burundi, Côte d'Ivoire, Haiti, and again in eastern Congo.[27] In this sequence of urgent deployments, DPKO's flow of new forces to the field reached but rarely exceeded 3,000 troops per month, suggesting a maximum surge rate for its logistics system, given the need simultaneously to support 30,000 troops and several thousand civilian personnel already in the field elsewhere.

That logistics system had been bolstered by a 2001 General Assembly decision to upgrade a UN supply base at Brindisi, Italy, with enough materiel to implement one new complex operation per year. The system began to choke when it had to implement the equivalent of four new complex operations in less than one year. No regional organization at that time would have done much better, however, at deploying 24,000 troops and other mission infrastructure in three widely separated locations.

Police in Peace Operations: Recruiting and Deployment Crises

For more than a decade, the United Nations' PSO mission plans have included deployment of police personnel. The Security Council has built them into its mandated forces as though the demand for police in peace operations would itself create the supply. But there are no international police outside such missions, and historically there has been no reserve force waiting to be called up to staff them. Instead, there are thousands of domestic police forces, all fully engaged in what they do for a living, "deploying" daily, some armed, many not. Each has its own local, provincial, or national laws to enforce and specified procedures for enforcing them. Their legal code may derive from one of two Western traditions (common or civil law), may be based on Islamic sharia, or may have some other foundation.[28]

When the United Nations seeks police for one of its operations, countries will recruit and nominate officers, who traditionally have had to pass just three relatively simple UN tests: they must have some years of experience as police; they must know how to drive a motor vehicle; and they must read and speak English (the usual mission language). The tiny Police Division in DPKO is kept busy administering these tests—ideally in the candidates' home countries but sometimes in the mission area. Many UN member states are not making even the minimal effort necessary to avoid wasting the division's limited time with unqualified candidates and, as a result, a high percentage of candidates offered to the United Nations have failed these simple competency tests and have been turned away. Recruiting appropriate police specialties—training officers, administrators, or forensic investigators, for example—is even more difficult.[29]

Every new mission with a substantial police force wastes a good deal of time training its members and making up strategy and procedures for the force. Absent such training, police draw upon the training that they have and, since a mission such as Kosovo may draw its police from four or five dozen countries and several legal traditions, there is little likelihood that criminal investigations by UN police will produce evidence justiciable in host-country courts. If their mandate includes restructuring and retraining local police forces, the need for consistent strategy and program content becomes rather acute. The International Police Task Force (IPTF) in Bosnia was required by its mandate to train Bosnian police to "internationally recognized standards of law enforcement" but, as Cousens and Harland note, "there was no text, convention or otherwise recognized statement" as to what those standards might be; so the IPTF drafted some.

Sometimes the need for crowd control or to combat organized criminals is such that more specialized forces are required. The United Nations (and NATO) have opted in those circumstances for special police, who wear different monikers in different countries: *carabinieri* in Italy, *guardia civil* in Spain, *gendarmerie* in France, and *national gendarmerie* in Argentina. Whereas police normally deploy to UN missions as individuals, special police deploy as formed units, which are like military contingents but are usually in company-sized lots (100 to 150 officers), with heavier weaponry than the usual police pistol and often with armored transport. In a first step toward expanding the global supply of such constabulary-type forces, the G-8 agreed in June 2004 to support a Center of Excellence for Stability Police Units in Vicenza, Italy, to train constabulary-type forces from many countries.[30]

Police are, of course, not the only element of a criminal justice or law enforcement capability that is in short supply internationally. Prosecutors, judges, defense lawyers, court clerks, and jailers are even harder to come by in quantity, either to implement justice directly or to train others. Yet each of these specialties is necessary in a mission with executive authority, and some number of each may be necessary in a mission with a lighter footprint if the mandate includes security sector reform. As of this writing, the European Union has developed a roster of jurists; the United Nations has for some years been trying to fill out a "rule of law" rapid deployment roster, but without much success. States have been reluctant to provide names for this roster, promising instead to provide designated skill sets should the need arise and the United Nations ask for them. Having placeholders instead of people, however, keeps the United Nations from pretraining those who may eventually be called upon to serve, and from devising exercises that might simulate their working together.

Elections: Conduct and Political Role

The United Nations began the era of complex peace operations with mandates that culminated in national elections—for constituent assemblies, national legislatures, or presidents—the successful conduct of which signaled the operation's exit. Good experiences with electoral mission capstones in Namibia, Nicaragua, Mozambique, and (for the most part) Cambodia contrasted, however, with postelection disaster in Angola, preelection putsches in Somalia and Rwanda, the long decay of political life in Haiti, and electoral reinforcement of nationalist parties in Bosnia.

No longer seen as the magic sign marking the international exit, elections are now just one more tool in the peacebuilding kit, essential to popular expression of political will but recognized as not enough, in themselves, to create public security or local government legitimacy, to promote economic recovery or community reconciliation, or to account for war crimes and crimes against humanity. Electoral results also cannot be sustained without supporting institutions. Institutions, in turn, require trained people, sustained international attention, and protection against organized crime and corruption.[31]

Long-term electoral assistance falls to the UN Development Program or to various quasi-public institutions, such as the International Institute for Democracy Assistance, the U.S. National Endowment for Democracy, and the International Foundation for Electoral Systems.[32]

Planning and Executing Transitional Administration

Operations with full executive authority attempt to do, in a short time and for a foreign people and culture, what national governments have trouble enough doing over decades for their own polities even when they have *not* been torn apart by war. Few country experts know how to fit together the various moving parts of a polity or an economy or how to sequence them properly (if, indeed, sequencing and not simultaneity is what is required). Some things are true everywhere: water runs downhill; copper conducts electricity; and people need air, water, food, and shelter. Beyond such basics of physics and biology, however, is a great deal of uncertainty, trial, and error.

Few organizations were less well prepared to run a country than the UN Secretariat in 1999. It did not volunteer to take on Kosovo and East Timor, and it has not volunteered since for anyplace else. The secretary-general wanted no more than a UN advisory role in Afghanistan and was reluctant to engage politically in postinvasion Iraq even before he lost many of his team to a Baghdad suicide bomber.

The United States also hoped not to involve itself too deeply in rebuilding Afghanistan and wished fervently for Iraq to rebuild itself once Saddam and his cronies had been driven from office. But, as Alexander Thier concluded from observing Afghanistan up close, "War, or regime removal, is not a policy in itself but a means of achieving a policy, which must be to create secure, stable environments in which the local population can (re)develop self-governance."

The task of creating a legitimate and effective government delivering acceptable types and quantities of public services is extremely difficult. The difficulty is compounded by the reluctance of the most likely appointed governors (the United Nations and regional organizations) to plan for or to take on these tasks, the colonial opprobrium that attaches to trusteeship managed by a single state, and donors who prefer not to give budgetary support to the local institutions that the reluctant governors try to build.

Cousens and Harland conclude from Bosnia that the only thing worse than attempting transitional governance in a strong and forthright manner is to acquire the job by default as local capacity fails. Incremental international involvement in local politics allows local politicians to continue high-handed (and lucrative) wartime practices. If and when international control is increased to compensate, it then appears to undermine the very democratic accountability and local responsibility for governance that it is supposed to be promoting.

As Smith and Dee argue, the dilemma of enforcing change by fiat in the interest of promoting democracy—and the political hypocrisy that it seems to embody—can be eased if outsiders have a strategy from the outset to shift governmental authority back to local hands. Ideally, such a strategy would be adopted with the input and concurrence of local actors. Just which local actors, with what bona fides, as defined and chosen by whom, will vary case by case according to the mandate of the international mission, the character of the local political "market," and the local actors' links to outside patrons and resources.

A competent and well-resourced peace operation needs time to achieve its results. In most cases, the moderate, nonviolent sectors of politics and society are the least likely to dominate if a peace operation comes and goes quickly. Most of the cases in this volume indicate that drawdown and departure of an operation should be keyed to achievement of peace implementation milestones. Fixed timelines, often designed to reassure skeptical domestic audiences in troop-contributing countries, work only if all local parties are committed to peace and will therefore do worse if the operation leaves than if it stays. Stedman dubbed the timeline approach the "departing train" strategy, and it was used to good effect in Mozambique because the parties there had no access to income-producing commodities trade and thus no incentive to prolong implementation beyond the point at which the United Nations would leave.[33] It is one of many potential approaches designed to constrain those who seek to derail a peace process.

Managing Spoilers

It has been the experience of most peace operations in most places that local parties continue jockeying for position and advantage long after formal peace talks have ended and accords have been inked. Terms are reinterpreted; promised facilities are not provided or, if provided, are in terrible repair; and weapons or troops fail to show up at agreed assembly points. It is important, in other words, not to romanticize either the process of peace implementation or the local politicians and factional leaders with whom peace operations work. Conflicts in the developing world have millions of victims, but the leaders of belligerent factions and political parties, provided they survive the war, usually manage to prosper in the ensuing peace.

Factions that have independent access to high-value commodities such as precious gems, minerals, or narcotics are likely to maintain the extraction and trading networks that they established during the war unless those networks are severed by superior countervailing local power. Of the countries whose cases are detailed in this volume, Afghanistan, Sierra Leone, and the DRC were most heavily damaged by illicit commodities trade during and after their respective wars. As of this writing, only Sierra Leone's diamond trade is close to being regulated, partly because RUF leader Foday Sankoh was arrested and subsequently died, and partly because his mentor and partner in crime, Liberian president Charles Taylor, was driven into exile. The illicit trade in Congolese gold, diamonds, and coltan (a high-value microelectronics component) has continued, however, long after the formal withdrawal of all foreign armies from the DRC.[34] And the opium poppy crop in Afghanistan rebounded from almost total suppression in the Taliban's final year to nearly 4,200 tons of opium gum in 2004 (87 percent of world production). More than 356,000 Afghan households cultivated opium poppy, 90,000 more than in 2003. And the news could have been worse:

the crop would have been larger but for bad weather that reduced yields by almost 30 percent.[35]

In both Congo and Afghanistan, fragile central governments were attempting to reassert legitimate control over their national territories, with international assistance. These goals will not be achieved, however, as long as illicit minerals and illegal drugs continue to fuel regional power centers, power brokers, and criminal distribution networks.

The Need for Accountability in International Operations

Effective immunity from local criminal jurisdiction is the common national precondition for states' contributions of forces to UN operations. Indeed, fearing the potential jurisdiction of the International Criminal Court (ICC), the Bush administration demanded that countries large and small agree never to seek ICC prosecution of American citizens, however grievous their alleged crimes might be, even if the United States takes no action to indict or prosecute them in its own courts.[36] The ICC notwithstanding, the United States, the United Nations, and other providers of peace operations forces routinely require that host governments sign status-of-forces agreements granting peacekeepers immunity from local arrest, detention, and prosecution.[37]

Such immunity also affects the ability of the United Nations to discipline its troops (and police), who are not UN employees but are on loan from member states. Unlike those states, which can arrest and try their police or soldiers for criminal behavior if they so choose, the United Nations' only immediate option is to deport bad actors to their home countries and rely on their governments' willingness to initiate proceedings. Although the United Nations is reluctant to name names, either of individuals or of countries, in public reports generated directly for the secretary-general's signature, reports by third parties (including UN-appointed panels of experts or commissions of inquiry) have done so, and the organization could readily maintain a list of individuals that it deems unacceptable for UN service, based on past behavior.[38] (Such performance tracking could assist its quality management in many other areas as well, preventing the rehiring of individuals with poor records in prior UN missions.)

UN operations also sign status-of-mission agreements with host governments, based on the 1946 Convention on UN Privileges and

Immunities, which shields UN personnel from local liability while in the performance of their official duties.[39] The 1994 Convention on the Safety of United Nations and Associated Personnel also attempts to protect international personnel from harm in dangerous places; it was enacted in response to growing numbers of attacks against UN staff in conflict zones such as Bosnia and Somalia in the early 1990s.[40]

The United Nations has no machinery for bringing criminal prosecutions against international civil servants assigned to field missions; the best it can do internally is impose administrative discipline. The secretary-general can waive staff immunity, making possible local prosecution, but in a failed state, the collapse of local law enforcement may render such prosecution unlikely.

In the most recent example of the need for better accountability mechanisms, some of the troops and civilians of MONUC began to prey on those whom they had been sent to protect. In response to reports of sexual exploitation and abuse, the United Nations sent an investigative team from its Office of Internal Oversight Services, a second team headed by an assistant secretary-general to develop proactive measures to prevent recurrences, and a special envoy to meet with troop contributors to deal with the issue at its source. By mid-2005, indications were that the system had begun to make progress against this problem.[41]

The Road from Here

The Stimson Center's first volume on UN peacekeeping was published just after the Security Council shifted the United Nations' focus from traditional to complex operations—that is, from border monitoring to political engineering. The second volume, looking back on the results of that shift, observed that, in the mid-1990s, "the Security Council explored, reached, and exceeded the United Nations' capacity to undertake UN-run military and military-related field operations."[42] As this third volume is completed, the council has created mandates and missions for the United Nations that have once again seriously overtaxed the ability of its Department of Peacekeeping Operations to effectively plan, manage, staff, and support them. By the end of 2005, DPKO was deploying troops and police at nearly mid-1990s levels, without much help from Western military establishments.

Of the six cases detailed in this volume, one (East Timor) finished as a PSO in May 2005 and another (Sierra Leone) was moving toward termination at the end of 2005, leaving behind reasonably stable but still-troubled states. The peacekeeping force in post-Dayton Bosnia had shrunk to a small fraction of its original size and been transferred to the European Union, but peacekeepers showed no signs of leaving altogether. The operation in nearby Kosovo was still treading water, awaiting a viable political outcome, while the military elements of PSOs in the Congo and Afghanistan had expanded considerably. MONUC had grown to nearly 17,000 troops and police as factional instability and meddling neighbors continued to plague the eastern third of the country. The NATO-managed PSO in Afghanistan, ISAF, roughly doubled in size during the Afghan presidential elections of October 2004 and was slowly establishing, or taking control of and augmenting, Provincial Reconstruction Teams in the less politically violent but increasingly poppy-ridden northern and western parts of the country. Its future depended on the country's continued political and economic development, the pace of training and deployment of Afghan military and police units, and the state of the continuing U.S.-led fight against the Taliban and al Qaeda supporters in the south-central and southeastern parts of the country.

In the wake of the Brahimi Report, the need for robust peace support operations penetrated UN circles and, as operations have become more robust, fair and firm peace implementation is seen to *generate* local consent as it generates tranquility; as the *defining characteristic* of operational impartiality; and as *justification* for a fairly broad-spectrum authority to use force. PSOs are also increasingly being "mainstreamed" into the military doctrine and practice of the world's only powers capable of waging "expeditionary" warfare.

Is this a good thing? The answer might seem to depend on whether peace support is invited or imposed, yet an imposed peace would have been a good thing in Rwanda in 1994 or in Darfur in 2004. The key characteristic distinguishing such peace enforcement from other forceful military operations would therefore seem to be international legitimation: that somebody other than the decision makers of the force-wielding state believed the undertaking to be a good idea. The authority could come from the UN Security Council or from the governing body of the relevant regional organization. Peace support operations, in other words, should be defined not just in terms of tasks but in terms of political context, if only to differentiate—and protect—invitational operations.

Ideally, an invitational PSO will enjoy the consent of all local parties initially, but it should be able to work with partial absence of consent and should be prepared to deal with decayed consent. A PSO should use the minimum force needed to protect and advance its mission objectives, even if that use is on occasion proactive rather than reactive. Combat should not be its baseline stance, however, and should it become so, then an operation has transitioned from a PSO to something else, regardless of who mandated it or what that initial mandate said.

In the case of imposed peace, international authorization substitutes politically for the consent of the "host" government and renders the action to be taken legitimate (that is, politically acceptable) in the eyes of the broader international community. Such endorsement can also validate direct appeals for help from civil society actors, endowing private requests with alternative public authority. The utility of such endorsement seemed apparent even in post-9/11 Washington, where decision makers have otherwise neither looked to nor seen much value in any higher temporal authority. Yet the Bush administration returned to the Security Council after that body's initial refusal to sanction the invasion of Iraq, both to undo prior Council decisions rendered moot by the downfall of Saddam Hussein and for the added legitimacy that a Council resolution could confer upon the occupation (some troop contributors would not leave home without it).

U.S. preoccupation with Iraq and the other elements of the post-9/11 agenda tended to obscure the fact—for American audiences, at least—that most PSOs do not just barge into the places where they operate. Even post-9/11, most peacekeepers in most places have been invited in to provide the basic security and stability that civilian peacebuilding efforts require.

Almost everywhere military peacekeepers have deployed, however, they arrive much sooner than the civilian components of the operation. Although elements within military forces may be able to undertake civilian-related activities within a limited time and space, the military is always an awkward substitute for civilian capacity and, on the whole, is no more suited to creating good governance than a dental drill is to *filling* a cavity.

The United Nations, the OSCE, and the European Union all recognize this, as has the U.S. government, somewhat belatedly. In mid-2004, the U.S. State Department created the Office of the Coordinator for Reconstruction and Stabilization, reporting directly to the Secretary of State. The coordinator's job was to assemble and coordinate civilian capacity for postconflict reconstruction across the federal government. Cognizant of both the need to work well in multinational settings and the political value of international mandates, the new office may offer a small but visible counterweight to Pentagon dominance in funding and personnel for postconflict policy and strategy, and offer ready civilian expertise to future international peace operations. Initial operational planning, however, seemed to risk making the office and its field staff merely valued but distinctly adjunct advisers to U.S. military enterprises, rather than policy coequals.[43]

Serious civilian capacity for reinstituting or reforming government in war-ravaged states is the key to outside military forces' exit from such countries in such a way that they do not find themselves soon reengaged, in a Kafkaesque version of the movie *Groundhog Day*. Yet civilian *postconflict* capacity, while needed, is not enough. Imposed and invited operations alike deploy late in the life of a failed, failing, or conflict-ridden state, usually after thousands to millions of people have died. States and international institutions have recognized in recent years that reinforcing government in states at risk of failure, rather than rebuilding government once it has fallen in on its people, is by far the preferable alternative. Governments at risk must see the need for help, however, and international providers must also see the need and have the tools *to* help. They must have at their disposal both serious carrots and capable sticks, inasmuch as bad government often owes as much to malfeasance as it does to bad luck.

The persuasive tools need not be military, however. They may comprise very good financial tracking networks and better cooperation between banking systems and law enforcement to implement sanctions targeted at individuals' offshore bank accounts, together with credible threats of the seizure of same. They may involve regional and global cooperation in tracking and intercepting the black-market commodities trade that finances many wars (although the national record in the "drug war" gives one pause). They may involve aid- and trade-linked incentives for good governance, including mandatory international audits of national books.[44] How much would such things cost? Not clear, but much of the needed infrastructure and networking ought to have been built already as a by-product of the "war on terror." What better use for it than encouraging the open and honest government that President Bush, in his second inaugural speech, characterized as a major impediment to terrorist groups' appeal?

Effective, legitimate governance is the appropriate strategic objective. The immediate operational need, however, is for states to bolster the institutions that organize and manage PSOs and to improve the training and competence of the people and forces that they send to serve in them. UN DPKO is seeing demand for its services outstrip its capacity for the third time in a decade. The Global Peace Operations Initiative discussed by the G-8 at their 2004 Sea Island Summit promised more help to build up, train, and support capable peacekeepers within the African Union; that initiative deserves sustained implementation. NATO has been shifting its focus to peace support and stability operations; its members, including the United States, should be encouraged to structure and prepare their military forces to undertake these missions. A long-awaited U.S. Department of Defense directive, issued in November 2005, has defined stability operations as "a core U.S. military mission" and directed U.S. Joint Forces Command to "explore new stability operations concepts and capabilities."[45] Other NATO members should restructure their forces to make a much higher fraction of them deployable.[46] The European Union is developing a military and policing capacity suitable for PSOs, together with civilian "crisis management" capacities equally suited to postconflict situations; it should be able to undertake complex peace operations without U.S. involvement and its operation in Bosnia is a step in that direction. African Union initiatives to create, manage, and supply regional forces capable of robust peace operations deserve expanded donor support designed to ensure the sustainable use of resources contributed. Until such time as those forces are available and regionally sustainable, the

United Nations will continue to be the PSO provider of choice throughout much of sub-Saharan Africa. Indeed, until conflict prevention tools are perfected, no single institution will be able to meet all the needs of postconflict societies. To leave those needs unmet is to leave these societies vulnerable to the forces that thrive in the absence of law, so each institution's contribution is needed. The outside world cannot solve all the problems of every society; indeed, those who contribute to PSOs have problems of their own. But outside aid may do enough, if channeled wisely, with a focus on effective, legitimate governance, that the peace operations industry might work itself out of a job in, say, the next twenty years. At least that would be a worthwhile goal.

Notes

1. See, for example, Mary B. Anderson, *Do No Harm: How Aid Can Support Peace—or War* (Boulder, CO: Lynne Rienner, 1999).

2. See, for example, James Fallows, "Bush's Lost Year," *Atlantic Monthly*, October 2004.

3. United Nations, *A More Secure World: Our Shared Responsibility—Report of the Secretary-General's High-Level Panel on Threats, Challenges, and Change* (New York: United Nations, 2004), 65–67. See also International Commission on Intervention and State Sovereignty, "The Responsibility to Protect" (report, International Development Research Centre, Ottawa, December 2001). The report expands the definition of sovereign responsibility to include the protection of individuals within states. If a state will not or cannot protect the people within its borders from serious harm, "the principle of nonintervention yields to the international responsibility to protect" (ibid., xi).

4. United Nations, *Report of the Panel on United Nations Peace Operations* (Brahimi Report), A/55/305-S/2000/809, August 21, 2000, para. 64d.

5. United Nations, *Third Special Report of the Secretary-General on the United Nations Organization Mission in the Democratic Republic of Congo*, S/2004/650, August 14, 2004, paras. 79–102.

6. For details see Michael Carnahan, William Durch, and Scott Gilmore, "Economic Impact of Peacekeeping" (report for the UN Department of Peacekeeping Operations Best Practices Section), Ottawa: Peace Dividend Trust, 2006.

7. Julian Lindley-French and Franco Algieri, *European Defence Strategy* (Gütersloh, Germany: Bertelsman Foundation, 2004), 30–33, 68.

8. Victoria K. Holt, "The Responsibility to Protect: Considering the Operational Capacity for Civilian Protection" (revised discussion paper prepared for Foreign Affairs Canada), Washington, DC: Henry L. Stimson Center, January 2005, 16.

9. Vanessa Kent and Mark Malan, "The African Standby Force: Progress and Prospects," *African Security Review* 12, no. 3 (2003): 74–75.

10. See the NATO International Military Staff Web page at www.nato .int/ims/docu/force-structure.htm.

11. For numbers and national contributors, see UN General Assembly, *Gratis Personnel Provided by Governments and Other Entities, Report of the Secretary-General,* A/C.5/53/54, February 26, 1999, Annexes III–VII. On indirect costs see United Nations, *Financing of the International Tribunal for the Prosecution of Persons Responsible for Serious Violations of International Humanitarian Law Committed in the Territory of the Former Yugoslavia since 1991,* A/C.5/51/30, November 15, 1996, Annex I.

12. UN General Assembly, *Gratis Personnel Provided by Governments and Other Entities,* A/RES/51/243, September 15, 1997.

13. For details on staff growth, see William J. Durch et al., *The Brahimi Report and the Future of Peace Operations* (Washington, DC: Henry L. Stimson Center, 2003), chap. 3.

14. William J. Durch, "Strengthening UN Secretariat Capacity for Civilian Post-Conflict Management" (report prepared for the Center on International Cooperation, New York University, for discussion at the Copenhagen Seminar on Civilian Crisis Management, June 8–9, 2004). Final revised draft, June 21, 2004, www.um.dk/en/servicemenu/News/TheCopenhagen SeminarOnCivilianCrisisManagement.htm.

15. Brahimi Report, paras. 202, 210.

16. The UN bureaucratic hierarchy, in descending order, is as follows: department (or fund, program, or agency) , led by an undersecretary-general; office, led by an assistant secretary-general; division, led by a level 2 director ("D2"); service, led by a level 1 director ("D1"); section; and unit.

17. UN DPKO has been doing better at mission planning inside the department, however, convening an "integrated mission planning team" for each new operation. The team includes planners from its police and military divisions and from its logistics, transport, and communications services, plus representatives from other parts of DPKO as needed. The team is chaired by the desk officer from Operations, who serves as DPKO's primary, day-to-day point of contact with the operation once it deploys. If there is an interdepartmental working group or task force for the operation, the same officer will be DPKO's representative on it. For further discussion, see Durch et al., *The Brahimi Report and the Future of Peace Operations*, 47–50.

18. See UN DPKO, Peacekeeping Best Practices Unit, "Lessons Learned Study on the Start-up Phase of the United Nations Mission in Liberia," New York, April 2004, 9, www.un.org/Depts/dpko/lessons/.

19. Ibid., 15.

20. In December 2000, the secretary-general issued general guidance to the UN community, giving representatives and special representatives responsibility for "political guidance to the overall UN presence" in countries where a Security Council–mandated mission is deployed. See UN DPKO, "Civil-Military Coordination Policy," September 2002, Annex, www.un.org/Depts/dpko/milad/oma/oma_policy.htm.

21. Durch, "Strengthening UN Secretariat Capacity," 12–13.

22. Humanitarian agencies and human rights advocates may disagree on the virtues of strict neutrality, especially where one or more local fighting factions are known to be committing atrocities. The humanitarian argument for distributing aid even among populations controlled by or supportive of such factions rests on the argument that a greater good, overall, is done by keeping more people alive with aid than is done by employing a selective approach that may lead the slighted faction to embargo all aid. For discussion of the issues involved, see Durch, "Strengthening UN Secretariat Capacity," 5–6.

23. Negative peace "is the absence of direct violence (physical, verbal, and psychological) between individuals, groups, and governments." Positive peace "is more than the absence of violence; it is the presence of social justice through equal opportunity, a fair distribution of power and resources, equal protection and impartial enforcement of law." See Educators for Social Responsibility, "What Is Peace?" www.esrnational.org/sp/we/uw/peacewhatis.htm.

24. Stimson Center interviews, Bukavu, Democratic Republic of the Congo, August 2003; Fondation Hirondelle, "Media for Peace and Human Dignity," www.hirondelle.org. Fondation Hirondelle receives primary funding from the governments of Switzerland, the United States, the Netherlands, Sweden, Great Britain, France, Canada, Germany, and Japan as well as the European Community.

25. Brahimi Report, para. 87.

26. United Nations, *Budget for the Support Account for Peacekeeping Operations for 1 July 2004 to 30 June 2005, Report of the Secretary-General,*

A/58/715, February 17, 2004, para. 1; and United Nations, *Implementation of the Recommendations of the Special Committee on Peacekeeping Operations, Report of the Secretary-General,* A/58/694, January 26, 2004, para. 20.

27. United Nations, *Fourth Progress Report of the Secretary-General on the UN Mission in Liberia,* S/2004/725, September 10, 2004, 1; and United Nations, *Fourteenth Report of the Secretary-General on the United Nations Mission Operation in the Democratic Republic of Congo,* November 17, 2003, 3. See also UN DPKO, Peacekeeping Best Practices Unit, "Lessons Learned Study," 6. DPKO was, at the same time, planning to implement a peace agreement for southern Sudan, and Darfur (in western Sudan) was looming as a genocidal crisis. For discussion, see Victoria K. Holt, "Peacekeeping in Africa: Challenges and Opportunities," testimony before the U.S. Congress, House International Relations Committee, Subcommittee on Africa, October 8, 2004, www.stimson.org/fopo/?SN=FP20041006723.

28. Michael J. Dziedzic, "Introduction," in *Policing the New World Disorder,* ed. Robert B. Oakley, Michael J. Dziedzic, and Eliot M. Greenberg (Washington, DC: National Defense University Press, 1998), 6–15; and Charles Call and William Stanley, "Civilian Security," in *Ending Civil Wars: The Implementation of Peace Agreements,* ed. Stephen John Stedman, Donald Rothchild, and Elizabeth M. Cousens (Boulder, CO: Lynne Rienner, 2002), 303–23.

29. Durch et al., *The Brahimi Report and the Future of Peace Operations,* 80. See also United Nations, *Implementation of the Recommendations of the Special Committee,* A/58/694, paras. 25, 31–34.

30. "G-8 Action Plan: Expanding Global Capability for Peace Support Operations" (proceedings of the G-8 Summit at Sea Island, GA, June 10, 2004), www.g8usa.gov/d_061004c.htm. The United States agreed to contribute $10 million to the new center under its Global Peace Operations Initiative.

31. Michael Dziedzic, Laura Rozen, and Phil Williams, "Lawless Rule versus Rule of Law in the Balkans," Special Report no. 97 (Washington, DC: United States Institute of Peace, 2002).

32. For more information, see these organizations' respective Web sites: www.undp.org/governance, www.idea.int/institute/inst-intro.html, www.ned.org, and www.ifes.org.

33. Stedman, "Spoiler Problems in Peace Processes," *International Security* (Fall 1997), 5–53.

34. Christian Dietrich, ed., *Diamond Industry Annual Review—Democratic Republic of Congo, 2004* (Ottawa: Partnership Africa-Canada, 2004), 10. Estimates as to the annual value of just the illicit diamond trade in the DRC are about $350 million of a total market valued at about $1 billion. See Ian Smillie, ed., *Rich Man, Poor Man: Development Diamonds and Poverty Diamonds* (Ottawa: Partnership Africa-Canada; Washington, DC: Global Witness Publishing, 2004), 25. Both studies are available at www.pacweb.org/e/.

35. "UN Drugs Office Reports Major Increase in Opium Cultivation in Afghanistan," *UN Information Service* (press release UNIS/NAR/867), November 18, 2004, www.unis.unvienna.org/unis/pressrels/2004/unisnar867.html.

36. For discussion of the treaty, see Human Rights Watch, "The United States and the International Criminal Court," www.hrw.org/campaigns/icc/us.htm. For the Bush administration's position, see remarks by Secretary of Defense Donald Rumsfeld, "Secretary Rumsfeld Statement on the ICC Treaty" (press release), Washington, DC: U.S. Department of Defense, May 6, 2002.

37. Language in the agreement between the Interim Administration of Afghanistan and the International Security Assistance Force, excerpted here, is common in status-of-forces agreements: "The ISAF and supporting personnel, including associated liaison personnel, will under all circumstances and at all times be subject to the exclusive jurisdiction of their respective national elements in respect of any criminal or disciplinary offences which may be committed by them on the territory of Afghanistan" (Annex A, para. 3). "The ISAF and supporting personnel, including associated liaison personnel, will be immune from personal arrest or detention" (Annex A, para. 4). Concern about the International Criminal Court was nonetheless reflected in the same paragraph: "The Interim Administration agree that ISAF and supporting personnel, including associated liaison personnel, may not be surrendered to, or otherwise transferred to the custody of, an international tribunal or any other entity or State without the express consent of the contributing nation." In return, ISAF troops would "respect the laws and culture of Afghanistan." See "Military Technical Agreement Between the International Security Assistance Force and the Interim Administration of Afghanistan," Annex A: Arrangements Regarding the Status of the International Security Assistance Force, www.operations.mod.uk/isafmta.pdf.

38. "Peacekeepers' Sexual Abuse of Local Girls Continuing in DR of Congo, UN Finds," *UN News Service,* January 7, 2005, www.un.org/apps/news/story.asp?NewsID=12990&Cr=democratic&Cr1=congo.

39. United Nations, *Convention on the Privileges and Immunities of the United Nations,* UN Treaty Series 15, February 13, 1946 (accessed via the University of Minnesota Human Rights Library, www1.umn.edu/humanrts/instree/p&i-convention.htm).

40. UN Office of Legal Affairs, Codification Division, *Convention on the Safety of United Nations and Associated Personnel,* www.un.org/law/cod/safety.htm.

41. United Nations, "Problem of Sexual Abuse by Peacekeepers Now Openly Recognized, Broad Strategy in Place to Address It, Security Council Told," transcript SC/8649, 5379th Meeting of the Security Council (AM) (New York: UN Department of Public Information, February 23, 2006).

42. William J. Durch, "Keeping the Peace," in *UN Peacekeeping, American Policy, and the Uncivil Wars of the 1990s,* ed. Durch (New York: St. Martin's, 1996), 28.

43. What the Office of the Coordinator for Reconstruction and Stabilization (S/CRS) called "Advance Civilian Teams" would "deploy with military at brigade or division level" and serve as the "foundation for PRTs" (Provincial Reconstruction Teams, a concept term coined for elements of the U.S. operation in Afghanistan). U.S. Department of State, "Office of the Coordinator for Reconstruction and Stabilization" (briefing), December 2004.

44. David Cortright and George A. Lopez, *The Sanctions Decade: Assessing UN Strategies in the 1990s* (Boulder, CO: Lynne Rienner, 2000), 247–49.

45. U.S. Department of Defense, Office of the Undersecretary of Defense for Policy, "Military Support for Stability, Security, Transition, and Reconstruction (SSTR) Operations," Directive No. 3000.05, Washington, DC, November 28, 2005.

46. For suggestions, see Hans Binnendijk and Stuart E. Johnson, *Transforming for Stabilization and Reconstruction Operations* (Washington, DC: National Defense University Press for the Center for Technology and National Security Policy, 2004). See also Lindley-French and Algieri, *European Defence Strategy.*

Selected Bibliography

For a complete bibliography online, go to http://www.stimson.org/fopo.

Reports, Books, and Articles

Amnesty International reports online. http://web.amnesty.org/library/engindex.

Anderson, Mary B. *Do No Harm: How Aid Can Support Peace—or War.* Boulder, CO: Lynne Rienner, 1999.

Bellamy, Alex J., Paul Williams, and Stuart Griffin. *Understanding Peacekeeping.* Cambridge: Polity, 2004.

Berman, Eric G., and Katie E. Sams. *Peacekeeping in Africa: Capabilities and Culpabilities.* Geneva: UN Institute for Disarmament Research, 2000.

Bi-partisan Commission on Post-conflict Reconstruction. "Play to Win: Report of the Bi-partisan Commission on Post-conflict Reconstruction." Washington, DC: Center for Strategic and International Studies and Association of the U.S. Army, January 2003.

Blechman, Barry M., William J. Durch, Wendy Eaton, and Julie Werbel. "Effective Transitions from Peace Operations to Sustainable Peace, Final Report." Prepared for the Office of the Assistant Secretary of Defense for Strategy and Resources, Office of Peacekeeping and Humanitarian Affairs. Washington, DC: DFI International, September 1997.

Chesterman, Simon. *You, the People: The United Nations, Transitional Administrations, and State Building.* New York: Oxford University Press, 2004.

Chopra, Jarat. *The Politics of Peace Maintenance.* Boulder, CO: Lynne Rienner, 1998.

Cilliers, Jakkie, and Peggy Mason, eds. *Peace, Profit or Plunder? The Privatisation of Security in War-Torn African Societies.* Pretoria: Institute for Security Studies, 1999.

Coghlan, Ben, Rick Brennan, Pascal Ngoy, David Dofara, Brad Otto, and Tony Stewart. "Mortality in the Democratic Republic of Congo: Results from a Nationwide Survey Conducted April–July 2004." Melbourne and New York: Burnet Institute and International Rescue Committee, December 2004.

Cousens, Elizabeth, and Chetan Kumar, with Karen Wermester, eds. *Peacebuilding as Politics: Cultivating Peace in Fragile Societies.* Boulder, CO: Lynne Rienner, 2001.

Covey, Jock, Michael J. Dziedzic, and Len Hawley, eds. *The Quest for Viable Peace: International Intervention and Strategies for Conflict Transformation.* Washington, DC: United States Institute of Peace Press, 2005.

Crocker, Chester A., Fen Osler Hampson, and Pamela Aall, eds. *Turbulent Peace: The Challenges of Managing International Conflict.* Washington, DC: United States Institute of Peace Press, 2001.

Diehl, Paul F. *International Peacekeeping.* Baltimore: Johns Hopkins University Press, 1993.

Dobbins, James, Seth G. Jones, Keith Crane, Andrew Rathmell, Brett Steele, Richard Teltschik, Anga Timilsina. *The UN's Role in Nation-Building: From the Congo to Iraq.* Santa Monica, CA: RAND, 2005.

Durch, William J., ed. *The Evolution of UN Peacekeeping: Case Studies and Comparative Analysis.* New York: St. Martin's, 1993.

———. *UN Peacekeeping, American Policy, and the Uncivil Wars of the 1990s.* New York: St. Martin's, 1996.

Durch, William J., Victoria K. Holt, Caroline R. Earle, and Moira K. Shanahan. *The Brahimi Report and the Future of Peace Operations.* Washington, DC: Henry L. Stimson Center, 2003.

Findlay, Trevor. *The Use of Force in UN Peace Operations.* Oxford: Oxford University Press, 2002.

Fishel, John T., ed. *The "Savage Wars of Peace": Toward a New Paradigm of Peace Operations.* Boulder, CO: Westview Press, 1998.

Fondation Hirondelle. "Media for Peace and Human Dignity." http://www.hirondelle.org.

Goldstone, Jack A., Robert H. Bates, Ted Robert Gurr, Michael Lustik, Monty G. Marshall, Jay Ulfelder, and Mark Woodward. "A Global Forecasting Model of Political Instability." Paper presented at the annual meeting of the American Political Science Association, Washington, DC, September 3, 2005. http://globalpolicy.gmu.edu/pitf/pitfp5.htm.

Gregoire, Joseph P. "The Bases of French Peace Operations Doctrine." Carlisle Papers in Security Strategy Series. Carlisle, PA: U.S. Army War College, Strategic Studies Institute, September 2002.

Hohe, Tanja. "The Clash of Paradigms: International Administration and Local Political Legitimacy in East Timor." *Contemporary Southeast Asia* 24, no. 3 (December 2002).

Human Rights Research and Advocacy Consortium. http://www.afghan advocacy.org/ourWork/.

Human Rights Watch reports online. http://www.hrw.org/doc/?t=pubs.

International Crisis Group reports online. http://www.crisisgroup.org/home/index.cfm.

King, Charles. *Ending Civil Wars.* Adelphi Paper no. 308. London: International Institute for Security Studies, 1997.

Ku, Charlotte, and Harold Jacobson, eds. *Domestic Accountability and the Use of Force in International Law.* Cambridge: Cambridge University Press, 2002.

Mackinlay, John, and Jarat Chopra. "Second Generation Multinational Operations." *Washington Quarterly* (Summer 1992): 113–31.

Maley, William, Charles Sampford, and Ramesh Thakur, eds. *From Civil Strife to Civil Society: Civil and Military Responsibilities to Disrupted States.* New York: United Nations Institute Press, 2003.

Manwaring, Max G., and Anthony James Joes, eds. *Beyond Declaring Victory and Coming Home: The Challenges of Peace and Stability Operations.* Westport, CT: Praeger Publishers, 2000.

Marshall, Monty G., and Ted Robert Gurr. *Peace and Conflict 2005.* College Park, MD: Center for International Development and Conflict Management, 2005.

Martin, Ian. *Self-Determination in East Timor: The United Nations, the Ballot and International Intervention.* Boulder, CO: Lynne Rienner, 2001.

Moskos, Charles C., Jr. *Peace Soldiers: The Sociology of a United Nations Military Force.* Chicago: University of Chicago Press, 1976.

Nzongola-Ntalaja, Georges. *The Congo: From Leopold to Kabila.* London: Zed, 2002.

Oakley, Robert B., Michael J. Dziedzic, and Eliot M. Goldberg, eds. *Policing the New World Disorder.* Washington, DC: National Defense University Press, 1998.

Orr, Robert C., ed. *Winning the Peace: An American Strategy for Post-conflict Reconstruction.* Washington, DC: CSIS Press, 2004.

Paris, Roland. *At War's End: Building Peace after Civil Conflict.* New York: Cambridge University Press, 2004.

Rashid, Ahmed. *Taliban: Islam, Oil and the New Great Game in Central Asia.* New Haven, CT: Yale University Press, 2000.

Reno, William. *Warlord Politics and African States.* Boulder, CO: Lynne Rienner, 1998.

Rikhye, Indar Jit. *Theory and Practice of Peacekeeping.* New York: St. Martin's Press, 1984.

Rubin, Barnett R. *The Search for Peace in Afghanistan.* New Haven, CT: Yale University Press, 1995.

Sell, Louis. *Slobodan Milosevic and the Destruction of Yugoslavia.* Durham and London: Duke University Press, 2002.

Singer, P. W. *Corporate Warriors: The Rise of the Privatized Military Industry.* Ithaca, NY: Cornell University Press, 2003.

Smillie, Ian, ed. *Rich Man, Poor Man: Development Diamonds and Poverty Diamonds.* Ottawa: Partnership Africa-Canada; Washington, DC: Global Witness Publishing, 2004.

Smith, Michael G., with Moreen Dee. *Peacekeeping in East Timor: The Path to Independence.* Boulder, CO: Lynne Rienner, 2003.

Stedman, Stephen John, Donald Rothchild, and Elizabeth M. Cousens, eds. *Ending Civil Wars: The Implementation of Peace Agreements.* Boulder, CO: Lynne Rienner, 2002.

Stedman, Stephen John, and Fred Tanner, eds. *Refugee Manipulation: War, Politics, and the Abuse of Human Suffering.* Washington, DC: Brookings Institution, 2003.

Tardy, Thierry. "French Policy towards Peace Support Operations." *International Peacekeeping* 6, no. 1 (Spring 1999).

United States Institute of Peace. "Peace Agreements Digital Collection." http://www.usip.org/library/pa.html.

Wilkinson, Philip. "Sharpening the Weapons of Peace: Peace Support Operations and Complex Emergencies." In *Peacekeeping and Conflict Resolution,* edited by Tom Woodhouse and Oliver Ramsbotham. Portland, OR: Frank Cass, 2000.

Woodward, David. *The IMF, the World Bank and Economic Policy in Bosnia.* Oxford: Oxfam, 1998.

Zanini, Michele, and Jennifer Morrison Taw. *The Army and Multinational Force Compatibility.* Santa Monica, CA: RAND, 2000.

Government Documents

Agreement on Provisional Arrangements in Afghanistan Pending the Re-establishment of Permanent Government Institutions ("Bonn Agreement"). December 5, 2001. http://www.runiceurope.org/german/frieden/afghanistan/talks/agreement.pdf.

Government of Sierra Leone. "Special Court Agreement, 2002 (Ratification Act)." March 19, 2002. http://www.sierra-leone.org/specialcourtagreement.html.

Republic of Bosnia and Herzegovina, Republic of Croatia, and Federal Republic of Yugoslavia. *Agreement on Sub-regional Arms Control* ("Florence Agreement"). June 14, 1996. http://www.morh.hr/hvs/SPORAZUMI/tekstovi/SSKN-engleski.pdf.

Sierra Leone Truth and Reconciliation Commission. *Final Report.* February 2005. http://www.usip.org/library/tc/tc_regions/tc_sl.html.

Transitional Islamic Government of Afghanistan, Asian Development Bank, UNAMA, UN Development Program, and World Bank Group. *Securing Afghanistan's Future: Accomplishments and the Strategic Path Forward.* Kabul, March 17, 2004. http://www.adb.org/Documents/Papers/Securing-AFG-Future/default.asp.

UK Ministry of Defence. *Interim Agreement for Peace and Self-Government in Kosovo* ("Rambouillet Accords"). February 23, 1999. http://www.kosovo.mod.uk/rambouillet_text.htm.

———. *Military Technical Agreement between the International Security Assistance Force and the Interim Administration of Afghanistan.* Kabul, January 2002. http://www.operations.mod.uk/isafmta.doc.

UK Ministry of Defence. Joint Doctrine and Concepts Centre. *The Military Contribution to Peace Support Operations.* Joint Warfare Publication 3-50. 2nd ed. Shrivenham, UK, 2004.

U.S. Army. *Peace Operations.* Field Manual 100-23. Fort Leavenworth, KS: U.S. Army Training and Doctrine Command, December 1994.

———. *Stability Operations and Support Operations.* Field Manual FM 3-07. Fort Leavenworth, KS: U.S. Army Training and Doctrine Command, February 2003.

U.S. Congress. Senate. *Authorization for Use of Military Force.* S.J. Res. 23. 107th Cong., 1st sess., September 14, 2001.

U.S. Department of Defense. Office of the Undersecretary of Defense for Policy. "Military Support for Stability, Security, Transition, and Reconstruction (SSTR) Operations." Directive no. 3000.05. Washington, DC, November 28, 2005.

United Nations and Other International Organization Documents

General

Boutros-Ghali, Boutros. *An Agenda for Peace.* New York: United Nations, 1992.

United Nations. Department of Peacekeeping Operations. Best Practices Section. Lessons learned reports online. http://www.un.org/Depts/dpko/lessons/.

United Nations. General Assembly. *A More Secure World: Our Shared Responsibility—Report of the Secretary-General's High-Level Panel on Threats, Challenges, and Change.* New York: United Nations, 2004.

United Nations. General Assembly and Security Council. *Report of the Panel on United Nations Peace Operations* (Brahimi Report). A/55/305-S/2000/809. August 21, 2000.

———. *Supplement to an Agenda for Peace.* A/50/60-S/1995/1. January 25, 1995.

United Nations. Security Council. *Report of the Commission of Inquiry Established Pursuant to Security Council Resolution 885 (1993) to Investigate Armed Attacks on UNOSOM II Personnel Which Led to Casualties among Them* (Somalia Commission of Inquiry). S/1994/653. June 1, 1994.

———. *Report of the Independent Inquiry into the Actions of the United Nations during the 1994 Genocide in Rwanda, Letter from the Secretary-General Addressed to the President of the Security Council.* S/1999/1257. December 16, 1999.

Afghanistan

United Nations. Economic and Social Council. *Report of the Independent Expert on the Situation of Human Rights in Afghanistan, M. Cherif Bassiouni.* E/CN.4/2005/122. March 11, 2005.

United Nations. General Assembly. *Report of the Secretary-General Pursuant to General Assembly Resolution 53/35. The Fall of Srebrenica.* A/54/549. November 15, 1999.

United Nations. General Assembly and Security Council. *The Situation in Afghanistan and Its Implications for International Peace and Security. Report of the Secretary-General.* A/56/875-S/2002/278. March 18, 2002; A/57/762-S/2003/333. March 18, 2003; A/57/850-S/2003/754. July 23, 2003; S/2003/1212. December 30, 2003; A/58/742-S/2004/230. March 19, 2004; A/58/868-S/2004/634. August 12, 2004; A/59/581-S/2004/925. November 26, 2004; A/59/744-S/2005/183. March 18, 2005; A/60/224-S/2005/525. August 12, 2005.

United Nations. Office on Drugs and Crime and Government of Afghanistan Counter Narcotics Directorate. *Afghanistan Opium Survey.* Vienna, November 2004. http://www.unodc.org/afg/en/reports_surveys.html.

United Nations. Security Council. (Resolutions on the situation in Afghanistan.) S/RES/1373. September 28, 2001; S/RES/1378. November 14, 2001; S/RES/1383. December 6, 2001; S/RES/1386. December 20, 2001; S/RES/1401. March 28, 2002; S/RES/1413. May 23, 2002; S/RES/1444. November 27, 2002; S/RES/1510. October 13, 2003; S/RES/1563. September 17, 2004.

Bosnia and Herzegovina

Office of the High Representative, Sarajevo. *General Framework Agreement for Peace in Bosnia and Herzegovina* ("Dayton Peace Agreement"). December 14, 1995. http://www.ohr.int/dpa/default.asp?content_id=380.

———. *Constitution of the Federation of Bosnia and Herzegovina.* Sarajevo, September 2001. http://www.ohr.int/const/bih-fed.

United Nations. Security Council. *Report of the Secretary-General on the United Nations Mission in Bosnia and Herzegovina (UNMIBH).* S/1997/468. June 16, 1997; S/1997/966. December 10, 1997; S/1999/284. March 16, 1999; S/1999/989. September 17, 1999; S/1999/1260. December 17, 1999; S/2000/215. March 15, 2000; S/2000/1137. November 30, 2000; S/2001/571. June 7, 2001; S/2001/571/Corr.1. June 21, 2001; S/2001/1132. November 29, 2001; S/2001/1132/Corr.1. December 3, 2001.

———. *Report of the Secretary-General Pursuant to Security Council Resolution 1035 (1995).* S/1996/210. March 29, 1996; S/1996/1017. December 9, 1996.

———. (Resolutions on Bosnia-Herzegovina.) S/RES/713. September 25, 1991; S/RES/743. February 21, 1992; S/RES/1031. December 15, 1995; S/RES/1035. December 21, 1995; S/RES/1088. December 12, 1996; S/RES/1103. March 31, 1997; S/RES/1107. May 16, 1997; S/RES/1168. May 21, 1998.

———. *The Situation in the Former Yugoslavia. Report of the Secretary-General.* S/1995/1031. December 13, 1995.

Democratic Republic of the Congo

United Nations. Security Council. *Report of the Secretary-General on the United Nations Organization Mission in the Democratic Republic of the Congo.* S/2000/30. January 17, 2000; 2nd, S/2000/330. April 18, 2000; 3rd, S/2000/566. June 12, 2000; 4th, S/2000/888. September 21, 2000; 6th, S/2001/128. February 12, 2001; 7th, S/2001/373. April 17, 2001; 8th, S/2001/572. June 12, 2001; 9th, S/2001/970. October 16, 2001; 10th, S/2002/169. February 15, 2002; 11th, S/2002/621. June 5, 2002; 12th, S/2002/1180. October 18, 2002; 13th, S/2003/211. February 21, 2003; 14th, S/2003/1098. November 17, 2003; 15th, S/2004/251. March 25, 2004; 16th, S/2004/1034. December 31, 2004; 18th, S/2005/506. August 2, 2005.

———. *Report of the Secretary-General on the United Nations Preliminary Deployment in the Democratic Republic of the Congo.* S/1999/790. July 15, 1999.

———. (Resolutions on the Democratic Republic of the Congo.) S/RES/1258. August 6, 1999; S/RES/1291. February 25, 2000; S/RES/1355. June 15, 2001; S/RES/1376. November 9, 2001; S/RES/1468. March 20, 2003; S/RES/1484. May 30, 2003; S/RES/1493. July 28, 2003; S/RES/1533. March 12, 2004; S/RES/1621. September 6, 2005.

———. *Special Report of the Secretary-General on the United Nations Organization Mission in the Democratic Republic of the Congo.* S/2002/1005. September 10, 2002; 2nd, S/2003/566. May 27, 2003; 3rd, S/2004/650. August 16, 2004; 4th, S/2005/320. May 26, 2005.

Kosovo

North Atlantic Treaty Organization. *Military Technical Agreement between the International Security Force (KFOR) and the Governments of the Federal Republic of Yugoslavia and the Republic of Serbia.* June 9, 1999. http://www.nato.int/kosovo/docu/a990609a.htm.

United Nations. Security Council. *Report of the Secretary-General on the United Nations Interim Administration Mission in Kosovo.* S/1999/779.

July 12, 1999; S/2004/348. April 30, 2004; S/2005/335. May 23, 2005; S/2005/335/Corr.1. May 26, 2005.

————. *Report of the Secretary-General Pursuant to Paragraph 10 of Security Council Resolution 1244 (1999).* S/1999/672. June 12, 1999.

————. (Resolutions on Kosovo.) S/RES/1160. March 31, 1998; S/RES/1199. September 23, 1998; S/RES/1244, June 10, 1999.

Sierra Leone

United Nations Children's Fund. *Report for the Children of Sierra Leone.* 2004. http://www.unicef.org/infobycountry/files/TRCCF9SeptFINAL.pdf.

United Nations. Security Council. *Progress Report of the Secretary-General on the United Nations Observer Mission in Sierra Leone.* S/1998/750. August 12, 1998; 2nd, S/1998/960. October 16, 1998; 3rd, S/1998/1176. December 16, 1998; 6th, S/1999/645. June 4, 1999; 7th, S/1999/836/Add.1. August 11, 1999.

————. *Report of the Secretary-General on the Establishment of a Special Court for Sierra Leone.* S/2000/915. October 4, 2000. Enclosure: "Statute of the Special Court for Sierra Leone."

————. *Report of the Secretary-General on the Situation in Sierra Leone.* 3rd, S/1998/103. February 5, 1998; 4th, S/1998/249. March 18, 1998; 5th, S/1998/486. June 9, 1998.

————. *Report of the Secretary-General on the United Nations Mission in Sierra Leone.* S/1999/1223. December 9, 1999; 2nd, S/2000/13. January 11, 2000; 3rd, S/2000/186. March 7, 2000; 4th, S/2000/455. May 19, 2000; 5th, S/2000/751. July 31, 2000; 6th, S/2000/832. August 24, 2000; 7th, S/2000/1055. October 31, 2000; 8th, S/2000/1199. December 15, 2000; 9th, S/2001/228. March 14, 2001; 10th, S/2001/627. June 25, 2001; 11th, S/2001/857. September 7, 2001; 12th, S/2001/1195. December 13, 2001; 13th, S/2002/267. March 14, 2002; 14th, S/2002/679. June 19, 2002; 15th, S/2002/987. September 5, 2002; 16th, S/2002/1417. December 24, 2002; 17th, S/2003/321. March 17, 2003; 18th, S/2003/663. June 23, 2003; 20th, S/2003/1201. December 23, 2003; 21st, S/2004/228. March 19, 2004; 22nd, S/2004/536. July 6, 2004; 23rd, S/2004/724. September 9, 2004; 24th, S/2004/965. December 10, 2004; 25th, S/2005/273. April 26, 2005.

————. (Resolutions on Sierra Leone.) S/RES/1132. October 8, 1997; S/RES/1162. April 17, 1998; S/RES/1181. July 13, 1998; S/RES/1260. August 20, 1999; S/RES/1270. October 22, 1999; S/RES/1289. February 7, 2000;

S/RES/1299. May 19, 2000; S/RES/1306. July 5, 2000; S/RES/1313. August 4, 2000; S/RES/1315. August 14, 2000; S/RES/1343. March 7, 2001; S/RES/1370. September 18, 2001; S/RES/1385. December 19, 2001; S/RES/1436. September 24, 2002; S/RES/1537. March 30, 2004.

————. *Special Report of the Secretary-General on the United Nations Observer Mission in Sierra Leone.* S/1999/20. January 7, 1999.

East Timor (Timor-Leste)

United Nations. Security Council. *End of Mandate Report of the Secretary-General on the United Nations Mission of Support in East Timor (for the period from 17 February to 11 May 2005).* S/2005/310. May 12, 2005.

————. *Progress Report of the Secretary-General on the United Nations Transitional Administration in East Timor.* S/2001/719. July 24, 2001.

————. *Question of East Timor: Report of the Secretary-General.* S/1999/595. May 22, 1999; S/1999/705. June 22, 1999; S/1999/803. July 20, 1999.

————. *Report of the Secretary-General on the Situation in East Timor.* S/1999/1024. October 4, 1999.

————. *Report of the Secretary-General on the United Nations Mission of Support in East Timor.* S/2002/1223. November 6, 2002; S/2004/333. April 29, 2004.

————. *Report of the Secretary-General on the United Nations Transitional Administration in East Timor.* S/2001/983. October 18, 2001; S/2002/432. April 17, 2002.

————. (Resolutions on East Timor.) S/RES/1246. June 11, 1999; S/RES/1264. September 15, 1999; S/RES/1272. October 22, 1999; S/RES/1319. September 8, 2000; S/RES/1338. January 31, 2001; S/RES/1392. January 31, 2002; S/RES/1410. May 17, 2002; S/RES/1473. April 4, 2003; S/RES/1480. May 19, 2003.

Index

United States Institute of Peace

The United States Institute of Peace is an independent, nonpartisan institution established and funded by Congress. Its goals are to help prevent and resolve violent conflicts, promote post-conflict peacebuilding, and increase conflict-management tools, capacity, and intellectual capital worldwide. The Institute does this by empowering others with knowledge, skills, and resources, as well as by its direct involvement in conflict zones around the globe.

Twenty-First-Century Peace Operations

This book is set in Minion; the display type is Frutiger. Jeff Urbancic designed the book's cover. Helene Y. Redmond designed the interior and made up the pages. Sherri Schultz and Wesley Palmer copyedited the text, which was proofread by EEI Communications. The index was prepared by Sonsie Conroy. The book's editor was Nigel Quinney.